Contents

		Page
1	**Introduction**	1
2	**The 1991 Census**	2
3	**Local results from the Census**	2
4	**The range of information in the Report**	2
5	**Finding information in the Report**	3
6	**The populations covered in the Report**	4
7	**Definitions and explanatory notes**	6
8	**The '10 per cent' sample**	6
9	**Evaluation of the results**	6
10	**Comparisons of results with those of earlier censuses**	7
11	**Further results from the 1991 Census**	8
12	**Copyright and reproduction of material from this Report**	8
13	**Further information**	9
14	**Reference map**	9
15	**Summary of the 1991 Census results for Avon**	11
	Tables A - L	
16	**Indexes and main tables**	
	Tables by key word title (Parts 1 and 2)	27
	Topic and key word index (Part 1)	29
	Full table titles (Parts 1 and 2)	35
	Tables 1 - 66	
	Annexes	
	A 1981-91 boundary changes (if applicable)	397
	B How to obtain 1991 Census results	399
	C Explanatory notes - Tables A - L - Tables 1 - 66	403

OFFICE OF POPULATION CENSUSES AND SURVEYS

1991 Census

County report

Laid before Parliament pursuant to Section 4(1)
Census Act 1920

Avon

part 1

London: HMSO

First published 1993

ISBN 0 11 691408 4

HMSO
Standing order service

Placing a standing order with HMSO BOOKS enables a customer to receive future titles in this series automatically as published. This saves the time, trouble and expense of placing individual orders and avoids the problem of knowing when to do so. For details please write to HMSO BOOKS (PC 13A/1), Publications Centre, PO Box 276, London SW8 5DT quoting reference 02 02 009. The standing order service also enables customers to receive automatically as published all material of their choice which additionally saves extensive catalogue research. The scope and selectivity of the service has been extended by new techniques, and there are more than 3,500 classifications to choose from. A special leaflet describing the service in detail may be obtained on request.

Cover illustration by Guy Eves

1 Introduction

1.1 This volume is the first part of the Report for Avon from the Census of Great Britain which took place on 21 April 1991. It is published and laid before Parliament under the authority of, and to meet the requirements of, section 4(1) of the Census Act 1920.

1.2 The 1991 Census was the nineteenth in a series begun in 1801, and carried out every tenth year except 1941, and the ninth in which there have been reports for each county.

1.3 The Report contains statistical tables on all topics covered by the 1991 Census. Part 1 includes the results based on processing all Census returns, prefaced by a summary of the main results. Part 2 includes results based on the subsequent processing of a one in ten sample of the returns, and is published separately and later. Each of the main tables is presented for the county as a whole and for each local authority district within the county.

1.4 A similar Report is being made for each county in England and Wales, and for each Region and Islands Area in Scotland. These are being published in a series during 1992 and 1993. To complete the series, there will be a Report for Great Britain as a whole, including figures for Scotland as a whole, Wales as a whole, and for each of the standard statistical regions in England.

1.5 The contents of the Reports were designed, after extensive consultations, to meet needs for statistical facts in consistent form over the whole country on population, housing, employment, health, education, and transport. The series of Reports will serve: local and health authorities; the elected representatives of the community; business and commerce; academic research; education and teaching; local community groups; and, taking the series of Reports as a whole, central government and other national organisations.

1.6 In addition, the forms of table included in this Report were designed to be the basis of standard sets of *statistical abstracts* available, under the terms of section 4(2) of the Census Act 1920, for areas such as wards which are smaller than a local authority. Thus the results of the Census can be analysed for counties, for local authority areas, and for still smaller local areas with comparability throughout Great Britain.

1.7 The text of this Report gives brief background information on the 1991 Census, an introduction to the detailed content of the report, and guidance to assist the user. It also includes a summary of the complete programme of reports and other results from the Census. There is guidance on how to obtain further information.

1.8 This Report was made possible by the co-operation of the households and other members of the public in Avon in responding to the Census, by the hard work of the many members of the temporary Census field staff who delivered and collected the Census forms, and by other help given locally. The Registrar General is most grateful for all these contributions. They will be repaid by the value of the results of the Census both to people and organisations in Avon and more widely.

2 The 1991 Census

2.1 The Census was held on Sunday 21 April 1991, when every household in Great Britain was required by law to complete a census form. In England there were five questions on housing and 19 questions on each person, while in Wales there was one additional question, and in Scotland two further questions. People in communal establishments such as hospitals, hotels, and prisons were also included. The forms were delivered shortly before Census day by some 118,000 'enumerators', each responsible for a precisely defined area, and then collected in the following days. Enumeration went well over Britain as a whole, although some households, mainly in inner city areas, proved difficult to contact.

2.2 The first results of the Census were published in July 1991 in *Preliminary Reports* for England and Wales and for Scotland. These results were derived from summary records made by the field staff. The main processing of the Census began in June 1991. The publication of County and Region Reports is scheduled to be completed during 1993.

2.3 Preparations for the Census began well in advance, and included trials in the field. Consultation on the topics to be included took place in 1987/8 and the Government issued its plans in a Parliamentary White Paper in July 1988[1]. Parliament debated and approved plans for the Census at the end of 1989 and they became law shortly afterwards. Consultation on the form of statistical output began in August 1988, and, for the County Reports, was completed by mid 1990.

The 1991 Census Reports to Parliament will be concluded by a ***General Report*** *covering all aspects of the conduct of the Census; in the meantime more information may be obtained from the addresses given in section 13.*

3 Local results from the Census

3.1 Results have been published for local areas of Great Britain from every census since the first in 1801. Reports for each county have been published from censuses in this century. These reports have covered most of the questions asked in each successive census, but there were innovations in the way the 1991 Census County Reports were prepared.

3.2 The Census Offices planned from the outset that the 1991 County Reports should provide results from *all* the topics covered by the Census, and that there should be a single base of standard statistical tables for the Reports and for the associated statistical abstracts which would be made available for smaller areas. It was therefore possible, for the first time, to consult with users of local statistics with a focus on one main objective.

3.3 The Census Offices prepared initial proposals for the local statistics based on those produced from the 1981 Census, and invited comment from advisory groups representing government departments and local and health authorities. Meetings, which were open to all those with an interest, were also held in various parts of the country to discuss the proposals, and written comments were invited. The form of the local statistics was then developed and refined through two further rounds of consultations.

3.4 It was decided to produce two tiers of local statistics. The upper tier is the set of main tables appearing in this Report - they are also known as the 'Local Base Statistics'. This upper tier is also available as statistical abstracts for wards in England and Wales and for postcode sectors in Scotland, provided that the wards or sectors are above a minimum population size. The lower tier - known as the 'Small Area Statistics' (SAS) - is a set of some 80 tables which, for comparability, are either whole or abbreviated versions of the upper tier tables. The SAS are available as statistical abstracts for smaller areas. More information is given in Annex B.

4 The range of information in the Report

4.1 This Report gives Census results for Avon, and for the local authority districts within it, *as constituted on 21 April 1991*. The county and district boundaries are shown on the map which forms section 14. There have been changes in the boundaries of Bristol, Northavon, Wansdyke, and Woodspring districts since the Census on 5 April 1981, and these are summarised in Annex A which follows the main tables.

4.2 The starting point of the topics covered in this Report is the Census form itself. There are facsimiles of the forms used in the Census in the volume of *1991 Census Definitions* - see section 7. All the topics in the 1981 Census were included in the 1991 Census, with the exception of a separate question on outside WCs. However, the answer categories in questions like tenure and economic position (whether in work, etc) were updated. There were also new questions on ethnic group, limiting long-term illness, term-time address of students and schoolchildren, and central heating; a question on weekly hours worked was reintroduced; and information was collected to give a count of dwellings and building types. As in the 1981 and previous censuses, a number of 'hard to code' questions, such as occupation, name and business of employer, and workplace, have been processed only for a 10 per cent sample of households - see section 8.2.

---
[1] *1991 Census of Population* (Cm 430). HMSO, 1988 ISBN 010 104302 3

4.3 The Census questions for all people, whether they were in households or in communal establishments like hospitals and hotels, were:

age (date of birth)
sex
marital status
relationship to head of household*/position in establishment
whereabouts on Census night - asked in households only
usual address
term-time address of students and schoolchildren
usual address one year ago (migration)
country of birth
ethnic group
long-term illness;

and for all those aged 16 or over:

economic activity in preceding week and employment status (self-employed, employee, etc)
hours worked weekly*
occupation*
industry of employment (name and business of employer)*
address of work-place*
means of daily journey to work*
higher qualifications*.

* Analysed for a 10 per cent sample of the population - see section 8.

In Wales there was a question on the Welsh language and in Scotland a question on Gaelic.

4.4 In addition, the person filling in the form in each household was asked about:

number of rooms
'shared' accommodation
tenure
amenities (WC, bath, central heating)
number of cars and vans available
lowest floor of accommodation - Scotland only.

The name and address of the household was recorded on the form, but, apart from the postcode of the address, this information was not included in the processing operation.

4.5 If a household was absent, or no contact was made with a household which appeared to be present on Census day, the census enumerators recorded the type of accommodation and an estimate of the number of rooms and the number of residents. Absent households were asked to complete a census form voluntarily on return. Where they did so, the data from the forms have been included in the results; where they did not, data about such households have been imputed.

4.6 Each topic on the Census form is covered by tables in this Report. But one of the strengths of the Census is the facility to derive additional variables from a number of questions asked at one time. Examples of derived variables for individuals are 'socio-economic group' and 'social class' (based on occupation) and, for households, an example is the type of household by composition.

5 Finding information in the Report

The tables

5.1 Each Report contains the following tables:

Summary tables in (Part 1)

A to L All parts of Great Britain

M Areas in Wales or Scotland only (Welsh or Gaelic language)

Main tables in (Part 1)

1 to 66 All parts of Great Britain

67 Areas in Wales or Scotland only (Welsh or Gaelic language)

68-70 Areas in Scotland only (special housing tables)

Main tables in (Part 2)

71-99 All parts of Great Britain

The *main tables* are either *cross-tabulations*, that is where each element in the population is counted only once in the matrix of table *cells*, or groupings of two or more cross-tabulations of related statistics. Some additional counts are given in *single cells* which do not form part of the matrix of a cross-tabulation.

5.2 Each of the main tables has a short *key word title* which appears at the head of each page and indicates the main feature of the table, but not necessarily every aspect included. These key word titles are listed in table number order in section 16. The tables are grouped into six main subject areas:

in part 1 of the Report:

1-18 Demographic and economic characteristics

19-27 Housing

28-53 Households and household composition

54-66 Household spaces and dwellings

67-70 Scotland and Wales only tables;

and, in part 2 of the Report:

71-99 Socio-economic characteristics (tables based on the 10 per cent sample)

The *Topic and key word index* in section 16 shows where topics and cross-tabulations of topics are found.

Table conventions

5.3 In each table, the figures for the county as a whole are given first, with the local authority areas following in alphabetical order. In the larger tables, the margins are repeated for each area. To make the table content clear, the wording in the table margins is as comprehensive as possible, and abbreviations have been kept to a minimum. There are also a number of standard conventions used in the tables.

Margins (row and column headings)

The *population base* or *bases* for each table - see section 6, are shown in the banner heading over the column headings; when the table contains two or more bases, these are separated by semi-colons.

Indentation in row headings indicates that counts in that row are *sub-totals* of counts in the previous non-indented rows (equivalent to the sub-divisions of column headings).

Text set in italics signifies either that no counts will appear for that row/column, or that counts in that row/column are a *sub-set* of a previous row/column and should not be added to other rows/columns when totalling.

Total rows/columns are indicated by text in capital letters.

Counts

Counts based on full processing (Tables 1 to 70) are given without modification; a cell where the count is zero, but where a non-zero count was possible, is shown with a dash, whereas a cell for which a non-zero count is impossible is left blank. Some cells obviously duplicating others are also left blank.

Counts based on the one in ten sample of returns (Tables 71 to 99) are given as the count obtained in the sample without modification; the count must be multiplied by ten to provide an estimated figure for the enumerated population as a whole; a cell with no member of the sample population is shown with a dash, but this is not necessarily an estimate of a nil value in the population as a whole. (part 2 of the Report gives fuller guidance.)

Cross-tabulations, that is where an element of the population is counted only once, are separated by *ruled lines* within tables, as are single cell counts; where a table has a total row or column common to a number of cross-tabulations, it is usually shown only for the first cross-tabulation.

6 The populations covered in the Report

6.1 Each cross-tabulation in this Report has a *population base*, that is the total population distributed among the tabulation cells - using the term 'population' in the wider statistical sense of the items being counted. Most of the bases count people or households, but some count other items, and many tabulations have bases which are sub-sets of populations as a whole.

6.2 The tabulations count people in an area in one of two basic ways - those who were *present* on Census night, and those who were *resident* whether or not they were present. The method of counting people present is unchanged from previous censuses; the method of enumerating people resident was revised for the 1991 Census to provide a more complete count.

6.3 The Census placed a legal obligation on every household in which someone was present on Census night, and on every person present in a communal establishment, to complete a census form whether they were resident there or a visitor resident elsewhere in Great Britain or outside Britain. Additionally in 1991, for the first time in a British census, there was an arrangement to enumerate, on a voluntary basis, households where nobody was present on Census night - 'wholly absent households'. Census forms and reply paid envelopes were left for completion on the return of such households. (This part of the enumeration was on a voluntary basis because members of the absent households either would have fulfilled their legal obligation by filling in forms if they were elsewhere in Britain, or, if they were outside Britain, had no such obligation.)

6.4 In all cases of wholly absent households, or where no contact was made with a household which appeared to have been present on Census day, the census enumerator recorded the type of accommodation and an estimate of the number of rooms and residents. Where a wholly absent household did not subsequently return a form or where no contact was made with a household, values for the fully processed parts of the Census form were imputed during computer processing using the basic information returned and data on households nearby. The number of people in an area, included either on the basis of voluntary returns or by imputation, is shown in Table 1, with more detail in Table 18; the number of households included by imputation is shown in Table 19.

6.5 The addition of data from wholly absent households and non-contacted households is an improvement compared with the 1981 Census, when people from absent households were only enumerated where they were present on Census night (if in Britain). In 1981, people in wholly absent households, although included in the counts of people present, were excluded from the tables with a base of residents in the 1981 County Reports. The change to the base does, however, slightly affect comparisons between 1981 and 1991 - see section 10.

Population bases

6.6 The main population bases used in cross-tabulations in this Report are defined in full in the volume *1991 Census Definitions* - see section 7. In summary they are as follows:

Persons present in the area on the night of 21 April 1991.

Residents of the area, who are:

- people both present and resident in a household or communal establishment;
- people resident in, but absent on the night of 21 April 1991, from a household in which one or more other people were present (people resident in communal establishments but absent on Census night are *not* included since the Census forms for communal establishments covered only those people present on Census night);
- people resident in wholly absent households who returned a census form; and
- people imputed as resident in wholly absent households and in households where no contact was made (Tables A to M and 1 to 70 only).

Households with residents.

Households with people present but no residents.

Household spaces occupied by a household, or unoccupied.

Dwellings - structurally separate premises (a building or part of one) designed for occupation by a single household.

Figure 1 below shows the relationship between the elements in the population bases of *persons present* and *residents*.

6.7 In addition, there are bases of: *families* of resident persons; units of *non-permanent accommodation*; units of *converted or shared accommodation*; *rooms*; *cars in* (available to) *households*; and *communal establishments*.

6.8 Many tabulations count sub-sets of the main bases, for example, residents in households (that is, excluding those in communal establishments). Two tabulations - Tables 10 and 26 - combine more than one sub-set by including both students who were residents and those whose usual addresses were elsewhere. *Bases should therefore be checked before making comparisons between tabulations.*

Fig 1 Inter-relationship of population bases

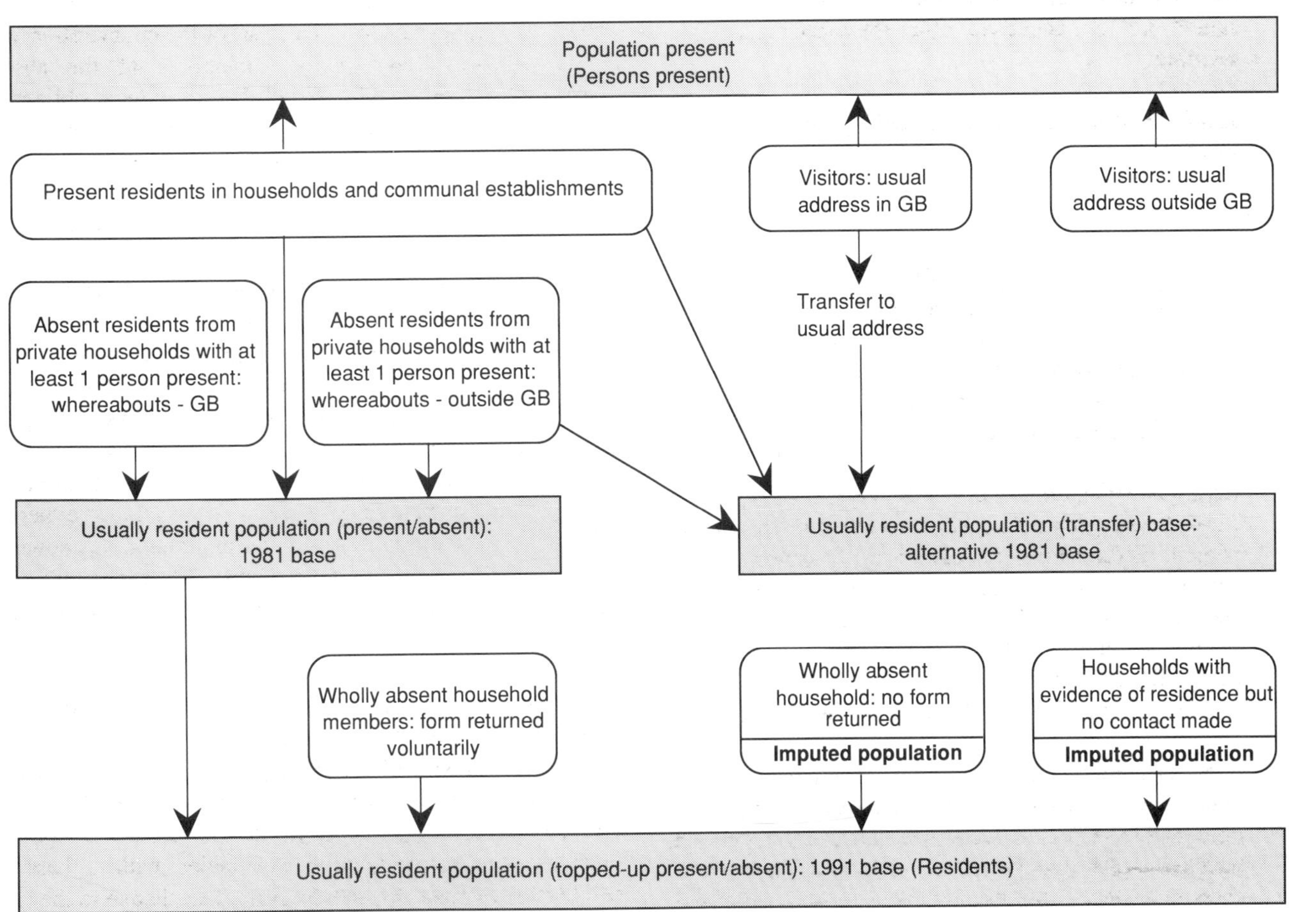

7 Definitions and explanatory notes

7.1 Definitions of all the terms used in the tables in this Report are given in *1991 Census Definitions* published by HMSO[2]. There are too many such definitions for them to be included in the text of this Report, although the terms used in the summary tables in section 15 are defined in Annex C after the main tables.

7.2 The margins of tables in this Report have been made as self-explanatory as possible, with as few abbreviations as possible. But they do not provide a complete definition of the statistics tabulated, and reference should also be made to the *1991 Census Definitions*. Reference may also need to be made to the volumes of *Definitions* for previous censuses if comparisons are being made, or to the appropriate definitions of terms in non-census sources.

7.3 Explanatory notes for the main tables, where they are necessary, are given in Annex C after the main tables.

8 The '10 per cent' sample
(Tables 71-99 in part 2 of the Report)

8.1 The answers to certain census questions, mainly those which are difficult to code because of a wide range of written responses, have been processed for a sample of a nominal one in ten returns. The questions are identified in the list in section 4. The sample is drawn from the edited records prepared during the processing of all the returns. Thus the processing of the sample follows after the full processing, and the results are published somewhat later.

8.2 The sample is drawn by randomly selecting one complete enumerated (but not imputed) household from each 'stratum' of ten sequentially numbered forms, together with one person randomly selected from each stratum of ten sequentially numbered individual forms in communal establishments. This method of sampling avoids the types of bias that can occur in field sampling, and the stratification improves the geographical spread of households included in the sample. However, the clustering of people within households tends to reduce the precision of estimates for variables such as migration or mode of travel to work where the characteristics of individuals within the same household tend to be inter-dependent. Data are not imputed for the sampled topics. *Imputed wholly absent households - see section 6 - are therefore not included in the '10 per cent' tables and the sample is therefore slightly fewer than 10 per cent* of the households included in the '100 per cent' tables. The 'sampling fraction' varies slightly from one area to another according to the proportion of imputed wholly absent households in the area.

[2]OPCS/GRO(S). *1991 Census Definitions, Great Britain.* HMSO, 1992

9 Evaluation of the results

9.1 The results presented in this Report will inevitably contain some inaccuracies arising from deficiencies and errors in coverage or response. The main causes are:

(a) failure to identify all residential accommodation;

(b) failure to identify all households and household spaces within accommodation;

(c) failure to enumerate all persons present or resident within households or communal establishments;

(d) errors in the estimates of numbers of persons in wholly absent households or where no contact was made;

(e) mis-classification of accommodation, for example, classifying wholly absent households as vacant, or vice versa;

(f) errors of double counting persons recorded as resident at more than one address;

(g) incorrect information supplied by filling in the forms, including missing responses; and

(h) errors introduced when processing the forms, including the imputation of data.

Steps are taken to assess the prevalence of these inaccuracies; but, because of the impracticability of conducting a very large number of one-to-one checks, the results are fairly broad estimates. These provide the basis of allowances for inaccuracies in the Census when the Registrar General's mid-year population estimates are made, and provide users of the Census with indications of the degree of confidence that may be placed in the Census results. The figures in Census Reports themselves are *not* adjusted.

9.2 The main check on the completeness and quality of response to the 1991 Census is provided by a Census Validation Survey (CVS). This was a voluntary sample survey conducted soon after the Census in 1,200 Census Enumeration Districts by interviewers employed in the Social Survey by the Office of Population Censuses and Surveys (OPCS). The sampling fraction for the CVS was higher in Inner and Outer London, and in the Metropolitan Counties and Glasgow.

9.3 The checks on *coverage* assessed whether:

(a) any household spaces in accommodation in the sampled areas had been missed;

(b) any of a sample of unoccupied household spaces had been mis-classified;

(c) any household in a sample of multi-occupied buildings had been missed; and whether

(d) anyone was present on Census night in a sample of households reported to have been wholly absent.

A sample of households where no contact had been made was also checked. On the basis of the coverage checks, estimates of under- or over-enumeration are being made for Inner London, Outer London, Glasgow, other Metropolitan Counties as a whole, the remaining parts of England and Wales as a whole, and the remaining parts of Scotland as a whole.

9.4 The check on the *quality* of response is provided by a further sample of households taken in the sampled Enumeration Districts. As well as checking whether everybody in the household had been included on the Census form (as part of the coverage check), the interviewer checked the accuracy of responses on the form by asking further questions, noting any explanations for differences. Analyses of gross and net differences will be prepared.

9.5 All estimates from the CVS will, of course, be subject to sampling error. Also, the CVS cannot provide a complete check on coverage and quality, even for the households included in the sample, because of changes in the circumstances of respondents between the Census and the CVS and because of incomplete response to the CVS. Despite these inherent limitations, the CVS is expected to provide much valuable information about the coverage and quality of the Census.

9.6 Results of the CVS are published as they become available, starting in summer 1992 with the first results on coverage. The full report on the CVS is scheduled to be published early in 1994. The *Census Newsletter* - see section 13, will include summaries of the main findings.

9.7 The Registrar General's mid-year estimates for local authorities in 1991 and subsequent years will take the Census counts of usual residents given in the County Reports as the starting point. The Census counts will be adjusted as necessary, the main adjustments being as follows:

(a) allowances for any estimated under- (or over-) enumeration indicated by the CVS and any other appropriate evidence;

(b) allowances for differences in the definition of 'residents' between the Census and the estimates; in particular, students are included in the estimates at term-time addresses (an extra question was included in the 1991 Census to provide a better basis for this adjustment);

(c) allowances in respect of armed forces personnel and their dependants; and

(d) the lapse of time between the Census and mid-year 1991.

The counts of residents in this Report and the 1991 mid-year population estimates will therefore not be identical. Differences should be interpreted in the light of the adjustments described above.

10 Comparisons of results with those of earlier censuses

10.1 The population of Avon at successive censuses from 1891 to 1991 is given in summary Table A in section 15. Comparisons between 1981 and 1991 are also given for selected variables in other tables in section 15.

10.2 Further comparisons between censuses are affected by changes in: the geographic base; the topics included in the censuses; and the definition of counts presented in the tables. The detail of changes over the long series of censuses is complex, and there is no single guide for users. Reports since the 1901 Census have listed intercensal boundary changes - on the lines of Annex A in this Report, and the *Guide to Census Reports*[3] describes the general changes in censuses up to 1966.

10.3 A guide to the detailed comparability of the 1971 and 1981 Census Small Area Statistics was issued after the 1981 Census (OPCS *1981 User Guide 84*[4]), but it does not cover comparison between 1971 and 1981 County Reports where they differ from the Small Area Statistics for those years. There is a similar guide on the detailed comparability of 1981 Small Area Statistics and 1991 Local and Small Area Statistics (OPCS/GRO(S) *1991 User Guide 28*[5]), and, although the Guide is not specific to the 1981 County Reports - the content of which differed somewhat from the Small Area Statistics, OPCS *1981 User Guide 86*[6] gives the link between 1981 SAS and 1981 County Report tables. It is therefore possible to determine where comparisons can be made between figures in the 1981 and 1991 County Report tables, and where comparisons must be qualified.

[3]OPCS/GRO(S). *Guide to Census reports, Great Britain 1801-1966.* HMSO, 1977. ISBN 0 11 690638 3

[4]OPCS. *Guide to Statistical Comparability 1971-81: England and Wales.* User Guide 84, OPCS Census Customer Services, 1984

[5]OPCS. *Guide to Statistical Comparability of 1981 Small Area Statistics and 1991 Local Base and Small Area Statistics - Prospectus.* User Guide 28, OPCS Census Customer Services, 1992

[6]OPCS. *1981 Small Area Statistics/County Reports. A guide to comparison. User Guide 86,* OPCS Census Customer Services, 1982

11 Further results from the 1991 Census

11.1 The results of the Census are made available in two ways:

(a) in printed reports made to Parliament and sold by HMSO bookshops (or, in a few cases, directly from the Census Offices); or

(b) in statistical abstracts available, on request and for a charge, from the Census Offices.

11.2 The results also tend to fall into two broad types: local statistics which cover the full range of census topics - such as this Report - or a summary selection of all topics; and topic statistics which focus on a particular census topic in more detail, mainly at national and regional level. There are also other products which provide further information from the Census. All the main results and products are described in *Prospectuses* in the OPCS/GRO(S) 1991 *User Guide* series, available from the addresses given in section 13. A brief guide to sources of comparable local statistics for other areas, and to sources of more detailed results on particular census topics, together with relevant *Prospectuses,* is included at Annex B.

12 Copyright and reproduction of material from this Report

12.1 All text, statistical and other material in this Report and information of any kind derived from the statistics or other material in the Report is CROWN COPYRIGHT and may be reproduced only with the permission of the Office of Population Censuses and Surveys (OPCS).

12.2 OPCS is prepared to allow extracts of statistics or other material from this Report to be reproduced without a licence provided that these form part of a larger work not primarily designed to reproduce the extracts *and* provided that any extract of statistics represents only a limited part of a table or tables *and* provided that Crown Copyright and the source are prominently acknowledged. OPCS reserves its rights in all circumstances and should be consulted in any case of uncertainty. Enquiries about the reproduction of material should be directed to OPCS at the address given in section 13, and reproduction may require a licence and payment of fees.

13 Further information

13.1 Any *queries* about the content of this Report or on the interpretation of the results in the Report should be made to:

Census Division
OPCS
St Catherine's House
10 Kingsway
London WC2B 6JP

telephone 071 396 2008

13.2 All *Prospectuses/User Guides* mentioned in this Report may be obtained (by those in England and Wales, or outside Great Britain) from:

Census Customer Services
OPCS
Segensworth Road
Titchfield
Fareham
Hants PO15 5RR

telephone 0329 813800

or (by those in Scotland) from:

Census Customer Services
General Register Office for Scotland
Ladywell House
Ladywell Road
Edinburgh EH12 7TF

telephone 031 314 4254

Census Customer Services will also arrange the supply of any statistical abstracts required.

Request to reproduce material from this Report - see section 12, should be made to Census Customer Services at OPCS.

Reports published by HMSO may be purchased from the addresses shown on the back cover of this Report.

Census Newsletter

News on all aspects of the Census, including the availability of results, is provided by the ***Census Newsletter*** *issued several times a year by the Census Offices and distributed without charge. Names may be added to the mailing list by contacting Census Customer Services. It is also possible to register with Census Customer Services as a user of the Census to obtain details of relevant products automatically and to ensure inclusion in consultation over future developments.*

14 Reference map

14.1 The map on the following page shows the boundaries of districts covered by this Report, and the boundaries of neighbouring counties. The map is reproduced from the Ordnance Survey 1:250,000 map with the permission of the Controller of Her Majesty's Stationery Office, Crown Copyright reserved.

14.2 The highlighted county/county district boundary lines were drawn by OPCS and reflect, as accurately as possible, the boundaries as constituted at 21 April 1991. As the base maps supplied by Ordnance Survey may not always reflect the latest boundary changes, the county boundary lines on the base map and the highlighted boundaries will not always correspond exactly.

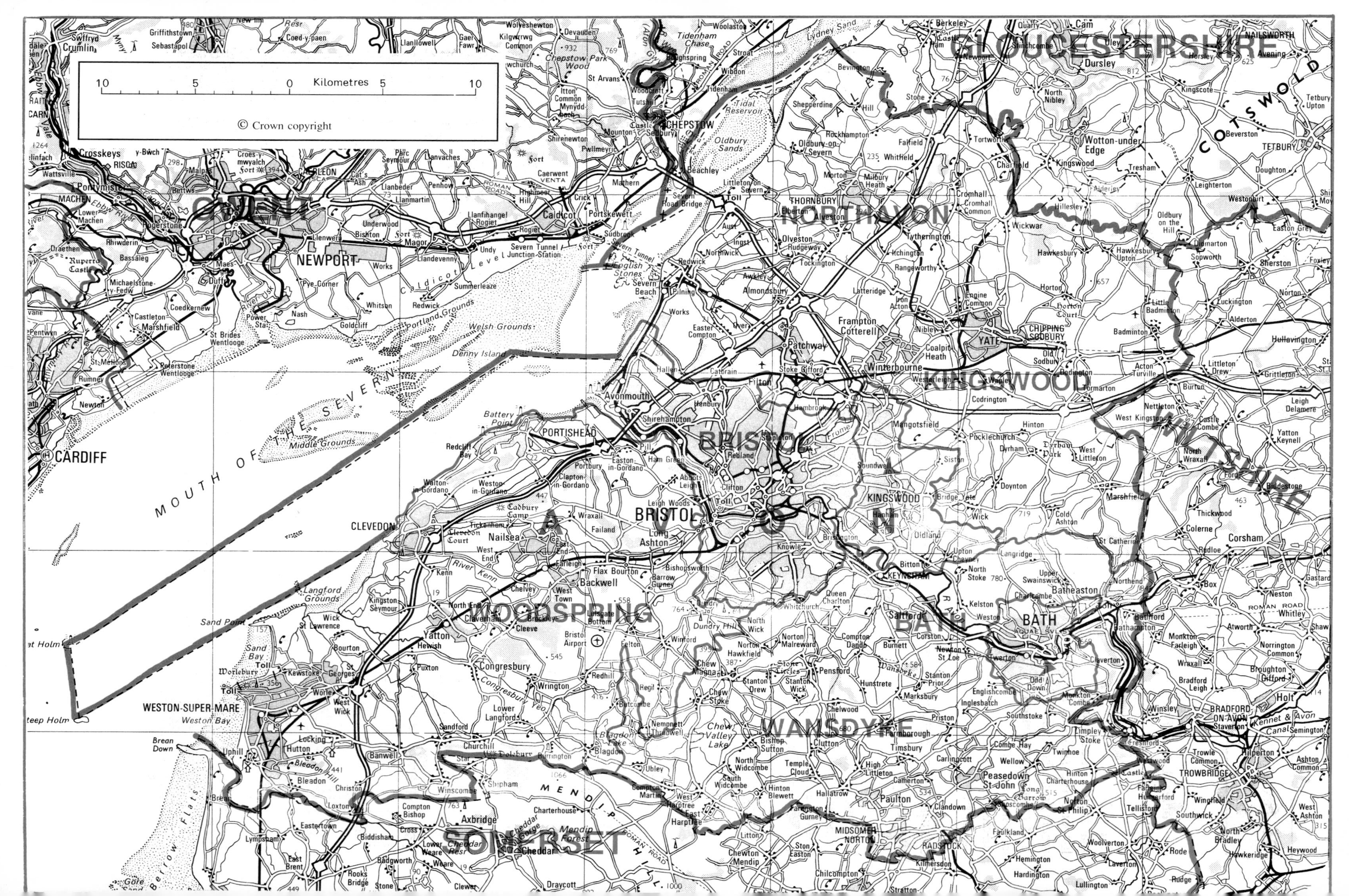

GLOUCESTERSHIRE
COTSWOLD
GWENT
NEWPORT
CARDIFF
CHEPSTOW
NORTHAVON
THORNBURY
KINGSWOOD
YATE
CHIPPING SODBURY
WILTSHIRE
BRISTOL
AVON
PORTISHEAD
CLEVEDON
WOODSPRING
WESTON-SUPER-MARE
BATH
WANSDYKE
SOMERSET
MENDIP HILLS
TROWBRIDGE
BRADFORD-ON-AVON
MIDSOMER NORTON
KEYNSHAM
Avonmouth
MOUTH OF THE SEVERN
10 5 0 Kilometres 5 10
© Crown copyright

15 Summary of 1991 Census results for Avon

The Tables A to L in this section were first published in 1992: Avon, County Monitor in August 1992.

15.1 This section of the Report contains a summary of the final figures of the population and housing in Avon and its districts. The statistics in the summary tables are derived largely from the main tables in the Report, and there is a short commentary on each summary table. In addition, the section contains: population counts from 1891 to 1991; selected measures of changes between 1981 to 1991; and a size in hectares and population density figures.

Comparisons between 1981 and 1991; terms and abbreviations

15.2 Section 6 explains the differences between the population bases used in the 1981 and 1991 Reports. The difference has necessitated the use of particular population bases in the parts of the summary tables showing change, and these are explained in Annex C after the main tables. Annex C also explains the terms and conventions used in the summary tables.

Population present on Census night (Tables A and B)

15.3 The figures of population *present* in an area include visitors to a household on Census night and exclude any residents who were away from the area on Census night. The 1991 Census showed that the population present on Census night in Avon was 924,459, an increase of about 15,600 compared with the rounded figure for 1981 - see Annex C. This represents an increase of 0.17 per cent per year in the population of the county during the decade, compared with virtually no change for England and Wales as a whole (based on preliminary figures), and with an increase of 0.04 per cent per year for the county over the period 1971-81.

15.4 The period in which there was the greatest rate of change in the county over the last century was 1891-1901, with an increase of 1.08 per cent per year. The changing size of the population present from 1891 to 1991 is illustrated by the diagram below.

Resident population (Tables C and D)

15.5 The number of people *resident* in Avon on Census night (that is, excluding visitors but including residents who were recorded as absent on Census night) was 932,674 (Table D). There was an increase of 0.4 per cent since 1981 (using the 1981 population base in each year - see Annex C). This change results principally from there being more births than deaths in the county, despite a net loss due to migration.

Population present 1891-1991 Avon

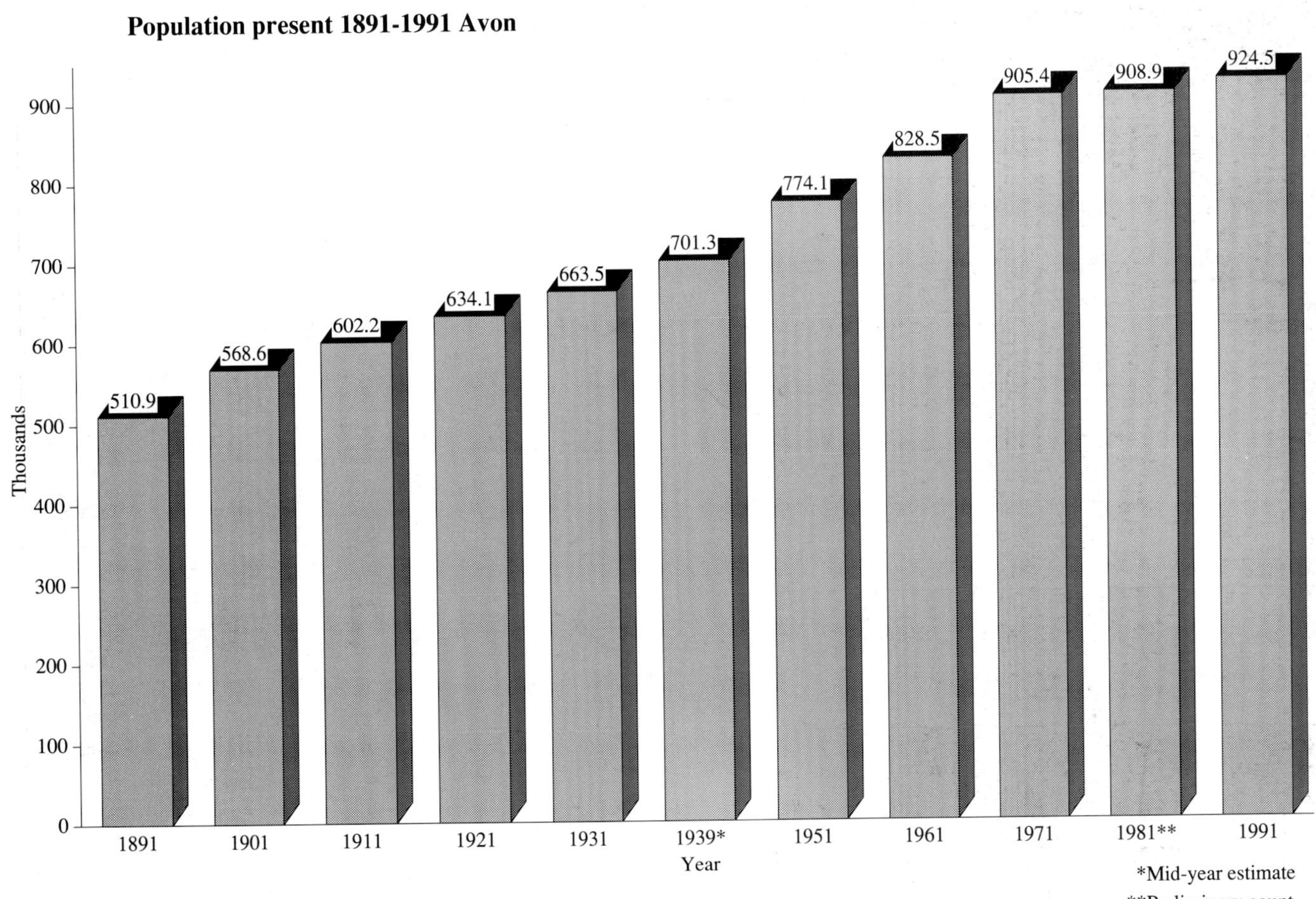

*Mid-year estimate
**Preliminary count

Percentage change in resident population (1981 population base) 1981-91: districts in Avon

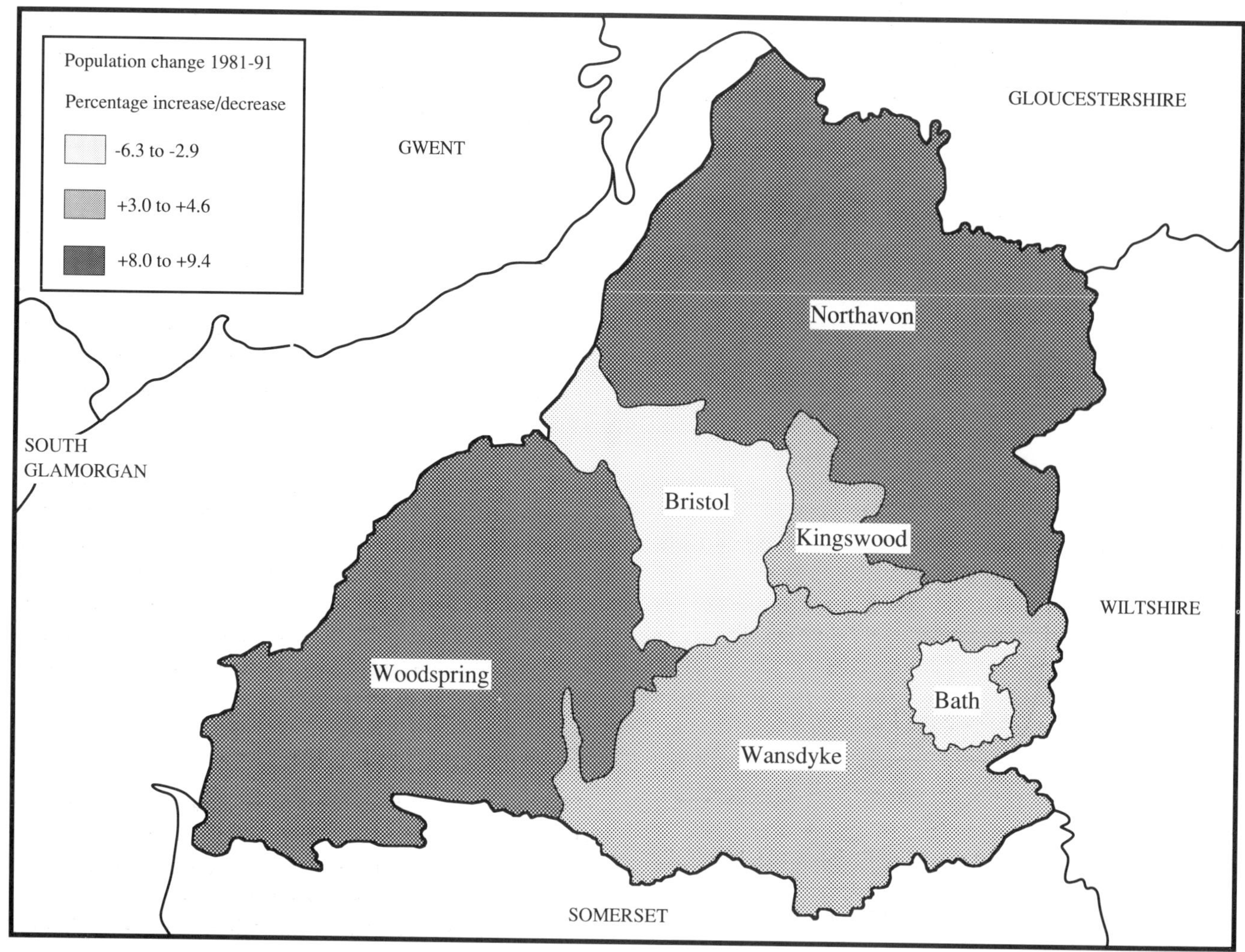

15.6 The changes between 1981 and 1991 in the resident population of the districts in Avon varied from a decrease of 6.3 per cent in Bristol to an increase of 9.4 per cent in Northavon. These changes are illustrated by the map above. The shading classes in the map have been chosen to highlight the pattern of population change in Avon, and will not necessarily be the same as those used for other counties.

15.7 The district with the largest proportion of people resident in communal establishments was Woodspring, with a figure of 2.6 per cent; this compares with 1.7 per cent for Avon as a whole.

Density of population (Table D)

15.8 People in Avon were living at an average density of 7.0 persons per hectare on Census night, compared with a provisional figure of 3.2 for England and Wales as a whole. Bristol was the most densely populated district (34.3 persons per hectare) and Wansdyke the least densely populated (2.5).

15.9 OPCS acknowledges the use of hectare figures supplied by Ordnance Survey in this table.

Children and young adults (Tables E and K)

15.10 At the 1991 Census, children (people aged under 16) made up 19.2 per cent of the population resident in Avon. The proportion was highest in Northavon (20.3 per cent) and lowest in Bath (16.7 per cent).

15.11 The proportion of the total population in households who were young adults (people aged 16-24) was highest in Northavon (13.5 per cent) and lowest in Woodspring (11.7 per cent). The proportion of young adults in households who were lone parents in 1991 was highest in Bristol (2.4 per cent).

15.12 Bath had the highest proportion of people aged 16-24 resident in households who were full-time students, 30.7 per cent, compared with 24.8 per cent for the county as a whole. Bristol was the district with the highest proportion of young adults who were unemployed, 11.2 per cent, compared with the county figure of 9.0 per cent.

Pensioners (Tables E and L)

15.13 People of pensionable age (that is, 65 years and over for men and 60 years and over for women) made up 19.4 per cent of the population of Avon in 1991, an increase of 0.8 percentage points since 1981 (using the 1981 population base in each year - see Annex C). The proportion of men and women who were aged 75 years and over increased, respectively, by 0.6 percentage points and 0.8 percentage points between 1981 and 1991. The proportion who were aged 85 years and over increased by 0.5 percentage points in the intercensal period.

15.14 The proportion of people of pensionable age in 1991 was highest in Bath (23.4 per cent) and lowest in Northavon (14.1 per cent).

15.15 In 1991, the total number of households containing at least one pensioner in Avon was 126,696. This was 33.6 per cent of all households in the county, a decrease of 1.4 percentage points from the figure in 1981. Bath, with 38.3 per cent, was the district with the highest proportion of such households in 1991.

15.16 Of all households in Avon in 1991, 25.2 per cent consisted only of pensioners; an increase of 0.6 percentage points since 1981. The districts with the highest proportion of households with at least one pensioner and which either lacked or shared basic amenities (bath/shower; inside WC) were Bath and Bristol, with 1.4 per cent.

Economic characteristics (Table F)

15.17 In Avon, 79.7 per cent of men aged 16-64 and 66.8 per cent of women aged 16-59 were in employment (full-time or part-time employees, self-employed, or on a Government scheme) at some time in the week before the Census. This was a fall of 2.8 percentage points for men and a rise of 8.5 percentage points for women since 1981 (using the 1981 population base, and the 1981 definition of students, in each year - see Annex C). At the 1991 Census 8.5 per cent of men and 4.1 per cent of women were unemployed (that is, seeking work, prevented by temporary sickness from seeking work, or waiting to take up a job already accepted). The remaining 11.8 per cent of men and 29.1 per cent of women were economically inactive. (See Annex C for further definitions.)

15.18 The proportion of men aged 16-64 who were economically active but unemployed in the week before the Census in 1991 was highest in Bristol (11.3 per cent) and lowest in Northavon (5.5 per cent). The corresponding figures for women were 5.2 per cent in Bristol and 2.7 per cent in Wansdyke.

Tenure (Table G)

15.19 The 1991 Census showed that 72.2 per cent of households in Avon were living in owner occupied accommodation (either owned outright or buying) and 16.6 per cent in accommodation that was rented from a local authority or new town association. This represents a rise of 9.6 percentage points and a fall of 8.6 percentage points respectively since 1981 (using the 1981 population base in each year - see Annex C). The proportion in owner occupied accommodation ranged from 83.3 per cent in Northavon to 63.6 per cent in Bristol.

Amenities (Table G)

15.20 In the county as a whole, 1.2 per cent of households lacked, or had to share with another household, the use of either a bath/shower or an inside WC. This represented an improvement since 1981 when the figure was 2.5 percentage points higher (using the 1981 population base in each year - see Annex C). The district with the highest proportion of such households was Bristol (1.8 per cent). The lowest proportion was in Kingswood, with 0.4 per cent.

15.21 The 1991 Census showed that 14.6 per cent of households in Avon had no central heating in any rooms though over nine-tenths of these had exclusive use of bath/shower and WC. The district with the highest proportion of accommodation without central heating was Bristol (20.0 per cent) and the lowest was in Kingswood with 7.2 per cent.

15.22 Bath had the highest proportion of households with no car available in 1991 (35.6 per cent). Northavon had the highest proportion with two or more cars (38.1 per cent). These compare with respective figures of 27.0 per cent and 27.3 per cent for Avon as a whole in 1991. Car availability had generally increased since the 1981 Census when the proportion of households with no car was 6.1 percentage points higher, and that with two or more cars 9.3 percentage points lower, than in 1991.

Overcrowding (Table G)

15.23 In 1991, 1.5 per cent of households in the county were living at a density of more than one person per room. This represents a decrease of 0.7 percentage points since 1981 (using the 1981 population base in each year - see Annex C). This figure varied throughout the county from a high of 2.0 per cent in Bristol to 0.8 per cent in Wansdyke.

Dwellings (Table H)

15.24 There were 390,113 dwellings in Avon in 1991. Of these, 17.3 per cent were detached household spaces, 29.4 per cent semi-detached, and 32.6 per cent terraced housing. 0.4 per cent of dwellings were shared - see Annex C.

Household composition (Table I)

15.25 There were 376,522 households in Avon at the 1991 Census. Of these, 12.1 per cent had at least one child aged under 5, 4.4 per cent had three or more children aged under 16, and 26.7 per cent had one person living alone. Compared with the 1981 Census, the proportion of households with a young family had increased by 0.4 percentage points; the proportion with large families decreased by 0.6 percentage points; and the proportion of single person households increased by 3.8 percentage points (using the 1981 population base in each year - see Annex C). Northavon was the district with the highest proportion of households with a young family, while Bristol had the greatest proportion with large families and Bath the largest proportion of single person households.

Limiting long-term illness (Tables E and I)

15.26 A question on long-term illness was asked in the 1991 Census for the first time. Bristol had the highest proportion of households containing at least one person with a long-term illness (23.5 per cent) while Northavon, with 17.4 per cent, had the lowest. These figures compare with 21.8 per cent for the county as a whole.

15.27 In Avon, 11.9 per cent of people had a long-term illness. This figure ranged from 13.1 per cent of persons in Bristol, the district with the highest proportion, to 8.9 per cent in Northavon, the district with the lowest.

Ethnic group (Table J)

15.28 The 1991 Census included, for the first time, a question on ethnic group. In Avon the White group formed 97.2 per cent of the population.

Summary Tables

Explanatory notes for the tables begin on the first page of Annex C, after the main tables

Table A Population present 1891 - 1991

Notes: (1) From 1961 to 1991 the figures relate to the county as constituted at 21 April 1991 and from 1891 to 1951 as closely as is possible.
(2) § Based on preliminary counts (rounded to the nearest hundred) - see notes.

Date of census	Population present	Intercensal increase or decrease (–)	
		Amount	Per cent per year
1891, April 5/6	510,881		
1901, March 31/April 1	568,564	57,683	1.08
1911, April 2/3	602,189	33,625	0.58
1921, June 19/20	634,098	31,909	0.51
1931, April 26/27	663,530	29,432	0.46
1939, Mid-year estimate	*701,257*	*37,727*	*0.68*
1951, April 8/9	774,126	72,869	0.84
1961, April 23/24	828,477	54,351	0.68
1971, April 25/26	905,368	76,891	0.89
1981, April 5/6	908,900 §	3,500 §	0.04
1991, April 21/22	924,459	15,600 §	0.17

Table B Population present 1971 - 91

Notes: (1) All figures relate to the areas as constituted at 21 April 1991.
(2) Changes since 1981 are denoted by:
* boundary
† name
\# denotes that the district has been granted borough status.
(3) § Based on preliminary counts (rounded to the nearest hundred) - see notes.

Area	Population present							Intercensal increase or decrease (–)		
	1971	1981 §			1991			Amount §	Per cent per year	
	Total persons	Total persons	Males	Females	Total persons	Males	Females	1981 - 1991	1971 - 1981	1981 - 1991
AVON *	**905,368**	**908,900**	**439,600**	**469,200**	**924,459**	**448,372**	**476,087**	**15,600**	**0.04**	**0.17**
Districts										
Bath	84,670	80,000	37,400	42,500	80,689	38,372	42,317	700	– 0.57	0.09
Bristol *	426,657	388,000	187,200	200,800	372,088	180,094	191,994	– 15,900	– 0.95	– 0.42
Kingswood #	77,808	84,000	41,400	42,700	87,754	42,809	44,945	3,700	0.78	0.43
Northavon *	104,644	118,300	58,900	59,500	129,617	64,479	65,138	11,300	1.24	0.91
Wansdyke *	70,870	76,300	37,200	39,200	79,225	38,589	40,636	2,900	0.75	0.37
Woodspring *	140,719	162,200	77,600	84,600	175,086	84,029	91,057	12,800	1.44	0.76

Table C Resident population - 1981 base

Note: The 1981 population base excludes households wholly absent on Census night.

Area	Residents (1981 population base)		Percentage increase or decrease (–) 1981 - 91		
	1981	1991	Total	By births and deaths	Migration and other changes
AVON	**900,416**	**903,870**	**0.4**	**1.5**	**– 1.1**
Districts					
Bath	77,959	75,678	– 2.9	– 2.0	– 0.9
Bristol	384,875	360,597	– 6.3	1.5	– 7.8
Kingswood	84,172	88,068	4.6	3.6	1.0
Northavon	117,011	128,054	9.4	5.7	3.7
Wansdyke	76,094	78,390	3.0	0.8	2.2
Woodspring	160,305	173,083	8.0	– 0.8	8.7

Table D Resident population and area

Note: A hectare is equivalent to 2.471 acres.

Area	Area (hectares)	Persons per hectare	Total persons = 100 per cent	Residents				
				Males	Females	In households	In communal establishments	
							Number	Percentage of total
AVON	**133,244**	**7.0**	**932,674**	**452,094**	**480,580**	**916,973**	**15,701**	**1.7**
Districts								
Bath	2,868	27.4	78,689	37,115	41,574	76,876	1,813	2.3
Bristol	10,959	34.3	376,146	181,644	194,502	370,131	6,015	1.6
Kingswood *	4,785	18.7	89,717	43,883	45,834	88,916	801	0.9
Northavon *	44,910	2.9	130,647	65,017	65,630	129,084	1,563	1.2
Wansdyke	32,245	2.5	80,003	39,058	40,945	79,122	881	1.1
Woodspring	37,478	4.7	177,472	85,377	92,095	172,844	4,628	2.6

* The Ordnance Survey area measurement (hectares) was revised after publication in the County Monitor. The figure in the persons per hectare column has been adjusted as necessary.

Table E Residents by age

Note: The 1981 population base excludes households wholly absent on Census night.

Area	Total persons = 100 per cent	Percentage aged:											Percentage of all persons with limiting long-term illness
		0 - 4	5 - 15	16 - 17	18 - 29	30 - 44	45 up to pensionable age	Pensionable age to 74	75 - 84	85 and over	75 and over		
											Males	Females	
Residents - 1991 population base													
AVON	**932,674**	**6.4**	**12.8**	**2.4**	**18.4**	**21.2**	**19.3**	**11.9**	**5.8**	**1.7**	**2.6**	**5.0**	**11.9**
Districts													
Bath	78,689	5.6	11.1	2.2	19.0	19.9	18.7	13.8	7.4	2.2	3.2	6.5	12.1
Bristol	376,146	6.9	12.5	2.2	20.1	21.1	17.5	12.0	5.9	1.7	2.6	5.1	13.1
Kingswood	89,717	6.6	13.3	2.5	17.4	22.0	21.0	11.1	4.8	1.3	2.2	4.0	10.4
Northavon	130,647	6.7	13.6	2.7	19.5	22.6	20.7	9.1	4.0	1.0	1.9	3.2	8.9
Wansdyke	80,003	5.9	13.3	2.7	15.6	21.3	21.2	12.5	5.8	1.7	2.8	4.7	10.3
Woodspring	177,472	5.8	13.1	2.7	15.5	20.7	20.4	12.9	6.7	2.3	3.0	6.0	12.9
Residents - 1981 population base													
Avon													
1981	900,416	5.7	15.7	3.4	17.3	19.7	19.8	12.2	5.0	1.2	2.0	4.2	
1991	903,870	6.5	13.0	2.5	18.3	21.3	19.3	11.7	5.8	1.7	2.6	5.0	11.8

Table F Economic characteristics

Notes: (1) * 1991 base counts include students who were also in employment, or seeking work, in the week before the Census. 1981 base counts categorise all students as economically inactive.
(2) The 1981 population base excludes households wholly absent on Census night.

Area	Total males aged 16 - 64 = 100 per cent	Percentage of males aged 16 - 64								
		Economically active*							Economically inactive	Students (economically active or inactive)
		Total	Employees		Self-employed	On a Government scheme	Unemployed			
			Full-time	Part-time						
		Residents - 1991 population base								
AVON	**297,480**	**88.2**	**62.8**	**2.5**	**13.4**	**0.9**	**8.5**		**11.8**	**5.5**
Districts										
Bath	24,232	86.2	58.0	3.3	14.8	1.0	9.0		13.8	7.8
Bristol	119,017	87.3	60.8	2.5	11.6	1.1	11.3		12.7	5.5
Kingswood	29,367	90.5	67.7	2.1	13.3	0.8	6.6		9.5	4.0
Northavon	44,703	90.1	68.5	2.0	13.4	0.7	5.5		9.9	4.9
Wansdyke	25,375	89.1	63.1	2.3	17.3	0.7	5.7		10.9	5.6
Woodspring	54,786	87.6	62.1	2.5	15.1	0.8	7.0		12.4	5.9
		Residents - 1981 population base								
Avon										
1981	282,423	90.4	69.9	1.8	10.2		8.5		9.6	5.5
1991	287,759	87.5	62.9	1.9	13.4	0.9	8.4		12.5	5.5

Total females aged 16 - 59 = 100 per cent	Percentage of females aged 16 - 59								Area
	Economically active*						Economically inactive	Students (economically active or inactive)	
	Total	Employees		Self-employed	On a Government scheme	Unemployed			
		Full-time	Part-time						
274,700	**70.9**	**36.8**	**25.1**	**4.2**	**0.8**	**4.1**	**29.1**	**6.0**	**AVON**
									Districts
22,911	72.1	36.6	24.7	5.2	0.9	4.6	27.9	8.3	Bath
110,252	70.3	38.0	22.7	3.5	0.9	5.2	29.7	5.7	Bristol
27,021	73.2	36.7	29.6	3.1	0.8	3.1	26.8	4.3	Kingswood
40,923	72.7	38.6	26.3	4.1	0.6	3.0	27.3	5.5	Northavon
23,269	70.1	34.4	26.9	5.3	0.8	2.7	29.9	6.5	Wansdyke
50,324	69.2	33.9	26.2	5.2	0.5	3.4	30.8	6.4	Woodspring
259,013	61.0	30.9	23.9	2.6		3.6	39.0	5.6	1981
266,111	69.9	36.5	24.5	4.1	0.8	4.0	30.1	6.0	1991

Table G Tenure and amenities: selected categories

Note: The 1981 population base excludes households wholly absent on Census night.

Area	Total households = 100 per cent	Percentage of households									
		Owner occupied (owned outright or buying)	Rented privately, from a housing association, or with a job	Rented from a local authority or new town	Over 1.0 person per room	Lacking or sharing use of bath/ shower and/or inside WC		Exclusive use of bath/shower and inside WC		No car	2 or more cars
						With central heating	No central heating	With central heating	No central heating		
Households with residents - 1991 population base											
AVON	**376,522**	**72.2**	**11.3**	**16.6**	**1.5**	**0.5**	**0.7**	**84.9**	**13.9**	**27.0**	**27.3**
Districts											
Bath	34,128	64.7	17.1	18.2	1.7	0.6	1.0	85.4	13.0	35.6	19.6
Bristol	156,778	63.6	14.2	22.2	2.0	0.7	1.1	79.4	18.9	34.2	20.3
Kingswood	34,657	81.5	5.5	13.0	1.0	0.2	0.2	92.6	7.0	20.3	32.8
Northavon	49,626	83.3	6.7	10.1	1.0	0.2	0.3	91.2	8.3	14.8	38.1
Wansdyke	30,814	78.8	7.3	13.9	0.8	0.3	0.5	87.9	11.3	18.6	36.9
Woodspring	70,519	79.5	9.7	10.8	1.0	0.4	0.6	87.4	11.7	22.6	32.3
Households with residents - 1981 population base											
Avon											
1981	333,597	63.0	11.8	25.2	2.2	3.6		96.4		32.8	18.5
1991	360,440	72.6	10.8	16.6	1.5	0.4	0.7	85.1	13.8	26.7	27.8

Table H Dwellings

Note: No comparable statistics available for 1981.

Area	Total dwellings = 100 per cent	Percentage of dwellings					
		Unshared dwellings					Shared dwellings
		Detached house	Semi-detached house	Terraced house	Purpose-built flat	In converted or partly converted accommodation	
AVON	**390,113**	**17.3**	**29.4**	**32.6**	**12.6**	**7.7**	**0.4**
Districts							
Bath	35,901	10.0	21.9	35.8	14.0	17.7	0.7
Bristol	162,501	5.3	26.3	41.1	16.9	9.7	0.7
Kingswood	35,595	15.5	39.0	35.3	9.2	0.9	0.1
Northavon	51,086	28.9	33.8	28.9	7.7	0.6	0.1
Wansdyke	31,914	31.8	32.7	26.0	7.7	1.8	0.1
Woodspring	73,116	33.9	30.7	16.2	9.7	9.1	0.3

Table I Household composition: selected categories

Notes: (1) * See introductory notes for the definition of a 'dependant'.
(2) The 1981 population base excludes households wholly absent on Census night.

Area	Total households = 100 per cent	Percentage of households with:					
		Child(ren) aged under 5	3 or more children aged under 16	Only 1 person aged 16 or over with child(ren) aged 0 - 15	1 person living alone	1 or more person(s) with limiting long-term illness	Only 'dependants' *
Households with residents - 1991 population base							
AVON	**376,522**	**12.1**	**4.4**	**3.3**	**26.7**	**21.8**	**7.6**
Districts							
Bath	34,128	9.7	3.6	3.4	32.8	21.2	8.3
Bristol	156,778	12.5	4.7	4.2	30.4	23.5	8.6
Kingswood	34,657	12.9	4.2	2.7	21.2	20.3	6.7
Northavon	49,626	13.4	4.4	2.3	20.1	17.4	5.0
Wansdyke	30,814	11.6	4.3	1.9	21.6	20.0	6.1
Woodspring	70,519	11.2	4.1	2.5	25.1	22.6	7.9
Households with residents - 1981 population base							
Avon							
1981	333,597	11.9	5.1	2.1	21.9		
1991	360,440	12.3	4.5	3.3	25.7	21.9	7.5

Table J Ethnic group of residents

Note: No comparable statistics available for 1981.

Area	Total persons = 100 per cent	Ethnic group - percentage									
		White	Black Carib-bean	Black African	Black other	Indian	Pakis-tani	Bangla-deshi	Chinese	Other groups	
										Asian	Other
AVON	**932,674**	**97.2**	**0.8**	**0.1**	**0.3**	**0.4**	**0.3**	**0.1**	**0.2**	**0.1**	**0.4**
Districts											
Bath	78,689	97.4	0.7	0.1	0.3	0.3	0.0	0.1	0.4	0.2	0.5
Bristol	376,146	94.9	1.6	0.2	0.6	0.7	0.7	0.1	0.3	0.2	0.6
Kingswood	89,717	98.9	0.3	0.0	0.1	0.2	0.0	0.0	0.2	0.1	0.2
Northavon	130,647	98.8	0.2	0.0	0.1	0.3	0.0	0.0	0.2	0.1	0.2
Wansdyke	80,003	99.4	0.0	0.0	0.0	0.1	0.0	0.0	0.1	0.0	0.2
Woodspring	177,472	99.2	0.1	0.0	0.1	0.1	0.0	0.0	0.1	0.1	0.2

Table K Young adults: selected categories

Notes: (1) * 1991 base counts include students who were also in employment, or seeking work, in the week before the Census. 1981 base counts categorise all students as economically inactive.
(2) The 1981 population base excludes households wholly absent on Census night.

Area	Total persons aged 16 - 24 in households = 100 per cent	Percentage of persons aged 16 - 24 in households who are:					
		Married	The only adult in household with child(ren) aged 0 - 15	Students (economically active or inactive)	Economically active*	On a Government scheme	Unemployed*
		Residents - 1991 population base					
AVON	**116,395**	**9.6**	**1.7**	**24.8**	**73.1**	**2.5**	**9.0**
Districts							
Bath	10,062	6.5	2.0	30.7	68.1	2.3	9.2
Bristol	48,365	9.1	2.4	21.8	73.6	2.7	11.2
Kingswood	10,800	9.4	1.1	20.5	78.6	2.5	7.6
Northavon	17,417	12.6	0.9	24.1	75.6	2.1	6.3
Wansdyke	9,455	9.2	0.8	28.8	71.1	2.4	6.8
Woodspring	20,296	9.8	1.3	29.9	70.1	2.2	8.0
		Residents - 1981 population base					
Avon							
1981	122,079	18.7		22.9	69.8		9.3
1991	112,622	9.5	1.6	24.8	69.4	2.5	8.9

Table L Pensioners: selected categories

Note: The 1981 population base excludes households wholly absent on Census night.

Area	All households			Households with pensioners				
		Percentage with:				Percentage of households which:		
	Total households = 100 per cent	1 pensioner living alone	2 or more pensioners and no other person(s)	Total households = 100 per cent	Total pensioners	Lack or share use of bath/ shower and/or inside WC	Have no central heating	Have no car
Households and residents - 1991 population base								
AVON	**376,522**	**14.8**	**10.4**	**126,696**	**172,148**	**1.2**	**18.1**	**48.8**
Districts								
Bath	34,128	18.3	11.7	13,078	17,668	1.4	16.3	54.5
Bristol	156,778	15.6	9.6	52,842	70,561	1.4	23.7	55.8
Kingswood	34,657	13.0	10.0	10,904	14,949	0.6	10.7	45.9
Northavon	49,626	10.4	8.4	13,037	17,856	0.7	13.7	38.5
Wansdyke	30,814	14.1	12.0	11,001	15,304	1.2	15.9	39.5
Woodspring	70,519	15.6	12.6	25,834	35,810	0.9	13.8	42.1
Households and residents - 1981 population base								
Avon								
1981	333,597	14.0	10.5	117,259	159,265	5.0		56.4
1991	360,440	14.6	10.5	121,388	165,229	1.1	18.2	48.8

16 Indexes and main tables

Tables by key word title

Summary tables

A Population present 1891-1991
B Population present 1971-91
C Resident population 1981 base
D Resident population and area
E Residents by age
F Economic characteristics
G Tenure and amenities: selected categories
H Dwellings
I Household composition: selected categories
J Ethnic group of residents
K Young adults: selected categories
L Pensioners: selected categories
M Born in Wales/Welsh speakers (Wales only)

Main tables (Part 1)

I Demographic and Economic characteristics

1 Population bases
2 Age and marital status
3 Communal establishments
4 Medical and care establishments
5 Hotels and other establishments

6 Ethnic group
7 Country of birth
8 Economic position
9 Economic position and ethnic group
10 Term-time address

11 Persons present
12 Long-term illness in households
13 Long-term illness in communal establishments
14 Long-term illness and economic position

15 Migrants
16 Wholly moving households
17 Ethnic group of migrants
18 Imputed residents

II Housing

19 Imputed households
20 Tenure and amenities
21 Car availability
22 Rooms and household size
23 Persons per room

24 Residents 18 and over
25 Visitor households
26 Students in households
27 Households: 1971/81/91 bases

III Households and household composition

28 Dependants in households
29 Dependants and long-term illness
30 'Carers'
31 Dependent children in households
32 Children aged 0-15 in households

33 Women in 'couples': economic position
34 Economic position of household residents
35 Age and marital status of household residents
36 'Earners' and dependent children
37 Young adults

38 Single years of age
39 Headship
40 Lone 'parents'
41 Shared accommodation
42 Household composition and housing

43 Household composition and ethnic group
44 Household composition and long-term illness
45 Migrant household heads
46 Households with dependent children: housing
47 Households with pensioners: housing

48 Households with dependants: housing
49 Ethnic group: housing
50 Country of birth: household heads and residents
51 Country of birth and ethnic group
52 Language indicators
53 'Lifestages'

IV Household spaces and dwellings

54 Occupancy (occupied, vacant and other accommodation)
55 Household spaces and occupancy
56 Household space type and occupancy
57 Household space type: rooms and household size
58 Household space type: tenure and amenities

59 Household space type: household composition
60 Dwellings and household spaces
61 Dwelling type and occupancy
62 Occupancy and tenure of dwellings

63 Dwelling type and tenure
64 Tenure of dwellings and household spaces
65 Occupancy of dwellings and household spaces
66 Shared dwellings

V Scotland and Wales only tables

67 Welsh language
67 Gaelic language
68 Floor level of accommodation
69 Occupancy norm: households
70 Occupancy norm: residents

Main tables (Part 2)

VI 10 per cent topics

71 Comparison of 100% and 10% counts
72 Economic and employment status (10% sample)
73 Industry (10% sample)
74 Occupation (10% sample)
75 Hours worked (10% sample)

76 Occupation and industry (10% sample)
77 Industry and hours worked (10% sample)
78 Occupation and hours worked (10% sample)
79 Industry and employment status (10% sample)
80 Working parents: hours worked (10% sample)

81 Occupation and employment status (10% sample)
82 Travel to work and SEG (10% sample)
83 Travel to work and car availability (10% sample)
84 Qualified manpower (10% sample)
85 Ethnic group of qualified manpower (10% sample)

86 SEG of households and families (10% sample)
87 Family type and tenure (10% sample)
88 'Concealed' families (10% sample)
89 Family composition (10% sample)
90 Social class of households (10% sample)

91 Social class and economic position (10% sample)
92 SEG and economic position (10% sample)
93 SEG, social class and ethnic group (10% sample)
94 Former industry of unemployed (10% sample)
95 Former occupation of unemployed (10% sample)

96 Armed forces (10% sample)
97 Armed forces: households (10% sample)
98 Occupation orders: 1980 classification (10% sample)
99 Occupation: Standard Occupational Classification (10% sample)

Topic and key word index (Part 1)

The numerical and alpha references in this index refer to county report and summary tables respectively

Absent residents
- in households *1*
- students *10*
- imputed *18, 19*

Absent households *19*

Adults
- amenities in households *42*
- economically active *36, 37*
- ethnic group of head of household *43*
- in employment *36*
- in household with long-term illness *44*
- tenure of household *46*
- unemployed *37*
- with/without (dependent) children *31, 36, 37, 42, 43, 46, 59*

Age
- all residents *2, 52, (E)*
- 'carers' *30*
- children aged 0-15 *32, 40*
- country of birth *50, 52*
- dependants *28-30, 48*
- dependent children *31, 46, 68*
- economic position *8, 14*
- ethnic group *6, 43*
- head of household *39, 45, 53*
- headship *39*
- imputed residents *18*
- in communal establishments (not in households) *4, 5, 11, 13*
- lifestage *53*
- long-term illness *12-14, 44, (E)*
- marital status *2, 35, 37, 39*
- migrants *15, 45*
- non-dependants *30*
- not in households *4, 5, 11, 13, 67*
- pensioners *47, (E)*
- persons present *11, 13*
- single years of age *38*
- students *10*
- Welsh speakers (Wales only) *67*
- young adults *37*
- 1981/1991 population base *(E)*

Amenities
- ethnic group of head of household *49*
- household composition *42*
- household space type *58*
- households with dependants *48*
- households with dependent children *46*
- households with pensioners *47, (L)*
- imputed households *19*
- no car *20*
- non permanent accommodation *20*
- selected categories *(G)*

Amenities - *continued*
- shared accommodation *41*
- student households *26*
- tenure *20*
- visitor households *25*
- 1981/1991 population base *(G)*

Area (hectares) *(D)*

Availability of cars - see *Car availability*

Bath/shower - see *Amenities*

Bedsit - see *Household space type*

Born
- in Ireland *6, 7, 9, 17, 43, 50, 51*
- in New Commonwealth *7, 50-52*
- in Scotland *7, 50, 51, (M)*
- in UK *6, 7, 50, 51*
- in Wales *7, 50, 51, 67, (M)*
- outside UK *7, 10, 50, 51*

Campers *3, 5*

Car availability
- no car
  - amenities *20*
  - ethnic group of head of household *49*
  - household composition *42*
  - households with dependants *48*
  - households with dependent children *46*
  - household with pensioners *47, (L)*
  - imputed households *19*
  - number of persons aged 17 and over in household *21*
  - shared accommodation *41*
  - tenure *20*
- number of cars *21*
- total cars *21, 25, 26*
- two or more cars *42, (G)*
- 1981/1991 population base *(G)*

'Carers' *30*

Central heating - see *Amenities*

Communal establishments *3-5, 13*

Converted flat - see *Household space type*

Converted/shared accommodation - see *Dwelling type*

Country of birth
all residents *7, 50-52*
born in Ireland *6, 7, 9, 17, 43, 49-51*
born in Scotland *7, 50, 51, (M)*
born in UK *6, 7, 50, 51*
born in Wales *7, 50, 51, 67, (M)*
born outside UK *7, 10, 50*
ethnic group *51*
household heads *49-52*

Couples
household heads *53*
women in 'couples' *33*

Density (persons per hectare) *(D)*

Dependants
age *28-30, 48*
age of non-dependants *30*
amenities *48*
household composition *29*

Dependent children/Children aged 0-15
age *31-33, 35, 40, 42, 46, 53, 59*
amenities *42, 46*
availability of car *42, 46*
economic activity of adults *36, 40*
ethnic group of head of household *43*
household composition *42, 43*
household space type *59*
in households with long-term illness *44*
non-permanent accommodation *59*
not self-contained accommodation *42, 46, 59*
persons per room *42, 46*
tenure *42, 46*

Different address one year before the Census - see *Migrants*

Dwellings
converted/shared accommodation *60, 66*
household space type *61, 63, (H)*
number of household spaces *55, 60*
occupancy type *61, 62, 65*
tenure *62-64*
type of dwelling *60, 61, 63*

'Earners' *36*

Economic activity
age *8*
ethnic group *9*
households with dependent children *31, 32, 36*
imputed residents *18*
in communal establishments *5*
lifestage *53*
lone 'parents' *40*
long-term illness *14, 44*
marital status *8, 34*
migrant heads of household *45*

Economic activity - *continued*
non-dependants *28*
women in 'couples' *33*
young adults *37, (K)*
1981/1991 population base *(F), (K)*

Economically inactive - see *Economic activity*

Economic position
age *8*
ethnic group *9*
lone 'parents' *40*
long-term illness *14*
marital status *8, 34*
women in 'couples' *33*
1981/1991 population base *(F)*

Employees - see *Economic position*

Establishments - see *Communal establishments*

Ethnic group
age *6*
country of birth *51*
economic position *9*
head of household *43, 49, 51*
household composition *43*
housing characteristics *49*
imputed residents *18*
in communal establishments *4, 5*
long-term illness *6*
migrants *17*
percentage distribution *(J)*

Exclusive use of amenities - see *Amenities*

Full-time/part-time employees - see *Economic position*

Government scheme, on a *8, 9, 14, 34, 37, (F), (K)*

Head of household
age *39, 45, 53*
age of residents in household *50*
birthplace of residents in household *50, 51*
country of birth *50, 51*
ethnic group *43, 49, 51*
lifestage *53*
marital status *39*
migrants *45, 57, 59*
tenure *45*

Headship *39*

Hectares *(D)*

Holiday accommodation *54, 55, 61, 64, 65*

Hotels and boarding houses *3, 5*

Household composition
amenities *42, 46-48*
car availability/no car *21, 42, 46-48*
children aged 0-15 *32, 33, 46*
dependants *28-30, 48*
dependent children *31, 36, 42, 44, 46, 59*
ethnic group of head of household *43*
household size *24*
household space type *59*
lifestage *53*
lone 'parents' *40*
migrant heads of household *59*
not in self-contained accommodation *46-48*
persons of pensionable age *43, 47, 59*
persons per room *42, 46, 48*
persons with long-term illness *29, 44, 47*
students *25, 26*
tenure *42, 46, 47*
wholly moving households *16*
1981/1991 population base *(I)*

Households
age of dependants/non-dependants *28-30*
age of head *45*
age of residents *39*
amenities *20, 41, 42, 46-49, 58*
car availability/no car *20, 21, 41, 42, 46-48*
economic activity/position *33, 34, 36, 44, 45*
ethnic group of head of household *43, 49*
household size (number of persons) *19, 22, 24, 26, 29, 31, 32, 36, 41-43, 57*
household space type *57-59*
imputed *19*
in not self-contained/shared accommodation *41, 42, 46-49, 57*
lone 'parent' *40*
migrant heads *45, 57, 59*
number of dependants/non-dependants *28-30, 48*
number of rooms *22, 57*
persons per room *23, 41, 42, 46-49, 57*
tenure *19, 20, 22, 23, 25, 26, 42, 45-47, 49, 58*
wholly moving *16*
with long-term illness *29, 44, 47, 49, (I)*
with no children aged 0-15 *32, 33*
with no residents *25*
with one person living alone *(I)*
with persons of pensionable age *43, 47, 48, 59, (L)*
with students *25, 26*
with/without children aged 0-15 *32, 33, (I)*
with/without dependants *28-30, 48, (I)*
with/without dependent children *31, 36, 42-44, 46, 59*
1971/81/91 bases *27*

Household size - see *Number of persons in household*

Household spaces
in dwellings *55, 60, 64-66*
occupancy type *54-56, 65*
tenure *64*

Household space type *56-61, 63, 66*

Imputed absent households *19*

Imputed absent residents *1, 18*

In employment - see *Economic activity*

Intercensal change in population
present *(A), (B)*
resident *(C)*

Irish (born in Ireland) - see *Ethnic group*

Language indicator *52*

Lifestage *53*

(Limiting) Long-term illness
age *12-14*
dependants *29*
economic position *14*
ethnic group of head of household *49*
household composition *44*
housing characteristics *47*
imputed residents *18*
in communal establishments *4, 13*
in households *12*
pensioners *47*
percentage of households *(I)*
percentage of residents *(E)*

Living alone *(I), (L)*

Lone 'parent(s)'
age *37, 48*
amenities *42, 46, 48*
economic activity *40*
ethnic group *43*
household space type *59*
imputed *19*
long-term illness *44*
migrant head of household *59*
tenure *42, 46*

Marital status
age *2, 35, 37, 39*
economic position *8, 34*
imputed residents *18*

Medical and care establishments *3, 4, 13*

Migrants
age *15*
ethnic group *17*
heads of household *45, 57, 59*
in communal establishments *4, 5*
type of move *15, 16*
wholly moving households *16*

New Commonwealth head of household *49-52*

No car - see *Car availability*

No central heating - see *Amenities*

Non-dependants *28-30, 48*

Non-permanent accommodation
- amenities *20, 58*
- household composition *59*
- household size *57*
- number of rooms *57*
- occupancy type *56, 61*
- persons per room *23, 57*
- tenure *58, 63*

Not in households
- age *4, 5, 11*
- economic activity *5*
- ethnic group *4, 5*
- long-term illness *4, 13*
- migrants *4, 5*
- non-staff *4, 5*
- persons of pensionable age *4, 5*
- persons present *3, 11*
- residents *1, 4, 5, (D)*
- staff *11*
- students *10*
- type of establishment *3-5*
- visitors (not resident) *1, 3*
- Welsh language (Wales only) *67*

Not self-contained/shared accommodation
- amenities *58*
- dependants *48*
- dwelling type *60*
- ethnic group of head of household *49*
- household composition *42, 47, 59*
- household size *41, 57*
- household spaces in shared dwellings *66*
- households with dependent children *46, 59*
- no car *41*
- number of rooms *41, 57*
- occupancy type *56, 61, 65*
- pensioners *47, 59*
- persons per room *41, 57*
- students *26*
- tenure *58, 63, 64*
- visitor households *25*

Number of persons in household (household size)
- amenities *41, 42, 48*
- ethnic group of head of household *43*
- household space type *57*
- imputed households *19*
- in employment *28, 36, 44*
- in shared accommodation *41*
- number of dependants/non-dependants *29, 30*
- number of persons aged 18 and over *24*
- number of rooms *22*
- number of students *26*
- tenure *22, 42*

Number of persons in household (household size) - *continued*
- with migrant head *57*
- 1971/81/91 population bases *27*

Occupancy type
- dwellings *61, 62, 64, 65*
- household spaces *54-56, 65*
- household space type *56, 61*
- rooms *54*
- tenure *62, 64*

On a Government scheme - see *Government scheme, on a*

Owner occupied - see *Tenure*

Part-time employees - see *Economic position*

Permanently sick *8, 9, 14, 34*

Persons aged
- 17 and over *21*
- 18 and over *24*

Persons of pensionable age
- age *43, 47, 50, 53, 59, (E)*
- 'carers' *30*
- country of birth *50, 52*
- dependants *28, 30*
- ethnic group of head of household *43*
- household space type *59*
- housing characteristics *47, 48, (L)*
- imputed residents *18*
- migrant head of household *59*
- no car *47, 48*
- with long-term illness *14, 47*
- 1981/1991 population base *(E), (L)*

Persons per hectare *(D)*

Persons per room
- ethnic group of head of household *49*
- household composition *42, 46-48*
- household size *41*
- household space type *57*
- households with migrant head *57*
- non-permanent accommodation *23*
- not self-contained accommodation *41*
- tenure *23*
- 1981/1991 population base *(G)*

Persons present
- in households *1, 11, 25-27*
- not in households *1, 3, 11, 13*
- 1891-1991 *(A)*
- 1971-1991 *(B)*

Persons sleeping rough *3, 5*

Population bases *1, 27*

Present residents *1, 3-5, 11, 13*

Purpose built flat - see *Household space type*

Rented accommodation - see *Tenure*

Resident outside UK *1*

Residents
- absent *1, 10, 18, 19*
- aged 1 and over *17*
- aged 16-24 *37*
- aged 16 and over *8, 9, 14, 34*
- aged 17 and over *21*
- aged 18 and over *24*
- imputed *18, 19*
- in communal establishments (not in households) *3-5, 13, (D)*
- present *1, 3-5, 11, 13*
- students *10, 26*
- with different address one year before Census - see *Migrants*
- 1981 base *(C)*

Rooms (number of)
- dwelling type *60*
- hotels and boarding houses *54*
- household size *22*
- household space type *57*
- in households with migrant head *57*
- occupancy type *54*
- shared accommodation *41*
- student households *26*
- tenure *22*
- visitor households *25*
- 1971/81/91 population bases *27*

Second residences *54, 55, 61, 64, 65*

Self-employed - see *Economic position*

Shared accommodation/dwellings - see *Not self-contained/ shared accommodation*

Shared/lacking use of amenities - see *Amenities*

Ships *3, 5*

Single years of age *38*

Student accommodation *54, 55, 61, 64, 65*

Students
- economically active - see *Economic activity*
- in households *10, 25, 26, 37*
- not in households *10*
- term-time address *10*

Tenure
- amenities *20*
- dependent children *42*

Tenure - *continued*
- dwellings *62-64*
- economic activity of head of household *45*
- ethnic group of head of household *49*
- household composition *42, 46, 47*
- household size *22*
- household space type *58*
- imputed households *19*
- migrant heads of household *45*
- number of persons per room *23*
- number of rooms *22*
- occupancy type *62, 64*
- pensioner households *47*
- student households *26*
- visitor households *25*
- 1981/1991 population base *(G)*

Term-time address *10*

Type of move *15, 16*

Unattached household spaces *55, 60*

Unemployed - see *Economic activity*

Unshared dwellings
- amenities *58*
- household composition *59*
- household size *57*
- household space type *60*
- number of rooms *57*
- occupancy type *56, 61, 63, 65*
- percentage of dwellings *(H)*
- persons per room *57*
- tenure *58, 63, 64*

Usual residents - see *Residents*

Use of amenities - see *Amenities*

Vacant accommodation *54-56, 61, 64, 65*

Visitors (not resident) *1, 3, 25, 26*

WC - see *Amenities*

Welsh language (Wales only) *67, (M)*

Wholly moving households *16*

Women in 'couples' *33*

Young adults *37, (K)*

1971 population base *1, 27*

1981 population base *1, 27, (B), (C), (E-G), (I), (K-M)*

Full table titles

The following notes describe how to interpret the titles, which are constructed in standard forms. Titles of simple tables which are generally a *cross-tabulation* with a single variable in the rows, but possibly have more than one variable in the columns, follow the form:

(row variable) "by" (column variable(s))

Table 7 is an example.

Titles of tables with more than one variable in the rows have the general form:

(row variables) "all by" (column variable(s))

Where cross-tabulations share a common set of total counts, this 'concatenation' is separated by a comma. Different tabulations *within* a table are separated by a semi-colon (for example, where a set of counts shares only the same population base but no common variables). Table 47 illustrates these features:

An example of a complex table illustrates these features.

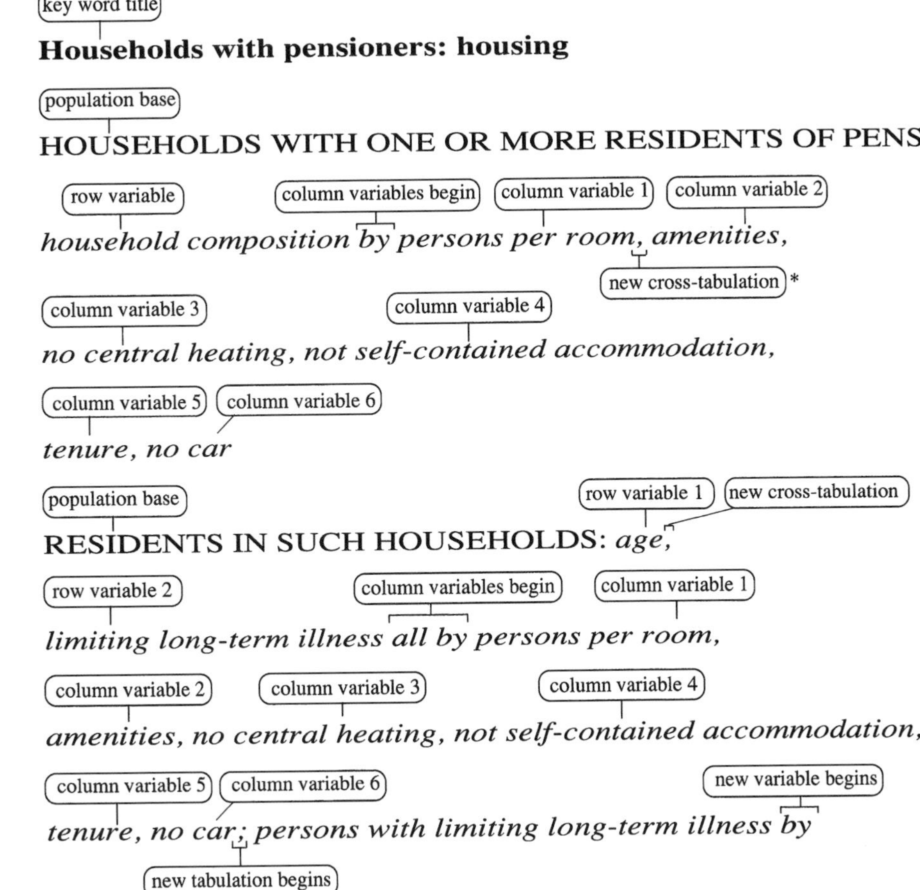

household composition

*** refers to all commas**

Where row or column variables are 'nested', that is where one variable is broken down by another along one axis of a table, they are separated by the word "by". Where this 'nesting' occurs in the rows axis, the 'nested' variables will be followed by "all by". Table 73 illustrates these features:

key word title

73 **Industry (10% sample)**

population base

RESIDENTS AGED 16 AND OVER, EMPLOYEES AND SELF-EMPLOYED:

nested variables | column variables begin

sex by age all by industry divisions

Main tables (Part 1)

Page

I ***Demographic and Economic characteristics***

1 **Population bases** 49

PERSONS PRESENT PLUS ABSENT RESIDENTS IN HOUSEHOLDS: *whether present or absent residents or visitors, 1971, 1981 and 1991 population base counts by whether in a household by sex*

2 **Age and marital status** 51

RESIDENTS: *age by sex by marital status*

3 **Communal establishments** 55

ESTABLISHMENTS: *number of establishments by type*
PERSONS PRESENT NOT IN HOUSEHOLDS: *type of establishment by status in establishment by sex*

4 **Medical and care establishments** 62

RESIDENTS (NON-STAFF) PRESENT NOT IN HOUSEHOLDS: *type of establishment by age by sex, migrants, limiting long-term illness, ethnic group*

5 **Hotels and other establishments** 66

RESIDENTS (NON-STAFF) PRESENT NOT IN HOUSEHOLDS: *type of establishment by age by sex, economic position, migrants, ethnic group*

6 **Ethnic group** 70

RESIDENTS: *age by sex, born in UK, limiting long-term illness by sex all by ethnic group, born in Ireland*

7 **Country of birth** 77

RESIDENTS: *country of birth by sex*

8 **Economic position** 84

RESIDENTS AGED 16 AND OVER: *sex by marital status for females by economic position all by age*

9 **Economic position and ethnic group** 108

RESIDENTS AGED 16 AND OVER: *sex by economic position all by ethnic group, born in Ireland*

10 **Term-time address** 115

STUDENTS (16 AND OVER) PRESENT PLUS ABSENT RESIDENT STUDENTS (16 AND OVER): *residence status by term-time address all by age, born outside UK*

11 **Persons present** 119

PERSONS PRESENT: *age by whether enumerated in a household or not by sex, status if not in a household by sex*

12 **Long-term illness in households** 123

RESIDENTS IN HOUSEHOLDS WITH LIMITING LONG-TERM ILLNESS: *age by sex*

Main tables (Part 1) - *continued*

Page

13 **Long-term illness in communal establishments** 124

PERSONS PRESENT NOT IN HOUSEHOLDS WITH LIMITING LONG-TERM ILLNESS: *age by type of establishment by sex, status in establishment by sex for residents*

14 **Long-term illness and economic position** 126

RESIDENTS AGED 16 AND OVER WITH LIMITING LONG-TERM ILLNESS: *economic position by age*

15 **Migrants** 130

RESIDENTS WITH DIFFERENT ADDRESS ONE YEAR BEFORE CENSUS: *all migrants by age, migrants in households by age, all by type of move by sex*

16 **Wholly moving households** 144

WHOLLY MOVING HOUSEHOLDS: *type of household by type of move*
RESIDENTS IN SUCH HOUSEHOLDS: *type of household by type of move*

17 **Ethnic group of migrants** 148

RESIDENTS AGED 1 AND OVER: *total persons, migrants all by ethnic group, born in Ireland*

18 **Imputed residents** 149

IMPUTED RESIDENTS OF WHOLLY ABSENT HOUSEHOLDS: *age, marital status, limiting long-term illness, economic position, ethnic group all by sex*

II Housing

19 **Imputed households** 151

WHOLLY ABSENT HOUSEHOLDS WITH IMPUTED RESIDENTS: *tenure, amenities, no central heating, no car, lone 'parent' households all by number of persons in household*
IMPUTED RESIDENTS IN SUCH HOUSEHOLDS: *tenure, amenities, central heating, no car, lone 'parent' households*

20 **Tenure and amenities** 154

HOUSEHOLDS WITH RESIDENTS: *amenities, no car all by tenure of households in permanent accommodation, non-permanent accommodation, no car*
RESIDENTS IN HOUSEHOLDS: *amenities, no car all by tenure of households in permanent accommodation, non-permanent accommodation, no car*

21 **Car availability** 168

HOUSEHOLDS WITH RESIDENTS: *household composition, by number of cars available*
RESIDENTS IN HOUSEHOLDS: *household composition; all persons and persons aged 17 and over all by number of cars available*
CARS IN HOUSEHOLDS: *household composition*

Page

22 **Rooms and household size** 170

HOUSEHOLDS WITH RESIDENTS: *tenure by number of persons all by number of rooms*
RESIDENTS IN HOUSEHOLDS: *tenure by number of rooms*
ROOMS IN HOUSEHOLD SPACES: *tenure by number of persons*

23 **Persons per room** 182

HOUSEHOLDS WITH RESIDENTS: *tenure of households in permanent buildings, non-permanent accommodation all by number of persons per room*
RESIDENTS IN HOUSEHOLDS: *tenure of households in permanent buildings, non-permanent accommodation all by number of persons per room*

24 **Residents 18 and over** 186

HOUSEHOLDS WITH RESIDENTS: *number of persons by number of persons aged 18 and over*
RESIDENTS IN HOUSEHOLDS: *total persons by number of persons aged 18 and over; total persons aged 18 and over by number of persons*

25 **Visitor households** 188

HOUSEHOLDS WITH PERSONS PRESENT BUT NO RESIDENTS: *household composition by amenities, no central heating, not self-contained accommodation, tenure*
PERSONS PRESENT IN SUCH HOUSEHOLDS: *total persons, total students all by amenities, no central heating, not self-contained accommodation, tenure; total students by household composition*
CARS IN SUCH HOUSEHOLDS: *household composition*
ROOMS IN SUCH HOUSEHOLDS: *household composition*

26 **Students in households** 190

HOUSEHOLDS WITH RESIDENTS: *household composition, number of students in household all by amenities, no central heating, not self-contained accommodation, tenure, number of persons present or resident*
RESIDENTS IN HOUSEHOLDS, PERSONS PRESENT IN HOUSEHOLDS: *total persons present or resident, total students present or resident all by amenities, no central heating, not self-contained accommodation, tenure, number of persons present or resident, household composition, number of students in household all by total student visitors, total student residents*
ROOMS IN HOUSEHOLD SPACES: *household composition, number of students in household*
CARS IN HOUSEHOLDS: *household composition, number of students in household*

27 **Households: 1971/81/91 bases** 196

HOUSEHOLDS WITH PERSONS PRESENT (1971 POPULATION BASE): *number of persons*
HOUSEHOLDS (1981 POPULATION BASE): *number of persons*
HOUSEHOLDS ENUMERATED OR ABSENT (1991 POPULATION BASE): *number of persons*
PRESENT RESIDENTS AND VISITORS (1971 POPULATION BASE): *total*
PRESENT AND ABSENT RESIDENTS (1981 POPULATION BASE): *total*
PRESENT AND ABSENT RESIDENTS AND IMPUTED MEMBERS OF WHOLLY ABSENT HOUSEHOLDS (1991 POPULATION BASE): *total*
ROOMS: *in 1971, 1981, and 1991 population base households*

Main tables (Part 1) - *continued*

Page

III Households and household composition

28 **Dependants in households** 198

HOUSEHOLDS WITH RESIDENTS: *household composition by economic position of non-dependants*
RESIDENTS IN HOUSEHOLDS: *non-dependants, dependants all by economic position of non-dependants*

29 **Dependants and long-term illness** 212

HOUSEHOLDS WITH RESIDENTS: *household composition*
DEPENDANTS IN HOUSEHOLDS: *household composition by dependency type*

30 **'Carers'** 214

HOUSEHOLDS WITH RESIDENTS: *number of non-dependants by sex by age all by ages in combination of dependants*
RESIDENTS IN HOUSEHOLDS WITH DEPENDANTS: non-dependants, dependants all by number, age and sex of non-dependants

31 **Dependent children in households** 218

HOUSEHOLDS WITH RESIDENTS: *number of adults by sex all by number of dependent children by age*
RESIDENTS IN HOUSEHOLDS: *number of adults in household by sex all by whether dependent children in household by economic activity*

32 **Children aged 0-15 in households** 221

HOUSEHOLDS WITH RESIDENTS: *number of persons aged 16 and over by sex all by number of persons aged 0-15 by age*
RESIDENTS IN HOUSEHOLDS: *number of persons aged 16 and over in household by sex all by whether persons aged 0-15 in household by economic activity*

33 **Women in 'couples': economic position** 224

FEMALES RESIDENT IN HOUSEHOLDS OF ONE MALE AGED 16 OR OVER AND ONE FEMALE AGED 16 OR OVER WITH OR WITHOUT PERSONS AGED 0-15: *ages in combination of persons aged under 16 by economic activity*
PERSONS AGED 0-15 IN SUCH HOUSEHOLDS: *age by economic position of female aged 16 or over*

34 **Economic position of household residents** 226

RESIDENTS AGED 16 AND OVER IN HOUSEHOLDS: *economic position by sex by marital status*

35 **Age and marital status of household residents** 229

RESIDENTS IN HOUSEHOLDS: *age by sex by marital status*

36 **'Earners' and dependent children** 233

HOUSEHOLDS WITH RESIDENTS: *number and economic position of adults all by number of dependent children*
RESIDENT ADULTS: *economic position by number of dependent children in household*
RESIDENT DEPENDENT CHILDREN: *number and economic position of adults in household*

Main tables (Part 1) - *continued*

Page

37 **Young adults** 236

RESIDENTS AGED 16-24 IN HOUSEHOLDS: *age by marital status, lone 'parents' with children aged 0-15, economic position*

38 **Single years of age** 238

RESIDENTS IN HOUSEHOLDS: *age by sex*

39 **Headship** 245

RESIDENTS IN HOUSEHOLDS: *age by sex by marital status; persons by household head's age, sex and marital status*

40 **Lone 'parents'** 249

LONE 'PARENTS' AGED 16 AND OVER IN HOUSEHOLDS OF ONE PERSON AGED 16 AND OVER WITH PERSON(S) AGED 0-15: *ages of children in combination by sex by economic position*
PERSONS AGED 0-15 IN SUCH HOUSEHOLDS: *age by sex by economic position of lone 'parent'*

41 **Shared accommodation** 252

HOUSEHOLDS WITH RESIDENTS NOT IN SELF-CONTAINED ACCOMMODATION: *number of persons by persons per room, amenities, central heating, no car*
ROOMS IN SUCH HOUSEHOLDS: *number of persons*

42 **Household composition and housing** 254

HOUSEHOLDS WITH RESIDENTS: *household composition by persons per room, amenities, no central heating, not self-contained accommodation, tenure, car availability*
DEPENDENT CHILDREN IN HOUSEHOLDS: *age by persons per room, amenities, no central heating, not self-contained accommodation, tenure, car availability*

43 **Household composition and ethnic group** 260

HOUSEHOLDS WITH RESIDENTS: *household composition, pensioner households all by ethnic group of head of household, household head born in Ireland*
RESIDENTS IN HOUSEHOLDS: *age by ethnic group of head of household, household head born in Ireland*

44 **Household composition and long-term illness** 268

HOUSEHOLDS CONTAINING PERSONS WITH LIMITING LONG-TERM ILLNESS: *household composition, economic position of household members*
RESIDENTS IN SUCH HOUSEHOLDS: *household composition, economic position of household members, economic position all by limiting long-term illness by age by sex*

45 **Migrant household heads** 276

HOUSEHOLDS WITH RESIDENTS: *tenure by household heads, economic activity all by age by sex of migrant heads, age by sex of all household heads*

Main tables (Part 1) - *continued*

Page

46 **Households with dependent children: housing** 284

HOUSEHOLDS WITH DEPENDENT CHILDREN: *household composition by persons per room, amenities, no central heating, not self-contained accommodation, tenure, no car*
RESIDENTS IN SUCH HOUSEHOLDS: *household composition by age all by persons per room, amenities, no central heating, not self-contained accommodation, tenure, no car; household composition*

47 **Households with pensioners: housing** 292

HOUSEHOLDS WITH ONE OR MORE RESIDENTS OF PENSIONABLE AGE: *household composition by persons per room, amenities, no central heating, not self-contained accommodation, tenure, no car*
RESIDENTS IN SUCH HOUSEHOLDS: *age, limiting long-term illness all by persons per room, amenities, no central heating, not self-contained accommodation, tenure, no car; persons with limiting long-term illness by household composition*

48 **Households with dependants: housing** 300

HOUSEHOLDS WITH RESIDENTS: *non-dependants and dependants by age of youngest and oldest dependants in combination all by persons per room, amenities, no central heating, not self-contained accommodation, no car*

49 **Ethnic group: housing** 307

HOUSEHOLDS WITH RESIDENTS: *persons per room, tenure, amenities, no central heating, not self-contained accommodation, no car, containing person(s) with limiting long-term illness all by ethnic group of household head, country of birth of household head*
RESIDENTS IN HOUSEHOLDS: persons per room, amenities, no central heating, not self-contained accommodation, no car all by ethnic group of household head, country of birth of household head

50 **Country of birth: household heads and residents** 314

RESIDENTS IN HOUSEHOLDS: *country of birth of household head by age, by country of birth of persons*
HOUSEHOLD HEADS: *country of birth*

51 **Country of birth and ethnic group** 322

RESIDENTS IN HOUSEHOLDS: *country of birth by ethnic group; country of birth of household heads by ethnic group of persons*
HOUSEHOLD HEADS: *country of birth by ethnic group*

52 **Language indicators** 333

RESIDENTS: *whether in a household by age all by country of birth, country of birth of household head*

53 **'Lifestages'** 335

RESIDENTS AGED 16 AND OVER IN HOUSEHOLDS: *age and household composition (lifestage category) all by whether in a 'couple' household*

Main tables (Part 1) - *continued* **Page**

IV Household spaces and dwellings

54 **Occupancy (occupied, vacant, and other accommodation)** 338

HOUSEHOLD SPACES: *occupancy type*
ROOMS IN HOUSEHOLD SPACES: *occupancy type*
ROOMS IN HOTELS AND BOARDING HOUSES: *total*

55 **Household spaces and occupancy** 340

HOUSEHOLD SPACES IN PERMANENT BUILDINGS: *occupancy type by number of household spaces in dwelling, unattached household spaces (not in a dwelling)*
DWELLINGS: *number of household spaces in dwelling*

56 **Household space type and occupancy** 344

HOUSEHOLD SPACES: *occupancy type by household space type in permanent buildings, non-permanent accommodation*

57 **Household space type: rooms and household size** 348

HOUSEHOLDS WITH RESIDENTS: *number of rooms, number of persons, persons per room all by household space type in permanent buildings, non-permanent accommodation, with migrant head*
RESIDENTS IN HOUSEHOLDS: *household space type in permanent buildings, non-permanent accommodation, with migrant head*
ROOMS IN HOUSEHOLD SPACES: *household space type in permanent buildings, non-permanent accommodation, with migrant head*

58 **Household space type: tenure and amenities** 355

HOUSEHOLDS WITH RESIDENTS: *tenure, amenities all by household space type in permanent buildings, non-permanent accommodation*

59 **Household space type: household composition** 362

HOUSEHOLDS WITH RESIDENTS: *household composition, pensioner households all by household space type in permanent buildings, non-permanent accommodation, with migrant head*
RESIDENTS IN HOUSEHOLDS: *age by household space type in permanent buildings, non-permanent accommodation, with migrant head; persons in households with migrant head by household composition, pensioner households*

60 **Dwellings and household spaces** 370

CONVERTED OR SHARED ACCOMMODATION (MULTI-OCCUPIED BUILDINGS): *number and type of dwellings*
DWELLINGS: *number and type in building by number of household spaces*
HOUSEHOLD SPACES: *number and type of dwellings in building by unattached household spaces, household space type*
ROOMS IN SUCH ACCOMMODATION: *number and type of dwellings in building*

61 **Dwelling type and occupancy** 374

DWELLINGS: *occupancy type by type of dwelling*
NON-PERMANENT ACCOMMODATION: *occupancy type*

Main tables (Part 1) - *continued*

Page

62 **Occupancy and tenure of dwellings** 378

DWELLINGS WITH PERSONS PRESENT OR RESIDENT: *occupancy type by tenure*

63 **Dwelling type and tenure** 380

DWELLINGS WITH RESIDENTS: *tenure by type of dwelling*
NON-PERMANENT ACCOMMODATION: *tenure*

64 **Tenure of dwellings and household spaces** 383

DWELLINGS: *tenure or occupancy type by type of dwelling*
HOUSEHOLD SPACES IN DWELLINGS: *tenure or occupancy type of dwelling by tenure or occupancy type of household spaces*

65 **Occupancy of dwellings and household spaces** 387

DWELLINGS: *occupancy type by type of dwelling*
HOUSEHOLD SPACES IN DWELLINGS: *occupancy type of dwelling by occupancy type of household spaces*

66 **Shared dwellings** 394

SHARED DWELLINGS: *number of household spaces within dwelling*
HOUSEHOLD SPACES IN SHARED DWELLINGS: *number of household spaces in dwelling by type of household spaces*

V Wales only tables

67 **Welsh language**

RESIDENTS: *age, not in households, born in Wales all by speaking, reading, writing Welsh, sex*

Main Tables (Part 2)

VI 10 per cent topics

Page numbers for tables are given in Part 2 of the report published separately and later.

71 **Comparison of 100% and 10% counts**

RESIDENTS: *100% and 10% sample counts all by whether in households, whether imputed residents in a wholly absent household*
HOUSEHOLDS WITH RESIDENTS: *100% and 10% counts all by whether imputed wholly absent households*

72 **Economic and employment status (10% sample)**

RESIDENTS AGED 16 AND OVER: *economic position and employment status all by sex, students (economically active or inactive)*

73 **Industry (10% sample)**

RESIDENTS AGED 16 AND OVER, EMPLOYEES AND SELF-EMPLOYED: *sex, by age all by industry divisions*

Main tables (Part 2) - *continued*

74 **Occupation (10% sample)**

RESIDENTS AGED 16 AND OVER, EMPLOYEES AND SELF-EMPLOYED: *Standard Occupational Classification sub-major groups by sex, by age*

75 **Hours worked (10% sample)**

RESIDENTS AGED 16 AND OVER, EMPLOYEES AND SELF-EMPLOYED: *sex, by age, sex by marital status, limiting long-term illness by sex all by hours worked weekly*

76 **Occupation and industry (10% sample)**

RESIDENTS AGED 16 AND OVER, EMPLOYEES AND SELF-EMPLOYED: *Standard Occupational Classification sub-major groups, working outside district of usual residence all by industry divisions, working outside district of usual residence*

77 **Industry and hours worked (10% sample)**

RESIDENTS AGED 16 AND OVER, EMPLOYEES AND SELF-EMPLOYED: *hours worked weekly by industry divisions*

78 **Occupation and hours worked (10% sample)**

RESIDENTS AGED 16 AND OVER, EMPLOYEES AND SELF-EMPLOYED: *Standard Occupational Classification sub-major groups, working outside district of usual residence all by hours worked weekly*

79 **Industry and employment status (10% sample)**

RESIDENTS AGED 16 AND OVER, EMPLOYEES AND SELF-EMPLOYED: *sex, by employment status all by industry divisions*

80 **Working parents: hours worked (10% sample)**

WOMEN IN COUPLE FAMILIES AND LONE PARENTS IN EMPLOYMENT: *family composition by hours worked weekly*

81 **Occupation and employment status (10% sample)**

RESIDENTS AGED 16 AND OVER, EMPLOYEES AND SELF-EMPLOYED: *sex, by employment status all by Standard Occupational Classification major groups*

82 **Travel to work and SEG (10% sample)**

RESIDENTS AGED 16 AND OVER, EMPLOYEES AND SELF-EMPLOYED: *socio-economic group, working outside district of usual residence, car availability by means of transport to work, working outside district of usual residence*

83 **Travel to work and car availability (10% sample)**

HOUSEHOLDS WITH RESIDENTS AGED 16 AND OVER, EMPLOYEES AND SELF-EMPLOYED: *car availability by number of resident employees or self-employed aged 16 and over by means of transport to work*

84 **Qualified manpower (10% sample)**

RESIDENTS AGED 18 AND OVER: *level of highest qualification, by age, economic position all by sex*

85 **Ethnic group of qualified manpower (10% sample)**

RESIDENTS AGED 16 AND OVER: *whether qualified, by age, economic position all by ethnic group, born in Ireland*

86 **SEG of households and families (10% sample)**

HOUSEHOLDS WITH RESIDENTS: *socio-economic group by tenure, migrant head of household, no car*
RESIDENTS IN HOUSEHOLDS: *total, economically active, dependent children all by tenure, migrant head of household, no car, in families, in lone parent with dependent child(ren) families; socio-economic group by economically active, dependent children, adults with limiting long-term illness*
FAMILIES OF RESIDENT PERSONS: *socio-economic group by total, lone parent families with dependent child(ren) by socio-economic group*

87 **Family type and tenure (10% sample)**

HOUSEHOLDS WITH RESIDENTS: *household and family composition by tenure, migrant head of household, car availability*
RESIDENTS IN HOUSEHOLDS: *dependent children aged 0-17 in lone parent families by tenure, migrant head of household, car availability; household and family composition by total, dependent children*

88 **'Concealed' families (10% sample)**

FAMILIES OF RESIDENT PERSONS: *family composition by age of head of household; composition of concealed families by age of head of family*

89 **Family composition (10% sample)**

FAMILIES OF RESIDENT PERSONS: *family composition, in households with two or more families by type of family*

90 **Social class of households (10% sample)**

HOUSEHOLDS WITH RESIDENTS: *social class based on occupation of household head, household head on a Government scheme, economic position of economically inactive heads*
RESIDENTS IN HOUSEHOLDS: *social class based on occupation of household head, household head on a Government scheme, economic position of economically inactive heads all by age, females in couples*

91 **Social class and economic position (10% sample)**

RESIDENTS AGED 16 AND OVER IN HOUSEHOLDS: *social class based on occupation, on a Government scheme, economic position of the economically inactive all by economic position, by sex, females in a couple*

92 **SEG and economic position (10% sample)**

ECONOMICALLY ACTIVE RESIDENTS: *socio-economic group, on a Government scheme all by economic position by sex , migrants, by sex*

93 **SEG, social class and ethnic group (10% sample)**

RESIDENTS AGED 16 AND OVER, EMPLOYEES AND SELF-EMPLOYED: *socio-economic group, social class based on occupation all by ethnic group, born in Ireland*

Main tables (Part 2) - *continued*

94 **Former industry of unemployed (10% sample)**

RESIDENTS ON A GOVERNMENT SCHEME OR UNEMPLOYED: *sex, by industry division of most recent job in last 10 years*

95 **Former occupation of unemployed (10% sample)**

RESIDENTS ON A GOVERNMENT SCHEME OR UNEMPLOYED: *sex by Standard Occupational Classification major group of most recent job in last 10 years*

96 **Armed forces (10% sample)**

RESIDENT ARMED FORCES, IN EMPLOYMENT: *age by whether in households by sex; age of migrants by type of move by whether in households*

97 **Armed forces: households (10% sample)**

RESIDENTS IN HOUSEHOLDS WITH HEAD IN EMPLOYMENT IN ARMED FORCES: *household heads: age, migrants all by marital status by sex; all persons: age, migrants all by marital status, by sex*

98 **Occupation orders: 1980 classification (10% sample)**

RESIDENTS AGED 16 AND OVER, EMPLOYEES AND SELF-EMPLOYED: *1980 occupation orders by sex*

99 **Occupation: Standard Occupational Classification (10% sample)**

RESIDENTS AGED 16 AND OVER, EMPLOYEES AND SELF EMPLOYED: *Standard Occupational Classification minor groups by sex*

Main Tables

Explanatory notes for tables appear in Annex C, after the tables. Notes are in the numerical order of the tables.

Table 1 Population bases

County, districts

Note: * All tables for residents on 100% topics are on this population base

1. Persons present plus absent residents, in households

	TOTAL PERSONS	In households			Not in households		
		Total	Males	Females	Total	Males	Females
a	b	c	d	e	f	g	h
AVON							
1 Present residents	887,639	871,938	423,089	448,849	15,701	6,345	9,356
2 Absent residents (part of household present)	16,231	16,231	8,906	7,325			
3 Absent residents (wholly absent household - enumerated)	12,149	12,149	5,753	6,396			
4 Absent residents (wholly absent household - imputed)	16,655	16,655	8,001	8,654			
5 Visitors	36,820	22,333	11,158	11,175	14,487	7,780	6,707
Resident in UK	32,008	19,389	9,754	9,635	12,619	6,693	5,926
Resident outside UK	4,812	2,944	1,404	1,540	1,868	1,087	781
PERSONS PRESENT 1991: 1971 BASE (1+5)	924,459	894,271	434,247	460,024	30,188	14,125	16,063
RESIDENTS 1991: 1981 BASE (1+2)	903,870	888,169	431,995	456,174	15,701	6,345	9,356
RESIDENTS 1991: 1991 BASE (1+2+3+4)*	932,674	916,973	445,749	471,224	15,701	6,345	9,356
Bath							
1 Present residents	73,808	71,995	34,114	37,881	1,813	686	1,127
2 Absent residents (part of household present)	1,870	1,870	969	901			
3 Absent residents (wholly absent household - enumerated)	1,286	1,286	565	721			
4 Absent residents (wholly absent household - imputed)	1,725	1,725	781	944			
5 Visitors	6,881	3,432	1,628	1,804	3,449	1,944	1,505
Resident in UK	5,814	2,870	1,377	1,493	2,944	1,670	1,274
Resident outside UK	1,067	562	251	311	505	274	231
PERSONS PRESENT 1991: 1971 BASE (1+5)	80,689	75,427	35,742	39,685	5,262	2,630	2,632
RESIDENTS 1991: 1981 BASE (1+2)	75,678	73,865	35,083	38,782	1,813	686	1,127
RESIDENTS 1991: 1991 BASE (1+2+3+4)*	78,689	76,876	36,429	40,447	1,813	686	1,127
Bristol							
1 Present residents	354,791	348,776	168,380	180,396	6,015	2,605	3,410
2 Absent residents (part of household present)	5,806	5,806	3,147	2,659			
3 Absent residents (wholly absent household - enumerated)	4,969	4,969	2,363	2,606			
4 Absent residents (wholly absent household - imputed)	10,580	10,580	5,149	5,431			
5 Visitors	17,297	11,159	5,776	5,383	6,138	3,333	2,805
Resident in UK	15,247	9,986	5,232	4,754	5,261	2,814	2,447
Resident outside UK	2,050	1,173	544	629	877	519	358
PERSONS PRESENT 1991: 1971 BASE (1+5)	372,088	359,935	174,156	185,779	12,153	5,938	6,215
RESIDENTS 1991: 1981 BASE (1+2)	360,597	354,582	171,527	183,055	6,015	2,605	3,410
RESIDENTS 1991: 1991 BASE (1+2+3+4)*	376,146	370,131	179,039	191,092	6,015	2,605	3,410
Kingswood							
1 Present residents	86,833	86,032	42,027	44,005	801	321	480
2 Absent residents (part of household present)	1,235	1,235	738	497			
3 Absent residents (wholly absent household - enumerated)	938	938	457	481			
4 Absent residents (wholly absent household - imputed)	711	711	340	371			
5 Visitors	921	884	445	439	37	16	21
Resident in UK	807	772	394	378	35	14	21
Resident outside UK	114	112	51	61	2	2	-
PERSONS PRESENT 1991: 1971 BASE (1+5)	87,754	86,916	42,472	44,444	838	337	501
RESIDENTS 1991: 1981 BASE (1+2)	88,068	87,267	42,765	44,502	801	321	480
RESIDENTS 1991: 1991 BASE (1+2+3+4)*	89,717	88,916	43,562	45,354	801	321	480

Note: * All tables for residents on 100% topics are on this population base

1. Persons present plus absent residents, in households

	TOTAL PERSONS	In households			Not in households		
		Total	Males	Females	Total	Males	Females
a	b	c	d	e	f	g	h
Northavon							
1 Present residents	125,725	124,162	61,699	62,463	1,563	740	823
2 Absent residents (part of household present)	2,329	2,329	1,311	1,018			
3 Absent residents (wholly absent household - enumerated)	1,510	1,510	743	767			
4 Absent residents (wholly absent household - imputed)	1,083	1,083	524	559			
5 Visitors	3,892	2,152	1,045	1,107	1,740	995	745
Resident in UK	3,300	1,820	877	943	1,480	839	641
Resident outside UK	592	332	168	164	260	156	104
PERSONS PRESENT 1991: 1971 BASE (1+5)	129,617	126,314	62,744	63,570	3,303	1,735	1,568
RESIDENTS 1991: 1981 BASE (1+2)	128,054	126,491	63,010	63,481	1,563	740	823
RESIDENTS 1991: 1991 BASE (1+2+3+4)*	130,647	129,084	64,277	64,807	1,563	740	823
Wansdyke							
1 Present residents	76,874	75,993	37,259	38,734	881	204	677
2 Absent residents (part of household present)	1,516	1,516	828	688			
3 Absent residents (wholly absent household - enumerated)	1,016	1,016	482	534			
4 Absent residents (wholly absent household - imputed)	597	597	285	312			
5 Visitors	2,351	1,463	709	754	888	417	471
Resident in UK	2,039	1,251	601	650	788	350	438
Resident outside UK	312	212	108	104	100	67	33
PERSONS PRESENT 1991: 1971 BASE (1+5)	79,225	77,456	37,968	39,488	1,769	621	1,148
RESIDENTS 1991: 1981 BASE (1+2)	78,390	77,509	38,087	39,422	881	204	677
RESIDENTS 1991: 1991 BASE (1+2+3+4)*	80,003	79,122	38,854	40,268	881	204	677
Woodspring							
1 Present residents	169,608	164,980	79,610	85,370	4,628	1,789	2,839
2 Absent residents (part of household present)	3,475	3,475	1,913	1,562			
3 Absent residents (wholly absent household - enumerated)	2,430	2,430	1,143	1,287			
4 Absent residents (wholly absent household - imputed)	1,959	1,959	922	1,037			
5 Visitors	5,478	3,243	1,555	1,688	2,235	1,075	1,160
Resident in UK	4,801	2,690	1,273	1,417	2,111	1,006	1,105
Resident outside UK	677	553	282	271	124	69	55
PERSONS PRESENT 1991: 1971 BASE (1+5)	175,086	168,223	81,165	87,058	6,863	2,864	3,999
RESIDENTS 1991: 1981 BASE (1+2)	173,083	168,455	81,523	86,932	4,628	1,789	2,839
RESIDENTS 1991: 1991 BASE (1+2+3+4)*	177,472	172,844	83,588	89,256	4,628	1,789	2,839

2. Residents

Age	TOTAL PERSONS	Males					Females				
		Total	Single	Married	Widowed	Divorced	Total	Single	Married	Widowed	Divorced
a	b	c	d	e	f	g	h	i	j	k	l
					AVON						
ALL AGES	**932,674**	**452,094**	**201,250**	**218,293**	**12,711**	**19,840**	**480,580**	**179,692**	**220,044**	**53,768**	**27,076**
0 - 4	59,984	30,811	30,811				29,173	29,173			
5 - 9	55,604	28,497	28,497				27,107	27,107			
10 - 14	53,176	27,260	27,260				25,916	25,916			
15	10,557	5,412	5,412				5,145	5,145			
16 - 17	22,569	11,611	11,585	23	1	2	10,958	10,910	39	3	6
18 - 19	25,057	12,749	12,653	82	1	13	12,308	12,008	285	4	11
20 - 24	71,000	35,464	31,889	3,398	7	170	35,536	27,646	7,367	40	483
25 - 29	75,814	37,663	21,039	15,476	20	1,128	38,151	15,294	20,661	76	2,120
30 - 34	67,661	33,633	9,697	21,584	42	2,310	34,028	6,579	23,966	130	3,353
35 - 39	62,032	30,897	5,462	22,580	65	2,790	31,135	3,412	23,831	211	3,681
40 - 44	68,417	34,113	4,131	26,593	139	3,250	34,304	2,231	27,204	443	4,426
45 - 49	58,706	29,453	2,719	23,668	237	2,829	29,253	1,486	23,513	731	3,523
50 - 54	50,372	25,271	1,991	20,652	313	2,315	25,101	1,228	20,127	1,140	2,606
55 - 59	47,500	23,574	1,874	19,459	500	1,741	23,926	1,253	18,371	2,173	2,129
60 - 64	47,469	23,052	1,898	18,791	1,021	1,342	24,417	1,560	17,118	4,119	1,620
65 - 69	47,120	21,659	1,666	17,381	1,690	922	25,461	1,760	15,388	7,005	1,308
70 - 74	39,115	16,814	1,121	12,977	2,140	576	22,301	1,722	10,894	8,828	857
75 - 79	32,325	12,824	789	9,285	2,466	284	19,501	1,898	6,790	10,247	566
80 - 84	22,007	7,414	494	4,569	2,225	126	14,593	1,678	3,194	9,468	253
85 - 89	11,449	3,051	201	1,504	1,309	37	8,398	1,095	1,058	6,135	110
90 and over	4,740	872	61	271	535	5	3,868	591	238	3,015	24
					Bath						
ALL AGES	**78,689**	**37,115**	**17,030**	**17,254**	**1,140**	**1,691**	**41,574**	**16,113**	**17,458**	**5,245**	**2,758**
0 - 4	4,372	2,231	2,231				2,141	2,141			
5 - 9	4,003	2,054	2,054				1,949	1,949			
10 - 14	3,866	1,957	1,957				1,909	1,909			
15	845	410	410				435	435			
16 - 17	1,745	931	927	4	-	-	814	809	5	-	-
18 - 19	2,146	1,018	1,008	8	-	2	1,128	1,106	19	2	1
20 - 24	6,632	3,248	3,038	196	-	14	3,384	2,902	432	5	45
25 - 29	6,198	3,097	2,125	899	1	72	3,101	1,651	1,288	8	154
30 - 34	5,356	2,669	1,005	1,489	3	172	2,687	686	1,683	15	303
35 - 39	4,938	2,406	541	1,640	3	222	2,532	387	1,749	20	376
40 - 44	5,380	2,653	423	1,927	8	295	2,727	242	2,027	21	437
45 - 49	4,614	2,264	275	1,751	9	229	2,350	168	1,764	58	360
50 - 54	4,106	2,032	210	1,593	27	202	2,074	154	1,584	87	249
55 - 59	4,006	1,892	168	1,540	41	143	2,114	141	1,574	180	219
60 - 64	4,366	2,022	188	1,627	80	127	2,344	187	1,586	355	216
65 - 69	4,591	2,082	190	1,656	143	93	2,509	229	1,435	670	175
70 - 74	3,941	1,648	120	1,270	199	59	2,293	279	1,083	828	103
75 - 79	3,421	1,329	82	959	252	36	2,092	283	733	1,006	70
80 - 84	2,398	785	55	502	208	20	1,613	236	343	993	41
85 - 89	1,221	297	20	159	115	3	924	128	123	665	8
90 and over	544	90	3	34	51	2	454	91	30	332	1

2. Residents

Age	TOTAL PERSONS	Males					Females				
		Total	Single	Married	Widowed	Divorced	Total	Single	Married	Widowed	Divorced
a	b	c	d	e	f	g	h	i	j	k	l
					Bristol						
ALL AGES	**376,146**	**181,644**	**87,851**	**79,115**	**5,412**	**9,266**	**194,502**	**79,150**	**80,081**	**22,790**	**12,481**
0 - 4	25,835	13,237	13,237				12,598	12,598			
5 - 9	22,821	11,672	11,672				11,149	11,149			
10 - 14	20,383	10,441	10,441				9,942	9,942			
15	3,945	2,015	2,015				1,930	1,930			
16 - 17	8,201	4,193	4,179	13	1	-	4,008	3,979	22	3	4
18 - 19	9,517	4,746	4,695	44	-	7	4,771	4,625	139	-	7
20 - 24	31,400	15,498	14,053	1,354	5	86	15,902	12,799	2,858	18	227
25 - 29	34,866	17,070	10,479	6,071	13	507	17,796	8,503	8,230	34	1,029
30 - 34	29,249	14,557	5,084	8,406	14	1,053	14,692	3,865	9,162	68	1,597
35 - 39	24,859	12,574	3,007	8,239	34	1,294	12,285	1,902	8,556	92	1,735
40 - 44	25,231	12,763	2,186	9,022	60	1,495	12,468	1,285	9,052	199	1,932
45 - 49	20,687	10,445	1,431	7,650	95	1,269	10,242	738	7,670	285	1,549
50 - 54	18,411	9,264	1,041	7,030	124	1,069	9,147	595	6,850	475	1,227
55 - 59	17,802	8,861	1,004	6,804	198	855	8,941	576	6,515	896	954
60 - 64	18,773	9,046	1,034	6,868	483	661	9,727	769	6,367	1,818	773
65 - 69	19,155	8,692	879	6,599	756	458	10,463	789	6,008	3,085	581
70 - 74	16,226	6,887	616	5,038	938	295	9,339	776	4,284	3,868	411
75 - 79	13,316	5,196	428	3,583	1,046	139	8,120	851	2,632	4,365	272
80 - 84	9,018	2,931	249	1,717	905	60	6,087	763	1,248	3,961	115
85 - 89	4,593	1,227	93	591	526	17	3,366	473	397	2,439	57
90 and over	1,858	329	28	86	214	1	1,529	243	91	1,184	11
					Kingswood						
ALL AGES	**89,717**	**43,883**	**18,092**	**23,007**	**1,108**	**1,676**	**45,834**	**15,843**	**23,096**	**4,675**	**2,220**
0 - 4	5,940	3,068	3,068				2,872	2,872			
5 - 9	5,500	2,785	2,785				2,715	2,715			
10 - 14	5,323	2,689	2,689				2,634	2,634			
15	1,066	538	538				528	528			
16 - 17	2,242	1,141	1,140	-	-	1	1,101	1,100	1	-	-
18 - 19	2,399	1,249	1,245	3	-	1	1,150	1,131	19	-	-
20 - 24	6,192	3,140	2,845	282	-	13	3,052	2,298	710	2	42
25 - 29	7,018	3,475	1,594	1,747	1	133	3,543	1,032	2,310	9	192
30 - 34	6,802	3,389	687	2,455	5	242	3,413	430	2,661	7	315
35 - 39	6,285	3,106	319	2,529	8	250	3,179	220	2,614	18	327
40 - 44	6,628	3,345	300	2,772	12	261	3,283	116	2,762	38	367
45 - 49	5,940	2,946	196	2,493	29	228	2,994	94	2,545	62	293
50 - 54	5,266	2,652	132	2,317	32	171	2,614	74	2,238	116	186
55 - 59	5,278	2,586	139	2,250	54	143	2,692	87	2,182	250	173
60 - 64	4,782	2,338	123	2,050	80	85	2,444	80	1,799	433	132
65 - 69	4,328	2,089	132	1,749	136	72	2,239	96	1,442	613	88
70 - 74	3,227	1,413	66	1,097	212	38	1,814	90	922	753	49
75 - 79	2,545	1,023	48	753	198	24	1,522	77	530	887	28
80 - 84	1,751	627	33	382	201	11	1,124	81	262	762	19
85 - 89	889	233	10	113	108	2	656	58	85	507	6
90 and over	316	51	3	15	32	1	265	30	14	218	3

2. Residents

Age	TOTAL PERSONS	Males					Females				
		Total	Single	Married	Widowed	Divorced	Total	Single	Married	Widowed	Divorced
a	b	c	d	e	f	g	h	i	j	k	l
					Northavon						
ALL AGES	**130,647**	**65,017**	**27,828**	**33,404**	**1,399**	**2,386**	**65,630**	**23,817**	**33,492**	**5,357**	**2,964**
0 - 4	8,803	4,545	4,545				4,258	4,258			
5 - 9	8,000	4,151	4,151				3,849	3,849			
10 - 14	8,116	4,155	4,155				3,961	3,961			
15	1,643	885	885				758	758			
16 - 17	3,546	1,844	1,841	3	-	-	1,702	1,700	1	-	1
18 - 19	3,794	1,940	1,932	8	-	-	1,854	1,809	42	1	2
20 - 24	10,305	5,117	4,403	688	2	24	5,188	3,674	1,458	5	51
25 - 29	11,410	5,752	2,638	2,940	3	171	5,658	1,629	3,747	5	277
30 - 34	9,980	5,133	1,134	3,681	9	309	4,847	591	3,856	11	389
35 - 39	8,969	4,426	536	3,548	3	339	4,543	287	3,816	28	412
40 - 44	10,599	5,263	429	4,414	19	401	5,336	179	4,550	57	550
45 - 49	9,588	4,854	277	4,153	37	387	4,734	168	4,035	105	426
50 - 54	7,788	3,988	214	3,444	55	275	3,800	113	3,259	148	280
55 - 59	6,624	3,363	181	2,918	73	191	3,261	145	2,637	266	213
60 - 64	5,813	3,023	177	2,569	137	140	2,790	125	2,129	416	120
65 - 69	5,093	2,435	124	2,034	200	77	2,658	141	1,662	744	111
70 - 74	3,959	1,699	89	1,363	206	41	2,260	106	1,190	906	58
75 - 79	3,228	1,351	63	1,006	260	22	1,877	128	664	1,033	52
80 - 84	2,058	747	25	484	231	7	1,311	98	335	864	14
85 - 89	979	281	22	139	118	2	698	70	96	527	5
90 and over	352	65	7	12	46	-	287	28	15	241	3
					Wansdyke						
ALL AGES	**80,003**	**39,058**	**15,902**	**20,776**	**1,100**	**1,280**	**40,945**	**13,883**	**20,784**	**4,548**	**1,730**
0 - 4	4,706	2,413	2,413				2,293	2,293			
5 - 9	4,745	2,482	2,482				2,263	2,263			
10 - 14	4,892	2,541	2,541				2,351	2,351			
15	1,012	507	507				505	505			
16 - 17	2,122	1,070	1,067	2	-	1	1,052	1,049	3	-	-
18 - 19	2,250	1,165	1,159	6	-	-	1,085	1,069	15	-	1
20 - 24	5,143	2,641	2,370	262	-	9	2,502	1,887	584	2	29
25 - 29	5,121	2,589	1,312	1,200	1	76	2,532	791	1,593	9	139
30 - 34	5,194	2,532	618	1,771	1	142	2,662	323	2,154	8	177
35 - 39	5,413	2,699	345	2,164	3	187	2,714	202	2,261	15	236
40 - 44	6,464	3,176	242	2,719	13	202	3,288	136	2,808	34	310
45 - 49	5,529	2,746	166	2,365	22	193	2,783	95	2,389	69	230
50 - 54	4,734	2,348	135	2,030	20	163	2,386	101	1,998	102	185
55 - 59	4,547	2,282	140	1,983	41	118	2,265	92	1,806	208	159
60 - 64	4,429	2,127	124	1,857	80	66	2,302	105	1,755	354	88
65 - 69	4,268	2,022	98	1,699	154	71	2,246	126	1,449	587	84
70 - 74	3,426	1,507	66	1,246	164	31	1,919	138	1,001	735	45
75 - 79	2,777	1,172	47	879	235	11	1,605	138	594	847	26
80 - 84	1,878	684	51	436	190	7	1,194	109	289	780	16
85 - 89	931	277	14	133	127	3	654	81	68	501	4
90 and over	422	78	5	24	49	-	344	29	17	297	1

2. Residents

Age	TOTAL PERSONS	Males					Females				
		Total	Single	Married	Widowed	Divorced	Total	Single	Married	Widowed	Divorced
a	b	c	d	e	f	g	h	i	j	k	l
					Woodspring						
ALL AGES	**177,472**	**85,377**	**34,547**	**44,737**	**2,552**	**3,541**	**92,095**	**30,886**	**45,133**	**11,153**	**4,923**
0 - 4	10,328	5,317	5,317				5,011	5,011			
5 - 9	10,535	5,353	5,353				5,182	5,182			
10 - 14	10,596	5,477	5,477				5,119	5,119			
15	2,046	1,057	1,057				989	989			
16 - 17	4,713	2,432	2,431	1	-	-	2,281	2,273	7	-	1
18 - 19	4,951	2,631	2,614	13	1	3	2,320	2,268	51	1	-
20 - 24	11,328	5,820	5,180	616	-	24	5,508	4,086	1,325	8	89
25 - 29	11,201	5,680	2,891	2,619	1	169	5,521	1,688	3,493	11	329
30 - 34	11,080	5,353	1,169	3,782	10	392	5,727	684	4,450	21	572
35 - 39	11,568	5,686	714	4,460	14	498	5,882	414	4,835	38	595
40 - 44	14,115	6,913	551	5,739	27	596	7,202	273	6,005	94	830
45 - 49	12,348	6,198	374	5,256	45	523	6,150	223	5,110	152	665
50 - 54	10,067	4,987	259	4,238	55	435	5,080	191	4,198	212	479
55 - 59	9,243	4,590	242	3,964	93	291	4,653	212	3,657	373	411
60 - 64	9,306	4,496	252	3,820	161	263	4,810	294	3,482	743	291
65 - 69	9,685	4,339	243	3,644	301	151	5,346	379	3,392	1,306	269
70 - 74	8,336	3,660	164	2,963	421	112	4,676	333	2,414	1,738	191
75 - 79	7,038	2,753	121	2,105	475	52	4,285	421	1,637	2,109	118
80 - 84	4,904	1,640	81	1,048	490	21	3,264	391	717	2,108	48
85 - 89	2,836	736	42	369	315	10	2,100	285	289	1,496	30
90 and over	1,248	259	15	100	143	1	989	170	71	743	5

Table 3 Communal establishments

3. Establishments: persons present not in households

Type of establishment	Number of establish-ments	TOTAL PERSONS	Total males	Total females	Not resident			Residents					
								Staff			Other residents		
					Total	Males	Females	Total	Males	Females	Total	Males	Females
a	b	c	d	e	f	g	h	i	j	k	l	m	n
AVON													
ALL ESTABLISHMENTS	**1,099**	**30,188**	**14,125**	**16,063**	**14,487**	**7,780**	**6,707**	**1,383**	**600**	**783**	**14,318**	**5,745**	**8,573**
Medical and care sector	**633**	**15,985**	**5,328**	**10,657**	**4,157**	**1,711**	**2,446**	**599**	**184**	**415**	**11,229**	**3,433**	**7,796**
NHS hospitals/homes - psychiatric	9	961	486	475	353	143	210	1	-	1	607	343	264
NHS hospitals/homes - other	34	3,320	1,346	1,974	2,531	1,068	1,463	296	72	224	493	206	287
Non-NHS hospitals - psychiatric	1	5	2	3	-	-	-	-	-	-	5	2	3
Non-NHS hospitals - other	9	597	236	361	475	166	309	-	-	-	122	70	52
Local authority homes	117	3,052	1,079	1,973	276	102	174	45	21	24	2,731	956	1,775
Housing association homes and hostels	54	595	233	362	21	10	11	19	9	10	555	214	341
Nursing homes (non-NHS/LA/HA)	151	3,528	837	2,691	341	155	186	50	16	34	3,137	666	2,471
Residential homes (non-NHS/LA/HA)	235	3,773	1,026	2,747	136	55	81	180	63	117	3,457	908	2,549
Children's homes	23	154	83	71	24	12	12	8	3	5	122	68	54
Detention, defence and education	**90**	**9,302**	**5,775**	**3,527**	**7,461**	**4,356**	**3,105**	**193**	**98**	**95**	**1,648**	**1,321**	**327**
Prison service establishments	7	698	634	64	420	367	53	4	3	1	274	264	10
Defence establishments	1	786	690	96	201	177	24				585	513	72
Educational establishments	82	7,818	4,451	3,367	6,840	3,812	3,028	189	95	94	789	544	245
Other groups	**376**	**4,901**	**3,022**	**1,879**	**2,869**	**1,713**	**1,156**	**591**	**318**	**273**	**1,441**	**991**	**450**
Hotels, boarding houses etc	300	3,668	2,118	1,550	2,412	1,327	1,085	545	291	254	711	500	211
Hostels and common lodging houses (non-HA)	31	435	351	84	45	35	10	24	19	5	366	297	69
Other miscellaneous establishments	33	341	140	201	72	46	26	21	8	13	248	86	162
Persons sleeping rough		148	137	11	35	32	3				112	105	7
Campers		63	36	27	63	36	27				-	-	-
Civilian ships, boats and barges	12	246	240	6	242	237	5				4	3	1

Note: The 'All Establishments' and 'Other groups' rows include a female member of staff incorrectly enumerated as a resident.

Table 3 Communal establishments - continued

3. Establishments: persons present not in households

Type of establishment	Number of establish-ments	TOTAL PERSONS	Total males	Total females	Not resident			Residents					
								Staff			Other residents		
					Total	Males	Females	Total	Males	Females	Total	Males	Females
a	b	c	d	e	f	g	h	i	j	k	l	m	n
Bath													
ALL ESTABLISHMENTS	**160**	**5,262**	**2,630**	**2,632**	**3,449**	**1,944**	**1,505**	**454**	**179**	**275**	**1,359**	**507**	**852**
Medical and care sector	**62**	**2,016**	**629**	**1,387**	**827**	**330**	**497**	**217**	**49**	**168**	**972**	**250**	**722**
NHS hospitals/homes - psychiatric	3	209	72	137	145	47	98	-	-	-	64	25	39
NHS hospitals/homes - other	4	836	314	522	624	270	354	178	35	143	34	9	25
Non-NHS hospitals - psychiatric	-	-	-	-	-	-	-	-	-	-	-	-	-
Non-NHS hospitals - other	1	28	6	22	28	6	22	-	-	-	-	-	-
Local authority homes	14	247	62	185	11	2	9	-	-	-	236	60	176
Housing association homes and hostels	3	27	15	12	2	-	2	2	1	1	23	14	9
Nursing homes (non-NHS/LA/HA)	12	256	55	201	3	1	2	15	4	11	238	50	188
Residential homes (non-NHS/LA/HA)	23	398	96	302	11	2	9	22	9	13	365	85	280
Children's homes	2	15	9	6	3	2	1	-	-	-	12	7	5
Detention, defence and education	**10**	**2,075**	**1,354**	**721**	**1,742**	**1,118**	**624**	**85**	**51**	**34**	**248**	**185**	**63**
Prison service establishments	-	-	-	-	-	-	-	-	-	-	-	-	-
Defence establishments	-	-	-	-	-	-	-				-	-	-
Educational establishments	10	2,075	1,354	721	1,742	1,118	624	85	51	34	248	185	63
Other groups	**88**	**1,171**	**647**	**524**	**880**	**496**	**384**	**152**	**79**	**73**	**139**	**72**	**67**
Hotels, boarding houses etc	74	1,042	580	462	851	477	374	149	79	70	42	24	18
Hostels and common lodging houses (non-HA)	7	66	38	28	10	5	5	1	-	1	55	33	22
Other miscellaneous establishments	6	43	13	30	14	10	4	1	-	1	28	3	25
Persons sleeping rough		18	15	3	5	4	1				12	11	1
Campers		-	-	-	-	-	-				-	-	-
Civilian ships, boats and barges	1	2	1	1	-	-	-				2	1	1

Note: The 'All Establishments' and 'Other groups' rows include a female member of staff incorrectly enumerated as a resident.

Table 3 Communal establishments – continued

3. Establishments: persons present not in households

Type of establishment	Number of establish-ments	TOTAL PERSONS	Total males	Total females	Not resident			Residents					
								Staff			Other residents		
					Total	Males	Females	Total	Males	Females	Total	Males	Females
a	b	c	d	e	f	g	h	i	j	k	l	m	n
Bristol													
ALL ESTABLISHMENTS	**422**	**12,153**	**5,938**	**6,215**	**6,138**	**3,333**	**2,805**	**375**	**152**	**223**	**5,640**	**2,453**	**3,187**
Medical and care sector	**234**	**6,215**	**2,197**	**4,018**	**1,801**	**728**	**1,073**	**165**	**46**	**119**	**4,249**	**1,423**	**2,826**
NHS hospitals/homes - psychiatric	3	297	161	136	80	43	37	1	-	1	216	118	98
NHS hospitals/homes - other	14	1,567	638	929	1,231	515	716	83	27	56	253	96	157
Non-NHS hospitals - psychiatric	-	-	-	-	-	-	-	-	-	-	-	-	-
Non-NHS hospitals - other	5	281	84	197	261	81	180	-	-	-	20	3	17
Local authority homes	60	1,550	597	953	160	71	89	10	5	5	1,380	521	859
Housing association homes and hostels	24	284	129	155	5	-	5	7	5	2	272	124	148
Nursing homes (non-NHS/LA/HA)	37	811	155	656	25	9	16	8	2	6	778	144	634
Residential homes (non-NHS/LA/HA)	75	1,333	379	954	29	4	25	56	7	49	1,248	368	880
Children's homes	16	92	54	38	10	5	5	-	-	-	82	49	33
Detention, defence and education	**53**	**4,063**	**2,393**	**1,670**	**3,522**	**2,013**	**1,509**	**61**	**22**	**39**	**480**	**358**	**122**
Prison service establishments	3	227	221	6	148	148	-	1	-	1	78	73	5
Defence establishments	-	-	-	-	-	-	-				-	-	-
Educational establishments	50	3,836	2,172	1,664	3,374	1,865	1,509	60	22	38	402	285	117
Other groups	**135**	**1,875**	**1,348**	**527**	**815**	**592**	**223**	**149**	**84**	**65**	**911**	**672**	**239**
Hotels, boarding houses etc	96	1,041	673	368	466	279	187	113	59	54	462	335	127
Hostels and common lodging houses (non-HA)	16	267	233	34	14	10	4	23	19	4	230	204	26
Other miscellaneous establishments	12	140	50	90	10	7	3	13	6	7	117	37	80
Persons sleeping rough		130	122	8	30	28	2				100	94	6
Campers		53	31	22	53	31	22				-	-	-
Civilian ships, boats and barges	11	244	239	5	242	237	5				2	2	-

Table 3 Communal establishments – continued

3. Establishments: persons present not in households

Type of establishment	Number of establishments	TOTAL PERSONS	Total males	Total females	Not resident			Residents					
								Staff			Other residents		
					Total	Males	Females	Total	Males	Females	Total	Males	Females
a	b	c	d	e	f	g	h	i	j	k	l	m	n
					Kingswood								
ALL ESTABLISHMENTS	**43**	**838**	**337**	**501**	**37**	**16**	**21**	**16**	**10**	**6**	**785**	**311**	**474**
Medical and care sector	**34**	**771**	**296**	**475**	**34**	**13**	**21**	**15**	**9**	**6**	**722**	**274**	**448**
NHS hospitals/homes - psychiatric	1	190	133	57	2	1	1	-	-	-	188	132	56
NHS hospitals/homes - other	-	-	-	-	-	-	-	-	-	-	-	-	-
Non-NHS hospitals - psychiatric	1	5	2	3	-	-	-	-	-	-	5	2	3
Non-NHS hospitals - other	-	-	-	-	-	-	-	-	-	-	-	-	-
Local authority homes	9	161	62	99	14	6	8	-	-	-	147	56	91
Housing association homes and hostels	1	24	18	6	-	-	-	-	-	-	24	18	6
Nursing homes (non-NHS/LA/HA)	6	172	31	141	5	-	5	3	2	1	164	29	135
Residential homes (non-NHS/LA/HA)	14	197	39	158	3	1	2	12	7	5	182	31	151
Children's homes	2	22	11	11	10	5	5	-	-	-	12	6	6
Detention, defence and education	-	-	-	-	-	-	-	-	-	-	-	-	-
Prison service establishments	-	-	-	-	-	-	-	-	-	-	-	-	-
Defence establishments	-	-	-	-	-	-	-	-	-	-	-	-	-
Educational establishments	-	-	-	-	-	-	-	-	-	-	-	-	-
Other groups	**9**	**67**	**41**	**26**	**3**	**3**	-	**1**	**1**	-	**63**	**37**	**26**
Hotels, boarding houses etc	2	23	12	11	2	2	-	1	1	-	20	9	11
Hostels and common lodging houses (non-HA)	2	10	6	4	-	-	-	-	-	-	10	6	4
Other miscellaneous establishments	5	34	23	11	1	1	-	-	-	-	33	22	11
Persons sleeping rough		-	-	-	-	-	-				-	-	-
Campers		-	-	-	-	-	-				-	-	-
Civilian ships, boats and barges	-	-	-	-	-	-	-				-	-	-

Table 3 Communal establishments – **continued**

3. Establishments: persons present not in households

Type of establishment	Number of establish-ments	TOTAL PERSONS	Total males	Total females	Not resident			Residents					
								Staff			Other residents		
					Total	Males	Females	Total	Males	Females	Total	Males	Females
a	b	c	d	e	f	g	h	i	j	k	l	m	n
Northavon													
ALL ESTABLISHMENTS	**68**	**3,303**	**1,735**	**1,568**	**1,740**	**995**	**745**	**146**	**72**	**74**	**1,417**	**668**	**749**
Medical and care sector	**37**	**1,686**	**654**	**1,032**	**504**	**224**	**280**	**60**	**24**	**36**	**1,122**	**406**	**716**
NHS hospitals/homes - psychiatric	1	22	5	17	21	5	16	-	-	-	1	-	1
NHS hospitals/homes - other	3	495	226	269	427	205	222	23	6	17	45	15	30
Non-NHS hospitals - psychiatric	-	-	-	-	-	-	-	-	-	-	-	-	-
Non-NHS hospitals - other	2	102	66	36	2	-	2	-	-	-	100	66	34
Local authority homes	9	616	218	398	48	12	36	33	15	18	535	191	344
Housing association homes and hostels	1	12	1	11	1	-	1	-	-	-	11	1	10
Nursing homes (non-NHS/LA/HA)	9	198	54	144	2	-	2	-	-	-	196	54	142
Residential homes (non-NHS/LA/HA)	11	235	81	154	3	2	1	4	3	1	228	76	152
Children's homes	1	6	3	3	-	-	-	-	-	-	6	3	3
Detention, defence and education	**8**	**1,271**	**827**	**444**	**1,000**	**593**	**407**	**13**	**5**	**8**	**258**	**229**	**29**
Prison service establishments	3	464	406	58	272	219	53	-	-	-	192	187	5
Defence establishments	-	-	-	-	-	-	-				-	-	-
Educational establishments	5	807	421	386	728	374	354	13	5	8	66	42	24
Other groups	**23**	**346**	**254**	**92**	**236**	**178**	**58**	**73**	**43**	**30**	**37**	**33**	**4**
Hotels, boarding houses etc	20	272	186	86	197	142	55	73	43	30	2	1	1
Hostels and common lodging houses (non-HA)	2	55	52	3	20	20	-	-	-	-	35	32	3
Other miscellaneous establishments	1	13	13	-	13	13	-	-	-	-	-	-	-
Persons sleeping rough		-	-	-	-	-	-				-	-	-
Campers		6	3	3	6	3	3				-	-	-
Civilian ships, boats and barges	-	-	-	-	-	-	-				-	-	-

Table 3 Communal establishments – continued

3. Establishments: persons present not in households

Type of establishment	Number of establishments	TOTAL PERSONS	Total males	Total females	Not resident			Residents					
								Staff			Other residents		
					Total	Males	Females	Total	Males	Females	Total	Males	Females
a	b	c	d	e	f	g	h	i	j	k	l	m	n
					Wansdyke								
ALL ESTABLISHMENTS	**65**	**1,769**	**621**	**1,148**	**888**	**417**	**471**	**41**	**16**	**25**	**840**	**188**	**652**
Medical and care sector	**42**	**892**	**207**	**685**	**110**	**42**	**68**	**22**	**5**	**17**	**760**	**160**	**600**
NHS hospitals/homes - psychiatric	-	-	-	-	-	-	-	-	-	-	-	-	-
NHS hospitals/homes - other	3	84	31	53	74	29	45	-	-	-	10	2	8
Non-NHS hospitals - psychiatric	-	-	-	-	-	-	-	-	-	-	-	-	-
Non-NHS hospitals - other	-	-	-	-	-	-	-	-	-	-	-	-	-
Local authority homes	8	191	59	132	17	6	11	-	-	-	174	53	121
Housing association homes and hostels	3	26	9	17	-	-	-	1	-	1	25	9	16
Nursing homes (non-NHS/LA/HA)	13	346	52	294	11	3	8	8	1	7	327	48	279
Residential homes (non-NHS/LA/HA)	15	245	56	189	8	4	4	13	4	9	224	48	176
Children's homes	-	-	-	-	-	-	-	-	-	-	-	-	-
Detention, defence and education	**4**	**764**	**360**	**404**	**696**	**329**	**367**	**10**	**7**	**3**	**58**	**24**	**34**
Prison service establishments	-	-	-	-	-	-	-	-	-	-	-	-	-
Defence establishments	-	-	-	-	-	-	-				-	-	-
Educational establishments	4	764	360	404	696	329	367	10	7	3	58	24	34
Other groups	**19**	**113**	**54**	**59**	**82**	**46**	**36**	**9**	**4**	**5**	**22**	**4**	**18**
Hotels, boarding houses etc	17	85	48	37	71	40	31	8	4	4	6	4	2
Hostels and common lodging houses (non-HA)	-	-	-	-	-	-	-	-	-	-	-	-	-
Other miscellaneous establishments	2	28	6	22	11	6	5	1	-	1	16	-	16
Persons sleeping rough		-	-	-	-	-	-				-	-	-
Campers		-	-	-	-	-	-				-	-	-
Civilian ships, boats and barges	-	-	-	-	-	-	-				-	-	-

3. Establishments: persons present not in households

Type of establishment	Number of establish-ments	TOTAL PERSONS	Total males	Total females	Not resident			Residents					
								Staff			Other residents		
					Total	Males	Females	Total	Males	Females	Total	Males	Females
a	b	c	d	e	f	g	h	i	j	k	l	m	n
				Woodspring									
ALL ESTABLISHMENTS	**341**	**6,863**	**2,864**	**3,999**	**2,235**	**1,075**	**1,160**	**351**	**171**	**180**	**4,277**	**1,618**	**2,659**
Medical and care sector	**224**	**4,405**	**1,345**	**3,060**	**881**	**374**	**507**	**120**	**51**	**69**	**3,404**	**920**	**2,484**
NHS hospitals/homes - psychiatric	1	243	115	128	105	47	58	-	-	-	138	68	70
NHS hospitals/homes - other	10	338	137	201	175	49	126	12	4	8	151	84	67
Non-NHS hospitals - psychiatric	-	-	-	-	-	-	-	-	-	-	-	-	-
Non-NHS hospitals - other	1	186	80	106	184	79	105	-	-	-	2	1	1
Local authority homes	17	287	81	206	26	5	21	2	1	1	259	75	184
Housing association homes and hostels	22	222	61	161	13	10	3	9	3	6	200	48	152
Nursing homes (non-NHS/LA/HA)	74	1,745	490	1,255	295	142	153	16	7	9	1,434	341	1,093
Residential homes (non-NHS/LA/HA)	97	1,365	375	990	82	42	40	73	33	40	1,210	300	910
Children's homes	2	19	6	13	1	-	1	8	3	5	10	3	7
Detention, defence and education	**15**	**1,129**	**841**	**288**	**501**	**303**	**198**	**24**	**13**	**11**	**604**	**525**	**79**
Prison service establishments	1	7	7	-	-	-	-	3	3	-	4	4	-
Defence establishments	1	786	690	96	201	177	24				585	513	72
Educational establishments	13	336	144	192	300	126	174	21	10	11	15	8	7
Other groups	**102**	**1,329**	**678**	**651**	**853**	**398**	**455**	**207**	**107**	**100**	**269**	**173**	**96**
Hotels, boarding houses etc	91	1,205	619	586	825	387	438	201	105	96	179	127	52
Hostels and common lodging houses (non-HA)	4	37	22	15	1	-	1	-	-	-	36	22	14
Other miscellaneous establishments	7	83	35	48	23	9	14	6	2	4	54	24	30
Persons sleeping rough		-	-	-	-	-	-				-	-	-
Campers		4	2	2	4	2	2				-	-	-
Civilian ships, boats and barges	-	-	-	-	-	-	-				-	-	-

Table 4 Medical and care establishments

4. Residents (non-staff) present not in households

Type of establishment	TOTAL PERSONS	Total males	Total females	Age							
				0 - 15		16 - 44		45 up to pensionable age		Pensionable age - 74	
				Males	Females	Males	Females	Males	Females	Males	Females
a	b	c	d	e	f	g	h	i	j	k	l
			AVON								
ALL MEDICAL AND CARE ESTABLISHMENTS	**11,107**	**3,365**	**7,742**	**32**	**24**	**822**	**629**	**577**	**266**	**502**	**857**
NHS hospitals/homes - psychiatric	607	343	264	1	2	87	38	99	35	87	66
NHS hospitals/homes - other	493	206	287	10	7	80	144	49	30	31	29
Non-NHS hospitals - psychiatric	5	2	3	-	-	-	-	1	-	1	2
Non-NHS hospitals - other	122	70	52	2	-	37	25	26	13	5	10
Local authority homes	2,731	956	1,775	8	2	238	179	198	103	148	236
Housing association homes and hostels	555	214	341	4	2	85	39	56	15	25	28
Nursing homes (non-NHS/LA/HA)	3,137	666	2,471	3	4	49	49	28	16	92	226
Residential homes (non-NHS/LA/HA)	3,457	908	2,549	4	7	246	155	120	54	113	260
			Bath								
ALL MEDICAL AND CAPE ESTABLISHMENTS	**960**	**243**	**717**	**3**	**4**	**65**	**62**	**30**	**22**	**30**	**65**
NHS hospitals/homes - psychiatric	64	25	39	-	-	6	-	4	2	6	8
NHS hospitals/homes - other	34	9	25	-	-	6	21	-	-	2	2
Non-NHS hospitals - psychiatric	-	-	-	-	-	-	-	-	-	-	-
Non-NHS hospitals - other	-	-	-	-	-	-	-	-	-	-	-
Local authority homes	236	60	176	-	-	10	13	14	10	11	20
Housing association homes and hostels	23	14	9	-	-	10	4	4	3	-	2
Nursing homes (non-NHS/LA/HA)	238	50	188	3	4	4	7	3	1	2	15
Residential homes (non-NHS/LA/HA)	365	85	280	-	-	29	17	5	6	9	18
			Bristol								
ALL MEDICAL AND CARE ESTABLISHMENTS	**4,167**	**1,374**	**2,793**	**23**	**14**	**361**	**282**	**235**	**95**	**225**	**337**
NHS hospitals/homes - psychiatric	216	118	98	-	-	29	16	26	10	35	30
NHS hospitals/homes - other	253	96	157	10	7	38	94	18	12	13	14
Non-NHS hospitals - psychiatric	-	-	-	-	-	-	-	-	-	-	-
Non-NHS hospitals - other	20	3	17	2	-	1	3	-	4	-	7
Local authority homes	1,380	521	859	7	2	109	55	105	32	91	118
Housing association homes and hostels	272	124	148	1	-	50	25	30	9	19	11
Nursing homes (non-NHS/LA/HA)	778	144	634	-	-	17	16	8	7	25	65
Residential homes (non-NHS/LA/HA)	1,248	368	880	3	5	117	73	48	21	42	92
			Kingswood								
ALL MEDICAL AND CARE ESTABLISHMENTS	**710**	**268**	**442**	**-**	**-**	**42**	**13**	**81**	**26**	**51**	**54**
NHS hospitals/homes - psychiatric	188	132	56	-	-	27	4	54	18	30	14
NHS hospitals/homes - other	-	-	-	-	-	-	-	-	-	-	-
Non-NHS hospitals - psychiatric	5	2	3	-	-	-	-	1	-	1	2
Non-NHS hospitals - other	-	-	-	-	-	-	-	-	-	-	-
Local authority homes	147	56	91	-	-	8	5	14	6	10	11
Housing association homes and hostels	24	18	6	-	-	6	2	7	1	4	3
Nursing homes (non-NHS/LA/HA)	164	29	135	-	-	-	-	-	-	3	12
Residential homes (non-NHS/LA/HA)	182	31	151	-	-	1	2	5	1	3	12

Age				Migrants	With limiting long-term illness	Ethnic group				Type of establishment
75 - 84		85 and over				White	Black groups	Indian, Pakistani and Bangladeshi	Chinese and other groups	
Males	Females	Males	Females							
m	n	o	p	q	r	s	t	u	v	a
833	**2,493**	**599**	**3,473**	**2,540**	**10,110**	**10,988**	**77**	**19**	**23**	**ALL MEDICAL AND CARE ESTABLISHMENTS**
54	78	15	45	110	573	596	5	4	2	NHS hospitals/homes - psychiatric
26	40	10	37	169	300	470	13	6	4	NHS hospitals/homes - other
-	1	-	-	-	5	5	-	-	-	Non-NHS hospitals - psychiatric
-	4	-	-	10	89	119	3	-	-	Non-NHS hospitals - other
215	549	149	706	601	2,484	2,701	19	5	6	Local authority homes
22	110	22	147	106	466	547	4	2	2	Housing association homes and hostels
285	856	209	1,320	838	3,028	3,117	14	2	4	Nursing homes (non-NHS/LA/HA)
231	855	194	1,218	706	3,165	3,433	19	-	5	Residential homes (non-NHS/LA/HA)
60	**210**	**55**	**354**	**207**	**837**	**946**	**13**	**-**	**1**	**ALL MEDICAL AND CARE ESTABLISHMENTS**
4	17	5	12	28	64	63	1	-	-	NHS hospitals/homes - psychiatric
1	-	-	2	12	8	34	-	-	-	NHS hospitals/homes - other
-	-	-	-	-	-	-	-	-	-	Non-NHS hospitals - psychiatric
-	-	-	-	-	-	-	-	-	-	Non-NHS hospitals - other
11	57	14	76	46	187	234	1	-	1	Local authority homes
-	-	-	-	-	19	22	1	-	-	Housing association homes and hostels
24	57	14	104	72	211	236	2	-	-	Nursing homes (non-NHS/LA/HA)
20	79	22	160	49	348	357	8	-	-	Residential homes (non-NHS/LA/HA)
325	**929**	**205**	**1,136**	**978**	**3,706**	**4,101**	**45**	**10**	**11**	**ALL MEDICAL AND CARE ESTABLISHMENTS**
22	32	6	10	23	208	210	3	3	-	NHS hospitals/homes - psychiatric
14	19	3	11	93	115	236	13	2	2	NHS hospitals/homes - other
-	-	-	-	-	-	-	-	-	-	Non-NHS hospitals - psychiatric
-	3	-	-	3	6	20	-	-	-	Non-NHS hospitals - other
131	307	78	345	324	1,279	1,363	11	5	1	Local authority homes
13	32	11	71	74	234	268	2	-	2	Housing association homes and hostels
48	227	46	319	218	741	768	8	-	2	Nursing homes (non-NHS/LA/HA)
97	309	61	380	243	1,123	1,236	8	-	4	Residential homes (non-NHS/LA/HA)
65	**146**	**29**	**203**	**140**	**665**	**707**	**-**	**2**	**1**	**ALL MEDICAL AND CARE ESTABLISHMENTS**
20	11	1	9	24	188	187	-	-	1	NHS hospitals/homes - psychiatric
-	-	-	-	-	-	-	-	-	-	NHS hospitals/homes - other
-	1	-	-	-	5	5	-	-	-	Non-NHS hospitals - psychiatric
-	-	-	-	-	-	-	-	-	-	Non-NHS hospitals - other
13	25	11	44	21	134	147	-	-	-	Local authority homes
1	-	-	-	-	24	24	-	-	-	Housing association homes and hostels
17	48	9	75	45	157	162	-	2	-	Nursing homes (non-NHS/LA/HA)
14	61	8	75	50	157	182	-	-	-	Residential homes (non-NHS/LA/HA)

Table 4 Medical and care establishments - **continued**

4. Residents (non-staff) present not in households

Type of establishment	TOTAL PERSONS	Total males	Total females	Age 0 - 15 Males	Age 0 - 15 Females	Age 16 - 44 Males	Age 16 - 44 Females	Age 45 up to pensionable age Males	Age 45 up to pensionable age Females	Age Pensionable age - 74 Males	Age Pensionable age - 74 Females
a	b	c	d	e	f	g	h	i	j	k	l
Northavon											
ALL MEDICAL AND CARE ESTABLISHMENTS	**1,116**	**403**	**713**	**2**	**2**	**193**	**167**	**86**	**69**	**34**	**76**
NHS hospitals/homes - psychiatric	1	-	1	-	-	-	-	-	-	-	-
NHS hospitals/homes - other	45	15	30	-	-	4	11	3	4	7	3
Non-NHS hospitals - psychiatric	-	-	-	-	-	-	-	-	-	-	-
Non-NHS hospitals - other	100	66	34	-	-	36	22	25	9	5	3
Local authority homes	535	191	344	1	-	89	91	54	49	15	56
Housing association homes and hostels	11	1	10	-	-	-	-	-	-	1	3
Nursing homes (non-NHS/LA/HA)	196	54	142	-	-	15	11	1	2	4	9
Residential homes (non-NHS/LA/HA)	228	76	152	1	2	49	32	3	5	2	2
Wansdyke											
ALL MEDICAL AND CARE ESTABLISHMENTS	**760**	**160**	**600**	**3**	**2**	**24**	**22**	**17**	**11**	**19**	**54**
NHS hospitals/homes - psychiatric	-	-	-	-	-	-	-	-	-	-	-
NHS hospitals/homes - other	10	2	8	-	-	-	-	-	3	-	2
Non-NHS hospitals - psychiatric	-	-	-	-	-	-	-	-	-	-	-
Non-NHS hospitals - other	-	-	-	-	-	-	-	-	-	-	-
Local authority homes	174	53	121	-	-	11	8	4	4	7	8
Housing association homes and hostels	25	9	16	3	2	1	3	-	1	1	-
Nursing homes (non-NHS/LA/HA)	327	48	279	-	-	-	-	-	-	8	25
Residential homes (non-NHS/LA/HA)	224	48	176	-	-	12	11	13	3	3	19
Woodspring											
ALL MEDICAL AND CARE ESTABLISHMENTS	**3,394**	**917**	**2,477**	**1**	**2**	**137**	**83**	**128**	**43**	**143**	**271**
NHS hospitals/homes - psychiatric	138	68	70	1	2	25	18	15	5	16	14
NHS hospitals/homes - other	151	84	67	-	-	32	18	28	11	9	8
Non-NHS hospitals - psychiatric	-	-	-	-	-	-	-	-	-	-	-
Non-NHS hospitals - other	2	1	1	-	-	-	-	1	-	-	-
Local authority homes	259	75	184	-	-	11	7	7	2	14	23
Housing association homes and hostels	200	48	152	-	-	18	5	15	1	-	9
Nursing homes (non-NHS/LA/HA)	1,434	341	1,093	-	-	13	15	16	6	50	100
Residential homes (non-NHS/LA/HA)	1,210	300	910	-	-	38	20	46	18	54	117

Age				Migrants	With limiting long-term illness	Ethnic group				Type of establishment
75 - 84		85 and over				White	Black groups	Indian, Pakistani and Bangladeshi	Chinese and other groups	
Males	Females	Males	Females							
m	n	o	p	q	r	s	t	u	v	a
52	**179**	**36**	**220**	**254**	**1,008**	**1,101**	**9**	**1**	**5**	**ALL MEDICAL AND CARE ESTABLISHMENTS**
-	1	-	-	-	1	1	-	-	-	NHS hospitals/homes - psychiatric
1	10	-	2	22	33	43	-	1	1	NHS hospitals/homes - other
-	-	-	-	-	-	-	-	-	-	Non-NHS hospitals - psychiatric
-	-	-	-	6	81	97	3	-	-	Non-NHS hospitals - other
20	72	12	76	125	471	526	5	-	4	Local authority homes
-	5	-	2	2	7	11	-	-	-	Housing association homes and hostels
19	49	15	71	65	193	196	-	-	-	Nursing homes (non-NHS/LA/HA)
12	42	9	69	34	222	227	1	-	-	Residential homes (non-NHS/LA/HA)
54	**193**	**43**	**318**	**189**	**724**	**755**	**1**	**2**	**2**	**ALL MEDICAL AND CARE ESTABLISHMENTS**
-	-	-	-	-	-	-	-	-	-	NHS hospitals/homes - psychiatric
1	2	1	1	1	10	9	-	-	1	NHS hospitals/homes - other
-	-	-	-	-	-	-	-	-	-	Non-NHS hospitals - psychiatric
-	-	-	-	-	-	-	-	-	-	Non-NHS hospitals - other
16	39	15	62	25	161	173	1	-	-	Local authority homes
3	9	1	1	7	21	23	-	2	-	Housing association homes and hostels
25	93	15	161	110	320	327	-	-	-	Nursing homes (non-NHS/LA/HA)
9	50	11	93	46	212	223	-	-	1	Residential homes (non-NHS/LA/HA)
277	**836**	**231**	**1,242**	**772**	**3,170**	**3,378**	**9**	**4**	**3**	**ALL MEDICAL AND CARE ESTABLISHMENTS**
8	17	3	14	35	112	135	1	1	1	NHS hospitals/homes - psychiatric
9	9	6	21	41	134	148	-	3	-	NHS hospitals/homes - other
-	-	-	-	-	-	-	-	-	-	Non-NHS hospitals - psychiatric
-	1	-	-	1	2	2	-	-	-	Non-NHS hospitals - other
24	49	19	103	60	252	258	1	-	-	Local authority homes
5	64	10	73	23	161	199	1	-	-	Housing association homes and hostels
152	382	110	590	328	1,406	1,428	4	-	2	Nursing homes (non-NHS/LA/HA)
79	314	83	441	284	1,103	1,208	2	-	-	Residential homes (non-NHS/LA/HA)

Table 5 Hotels and other establishments

5. Residents (non-staff) present not in households

TOTAL PERSONS	Total males	Total females	Age											
			0 - 15		16 - 17		18 - 29		30 - 44		45 up to pensionable age		Pensionable age and over	
			Males	Females	Males	Females	Males	Females	Males	Females	Males	Females	Males	Females
a	b	c	d	e	f	g	h	i	j	k	l	m	n	o
							AVON							
3,211	**2,380**	**831**	**186**	**107**	**88**	**30**	**1,157**	**415**	**498**	**116**	**342**	**59**	**109**	**104**
122	68	54	68	54	-	-	-	-	-	-	-	-	-	-
274	264	10	-	-	-	-	47	2	131	3	76	3	10	2
585	513	72	-	-	33	6	452	62	26	4	2	-	-	-
789	544	245	35	3	32	2	371	189	101	38	5	6	-	7
711	500	211	51	37	7	10	151	84	118	41	124	21	49	18
366	297	69	9	4	4	8	74	33	77	9	96	9	37	6
248	86	162	23	9	12	4	19	42	7	17	12	19	13	71
112	105	7	-	-	-	-	42	3	37	3	26	1	-	-
-	-	-	-	-	-	-	-	-	-	-	-	-	-	-
4	3	1	-	-	-	-	1	-	1	1	1	-	-	-
							Bath							
399	**264**	**135**	**9**	**7**	**3**	**3**	**179**	**89**	**57**	**25**	**12**	**6**	**4**	**5**
12	7	5	7	5	-	-	-	-	-	-	-	-	-	-
-	-	-	-	-	-	-	-	-	-	-	-	-	-	-
-	-	-	-	-	-	-	-	-	-	-	-	-	-	-
248	185	63	-	-	2	1	145	50	37	12	1	-	-	-
42	24	18	1	1	1	-	8	7	8	5	6	3	-	2
55	33	22	1	1	-	2	19	13	7	5	2	1	4	-
28	3	25	-	-	-	-	3	19	-	1	-	2	-	3
12	11	1	-	-	-	-	4	-	4	1	3	-	-	-
-	-	-	-	-	-	-	-	-	-	-	-	-	-	-
2	1	1	-	-	-	-	-	-	1	1	-	-	-	-
							Bristol							
1,473	**1,079**	**394**	**110**	**60**	**30**	**12**	**379**	**168**	**254**	**60**	**215**	**38**	**91**	**56**
82	49	33	49	33	-	-	-	-	-	-	-	-	-	-
78	73	5	-	-	-	-	27	-	28	1	15	2	3	2
-	-	-	-	-	-	-	-	-	-	-	-	-	-	-
402	285	117	22	2	25	1	178	85	56	23	4	2	-	4
462	335	127	24	18	5	6	90	53	81	22	93	16	42	12
230	204	26	5	3	-	3	41	13	53	1	72	5	33	1
117	37	80	10	4	-	2	4	14	3	11	7	12	13	37
100	94	6	-	-	-	-	38	3	33	2	23	1	-	-
-	-	-	-	-	-	-	-	-	-	-	-	-	-	-
2	2	-	-	-	-	-	1	-	-	-	1	-	-	-
							Kingswood							
75	**43**	**32**	**20**	**12**	**13**	**1**	**7**	**11**	**1**	**3**	**2**	**2**	**-**	**3**
12	6	6	6	6	-	-	-	-	-	-	-	-	-	-
-	-	-	-	-	-	-	-	-	-	-	-	-	-	-
-	-	-	-	-	-	-	-	-	-	-	-	-	-	-
-	-	-	-	-	-	-	-	-	-	-	-	-	-	-
20	9	11	5	5	-	-	3	5	1	1	-	-	-	-
10	6	4	2	-	1	1	3	3	-	-	-	-	-	-
33	22	11	7	1	12	-	1	3	-	2	2	2	-	3
-	-	-	-	-	-	-	-	-	-	-	-	-	-	-
-	-	-	-	-	-	-	-	-	-	-	-	-	-	-
-	-	-	-	-	-	-	-	-	-	-	-	-	-	-

Type of establishment	In employment	Un-employed	Econ-omically inactive	Econ-omically active students	Migrants	Ethnic group: White	Ethnic group: Black groups	Ethnic group: Indian, Pakistani and Bangla-deshi	Ethnic group: Chinese and other groups
p	q	r	s	t	u	v	w	x	y
ALL HOTELS AND OTHER ESTABLISHMENTS	**997**	**548**	**1,373**	**51**	**1,833**	**2,810**	**167**	**57**	**177**
Children's homes	-	-	-	-	76	104	15	-	3
Prison service establishments	61	19	194	-	125	243	21	8	2
Defence establishments	582	1	2	4	342	582	-	2	1
Educational establishments	92	13	646	44	522	495	103	38	153
Hotels, boarding houses etc	167	266	190	2	385	683	10	6	12
Hostels and common lodging houses (non-HA)	43	178	132	-	193	347	12	1	6
Other miscellaneous establishments	45	20	151	1	100	242	4	2	-
Persons sleeping rough	4	50	58	-	90	110	2	-	-
Campers	-	-	-	-	-	-	-	-	-
Civilian ships, boats and barges	3	1	-	-	-	4	-	-	-
ALL HOTELS AND OTHER ESTABLISHMENTS	**71**	**58**	**254**	**15**	**246**	**304**	**23**	**14**	**58**
Children's homes	-	-	-	-	7	11	-	-	1
Prison service establishments	-	-	-	-	-	-	-	-	-
Defence establishments	-	-	-	-	-	-	-	-	-
Educational establishments	33	2	213	14	174	158	21	14	55
Hotels, boarding houses etc	15	8	17	-	18	40	-	-	2
Hostels and common lodging houses (non-HA)	2	41	10	-	29	53	2	-	-
Other miscellaneous establishments	18	2	8	1	9	28	-	-	-
Persons sleeping rough	2	4	6	-	9	12	-	-	-
Campers	-	-	-	-	-	-	-	-	-
Civilian ships, boats and barges	1	1	-	-	-	2	-	-	-
ALL HOTELS AND OTHER ESTABLISHMENTS	**221**	**339**	**743**	**17**	**819**	**1,251**	**109**	**25**	**88**
Children's homes	-	-	-	-	53	74	7	-	1
Prison service establishments	20	10	48	-	35	68	8	2	-
Defence establishments	-	-	-	-	-	-	-	-	-
Educational establishments	39	5	334	16	250	235	75	16	76
Hotels, boarding houses etc	121	172	127	1	241	440	8	6	8
Hostels and common lodging houses (non-HA)	24	101	97	-	120	217	9	1	3
Other miscellaneous establishments	13	5	85	-	39	117	-	-	-
Persons sleeping rough	2	46	52	-	81	98	2	-	-
Campers	-	-	-	-	-	-	-	-	-
Civilian ships, boats and barges	2	-	-	-	-	2	-	-	-
ALL HOTELS AND OTHER ESTABLISHMENTS	**14**	**7**	**22**	**-**	**52**	**64**	**7**	**1**	**3**
Children's homes	-	-	-	-	10	10	2	-	-
Prison service establishments	-	-	-	-	-	-	-	-	-
Defence establishments	-	-	-	-	-	-	-	-	-
Educational establishments	-	-	-	-	-	-	-	-	-
Hotels, boarding houses etc	2	4	4	-	18	19	-	-	1
Hostels and common lodging houses (non-HA)	6	2	-	-	7	7	1	-	2
Other miscellaneous establishments	6	1	18	-	17	28	4	1	-
Persons sleeping rough	-	-	-	-	-	-	-	-	-
Campers	-	-	-	-	-	-	-	-	-
Civilian ships, boats and barges	-	-	-	-	-	-	-	-	-

Table 5 Hotels and other establishments – **continued**

5. Residents (non-staff) present not in households

TOTAL PERSONS	Total males	Total females	Age 0 - 15 Males	Age 0 - 15 Females	Age 16 - 17 Males	Age 16 - 17 Females	Age 18 - 29 Males	Age 18 - 29 Females	Age 30 - 44 Males	Age 30 - 44 Females	Age 45 up to pensionable age Males	Age 45 up to pensionable age Females	Age Pensionable age and over Males	Age Pensionable age and over Females
a	b	c	d	e	f	g	h	i	j	k	l	m	n	o
							Northavon							
301	**265**	**36**	**8**	**4**	**8**	**2**	**51**	**26**	**118**	**3**	**76**	**1**	**4**	**-**
6	3	3	3	3	-	-	-	-	-	-	-	-	-	-
192	187	5	-	-	-	-	20	2	103	2	60	1	4	-
-	-	-	-	-	-	-	-	-	-	-	-	-	-	-
66	42	24	5	1	5	-	27	22	5	1	-	-	-	-
2	1	1	-	-	-	-	-	1	-	-	1	-	-	-
35	32	3	-	-	3	2	4	1	10	-	15	-	-	-
-	-	-	-	-	-	-	-	-	-	-	-	-	-	-
-	-	-	-	-	-	-	-	-	-	-	-	-	-	-
-	-	-	-	-	-	-	-	-	-	-	-	-	-	-
-	-	-	-	-	-	-	-	-	-	-	-	-	-	-
							Wansdyke							
80	**28**	**52**	**8**	**-**	**-**	**-**	**18**	**32**	**-**	**3**	**2**	**2**	**-**	**15**
-	-	-	-	-	-	-	-	-	-	-	-	-	-	-
-	-	-	-	-	-	-	-	-	-	-	-	-	-	-
-	-	-	-	-	-	-	-	-	-	-	-	-	-	-
58	24	34	8	-	-	-	16	31	-	2	-	-	-	1
6	4	2	-	-	-	-	2	1	-	1	2	-	-	-
-	-	-	-	-	-	-	-	-	-	-	-	-	-	-
16	-	16	-	-	-	-	-	-	-	-	-	2	-	14
-	-	-	-	-	-	-	-	-	-	-	-	-	-	-
-	-	-	-	-	-	-	-	-	-	-	-	-	-	-
-	-	-	-	-	-	-	-	-	-	-	-	-	-	-
							Woodspring							
883	**701**	**182**	**31**	**24**	**34**	**12**	**523**	**89**	**68**	**22**	**35**	**10**	**10**	**25**
10	3	7	3	7	-	-	-	-	-	-	-	-	-	-
4	4	-	-	-	-	-	-	-	-	-	1	-	3	-
585	513	72	-	-	33	6	452	62	26	4	2	-	-	-
15	8	7	-	-	-	-	5	1	3	-	-	4	-	2
179	127	52	21	13	1	4	48	17	28	12	22	2	7	4
36	22	14	1	-	-	-	7	3	7	3	7	3	-	5
54	24	30	6	4	-	2	11	6	4	3	3	1	-	14
-	-	-	-	-	-	-	-	-	-	-	-	-	-	-
-	-	-	-	-	-	-	-	-	-	-	-	-	-	-
-	-	-	-	-	-	-	-	-	-	-	-	-	-	-

Type of establishment	In employment	Un-employed	Econ-omically inactive	Econ-omically active students	Migrants	Ethnic group: White	Black groups	Indian, Pakistani and Bangla-deshi	Chinese and other groups
p	q	r	s	t	u	v	w	x	y
ALL HOTELS AND OTHER ESTABLISHMENTS	**53**	**33**	**203**	**7**	**168**	**252**	**18**	**13**	**18**
Children's homes	-	-	-	-	5	5	-	-	1
Prison service establishments	41	9	142	-	89	171	13	6	2
Defence establishments	-	-	-	-	-	-	-	-	-
Educational establishments	5	3	52	7	49	40	5	7	14
Hotels, boarding houses etc	-	2	-	-	2	1	-	-	1
Hostels and common lodging houses (non-HA)	7	19	9	-	23	35	-	-	-
Other miscellaneous establishments	-	-	-	-	-	-	-	-	-
Persons sleeping rough	-	-	-	-	-	-	-	-	-
Campers	-	-	-	-	-	-	-	-	-
Civilian ships, boats and barges	-	-	-	-	-	-	-	-	-

Type of establishment	In employment	Un-employed	Econ-omically inactive	Econ-omically active students	Migrants	Ethnic group: White	Black groups	Indian, Pakistani and Bangla-deshi	Chinese and other groups
ALL HOTELS AND OTHER ESTABLISHMENTS	**12**	**4**	**56**	**7**	**47**	**70**	**2**	**-**	**8**
Children's homes	-	-	-	-	-	-	-	-	-
Prison service establishments	-	-	-	-	-	-	-	-	-
Defence establishments	-	-	-	-	-	-	-	-	-
Educational establishments	6	2	42	7	43	48	2	-	8
Hotels, boarding houses etc	4	2	-	-	3	6	-	-	-
Hostels and common lodging houses (non-HA)	-	-	-	-	-	-	-	-	-
Other miscellaneous establishments	2	-	14	-	1	16	-	-	-
Persons sleeping rough	-	-	-	-	-	-	-	-	-
Campers	-	-	-	-	-	-	-	-	-
Civilian ships, boats and barges	-	-	-	-	-	-	-	-	-

Type of establishment	In employment	Un-employed	Econ-omically inactive	Econ-omically active students	Migrants	Ethnic group: White	Black groups	Indian, Pakistani and Bangla-deshi	Chinese and other groups
ALL HOTELS AND OTHER ESTABLISHMENTS	**626**	**107**	**95**	**5**	**501**	**869**	**8**	**4**	**2**
Children's homes	-	-	-	-	1	4	6	-	-
Prison service establishments	-	-	4	-	1	4	-	-	-
Defence establishments	582	1	2	4	342	582	-	2	1
Educational establishments	9	1	5	-	6	14	-	1	-
Hotels, boarding houses etc	25	78	42	1	103	177	2	-	-
Hostels and common lodging houses (non-HA)	4	15	16	-	14	35	-	-	1
Other miscellaneous establishments	6	12	26	-	34	53	-	1	-
Persons sleeping rough	-	-	-	-	-	-	-	-	-
Campers	-	-	-	-	-	-	-	-	-
Civilian ships, boats and barges	-	-	-	-	-	-	-	-	-

6. Residents

Age	TOTAL PERSONS	Ethnic group: White	Black Caribbean	Black African	Black other	Indian	Pakistani	Bangla-deshi	Chinese	Other groups: Asian	Other groups: Other	Persons born in Ireland
a	b	c	d	e	f	g	h	i	j	k	l	m
					AVON							
TOTAL PERSONS	**932,674**	**906,980**	**7,147**	**1,087**	**2,725**	**3,778**	**2,847**	**770**	**2,125**	**1,339**	**3,876**	**10,639**
Males, all ages	**452,094**	**439,206**	**3,481**	**625**	**1,320**	**1,886**	**1,471**	**409**	**1,058**	**611**	**2,027**	**5,076**
0 - 4	30,811	29,291	266	55	317	167	165	56	64	45	385	45
5 - 9	28,497	27,090	241	50	252	190	216	60	69	48	281	71
10 - 14	27,260	26,080	238	49	167	175	197	51	67	56	180	101
15	5,412	5,219	35	13	25	27	29	5	16	11	32	13
16 - 17	11,611	11,203	87	11	48	64	58	21	35	16	68	45
18 - 19	12,749	12,319	97	14	60	54	55	10	51	20	69	45
20 - 24	35,464	34,272	277	62	120	170	136	31	148	72	176	242
25 - 29	37,663	36,442	362	75	141	164	102	30	119	48	180	363
30 - 34	33,633	32,425	321	109	62	186	108	44	125	66	187	351
35 - 39	30,897	29,998	195	75	35	186	102	24	89	55	138	428
40 - 44	34,113	33,481	103	43	26	146	54	10	81	63	106	451
45 - 49	29,453	28,931	149	23	26	90	60	18	35	44	77	476
50 - 54	25,271	24,626	296	26	8	86	80	25	59	27	38	456
55 - 59	23,574	22,983	322	13	12	73	51	13	44	17	46	471
60 - 64	23,052	22,656	232	2	12	47	37	8	22	9	27	408
65 - 69	21,659	21,437	135	2	4	31	10	1	19	4	16	408
70 - 74	16,814	16,675	85	2	2	20	8	1	7	6	8	374
75 - 79	12,824	12,773	26	1	2	5	2	-	5	2	8	208
80 - 84	7,414	7,390	11	-	1	4	-	1	2	1	4	91
85 and over	3,923	3,915	3	-	-	1	1	-	1	1	1	29
Females, all ages	**480,580**	**467,774**	**3,666**	**462**	**1,405**	**1,892**	**1,376**	**361**	**1,067**	**728**	**1,849**	**5,563**
0 - 4	29,173	27,645	254	54	318	193	187	62	66	45	349	34
5 - 9	27,107	25,778	248	46	257	195	166	48	66	48	255	89
10 - 14	25,916	24,782	212	41	176	209	158	46	73	40	179	90
15	5,145	4,942	46	7	30	28	20	7	21	7	37	10
16 - 17	10,958	10,557	92	13	38	59	59	12	39	18	71	31
18 - 19	12,308	11,923	82	19	50	52	58	19	40	17	48	44
20 - 24	35,536	34,326	306	44	145	153	150	41	115	76	180	285
25 - 29	38,151	36,722	438	79	180	186	123	29	132	91	171	353
30 - 34	34,028	32,809	375	53	80	195	114	29	114	110	149	388
35 - 39	31,135	30,214	227	39	30	185	94	24	122	88	112	414
40 - 44	34,304	33,612	161	27	22	131	71	15	92	89	84	545
45 - 49	29,253	28,711	210	16	30	78	55	12	42	36	63	505
50 - 54	25,101	24,573	280	11	13	67	52	11	46	19	29	457
55 - 59	23,926	23,448	272	3	14	53	31	3	39	18	45	440
60 - 64	24,417	24,068	211	6	5	44	18	1	24	10	30	479
65 - 69	25,461	25,265	117	2	7	27	3	1	12	5	22	460
70 - 74	22,301	22,170	73	2	3	14	6	1	10	8	14	387
75 - 79	19,501	19,438	34	-	4	8	3	-	5	2	7	287
80 - 84	14,593	14,549	17	-	3	11	5	-	6	-	2	155
85 and over	12,266	12,242	11	-	-	4	3	-	3	1	2	110
Born in UK	889,505	876,223	3,565	364	2,499	1,703	1,475	287	602	248	2,539	3,410
With limiting long-term illness	**110,766**	**108,664**	**945**	**114**	**151**	**246**	**225**	**50**	**78**	**59**	**234**	**1,801**
Males	49,311	48,299	442	52	75	114	119	28	35	30	117	927
Females	61,455	60,365	503	62	76	132	106	22	43	29	117	874

6. Residents

Age	TOTAL PERSONS	Ethnic group: White	Black Caribbean	Black African	Black other	Indian	Pakistani	Bangla-deshi	Chinese	Other groups: Asian	Other groups: Other	Persons born in Ireland
a	b	c	d	e	f	g	h	i	j	k	l	m
					Bath							
TOTAL PERSONS	**78,689**	**76,628**	**551**	**79**	**241**	**203**	**29**	**74**	**300**	**159**	**425**	**1,076**
Males, all ages	**37,115**	**36,036**	**284**	**49**	**115**	**110**	**16**	**41**	**170**	**72**	**222**	**493**
0 - 4	2,231	2,141	15	1	26	5	1	5	5	6	26	3
5 - 9	2,054	1,956	19	3	20	6	1	4	9	5	31	3
10 - 14	1,957	1,875	13	2	11	10	2	5	14	6	19	7
15	410	393	2	2	2	3	-	-	2	1	5	-
16 - 17	931	905	6	-	4	1	-	4	2	1	8	4
18 - 19	1,018	982	10	2	6	3	-	2	7	4	2	3
20 - 24	3,248	3,112	24	12	12	8	3	3	32	16	26	37
25 - 29	3,097	2,965	35	5	17	9	3	1	27	6	29	36
30 - 34	2,669	2,551	31	7	4	15	3	6	23	7	22	27
35 - 39	2,406	2,345	8	7	5	6	-	3	10	5	17	49
40 - 44	2,653	2,590	10	5	1	11	1	1	13	6	15	39
45 - 49	2,264	2,213	14	3	2	12	-	3	6	2	9	39
50 - 54	2,032	1,982	26	-	2	5	1	2	7	3	4	38
55 - 59	1,892	1,845	32	-	-	7	-	-	3	3	2	28
60 - 64	2,022	1,984	19	-	2	5	1	2	5	-	4	35
65 - 69	2,082	2,066	9	-	-	3	-	-	4	-	-	41
70 - 74	1,648	1,638	7	-	-	1	-	-	-	1	1	49
75 - 79	1,329	1,324	3	-	1	-	-	-	-	-	1	37
80 - 84	785	783	1	-	-	-	-	-	-	-	1	14
85 and over	387	386	-	-	-	-	-	-	1	-	-	4
Females, all ages	**41,574**	**40,592**	**267**	**30**	**126**	**93**	**13**	**33**	**130**	**87**	**203**	**583**
0 - 4	2,141	2,033	18	2	31	3	1	6	4	6	37	3
5 - 9	1,949	1,868	18	1	23	3	-	3	5	8	20	6
10 - 14	1,909	1,845	9	3	12	8	-	3	9	3	17	3
15	435	418	3	1	3	4	-	-	1	-	5	2
16 - 17	814	775	9	2	7	6	-	1	5	1	8	4
18 - 19	1,128	1,098	7	2	6	-	1	-	3	5	6	8
20 - 24	3,384	3,273	31	4	20	6	3	4	15	6	22	33
25 - 29	3,101	2,987	27	7	11	9	1	3	21	13	22	31
30 - 34	2,687	2,600	18	3	4	8	1	6	9	17	21	42
35 - 39	2,532	2,454	10	3	3	11	1	2	24	10	14	30
40 - 44	2,727	2,673	9	-	2	13	3	2	11	10	4	47
45 - 49	2,350	2,309	18	1	-	7	1	-	5	-	9	51
50 - 54	2,074	2,032	21	1	2	6	-	2	6	1	3	46
55 - 59	2,114	2,066	30	-	-	3	1	1	5	4	4	48
60 - 64	2,344	2,312	22	-	-	2	-	-	3	-	5	63
65 - 69	2,509	2,490	10	-	1	2	-	-	1	1	4	43
70 - 74	2,293	2,283	4	-	-	1	-	-	1	2	2	46
75 - 79	2,092	2,089	1	-	1	-	-	-	1	-	-	40
80 - 84	1,613	1,611	-	-	-	1	-	-	1	-	-	22
85 and over	1,378	1,376	2	-	-	-	-	-	-	-	-	15
Born in UK	73,307	72,416	271	24	213	52	6	22	50	19	234	382
With limiting long-term illness	**9,521**	**9,376**	**63**	**5**	**14**	**14**	**2**	**6**	**14**	**4**	**23**	**154**
Males	4,012	3,937	34	4	7	7	1	5	5	1	11	78
Females	5,509	5,439	29	1	7	7	1	1	9	3	12	76

6. Residents

Age	TOTAL PERSONS	Ethnic group										Persons born in Ireland
		White	Black Caribbean	Black African	Black other	Indian	Pakistani	Bangla-deshi	Chinese	Other groups		
										Asian	Other	
a	b	c	d	e	f	g	h	i	j	k	l	m
					Bristol							
TOTAL PERSONS	**376,146**	**356,865**	**5,971**	**814**	**2,120**	**2,773**	**2,717**	**557**	**1,135**	**772**	**2,422**	**5,571**
Males, all ages	**181,644**	**172,010**	**2,872**	**469**	**1,029**	**1,368**	**1,395**	**285**	**573**	**365**	**1,278**	**2,784**
0 - 4	13,237	12,043	230	45	247	127	161	41	31	32	280	24
5 - 9	11,672	10,545	209	30	211	157	213	46	45	30	186	39
10 - 14	10,441	9,517	202	35	139	136	191	39	31	36	115	53
15	2,015	1,876	28	7	20	21	29	4	10	5	15	6
16 - 17	4,193	3,891	68	9	36	51	58	10	20	6	44	25
18 - 19	4,746	4,438	75	11	42	44	52	4	27	9	44	17
20 - 24	15,498	14,615	227	43	92	125	127	22	87	44	116	145
25 - 29	17,070	16,169	283	60	112	121	92	24	68	28	113	225
30 - 34	14,557	13,687	252	91	44	129	98	30	62	42	122	194
35 - 39	12,574	11,949	148	56	22	133	97	12	49	35	73	226
40 - 44	12,763	12,372	72	22	18	95	51	7	40	33	53	229
45 - 49	10,445	10,100	115	18	18	57	53	10	16	23	35	243
50 - 54	9,264	8,768	254	24	4	60	72	19	28	13	22	253
55 - 59	8,861	8,399	275	12	11	40	49	11	23	10	31	295
60 - 64	9,046	8,740	205	2	7	26	31	3	14	8	10	235
65 - 69	8,692	8,509	119	2	3	26	10	1	8	4	10	228
70 - 74	6,887	6,769	76	2	2	14	8	1	7	4	4	194
75 - 79	5,196	5,160	23	-	-	2	2	-	5	2	2	106
80 - 84	2,931	2,912	10	-	1	3	-	1	2	-	2	36
85 and over	1,556	1,551	1	-	-	1	1	-	-	1	1	11
Females, all ages	**194,502**	**184,855**	**3,099**	**345**	**1,091**	**1,405**	**1,322**	**272**	**562**	**407**	**1,144**	**2,787**
0 - 4	12,598	11,422	218	40	247	142	181	48	40	29	231	19
5 - 9	11,149	10,092	209	37	199	163	165	38	39	29	178	48
10 - 14	9,942	9,064	179	27	143	168	155	35	38	21	112	53
15	1,930	1,781	41	4	24	22	19	5	11	4	19	4
16 - 17	4,008	3,724	67	8	27	48	57	9	22	12	34	12
18 - 19	4,771	4,483	63	13	33	44	55	17	23	8	32	26
20 - 24	15,902	14,955	263	33	110	122	144	29	72	54	120	177
25 - 29	17,796	16,703	371	64	149	131	115	22	66	59	116	222
30 - 34	14,692	13,794	325	45	67	131	112	21	61	56	80	200
35 - 39	12,285	11,646	188	30	20	129	86	17	57	46	66	208
40 - 44	12,468	12,013	135	17	16	86	66	9	40	37	49	257
45 - 49	10,242	9,868	171	12	23	48	50	10	19	15	26	215
50 - 54	9,147	8,738	238	4	8	49	50	7	24	12	17	223
55 - 59	8,941	8,586	224	3	8	37	30	2	18	8	25	215
60 - 64	9,727	9,446	185	4	3	35	17	1	13	8	15	240
65 - 69	10,463	10,309	104	2	5	20	3	1	7	2	10	225
70 - 74	9,339	9,231	64	2	3	13	6	1	4	6	9	191
75 - 79	8,120	8,069	32	-	3	6	3	-	4	-	3	138
80 - 84	6,087	6,053	15	-	3	9	5	-	1	-	1	70
85 and over	4,895	4,878	7	-	-	2	3	-	3	1	1	44
Born in UK	353,028	342,662	2,961	257	1,963	1,351	1,436	222	348	167	1,661	1,508
With limiting long-term illness	**49,275**	**47,552**	**843**	**78**	**121**	**199**	**218**	**38**	**36**	**37**	**153**	**1,057**
Males	22,265	21,426	396	39	60	90	115	20	16	24	79	586
Females	27,010	26,126	447	39	61	109	103	18	20	13	74	471

6. Residents

Age	TOTAL PERSONS	Ethnic group: White	Black Caribbean	Black African	Black other	Indian	Pakistani	Bangla-deshi	Chinese	Other groups: Asian	Other groups: Other	Persons born in Ireland
a	b	c	d	e	f	g	h	i	j	k	l	m
					Kingswood							
TOTAL PERSONS	**89,717**	**88,731**	**226**	**32**	**95**	**165**	**28**	**30**	**154**	**74**	**182**	**612**
Males, all ages	**43,883**	**43,378**	**118**	**16**	**50**	**83**	**18**	**20**	**65**	**33**	**102**	**275**
0 - 4	3,068	3,000	11	1	16	12	-	2	7	2	17	1
5 - 9	2,785	2,741	2	3	5	6	-	3	7	1	17	5
10 - 14	2,689	2,639	9	1	8	6	3	2	6	1	14	7
15	538	531	1	1	1	-	-	1	1	1	1	1
16 - 17	1,141	1,121	6	-	3	5	-	1	2	-	3	1
18 - 19	1,249	1,231	3	-	2	1	1	2	4	2	3	3
20 - 24	3,140	3,099	12	2	5	6	2	1	6	2	5	7
25 - 29	3,475	3,427	13	2	3	8	2	3	4	5	8	19
30 - 34	3,389	3,343	15	-	3	8	2	-	6	4	8	22
35 - 39	3,106	3,067	13	-	1	8	-	1	5	3	8	28
40 - 44	3,345	3,316	6	3	-	3	-	-	7	4	6	31
45 - 49	2,946	2,916	7	1	3	4	2	3	2	5	3	27
50 - 54	2,652	2,626	8	1	-	5	3	1	3	2	3	25
55 - 59	2,586	2,566	7	-	-	5	1	-	4	-	3	28
60 - 64	2,338	2,327	4	-	-	4	2	-	-	1	-	17
65 - 69	2,089	2,085	1	-	-	1	-	-	1	-	1	26
70 - 74	1,413	1,411	-	-	-	1	-	-	-	-	1	17
75 - 79	1,023	1,021	-	1	-	-	-	-	-	-	1	5
80 - 84	627	627	-	-	-	-	-	-	-	-	-	2
85 and over	284	284	-	-	-	-	-	-	-	-	-	3
Females, all ages	**45,834**	**45,353**	**108**	**16**	**45**	**82**	**10**	**10**	**89**	**41**	**80**	**337**
0 - 4	2,872	2,807	6	3	12	11	-	1	9	1	22	1
5 - 9	2,715	2,675	8	-	6	3	-	-	6	5	12	10
10 - 14	2,634	2,586	9	4	8	8	1	3	7	2	6	5
15	528	517	1	-	1	-	-	1	4	-	4	1
16 - 17	1,101	1,087	4	1	2	-	-	-	3	-	4	1
18 - 19	1,150	1,136	6	-	-	3	1	-	3	-	1	-
20 - 24	3,052	3,029	2	1	4	3	1	1	5	4	2	9
25 - 29	3,543	3,495	10	1	6	8	2	-	12	3	6	15
30 - 34	3,413	3,363	9	1	3	10	-	-	10	10	7	23
35 - 39	3,179	3,134	14	-	1	10	1	2	12	3	2	33
40 - 44	3,283	3,241	7	4	-	11	1	2	8	5	4	33
45 - 49	2,994	2,971	10	-	1	2	1	-	1	5	3	32
50 - 54	2,614	2,595	9	1	-	5	2	-	-	1	1	29
55 - 59	2,692	2,665	11	-	1	5	-	-	6	1	3	37
60 - 64	2,444	2,436	2	-	-	1	-	-	1	1	3	33
65 - 69	2,239	2,239	-	-	-	-	-	-	-	-	-	29
70 - 74	1,814	1,813	-	-	-	-	-	-	1	-	-	17
75 - 79	1,522	1,522	-	-	-	-	-	-	-	-	-	12
80 - 84	1,124	1,123	-	-	-	-	-	-	1	-	-	8
85 and over	921	919	-	-	-	2	-	-	-	-	-	9
Born in UK	87,570	87,095	104	10	88	63	10	8	48	12	132	201
With limiting long-term illness	**9,291**	**9,253**	**4**	**3**	**2**	**9**	**2**	**1**	**7**	**2**	**8**	**76**
Males	4,244	4,225	2	1	-	5	1	-	2	-	8	35
Females	5,047	5,028	2	2	2	4	1	1	5	2	-	41

6. Residents

Age	TOTAL PERSONS	Ethnic group										Persons born in Ireland
		White	Black Caribbean	Black African	Black other	Indian	Pakistani	Bangla-deshi	Chinese	Other groups		
										Asian	Other	
a	b	c	d	e	f	g	h	i	j	k	l	m
					Northavon							
TOTAL PERSONS	**130,647**	**129,120**	**247**	**65**	**129**	**331**	**42**	**26**	**215**	**156**	**316**	**1,231**
Males, all ages	**65,017**	**64,266**	**122**	**43**	**60**	**168**	**24**	**16**	**95**	**71**	**152**	**580**
0 - 4	4,545	4,471	6	2	15	14	1	2	11	3	20	4
5 - 9	4,151	4,088	7	7	8	12	1	-	4	8	16	12
10 - 14	4,155	4,109	5	2	4	11	-	-	2	8	14	12
15	885	874	4	2	1	1	-	-	-	2	1	2
16 - 17	1,844	1,821	6	1	2	5	-	2	3	2	2	5
18 - 19	1,940	1,914	4	-	5	2	2	-	1	4	8	8
20 - 24	5,117	5,051	6	4	4	15	1	3	13	6	14	19
25 - 29	5,752	5,676	21	4	6	14	4	1	9	2	15	35
30 - 34	5,133	5,040	14	7	3	22	3	2	19	8	15	54
35 - 39	4,426	4,345	18	7	3	20	-	2	11	5	15	43
40 - 44	5,263	5,194	10	6	4	19	1	1	6	11	11	59
45 - 49	4,854	4,813	8	-	1	8	4	-	2	7	11	68
50 - 54	3,988	3,958	5	-	1	7	3	-	7	3	4	56
55 - 59	3,363	3,339	5	1	1	7	1	1	5	2	1	51
60 - 64	3,023	3,006	2	-	1	6	3	2	1	-	2	41
65 - 69	2,435	2,432	1	-	-	-	-	-	1	-	1	33
70 - 74	1,699	1,697	-	-	-	2	-	-	-	-	-	43
75 - 79	1,351	1,346	-	-	1	3	-	-	-	-	1	20
80 - 84	747	746	-	-	-	-	-	-	-	-	1	10
85 and over	346	346	-	-	-	-	-	-	-	-	-	5
Females, all ages	**65,630**	**64,854**	**125**	**22**	**69**	**163**	**18**	**10**	**120**	**85**	**164**	**651**
0 - 4	4,258	4,174	10	2	16	19	2	-	4	2	29	4
5 - 9	3,849	3,782	7	2	12	18	1	1	8	3	15	12
10 - 14	3,961	3,898	9	3	5	14	2	-	10	5	15	8
15	758	750	-	1	2	1	1	-	1	1	1	-
16 - 17	1,702	1,673	10	-	-	1	1	-	3	4	10	4
18 - 19	1,854	1,831	3	2	6	3	1	1	5	1	1	2
20 - 24	5,188	5,122	9	5	6	11	1	3	13	5	13	34
25 - 29	5,658	5,564	20	1	7	21	3	1	18	4	19	40
30 - 34	4,847	4,746	18	2	5	25	-	-	15	17	19	44
35 - 39	4,543	4,476	9	1	2	19	2	-	9	13	12	57
40 - 44	5,336	5,285	6	1	2	10	1	1	9	16	5	73
45 - 49	4,734	4,693	7	1	2	9	2	1	5	7	7	88
50 - 54	3,800	3,768	7	1	-	4	-	2	10	3	5	64
55 - 59	3,261	3,238	7	-	4	3	-	-	3	2	4	49
60 - 64	2,790	2,780	-	-	-	1	1	-	4	1	3	44
65 - 69	2,658	2,650	1	-	-	3	-	-	1	1	2	42
70 - 74	2,260	2,253	2	-	-	-	-	-	2	-	3	39
75 - 79	1,877	1,876	-	-	-	1	-	-	-	-	-	29
80 - 84	1,311	1,310	-	-	-	-	-	-	-	-	1	11
85 and over	985	985	-	-	-	-	-	-	-	-	-	7
Born in UK	126,308	125,637	132	25	108	125	11	9	60	27	174	474
With limiting long-term illness	**11,599**	**11,521**	**14**	**8**	**6**	**18**	**2**	**1**	**7**	**6**	**16**	**162**
Males	5,354	5,320	4	3	3	11	1	-	4	2	6	73
Females	6,245	6,201	10	5	3	7	1	1	3	4	10	89

6. Residents

Age	TOTAL PERSONS	Ethnic group										Persons born in Ireland
		White	Black Caribbean	Black African	Black other	Indian	Pakistani	Bangla-deshi	Chinese	Other groups		
										Asian	Other	
a	b	c	d	e	f	g	h	i	j	k	l	m
						Wansdyke						
TOTAL PERSONS	**80,003**	**79,551**	**39**	**36**	**39**	**65**	**5**	**2**	**75**	**39**	**152**	**571**
Males, all ages	**39,058**	**38,852**	**19**	**17**	**18**	**28**	**3**	**2**	**35**	**10**	**74**	**224**
0 - 4	2,413	2,385	3	5	4	-	-	-	2	-	14	-
5 - 9	2,482	2,462	2	3	3	4	-	-	2	-	6	1
10 - 14	2,541	2,524	2	2	-	2	-	2	5	-	4	9
15	507	504	-	-	-	1	-	-	-	-	2	2
16 - 17	1,070	1,062	-	-	1	1	-	-	2	1	3	2
18 - 19	1,165	1,160	1	-	-	-	-	-	1	-	3	2
20 - 24	2,641	2,632	1	-	-	3	-	-	2	1	2	11
25 - 29	2,589	2,569	2	2	-	3	-	-	3	2	8	18
30 - 34	2,532	2,516	2	1	3	-	1	-	4	1	4	16
35 - 39	2,699	2,675	2	3	3	3	1	-	4	-	8	20
40 - 44	3,176	3,162	-	1	1	3	-	-	4	2	3	19
45 - 49	2,746	2,733	3	-	-	1	-	-	3	1	5	21
50 - 54	2,348	2,338	-	-	1	1	1	-	2	2	3	23
55 - 59	2,282	2,277	-	-	-	3	-	-	-	-	2	14
60 - 64	2,127	2,121	-	-	1	1	-	-	-	-	4	15
65 - 69	2,022	2,016	1	-	1	1	-	-	1	-	2	25
70 - 74	1,507	1,506	-	-	-	1	-	-	-	-	-	15
75 - 79	1,172	1,171	-	-	-	-	-	-	-	-	1	5
80 - 84	684	684	-	-	-	-	-	-	-	-	-	6
85 and over	355	355	-	-	-	-	-	-	-	-	-	-
Females, all ages	**40,945**	**40,699**	**20**	**19**	**21**	**37**	**2**	**-**	**40**	**29**	**78**	**347**
0 - 4	2,293	2,276	-	4	3	3	-	-	4	-	3	2
5 - 9	2,263	2,245	1	2	5	1	-	-	3	-	6	2
10 - 14	2,351	2,329	3	1	2	2	-	-	-	2	12	4
15	505	500	-	-	-	1	-	-	2	1	1	1
16 - 17	1,052	1,040	1	1	-	3	-	-	1	-	6	2
18 - 19	1,085	1,072	-	1	3	-	-	-	2	2	5	2
20 - 24	2,502	2,484	-	1	2	2	-	-	4	4	5	10
25 - 29	2,532	2,506	5	3	3	4	-	-	3	5	3	17
30 - 34	2,662	2,644	1	2	-	4	-	-	3	2	6	21
35 - 39	2,714	2,691	3	1	1	4	2	-	4	1	7	35
40 - 44	3,288	3,257	2	2	-	4	-	-	8	6	9	30
45 - 49	2,783	2,768	1	-	-	3	-	-	2	2	7	30
50 - 54	2,386	2,379	2	-	1	1	-	-	1	1	1	26
55 - 59	2,265	2,255	-	-	-	2	-	-	2	2	4	31
60 - 64	2,302	2,298	-	1	1	2	-	-	-	-	-	21
65 - 69	2,246	2,242	-	-	-	-	-	-	1	-	3	39
70 - 74	1,919	1,919	-	-	-	-	-	-	-	-	-	30
75 - 79	1,605	1,604	-	-	-	-	-	-	-	1	-	18
80 - 84	1,194	1,192	1	-	-	1	-	-	-	-	-	12
85 and over	998	998	-	-	-	-	-	-	-	-	-	14
Born in UK	77,717	77,508	22	14	37	28	1	1	26	4	76	212
With limiting long-term illness	**8,233**	**8,208**	**3**	**4**	**4**	**1**	**-**	**2**	**1**	**2**	**8**	**84**
Males	3,661	3,651	-	1	2	-	-	2	1	-	4	35
Females	4,572	4,557	3	3	2	1	-	-	-	2	4	49

6. Residents

Age	TOTAL PERSONS	Ethnic group: White	Black Caribbean	Black African	Black other	Indian	Pakistani	Bangla-deshi	Chinese	Other groups: Asian	Other groups: Other	Persons born in Ireland
a	b	c	d	e	f	g	h	i	j	k	l	m
					Woodspring							
TOTAL PERSONS	**177,472**	**176,085**	**113**	**61**	**101**	**241**	**26**	**81**	**246**	**139**	**379**	**1,578**
Males, all ages	**85,377**	**84,664**	**66**	**31**	**48**	**129**	**15**	**45**	**120**	**60**	**199**	**720**
0 - 4	5,317	5,251	1	1	9	9	2	6	8	2	28	13
5 - 9	5,353	5,298	2	4	5	5	1	7	2	4	25	11
10 - 14	5,477	5,416	7	7	5	10	1	3	9	5	14	13
15	1,057	1,041	-	1	1	1	-	-	3	2	8	2
16 - 17	2,432	2,403	1	1	2	1	-	4	6	6	8	8
18 - 19	2,631	2,594	4	1	5	4	-	2	11	1	9	12
20 - 24	5,820	5,763	7	1	7	13	3	2	8	3	13	23
25 - 29	5,680	5,636	8	2	3	9	1	1	8	5	7	30
30 - 34	5,353	5,288	7	3	5	12	1	6	11	4	16	38
35 - 39	5,686	5,617	6	2	1	16	4	6	10	7	17	62
40 - 44	6,913	6,847	5	6	2	15	1	1	11	7	18	74
45 - 49	6,198	6,156	2	1	2	8	1	2	6	6	14	78
50 - 54	4,987	4,954	3	1	-	8	-	3	12	4	2	61
55 - 59	4,590	4,557	3	-	-	11	-	1	9	2	7	55
60 - 64	4,496	4,478	2	-	1	5	-	1	2	-	7	65
65 - 69	4,339	4,329	4	-	-	-	-	-	4	-	2	55
70 - 74	3,660	3,654	2	-	-	1	-	-	-	1	2	56
75 - 79	2,753	2,751	-	-	-	-	-	-	-	-	2	35
80 - 84	1,640	1,638	-	-	-	1	-	-	-	1	-	23
85 and over	995	993	2	-	-	-	-	-	-	-	-	6
Females, all ages	**92,095**	**91,421**	**47**	**30**	**53**	**112**	**11**	**36**	**126**	**79**	**180**	**858**
0 - 4	5,011	4,933	2	3	9	15	3	7	5	7	27	5
5 - 9	5,182	5,116	5	4	12	7	-	6	5	3	24	11
10 - 14	5,119	5,060	3	3	6	9	-	5	9	7	17	17
15	989	976	1	1	-	-	-	1	2	1	7	2
16 - 17	2,281	2,258	1	1	2	1	1	2	5	1	9	8
18 - 19	2,320	2,303	3	1	2	2	-	1	4	1	3	6
20 - 24	5,508	5,463	1	-	3	9	1	4	6	3	18	22
25 - 29	5,521	5,467	5	3	4	13	2	3	12	7	5	28
30 - 34	5,727	5,662	4	-	1	17	1	2	16	8	16	58
35 - 39	5,882	5,813	3	4	3	12	2	3	16	15	11	51
40 - 44	7,202	7,143	2	3	2	7	-	1	16	15	13	105
45 - 49	6,150	6,102	3	2	4	9	1	1	10	7	11	89
50 - 54	5,080	5,061	3	4	2	2	-	-	5	1	2	69
55 - 59	4,653	4,638	-	-	1	3	-	-	5	1	5	60
60 - 64	4,810	4,796	2	1	1	3	-	-	3	-	4	78
65 - 69	5,346	5,335	2	-	1	2	-	-	2	1	3	82
70 - 74	4,676	4,671	3	-	-	-	-	-	2	-	-	64
75 - 79	4,285	4,278	1	-	-	1	-	-	-	1	4	50
80 - 84	3,264	3,260	1	-	-	-	-	-	3	-	-	32
85 and over	3,089	3,086	2	-	-	-	-	-	-	-	1	21
Born in UK	171,575	170,905	75	34	90	84	11	25	70	19	262	633
With limiting long-term illness	**22,847**	**22,754**	**18**	**16**	**4**	**5**	**1**	**2**	**13**	**8**	**26**	**268**
Males	9,775	9,740	6	4	3	1	1	1	7	3	9	120
Females	13,072	13,014	12	12	1	4	-	1	6	5	17	148

7. Residents

Country of birth	TOTAL PERSONS	Males	Females
a	b	c	d
AVON			
ALL COUNTRIES OF BIRTH	**932,674**	**452,094**	**480,580**
Europe	906,698	439,422	467,276
European Community	903,870	438,013	465,857
United Kingdom	**889,505**	**431,677**	**457,828**
England	844,919	410,754	434,165
Scotland	11,899	6,022	5,877
Wales	29,233	13,181	16,052
Northern Ireland	3,410	1,696	1,714
United Kingdom (part not stated)	44	24	20
Outside United Kingdom	**43,169**	**20,417**	**22,752**
Channel Islands	454	203	251
Isle of Man	132	72	60
Irish Republic	7,222	3,378	3,844
Ireland (part not stated)	7	2	5
Old Commonwealth	**3,107**	**1,434**	**1,673**
Australia	1,295	605	690
Canada	1,233	530	703
New Zealand	579	299	280
New Commonwealth	**15,953**	**7,873**	**8,080**
Africa	2,682	1,364	1,318
Eastern Africa	1,772	876	896
Kenya	824	412	412
Malawi	108	51	57
Tanzania	204	102	102
Uganda	356	196	160
Zambia	280	115	165
Southern Africa	452	206	246
Zimbabwe	410	183	227
Botswana, Lesotho and Swaziland	42	23	19
Western Africa	458	282	176
Gambia	16	14	2
Ghana	142	90	52
Nigeria	276	164	112
Sierra Leone	24	14	10
Caribbean	4,079	1,950	2,129
Barbados	226	105	121
Jamaica	3,193	1,531	1,662
Trinidad and Tobago	142	60	82
Other Independent States	201	108	93
Caribbean Dependent Territories	71	30	41
West Indies (so stated)	92	45	47
Belize	18	5	13
Guyana	136	66	70
Asia	7,286	3,620	3,666
South Asia	4,839	2,437	2,402
Bangladesh	507	271	236
India	2,586	1,269	1,317
Pakistan	1,515	776	739
Sri Lanka	231	121	110
South East Asia	2,447	1,183	1,264
Hong Kong	1,208	595	613
Malaysia	625	312	313
Singapore	614	276	338
AVON - *continued*			
Remainder of New Commonwealth	1,906	939	967
Cyprus	793	412	381
Gibraltar	177	79	98
Malta and Gozo	569	264	305
Mauritius	214	120	94
Seychelles	31	12	19
Other New Commonwealth	122	52	70
European Community	**7,136**	**2,956**	**4,180**
Belgium	220	77	143
Denmark	181	75	106
France	917	335	582
Germany	3,322	1,287	2,035
Greece	168	95	73
Italy	1,379	695	684
Luxembourg	8	3	5
Netherlands	414	161	253
Portugal	123	58	65
Spain	404	170	234
Remainder of Europe	**2,242**	**1,134**	**1,108**
Albania	1	-	1
Austria	258	75	183
Bulgaria	20	7	13
Czechoslovakia	100	40	60
Finland	59	10	49
Hungary	246	149	97
Norway	107	40	67
Poland	966	623	343
Romania	43	27	16
Sweden	123	35	88
Switzerland	192	71	121
Yugoslavia	110	52	58
Other Europe	17	5	12
Turkey	**151**	**100**	**51**
U.S.S.R.	**247**	**142**	**105**
Africa	**2,063**	**1,040**	**1,023**
Algeria	90	52	38
Egypt	288	155	133
Libya	129	77	52
Morocco	54	34	20
Tunisia	29	19	10
South Africa, Republic of	1,207	556	651
Other Africa	266	147	119
America	**1,923**	**828**	**1,095**
United States of America	1,361	598	763
Caribbean	33	18	15
Central America	61	24	37
South America	468	188	280
Asia	**2,501**	**1,236**	**1,265**
Middle East	1,137	679	458
Iran	412	265	147
Israel	100	52	48
Other Middle East	625	362	263
Remainder of Asia	1,364	557	807
Burma (Myanmar, Union of)	222	100	122
China, Peoples Republic of	386	186	200
Japan	132	47	85
Philippines	156	19	137
Vietnam	210	118	92
Other Asia	258	87	171
Rest of the world and at sea/in the air	**31**	**19**	**12**

7. Residents

Country of birth	TOTAL PERSONS	Males	Females
a	b	c	d
Bath			
ALL COUNTRIES OF BIRTH	**78,689**	**37,115**	**41,574**
Europe	75,402	35,526	39,876
European Community	75,047	35,358	39,689
United Kingdom	**73,307**	**34,620**	**38,687**
England	69,162	32,770	36,392
Scotland	1,405	640	765
Wales	2,352	1,010	1,342
Northern Ireland	382	198	184
United Kingdom (part not stated)	6	2	4
Outside United Kingdom	**5,382**	**2,495**	**2,887**
Channel Islands	53	20	33
Isle of Man	7	3	4
Irish Republic	694	295	399
Ireland (part not stated)	-	-	-
Old Commonwealth	**525**	**233**	**292**
Australia	251	120	131
Canada	173	71	102
New Zealand	101	42	59
New Commonwealth	**1,657**	**834**	**823**
Africa	302	150	152
Eastern Africa	199	98	101
Kenya	90	46	44
Malawi	15	9	6
Tanzania	24	12	12
Uganda	34	18	16
Zambia	36	13	23
Southern Africa	63	28	35
Zimbabwe	53	23	30
Botswana, Lesotho and Swaziland	10	5	5
Western Africa	40	24	16
Gambia	2	1	1
Ghana	12	10	2
Nigeria	25	12	13
Sierra Leone	1	1	-
Caribbean	342	172	170
Barbados	85	41	44
Jamaica	186	99	87
Trinidad and Tobago	19	6	13
Other Independent States	14	12	2
Caribbean Dependent Territories	14	1	13
West Indies (so stated)	8	4	4
Belize	-	-	-
Guyana	16	9	7
Asia	816	417	399
South Asia	458	223	235
Bangladesh	51	29	22
India	318	147	171
Pakistan	57	29	28
Sri Lanka	32	18	14
South East Asia	358	194	164
Hong Kong	175	97	78
Malaysia	86	51	35
Singapore	97	46	51
Bath - *continued*			
Remainder of New Commonwealth	197	95	102
Cyprus	64	30	34
Gibraltar	25	15	10
Malta and Gozo	76	39	37
Mauritius	19	7	12
Seychelles	1	-	1
Other New Commonwealth	12	4	8
European Community	**1,046**	**443**	**603**
Belgium	33	11	22
Denmark	41	16	25
France	153	58	95
Germany	372	151	221
Greece	33	17	16
Italy	267	130	137
Luxembourg	2	1	1
Netherlands	61	22	39
Portugal	6	2	4
Spain	78	35	43
Remainder of Europe	**295**	**145**	**150**
Albania	-	-	-
Austria	40	10	30
Bulgaria	3	1	2
Czechoslovakia	10	7	3
Finland	6	3	3
Hungary	32	11	21
Norway	20	12	8
Poland	89	60	29
Romania	9	6	3
Sweden	27	6	21
Switzerland	36	16	20
Yugoslavia	22	12	10
Other Europe	1	1	-
Turkey	**40**	**24**	**16**
U.S.S.R.	**29**	**17**	**12**
Africa	**302**	**157**	**145**
Algeria	14	9	5
Egypt	63	37	26
Libya	33	22	11
Morocco	12	6	6
Tunisia	4	2	2
South Africa, Republic of	152	68	84
Other Africa	24	13	11
America	**346**	**145**	**201**
United States of America	272	115	157
Caribbean	4	1	3
Central America	10	6	4
South America	60	23	37
Asia	**387**	**178**	**209**
Middle East	164	91	73
Iran	64	38	26
Israel	6	3	3
Other Middle East	94	50	44
Remainder of Asia	223	87	136
Burma (Myanmar, Union of)	17	5	12
China, Peoples Republic of	89	46	43
Japan	25	9	16
Philippines	11	1	10
Vietnam	14	6	8
Other Asia	67	20	47
Rest of the world and at sea/in the air	**1**	**1**	**-**

7. Residents

Country of birth	TOTAL PERSONS	Males	Females
a	b	c	d
Bristol			
ALL COUNTRIES OF BIRTH	**376,146**	**181,644**	**194,502**
Europe	361,725	174,561	187,164
European Community	360,366	173,860	186,506
United Kingdom	**353,028**	**170,473**	**182,555**
England	336,355	162,512	173,843
Scotland	4,460	2,325	2,135
Wales	10,692	4,871	5,821
Northern Ireland	1,508	755	753
United Kingdom (part not stated)	13	10	3
Outside United Kingdom	**23,118**	**11,171**	**11,947**
Channel Islands	183	83	100
Isle of Man	47	25	22
Irish Republic	4,061	2,028	2,033
Ireland (part not stated)	2	1	1
Old Commonwealth	**1,255**	**567**	**688**
Australia	512	226	286
Canada	492	207	285
New Zealand	251	134	117
New Commonwealth	**9,843**	**4,823**	**5,020**
Africa	1,387	723	664
Eastern Africa	938	469	469
Kenya	446	224	222
Malawi	53	31	22
Tanzania	89	44	45
Uganda	211	116	95
Zambia	139	54	85
Southern Africa	176	77	99
Zimbabwe	157	66	91
Botswana, Lesotho and Swaziland	19	11	8
Western Africa	273	177	96
Gambia	13	12	1
Ghana	72	46	26
Nigeria	170	110	60
Sierra Leone	18	9	9
Caribbean	3,290	1,550	1,740
Barbados	109	48	61
Jamaica	2,733	1,298	1,435
Trinidad and Tobago	79	31	48
Other Independent States	157	78	79
Caribbean Dependent Territories	37	15	22
West Indies (so stated)	76	37	39
Belize	8	3	5
Guyana	91	40	51
Asia	4,382	2,178	2,204
South Asia	3,225	1,604	1,621
Bangladesh	364	184	180
India	1,449	704	745
Pakistan	1,308	664	644
Sri Lanka	104	52	52
South East Asia	1,157	574	583
Hong Kong	577	284	293
Malaysia	349	187	162
Singapore	231	103	128

Country of birth	TOTAL PERSONS	Males	Females
a	b	c	d
Bristol - *continued*			
Remainder of New Commonwealth	784	372	412
Cyprus	334	169	165
Gibraltar	55	21	34
Malta and Gozo	213	89	124
Mauritius	106	62	44
Seychelles	13	3	10
Other New Commonwealth	63	28	35
European Community	**3,275**	**1,358**	**1,917**
Belgium	91	33	58
Denmark	60	25	35
France	457	161	296
Germany	1,321	499	822
Greece	82	53	29
Italy	803	400	403
Luxembourg	4	-	4
Netherlands	177	70	107
Portugal	87	43	44
Spain	193	74	119
Remainder of Europe	**1,129**	**593**	**536**
Albania	-	-	-
Austria	114	34	80
Bulgaria	11	4	7
Czechoslovakia	56	22	34
Finland	20	2	18
Hungary	138	89	49
Norway	33	10	23
Poland	540	347	193
Romania	19	12	7
Sweden	62	16	46
Switzerland	67	27	40
Yugoslavia	55	26	29
Other Europe	14	4	10
Turkey	**92**	**64**	**28**
U.S.S.R.	**119**	**69**	**50**
Africa	**950**	**495**	**455**
Algeria	56	34	22
Egypt	97	52	45
Libya	61	36	25
Morocco	24	13	11
Tunisia	18	13	5
South Africa, Republic of	509	237	272
Other Africa	185	110	75
America	**871**	**392**	**479**
United States of America	553	253	300
Caribbean	19	14	5
Central America	30	11	19
South America	269	114	155
Asia	**1,270**	**662**	**608**
Middle East	609	367	242
Iran	229	144	85
Israel	60	34	26
Other Middle East	320	189	131
Remainder of Asia	661	295	366
Burma (Myanmar, Union of)	122	62	60
China, Peoples Republic of	176	86	90
Japan	66	22	44
Philippines	67	10	57
Vietnam	123	68	55
Other Asia	107	47	60
Rest of the world and at sea/in the air	**21**	**11**	**10**

7. Residents

Country of birth	TOTAL PERSONS	Males	Females
a	b	c	d
Kingswood			
ALL COUNTRIES OF BIRTH	**89,717**	**43,883**	**45,834**
Europe	88,532	43,320	45,212
European Community	88,348	43,215	45,133
United Kingdom	**87,570**	**42,901**	**44,669**
England	84,311	41,392	42,919
Scotland	707	354	353
Wales	2,350	1,051	1,299
Northern Ireland	201	104	97
United Kingdom (part not stated)	1	-	1
Outside United Kingdom	**2,147**	**982**	**1,165**
Channel Islands	26	16	10
Isle of Man	12	6	6
Irish Republic	409	170	239
Ireland (part not stated)	2	1	1
Old Commonwealth	**171**	**76**	**95**
Australia	63	24	39
Canada	79	38	41
New Zealand	29	14	15
New Commonwealth	**712**	**340**	**372**
Africa	148	75	73
Eastern Africa	102	51	51
Kenya	39	19	20
Malawi	5	-	5
Tanzania	23	12	11
Uganda	22	13	9
Zambia	13	7	6
Southern Africa	26	10	16
Zimbabwe	26	10	16
Botswana, Lesotho and Swaziland	-	-	-
Western Africa	20	14	6
Gambia	1	1	-
Ghana	9	5	4
Nigeria	9	7	2
Sierra Leone	1	1	-
Caribbean	138	66	72
Barbados	5	2	3
Jamaica	112	53	59
Trinidad and Tobago	5	3	2
Other Independent States	4	3	1
Caribbean Dependent Territories	1	1	-
West Indies (so stated)	3	2	1
Belize	4	1	3
Guyana	4	1	3
Asia	324	150	174
South Asia	175	88	87
Bangladesh	15	11	4
India	115	49	66
Pakistan	29	18	11
Sri Lanka	16	10	6
South East Asia	149	62	87
Hong Kong	92	43	49
Malaysia	20	8	12
Singapore	37	11	26
Kingswood - *continued*			
Remainder of New Commonwealth	102	49	53
Cyprus	32	16	16
Gibraltar	14	5	9
Malta and Gozo	32	16	16
Mauritius	15	7	8
Seychelles	1	1	-
Other New Commonwealth	8	4	4
European Community	**367**	**143**	**224**
Belgium	9	3	6
Denmark	6	2	4
France	37	10	27
Germany	192	74	118
Greece	6	3	3
Italy	70	33	37
Luxembourg	-	-	-
Netherlands	18	7	11
Portugal	5	1	4
Spain	24	10	14
Remainder of Europe	**146**	**83**	**63**
Albania	-	-	-
Austria	12	4	8
Bulgaria	-	-	-
Czechoslovakia	3	-	3
Finland	2	-	2
Hungary	13	10	3
Norway	3	1	2
Poland	92	61	31
Romania	2	1	1
Sweden	4	2	2
Switzerland	8	1	7
Yugoslavia	7	3	4
Other Europe	-	-	-
Turkey	**3**	**2**	**1**
U.S.S.R.	**13**	**6**	**7**
Africa	**98**	**50**	**48**
Algeria	6	4	2
Egypt	12	7	5
Libya	7	4	3
Morocco	3	2	1
Tunisia	2	1	1
South Africa, Republic of	62	28	34
Other Africa	6	4	2
America	**87**	**38**	**49**
United States of America	70	29	41
Caribbean	2	1	1
Central America	2	1	1
South America	13	7	6
Asia	**100**	**50**	**50**
Middle East	44	31	13
Iran	19	16	3
Israel	3	2	1
Other Middle East	22	13	9
Remainder of Asia	56	19	37
Burma (Myanmar, Union of)	11	3	8
China, Peoples Republic of	8	4	4
Japan	5	4	1
Philippines	12	-	12
Vietnam	6	4	2
Other Asia	14	4	10
Rest of the world and at sea/in the air	**1**	**1**	**-**

7. Residents

Country of birth	TOTAL PERSONS	Males	Females
a	b	c	d
Northavon			
ALL COUNTRIES OF BIRTH	**130,647**	**65,017**	**65,630**
Europe	128,181	63,779	64,402
European Community	127,931	63,670	64,261
United Kingdom	**126,308**	**62,940**	**63,368**
England	119,227	59,533	59,694
Scotland	1,610	838	772
Wales	4,990	2,348	2,642
Northern Ireland	474	218	256
United Kingdom (part not stated)	7	3	4
Outside United Kingdom	**4,339**	**2,077**	**2,262**
Channel Islands	48	18	30
Isle of Man	13	7	6
Irish Republic	757	362	395
Ireland (part not stated)	-	-	-
Old Commonwealth	**342**	**188**	**154**
Australia	140	78	62
Canada	135	69	66
New Zealand	67	41	26
New Commonwealth	**1,353**	**682**	**671**
Africa	324	173	151
Eastern Africa	203	105	98
Kenya	92	47	45
Malawi	8	2	6
Tanzania	27	13	14
Uganda	48	27	21
Zambia	28	16	12
Southern Africa	72	36	36
Zimbabwe	70	35	35
Botswana, Lesotho and Swaziland	2	1	1
Western Africa	49	32	17
Gambia	-	-	-
Ghana	17	13	4
Nigeria	31	19	12
Sierra Leone	1	-	1
Caribbean	156	75	81
Barbados	10	6	4
Jamaica	104	51	53
Trinidad and Tobago	13	4	9
Other Independent States	11	7	4
Caribbean Dependent Territories	6	4	2
West Indies (so stated)	1	-	1
Belize	3	-	3
Guyana	8	3	5
Asia	649	330	319
South Asia	353	194	159
Bangladesh	18	12	6
India	245	131	114
Pakistan	53	31	22
Sri Lanka	37	20	17
South East Asia	296	136	160
Hong Kong	142	70	72
Malaysia	62	26	36
Singapore	92	40	52
Northavon - *continued*			
Remainder of New Commonwealth	224	104	120
Cyprus	65	30	35
Gibraltar	17	8	9
Malta and Gozo	74	36	38
Mauritius	38	18	20
Seychelles	12	6	6
Other New Commonwealth	18	6	12
European Community	**866**	**368**	**498**
Belgium	25	8	17
Denmark	28	11	17
France	72	24	48
Germany	513	207	306
Greece	21	10	11
Italy	93	56	37
Luxembourg	1	1	-
Netherlands	68	31	37
Portugal	3	1	2
Spain	42	19	23
Remainder of Europe	**189**	**84**	**105**
Albania	1	-	1
Austria	18	5	13
Bulgaria	5	2	3
Czechoslovakia	5	2	3
Finland	7	-	7
Hungary	20	10	10
Norway	7	4	3
Poland	86	48	38
Romania	6	2	4
Sweden	8	3	5
Switzerland	20	5	15
Yugoslavia	6	3	3
Other Europe	-	-	-
Turkey	**6**	**5**	**1**
U.S.S.R.	**21**	**12**	**9**
Africa	**225**	**105**	**120**
Algeria	3	2	1
Egypt	33	16	17
Libya	11	8	3
Morocco	6	6	-
Tunisia	2	2	-
South Africa, Republic of	154	67	87
Other Africa	16	4	12
America	**223**	**107**	**116**
United States of America	178	85	93
Caribbean	3	-	3
Central America	7	3	4
South America	35	19	16
Asia	**291**	**134**	**157**
Middle East	145	84	61
Iran	45	29	16
Israel	12	6	6
Other Middle East	88	49	39
Remainder of Asia	146	50	96
Burma (Myanmar, Union of)	34	12	22
China, Peoples Republic of	33	16	17
Japan	7	1	6
Philippines	27	4	23
Vietnam	22	12	10
Other Asia	23	5	18
Rest of the world and at sea/in the air	**5**	**5**	**-**

7. Residents

Country of birth	TOTAL PERSONS	Males	Females
a	b	c	d
Wansdyke			
ALL COUNTRIES OF BIRTH	**80,003**	**39,058**	**40,945**
Europe	78,703	38,487	40,216
European Community	78,486	38,377	40,109
United Kingdom	**77,717**	**38,068**	**39,649**
England	74,720	36,689	38,031
Scotland	934	454	480
Wales	1,849	825	1,024
Northern Ireland	212	98	114
United Kingdom (part not stated)	2	2	-
Outside United Kingdom	**2,286**	**990**	**1,296**
Channel Islands	39	17	22
Isle of Man	16	8	8
Irish Republic	359	126	233
Ireland (part not stated)	-	-	-
Old Commonwealth	**258**	**111**	**147**
Australia	109	46	63
Canada	104	44	60
New Zealand	45	21	24
New Commonwealth	**627**	**277**	**350**
Africa	168	73	95
Eastern Africa	102	43	59
Kenya	42	21	21
Malawi	11	2	9
Tanzania	11	5	6
Uganda	12	7	5
Zambia	26	8	18
Southern Africa	36	14	22
Zimbabwe	33	12	21
Botswana, Lesotho and Swaziland	3	2	1
Western Africa	30	16	14
Gambia	-	-	-
Ghana	12	8	4
Nigeria	18	8	10
Sierra Leone	-	-	-
Caribbean	53	23	30
Barbados	8	3	5
Jamaica	23	11	12
Trinidad and Tobago	6	5	1
Other Independent States	6	1	5
Caribbean Dependent Territories	4	2	2
West Indies (so stated)	1	-	1
Belize	1	-	1
Guyana	4	1	3
Asia	307	129	178
South Asia	176	79	97
Bangladesh	3	3	-
India	138	60	78
Pakistan	22	11	11
Sri Lanka	13	5	8
South East Asia	131	50	81
Hong Kong	56	21	35
Malaysia	35	12	23
Singapore	40	17	23

Country of birth	TOTAL PERSONS	Males	Females
a	b	c	d
Wansdyke - *continued*			
Remainder of New Commonwealth	99	52	47
Cyprus	28	13	15
Gibraltar	21	11	10
Malta and Gozo	36	19	17
Mauritius	9	6	3
Seychelles	-	-	-
Other New Commonwealth	5	3	2
European Community	**410**	**183**	**227**
Belgium	11	4	7
Denmark	13	9	4
France	37	12	25
Germany	237	99	138
Greece	9	3	6
Italy	54	33	21
Luxembourg	-	-	-
Netherlands	27	10	17
Portugal	4	1	3
Spain	18	12	6
Remainder of Europe	**162**	**85**	**77**
Albania	-	-	-
Austria	22	7	15
Bulgaria	-	-	-
Czechoslovakia	10	4	6
Finland	4	1	3
Hungary	19	11	8
Norway	10	3	7
Poland	59	42	17
Romania	1	1	-
Sweden	5	2	3
Switzerland	26	13	13
Yugoslavia	5	1	4
Other Europe	1	-	1
Turkey	**1**	**1**	**-**
U.S.S.R.	**15**	**11**	**4**
Africa	**135**	**65**	**70**
Algeria	3	-	3
Egypt	21	11	10
Libya	6	3	3
Morocco	2	2	-
Tunisia	-	-	-
South Africa, Republic of	87	39	48
Other Africa	16	10	6
America	**137**	**46**	**91**
United States of America	104	36	68
Caribbean	1	1	-
Central America	-	-	-
South America	32	9	23
Asia	**125**	**59**	**66**
Middle East	60	36	24
Iran	20	13	7
Israel	8	3	5
Other Middle East	32	20	12
Remainder of Asia	65	23	42
Burma (Myanmar, Union of)	12	4	8
China, Peoples Republic of	18	9	9
Japan	10	2	8
Philippines	8	2	6
Vietnam	8	4	4
Other Asia	9	2	7
Rest of the world and at sea/in the air	**2**	**1**	**1**

7. Residents

Country of birth	TOTAL PERSONS	Males	Females
a	b	c	d
Woodspring			
ALL COUNTRIES OF BIRTH	**177,472**	**85,377**	**92,095**
Europe	174,155	83,749	90,406
European Community	173,692	83,533	90,159
United Kingdom	**171,575**	**82,675**	**88,900**
England	161,144	77,858	83,286
Scotland	2,783	1,411	1,372
Wales	7,000	3,076	3,924
Northern Ireland	633	323	310
United Kingdom (part not stated)	15	7	8
Outside United Kingdom	**5,897**	**2,702**	**3,195**
Channel Islands	105	49	56
Isle of Man	37	23	14
Irish Republic	942	397	545
Ireland (part not stated)	3	-	3
Old Commonwealth	**556**	**259**	**297**
Australia	220	111	109
Canada	250	101	149
New Zealand	86	47	39
New Commonwealth	**1,761**	**917**	**844**
Africa	353	170	183
Eastern Africa	228	110	118
Kenya	115	55	60
Malawi	16	7	9
Tanzania	30	16	14
Uganda	29	15	14
Zambia	38	17	21
Southern Africa	79	41	38
Zimbabwe	71	37	34
Botswana, Lesotho and Swaziland	8	4	4
Western Africa	46	19	27
Gambia	-	-	-
Ghana	20	8	12
Nigeria	23	8	15
Sierra Leone	3	3	-
Caribbean	100	64	36
Barbados	9	5	4
Jamaica	35	19	16
Trinidad and Tobago	20	11	9
Other Independent States	9	7	2
Caribbean Dependent Territories	9	7	2
West Indies (so stated)	3	2	1
Belize	2	1	1
Guyana	13	12	1
Asia	808	416	392
South Asia	452	249	203
Bangladesh	56	32	24
India	321	178	143
Pakistan	46	23	23
Sri Lanka	29	16	13
South East Asia	356	167	189
Hong Kong	166	80	86
Malaysia	73	28	45
Singapore	117	59	58

Country of birth	TOTAL PERSONS	Males	Females
a	b	c	d
Woodspring - *continued*			
Remainder of New Commonwealth	500	267	233
Cyprus	270	154	116
Gibraltar	45	19	26
Malta and Gozo	138	65	73
Mauritius	27	20	7
Seychelles	4	2	2
Other New Commonwealth	16	7	9
European Community	**1,172**	**461**	**711**
Belgium	51	18	33
Denmark	33	12	21
France	161	70	91
Germany	687	257	430
Greece	17	9	8
Italy	92	43	49
Luxembourg	1	1	-
Netherlands	63	21	42
Portugal	18	10	8
Spain	49	20	29
Remainder of Europe	**321**	**144**	**177**
Albania	-	-	-
Austria	52	15	37
Bulgaria	1	-	1
Czechoslovakia	16	5	11
Finland	20	4	16
Hungary	24	18	6
Norway	34	10	24
Poland	100	65	35
Romania	6	5	1
Sweden	17	6	11
Switzerland	35	9	26
Yugoslavia	15	7	8
Other Europe	1	-	1
Turkey	**9**	**4**	**5**
U.S.S.R.	**50**	**27**	**23**
Africa	**353**	**168**	**185**
Algeria	8	3	5
Egypt	62	32	30
Libya	11	4	7
Morocco	7	5	2
Tunisia	3	1	2
South Africa, Republic of	243	117	126
Other Africa	19	6	13
America	**259**	**100**	**159**
United States of America	184	80	104
Caribbean	4	1	3
Central America	12	3	9
South America	59	16	43
Asia	**328**	**153**	**175**
Middle East	115	70	45
Iran	35	25	10
Israel	11	4	7
Other Middle East	69	41	28
Remainder of Asia	213	83	130
Burma (Myanmar, Union of)	26	14	12
China, Peoples Republic of	62	25	37
Japan	19	9	10
Philippines	31	2	29
Vietnam	37	24	13
Other Asia	38	9	29
Rest of the world and at sea/in the air	**1**	**-**	**1**

Table 8 Economic position

8. Residents aged 16 and over

Sex, marital status and economic position	TOTAL AGED 16 AND OVER	Age								
		16	17	18	19	20	21 - 24	25 - 29	30 - 34	35 - 39
a	b	c	d	e	f	g	h	i	j	k
				AVON						
TOTAL PERSONS	**753,353**	**11,181**	**11,388**	**12,119**	**12,938**	**13,774**	**57,226**	**75,814**	**67,661**	**62,032**
Economically active	**471,091**	**3,610**	**6,889**	**8,591**	**9,845**	**10,588**	**47,032**	**63,191**	**55,413**	**52,566**
Employees - full time	291,279	1,214	3,387	5,374	7,159	7,993	35,931	44,779	34,423	30,763
- part time	84,317	1,364	1,602	1,283	765	708	2,599	6,415	9,828	11,186
Self-employed - with employees	17,561	2	3	9	11	24	308	1,184	2,020	2,604
- without employees	36,300	24	58	109	222	313	2,445	4,522	4,674	4,515
On a Government scheme	4,921	480	985	574	212	132	523	512	431	340
Unemployed	36,713	526	854	1,242	1,476	1,418	5,226	5,779	4,037	3,158
Economically active students (included above)	*4,761*	*1,147*	*1,216*	*881*	*322*	*306*	*468*	*178*	*86*	*69*
Economically inactive	**282,262**	**7,571**	**4,499**	**3,528**	**3,093**	**3,186**	**10,194**	**12,623**	**12,248**	**9,466**
Students	28,134	7,504	4,342	3,185	2,503	2,422	5,054	1,416	706	463
Permanently sick	22,154	19	31	47	97	110	590	1,021	983	1,209
Retired	144,860	-	1	5	3	6	23	31	29	84
Other inactive	87,114	48	125	291	490	648	4,527	10,155	10,530	7,710
Total males	**360,114**	**5,693**	**5,918**	**6,213**	**6,536**	**6,927**	**28,537**	**37,663**	**33,633**	**30,897**
Economically active	**267,185**	**1,844**	**3,767**	**4,606**	**5,165**	**5,586**	**25,325**	**36,048**	**32,402**	**29,698**
Employees - full time	188,132	697	1,950	2,906	3,627	4,085	18,756	26,767	23,835	21,591
- part time	9,446	556	698	522	271	240	509	534	424	404
Self-employed - with employees	13,231	2	3	7	8	19	230	893	1,535	1,975
- without employees	28,200	21	53	92	177	246	1,991	3,602	3,568	3,307
On a Government scheme	2,777	261	552	315	130	77	304	298	240	181
Unemployed	25,399	307	511	764	952	919	3,535	3,954	2,800	2,240
Economically active students (included above)	*2,146*	*473*	*541*	*398*	*156*	*146*	*238*	*84*	*39*	*35*
Economically inactive	**92,929**	**3,849**	**2,151**	**1,607**	**1,371**	**1,341**	**3,212**	**1,615**	**1,231**	**1,199**
Students	14,303	3,835	2,129	1,552	1,284	1,229	2,714	787	384	211
Permanently sick	12,813	10	15	28	54	66	330	551	557	667
Retired	63,286	-	-	1	1	3	12	7	13	38
Other inactive	2,527	4	7	26	32	43	156	270	277	283
Total females	**393,239**	**5,488**	**5,470**	**5,906**	**6,402**	**6,847**	**28,689**	**38,151**	**34,028**	**31,135**
Economically active	**203,906**	**1,766**	**3,122**	**3,985**	**4,680**	**5,002**	**21,707**	**27,143**	**23,011**	**22,868**
Employees - full time	103,147	517	1,437	2,468	3,532	3,908	17,175	18,012	10,588	9,172
- part time	74,871	808	904	761	494	468	2,090	5,881	9,404	10,782
Self-employed - with employees	4,330	-	-	2	3	5	78	291	485	629
- without employees	8,100	3	5	17	45	67	454	920	1,106	1,208
On a Government scheme	2,144	219	433	259	82	55	219	214	191	159
Unemployed	11,314	219	343	478	524	499	1,691	1,825	1,237	918
Economically active students (included above)	*2,615*	*674*	*675*	*483*	*166*	*160*	*230*	*94*	*47*	*34*
Economically inactive	**189,333**	**3,722**	**2,348**	**1,921**	**1,722**	**1,845**	**6,982**	**11,008**	**11,017**	**8,267**
Students	13,831	3,669	2,213	1,633	1,219	1,193	2,340	629	322	252
Permanently sick	9,341	9	16	19	43	44	260	470	426	542
Retired	81,574	-	1	4	2	3	11	24	16	46
Other inactive	84,587	44	118	265	458	605	4,371	9,885	10,253	7,427

Age 40 - 44	45 - 49	50 - 54	55 - 59	60 - 64	65 - 69	70 - 74	75 and over	Students (economically active or inactive)	Sex, marital status and economic position
l	m	n	o	p	q	r	s	t	a
68,417	**58,706**	**50,372**	**47,500**	**47,469**	**47,120**	**39,115**	**70,521**	**32,895**	**TOTAL PERSONS**
59,943	**51,146**	**41,264**	**33,273**	**19,789**	**4,676**	**1,893**	**1,382**	**4,761**	**Economically active**
35,315	30,484	23,934	18,625	10,218	983	335	362	427	Employees - full time
12,448	10,344	8,888	7,606	5,134	2,549	1,058	540	4,115	- part time
3,296	2,924	2,099	1,549	874	340	155	159	10	Self-employed - with employees
5,235	4,444	3,611	2,813	2,002	745	320	248	27	- without employees
268	211	135	80	24	4	4	6		On a Government scheme
3,381	2,739	2,597	2,600	1,537	55	21	67	182	Unemployed
45	*20*	*14*	*3*	*2*	*4*	-	-		*Economically active students (included above)*
8,474	**7,560**	**9,108**	**14,227**	**27,680**	**42,444**	**37,222**	**69,139**	**28,134**	**Economically inactive**
323	126	38	9	5	7	13	18	28,134	Students
1,704	1,945	2,487	3,590	4,223	1,542	637	1,919		Permanently sick
106	218	919	3,506	17,080	34,730	31,132	56,987		Retired
6,341	5,271	5,664	7,122	6,372	6,165	5,440	10,215		Other inactive
34,113	**29,453**	**25,271**	**23,574**	**23,052**	**21,659**	**16,814**	**24,161**	**16,449**	**Total males**
32,830	**28,094**	**23,420**	**19,852**	**13,661**	**2,871**	**1,181**	**835**	**2,146**	**Economically active**
23,624	20,199	16,584	13,702	8,635	725	230	219	243	Employees - full time
379	337	470	793	1,164	1,259	583	303	1,775	- part time
2,429	2,168	1,604	1,181	703	265	104	105	7	Self-employed - with employees
3,946	3,446	2,832	2,250	1,673	580	242	174	13	- without employees
141	120	80	51	16	4	4	3		On a Government scheme
2,311	1,824	1,850	1,875	1,470	38	18	31	108	Unemployed
12	*11*	*6*	*2*	*2*	*3*	-	-		*Economically active students (included above)*
1,283	**1,359**	**1,851**	**3,722**	**9,391**	**18,788**	**15,633**	**23,326**	**14,303**	**Economically inactive**
98	42	14	5	4	4	6	5	14,303	Students
875	994	1,305	2,098	3,386	1,085	315	477		Permanently sick
54	106	367	1,415	5,821	17,603	15,203	22,642		Retired
256	217	165	204	180	96	109	202		Other inactive
34,304	**29,253**	**25,101**	**23,926**	**24,417**	**25,461**	**22,301**	**46,360**	**16,446**	**Total females**
27,113	**23,052**	**17,844**	**13,421**	**6,128**	**1,805**	**712**	**547**	**2,615**	**Economically active**
11,691	10,285	7,350	4,923	1,583	258	105	143	184	Employees - full time
12,069	10,007	8,418	6,813	3,970	1,290	475	237	2,340	- part time
867	756	495	368	171	75	51	54	3	Self-employed - with employees
1,289	998	779	563	329	165	78	74	14	- without employees
127	91	55	29	8	-	-	3		On a Government scheme
1,070	915	747	725	67	17	3	36	74	Unemployed
33	*9*	*8*	*1*	-	*1*	-	-		*Economically active students (included above)*
7,191	**6,201**	**7,257**	**10,505**	**18,289**	**23,656**	**21,589**	**45,813**	**13,831**	**Economically inactive**
225	84	24	4	1	3	7	13	13,831	Students
829	951	1,182	1,492	837	457	322	1,442		Permanently sick
52	112	552	2,091	11,259	17,127	15,929	34,345		Retired
6,085	5,054	5,499	6,918	6,192	6,069	5,331	10,013		Other inactive

Table 8 Economic position - continued

8. Residents aged 16 and over

Sex, marital status and economic position	TOTAL AGED 16 AND OVER	Age								
		16	17	18	19	20	21 - 24	25 - 29	30 - 34	35 - 39
a	b	c	d	e	f	g	h	i	j	k
			AVON - *continued*							
Married females	**220,044**	**16**	**23**	**81**	**204**	**434**	**6,933**	**20,661**	**23,966**	**23,831**
Economically active	**120,872**	**5**	**9**	**41**	**98**	**268**	**4,635**	**13,245**	**15,354**	**17,233**
Employees - full time	47,270	2	5	21	59	174	3,245	7,296	5,379	5,741
- part time	60,177	2	1	7	18	54	903	4,538	8,128	9,519
Self-employed - with employees	3,505	-	-	-	-	1	31	195	389	527
- without employees	5,469	-	-	2	1	2	97	475	774	897
On a Government scheme	398	1	3	1	-	2	20	39	79	82
Unemployed	4,053	-	-	10	20	35	339	702	605	467
Economically active students (included above)	*85*	-	-	-	-	-	*5*	*15*	*21*	*19*
Economically inactive	**99,172**	**11**	**14**	**40**	**106**	**166**	**2,298**	**7,416**	**8,612**	**6,598**
Students	692	3	3	1	5	3	50	119	139	153
Permanently sick	3,809	-	-	-	1	-	31	98	135	224
Retired	33,562	-	-	2	-	-	1	7	10	22
Other inactive	61,109	8	11	37	100	163	2,216	7,192	8,328	6,199
Single, widowed or divorced females	**173,195**	**5,472**	**5,447**	**5,825**	**6,198**	**6,413**	**21,756**	**17,490**	**10,062**	**7,304**
Economically active	**83,034**	**1,761**	**3,113**	**3,944**	**4,582**	**4,734**	**17,072**	**13,898**	**7,657**	**5,635**
Employees - full time	55,877	515	1,432	2,447	3,473	3,734	13,930	10,716	5,209	3,431
- part time	14,694	806	903	754	476	414	1,187	1,343	1,276	1,263
Self-employed - with employees	825	-	-	2	3	4	47	96	96	102
- without employees	2,631	3	5	15	44	65	357	445	332	311
On a Government scheme	1,746	218	430	258	82	53	199	175	112	77
Unemployed	7,261	219	343	468	504	464	1,352	1,123	632	451
Economically active students (included above)	*2,530*	*674*	*675*	*483*	*166*	*160*	*225*	*79*	*26*	*15*
Economically inactive	**90,161**	**3,711**	**2,334**	**1,881**	**1,616**	**1,679**	**4,684**	**3,592**	**2,405**	**1,669**
Students	13,139	3,666	2,210	1,632	1,214	1,190	2,290	510	183	99
Permanently sick	5,532	9	16	19	42	44	229	372	291	318
Retired	48,012	-	1	2	2	3	10	17	6	24
Other inactive	23,478	36	107	228	358	442	2,155	2,693	1,925	1,228
			Bath							
TOTAL PERSONS	**65,603**	**838**	**907**	**978**	**1,168**	**1,328**	**5,304**	**6,198**	**5,356**	**4,938**
Economically active	**38,939**	**263**	**493**	**636**	**826**	**908**	**4,023**	**5,218**	**4,431**	**4,210**
Employees - full time	22,727	52	204	343	546	631	2,982	3,539	2,707	2,319
- part time	7,419	119	132	126	99	108	290	532	725	876
Self-employed - with employees	1,535	-	-	-	2	1	21	111	154	254
- without employees	3,541	4	6	15	17	16	241	449	417	423
On a Government scheme	451	35	79	34	27	12	47	47	48	34
Unemployed	3,266	53	72	118	135	140	442	540	380	304
Economically active students (included above)	*491*	*103*	*95*	*77*	*26*	*53*	*77*	*36*	*8*	*5*
Economically inactive	**26,664**	**575**	**414**	**342**	**342**	**420**	**1,281**	**980**	**925**	**728**
Students	3,291	568	406	316	296	352	869	254	105	54
Permanently sick	1,608	1	1	2	6	9	50	100	77	96
Retired	14,771	-	-	2	-	1	2	-	3	2
Other inactive	6,994	6	7	22	40	58	360	626	740	576

40 - 44	45 - 49	50 - 54	55 - 59	60 - 64	65 - 69	70 - 74	75 and over	Students (economically active or inactive)	Sex, marital status and economic position
Age									
l	m	n	o	p	q	r	s	t	a
27,204	**23,513**	**20,127**	**18,371**	**17,118**	**15,388**	**10,894**	**11,280**	**777**	**Married females**
21,393	**18,426**	**14,159**	**10,118**	**4,343**	**1,062**	**317**	**166**	**85**	**Economically active**
8,160	7,435	5,211	3,345	990	122	48	37	12	Employees - full time
10,833	9,015	7,457	5,689	2,945	778	214	76	61	- part time
743	670	425	304	131	47	19	23	1	Self-employed - with employees
992	786	625	414	234	110	35	25	6	- without employees
69	50	29	17	6	-	-	-		On a Government scheme
596	470	412	349	37	5	1	5	5	Unemployed
16	*4*	*4*	-	-	*1*	-	-		*Economically active students (included above)*
5,811	**5,087**	**5,968**	**8,253**	**12,775**	**14,326**	**10,577**	**11,114**	**692**	**Economically inactive**
147	50	14	2	1	-	-	2	692	Students
398	462	605	811	463	229	125	227		Permanently sick
26	60	388	1,448	7,161	9,754	7,233	7,450		Retired
5,240	4,515	4,961	5,992	5,150	4,343	3,219	3,435		Other inactive
7,100	**5,740**	**4,974**	**5,555**	**7,299**	**10,073**	**11,407**	**35,080**	**15,669**	**Single, widowed or divorced females**
5,720	**4,626**	**3,685**	**3,303**	**1,785**	**743**	**395**	**381**	**2,530**	**Economically active**
3,531	2,850	2,139	1,578	593	136	57	106	172	Employees - full time
1,236	992	961	1,124	1,025	512	261	161	2,279	- part time
124	86	70	64	40	28	32	31	2	Self-employed - with employees
297	212	154	149	95	55	43	49	8	- without employees
58	41	26	12	2	-	-	3		On a Government scheme
474	445	335	376	30	12	2	31	69	Unemployed
17	*5*	*4*	*1*	-	-	-	-		*Economically active students (included above)*
1,380	**1,114**	**1,289**	**2,252**	**5,514**	**9,330**	**11,012**	**34,699**	**13,139**	**Economically inactive**
78	34	10	2	-	3	7	11	13,139	Students
431	489	577	681	374	228	197	1,215		Permanently sick
26	52	164	643	4,098	7,373	8,696	26,895		Retired
845	539	538	926	1,042	1,726	2,112	6,578		Other inactive
5,380	**4,614**	**4,106**	**4,006**	**4,366**	**4,591**	**3,941**	**7,584**	**3,782**	**TOTAL PERSONS**
4,734	**4,054**	**3,457**	**2,962**	**1,813**	**533**	**225**	**153**	**491**	**Economically active**
2,597	2,286	1,893	1,630	857	84	23	34	56	Employees - full time
981	835	787	728	537	316	146	82	406	- part time
300	246	184	125	81	34	14	8	2	Self-employed - with employees
507	433	359	278	218	93	41	24	3	- without employees
30	22	19	13	2	1	-	1		On a Government scheme
319	232	215	188	118	5	1	4	24	Unemployed
4	*3*	*2*	*1*	*1*	-	-	-		*Economically active students (included above)*
646	**560**	**649**	**1,044**	**2,553**	**4,058**	**3,716**	**7,431**	**3,291**	**Economically inactive**
45	17	3	3	-	-	1	2	3,291	Students
134	142	185	212	292	110	45	146		Permanently sick
6	14	80	292	1,696	3,369	3,144	6,160		Retired
461	387	381	537	565	579	526	1,123		Other inactive

Table 8 Economic position - continued

8. Residents aged 16 and over

Sex, marital status and economic position	TOTAL AGED 16 AND OVER	Age 16	17	18	19	20	21 - 24	25 - 29	30 - 34	35 - 39
a	b	c	d	e	f	g	h	i	j	k
				Bath - *continued*						
Total males	**30,463**	**436**	**495**	**487**	**531**	**645**	**2,603**	**3,097**	**2,669**	**2,406**
Economically active	**21,388**	**144**	**283**	**329**	**389**	**467**	**2,101**	**2,875**	**2,537**	**2,309**
Employees - full time	14,146	29	122	171	255	317	1,503	1,997	1,811	1,538
- part time	1,050	52	61	49	29	42	77	76	42	54
Self-employed - with employees	1,128	-	-	-	2	1	16	83	114	189
- without employees	2,625	4	5	12	11	14	189	339	295	296
On a Government scheme	243	23	52	16	12	9	21	22	24	19
Unemployed	2,196	36	43	81	80	84	295	358	251	213
Economically active students (included above)	*224*	*48*	*49*	*29*	*13*	*23*	*38*	*12*	*4*	*2*
Economically inactive	**9,075**	**292**	**212**	**158**	**142**	**178**	**502**	**222**	**132**	**97**
Students	1,658	290	211	152	133	169	455	145	59	29
Permanently sick	925	-	-	2	6	7	32	57	47	46
Retired	6,286	-	-	1	-	1	1	-	1	-
Other inactive	206	2	1	3	3	1	14	20	25	22
Total females	**35,140**	**402**	**412**	**491**	**637**	**683**	**2,701**	**3,101**	**2,687**	**2,532**
Economically active	**17,551**	**119**	**210**	**307**	**437**	**441**	**1,922**	**2,343**	**1,894**	**1,901**
Employees - full time	8,581	23	82	172	291	314	1,479	1,542	896	781
- part time	6,369	67	71	77	70	66	213	456	683	822
Self-employed - with employees	407	-	-	-	-	-	5	28	40	65
- without employees	916	-	1	3	6	2	52	110	122	127
On a Government scheme	208	12	27	18	15	3	26	25	24	15
Unemployed	1,070	17	29	37	55	56	147	182	129	91
Economically active students (included above)	*267*	*55*	*46*	*48*	*13*	*30*	*39*	*24*	*4*	*3*
Economically inactive	**17,589**	**283**	**202**	**184**	**200**	**242**	**779**	**758**	**793**	**631**
Students	1,633	278	195	164	163	183	414	109	46	25
Permanently sick	683	1	1	-	-	2	18	43	30	50
Retired	8,485	-	-	1	-	-	1	-	2	2
Other inactive	6,788	4	6	19	37	57	346	606	715	554
Married females	**17,458**	**3**	**2**	**3**	**16**	**30**	**402**	**1,288**	**1,683**	**1,749**
Economically active	**9,294**	**-**	**1**	**2**	**10**	**16**	**243**	**885**	**1,104**	**1,277**
Employees - full time	3,314	-	1	1	6	9	146	458	378	395
- part time	4,802	-	-	-	2	3	64	317	560	709
Self-employed - with employees	304	-	-	-	-	-	3	16	30	48
- without employees	539	-	-	1	-	-	6	45	81	83
On a Government scheme	50	-	-	-	-	1	4	6	10	5
Unemployed	285	-	-	-	2	3	20	43	45	37
Economically active students (included above)	*10*	-	-	-	-	-	-	*5*	*2*	-
Economically inactive	**8,164**	**3**	**1**	**1**	**6**	**14**	**159**	**403**	**579**	**472**
Students	88	2	-	-	-	1	5	15	16	16
Permanently sick	242	-	-	-	-	-	-	5	10	17
Retired	3,234	-	-	-	-	-	-	-	1	2
Other inactive	4,600	1	1	1	6	13	154	383	552	437

Age 40 - 44	45 - 49	50 - 54	55 - 59	60 - 64	65 - 69	70 - 74	75 and over	Students (economically active or inactive)	Sex, marital status and economic position
l	m	n	o	p	q	r	s	t	a
2,653	**2,264**	**2,032**	**1,892**	**2,022**	**2,082**	**1,648**	**2,501**	**1,882**	**Total males**
2,561	**2,158**	**1,883**	**1,662**	**1,179**	**303**	**120**	**88**	**224**	**Economically active**
1,688	1,474	1,283	1,157	714	58	12	17	36	Employees - full time
46	39	40	68	113	142	70	50	177	- part time
217	177	128	93	66	29	10	3	1	Self-employed - with employees
369	317	274	216	171	70	27	16	-	- without employees
15	9	11	7	2	1	-	-		On a Government scheme
226	142	147	121	113	3	1	2	10	Unemployed
2	*1*	*1*	*1*	*1*	-	-	-		*Economically active students (included above)*
92	**106**	**149**	**230**	**843**	**1,779**	**1,528**	**2,413**	**1,658**	**Economically inactive**
8	4	1	1	-	-	1	-	1,658	Students
66	75	106	113	243	70	19	36		Permanently sick
1	9	34	98	589	1,700	1,497	2,354		Retired
17	18	8	18	11	9	11	23		Other inactive
2,727	**2,350**	**2,074**	**2,114**	**2,344**	**2,509**	**2,293**	**5,083**	**1,900**	**Total females**
2,173	**1,896**	**1,574**	**1,300**	**634**	**230**	**105**	**65**	**267**	**Economically active**
909	812	610	473	143	26	11	17	20	Employees - full time
935	796	747	660	424	174	76	32	229	- part time
83	69	56	32	15	5	4	5	1	Self-employed - with employees
138	116	85	62	47	23	14	8	3	- without employees
15	13	8	6	-	-	-	1		On a Government scheme
93	90	68	67	5	2	-	2	14	Unemployed
2	*2*	*1*	-	-	-	-	-		*Economically active students (included above)*
554	**454**	**500**	**814**	**1,710**	**2,279**	**2,188**	**5,018**	**1,633**	**Economically inactive**
37	13	2	2	-	-	-	2	1,633	Students
68	67	79	99	49	40	26	110		Permanently sick
5	5	46	194	1,107	1,669	1,647	3,806		Retired
444	369	373	519	554	570	515	1,100		Other inactive
2,027	**1,764**	**1,584**	**1,574**	**1,586**	**1,435**	**1,083**	**1,229**	**98**	**Married females**
1,613	**1,400**	**1,182**	**950**	**417**	**122**	**53**	**19**	**10**	**Economically active**
572	538	385	319	92	8	3	3	2	Employees - full time
829	691	656	530	290	97	41	13	6	- part time
67	55	44	27	9	3	2	-	1	Self-employed - with employees
92	76	62	45	24	14	7	3	-	- without employees
10	8	4	2	-	-	-	-		On a Government scheme
43	32	31	27	2	-	-	-	1	Unemployed
2	-	*1*	-	-	-	-	-		*Economically active students (included above)*
414	**364**	**402**	**624**	**1,169**	**1,313**	**1,030**	**1,210**	**88**	**Economically inactive**
22	10	-	1	-	-	-	-	88	Students
24	28	38	44	23	22	11	20		Permanently sick
1	2	33	131	676	893	700	795		Retired
367	324	331	448	470	398	319	395		Other inactive

Table 8 Economic position - **continued**

8. Residents aged 16 and over

Sex, marital status and economic position	TOTAL AGED 16 AND OVER	Age								
		16	17	18	19	20	21 - 24	25 - 29	30 - 34	35 - 39
a	b	c	d	e	f	g	h	i	j	k
			Bath - *continued*							
Single, widowed or divorced females	**17,682**	**399**	**410**	**488**	**621**	**653**	**2,299**	**1,813**	**1,004**	**783**
Economically active	**8,257**	**119**	**209**	**305**	**427**	**425**	**1,679**	**1,458**	**790**	**624**
Employees - full time	5,267	23	81	171	285	305	1,333	1,084	518	386
- part time	1,567	67	71	77	68	63	149	139	123	113
Self-employed - with employees	103	-	-	-	-	-	2	12	10	17
- without employees	377	-	1	2	6	2	46	65	41	44
On a Government scheme	158	12	27	18	15	2	22	19	14	10
Unemployed	785	17	29	37	53	53	127	139	84	54
Economically active students (included above)	*257*	*55*	*46*	*48*	*13*	*30*	*39*	*19*	*2*	*3*
Economically inactive	**9,425**	**280**	**201**	**183**	**194**	**228**	**620**	**355**	**214**	**159**
Students	1,545	276	195	164	163	182	409	94	30	9
Permanently sick	441	1	1	-	-	2	18	38	20	33
Retired	5,251	-	-	1	-	-	1	-	1	-
Other inactive	2,188	3	5	18	31	44	192	223	163	117
			Bristol							
TOTAL PERSONS	**303,162**	**4,080**	**4,121**	**4,512**	**5,005**	**5,582**	**25,818**	**34,866**	**29,249**	**24,859**
Economically active	**187,161**	**1,455**	**2,630**	**3,278**	**3,781**	**4,165**	**20,698**	**28,636**	**23,803**	**20,845**
Employees - full time	115,742	539	1,274	1,994	2,647	2,999	15,382	20,071	14,723	12,199
- part time	31,287	411	487	389	281	290	1,183	2,744	3,897	4,107
Self-employed - with employees	5,426	-	1	2	1	14	111	397	748	890
- without employees	12,939	6	24	35	66	110	889	1,818	1,931	1,757
On a Government scheme	2,404	214	414	248	86	62	303	321	238	187
Unemployed	19,363	285	430	610	700	690	2,830	3,285	2,266	1,705
Economically active students (included above)	*1,578*	*328*	*337*	*237*	*117*	*112*	*211*	*100*	*58*	*38*
Economically inactive	**116,001**	**2,625**	**1,491**	**1,234**	**1,224**	**1,417**	**5,120**	**6,230**	**5,446**	**4,014**
Students	11,313	2,592	1,395	1,040	904	978	2,530	873	455	269
Permanently sick	10,671	8	13	16	48	48	278	472	496	629
Retired	59,036	-	1	2	2	4	13	18	15	30
Other inactive	34,981	25	82	176	270	387	2,299	4,867	4,480	3,086
Total males	**144,279**	**2,060**	**2,133**	**2,244**	**2,502**	**2,745**	**12,753**	**17,070**	**14,557**	**12,574**
Economically active	**105,837**	**743**	**1,413**	**1,728**	**1,982**	**2,185**	**11,151**	**16,165**	**13,854**	**11,905**
Employees - full time	72,888	295	707	1,046	1,337	1,494	7,997	11,667	9,788	8,346
- part time	3,858	158	208	140	93	105	259	303	260	236
Self-employed - with employees	4,137	-	1	2	1	11	85	312	576	689
- without employees	10,075	6	23	31	55	86	730	1,430	1,491	1,299
On a Government scheme	1,360	120	226	135	52	38	176	180	133	107
Unemployed	13,519	164	248	374	444	451	1,904	2,273	1,606	1,228
Economically active students (included above)	*700*	*126*	*157*	*95*	*53*	*53*	*102*	*51*	*30*	*19*
Economically inactive	**38,442**	**1,317**	**720**	**516**	**520**	**560**	**1,602**	**905**	**703**	**669**
Students	5,850	1,313	709	493	476	499	1,362	490	269	136
Permanently sick	6,236	3	7	8	26	28	142	244	283	362
Retired	25,115	-	-	-	-	1	7	6	7	18
Other inactive	1,241	1	4	15	18	32	91	165	144	153

Age								Students (economically active or inactive)	Sex, marital status and economic position
40 - 44	45 - 49	50 - 54	55 - 59	60 - 64	65 - 69	70 - 74	75 and over		
l	m	n	o	p	q	r	s	t	a
700	**586**	**490**	**540**	**758**	**1,074**	**1,210**	**3,854**	**1,802**	**Single, widowed or divorced females**
560	**496**	**392**	**350**	**217**	**108**	**52**	**46**	**257**	**Economically active**
337	274	225	154	51	18	8	14	18	Employees - full time
106	105	91	130	134	77	35	19	223	- part time
16	14	12	5	6	2	2	5	-	Self-employed - with employees
46	40	23	17	23	9	7	5	3	- without employees
5	5	4	4	-	-	-	1		On a Government scheme
50	58	37	40	3	2	-	2	13	Unemployed
-	*2*	*-*	*-*	*-*	*-*	*-*	*-*		*Economically active students (included above)*
140	**90**	**98**	**190**	**541**	**966**	**1,158**	**3,808**	**1,545**	**Economically inactive**
15	3	2	1	-	-	-	2	1,545	Students
44	39	41	55	26	18	15	90		Permanently sick
4	3	13	63	431	776	947	3,011		Retired
77	45	42	71	84	172	196	705		Other inactive
25,231	**20,687**	**18,411**	**17,802**	**18,773**	**19,155**	**16,226**	**28,785**	**12,891**	**TOTAL PERSONS**
21,865	**17,785**	**14,877**	**12,383**	**7,827**	**1,832**	**731**	**570**	**1,578**	**Economically active**
12,844	10,585	8,661	6,911	4,140	435	160	178	161	Employees - full time
4,255	3,516	3,172	2,840	2,066	1,029	408	212	1,312	- part time
1,032	820	535	467	229	103	39	37	3	Self-employed - with employees
1,855	1,410	1,119	872	618	234	107	88	16	- without employees
136	98	59	22	12	-	2	2		On a Government scheme
1,743	1,356	1,331	1,271	762	31	15	53	86	Unemployed
24	*10*	*4*	*1*	*1*	*-*	*-*	*-*		*Economically active students (included above)*
3,366	**2,902**	**3,534**	**5,419**	**10,946**	**17,323**	**15,495**	**28,215**	**11,313**	**Economically inactive**
175	63	19	4	1	3	7	5	11,313	Students
849	954	1,226	1,733	2,022	750	305	824		Permanently sick
33	68	346	1,185	6,607	14,240	13,054	23,418		Retired
2,309	1,817	1,943	2,497	2,316	2,330	2,129	3,968		Other inactive
12,763	**10,445**	**9,264**	**8,861**	**9,046**	**8,692**	**6,887**	**9,683**	**6,550**	**Total males**
12,112	**9,789**	**8,376**	**7,269**	**5,283**	**1,102**	**453**	**327**	**700**	**Economically active**
8,479	6,904	5,869	4,998	3,422	319	107	113	90	Employees - full time
184	151	196	298	430	502	232	103	548	- part time
770	609	419	346	185	84	21	26	2	Self-employed - with employees
1,382	1,123	887	695	522	176	78	61	10	- without employees
75	60	35	14	6	-	2	1		On a Government scheme
1,222	942	970	918	718	21	13	23	50	Unemployed
7	*4*	*1*	*1*	*1*	*-*	*-*	*-*		*Economically active students (included above)*
651	**656**	**888**	**1,592**	**3,763**	**7,590**	**6,434**	**9,356**	**5,850**	**Economically inactive**
66	21	6	2	1	2	4	1	5,850	Students
453	505	656	1,017	1,600	512	154	236		Permanently sick
16	29	154	476	2,074	7,038	6,240	9,049		Retired
116	101	72	97	88	38	36	70		Other inactive

Table 8 Economic position - **continued**

8. Residents aged 16 and over

Sex, marital status and economic position	TOTAL AGED 16 AND OVER	Age								
		16	17	18	19	20	21 - 24	25 - 29	30 - 34	35 - 39
a	b	c	d	e	f	g	h	i	j	k
			Bristol - *continued*							
Total females	**158,883**	**2,020**	**1,988**	**2,268**	**2,503**	**2,837**	**13,065**	**17,796**	**14,692**	**12,285**
Economically active	**81,324**	**712**	**1,217**	**1,550**	**1,799**	**1,980**	**9,547**	**12,471**	**9,949**	**8,940**
Employees - full time	42,854	244	567	948	1,310	1,505	7,385	8,404	4,935	3,853
- part time	27,429	253	279	249	188	185	924	2,441	3,637	3,871
Self-employed - with employees	1,289	-	-	-	-	3	26	85	172	201
- without employees	2,864	-	1	4	11	24	159	388	440	458
On a Government scheme	1,044	94	188	113	34	24	127	141	105	80
Unemployed	5,844	121	182	236	256	239	926	1,012	660	477
Economically active students (included above)	*878*	*202*	*180*	*142*	*64*	*59*	*109*	*49*	*28*	*19*
Economically inactive	**77,559**	**1,308**	**771**	**718**	**704**	**857**	**3,518**	**5,325**	**4,743**	**3,345**
Students	5,463	1,279	686	547	428	479	1,168	383	186	133
Permanently sick	4,435	5	6	8	22	20	136	228	213	267
Retired	33,921	-	1	2	2	3	6	12	8	12
Other inactive	33,740	24	78	161	252	355	2,208	4,702	4,336	2,933
Married females	**80,081**	**9**	**13**	**44**	**95**	**187**	**2,671**	**8,230**	**9,162**	**8,556**
Economically active	**42,643**	**5**	**3**	**16**	**34**	**105**	**1,648**	**5,042**	**5,803**	**6,127**
Employees - full time	16,920	2	1	9	19	66	1,118	2,750	2,136	2,129
- part time	21,090	2	-	2	6	23	343	1,720	2,978	3,295
Self-employed - with employees	975	-	-	-	-	1	8	43	131	157
- without employees	1,724	-	-	1	-	1	25	174	262	300
On a Government scheme	164	1	2	1	-	-	8	19	31	36
Unemployed	1,770	-	-	3	9	14	146	336	265	210
Economically active students (included above)	*36*	-	-	-	-	-	*4*	*5*	*9*	*10*
Economically inactive	**37,438**	**4**	**10**	**28**	**61**	**82**	**1,023**	**3,188**	**3,359**	**2,429**
Students	341	-	1	1	3	2	32	71	66	69
Permanently sick	1,718	-	-	-	1	-	21	45	67	101
Retired	13,130	-	-	2	-	-	1	4	5	10
Other inactive	22,249	4	9	25	57	80	969	3,068	3,221	2,249
Single, widowed or divorced females	**78,802**	**2,011**	**1,975**	**2,224**	**2,408**	**2,650**	**10,394**	**9,566**	**5,530**	**3,729**
Economically active	**38,681**	**707**	**1,214**	**1,534**	**1,765**	**1,875**	**7,899**	**7,429**	**4,146**	**2,813**
Employees - full time	25,934	242	566	939	1,291	1,439	6,267	5,654	2,799	1,724
- part time	6,339	251	279	247	182	162	581	721	659	576
Self-employed - with employees	314	-	-	-	-	2	18	42	41	44
- without employees	1,140	-	1	3	11	23	134	214	178	158
On a Government scheme	880	93	186	112	34	24	119	122	74	44
Unemployed	4,074	121	182	233	247	225	780	676	395	267
Economically active students (included above)	*842*	*202*	*180*	*142*	*64*	*59*	*105*	*44*	*19*	*9*
Economically inactive	**40,121**	**1,304**	**761**	**690**	**643**	**775**	**2,495**	**2,137**	**1,384**	**916**
Students	5,122	1,279	685	546	425	477	1,136	312	120	64
Permanently sick	2,717	5	6	8	21	20	115	183	146	166
Retired	20,791	-	1	-	2	3	5	8	3	2
Other inactive	11,491	20	69	136	195	275	1,239	1,634	1,115	684

Age								Students (economically active or inactive)	Sex, marital status and economic position
40 - 44	45 - 49	50 - 54	55 - 59	60 - 64	65 - 69	70 - 74	75 and over		
l	m	n	o	p	q	r	s	t	a
12,468	**10,242**	**9,147**	**8,941**	**9,727**	**10,463**	**9,339**	**19,102**	**6,341**	**Total females**
9,753	**7,996**	**6,501**	**5,114**	**2,544**	**730**	**278**	**243**	**878**	**Economically active**
4,365	3,681	2,792	1,913	718	116	53	65	71	Employees - full time
4,071	3,365	2,976	2,542	1,636	527	176	109	764	- part time
262	211	116	121	44	19	18	11	1	Self-employed - with employees
473	287	232	177	96	58	29	27	6	- without employees
61	38	24	8	6	-	-	1		On a Government scheme
521	414	361	353	44	10	2	30	36	Unemployed
17	*6*	*3*	-	-	-	-	-		*Economically active students (included above)*
2,715	**2,246**	**2,646**	**3,827**	**7,183**	**9,733**	**9,061**	**18,859**	**5,463**	**Economically inactive**
109	42	13	2	-	1	3	4	5,463	Students
396	449	570	716	422	238	151	588		Permanently sick
17	39	192	709	4,533	7,202	6,814	14,369		Retired
2,193	1,716	1,871	2,400	2,228	2,292	2,093	3,898		Other inactive
9,052	**7,670**	**6,850**	**6,515**	**6,367**	**6,008**	**4,284**	**4,368**	**377**	**Married females**
7,043	**5,950**	**4,863**	**3,673**	**1,722**	**434**	**109**	**66**	**36**	**Economically active**
2,706	2,430	1,840	1,211	410	55	21	17	3	Employees - full time
3,507	2,931	2,560	2,097	1,192	329	73	32	27	- part time
209	185	96	95	31	11	4	4	-	Self-employed - with employees
341	211	175	114	66	35	11	8	2	- without employees
31	15	12	4	4	-	-	-		On a Government scheme
249	178	180	152	19	4	-	5	4	Unemployed
5	*3*	-	-	-	-	-	-		*Economically active students (included above)*
2,009	**1,720**	**1,987**	**2,842**	**4,645**	**5,574**	**4,175**	**4,302**	**341**	**Economically inactive**
66	20	9	1	-	-	-	-	341	Students
175	197	254	394	217	118	49	79		Permanently sick
10	25	125	446	2,666	3,916	2,933	2,987		Retired
1,758	1,478	1,599	2,001	1,762	1,540	1,193	1,236		Other inactive
3,416	**2,572**	**2,297**	**2,426**	**3,360**	**4,455**	**5,055**	**14,734**	**5,964**	**Single, widowed or divorced females**
2,710	**2,046**	**1,638**	**1,441**	**822**	**296**	**169**	**177**	**842**	**Economically active**
1,659	1,251	952	702	308	61	32	48	68	Employees - full time
564	434	416	445	444	198	103	77	737	- part time
53	26	20	26	13	8	14	7	1	Self-employed - with employees
132	76	57	63	30	23	18	19	4	- without employees
30	23	12	4	2	-	-	1		On a Government scheme
272	236	181	201	25	6	2	25	32	Unemployed
12	*3*	*3*	-	-	-	-	-		*Economically active students (included above)*
706	**526**	**659**	**985**	**2,538**	**4,159**	**4,886**	**14,557**	**5,122**	**Economically inactive**
43	22	4	1	-	1	3	4	5,122	Students
221	252	316	322	205	120	102	509		Permanently sick
7	14	67	263	1,867	3,286	3,881	11,382		Retired
435	238	272	399	466	752	900	2,662		Other inactive

Table 8 Economic position - **continued**

8. Residents aged 16 and over

Sex, marital status and economic position	TOTAL AGED 16 AND OVER	Age								
		16	17	18	19	20	21 - 24	25 - 29	30 - 34	35 - 39
a	b	c	d	e	f	g	h	i	j	k
			Kingswood							
TOTAL PERSONS	**71,888**	**1,099**	**1,143**	**1,167**	**1,232**	**1,265**	**4,927**	**7,018**	**6,802**	**6,285**
Economically active	**47,553**	**385**	**780**	**901**	**1,049**	**1,086**	**4,300**	**5,922**	**5,696**	**5,467**
Employees - full time	30,066	145	456	598	827	870	3,444	4,360	3,546	3,187
- part time	9,365	143	156	125	48	39	175	648	1,194	1,351
Self-employed - with employees	1,556	1	1	2	1	2	28	120	193	232
- without employees	3,368	1	3	14	25	36	256	402	442	431
On a Government scheme	436	48	102	67	16	14	33	34	32	24
Unemployed	2,762	47	62	95	132	125	364	358	289	242
Economically active students (included above)	*437*	*128*	*128*	*96*	*18*	*22*	*25*	*6*	*4*	*4*
Economically inactive	**24,335**	**714**	**363**	**266**	**183**	**179**	**627**	**1,096**	**1,106**	**818**
Students	1,918	710	356	243	146	138	215	51	20	19
Permanently sick	1,687	2	2	6	5	8	43	66	66	79
Retired	12,716	-	-	-	-	-	1	3	1	8
Other inactive	8,014	2	5	17	32	33	368	976	1,019	712
Total males	**34,803**	**548**	**593**	**601**	**648**	**682**	**2,458**	**3,475**	**3,389**	**3,106**
Economically active	**26,957**	**178**	**420**	**474**	**553**	**607**	**2,317**	**3,381**	**3,331**	**3,038**
Employees - full time	19,964	81	242	309	399	468	1,796	2,654	2,573	2,326
- part time	812	50	73	60	26	10	28	33	25	22
Self-employed - with employees	1,235	1	1	2	1	2	21	95	155	180
- without employees	2,785	-	3	11	21	32	207	342	365	329
On a Government scheme	230	24	56	29	10	9	16	25	16	9
Unemployed	1,931	22	45	63	96	86	249	232	197	172
Economically active students (included above)	*202*	*44*	*57*	*48*	*13*	*14*	*17*	*5*	*-*	*2*
Economically inactive	**7,846**	**370**	**173**	**127**	**95**	**75**	**141**	**94**	**58**	**68**
Students	977	369	173	121	92	70	106	30	9	4
Permanently sick	1,034	1	-	5	3	4	26	43	35	44
Retired	5,677	-	-	-	-	-	1	-	-	3
Other inactive	158	-	-	1	-	1	8	21	14	17
Total females	**37,085**	**551**	**550**	**566**	**584**	**583**	**2,469**	**3,543**	**3,413**	**3,179**
Economically active	**20,596**	**207**	**360**	**427**	**496**	**479**	**1,983**	**2,541**	**2,365**	**2,429**
Employees - full time	10,102	64	214	289	428	402	1,648	1,706	973	861
- part time	8,553	93	83	65	22	29	147	615	1,169	1,329
Self-employed - with employees	321	-	-	-	-	-	7	25	38	52
- without employees	583	1	-	3	4	4	49	60	77	102
On a Government scheme	206	24	46	38	6	5	17	9	16	15
Unemployed	831	25	17	32	36	39	115	126	92	70
Economically active students (included above)	*235*	*84*	*71*	*48*	*5*	*8*	*8*	*1*	*4*	*2*
Economically inactive	**16,489**	**344**	**190**	**139**	**88**	**104**	**486**	**1,002**	**1,048**	**750**
Students	941	341	183	122	54	68	109	21	11	15
Permanently sick	653	1	2	1	2	4	17	23	31	35
Retired	7,039	-	-	-	-	-	-	3	1	5
Other inactive	7,856	2	5	16	32	32	360	955	1,005	695

Age								Students (economically active or inactive)	Sex, marital status and economic position
40 - 44	45 - 49	50 - 54	55 - 59	60 - 64	65 - 69	70 - 74	75 and over		
l	m	n	o	p	q	r	s	t	a
6,628	**5,940**	**5,266**	**5,278**	**4,782**	**4,328**	**3,227**	**5,501**	**2,355**	**TOTAL PERSONS**
5,933	**5,282**	**4,359**	**3,752**	**2,053**	**377**	**129**	**82**	**437**	**Economically active**
3,496	3,176	2,552	2,131	1,158	82	13	25	34	Employees - full time
1,424	1,212	1,033	977	508	219	78	35	389	- part time
279	261	206	133	55	24	9	9	1	Self-employed - with employees
469	399	340	277	185	50	27	11	3	- without employees
27	15	11	8	3	1	-	1		On a Government scheme
238	219	217	226	144	1	2	1	10	Unemployed
3	*2*	*1*	-	-	-	-	-		*Economically active students (included above)*
695	**658**	**907**	**1,526**	**2,729**	**3,951**	**3,098**	**5,419**	**1,918**	**Economically inactive**
15	2	1	-	1	-	1	-	1,918	Students
132	123	209	324	372	125	33	92		Permanently sick
16	25	83	368	1,723	3,307	2,615	4,566		Retired
532	508	614	834	633	519	449	761		Other inactive
3,345	**2,946**	**2,652**	**2,586**	**2,338**	**2,089**	**1,413**	**1,934**	**1,179**	**Total males**
3,245	**2,859**	**2,498**	**2,222**	**1,451**	**234**	**91**	**58**	**202**	**Economically active**
2,435	2,155	1,854	1,586	999	60	11	16	22	Employees - full time
24	21	38	111	102	114	49	26	171	- part time
221	209	158	110	49	17	6	7	1	Self-employed - with employees
395	328	283	240	156	41	24	8	1	- without employees
14	5	8	5	3	1	-	-		On a Government scheme
156	141	157	170	142	1	1	1	7	Unemployed
-	*2*	-	-	-	-	-	-		*Economically active students (included above)*
100	**87**	**154**	**364**	**887**	**1,855**	**1,322**	**1,876**	**977**	**Economically inactive**
1	1	-	-	-	-	1	-	977	Students
70	55	110	198	301	97	18	24		Permanently sick
13	17	31	148	573	1,752	1,296	1,843		Retired
16	14	13	18	13	6	7	9		Other inactive
3,283	**2,994**	**2,614**	**2,692**	**2,444**	**2,239**	**1,814**	**3,567**	**1,176**	**Total females**
2,688	**2,423**	**1,861**	**1,530**	**602**	**143**	**38**	**24**	**235**	**Economically active**
1,061	1,021	698	545	159	22	2	9	12	Employees - full time
1,400	1,191	995	866	406	105	29	9	218	- part time
58	52	48	23	6	7	3	2	-	Self-employed - with employees
74	71	57	37	29	9	3	3	2	- without employees
13	10	3	3	-	-	-	1		On a Government scheme
82	78	60	56	2	-	1	-	3	Unemployed
3	-	*1*	-	-	-	-	-		*Economically active students (included above)*
595	**571**	**753**	**1,162**	**1,842**	**2,096**	**1,776**	**3,543**	**941**	**Economically inactive**
14	1	1	-	1	-	-	-	941	Students
62	68	99	126	71	28	15	68		Permanently sick
3	8	52	220	1,150	1,555	1,319	2,723		Retired
516	494	601	816	620	513	442	752		Other inactive

8. Residents aged 16 and over

Sex, marital status and economic position	TOTAL AGED 16 AND OVER	Age								
		16	17	18	19	20	21 - 24	25 - 29	30 - 34	35 - 39
a	b	c	d	e	f	g	h	i	j	k
		Kingswood - *continued*								
Married females	**23,096**	**1**	**-**	**5**	**14**	**29**	**681**	**2,310**	**2,661**	**2,614**
Economically active	**13,450**	**-**	**-**	**2**	**6**	**21**	**465**	**1,521**	**1,787**	**1,972**
Employees - full time	4,957	-	-	2	5	11	331	856	557	593
- part time	7,370	-	-	-	1	5	84	539	1,076	1,194
Self-employed - with employees	273	-	-	-	-	-	2	19	32	46
- without employees	445	-	-	-	-	-	17	34	64	87
On a Government scheme	37	-	-	-	-	1	3	3	7	7
Unemployed	368	-	-	-	-	4	28	70	51	45
Economically active students (included above)	*10*	-	-	-	-	-	-	*1*	*3*	*2*
Economically inactive	**9,646**	**1**	**-**	**3**	**8**	**8**	**216**	**789**	**874**	**642**
Students	41	-	-	-	-	-	5	7	5	12
Permanently sick	330	-	-	-	-	-	-	5	9	19
Retired	3,175	-	-	-	-	-	-	2	-	1
Other inactive	6,100	1	-	3	8	8	211	775	860	610
Single, widowed or divorced females	**13,989**	**550**	**550**	**561**	**570**	**554**	**1,788**	**1,233**	**752**	**565**
Economically active	**7,146**	**207**	**360**	**425**	**490**	**458**	**1,518**	**1,020**	**578**	**457**
Employees - full time	5,145	64	214	287	423	391	1,317	850	416	268
- part time	1,183	93	83	65	21	24	63	76	93	135
Self-employed - with employees	48	-	-	-	-	-	5	6	6	6
- without employees	138	1	-	3	4	4	32	26	13	15
On a Government scheme	169	24	46	38	6	4	14	6	9	8
Unemployed	463	25	17	32	36	35	87	56	41	25
Economically active students (included above)	*225*	*84*	*71*	*48*	*5*	*8*	*8*	-	*1*	-
Economically inactive	**6,843**	**343**	**190**	**136**	**80**	**96**	**270**	**213**	**174**	**108**
Students	900	341	183	122	54	68	104	14	6	3
Permanently sick	323	1	2	1	2	4	17	18	22	16
Retired	3,864	-	-	-	-	-	-	1	1	4
Other inactive	1,756	1	5	13	24	24	149	180	145	85
		Northavon								
TOTAL PERSONS	**104,085**	**1,780**	**1,766**	**1,947**	**1,847**	**2,007**	**8,298**	**11,410**	**9,980**	**8,969**
Economically active	**71,587**	**565**	**1,083**	**1,396**	**1,421**	**1,619**	**7,188**	**9,739**	**8,351**	**7,670**
Employees - full time	46,794	190	538	926	1,092	1,327	5,841	7,286	5,491	4,704
- part time	12,523	251	288	208	99	78	343	965	1,516	1,712
Self-employed - with employees	2,700	-	-	3	4	5	60	194	309	353
- without employees	5,302	7	11	21	27	57	408	701	612	606
On a Government scheme	559	67	144	90	32	8	42	43	34	26
Unemployed	3,709	50	102	148	167	144	494	550	389	269
Economically active students (included above)	*765*	*211*	*234*	*154*	*43*	*34*	*54*	*12*	*4*	*5*
Economically inactive	**32,498**	**1,215**	**683**	**551**	**426**	**388**	**1,110**	**1,671**	**1,629**	**1,299**
Students	3,723	1,205	667	511	352	309	479	78	41	32
Permanently sick	2,292	5	5	13	15	15	89	172	116	109
Retired	14,938	-	-	-	-	-	4	2	1	28
Other inactive	11,545	5	11	27	59	64	538	1,419	1,471	1,130

Age 40 - 44	45 - 49	50 - 54	55 - 59	60 - 64	65 - 69	70 - 74	75 and over	Students (economically active or inactive)	Sex, marital status and economic position
l	m	n	o	p	q	r	s	t	a
2,762	**2,545**	**2,238**	**2,182**	**1,799**	**1,442**	**922**	**891**	**51**	**Married females**
2,251	**2,044**	**1,577**	**1,232**	**451**	**98**	**14**	**9**	**10**	**Economically active**
784	779	536	383	103	13	1	3	2	Employees - full time
1,293	1,103	906	765	318	72	10	4	6	- part time
54	46	41	20	6	4	2	1	-	Self-employed - with employees
63	65	50	32	23	9	-	1	2	- without employees
6	7	2	1	-	-	-	-		On a Government scheme
51	44	42	31	1	-	1	-	-	Unemployed
3	-	*1*	-	-	-	-	-		*Economically active students (included above)*
511	**501**	**661**	**950**	**1,348**	**1,344**	**908**	**882**	**41**	**Economically inactive**
10	1	-	-	1	-	-	-	41	Students
37	42	68	71	48	15	9	7		Permanently sick
1	4	30	164	785	952	623	613		Retired
463	454	563	715	514	377	276	262		Other inactive
521	**449**	**376**	**510**	**645**	**797**	**892**	**2,676**	**1,125**	**Single, widowed or divorced females**
437	**379**	**284**	**298**	**151**	**45**	**24**	**15**	**225**	**Economically active**
277	242	162	162	56	9	1	6	10	Employees - full time
107	88	89	101	88	33	19	5	212	- part time
4	6	7	3	-	3	1	1	-	Self-employed - with employees
11	6	7	5	6	-	3	2	-	- without employees
7	3	1	2	-	-	-	1		On a Government scheme
31	34	18	25	1	-	-	-	3	Unemployed
-	-	-	-	-	-	-	-		*Economically active students (included above)*
84	**70**	**92**	**212**	**494**	**752**	**868**	**2,661**	**900**	**Economically inactive**
4	-	1	-	-	-	-	-	900	Students
25	26	31	55	23	13	6	61		Permanently sick
2	4	22	56	365	603	696	2,110		Retired
53	40	38	101	106	136	166	490		Other inactive
10,599	**9,588**	**7,788**	**6,624**	**5,813**	**5,093**	**3,959**	**6,617**	**4,488**	**TOTAL PERSONS**
9,409	**8,485**	**6,520**	**4,693**	**2,592**	**514**	**195**	**147**	**765**	**Economically active**
5,798	5,267	3,963	2,767	1,426	108	34	36	66	Employees - full time
1,990	1,688	1,375	1,009	580	262	110	49	675	- part time
503	456	369	218	141	39	22	24	1	Self-employed - with employees
766	733	535	383	275	98	29	33	-	- without employees
29	25	10	7	-	-	-	2		On a Government scheme
323	316	268	309	170	7	-	3	23	Unemployed
9	*1*	*2*	-	-	*2*	-	-		*Economically active students (included above)*
1,190	**1,103**	**1,268**	**1,931**	**3,221**	**4,579**	**3,764**	**6,470**	**3,723**	**Economically inactive**
25	10	5	-	2	2	-	5	3,723	Students
173	192	257	373	418	140	52	148		Permanently sick
27	50	127	553	2,017	3,749	3,102	5,278		Retired
965	851	879	1,005	784	688	610	1,039		Other inactive

Table 8 Economic position - **continued**

8. Residents aged 16 and over

Sex, marital status and economic position	TOTAL AGED 16 AND OVER	Age								
		16	17	18	19	20	21 - 24	25 - 29	30 - 34	35 - 39
a	b	c	d	e	f	g	h	i	j	k
			Northavon - *continued*							
Total males	**51,281**	**920**	**924**	**1,021**	**919**	**985**	**4,132**	**5,752**	**5,133**	**4,426**
Economically active	**40,867**	**296**	**604**	**769**	**727**	**812**	**3,791**	**5,594**	**5,007**	**4,293**
Employees - full time	30,757	115	331	510	542	651	3,014	4,463	4,003	3,379
- part time	1,139	107	123	90	35	20	45	41	39	28
Self-employed - with employees	2,050	-	-	1	2	4	45	141	238	265
- without employees	4,139	7	10	19	22	44	341	564	460	425
On a Government scheme	315	36	77	57	19	4	24	26	20	15
Unemployed	2,467	31	63	92	107	89	322	359	247	181
Economically active students (included above)	*343*	*89*	*100*	*74*	*19*	*14*	*31*	*8*	*2*	*2*
Economically inactive	**10,414**	**624**	**320**	**252**	**192**	**173**	**341**	**158**	**126**	**133**
Students	1,870	620	317	242	178	159	273	36	12	12
Permanently sick	1,305	3	2	7	9	9	47	89	66	60
Retired	6,859	-	-	-	-	-	2	-	1	12
Other inactive	380	1	1	3	5	5	19	33	47	49
Total females	**52,804**	**860**	**842**	**926**	**928**	**1,022**	**4,166**	**5,658**	**4,847**	**4,543**
Economically active	**30,720**	**269**	**479**	**627**	**694**	**807**	**3,397**	**4,145**	**3,344**	**3,377**
Employees - full time	16,037	75	207	416	550	676	2,827	2,823	1,488	1,325
- part time	11,384	144	165	118	64	58	298	924	1,477	1,684
Self-employed - with employees	650	-	-	2	2	1	15	53	71	88
- without employees	1,163	-	1	2	5	13	67	137	152	181
On a Government scheme	244	31	67	33	13	4	18	17	14	11
Unemployed	1,242	19	39	56	60	55	172	191	142	88
Economically active students (included above)	*422*	*122*	*134*	*80*	*24*	*20*	*23*	*4*	*2*	*3*
Economically inactive	**22,084**	**591**	**363**	**299**	**234**	**215**	**769**	**1,513**	**1,503**	**1,166**
Students	1,853	585	350	269	174	150	206	42	29	20
Permanently sick	987	2	3	6	6	6	42	83	50	49
Retired	8,079	-	-	-	-	-	2	2	-	16
Other inactive	11,165	4	10	24	54	59	519	1,386	1,424	1,081
Married females	**33,492**	**1**	**-**	**12**	**30**	**81**	**1,377**	**3,747**	**3,856**	**3,816**
Economically active	**20,319**	**-**	**-**	**9**	**17**	**55**	**1,050**	**2,552**	**2,561**	**2,805**
Employees - full time	8,584	-	-	4	12	43	801	1,503	917	956
- part time	9,645	-	-	3	2	7	169	805	1,345	1,547
Self-employed - with employees	550	-	-	-	-	-	5	38	60	82
- without employees	884	-	-	-	-	-	18	91	129	155
On a Government scheme	49	-	-	-	-	-	-	6	9	9
Unemployed	607	-	-	2	3	5	57	109	101	56
Economically active students (included above)	*13*	-	-	-	-	-	*1*	*2*	*1*	*2*
Economically inactive	**13,173**	**1**	**-**	**3**	**13**	**26**	**327**	**1,195**	**1,295**	**1,011**
Students	72	1	-	-	1	-	5	11	20	14
Permanently sick	438	-	-	-	-	-	5	18	14	20
Retired	3,813	-	-	-	-	-	-	-	-	1
Other inactive	8,850	-	-	3	12	26	317	1,166	1,261	976

Age 40 - 44	45 - 49	50 - 54	55 - 59	60 - 64	65 - 69	70 - 74	75 and over	Students (economically active or inactive)	Sex, marital status and economic position
l	m	n	o	p	q	r	s	t	a
5,263	**4,854**	**3,988**	**3,363**	**3,023**	**2,435**	**1,699**	**2,444**	**2,213**	**Total males**
5,104	**4,691**	**3,785**	**2,914**	**1,909**	**352**	**123**	**96**	**343**	**Economically active**
3,906	3,538	2,824	2,098	1,250	84	29	20	35	Employees - full time
32	26	57	99	154	151	61	31	291	- part time
375	337	288	176	113	31	17	17	1	Self-employed - with employees
580	580	426	310	229	81	16	25	-	- without employees
11	16	3	5	-	-	-	2		On a Government scheme
200	194	187	226	163	5	-	1	16	Unemployed
2	-	*1*	-	-	*1*	-	-		*Economically active students (included above)*
159	**163**	**203**	**449**	**1,114**	**2,083**	**1,576**	**2,348**	**1,870**	**Economically inactive**
9	4	4	-	2	1	-	1	1,870	Students
79	90	122	213	353	106	25	25		Permanently sick
17	22	47	214	744	1,961	1,532	2,307		Retired
54	47	30	22	15	15	19	15		Other inactive
5,336	**4,734**	**3,800**	**3,261**	**2,790**	**2,658**	**2,260**	**4,173**	**2,275**	**Total females**
4,305	**3,794**	**2,735**	**1,779**	**683**	**162**	**72**	**51**	**422**	**Economically active**
1,892	1,729	1,139	669	176	24	5	16	31	Employees - full time
1,958	1,662	1,318	910	426	111	49	18	384	- part time
128	119	81	42	28	8	5	7	-	Self-employed - with employees
186	153	109	73	46	17	13	8	-	- without employees
18	9	7	2	-	-	-	-		On a Government scheme
123	122	81	83	7	2	-	2	7	Unemployed
7	*1*	*1*	-	-	*1*	-	-		*Economically active students (included above)*
1,031	**940**	**1,065**	**1,482**	**2,107**	**2,496**	**2,188**	**4,122**	**1,853**	**Economically inactive**
16	6	1	-	-	1	-	4	1,853	Students
94	102	135	160	65	34	27	123		Permanently sick
10	28	80	339	1,273	1,788	1,570	2,971		Retired
911	804	849	983	769	673	591	1,024		Other inactive
4,550	**4,035**	**3,259**	**2,637**	**2,129**	**1,662**	**1,190**	**1,110**	**85**	**Married females**
3,644	**3,228**	**2,319**	**1,416**	**521**	**96**	**30**	**16**	**13**	**Economically active**
1,453	1,364	890	497	123	12	2	7	1	Employees - full time
1,814	1,545	1,207	778	331	67	20	5	12	- part time
113	110	75	35	22	5	3	2	-	Self-employed - with employees
165	124	91	55	38	11	5	2	-	- without employees
11	7	5	2	-	-	-	-		On a Government scheme
88	78	51	49	7	1	-	-	-	Unemployed
5	*1*	-	-	-	*1*	-	-		*Economically active students (included above)*
906	**807**	**940**	**1,221**	**1,608**	**1,566**	**1,160**	**1,094**	**72**	**Economically inactive**
14	4	1	-	-	-	-	1	72	Students
59	58	83	88	45	17	13	18		Permanently sick
4	8	58	261	896	1,073	802	710		Retired
829	737	798	872	667	476	345	365		Other inactive

8. Residents aged 16 and over

Sex, marital status and economic position	TOTAL AGED 16 AND OVER	Age								
		16	17	18	19	20	21 - 24	25 - 29	30 - 34	35 - 39
a	b	c	d	e	f	g	h	i	j	k
				Northavon - *continued*						
Single, widowed or divorced females	**19,312**	**859**	**842**	**914**	**898**	**941**	**2,789**	**1,911**	**991**	**727**
Economically active	**10,401**	**269**	**479**	**618**	**677**	**752**	**2,347**	**1,593**	**783**	**572**
Employees - full time	7,453	75	207	412	538	633	2,026	1,320	571	369
- part time	1,739	144	165	115	62	51	129	119	132	137
Self-employed - with employees	100	-	-	2	2	1	10	15	11	6
- without employees	279	-	1	2	5	13	49	46	23	26
On a Government scheme	195	31	67	33	13	4	18	11	5	2
Unemployed	635	19	39	54	57	50	115	82	41	32
Economically active students (included above)	*409*	*122*	*134*	*80*	*24*	*20*	*22*	*2*	*1*	*1*
Economically inactive	**8,911**	**590**	**363**	**296**	**221**	**189**	**442**	**318**	**208**	**155**
Students	1,781	584	350	269	173	150	201	31	9	6
Permanently sick	549	2	3	6	6	6	37	65	36	29
Retired	4,266	-	-	-	-	-	2	2	-	15
Other inactive	2,315	4	10	21	42	33	202	220	163	105
				Wansdyke						
TOTAL PERSONS	**64,648**	**1,085**	**1,037**	**1,093**	**1,157**	**1,117**	**4,026**	**5,121**	**5,194**	**5,413**
Economically active	**40,351**	**310**	**584**	**742**	**868**	**863**	**3,373**	**4,323**	**4,216**	**4,667**
Employees - full time	24,327	98	320	495	648	678	2,590	2,956	2,546	2,697
- part time	7,671	139	124	128	62	54	186	484	803	1,001
Self-employed - with employees	2,169	1	-	-	1	1	31	110	214	319
- without employees	3,762	1	6	7	33	40	229	430	454	449
On a Government scheme	351	47	83	46	14	11	23	22	33	22
Unemployed	2,071	24	51	66	110	79	314	321	166	179
Economically active students (included above)	*448*	*129*	*95*	*97*	*33*	*30*	*39*	*11*	*4*	*4*
Economically inactive	**24,297**	**775**	**453**	**351**	**289**	**254**	**653**	**798**	**978**	**746**
Students	2,491	769	447	337	247	215	325	60	26	24
Permanently sick	1,341	2	4	2	6	12	40	47	56	54
Retired	12,382	-	-	-	-	-	-	4	2	4
Other inactive	8,083	4	2	12	36	27	288	687	894	664
Total males	**31,115**	**558**	**512**	**568**	**597**	**586**	**2,055**	**2,589**	**2,532**	**2,699**
Economically active	**23,148**	**173**	**310**	**404**	**473**	**461**	**1,839**	**2,521**	**2,483**	**2,650**
Employees - full time	16,133	68	181	279	342	367	1,371	1,840	1,807	1,930
- part time	815	65	52	56	22	18	26	21	18	11
Self-employed - with employees	1,646	1	-	-	1	1	22	79	169	232
- without employees	2,940	-	5	6	29	24	180	358	345	346
On a Government scheme	172	22	48	24	9	3	13	12	15	5
Unemployed	1,442	17	24	39	70	48	227	211	129	126
Economically active students (included above)	*197*	*60*	*36*	*49*	*14*	*13*	*16*	*2*	*2*	*1*
Economically inactive	**7,967**	**385**	**202**	**164**	**124**	**125**	**216**	**68**	**49**	**49**
Students	1,216	383	199	162	118	116	184	30	7	5
Permanently sick	812	2	3	2	4	8	24	28	32	28
Retired	5,768	-	-	-	-	-	-	1	1	1
Other inactive	171	-	-	-	2	1	8	9	9	15

Age 40 - 44	45 - 49	50 - 54	55 - 59	60 - 64	65 - 69	70 - 74	75 and over	Students (economically active or inactive)	Sex, marital status and economic position
l	m	n	o	p	q	r	s	t	a
786	**699**	**541**	**624**	**661**	**996**	**1,070**	**3,063**	**2,190**	**Single, widowed or divorced females**
661	**566**	**416**	**363**	**162**	**66**	**42**	**35**	**409**	**Economically active**
439	365	249	172	53	12	3	9	30	Employees - full time
144	117	111	132	95	44	29	13	372	- part time
15	9	6	7	6	3	2	5	-	Self-employed - with employees
21	29	18	18	8	6	8	6	-	- without employees
7	2	2	-	-	-	-	-		On a Government scheme
35	44	30	34	-	1	-	2	7	Unemployed
2	*-*	*1*	*-*	*-*	*-*	*-*	*-*		*Economically active students (included above)*
125	**133**	**125**	**261**	**499**	**930**	**1,028**	**3,028**	**1,781**	**Economically inactive**
2	2	-	-	-	1	-	3	1,781	Students
35	44	52	72	20	17	14	105		Permanently sick
6	20	22	78	377	715	768	2,261		Retired
82	67	51	111	102	197	246	659		Other inactive
6,464	**5,529**	**4,734**	**4,547**	**4,429**	**4,268**	**3,426**	**6,008**	**2,939**	**TOTAL PERSONS**
5,684	**4,821**	**3,925**	**3,226**	**1,918**	**492**	**206**	**133**	**448**	**Economically active**
3,315	2,780	2,268	1,798	966	97	40	35	41	Employees - full time
1,219	993	829	725	516	253	103	52	386	- part time
389	388	297	203	122	50	23	20	2	Self-employed - with employees
542	485	394	322	216	90	39	25	2	- without employees
15	15	9	8	2	-	1	-		On a Government scheme
204	160	128	170	96	2	-	1	17	Unemployed
2	*1*	*2*	*-*	*-*	*1*	*-*	*-*		*Economically active students (included above)*
780	**708**	**809**	**1,321**	**2,511**	**3,776**	**3,220**	**5,875**	**2,491**	**Economically inactive**
24	9	2	-	-	1	3	2	2,491	Students
77	115	142	249	294	96	36	109		Permanently sick
5	13	79	321	1,530	3,016	2,644	4,764		Retired
674	571	586	751	687	663	537	1,000		Other inactive
3,176	**2,746**	**2,348**	**2,282**	**2,127**	**2,022**	**1,507**	**2,211**	**1,413**	**Total males**
3,115	**2,664**	**2,222**	**1,984**	**1,311**	**314**	**140**	**84**	**197**	**Economically active**
2,234	1,871	1,536	1,363	827	71	27	19	21	Employees - full time
34	32	47	76	115	134	59	29	166	- part time
283	290	242	157	96	38	19	16	2	Self-employed - with employees
418	364	302	261	179	70	34	19	1	- without employees
5	5	3	6	1	-	1	-		On a Government scheme
141	102	92	121	93	1	-	1	7	Unemployed
1	*1*	*1*	*-*	*-*	*1*	*-*	*-*		*Economically active students (included above)*
61	**82**	**126**	**298**	**816**	**1,708**	**1,367**	**2,127**	**1,216**	**Economically inactive**
6	4	2	-	-	-	-	-	1,216	Students
36	57	75	150	251	71	16	25		Permanently sick
1	8	33	135	549	1,625	1,339	2,075		Retired
18	13	16	13	16	12	12	27		Other inactive

Table 8 Economic position – **continued**

8. Residents aged 16 and over

Sex, marital status and economic position	TOTAL AGED 16 AND OVER	Age								
		16	17	18	19	20	21 - 24	25 - 29	30 - 34	35 - 39
a	b	c	d	e	f	g	h	i	j	k
				Wansdyke – *continued*						
Total females	**33,533**	**527**	**525**	**525**	**560**	**531**	**1,971**	**2,532**	**2,662**	**2,714**
Economically active	**17,203**	**137**	**274**	**338**	**395**	**402**	**1,534**	**1,802**	**1,733**	**2,017**
Employees - full time	8,194	30	139	216	306	311	1,219	1,116	739	767
- part time	6,856	74	72	72	40	36	160	463	785	990
Self-employed - with employees	523	-	-	-	-	-	9	31	45	87
- without employees	822	1	1	1	4	16	49	72	109	103
On a Government scheme	179	25	35	22	5	8	10	10	18	17
Unemployed	629	7	27	27	40	31	87	110	37	53
Economically active students (included above)	*251*	*69*	*59*	*48*	*19*	*17*	*23*	*9*	*2*	*3*
Economically inactive	**16,330**	**390**	**251**	**187**	**165**	**129**	**437**	**730**	**929**	**697**
Students	1,275	386	248	175	129	99	141	30	19	19
Permanently sick	529	-	1	-	2	4	16	19	24	26
Retired	6,614	-	-	-	-	-	-	3	1	3
Other inactive	7,912	4	2	12	34	26	280	678	885	649
Married females	**20,784**	**1**	**2**	**4**	**11**	**25**	**559**	**1,593**	**2,154**	**2,261**
Economically active	**11,382**	**-**	**1**	**4**	**4**	**18**	**372**	**1,014**	**1,345**	**1,646**
Employees - full time	4,321	-	-	-	1	10	257	537	458	547
- part time	5,740	-	-	1	2	6	82	368	722	896
Self-employed - with employees	438	-	-	-	-	-	6	22	37	74
- without employees	583	-	-	-	-	-	9	40	89	84
On a Government scheme	47	-	1	-	-	-	1	2	13	11
Unemployed	253	-	-	3	1	2	17	45	26	34
Economically active students (included above)	*7*	-	-	-	-	-	-	*1*	*2*	*3*
Economically inactive	**9,402**	**1**	**1**	**-**	**7**	**7**	**187**	**579**	**809**	**615**
Students	46	-	-	-	-	-	-	7	10	12
Permanently sick	239	-	-	-	-	-	3	5	6	13
Retired	2,927	-	-	-	-	-	-	1	1	3
Other inactive	6,190	1	1	-	7	7	184	566	792	587
Single, widowed or divorced females	**12,749**	**526**	**523**	**521**	**549**	**506**	**1,412**	**939**	**508**	**453**
Economically active	**5,821**	**137**	**273**	**334**	**391**	**384**	**1,162**	**788**	**388**	**371**
Employees - full time	3,873	30	139	216	305	301	962	579	281	220
- part time	1,116	74	72	71	38	30	78	95	63	94
Self-employed - with employees	85	-	-	-	-	-	3	9	8	13
- without employees	239	1	1	1	4	16	40	32	20	19
On a Government scheme	132	25	34	22	5	8	9	8	5	6
Unemployed	376	7	27	24	39	29	70	65	11	19
Economically active students (included above)	*244*	*69*	*59*	*48*	*19*	*17*	*23*	*8*	-	-
Economically inactive	**6,928**	**389**	**250**	**187**	**158**	**122**	**250**	**151**	**120**	**82**
Students	1,229	386	248	175	129	99	141	23	9	7
Permanently sick	290	-	1	-	2	4	13	14	18	13
Retired	3,687	-	-	-	-	-	-	2	-	-
Other inactive	1,722	3	1	12	27	19	96	112	93	62

Age								Students (economically active or inactive)	Sex, marital status and economic position
40 - 44	45 - 49	50 - 54	55 - 59	60 - 64	65 - 69	70 - 74	75 and over		
l	m	n	o	p	q	r	s	t	a
3,288	**2,783**	**2,386**	**2,265**	**2,302**	**2,246**	**1,919**	**3,797**	**1,526**	**Total females**
2,569	**2,157**	**1,703**	**1,242**	**607**	**178**	**66**	**49**	**251**	**Economically active**
1,081	909	732	435	139	26	13	16	20	Employees - full time
1,185	961	782	649	401	119	44	23	220	- part time
106	98	55	46	26	12	4	4	-	Self-employed - with employees
124	121	92	61	37	20	5	6	1	- without employees
10	10	6	2	1	-	-	-		On a Government scheme
63	58	36	49	3	1	-	-	10	Unemployed
1	-	*1*	-	-	-	-	-		*Economically active students (included above)*
719	**626**	**683**	**1,023**	**1,695**	**2,068**	**1,853**	**3,748**	**1,275**	**Economically inactive**
18	5	-	-	-	1	3	2	1,275	Students
41	58	67	99	43	25	20	84		Permanently sick
4	5	46	186	981	1,391	1,305	2,689		Retired
656	558	570	738	671	651	525	973		Other inactive
2,808	**2,389**	**1,998**	**1,806**	**1,755**	**1,449**	**1,001**	**968**	**53**	**Married females**
2,176	**1,821**	**1,400**	**972**	**465**	**100**	**34**	**10**	**7**	**Economically active**
844	696	543	311	93	13	8	3	3	Employees - full time
1,104	890	709	550	318	67	20	5	3	- part time
93	89	49	40	20	6	1	1	-	Self-employed - with employees
91	101	72	47	30	14	5	1	1	- without employees
6	6	4	2	1	-	-	-		On a Government scheme
38	39	23	22	3	-	-	-	-	Unemployed
-	-	*1*	-	-	-	-	-		*Economically active students (included above)*
632	**568**	**598**	**834**	**1,290**	**1,349**	**967**	**958**	**46**	**Economically inactive**
12	4	-	-	-	-	-	1	46	Students
22	33	35	60	28	12	9	13		Permanently sick
3	4	38	126	691	842	622	596		Retired
595	527	525	648	571	495	336	348		Other inactive
480	**394**	**388**	**459**	**547**	**797**	**918**	**2,829**	**1,473**	**Single, widowed or divorced females**
393	**336**	**303**	**270**	**142**	**78**	**32**	**39**	**244**	**Economically active**
237	213	189	124	46	13	5	13	17	Employees - full time
81	71	73	99	83	52	24	18	217	- part time
13	9	6	6	6	6	3	3	-	Self-employed - with employees
33	20	20	14	7	6	-	5	-	- without employees
4	4	2	-	-	-	-	-		On a Government scheme
25	19	13	27	-	1	-	-	10	Unemployed
1	-	-	-	-	-	-	-		*Economically active students (included above)*
87	**58**	**85**	**189**	**405**	**719**	**886**	**2,790**	**1,229**	**Economically inactive**
6	1	-	-	-	1	3	1	1,229	Students
19	25	32	39	15	13	11	71		Permanently sick
1	1	8	60	290	549	683	2,093		Retired
61	31	45	90	100	156	189	625		Other inactive

Table 8 Economic position - **continued**

8. Residents aged 16 and over

Sex, marital status and economic position	TOTAL AGED 16 AND OVER	Age 16	17	18	19	20	21 - 24	25 - 29	30 - 34	35 - 39
a	b	c	d	e	f	g	h	i	j	k
			Woodspring							
TOTAL PERSONS	**143,967**	**2,299**	**2,414**	**2,422**	**2,529**	**2,475**	**8,853**	**11,201**	**11,080**	**11,568**
Economically active	**85,500**	**632**	**1,319**	**1,638**	**1,900**	**1,947**	**7,450**	**9,353**	**8,916**	**9,707**
Employees - full time	51,623	190	595	1,018	1,399	1,488	5,692	6,567	5,410	5,657
- part time	16,052	301	415	307	176	139	422	1,042	1,693	2,139
Self-employed - with employees	4,175	-	1	2	2	1	57	252	402	556
- without employees	7,388	5	8	17	54	54	422	722	818	849
On a Government scheme	720	69	163	89	37	25	75	45	46	47
Unemployed	5,542	67	137	205	232	240	782	725	547	459
Economically active students (included above)	*1,042*	*248*	*327*	*220*	*85*	*55*	*62*	*13*	*8*	*13*
Economically inactive	**58,467**	**1,667**	**1,095**	**784**	**629**	**528**	**1,403**	**1,848**	**2,164**	**1,861**
Students	5,398	1,660	1,071	738	558	430	636	100	59	65
Permanently sick	4,555	1	6	8	17	18	90	164	172	242
Retired	31,017	-	-	1	1	1	3	4	7	12
Other inactive	17,497	6	18	37	53	79	674	1,580	1,926	1,542
Total males	**68,173**	**1,171**	**1,261**	**1,292**	**1,339**	**1,284**	**4,536**	**5,680**	**5,353**	**5,686**
Economically active	**48,988**	**310**	**737**	**902**	**1,041**	**1,054**	**4,126**	**5,512**	**5,190**	**5,503**
Employees - full time	34,244	109	367	591	752	788	3,075	4,146	3,853	4,072
- part time	1,772	124	181	127	66	45	74	60	40	53
Self-employed - with employees	3,035	-	1	2	1	-	41	183	283	420
- without employees	5,636	4	7	13	39	46	344	569	612	612
On a Government scheme	457	36	93	54	28	14	54	33	32	26
Unemployed	3,844	37	88	115	155	161	538	521	370	320
Economically active students (included above)	*480*	*106*	*142*	*103*	*44*	*29*	*34*	*6*	*1*	*9*
Economically inactive	**19,185**	**861**	**524**	**390**	**298**	**230**	**410**	**168**	**163**	**183**
Students	2,732	860	520	382	287	216	334	56	28	25
Permanently sick	2,501	1	3	4	6	10	59	90	94	127
Retired	13,581	-	-	-	1	1	1	-	3	4
Other inactive	371	-	1	4	4	3	16	22	38	27
Total females	**75,794**	**1,128**	**1,153**	**1,130**	**1,190**	**1,191**	**4,317**	**5,521**	**5,727**	**5,882**
Economically active	**36,512**	**322**	**582**	**736**	**859**	**893**	**3,324**	**3,841**	**3,726**	**4,204**
Employees - full time	17,379	81	228	427	647	700	2,617	2,421	1,557	1,585
- part time	14,280	177	234	180	110	94	348	982	1,653	2,086
Self-employed - with employees	1,140	-	-	-	1	1	16	69	119	136
- without employees	1,752	1	1	4	15	8	78	153	206	237
On a Government scheme	263	33	70	35	9	11	21	12	14	21
Unemployed	1,698	30	49	90	77	79	244	204	177	139
Economically active students (included above)	*562*	*142*	*185*	*117*	*41*	*26*	*28*	*7*	*7*	*4*
Economically inactive	**39,282**	**806**	**571**	**394**	**331**	**298**	**993**	**1,680**	**2,001**	**1,678**
Students	2,666	800	551	356	271	214	302	44	31	40
Permanently sick	2,054	-	3	4	11	8	31	74	78	115
Retired	17,436	-	-	1	-	-	2	4	4	8
Other inactive	17,126	6	17	33	49	76	658	1,558	1,888	1,515

Age								Students (economically active or inactive)	Sex, marital status and economic position
40 - 44	45 - 49	50 - 54	55 - 59	60 - 64	65 - 69	70 - 74	75 and over		
l	m	n	o	p	q	r	s	t	a
14,115	**12,348**	**10,067**	**9,243**	**9,306**	**9,685**	**8,336**	**16,026**	**6,440**	**TOTAL PERSONS**
12,318	**10,719**	**8,126**	**6,257**	**3,586**	**928**	**407**	**297**	**1,042**	**Economically active**
7,265	6,390	4,597	3,388	1,671	177	65	54	69	Employees - full time
2,579	2,100	1,692	1,327	927	470	213	110	947	- part time
793	753	508	403	246	90	48	61	1	Self-employed - with employees
1,096	984	864	681	490	180	77	67	3	- without employees
31	36	27	22	5	2	1	-		On a Government scheme
554	456	438	436	247	9	3	5	22	Unemployed
3	*3*	*3*	*1*	-	*1*	-	-		*Economically active students (included above)*
1,797	**1,629**	**1,941**	**2,986**	**5,720**	**8,757**	**7,929**	**15,729**	**5,398**	**Economically inactive**
39	25	8	2	1	1	1	4	5,398	Students
339	419	468	699	825	321	166	600		Permanently sick
19	48	204	787	3,507	7,049	6,573	12,801		Retired
1,400	1,137	1,261	1,498	1,387	1,386	1,189	2,324		Other inactive
6,913	**6,198**	**4,987**	**4,590**	**4,496**	**4,339**	**3,660**	**5,388**	**3,212**	**Total males**
6,693	**5,933**	**4,656**	**3,801**	**2,528**	**566**	**254**	**182**	**480**	**Economically active**
4,882	4,257	3,218	2,500	1,423	133	44	34	39	Employees - full time
59	68	92	141	250	216	112	64	422	- part time
563	546	369	299	194	66	31	36	-	Self-employed - with employees
802	734	660	528	416	142	63	45	1	- without employees
21	25	20	14	4	2	1	-		On a Government scheme
366	303	297	319	241	7	3	3	18	Unemployed
-	*3*	*2*	-	-	*1*	-	-		*Economically active students (included above)*
220	**265**	**331**	**789**	**1,968**	**3,773**	**3,406**	**5,206**	**2,732**	**Economically inactive**
8	8	1	2	1	1	-	3	2,732	Students
171	212	236	407	638	229	83	131		Permanently sick
6	21	68	344	1,292	3,527	3,299	5,014		Retired
35	24	26	36	37	16	24	58		Other inactive
7,202	**6,150**	**5,080**	**4,653**	**4,810**	**5,346**	**4,676**	**10,638**	**3,228**	**Total females**
5,625	**4,786**	**3,470**	**2,456**	**1,058**	**362**	**153**	**115**	**562**	**Economically active**
2,383	2,133	1,379	888	248	44	21	20	30	Employees - full time
2,520	2,032	1,600	1,186	677	254	101	46	525	- part time
230	207	139	104	52	24	17	25	1	Self-employed - with employees
294	250	204	153	74	38	14	22	2	- without employees
10	11	7	8	1	-	-	-		On a Government scheme
188	153	141	117	6	2	-	2	4	Unemployed
3	-	*1*	*1*	-	-	-	-		*Economically active students (included above)*
1,577	**1,364**	**1,610**	**2,197**	**3,752**	**4,984**	**4,523**	**10,523**	**2,666**	**Economically inactive**
31	17	7	-	-	-	1	1	2,666	Students
168	207	232	292	187	92	83	469		Permanently sick
13	27	136	443	2,215	3,522	3,274	7,787		Retired
1,365	1,113	1,235	1,462	1,350	1,370	1,165	2,266		Other inactive

Table 8 Economic position - **continued**

8. Residents aged 16 and over

Sex, marital status and economic position	TOTAL AGED 16 AND OVER	Age								
		16	17	18	19	20	21 - 24	25 - 29	30 - 34	35 - 39
a	b	c	d	e	f	g	h	i	j	k
		Woodspring - *continued*								
Married females	**45,133**	**1**	**6**	**13**	**38**	**82**	**1,243**	**3,493**	**4,450**	**4,835**
Economically active	**23,784**	**-**	**4**	**8**	**27**	**53**	**857**	**2,231**	**2,754**	**3,406**
Employees - full time	9,174	-	3	5	16	35	592	1,192	933	1,121
- part time	11,530	-	1	1	5	10	161	789	1,447	1,878
Self-employed - with employees	965	-	-	-	-	-	7	57	99	120
- without employees	1,294	-	-	-	1	1	22	91	149	188
On a Government scheme	51	-	-	-	-	-	4	3	9	14
Unemployed	770	-	-	2	5	7	71	99	117	85
Economically active students (included above)	*9*	-	-	-	-	-	-	*1*	*4*	*2*
Economically inactive	**21,349**	**1**	**2**	**5**	**11**	**29**	**386**	**1,262**	**1,696**	**1,429**
Students	104	-	2	-	1	-	3	8	22	30
Permanently sick	842	-	-	-	-	-	2	20	29	54
Retired	7,283	-	-	-	-	-	-	-	3	5
Other inactive	13,120	1	-	5	10	29	381	1,234	1,642	1,340
Single, widowed or divorced females	**30,661**	**1,127**	**1,147**	**1,117**	**1,152**	**1,109**	**3,074**	**2,028**	**1,277**	**1,047**
Economically active	**12,728**	**322**	**578**	**728**	**832**	**840**	**2,467**	**1,610**	**972**	**798**
Employees - full time	8,205	81	225	422	631	665	2,025	1,229	624	464
- part time	2,750	177	233	179	105	84	187	193	206	208
Self-employed - with employees	175	-	-	-	1	1	9	12	20	16
- without employees	458	1	1	4	14	7	56	62	57	49
On a Government scheme	212	33	70	35	9	11	17	9	5	7
Unemployed	928	30	49	88	72	72	173	105	60	54
Economically active students (included above)	*553*	*142*	*185*	*117*	*41*	*26*	*28*	*6*	*3*	*2*
Economically inactive	**17,933**	**805**	**569**	**389**	**320**	**269**	**607**	**418**	**305**	**249**
Students	2,562	800	549	356	270	214	299	36	9	10
Permanently sick	1,212	-	3	4	11	8	29	54	49	61
Retired	10,153	-	-	1	-	-	2	4	1	3
Other inactive	4,006	5	17	28	39	47	277	324	246	175

Age 40 - 44	45 - 49	50 - 54	55 - 59	60 - 64	65 - 69	70 - 74	75 and over	Students (economically active or inactive)	Sex, marital status and economic position
l	m	n	o	p	q	r	s	t	a
6,005	**5,110**	**4,198**	**3,657**	**3,482**	**3,392**	**2,414**	**2,714**	**113**	**Married females**
4,666	**3,983**	**2,818**	**1,875**	**767**	**212**	**77**	**46**	**9**	**Economically active**
1,801	1,628	1,017	624	169	21	13	4	1	Employees - full time
2,286	1,855	1,419	969	496	146	50	17	7	- part time
207	185	120	87	43	18	7	15	-	Self-employed - with employees
240	209	175	121	53	27	7	10	1	- without employees
5	7	2	6	1	-	-	-		On a Government scheme
127	99	85	68	5	-	-	-	-	Unemployed
1	-	*1*	-	-	-	-	-		*Economically active students (included above)*
1,339	**1,127**	**1,380**	**1,782**	**2,715**	**3,180**	**2,337**	**2,668**	**104**	**Economically inactive**
23	11	4	-	-	-	-	-	104	Students
81	104	127	154	102	45	34	90		Permanently sick
7	17	104	320	1,447	2,078	1,553	1,749		Retired
1,228	995	1,145	1,308	1,166	1,057	750	829		Other inactive
1,197	**1,040**	**882**	**996**	**1,328**	**1,954**	**2,262**	**7,924**	**3,115**	**Single, widowed or divorced females**
959	**803**	**652**	**581**	**291**	**150**	**76**	**69**	**553**	**Economically active**
582	505	362	264	79	23	8	16	29	Employees - full time
234	177	181	217	181	108	51	29	518	- part time
23	22	19	17	9	6	10	10	1	Self-employed - with employees
54	41	29	32	21	11	7	12	1	- without employees
5	4	5	2	-	-	-	-		On a Government scheme
61	54	56	49	1	2	-	2	4	Unemployed
2	-	-	*1*	-	-	-	-		*Economically active students (included above)*
238	**237**	**230**	**415**	**1,037**	**1,804**	**2,186**	**7,855**	**2,562**	**Economically inactive**
8	6	3	-	-	-	1	1	2,562	Students
87	103	105	138	85	47	49	379		Permanently sick
6	10	32	123	768	1,444	1,721	6,038		Retired
137	118	90	154	184	313	415	1,437		Other inactive

Table 9 Economic position and ethnic group

9. Residents aged 16 and over

Economic position	TOTAL PERSONS	Ethnic group										Persons born in Ireland
		White	Black Caribbean	Black African	Black other	Indian	Pakistani	Bangladeshi	Chinese	Other groups		
										Asian	Other	
a	b	c	d	e	f	g	h	i	j	k	l	m
AVON												
TOTAL PERSONS	**753,353**	**736,153**	**5,607**	**772**	**1,183**	**2,594**	**1,709**	**435**	**1,683**	**1,039**	**2,178**	**10,186**
Males 16 and over	**360,114**	**351,526**	**2,701**	**458**	**559**	**1,327**	**864**	**237**	**842**	**451**	**1,149**	**4,846**
Economically active	**267,185**	**260,562**	**2,151**	**289**	**463**	**1,086**	**662**	**196**	**587**	**314**	**875**	**3,318**
of which, aged under 25	*46,293*	*45,075*	*355*	*43*	*170*	*164*	*141*	*40*	*92*	*34*	*179*	*261*
Employees - full time	188,132	184,417	1,279	165	236	614	294	101	309	214	503	2,103
- part time	9,446	9,162	77	22	21	34	46	10	17	13	44	99
Self-employed - with employees	13,231	12,757	47	7	12	138	47	46	111	19	47	168
- without employees	28,200	27,548	153	19	42	147	77	11	100	19	84	410
On a Government scheme	2,777	2,614	46	14	23	19	13	1	5	8	34	19
Unemployed	25,399	24,064	549	62	129	134	185	27	45	41	163	519
of which, aged under 25	*6,988*	*6,600*	*153*	*12*	*61*	*44*	*46*	*4*	*12*	*4*	*52*	*53*
Economically active students (included above)	*2,146*	*2,071*	*16*	*7*	*9*	*8*	*7*	*1*	*7*	*2*	*18*	*7*
Economically inactive	**92,929**	**90,964**	**550**	**169**	**96**	**241**	**202**	**41**	**255**	**137**	**274**	**1,528**
Students	14,303	13,194	109	142	59	141	121	29	207	107	194	85
Permanently sick	12,813	12,511	168	5	17	33	34	8	7	7	23	322
Retired	63,286	62,862	236	5	10	53	27	3	36	15	39	1,049
Other inactive	2,527	2,397	37	17	10	14	20	1	5	8	18	72
Females 16 and over	**393,239**	**384,627**	**2,906**	**314**	**624**	**1,267**	**845**	**198**	**841**	**588**	**1,029**	**5,340**
Economically active	**203,906**	**199,006**	**1,884**	**177**	**412**	**721**	**274**	**62**	**471**	**321**	**578**	**2,689**
of which, aged under 25	*40,262*	*39,244*	*320*	*34*	*150*	*139*	*107*	*25*	*66*	*29*	*148*	*250*
Employees - full time	103,147	100,540	1,145	92	235	333	131	24	181	171	295	1,326
- part time	74,871	73,731	424	46	72	176	62	13	112	91	144	992
Self-employed - with employees	4,330	4,168	20	-	1	50	7	4	62	9	9	72
- without employees	8,100	7,865	30	5	12	57	16	2	74	11	28	101
On a Government scheme	2,144	2,006	44	5	15	22	8	4	6	8	26	18
Unemployed	11,314	10,696	221	29	77	83	50	15	36	31	76	180
of which, aged under 25	*3,754*	*3,537*	*78*	*9*	*36*	*21*	*14*	*8*	*10*	*6*	*35*	*30*
Economically active students (included above)	*2,615*	*2,557*	*16*	*5*	*5*	*6*	*5*	-	*9*	*1*	*11*	*5*
Economically inactive	**189,333**	**185,621**	**1,022**	**137**	**212**	**546**	**571**	**136**	**370**	**267**	**451**	**2,651**
Students	13,831	12,988	123	62	56	99	111	22	155	91	124	96
Permanently sick	9,341	9,043	165	9	16	31	30	2	10	6	29	167
Retired	81,574	81,039	314	2	15	69	21	3	42	17	52	1,303
Other inactive	84,587	82,551	420	64	125	347	409	109	163	153	246	1,085

9. Residents aged 16 and over

Economic position	TOTAL PERSONS	Ethnic group										Persons born in Ireland
		White	Black Caribbean	Black African	Black other	Indian	Pakistani	Bangladeshi	Chinese	Other groups		
										Asian	Other	
a	b	c	d	e	f	g	h	i	j	k	l	m
Bath												
TOTAL PERSONS	**65,603**	**64,099**	**454**	**64**	**113**	**161**	**24**	**48**	**251**	**124**	**265**	**1,049**
Males 16 and over	**30,463**	**29,671**	**235**	**41**	**56**	**86**	**12**	**27**	**140**	**54**	**141**	**480**
Economically active	**21,388**	**20,829**	**200**	**23**	**36**	**65**	**5**	**20**	**87**	**23**	**100**	**301**
of which, aged under 25	*3,713*	*3,622*	*36*	*5*	*10*	*2*	*1*	*7*	*12*	*2*	*16*	*30*
Employees - full time	14,146	13,814	126	13	16	36	4	12	61	16	48	190
- part time	1,050	1,019	11	3	3	2	-	-	3	2	7	21
Self-employed - with employees	1,128	1,080	7	-	2	6	-	6	13	2	12	10
- without employees	2,625	2,586	9	1	3	12	-	1	6	-	7	34
On a Government scheme	243	226	3	3	-	1	-	-	-	2	8	-
Unemployed	2,196	2,104	44	3	12	8	1	1	4	1	18	46
of which, aged under 25	*619*	*594*	*16*	-	*3*	*1*	-	-	*2*	-	*3*	*8*
Economically active students (included above)	*224*	*214*	*3*	*2*	-	-	*1*	-	*2*	*1*	*1*	*2*
Economically inactive	**9,075**	**8,842**	**35**	**18**	**20**	**21**	**7**	**7**	**53**	**31**	**41**	**179**
Students	1,658	1,490	5	18	12	15	7	4	46	28	33	17
Permanently sick	925	902	12	-	4	2	-	3	1	-	1	23
Retired	6,286	6,253	17	-	2	4	-	-	5	1	4	137
Other inactive	206	197	1	-	2	-	-	-	1	2	3	2
Females 16 and over	**35,140**	**34,428**	**219**	**23**	**57**	**75**	**12**	**21**	**111**	**70**	**124**	**569**
Economically active	**17,551**	**17,153**	**147**	**9**	**33**	**48**	**5**	**8**	**61**	**30**	**57**	**290**
of which, aged under 25	*3,436*	*3,354*	*28*	*3*	*23*	*6*	-	*2*	*7*	-	*13*	*30*
Employees - full time	8,581	8,404	68	5	18	21	3	2	18	15	27	131
- part time	6,369	6,256	51	1	8	14	1	2	15	8	13	118
Self-employed - with employees	407	382	7	-	-	3	-	2	11	1	1	6
- without employees	916	896	1	-	2	4	-	-	6	2	5	13
On a Government scheme	208	191	4	1	1	5	-	-	1	2	3	1
Unemployed	1,070	1,024	16	2	4	1	1	2	10	2	8	21
of which, aged under 25	*341*	*323*	*7*	*1*	*4*	-	-	*1*	*2*	-	*3*	*3*
Economically active students (included above)	*267*	*256*	*4*	*1*	*2*	*1*	-	-	*1*	-	*2*	*2*
Economically inactive	**17,589**	**17,275**	**72**	**14**	**24**	**27**	**7**	**13**	**50**	**40**	**67**	**279**
Students	1,633	1,521	11	10	11	9	4	2	22	21	22	12
Permanently sick	683	658	14	-	2	2	1	-	2	-	4	14
Retired	8,485	8,444	18	-	1	5	-	-	6	3	8	159
Other inactive	6,788	6,652	29	4	10	11	2	11	20	16	33	94

Table 9 Economic position and ethnic group – continued

9. Residents aged 16 and over

Economic position	TOTAL PERSONS	Ethnic group										Persons born in Ireland
		White	Black Caribbean	Black African	Black other	Indian	Pakistani	Bangladeshi	Chinese	Other groups		
										Asian	Other	
a	b	c	d	e	f	g	h	i	j	k	l	m
Bristol												
TOTAL PERSONS	**303,162**	**290,525**	**4,655**	**589**	**890**	**1,837**	**1,603**	**301**	**890**	**586**	**1,286**	**5,325**
Males 16 and over	**144,279**	**138,029**	**2,203**	**352**	**412**	**927**	**801**	**155**	**456**	**262**	**682**	**2,662**
Economically active	**105,837**	**101,056**	**1,731**	**221**	**345**	**754**	**613**	**128**	**303**	**181**	**505**	**1,809**
of which, aged under 25	*19,202*	*18,275*	*288*	*34*	*128*	*127*	*137*	*22*	*51*	*22*	*118*	*153*
Employees - full time	72,888	70,334	992	123	170	415	259	59	152	119	265	1,083
- part time	3,858	3,641	62	17	17	23	45	9	10	7	27	51
Self-employed - with employees	4,137	3,858	30	4	5	85	44	27	51	10	23	72
- without employees	10,075	9,591	122	18	30	108	74	8	65	10	49	229
On a Government scheme	1,360	1,239	41	7	21	13	11	1	2	4	21	17
Unemployed	13,519	12,393	484	52	102	110	180	24	23	31	120	357
of which, aged under 25	*3,585*	*3,252*	*130*	*11*	*51*	*40*	*45*	*4*	*4*	*3*	*45*	*29*
Economically active students (included above)	*700*	*649*	*12*	*3*	*8*	*6*	*6*	*1*	*4*	*1*	*10*	*4*
Economically inactive	**38,442**	**36,973**	**472**	**131**	**67**	**173**	**188**	**27**	**153**	**81**	**177**	**853**
Students	5,850	5,065	83	114	43	104	108	19	126	59	129	44
Permanently sick	6,236	5,984	149	3	12	27	33	4	2	4	18	216
Retired	25,115	24,773	208	4	5	38	27	3	23	13	21	545
Other inactive	1,241	1,151	32	10	7	4	20	1	2	5	9	48
Females 16 and over	**158,883**	**152,496**	**2,452**	**237**	**478**	**910**	**802**	**146**	**434**	**324**	**604**	**2,663**
Economically active	**81,324**	**77,758**	**1,574**	**136**	**314**	**491**	**252**	**44**	**238**	**178**	**339**	**1,369**
of which, aged under 25	*16,805*	*16,005*	*273*	*27*	*107*	*113*	*105*	*19*	*40*	*24*	*92*	*159*
Employees - full time	42,854	40,898	968	64	175	238	118	17	107	89	180	687
- part time	27,429	26,649	338	38	53	113	58	9	47	50	74	470
Self-employed - with employees	1,289	1,214	9	-	1	27	5	2	23	6	2	32
- without employees	2,864	2,705	27	4	8	38	15	2	43	5	17	53
On a Government scheme	1,044	944	35	4	14	12	8	2	3	5	17	13
Unemployed	5,844	5,348	197	26	63	63	48	12	15	23	49	114
of which, aged under 25	*1,960*	*1,786*	*68*	*8*	*27*	*15*	*14*	*6*	*5*	*6*	*25*	*23*
Economically active students (included above)	*878*	*847*	*8*	*4*	*2*	*3*	*5*	*-*	*5*	*-*	*4*	*1*
Economically inactive	**77,559**	**74,738**	**878**	**101**	**164**	**419**	**550**	**102**	**196**	**146**	**265**	**1,294**
Students	5,463	4,886	91	42	38	72	103	16	92	50	73	48
Permanently sick	4,435	4,200	141	6	9	24	27	2	6	3	17	106
Retired	33,921	33,483	287	2	12	52	21	3	20	11	30	629
Other inactive	33,740	32,169	359	51	105	271	399	81	78	82	145	511

9. Residents aged 16 and over

Economic position	TOTAL PERSONS	Ethnic group										Persons born in Ireland
		White	Black Caribbean	Black African	Black other	Indian	Pakistani	Bangladeshi	Chinese	Other groups		
										Asian	Other	
a	b	c	d	e	f	g	h	i	j	k	l	m
Kingswood												
TOTAL PERSONS	**71,888**	**71,235**	**179**	**19**	**38**	**119**	**24**	**17**	**107**	**61**	**89**	**581**
Males 16 and over	**34,803**	**34,467**	**95**	**10**	**20**	**59**	**15**	**12**	**44**	**28**	**53**	**261**
Economically active	**26,957**	**26,670**	**83**	**8**	**18**	**50**	**14**	**8**	**38**	**27**	**41**	**197**
of which, aged under 25	*4,549*	*4,501*	*13*	*1*	*8*	*8*	*2*	-	*8*	*3*	*5*	*10*
Employees - full time	19,964	19,790	58	5	11	22	9	4	19	22	24	141
- part time	812	803	-	1	-	4	1	-	1	1	1	6
Self-employed - with employees	1,235	1,195	7	1	-	14	1	4	9	-	4	13
- without employees	2,785	2,752	9	-	2	6	1	-	7	2	6	22
On a Government scheme	230	227	-	-	1	1	-	-	-	-	1	-
Unemployed	1,931	1,903	9	1	4	3	2	-	2	2	5	15
of which, aged under 25	*561*	*546*	*6*	*1*	*3*	*1*	*1*	-	*2*	-	*1*	*3*
Economically active students (included above)	*202*	*200*	-	-	-	-	-	-	*1*	-	*1*	-
Economically inactive	**7,846**	**7,797**	**12**	**2**	**2**	**9**	**1**	**4**	**6**	**1**	**12**	**64**
Students	977	945	8	1	2	4	1	4	4	1	7	1
Permanently sick	1,034	1,030	1	-	-	2	-	-	-	-	1	10
Retired	5,677	5,668	1	1	-	2	-	-	2	-	3	51
Other inactive	158	154	2	-	-	1	-	-	-	-	1	2
Females 16 and over	**37,085**	**36,768**	**84**	**9**	**18**	**60**	**9**	**5**	**63**	**33**	**36**	**320**
Economically active	**20,596**	**20,381**	**66**	**8**	**13**	**41**	**6**	**1**	**37**	**18**	**25**	**174**
of which, aged under 25	*3,952*	*3,930*	*8*	*1*	*3*	*3*	*1*	-	*2*	*1*	*3*	*6*
Employees - full time	10,102	9,980	50	8	9	16	3	-	9	13	14	84
- part time	8,553	8,507	9	-	1	10	1	1	13	5	6	71
Self-employed - with employees	321	311	1	-	-	4	-	-	4	-	1	5
- without employees	583	568	-	-	-	6	1	-	6	-	2	6
On a Government scheme	206	201	4	-	-	-	-	-	1	-	-	1
Unemployed	831	814	2	-	3	5	1	-	4	-	2	7
of which, aged under 25	*264*	*262*	*1*	-	-	*1*	-	-	-	-	-	-
Economically active students (included above)	*235*	*233*	*1*	-	-	-	-	-	*1*	-	-	-
Economically inactive	**16,489**	**16,387**	**18**	**1**	**5**	**19**	**3**	**4**	**26**	**15**	**11**	**146**
Students	941	913	4	1	1	3	1	1	11	2	4	4
Permanently sick	653	648	1	-	2	-	1	-	1	-	-	8
Retired	7,039	7,032	1	-	1	3	-	-	1	-	1	66
Other inactive	7,856	7,794	12	-	1	13	1	3	13	13	6	68

Table 9 Economic position and ethnic group – **continued**

9. Residents aged 16 and over

Economic position	TOTAL PERSONS	Ethnic group										Persons born in Ireland
		White	Black Caribbean	Black African	Black other	Indian	Pakistani	Bangladeshi	Chinese	Other groups		
										Asian	Other	
a	b	c	d	e	f	g	h	i	j	k	l	m
Northavon												
TOTAL PERSONS	**104,085**	**102,974**	**199**	**44**	**66**	**241**	**34**	**23**	**175**	**124**	**205**	**1,177**
Males 16 and over	**51,281**	**50,724**	**100**	**30**	**32**	**130**	**22**	**14**	**78**	**50**	**101**	**550**
Economically active	**40,867**	**40,411**	**85**	**18**	**29**	**106**	**18**	**13**	**60**	**40**	**87**	**404**
of which, aged under 25	*6,999*	*6,936*	*10*	*1*	*10*	*12*	-	*4*	*9*	*3*	*14*	*25*
Employees - full time	30,757	30,435	64	10	20	74	13	8	35	30	68	275
- part time	1,139	1,130	2	1	1	2	-	1	1	1	-	5
Self-employed - with employees	2,050	2,011	2	2	-	11	1	3	16	2	2	27
- without employees	4,139	4,098	10	-	3	14	2	-	3	2	7	51
On a Government scheme	315	304	1	3	-	1	1	-	1	1	3	-
Unemployed	2,467	2,433	6	2	5	4	1	1	4	4	7	46
of which, aged under 25	*704*	*701*	-	-	*1*	-	-	-	*2*	-	-	*6*
Economically active students (included above)	*343*	*337*	*1*	*2*	*1*	-	-	-	-	-	*2*	-
Economically inactive	**10,414**	**10,313**	**15**	**12**	**3**	**24**	**4**	**1**	**18**	**10**	**14**	**146**
Students	1,870	1,810	7	4	1	10	4	1	13	9	11	6
Permanently sick	1,305	1,296	4	1	-	2	-	-	2	-	-	26
Retired	6,859	6,847	2	-	2	4	-	-	2	-	2	103
Other inactive	380	360	2	7	-	8	-	-	1	1	1	11
Females 16 and over	**52,804**	**52,250**	**99**	**14**	**34**	**111**	**12**	**9**	**97**	**74**	**104**	**627**
Economically active	**30,720**	**30,376**	**67**	**7**	**29**	**63**	**5**	**5**	**56**	**47**	**65**	**340**
of which, aged under 25	*6,273*	*6,212*	*10*	*1*	*11*	*7*	*1*	*3*	*9*	*1*	*18*	*28*
Employees - full time	16,037	15,853	42	4	20	27	4	3	22	27	35	172
- part time	11,384	11,288	15	2	5	19	1	-	19	17	18	136
Self-employed - with employees	650	632	2	-	-	4	-	-	9	-	3	6
- without employees	1,163	1,153	1	1	1	4	-	-	2	1	-	9
On a Government scheme	244	236	1	-	-	2	-	2	1	-	2	1
Unemployed	1,242	1,214	6	-	3	7	-	-	3	2	7	16
of which, aged under 25	*401*	*391*	*2*	-	*2*	*2*	-	-	*1*	-	*3*	*2*
Economically active students (included above)	*422*	*413*	*2*	-	*1*	*1*	-	-	-	*1*	*4*	*1*
Economically inactive	**22,084**	**21,874**	**32**	**7**	**5**	**48**	**7**	**4**	**41**	**27**	**39**	**287**
Students	1,853	1,794	12	6	1	7	1	1	14	9	8	7
Permanently sick	987	974	6	-	1	3	1	-	-	-	2	12
Retired	8,079	8,059	1	-	-	4	-	-	6	2	7	122
Other inactive	11,165	11,047	13	1	3	34	5	3	21	16	22	146

9. Residents aged 16 and over

Economic position	TOTAL PERSONS	Ethnic group										Persons born in Ireland
		White	Black Caribbean	Black African	Black other	Indian	Pakistani	Bangladeshi	Chinese	Other groups		
										Asian	Other	
a	b	c	d	e	f	g	h	i	j	k	l	m
					Wansdyke							
TOTAL PERSONS	**64,648**	**64,326**	**28**	**19**	**22**	**51**	**5**	**-**	**57**	**36**	**104**	**550**
Males 16 and over	**31,115**	**30,977**	**12**	**7**	**11**	**21**	**3**	**-**	**26**	**10**	**48**	**212**
Economically active	**23,148**	**23,034**	**11**	**5**	**9**	**17**	**3**	**-**	**22**	**8**	**39**	**155**
of which, aged under 25	*3,660*	*3,648*	*2*	-	*1*	*3*	-	-	*1*	-	*5*	*9*
Employees - full time	16,133	16,062	9	5	8	11	3	-	6	3	26	111
- part time	815	811	2	-	-	-	-	-	-	1	1	6
Self-employed - with employees	1,646	1,634	-	-	-	4	-	-	6	1	1	6
- without employees	2,940	2,926	-	-	-	1	-	-	7	2	4	17
On a Government scheme	172	169	-	-	1	-	-	-	-	1	1	-
Unemployed	1,442	1,432	-	-	-	1	-	-	3	-	6	15
of which, aged under 25	*425*	*423*	-	-	-	*1*	-	-	-	-	*1*	*2*
Economically active students (included above)	*197*	*197*	-	-	-	-	-	-	-	-	-	-
Economically inactive	**7,967**	**7,943**	**1**	**2**	**2**	**4**	**-**	**-**	**4**	**2**	**9**	**57**
Students	1,216	1,203	-	2	-	1	-	-	4	2	4	7
Permanently sick	812	811	-	-	-	-	-	-	-	-	1	5
Retired	5,768	5,760	1	-	1	3	-	-	-	-	3	43
Other inactive	171	169	-	-	1	-	-	-	-	-	1	2
Females 16 and over	**33,533**	**33,349**	**16**	**12**	**11**	**30**	**2**	**-**	**31**	**26**	**56**	**338**
Economically active	**17,203**	**17,084**	**12**	**5**	**8**	**22**	**2**	**-**	**21**	**14**	**35**	**155**
of which, aged under 25	*3,080*	*3,061*	*1*	*1*	*4*	*3*	-	-	*2*	*1*	*7*	*7*
Employees - full time	8,194	8,142	9	3	4	6	1	-	6	11	12	77
- part time	6,856	6,817	3	2	1	9	1	-	5	3	15	61
Self-employed - with employees	523	519	-	-	-	2	-	-	2	-	-	4
- without employees	822	810	-	-	-	3	-	-	6	-	3	8
On a Government scheme	179	175	-	-	-	1	-	-	-	-	3	1
Unemployed	629	621	-	-	3	1	-	-	2	-	2	4
of which, aged under 25	*219*	*213*	-	-	*3*	*1*	-	-	*2*	-	-	-
Economically active students (included above)	*251*	*249*	*1*	-	-	-	-	-	-	-	*1*	*1*
Economically inactive	**16,330**	**16,265**	**4**	**7**	**3**	**8**	**-**	**-**	**10**	**12**	**21**	**183**
Students	1,275	1,248	2	2	1	3	-	-	6	6	7	10
Permanently sick	529	522	1	2	2	-	-	-	-	2	-	5
Retired	6,614	6,612	-	-	-	1	-	-	-	-	1	97
Other inactive	7,912	7,883	1	3	-	4	-	-	4	4	13	71

Table 9 Economic position and ethnic group – **continued**

9. Residents aged 16 and over

Economic position	TOTAL PERSONS	Ethnic group										Persons born in Ireland
		White	Black Caribbean	Black African	Black other	Indian	Pakistani	Bangladeshi	Chinese	Other groups		
										Asian	Other	
a	b	c	d	e	f	g	h	i	j	k	l	m
Woodspring												
TOTAL PERSONS	**143,967**	**142,994**	**92**	**37**	**54**	**185**	**19**	**46**	**203**	**108**	**229**	**1,504**
Males 16 and over	**68,173**	**67,658**	**56**	**18**	**28**	**104**	**11**	**29**	**98**	**47**	**124**	**681**
Economically active	**48,988**	**48,562**	**41**	**14**	**26**	**94**	**9**	**27**	**77**	**35**	**103**	**452**
of which, aged under 25	*8,170*	*8,093*	*6*	*2*	*13*	*12*	*1*	*7*	*11*	*4*	*21*	*34*
Employees - full time	34,244	33,982	30	9	11	56	6	18	36	24	72	303
- part time	1,772	1,758	-	-	-	3	-	-	2	1	8	10
Self-employed - with employees	3,035	2,979	1	-	5	18	1	6	16	4	5	40
- without employees	5,636	5,595	3	-	4	6	-	2	12	3	11	57
On a Government scheme	457	449	1	1	-	3	1	-	2	-	-	2
Unemployed	3,844	3,799	6	4	6	8	1	1	9	3	7	40
of which, aged under 25	*1,094*	*1,084*	*1*	-	*3*	*1*	-	-	*2*	*1*	*2*	*5*
Economically active students (included above)	*480*	*474*	-	-	-	*2*	-	-	-	-	*4*	*1*
Economically inactive	**19,185**	**19,096**	**15**	**4**	**2**	**10**	**2**	**2**	**21**	**12**	**21**	**229**
Students	2,732	2,681	6	3	1	7	1	1	14	8	10	10
Permanently sick	2,501	2,488	2	1	1	-	1	1	2	3	2	42
Retired	13,581	13,561	7	-	-	2	-	-	4	1	6	170
Other inactive	371	366	-	-	-	1	-	-	1	-	3	7
Females 16 and over	**75,794**	**75,336**	**36**	**19**	**26**	**81**	**8**	**17**	**105**	**61**	**105**	**823**
Economically active	**36,512**	**36,254**	**18**	**12**	**15**	**56**	**4**	**4**	**58**	**34**	**57**	**361**
of which, aged under 25	*6,716*	*6,682*	-	*1*	*2*	*7*	-	*1*	*6*	*2*	*15*	*20*
Employees - full time	17,379	17,263	8	8	9	25	2	2	19	16	27	175
- part time	14,280	14,214	8	3	4	11	-	1	13	8	18	136
Self-employed - with employees	1,140	1,110	1	-	-	10	2	-	13	2	2	19
- without employees	1,752	1,733	1	-	1	2	-	-	11	3	1	12
On a Government scheme	263	259	-	-	-	2	-	-	-	1	1	1
Unemployed	1,698	1,675	-	1	1	6	-	1	2	4	8	18
of which, aged under 25	*569*	*562*	-	-	-	*2*	-	*1*	-	-	*4*	*2*
Economically active students (included above)	*562*	*559*	-	-	-	*1*	-	-	*2*	-	-	-
Economically inactive	**39,282**	**39,082**	**18**	**7**	**11**	**25**	**4**	**13**	**47**	**27**	**48**	**462**
Students	2,666	2,626	3	1	4	5	2	2	10	3	10	15
Permanently sick	2,054	2,041	2	1	-	2	-	-	1	1	6	22
Retired	17,436	17,409	7	-	1	4	-	-	9	1	5	230
Other inactive	17,126	17,006	6	5	6	14	2	11	27	22	27	195

10. Students (16 and over) present plus absent resident students (16 and over)

	TOTAL STUDENTS	Age											Born outside UK
		16	17	18	19	20	21	22	23	24	25 - 34	35 and over	
a	b	c	d	e	f	g	h	i	j	k	l	m	n
AVON													
TOTAL STUDENTS	**46,826**	**9,115**	**6,003**	**5,333**	**5,936**	**6,051**	**4,596**	**3,064**	**1,517**	**889**	**3,013**	**1,309**	**4,882**
Students in households	**40,300**	**8,744**	**5,641**	**4,295**	**3,921**	**4,949**	**4,161**	**2,749**	**1,307**	**770**	**2,593**	**1,170**	**3,311**
Present residents	25,434	8,286	5,217	3,416	1,438	1,244	1,077	917	566	403	1,850	1,020	1,760
Term-time address - this address	24,067	8,251	5,182	3,295	1,132	909	844	800	527	374	1,772	981	1,679
- elsewhere	1,367	35	35	121	306	335	233	117	39	29	78	39	81
Absent residents	6,661	330	315	598	1,283	1,397	1,109	728	326	175	328	72	440
Term-time address - this address	1,852	194	154	173	247	281	260	187	100	79	141	36	178
- elsewhere	4,809	136	161	425	1,036	1,116	849	541	226	96	187	36	262
Non-residents	8,205	128	109	281	1,200	2,308	1,975	1,104	415	192	415	78	1,111
Term-time address - this address	7,246	55	46	209	1,085	2,127	1,831	1,007	364	157	306	59	916
- elsewhere	959	73	63	72	115	181	144	97	51	35	109	19	195
Students not in households	**6,526**	**371**	**362**	**1,038**	**2,015**	**1,102**	**435**	**315**	**210**	**119**	**420**	**139**	**1,571**
Present residents	800	35	26	52	104	87	42	68	60	51	208	67	383
Term-time address - this address	772	34	26	50	97	83	41	67	58	50	203	63	378
- elsewhere	28	1	-	2	7	4	1	1	2	1	5	4	5
Non-residents	5,726	336	336	986	1,911	1,015	393	247	150	68	212	72	1,188
Term-time address - this address	5,504	325	334	957	1,855	983	373	237	138	62	190	50	1,129
- elsewhere	222	11	2	29	56	32	20	10	12	6	22	22	59
Bath													
TOTAL STUDENTS	**7,086**	**729**	**556**	**687**	**1,037**	**1,171**	**902**	**764**	**337**	**179**	**557**	**167**	**1,162**
Students in households	**5,298**	**682**	**513**	**415**	**518**	**901**	**748**	**608**	**236**	**134**	**402**	**141**	**701**
Present residents	2,691	634	448	302	160	211	188	185	111	58	274	120	324
Term-time address - this address	2,538	627	443	289	134	172	164	171	108	55	262	113	312
- elsewhere	153	7	5	13	26	39	24	14	3	3	12	7	12
Absent residents	853	35	48	78	135	171	153	111	38	22	56	6	95
Term-time address - this address	259	17	23	26	29	42	50	37	8	10	16	1	40
- elsewhere	594	18	25	52	106	129	103	74	30	12	40	5	55
Non-residents	1,754	13	17	35	223	519	407	312	87	54	72	15	282
Term-time address - this address	1,603	4	9	23	210	493	377	296	79	43	57	12	235
- elsewhere	151	9	8	12	13	26	30	16	8	11	15	3	47
Students not in households	**1,788**	**47**	**43**	**272**	**519**	**270**	**154**	**156**	**101**	**45**	**155**	**26**	**461**
Present residents	238	2	5	13	27	23	13	26	27	14	73	15	111
Term-time address - this address	225	2	5	11	22	20	13	25	26	14	73	14	110
- elsewhere	13	-	-	2	5	3	-	1	1	-	-	1	1
Non-residents	1,550	45	38	259	492	247	141	130	74	31	82	11	350
Term-time address - this address	1,429	44	38	238	450	225	132	128	68	26	71	9	320
- elsewhere	121	1	-	21	42	22	9	2	6	5	11	2	30

Table 10 Term-time address – continued

10. Students (16 and over) present plus absent resident students (16 and over)

	TOTAL STUDENTS	Age 16	17	18	19	20	21	22	23	24	25 - 34	35 and over	Born outside UK
a	b	c	d	e	f	g	h	i	j	k	l	m	n
Bristol													
TOTAL STUDENTS	**21,381**	**3,119**	**1,923**	**1,975**	**2,926**	**3,326**	**2,626**	**1,586**	**848**	**510**	**1,835**	**707**	**2,675**
Students in households	**18,105**	**2,946**	**1,761**	**1,428**	**1,829**	**2,689**	**2,428**	**1,501**	**784**	**464**	**1,645**	**630**	**1,920**
Present residents	10,199	2,776	1,606	1,087	579	606	620	534	353	269	1,230	539	1,010
Term-time address - this address	9,809	2,770	1,596	1,060	496	517	539	504	343	263	1,198	523	975
- elsewhere	390	6	10	27	83	89	81	30	10	6	32	16	35
Absent residents	2,305	126	114	161	396	440	366	266	151	86	152	47	207
Term-time address - this address	1,020	95	73	69	120	152	143	108	77	53	101	29	119
- elsewhere	1,285	31	41	92	276	288	223	158	74	33	51	18	88
Non-residents	5,601	44	41	180	854	1,643	1,442	701	280	109	263	44	703
Term-time address - this address	5,182	22	19	152	802	1,549	1,380	655	260	96	209	38	620
- elsewhere	419	22	22	28	52	94	62	46	20	13	54	6	83
Students not in households	**3,276**	**173**	**162**	**547**	**1,097**	**637**	**198**	**85**	**64**	**46**	**190**	**77**	**755**
Present residents	387	18	12	29	46	44	18	29	23	26	104	38	216
Term-time address - this address	382	17	12	29	46	44	18	29	23	26	102	36	214
- elsewhere	5	1	-	-	-	-	-	-	-	-	2	2	2
Non-residents	2,889	155	150	518	1,051	593	180	56	41	20	86	39	539
Term-time address - this address	2,840	149	149	515	1,041	587	175	55	38	19	81	31	516
- elsewhere	49	6	1	3	10	6	5	1	3	1	5	8	23
Kingswood													
TOTAL STUDENTS	**2,448**	**846**	**490**	**347**	**182**	**176**	**127**	**88**	**31**	**22**	**86**	**53**	**72**
Students in households	**2,436**	**840**	**484**	**347**	**182**	**176**	**127**	**88**	**31**	**22**	**86**	**53**	**72**
Present residents	1,956	817	463	310	89	62	42	46	8	10	61	48	52
Term-time address - this address	1,856	816	463	303	64	34	27	33	7	8	56	45	51
- elsewhere	100	1	-	7	25	28	15	13	1	2	5	3	1
Absent residents	387	15	15	29	75	98	72	38	17	7	20	1	13
Term-time address - this address	67	13	5	9	8	12	8	5	2	2	3	-	2
- elsewhere	320	2	10	20	67	86	64	33	15	5	17	1	11
Non-residents	93	8	6	8	18	16	13	4	6	5	5	4	7
Term-time address - this address	51	3	3	5	12	10	10	2	2	2	2	-	4
- elsewhere	42	5	3	3	6	6	3	2	4	3	3	4	3
Students not in households	**12**	**6**	**6**	-	-	-	-	-	-	-	-	-	-
Present residents	12	6	6	-	-	-	-	-	-	-	-	-	-
Term-time address - this address	12	6	6	-	-	-	-	-	-	-	-	-	-
- elsewhere	-	-	-	-	-	-	-	-	-	-	-	-	-
Non-residents	-	-	-	-	-	-	-	-	-	-	-	-	-
Term-time address - this address	-	-	-	-	-	-	-	-	-	-	-	-	-
- elsewhere	-	-	-	-	-	-	-	-	-	-	-	-	-

10. Students (16 and over) present plus absent resident students (16 and over)

	TOTAL STUDENTS	Age											Born outside UK
		16	17	18	19	20	21	22	23	24	25 - 34	35 and over	
a	b	c	d	e	f	g	h	i	j	k	l	m	n
Northavon													
TOTAL STUDENTS	**5,350**	**1,474**	**955**	**776**	**641**	**488**	**317**	**217**	**117**	**64**	**188**	**113**	**397**
Students in households	**4,689**	**1,431**	**915**	**682**	**426**	**383**	**279**	**174**	**93**	**50**	**156**	**100**	**201**
Present residents	3,467	1,368	853	550	176	125	83	65	39	25	94	89	120
Term-time address - this address	3,223	1,361	844	529	120	66	40	42	28	20	86	87	110
- elsewhere	244	7	9	21	56	59	43	23	11	5	8	2	10
Absent residents	941	42	47	110	205	205	158	82	44	16	27	5	40
Term-time address - this address	153	19	22	21	29	16	16	13	2	4	10	1	5
- elsewhere	788	23	25	89	176	189	142	69	42	12	17	4	35
Non-residents	281	21	15	22	45	53	38	27	10	9	35	6	41
Term-time address - this address	182	9	7	15	36	38	25	19	4	5	22	2	24
- elsewhere	99	12	8	7	9	15	13	8	6	4	13	4	17
Students not in households	**661**	**43**	**40**	**94**	**215**	**105**	**38**	**43**	**24**	**14**	**32**	**13**	**196**
Present residents	80	6	1	5	14	13	4	4	6	7	14	6	34
Term-time address - this address	76	6	1	5	13	12	4	4	5	7	13	6	33
- elsewhere	4	-	-	-	1	1	-	-	1	-	1	-	1
Non-residents	581	37	39	89	201	92	34	39	18	7	18	7	162
Term-time address - this address	553	36	39	85	197	89	29	35	17	7	15	4	159
- elsewhere	28	1	-	4	4	3	5	4	1	-	3	3	3
Wansdyke													
TOTAL STUDENTS	**3,692**	**974**	**637**	**540**	**452**	**364**	**266**	**146**	**60**	**39**	**131**	**83**	**229**
Students in households	**3,108**	**919**	**554**	**448**	**294**	**283**	**225**	**125**	**52**	**30**	**106**	**72**	**140**
Present residents	2,181	862	512	369	121	75	57	27	18	13	63	64	71
Term-time address - this address	2,012	855	509	345	84	40	28	15	11	10	54	61	66
- elsewhere	169	7	3	24	37	35	29	12	7	3	9	3	5
Absent residents	700	36	29	62	149	164	125	69	22	14	25	5	29
Term-time address - this address	107	12	10	13	17	26	14	4	4	3	3	1	-
- elsewhere	593	24	19	49	132	138	111	65	18	11	22	4	29
Non-residents	227	21	13	17	24	44	43	29	12	3	18	3	40
Term-time address - this address	124	9	6	4	14	24	27	22	6	1	9	2	16
- elsewhere	103	12	7	13	10	20	16	7	6	2	9	1	24
Students not in households	**584**	**55**	**83**	**92**	**158**	**81**	**41**	**21**	**8**	**9**	**25**	**11**	**89**
Present residents	58	-	1	3	10	6	6	7	3	3	13	6	18
Term-time address - this address	58	-	1	3	10	6	6	7	3	3	13	6	18
- elsewhere	-	-	-	-	-	-	-	-	-	-	-	-	-
Non-residents	526	55	82	89	148	75	35	14	5	6	12	5	71
Term-time address - this address	524	55	82	89	148	75	35	14	5	6	12	3	71
- elsewhere	2	-	-	-	-	-	-	-	-	-	-	2	-

Table 10 Term-time address – **continued**

10. Students (16 and over) present plus absent resident students (16 and over)

	TOTAL STUDENTS	Age											Born outside UK
		16	17	18	19	20	21	22	23	24	25 - 34	35 and over	
a	b	c	d	e	f	g	h	i	j	k	l	m	n
					Woodspring								
TOTAL STUDENTS	**6,869**	**1,973**	**1,442**	**1,008**	**698**	**526**	**358**	**263**	**124**	**75**	**216**	**186**	**347**
Students in households	**6,664**	**1,926**	**1,414**	**975**	**672**	**517**	**354**	**253**	**111**	**70**	**198**	**174**	**277**
Present residents	4,940	1,829	1,335	798	313	165	87	60	37	28	128	160	183
Term-time address - this address	4,629	1,822	1,327	769	234	80	46	35	30	18	116	152	165
- elsewhere	311	7	8	29	79	85	41	25	7	10	12	8	18
Absent residents	1,475	76	62	158	323	319	235	162	54	30	48	8	56
Term-time address - this address	246	38	21	35	44	33	29	20	7	7	8	4	12
- elsewhere	1,229	38	41	123	279	286	206	142	47	23	40	4	44
Non-residents	249	21	17	19	36	33	32	31	20	12	22	6	38
Term-time address - this address	104	8	2	10	11	13	12	13	13	10	7	5	17
- elsewhere	145	13	15	9	25	20	20	18	7	2	15	1	21
Students not in households	**205**	**47**	**28**	**33**	**26**	**9**	**4**	**10**	**13**	**5**	**18**	**12**	**70**
Present residents	25	3	1	2	7	1	1	2	1	1	4	2	4
Term-time address - this address	19	3	1	2	6	1	-	2	1	-	2	1	3
- elsewhere	6	-	-	-	1	-	1	-	-	1	2	1	1
Non-residents	180	44	27	31	19	8	3	8	12	4	14	10	66
Term-time address - this address	158	41	26	30	19	7	2	5	10	4	11	3	63
- elsewhere	22	3	1	1	-	1	1	3	2	-	3	7	3

11. Persons present

Age	TOTAL PERSONS	In households			Not in households						
		Total	Males	Females	Persons present			Residents			
					Total	Males	Females	Staff		Other	
								Males	Females	Males	Females
a	b	c	d	e	f	g	h	i	j	k	l
					AVON						
ALL AGES	**924,459**	**894,271**	**434,247**	**460,024**	**30,188**	**14,125**	**16,063**	**600**	**783**	**5,745**	**8,573**
0 - 4	59,006	58,584	30,091	28,493	422	239	183	15	21	69	50
5 - 9	54,940	54,714	28,063	26,651	226	137	89	14	10	35	24
10 - 14	53,188	52,086	26,616	25,470	1,102	634	468	18	21	81	41
15	10,709	10,301	5,264	5,037	408	228	180	6	6	33	16
16 - 17	22,816	21,901	11,212	10,689	915	544	371	15	8	94	41
18 - 19	27,459	23,770	12,115	11,655	3,689	2,056	1,633	28	72	341	141
20 - 24	74,267	70,228	34,998	35,230	4,039	2,187	1,852	127	247	714	403
25 - 29	74,207	72,380	35,824	36,556	1,827	1,111	716	99	96	453	241
30 - 34	66,167	64,988	32,115	32,873	1,179	770	409	50	39	351	143
35 - 39	60,787	59,836	29,607	30,229	951	629	322	35	38	289	123
40 - 44	67,113	66,157	32,727	33,430	956	651	305	42	44	323	98
45 - 49	57,295	56,469	28,240	28,229	826	539	287	39	49	261	105
50 - 54	49,143	48,449	24,150	24,299	694	414	280	44	44	210	102
55 - 59	46,212	45,501	22,524	22,977	711	393	318	35	42	208	118
60 - 64	46,195	45,342	21,988	23,354	853	453	400	24	17	240	187
65 - 69	46,047	44,947	20,621	24,326	1,100	551	549	5	11	288	274
70 - 74	38,522	37,233	16,026	21,207	1,289	541	748	2	8	294	450
75 - 79	32,044	30,191	12,070	18,121	1,853	625	1,228	-	2	379	915
80 - 84	22,021	19,445	6,756	12,689	2,576	690	1,886	1	2	480	1,605
85 - 89	11,518	8,946	2,604	6,342	2,572	482	2,090	1	4	385	1,869
90 and over	4,803	2,803	636	2,167	2,000	251	1,749	-	2	217	1,627
					Bath						
ALL AGES	**80,689**	**75,427**	**35,742**	**39,685**	**5,262**	**2,630**	**2,632**	**179**	**275**	**507**	**852**
0 - 4	4,340	4,262	2,170	2,092	78	41	37	4	1	4	4
5 - 9	3,997	3,955	2,029	1,926	42	31	11	3	3	2	1
10 - 14	3,917	3,751	1,891	1,860	166	132	34	5	7	5	5
15	871	814	395	419	57	30	27	1	1	1	1
16 - 17	1,780	1,671	882	789	109	70	39	7	2	4	3
18 - 19	2,937	2,062	981	1,081	875	522	353	9	40	36	16
20 - 24	8,170	7,051	3,468	3,583	1,119	563	556	47	115	107	75
25 - 29	6,289	5,816	2,883	2,933	473	281	192	36	40	69	44
30 - 34	5,321	5,074	2,515	2,559	247	155	92	14	10	44	15
35 - 39	4,918	4,739	2,301	2,438	179	118	61	9	10	25	15
40 - 44	5,386	5,225	2,555	2,670	161	93	68	12	8	19	11
45 - 49	4,537	4,406	2,168	2,238	131	66	65	7	10	9	12
50 - 54	4,035	3,924	1,936	1,988	111	59	52	10	9	16	8
55 - 59	3,916	3,792	1,806	1,986	124	60	64	10	11	5	8
60 - 64	4,255	4,150	1,933	2,217	105	52	53	4	6	12	6
65 - 69	4,458	4,327	1,967	2,360	131	57	74	1	-	17	24
70 - 74	3,890	3,747	1,570	2,177	143	62	81	-	2	17	37
75 - 79	3,412	3,201	1,255	1,946	211	72	139	-	-	15	67
80 - 84	2,448	2,151	717	1,434	297	85	212	-	-	45	145
85 - 89	1,238	975	248	727	263	55	208	-	-	36	164
90 and over	574	334	72	262	240	26	214	-	-	19	191

11. Persons present

Age	TOTAL PERSONS	In households			Not in households						
					Persons present			Residents			
								Staff		Other	
		Total	Males	Females	Total	Males	Females	Males	Females	Males	Females
a	b	c	d	e	f	g	h	i	j	k	l
					Bristol						
ALL AGES	**372,088**	**359,935**	**174,156**	**185,779**	**12,153**	**5,938**	**6,215**	**152**	**223**	**2,453**	**3,187**
0 - 4	25,173	24,926	12,755	12,171	247	149	98	6	9	43	30
5 - 9	22,276	22,189	11,370	10,819	87	48	39	4	2	20	12
10 - 14	20,285	19,776	10,108	9,668	509	277	232	2	1	47	21
15	4,013	3,814	1,936	1,878	199	102	97	-	1	23	11
16 - 17	8,316	7,932	4,059	3,873	384	201	183	1	1	33	20
18 - 19	11,433	9,661	4,840	4,821	1,772	971	801	4	15	82	55
20 - 24	34,425	32,765	16,249	16,516	1,660	908	752	35	61	256	190
25 - 29	33,536	32,833	16,031	16,802	703	423	280	26	30	204	103
30 - 34	28,207	27,673	13,655	14,018	534	349	185	10	13	181	67
35 - 39	24,070	23,703	11,900	11,803	367	255	112	15	12	125	40
40 - 44	24,546	24,164	12,161	12,003	382	262	120	12	14	143	47
45 - 49	20,024	19,685	9,895	9,790	339	245	94	9	11	134	43
50 - 54	17,813	17,540	8,784	8,756	273	174	99	8	12	98	44
55 - 59	17,177	16,910	8,369	8,541	267	163	104	7	16	108	46
60 - 64	18,049	17,739	8,539	9,200	310	184	126	10	6	110	76
65 - 69	18,538	18,111	8,194	9,917	427	233	194	1	8	151	113
70 - 74	15,758	15,269	6,492	8,777	489	223	266	1	5	141	175
75 - 79	13,055	12,364	4,848	7,516	691	245	446	-	1	164	343
80 - 84	8,922	7,965	2,658	5,307	957	266	691	1	2	184	598
85 - 89	4,609	3,720	1,063	2,657	889	174	715	-	3	133	619
90 and over	1,863	1,196	250	946	667	86	581	-	-	73	534
					Kingswood						
ALL AGES	**87,754**	**86,916**	**42,472**	**44,444**	**838**	**337**	**501**	**10**	**6**	**311**	**474**
0 - 4	5,866	5,854	3,029	2,825	12	7	5	-	-	7	5
5 - 9	5,449	5,444	2,755	2,689	5	3	2	-	-	3	2
10 - 14	5,261	5,251	2,648	2,603	10	5	5	1	-	3	4
15	1,062	1,054	529	525	8	7	1	-	-	7	1
16 - 17	2,220	2,206	1,121	1,085	14	13	1	-	-	13	1
18 - 19	2,303	2,291	1,191	1,100	12	6	6	2	-	2	6
20 - 24	5,899	5,888	2,966	2,922	11	7	4	3	-	4	2
25 - 29	6,880	6,863	3,375	3,488	17	13	4	-	-	11	4
30 - 34	6,659	6,641	3,296	3,345	18	11	7	-	1	10	3
35 - 39	6,163	6,151	3,037	3,114	12	4	8	-	-	3	6
40 - 44	6,506	6,475	3,233	3,242	31	23	8	-	-	20	6
45 - 49	5,816	5,789	2,864	2,925	27	20	7	-	2	19	2
50 - 54	5,141	5,113	2,554	2,559	28	13	15	1	1	12	12
55 - 59	5,146	5,102	2,499	2,603	44	28	16	1	2	27	14
60 - 64	4,659	4,617	2,249	2,368	42	27	15	2	-	25	15
65 - 69	4,180	4,142	1,990	2,152	38	27	11	-	-	27	11
70 - 74	3,144	3,089	1,349	1,740	55	24	31	-	-	24	30
75 - 79	2,485	2,397	963	1,434	88	32	56	-	-	32	55
80 - 84	1,726	1,599	576	1,023	127	34	93	-	-	33	92
85 - 89	881	740	211	529	141	21	120	-	-	18	118
90 and over	308	210	37	173	98	12	86	-	-	11	85

11. Persons present

Age	TOTAL PERSONS	In households			Not in households						
					Persons present			Residents			
								Staff		Other	
		Total	Males	Females	Total	Males	Females	Males	Females	Males	Females
a	b	c	d	e	f	g	h	i	j	k	l
					Northavon						
ALL AGES	**129,617**	**126,314**	**62,744**	**63,570**	**3,303**	**1,735**	**1,568**	**72**	**74**	**668**	**749**
0 - 4	8,739	8,721	4,514	4,207	18	12	6	4	4	-	-
5 - 9	7,988	7,954	4,129	3,825	34	25	9	3	2	3	-
10 - 14	8,172	8,026	4,093	3,933	146	58	88	3	5	6	4
15	1,667	1,622	871	751	45	22	23	1	-	1	2
16 - 17	3,563	3,455	1,781	1,674	108	68	40	3	1	9	4
18 - 19	3,888	3,484	1,802	1,682	404	233	171	5	9	20	14
20 - 24	10,129	9,667	4,783	4,884	462	226	236	17	30	56	60
25 - 29	11,322	11,071	5,534	5,537	251	161	90	14	7	75	44
30 - 34	9,876	9,720	4,985	4,735	156	115	41	2	7	62	20
35 - 39	8,866	8,686	4,250	4,436	180	121	59	2	2	76	37
40 - 44	10,451	10,284	5,058	5,226	167	136	31	6	1	72	19
45 - 49	9,419	9,265	4,663	4,602	154	103	51	3	4	55	25
50 - 54	7,656	7,541	3,819	3,722	115	82	33	5	2	45	17
55 - 59	6,536	6,433	3,258	3,175	103	53	50	2	-	31	28
60 - 64	5,710	5,608	2,909	2,699	102	63	39	-	-	31	23
65 - 69	5,008	4,908	2,340	2,568	100	50	50	1	-	22	26
70 - 74	3,925	3,829	1,635	2,194	96	44	52	-	-	16	27
75 - 79	3,236	3,088	1,300	1,788	148	58	90	-	-	23	71
80 - 84	2,096	1,896	706	1,190	200	54	146	-	-	29	108
85 - 89	1,003	816	254	562	187	40	147	1	-	29	118
90 and over	367	240	60	180	127	11	116	-	-	7	102
					Wansdyke						
ALL AGES	**79,225**	**77,456**	**37,968**	**39,488**	**1,769**	**621**	**1,148**	**16**	**25**	**188**	**652**
0 - 4	4,673	4,664	2,394	2,270	9	4	5	-	-	-	-
5 - 9	4,741	4,734	2,475	2,259	7	7	-	-	-	3	-
10 - 14	4,908	4,786	2,477	2,309	122	91	31	-	1	8	2
15	1,039	987	489	498	52	52	-	1	-	-	-
16 - 17	2,227	2,088	1,042	1,046	139	104	35	-	1	-	1
18 - 19	2,295	2,037	1,066	971	258	58	200	1	1	7	11
20 - 24	4,964	4,784	2,450	2,334	180	52	128	3	4	14	17
25 - 29	5,076	5,030	2,570	2,460	46	17	29	1	2	4	11
30 - 34	5,167	5,131	2,496	2,635	36	19	17	3	-	8	10
35 - 39	5,353	5,333	2,642	2,691	20	4	16	-	2	4	6
40 - 44	6,341	6,319	3,078	3,241	22	13	9	1	2	5	1
45 - 49	5,424	5,404	2,694	2,710	20	12	8	1	2	7	2
50 - 54	4,642	4,621	2,284	2,337	21	6	15	-	2	2	7
55 - 59	4,412	4,385	2,206	2,179	27	10	17	2	5	3	4
60 - 64	4,347	4,315	2,078	2,237	32	15	17	2	-	7	8
65 - 69	4,189	4,153	1,954	2,199	36	14	22	-	1	5	21
70 - 74	3,409	3,346	1,480	1,866	63	19	44	1	-	14	34
75 - 79	2,765	2,650	1,133	1,517	115	31	84	-	1	19	69
80 - 84	1,882	1,703	647	1,056	179	42	137	-	-	35	130
85 - 89	946	744	253	491	202	32	170	-	1	26	162
90 and over	425	242	60	182	183	19	164	-	-	17	156

11. Persons present

Age	TOTAL PERSONS	In households			Not in households						
					Persons present			Residents			
								Staff		Other	
		Total	Males	Females	Total	Males	Females	Males	Females	Males	Females
a	b	c	d	e	f	g	h	i	j	k	l
					Woodspring						
ALL AGES	**175,086**	**168,223**	**81,165**	**87,058**	**6,863**	**2,864**	**3,999**	**171**	**180**	**1,618**	**2,659**
0 - 4	10,215	10,157	5,229	4,928	58	26	32	1	7	15	11
5 - 9	10,489	10,438	5,305	5,133	51	23	28	4	3	4	9
10 - 14	10,645	10,496	5,399	5,097	149	71	78	7	7	12	5
15	2,057	2,010	1,044	966	47	15	32	3	4	1	1
16 - 17	4,710	4,549	2,327	2,222	161	88	73	4	3	35	12
18 - 19	4,603	4,235	2,235	2,000	368	266	102	7	7	194	39
20 - 24	10,680	10,073	5,082	4,991	607	431	176	22	37	277	59
25 - 29	11,104	10,767	5,431	5,336	337	216	121	22	17	90	35
30 - 34	10,937	10,749	5,168	5,581	188	121	67	21	8	46	28
35 - 39	11,417	11,224	5,477	5,747	193	127	66	9	12	56	19
40 - 44	13,883	13,690	6,642	7,048	193	124	69	11	19	64	14
45 - 49	12,075	11,920	5,956	5,964	155	93	62	19	20	37	21
50 - 54	9,856	9,710	4,773	4,937	146	80	66	20	18	37	14
55 - 59	9,025	8,879	4,386	4,493	146	79	67	13	8	34	18
60 - 64	9,175	8,913	4,280	4,633	262	112	150	6	5	55	59
65 - 69	9,674	9,306	4,176	5,130	368	170	198	2	2	66	79
70 - 74	8,396	7,953	3,500	4,453	443	169	274	-	1	82	147
75 - 79	7,091	6,491	2,571	3,920	600	187	413	-	-	126	310
80 - 84	4,947	4,131	1,452	2,679	816	209	607	-	-	154	532
85 - 89	2,841	1,951	575	1,376	890	160	730	-	-	143	688
90 and over	1,266	581	157	424	685	97	588	-	2	90	559

12. Residents in households with limiting long-term illness

Age	TOTAL PERSONS	Males	Females
a	b	c	d
AVON			
ALL AGES	**100,124**	**45,867**	**54,257**
0 - 4	1,064	641	423
5 - 15	2,686	1,528	1,158
16 - 17	489	269	220
18 - 29	5,210	2,745	2,465
30 - 44	9,215	4,713	4,502
45 - 54	9,667	4,839	4,828
55 - 59	7,391	3,858	3,533
60 - 64	10,403	5,836	4,567
65 - 74	24,716	11,613	13,103
75 - 84	21,971	7,993	13,978
85 and over	7,312	1,832	5,480
Bath			
ALL AGES	**8,639**	**3,772**	**4,867**
0 - 4	84	52	32
5 - 15	151	94	57
16 - 17	36	20	16
18 - 29	448	236	212
30 - 44	767	388	379
45 - 54	747	392	355
55 - 59	505	248	257
60 - 64	749	424	325
65 - 74	2,134	958	1,176
75 - 84	2,202	764	1,438
85 and over	816	196	620
Bristol			
ALL AGES	**45,246**	**20,808**	**24,438**
0 - 4	573	353	220
5 - 15	1,352	773	579
16 - 17	203	106	97
18 - 29	2,625	1,362	1,263
30 - 44	4,540	2,367	2,173
45 - 54	4,419	2,238	2,181
55 - 59	3,352	1,761	1,591
60 - 64	4,752	2,661	2,091
65 - 74	10,855	5,103	5,752
75 - 84	9,432	3,333	6,099
85 and over	3,143	751	2,392
Kingswood			
ALL AGES	**8,620**	**3,988**	**4,632**
0 - 4	78	46	32
5 - 15	208	107	101
16 - 17	44	21	23
18 - 29	414	240	174
30 - 44	741	403	338
45 - 54	801	391	410
55 - 59	727	378	349
60 - 64	995	541	454
65 - 74	2,182	1,049	1,133
75 - 84	1,797	661	1,136
85 and over	633	151	482
Northavon			
ALL AGES	**10,531**	**4,930**	**5,601**
0 - 4	113	63	50
5 - 15	311	184	127
16 - 17	73	43	30
18 - 29	593	296	297
30 - 44	1,012	493	519
45 - 54	1,149	570	579
55 - 59	854	450	404
60 - 64	1,149	683	466
65 - 74	2,480	1,142	1,338
75 - 84	2,168	846	1,322
85 and over	629	160	469
Wansdyke			
ALL AGES	**7,497**	**3,508**	**3,989**
0 - 4	53	24	29
5 - 15	193	117	76
16 - 17	43	26	17
18 - 29	312	171	141
30 - 44	558	269	289
45 - 54	648	327	321
55 - 59	587	312	275
60 - 64	823	457	366
65 - 74	1,952	944	1,008
75 - 84	1,749	691	1,058
85 and over	579	170	409
Woodspring			
ALL AGES	**19,591**	**8,861**	**10,730**
0 - 4	163	103	60
5 - 15	471	253	218
16 - 17	90	53	37
18 - 29	818	440	378
30 - 44	1,597	793	804
45 - 54	1,903	921	982
55 - 59	1,366	709	657
60 - 64	1,935	1,070	865
65 - 74	5,113	2,417	2,696
75 - 84	4,623	1,698	2,925
85 and over	1,512	404	1,108

13. Persons present not in households with limiting long-term illness

Age	Medical and care establishments				Other			
	Total persons	Non-residents	Residents		Total persons	Non-residents	Residents	
			Males	Females			Males	Females
a	b	c	d	e	f	g	h	i
AVON								
ALL AGES	**12,680**	**2,523**	**3,086**	**7,071**	**1,010**	**525**	**358**	**127**
0 - 4	45	39	3	3	5	-	4	1
5 - 15	90	55	22	13	34	28	6	-
16 - 17	32	21	5	6	19	12	4	3
18 - 29	612	163	266	183	219	126	61	32
30 - 44	813	172	424	217	166	48	98	20
45 - 54	553	148	241	164	121	33	76	12
55 - 59	321	93	136	92	67	31	29	7
60 - 64	473	139	177	157	76	41	30	5
65 - 74	1,654	546	474	634	163	115	35	13
75 - 84	3,825	739	768	2,318	110	78	13	19
85 and over	4,262	408	570	3,284	30	13	2	15
Bath								
ALL AGES	**1,337**	**493**	**218**	**626**	**121**	**83**	**22**	**16**
0 - 4	2	2	-	-	-	-	-	-
5 - 15	2	1	1	-	9	8	1	-
16 - 17	1	1	-	-	1	1	-	-
18 - 29	66	16	27	23	42	27	9	6
30 - 44	74	31	29	14	13	3	6	4
45 - 54	68	37	15	16	5	3	2	-
55 - 59	36	27	3	6	8	5	1	2
60 - 64	44	29	9	6	8	6	2	-
65 - 74	174	96	28	50	19	17	1	1
75 - 84	408	171	53	184	12	10	-	2
85 and over	462	82	53	327	4	3	-	1
Bristol								
ALL AGES	**4,793**	**1,064**	**1,227**	**2,502**	**425**	**125**	**230**	**70**
0 - 4	41	35	3	3	4	-	3	1
5 - 15	65	45	14	6	6	4	2	-
16 - 17	23	17	3	3	8	6	1	1
18 - 29	247	65	108	74	104	50	37	17
30 - 44	302	53	170	79	92	23	59	10
45 - 54	211	57	97	57	69	17	45	7
55 - 59	121	37	56	28	32	7	21	4
60 - 64	171	45	66	60	30	8	20	2
65 - 74	681	225	210	246	44	9	29	6
75 - 84	1,477	304	304	869	24	1	12	11
85 and over	1,454	181	196	1,077	12	-	1	11
Kingswood								
ALL AGES	**683**	**15**	**255**	**413**	**3**	**-**	**1**	**2**
0 - 4	-	-	-	-	1	-	1	-
5 - 15	3	-	2	1	-	-	-	-
16 - 17	-	-	-	-	-	-	-	-
18 - 29	13	2	10	1	-	-	-	-
30 - 44	47	3	32	12	-	-	-	-
45 - 54	44	-	30	14	-	-	-	-
55 - 59	38	-	26	12	1	-	-	1
60 - 64	38	-	25	13	-	-	-	-
65 - 74	85	-	49	36	-	-	-	-
75 - 84	193	3	55	135	1	-	-	1
85 and over	222	7	26	189	-	-	-	-

Table 13 Long-term illness in communal establishments - **continued**

13. Persons present not in households with limiting long-term illness

Age	Medical and care establishments				Other			
	Total persons	Non-residents	Residents		Total persons	Non-residents	Residents	
			Males	Females			Males	Females
a	b	c	d	e	f	g	h	i
Northavon								
ALL AGES	**1,310**	**300**	**370**	**640**	**143**	**85**	**54**	**4**
0 - 4	2	2	-	-	-	-	-	-
5 - 15	12	7	1	4	2	2	-	-
16 - 17	4	1	1	2	4	2	1	1
18 - 29	157	17	84	56	39	36	2	1
30 - 44	165	19	84	62	40	16	23	1
45 - 54	104	22	43	39	26	9	16	1
55 - 59	56	12	17	27	13	6	7	-
60 - 64	63	18	24	21	9	6	3	-
65 - 74	145	61	33	51	7	5	2	-
75 - 84	303	87	48	168	3	3	-	-
85 and over	299	54	35	210	-	-	-	-
Wansdyke								
ALL AGES	**810**	**83**	**153**	**574**	**24**	**15**	**-**	**9**
0 - 4	-	-	-	-	-	-	-	-
5 - 15	5	-	3	2	4	4	-	-
16 - 17	1	-	-	1	1	1	-	-
18 - 29	15	1	7	7	8	7	-	1
30 - 44	35	3	17	15	3	1	-	2
45 - 54	19	2	8	9	1	1	-	-
55 - 59	8	2	2	4	-	-	-	-
60 - 64	20	6	7	7	-	-	-	-
65 - 74	78	15	19	44	4	1	-	3
75 - 84	262	34	48	180	2	-	-	2
85 and over	367	20	42	305	1	-	-	1
Woodspring								
ALL AGES	**3,747**	**568**	**863**	**2,316**	**294**	**217**	**51**	**26**
0 - 4	-	-	-	-	-	-	-	-
5 - 15	3	2	1	-	13	10	3	-
16 - 17	3	2	1	-	5	2	2	1
18 - 29	114	62	30	22	26	6	13	7
30 - 44	190	63	92	35	18	5	10	3
45 - 54	107	30	48	29	20	3	13	4
55 - 59	62	15	32	15	13	13	-	-
60 - 64	137	41	46	50	29	21	5	3
65 - 74	491	149	135	207	89	83	3	3
75 - 84	1,182	140	260	782	68	64	1	3
85 and over	1,458	64	218	1,176	13	10	1	2

14. Residents aged 16 and over with limiting long-term illness

Economic position	TOTAL AGED 16 AND OVER	Age						Students (economically active or inactive)
		16 - 17	18 - 19	20 - 29	30 - 44	45 up to pensionable age	Pensionable age and over	
a	b	c	d	e	f	g	h	i
			AVON					
TOTAL PERSONS	**106,964**	**507**	**643**	**5,109**	**9,974**	**23,858**	**66,873**	**723**
Economically active	**18,073**	**178**	**347**	**2,748**	**4,858**	**8,285**	**1,657**	**71**
Employees - full time	8,719	65	175	1,577	2,475	4,044	383	6
- part time	3,550	34	30	239	892	1,544	811	52
Self-employed - with employees	713	-	1	20	151	394	147	-
- without employees	1,506	2	1	113	360	779	251	2
On a Government scheme	430	38	41	136	127	83	5	
Unemployed	3,155	39	99	663	853	1,441	60	11
Economically active students (included above)	*71*	*28*	*15*	*12*	*11*	*4*	*1*	
Economically inactive	**88,891**	**329**	**296**	**2,361**	**5,116**	**15,573**	**65,216**	**652**
Students	652	274	129	167	64	16	2	652
Permanently sick	22,152	48	144	1,721	3,896	11,408	4,935	
Retired	53,922	-	2	17	102	2,130	51,671	
Other inactive	12,165	7	21	456	1,054	2,019	8,608	
			Bath					
TOTAL PERSONS	**9,284**	**36**	**55**	**458**	**820**	**1,732**	**6,183**	**72**
Economically active	**1,500**	**11**	**31**	**243**	**425**	**654**	**136**	**7**
Employees - full time	691	4	17	130	210	300	30	1
- part time	316	2	3	24	71	141	75	5
Self-employed - with employees	50	-	-	3	14	27	6	-
- without employees	147	1	-	11	37	75	23	-
On a Government scheme	32	2	3	11	11	5	-	
Unemployed	264	2	8	64	82	106	2	1
Economically active students (included above)	*7*	*3*	*2*	*1*	*1*	-	-	
Economically inactive	**7,784**	**25**	**24**	**215**	**395**	**1,078**	**6,047**	**65**
Students	65	23	14	23	4	-	1	65
Permanently sick	1,607	1	8	159	307	782	350	
Retired	5,094	-	1	1	4	168	4,920	
Other inactive	1,018	1	1	32	80	128	776	
			Bristol					
TOTAL PERSONS	**47,318**	**211**	**275**	**2,586**	**4,858**	**10,833**	**28,555**	**311**
Economically active	**8,285**	**81**	**155**	**1,414**	**2,301**	**3,598**	**736**	**29**
Employees - full time	3,953	32	71	767	1,126	1,749	208	2
- part time	1,524	10	11	121	386	640	356	18
Self-employed - with employees	224	-	-	3	62	121	38	-
- without employees	552	-	1	54	144	267	86	1
On a Government scheme	241	20	18	81	81	39	2	
Unemployed	1,791	19	54	388	502	782	46	8
Economically active students (included above)	*29*	*5*	*6*	*8*	*7*	*3*	-	
Economically inactive	**39,033**	**130**	**120**	**1,172**	**2,557**	**7,235**	**27,819**	**282**
Students	282	105	44	88	34	10	1	282
Permanently sick	10,671	21	64	798	1,974	5,513	2,301	
Retired	22,936	-	-	11	23	850	22,052	
Other inactive	5,144	4	12	275	526	862	3,465	

14. Residents aged 16 and over with limiting long-term illness

Economic position	TOTAL AGED 16 AND OVER	Age						Students (economically active or inactive)
		16 - 17	18 - 19	20 - 29	30 - 44	45 up to pensionable age	Pensionable age and over	
a	b	c	d	e	f	g	h	i
Kingswood								
TOTAL PERSONS	**9,001**	**44**	**61**	**364**	**785**	**2,177**	**5,570**	**53**
Economically active	**1,560**	**16**	**33**	**209**	**412**	**770**	**120**	**5**
Employees - full time	815	6	17	139	217	411	25	-
- part time	315	3	2	12	79	150	69	4
Self-employed - with employees	52	-	-	4	11	32	5	-
- without employees	122	-	-	7	34	61	20	1
On a Government scheme	36	2	4	8	14	7	1	
Unemployed	220	5	10	39	57	109	-	-
Economically active students (included above)	*5*	*2*	*2*	-	*1*	-	-	
Economically inactive	**7,441**	**28**	**28**	**155**	**373**	**1,407**	**5,450**	**48**
Students	48	24	16	8	-	-	-	48
Permanently sick	1,687	4	11	117	277	957	321	
Retired	4,672	-	-	-	23	244	4,405	
Other inactive	1,034	-	1	30	73	206	724	
Northavon								
TOTAL PERSONS	**11,170**	**78**	**92**	**644**	**1,182**	**2,863**	**6,311**	**88**
Economically active	**2,245**	**27**	**42**	**319**	**593**	**1,087**	**177**	**9**
Employees - full time	1,196	9	24	210	340	583	30	1
- part time	417	7	6	28	114	184	78	8
Self-employed - with employees	114	-	-	7	20	56	31	-
- without employees	204	-	-	15	51	108	30	-
On a Government scheme	47	9	7	19	4	7	1	
Unemployed	267	2	5	40	64	149	7	-
Economically active students (included above)	*9*	*6*	*1*	-	*1*	-	*1*	
Economically inactive	**8,925**	**51**	**50**	**325**	**589**	**1,776**	**6,134**	**79**
Students	79	42	20	12	5	-	-	79
Permanently sick	2,291	9	28	276	398	1,175	405	
Retired	5,180	-	-	1	45	323	4,811	
Other inactive	1,375	-	2	36	141	278	918	
Wansdyke								
TOTAL PERSONS	**7,982**	**44**	**47**	**280**	**592**	**1,722**	**5,297**	**68**
Economically active	**1,336**	**12**	**25**	**159**	**314**	**657**	**169**	**8**
Employees - full time	624	3	12	99	166	309	35	2
- part time	317	2	3	22	73	129	88	4
Self-employed - with employees	76	-	-	1	10	44	21	-
- without employees	141	-	-	8	25	84	24	-
On a Government scheme	13	3	2	2	2	4	-	
Unemployed	165	4	8	27	38	87	1	2
Economically active students (included above)	*8*	*2*	*2*	*2*	*1*	*1*	-	
Economically inactive	**6,646**	**32**	**22**	**121**	**278**	**1,065**	**5,128**	**60**
Students	60	26	13	6	13	2	-	60
Permanently sick	1,341	6	8	99	187	757	284	
Retired	4,215	-	-	1	1	143	4,070	
Other inactive	1,030	-	1	15	77	163	774	

Table 14 Long-term illness and economic position – continued

14. Residents aged 16 and over with limiting long-term illness

Economic position	TOTAL AGED 16 AND OVER	Age						Students (economically active or inactive)
		16 - 17	18 - 19	20 - 29	30 - 44	45 up to pensionable age	Pensionable age and over	
a	b	c	d	e	f	g	h	i
			Woodspring					
TOTAL PERSONS	**22,209**	**94**	**113**	**777**	**1,737**	**4,531**	**14,957**	**131**
Economically active	**3,147**	**31**	**61**	**404**	**813**	**1,519**	**319**	**13**
Employees - full time	1,440	11	34	232	416	692	55	-
- part time	661	10	5	32	169	300	145	13
Self-employed - with employees	197	-	1	2	34	114	46	-
- without employees	340	1	-	18	69	184	68	-
On a Government scheme	61	2	7	15	15	21	1	
Unemployed	448	7	14	105	110	208	4	-
Economically active students (included above)	*13*	*10*	*2*	*1*	-	-	-	
Economically inactive	**19,062**	**63**	**52**	**373**	**924**	**3,012**	**14,638**	**118**
Students	118	54	22	30	8	4	-	118
Permanently sick	4,555	7	25	272	753	2,224	1,274	
Retired	11,825	-	1	3	6	402	11,413	
Other inactive	2,564	2	4	68	157	382	1,951	

Table 15 Migrants

15. Residents with different address one year before census

Age	TOTAL PERSONS	Total males	Total females	Moved within wards		Between wards but within district		Between districts but within county	
				Males	Females	Males	Females	Males	Females
a	b	c	d	e	f	g	h	i	j
				AVON					
All migrants									
ALL AGES 1 AND OVER	**96,764**	**48,000**	**48,764**	**10,036**	**10,107**	**18,312**	**19,283**	**6,917**	**7,046**
1 - 4	6,917	3,605	3,312	889	814	1,552	1,398	394	359
5 - 9	5,034	2,528	2,506	612	607	985	1,037	275	251
10 - 14	3,534	1,856	1,678	437	377	731	680	218	195
15	594	298	296	63	60	124	140	47	41
16	685	327	358	75	81	132	157	49	43
17	940	402	538	69	120	160	226	54	84
18 - 19	3,906	1,615	2,291	310	489	539	894	196	336
20 - 24	21,322	9,950	11,372	1,977	2,087	3,745	4,611	1,404	1,771
25 - 28	15,415	7,981	7,434	1,518	1,412	3,119	2,908	1,278	1,152
29	2,855	1,490	1,365	297	303	583	495	236	193
30 - 34	9,875	5,333	4,542	1,064	866	1,970	1,658	807	617
35 - 39	6,199	3,434	2,765	702	552	1,206	984	464	366
40 - 44	4,841	2,608	2,233	554	431	934	865	393	338
45 - 49	3,217	1,798	1,419	384	288	647	517	272	235
50 - 54	2,160	1,170	990	263	218	400	340	207	180
55 - 59	1,535	789	746	166	167	294	287	159	126
60 - 64	1,436	689	747	154	187	276	268	124	127
65 - 69	1,475	638	837	143	198	251	341	108	113
70 - 74	1,219	500	719	122	179	226	309	69	89
75 - 84	2,363	758	1,605	195	415	325	700	117	254
85 and over	1,242	231	1,011	42	256	113	468	46	176
Migrants in households									
All ages 1 and over	**91,629**	**45,573**	**46,056**	**9,623**	**9,635**	**17,740**	**18,264**	**6,543**	**6,529**
1 - 4	6,861	3,575	3,286	887	812	1,546	1,391	383	352
5 - 9	4,990	2,504	2,486	605	604	977	1,030	269	246
10 - 14	3,467	1,813	1,654	424	377	719	665	213	190
15	565	279	286	59	58	122	134	39	40
16	664	316	348	73	79	132	154	47	40
17	868	359	509	69	115	155	217	54	79
18 - 19	3,499	1,366	2,133	297	475	523	876	184	318
20 - 24	20,489	9,478	11,011	1,911	2,052	3,670	4,550	1,378	1,720
25 - 28	15,022	7,749	7,273	1,483	1,394	3,078	2,876	1,252	1,135
29	2,800	1,452	1,348	293	301	570	493	232	192
30 - 34	9,645	5,179	4,466	1,036	856	1,950	1,644	787	607
35 - 39	6,003	3,295	2,708	675	547	1,186	967	443	352
40 - 44	4,670	2,479	2,191	523	428	904	848	370	327
45 - 49	3,070	1,685	1,385	357	285	627	507	251	226
50 - 54	2,044	1,090	954	236	212	385	331	187	164
55 - 59	1,457	736	721	155	164	283	281	139	116
60 - 64	1,337	638	699	145	177	261	256	104	110
65 - 69	1,354	580	774	134	185	230	309	86	102
70 - 74	1,032	420	612	107	157	188	260	50	64
75 - 84	1,470	508	962	139	282	211	382	60	126
85 and over	322	72	250	15	75	23	93	15	23

Between counties but within region		Between regions or from Scotland		From outside GB		Between neighbouring districts		Between neighbouring counties/Scottish Regions		Age
Males	Females	Males	Females	Males	Females	Males	Females	Males	Females	
k	l	m	n	o	p	q	r	s	t	a
										All migrants
2,831	**2,738**	**7,633**	**7,237**	**2,271**	**2,353**	**6,189**	**6,334**	**2,034**	**1,948**	**ALL AGES 1 AND OVER**
159	144	444	455	167	142	365	339	117	110	1 - 4
114	114	392	378	150	119	239	240	71	82	5 - 9
91	74	283	242	96	110	200	191	66	53	10 - 14
11	10	40	35	13	10	49	35	10	5	15
10	24	49	38	12	15	46	39	7	17	16
41	25	67	66	11	17	52	84	34	19	17
140	168	355	301	75	103	182	320	98	116	18 - 19
628	657	1,796	1,712	400	534	1,274	1,609	410	456	20 - 24
466	423	1,206	1,139	394	400	1,148	1,035	358	328	25 - 28
81	85	224	211	69	78	210	155	67	53	29
312	257	884	846	296	298	696	528	221	174	30 - 34
212	155	636	508	214	200	421	325	151	116	35 - 39
171	130	423	358	133	111	365	314	128	95	40 - 44
126	102	277	212	92	65	233	217	92	67	45 - 49
72	68	172	139	56	45	186	150	57	46	50 - 54
36	43	104	95	30	28	136	110	28	28	55 - 59
37	44	74	95	24	26	102	114	27	26	60 - 64
44	56	73	105	19	24	89	99	34	40	65 - 69
28	38	46	91	9	13	51	75	17	30	70 - 74
40	75	72	146	9	15	106	206	33	56	75 - 84
12	46	16	65	2	-	39	149	8	31	85 and over
										Migrants in households
2,621	**2,565**	**6,972**	**6,866**	**2,074**	**2,197**	**5,871**	**5,916**	**1,901**	**1,826**	**All ages 1 and over**
155	141	439	450	165	140	354	331	114	108	1 - 4
112	113	391	374	150	119	235	237	70	81	5 - 9
87	71	276	241	94	110	197	184	65	50	10 - 14
10	9	37	35	12	10	43	34	9	4	15
8	22	44	38	12	15	44	36	6	15	16
34	25	38	59	9	14	52	79	32	19	17
113	141	195	244	54	79	169	307	80	101	18 - 19
584	619	1,586	1,588	349	482	1,252	1,568	382	434	20 - 24
443	411	1,135	1,086	358	371	1,127	1,021	343	318	25 - 28
76	82	214	207	67	73	207	154	65	52	29
297	252	846	827	263	280	678	519	215	170	30 - 34
199	151	604	501	188	190	402	316	144	112	35 - 39
157	128	402	353	123	107	342	306	118	94	40 - 44
109	98	255	206	86	63	209	211	79	64	45 - 49
65	65	161	137	56	45	169	136	53	44	50 - 54
34	41	97	93	28	26	117	100	26	26	55 - 59
35	41	70	92	23	23	85	101	25	23	60 - 64
40	52	72	103	18	23	75	92	30	36	65 - 69
24	32	42	86	9	13	38	57	15	25	70 - 74
30	50	60	108	8	14	60	105	24	34	75 - 84
9	21	8	38	2	-	16	22	6	16	85 and over

Table 15 Migrants - continued

15. Residents with different address one year before census

Age	TOTAL PERSONS	Total males	Total females	Moved within wards		Between wards but within district		Between districts but within county	
				Males	Females	Males	Females	Males	Females
a	b	c	d	e	f	g	h	i	j
				Bath					
All migrants									
ALL AGES 1 AND OVER	**9,636**	**4,695**	**4,941**	**824**	**916**	**1,894**	**1,939**	**361**	**386**
1 - 4	573	306	267	66	56	129	125	21	8
5 - 9	348	174	174	32	42	71	59	15	14
10 - 14	278	146	132	29	23	68	58	8	9
15	49	21	28	4	6	9	13	2	4
16	48	25	23	3	3	11	8	3	3
17	85	32	53	7	7	9	22	2	6
18 - 19	496	200	296	34	54	66	105	17	33
20 - 24	2,508	1,161	1,347	173	214	483	529	96	109
25 - 28	1,556	785	771	129	130	310	306	64	63
29	272	144	128	22	27	59	45	16	12
30 - 34	966	507	459	81	81	201	167	44	30
35 - 39	585	317	268	58	48	127	96	16	20
40 - 44	424	236	188	44	31	93	70	14	17
45 - 49	314	181	133	42	26	59	45	7	6
50 - 54	216	119	97	30	27	37	27	13	5
55 - 59	142	72	70	16	23	27	22	4	6
60 - 64	153	68	85	18	17	28	36	4	9
65 - 69	166	68	98	7	15	34	49	8	5
70 - 74	124	54	70	13	20	30	31	3	5
75 - 84	218	61	157	14	44	32	73	2	17
85 and over	115	18	97	2	22	11	53	2	5
Migrants in households									
All ages 1 and over	**8,947**	**4,380**	**4,567**	**783**	**867**	**1,820**	**1,819**	**343**	**355**
1 - 4	569	303	266	66	56	129	125	21	8
5 - 9	344	172	172	32	42	71	59	14	13
10 - 14	274	144	130	29	23	68	57	6	9
15	46	20	26	4	6	9	12	1	3
16	47	25	22	3	3	11	8	3	3
17	79	29	50	7	6	8	21	2	6
18 - 19	427	169	258	33	51	65	101	16	27
20 - 24	2,316	1,065	1,251	156	205	466	516	93	104
25 - 28	1,461	735	726	123	125	299	300	63	61
29	265	139	126	21	27	57	45	16	12
30 - 34	924	480	444	80	78	198	166	42	29
35 - 39	556	297	259	54	47	123	94	15	18
40 - 44	412	230	182	44	30	92	68	14	17
45 - 49	303	175	128	40	26	59	45	7	6
50 - 54	204	109	95	26	27	35	27	12	5
55 - 59	135	67	68	16	23	26	22	3	6
60 - 64	147	65	82	18	16	26	36	3	9
65 - 69	153	62	91	7	14	31	45	8	4
70 - 74	108	49	59	12	18	26	24	3	3
75 - 84	140	40	100	11	35	19	36	1	11
85 and over	37	5	32	1	9	2	12	-	1

Between counties but within region		Between regions or from Scotland		From outside GB		Between neighbouring districts		Between neighbouring counties/Scottish Regions		Age
Males	Females	Males	Females	Males	Females	Males	Females	Males	Females	
k	l	m	n	o	p	q	r	s	t	a
										All migrants
433	**467**	**849**	**891**	**334**	**342**	**194**	**228**	**344**	**352**	**ALL AGES 1 AND OVER**
27	16	46	40	17	22	11	4	20	12	1 - 4
11	14	29	29	16	16	10	9	8	12	5 - 9
16	10	17	20	8	12	5	9	14	10	10 - 14
-	1	2	2	4	2	2	3	-	1	15
1	4	5	5	2	-	2	-	1	4	16
9	5	4	10	1	3	1	5	8	6	17
32	47	36	40	15	17	10	17	24	32	18 - 19
99	145	245	283	65	67	56	69	73	97	20 - 24
78	70	145	140	59	62	27	34	60	52	25 - 28
7	5	27	24	13	15	6	5	6	2	29
34	31	94	102	53	48	17	14	28	28	30 - 34
30	27	66	51	20	26	8	11	26	23	35 - 39
21	15	41	36	23	19	9	12	19	14	40 - 44
26	15	32	29	15	12	5	4	20	12	45 - 49
11	16	19	15	9	7	9	3	9	10	50 - 54
8	6	12	10	5	3	3	4	6	5	55 - 59
6	8	8	12	4	3	2	6	5	4	60 - 64
9	10	7	16	3	3	6	2	8	8	65 - 69
2	3	4	6	2	5	1	4	2	3	70 - 74
5	10	8	13	-	-	2	10	6	10	75 - 84
1	9	2	8	-	-	2	3	1	7	85 and over
										Migrants in households
399	**412**	**751**	**796**	**284**	**318**	**182**	**216**	**315**	**314**	**All ages 1 and over**
27	16	43	39	17	22	11	4	20	12	1 - 4
11	14	28	28	16	16	10	9	8	12	5 - 9
16	9	17	20	8	12	5	9	14	9	10 - 14
-	1	2	2	4	2	1	3	-	1	15
1	3	5	5	2	-	2	-	1	3	16
9	5	2	10	1	2	1	5	8	6	17
26	31	22	34	7	14	9	16	19	23	18 - 19
93	130	206	237	51	59	55	68	68	90	20 - 24
72	65	129	120	49	55	26	33	55	49	25 - 28
7	5	25	23	13	14	6	5	6	2	29
33	31	84	94	43	46	15	13	28	27	30 - 34
27	27	63	49	15	24	7	11	24	23	35 - 39
20	15	39	33	21	19	9	12	18	14	40 - 44
24	12	31	27	14	12	5	4	18	9	45 - 49
8	14	19	15	9	7	9	3	6	8	50 - 54
7	4	10	10	5	3	2	4	5	3	55 - 59
6	7	8	11	4	3	1	6	5	3	60 - 64
6	9	7	16	3	3	6	2	5	7	65 - 69
2	3	4	6	2	5	1	2	2	3	70 - 74
3	6	6	12	-	-	1	6	4	6	75 - 84
1	5	1	5	-	-	-	1	1	4	85 and over

Table 15 Migrants - continued

15. Residents with different address one year before census

Age	TOTAL PERSONS	Total males	Total females	Moved within wards		Between wards but within district		Between districts but within county	
				Males	Females	Males	Females	Males	Females
a	b	c	d	e	f	g	h	i	j
Bristol									
All migrants									
ALL AGES 1 AND OVER	**41,822**	**20,932**	**20,890**	**5,120**	**4,885**	**8,786**	**9,239**	**2,097**	**2,124**
1 - 4	2,874	1,498	1,376	436	373	713	689	105	91
5 - 9	1,971	1,012	959	287	268	460	478	59	55
10 - 14	1,352	691	661	192	169	303	304	54	54
15	241	126	115	30	22	62	64	17	12
16	275	136	139	32	39	65	62	18	17
17	385	146	239	33	63	70	103	19	46
18 - 19	1,743	700	1,043	164	247	248	407	78	149
20 - 24	10,679	5,086	5,593	1,189	1,176	1,978	2,394	537	651
25 - 28	7,451	3,862	3,589	851	769	1,630	1,562	431	351
29	1,327	692	635	152	169	306	265	71	47
30 - 34	4,283	2,348	1,935	551	424	989	829	213	171
35 - 39	2,446	1,373	1,073	329	256	546	438	117	89
40 - 44	1,863	1,024	839	253	191	420	360	119	94
45 - 49	1,081	609	472	152	105	257	199	64	65
50 - 54	741	412	329	117	95	160	127	55	40
55 - 59	538	283	255	86	56	111	124	39	27
60 - 64	463	233	230	64	67	119	101	23	31
65 - 69	470	190	280	60	79	86	123	20	27
70 - 74	436	187	249	54	65	94	125	21	27
75 - 84	806	255	551	72	157	127	300	30	47
85 and over	397	69	328	16	95	42	185	7	33
Migrants in households									
All ages 1 and over	**39,758**	**19,936**	**19,822**	**4,885**	**4,695**	**8,508**	**8,768**	**1,949**	**1,957**
1 - 4	2,841	1,483	1,358	435	371	709	685	100	86
5 - 9	1,950	999	951	282	266	453	473	58	55
10 - 14	1,309	661	648	182	169	292	293	54	52
15	226	117	109	27	21	60	59	15	12
16	266	134	132	32	37	65	59	17	16
17	368	141	227	33	62	69	99	19	41
18 - 19	1,627	641	986	155	240	239	401	73	142
20 - 24	10,338	4,901	5,437	1,153	1,158	1,937	2,359	521	619
25 - 28	7,272	3,754	3,518	829	762	1,611	1,543	416	343
29	1,303	673	630	150	169	299	265	68	47
30 - 34	4,171	2,275	1,896	531	420	977	821	204	166
35 - 39	2,347	1,299	1,048	313	254	536	429	104	84
40 - 44	1,781	966	815	233	190	409	351	108	88
45 - 49	1,003	547	456	134	104	247	193	53	60
50 - 54	678	372	306	100	90	150	120	46	32
55 - 59	499	257	242	81	54	105	120	30	23
60 - 64	423	216	207	59	61	113	98	18	22
65 - 69	427	167	260	55	76	77	111	12	25
70 - 74	353	148	205	47	55	71	102	15	20
75 - 84	476	163	313	49	105	78	154	15	21
85 and over	100	22	78	5	31	11	33	3	3

Between counties but within region		Between regions or from Scotland		From outside GB		Between neighbouring districts		Between neighbouring counties/Scottish Regions		Age
Males	Females	Males	Females	Males	Females	Males	Females	Males	Females	
k	l	m	n	o	p	q	r	s	t	a
										All migrants
882	**785**	**2,943**	**2,674**	**1,104**	**1,183**	**1,998**	**2,002**	**550**	**476**	**ALL AGES 1 AND OVER**
32	32	129	118	83	73	103	83	19	20	1 - 4
34	19	100	92	72	47	56	52	16	13	5 - 9
29	18	76	66	37	50	54	53	19	10	10 - 14
5	4	8	10	4	3	17	11	4	1	15
3	9	13	7	5	5	18	16	1	4	16
8	5	12	15	4	7	19	45	6	4	17
47	51	129	142	34	47	76	142	28	36	18 - 19
267	221	925	864	190	287	511	612	158	134	20 - 24
143	146	587	526	220	235	401	321	97	100	25 - 28
33	32	95	84	35	38	67	40	25	15	29
91	68	343	288	161	155	199	164	57	36	30 - 34
64	47	206	149	111	94	114	84	39	28	35 - 39
48	38	133	104	51	52	112	88	28	25	40 - 44
24	25	72	56	40	22	61	63	18	11	45 - 49
16	13	41	33	23	21	54	38	11	10	50 - 54
9	10	27	26	11	12	38	27	5	5	55 - 59
6	6	13	15	8	10	21	31	5	2	60 - 64
5	12	11	24	8	15	19	27	5	5	65 - 69
6	7	8	20	4	5	21	26	4	6	70 - 74
11	17	13	25	2	5	30	46	5	9	75 - 84
1	5	2	10	1	-	7	33	-	2	85 and over
										Migrants in households
819	**747**	**2,767**	**2,556**	**1,008**	**1,099**	**1,855**	**1,839**	**509**	**451**	**All ages 1 and over**
29	30	128	115	82	71	98	78	16	19	1 - 4
34	19	100	91	72	47	55	52	16	13	5 - 9
26	18	71	66	36	50	54	51	19	10	10 - 14
4	4	8	10	3	3	15	11	4	1	15
2	8	13	7	5	5	17	15	-	3	16
7	5	9	14	4	6	19	40	6	4	17
43	48	103	119	28	36	71	135	25	34	18 - 19
251	212	872	828	167	261	495	581	149	129	20 - 24
134	141	560	510	204	219	386	313	90	95	25 - 28
30	31	92	81	34	37	64	40	23	15	29
89	67	330	279	144	143	191	159	55	35	30 - 34
59	46	191	145	96	90	101	80	36	27	35 - 39
45	36	127	102	44	48	102	83	25	24	40 - 44
17	24	61	54	35	21	51	58	14	11	45 - 49
16	12	37	31	23	21	45	30	11	10	50 - 54
8	10	24	25	9	10	30	23	4	5	55 - 59
5	4	13	15	8	7	17	22	4	-	60 - 64
5	11	11	23	7	14	11	25	5	4	65 - 69
5	4	6	19	4	5	15	19	3	4	70 - 74
9	13	10	15	2	5	15	21	4	6	75 - 84
1	4	1	7	1	-	3	3	-	2	85 and over

15. Residents with different address one year before census

Age	TOTAL PERSONS	Total males	Total females	Moved within wards		Between wards but within district		Between districts but within county	
				Males	Females	Males	Females	Males	Females
a	b	c	d	e	f	g	h	i	j
				Kingswood					
All migrants									
ALL AGES 1 AND OVER	**7,194**	**3,493**	**3,701**	**495**	**526**	**1,254**	**1,361**	**1,240**	**1,308**
1 - 4	596	280	316	43	50	127	117	79	102
5 - 9	426	213	213	40	31	86	103	58	57
10 - 14	257	141	116	23	18	63	49	43	36
15	49	32	17	6	2	7	6	15	5
16	53	24	29	2	8	13	15	4	4
17	72	33	39	6	6	15	18	8	12
18 - 19	200	76	124	10	22	27	48	24	43
20 - 24	1,346	580	766	74	81	186	258	215	304
25 - 28	1,226	643	583	80	68	198	189	263	238
29	224	127	97	21	13	41	34	47	35
30 - 34	756	397	359	55	57	133	126	147	110
35 - 39	498	266	232	34	34	104	92	92	74
40 - 44	334	176	158	25	14	64	69	70	56
45 - 49	248	134	114	15	22	46	37	50	38
50 - 54	160	84	76	15	11	27	22	24	32
55 - 59	152	80	72	11	13	29	28	31	24
60 - 64	111	36	75	5	17	12	23	16	32
65 - 69	118	49	69	11	13	21	30	11	17
70 - 74	87	37	50	5	10	19	25	12	12
75 - 84	194	71	123	12	24	33	49	24	44
85 and over	87	14	73	2	12	3	23	7	33
Migrants in households									
All ages 1 and over	**6,998**	**3,426**	**3,572**	**491**	**515**	**1,241**	**1,327**	**1,198**	**1,227**
1 - 4	587	274	313	43	50	127	116	73	100
5 - 9	421	210	211	40	31	86	103	56	55
10 - 14	251	138	113	21	18	63	48	42	34
15	42	25	17	6	2	7	6	10	5
16	47	19	28	2	8	13	15	3	3
17	71	32	39	6	6	15	18	8	12
18 - 19	194	75	119	10	21	27	46	23	41
20 - 24	1,343	579	764	74	81	185	256	215	304
25 - 28	1,220	640	580	80	68	197	188	261	236
29	223	127	96	21	13	41	34	47	34
30 - 34	753	396	357	55	57	132	125	147	109
35 - 39	496	266	230	34	34	104	92	92	72
40 - 44	329	173	156	25	14	63	68	68	55
45 - 49	246	132	114	15	22	46	37	48	38
50 - 54	153	82	71	15	11	26	22	23	27
55 - 59	145	78	67	11	13	29	28	29	19
60 - 64	105	35	70	5	17	12	22	15	28
65 - 69	115	47	68	11	12	21	30	9	17
70 - 74	80	33	47	5	9	17	24	10	11
75 - 84	145	60	85	11	20	30	39	17	21
85 and over	32	5	27	1	8	-	10	2	6

Between counties but within region		Between regions or from Scotland		From outside GB		Between neighbouring districts		Between neighbouring counties/Scottish Regions		Age
Males	Females	Males	Females	Males	Females	Males	Females	Males	Females	
k	l	m	n	o	p	q	r	s	t	a
										All migrants
127	**125**	**303**	**299**	**74**	**82**	**1,146**	**1,231**	**84**	**77**	**ALL AGES 1 AND OVER**
11	7	17	32	3	8	76	99	5	5	1 - 4
3	6	18	13	8	3	53	54	2	2	5 - 9
4	3	5	8	3	2	41	36	2	1	10 - 14
-	1	4	3	-	-	13	4	1	-	15
-	2	5	-	-	-	4	4	-	1	16
-	-	2	3	2	-	8	12	-	-	17
3	4	9	5	3	2	24	40	1	1	18 - 19
17	35	74	64	14	24	195	284	12	20	20 - 24
31	20	61	53	10	15	246	219	27	20	25 - 28
5	4	11	7	2	4	45	32	4	4	29
16	17	39	41	7	8	131	104	12	10	30 - 34
10	4	19	22	7	6	86	71	4	2	35 - 39
5	3	10	12	2	4	64	53	4	1	40 - 44
10	6	10	10	3	1	46	33	4	2	45 - 49
5	2	7	6	6	3	20	29	2	1	50 - 54
2	2	6	4	1	1	28	23	1	-	55 - 59
2	1	-	1	1	1	16	31	1	-	60 - 64
1	2	3	7	2	-	11	17	1	2	65 - 69
-	2	1	1	-	-	11	11	-	1	70 - 74
2	1	-	5	-	-	21	42	1	1	75 - 84
-	3	2	2	-	-	7	33	-	3	85 and over
										Migrants in households
126	**123**	**296**	**298**	**74**	**82**	**1,106**	**1,150**	**82**	**76**	**All ages 1 and over**
11	7	17	32	3	8	70	97	5	5	1 - 4
2	6	18	13	8	3	51	52	1	2	5 - 9
4	3	5	8	3	2	40	34	2	1	10 - 14
-	1	2	3	-	-	10	4	-	-	15
-	2	1	-	-	-	3	3	-	1	16
-	-	1	3	2	-	8	12	-	-	17
3	4	9	5	3	2	23	38	1	1	18 - 19
17	35	74	64	14	24	195	284	12	20	20 - 24
31	20	61	53	10	15	244	217	27	20	25 - 28
5	4	11	7	2	4	45	31	4	4	29
16	17	39	41	7	8	131	103	12	10	30 - 34
10	4	19	22	7	6	86	69	4	2	35 - 39
5	3	10	12	2	4	62	52	4	1	40 - 44
10	6	10	10	3	1	44	33	4	2	45 - 49
5	2	7	6	6	3	19	24	2	1	50 - 54
2	2	6	4	1	1	26	18	1	-	55 - 59
2	1	-	1	1	1	15	27	1	-	60 - 64
1	2	3	7	2	-	9	17	1	2	65 - 69
-	2	1	1	-	-	9	10	-	1	70 - 74
2	1	-	4	-	-	14	19	1	1	75 - 84
-	1	2	2	-	-	2	6	-	2	85 and over

Table 15 Migrants - continued

15. Residents with different address one year before census

Age	TOTAL PERSONS	Total males	Total females	Moved within wards		Between wards but within district		Between districts but within county	
				Males	Females	Males	Females	Males	Females
a	b	c	d	e	f	g	h	i	j
				Northavon					
All migrants									
ALL AGES 1 AND OVER	**13,941**	**6,978**	**6,963**	**1,243**	**1,280**	**2,215**	**2,326**	**1,598**	**1,523**
1 - 4	1,104	592	512	122	132	223	160	94	78
5 - 9	870	437	433	99	100	150	161	60	53
10 - 14	589	299	290	65	58	105	112	59	41
15	85	38	47	12	8	12	21	9	9
16	113	54	59	16	9	14	30	12	9
17	120	63	57	9	9	26	28	12	7
18 - 19	451	167	284	27	56	63	100	27	66
20 - 24	2,609	1,146	1,463	175	220	367	501	323	406
25 - 28	2,172	1,129	1,043	166	175	383	317	276	272
29	407	216	191	46	37	55	52	56	49
30 - 34	1,557	859	698	139	118	247	201	199	146
35 - 39	950	522	428	93	74	124	129	120	77
40 - 44	798	441	357	84	65	115	128	105	79
45 - 49	564	325	239	65	41	111	82	67	53
50 - 54	355	183	172	31	29	47	63	48	36
55 - 59	241	126	115	14	20	47	42	31	23
60 - 64	211	111	100	21	30	33	28	31	17
65 - 69	198	88	110	18	25	30	40	23	20
70 - 74	134	49	85	15	21	19	27	8	12
75 - 84	305	100	205	22	37	36	73	24	53
85 and over	108	33	75	4	16	8	31	14	17
Migrants in households									
All ages 1 and over	**13,452**	**6,694**	**6,758**	**1,202**	**1,258**	**2,181**	**2,262**	**1,519**	**1,473**
1 - 4	1,102	591	511	122	132	223	160	94	78
5 - 9	867	435	432	98	100	150	161	59	53
10 - 14	583	296	287	64	58	105	111	58	41
15	83	37	46	11	7	12	21	9	9
16	110	52	58	14	9	14	30	12	8
17	115	59	56	9	9	24	27	12	7
18 - 19	417	150	267	27	55	60	98	26	64
20 - 24	2,538	1,117	1,421	172	217	362	496	321	399
25 - 28	2,134	1,107	1,027	163	172	381	316	274	270
29	401	211	190	45	36	55	52	56	49
30 - 34	1,530	836	694	136	117	246	201	194	146
35 - 39	919	498	421	90	73	123	128	115	76
40 - 44	761	407	354	78	65	113	126	98	78
45 - 49	540	304	236	60	41	111	80	63	52
50 - 54	335	166	169	28	29	47	62	41	34
55 - 59	224	111	113	9	20	46	40	23	23
60 - 64	198	98	100	21	30	33	28	20	17
65 - 69	187	81	106	17	24	28	38	20	19
70 - 74	124	44	80	15	20	16	26	6	10
75 - 84	233	77	156	20	33	30	48	10	39
85 and over	51	17	34	3	11	2	13	8	1

Between counties but within region		Between regions or from Scotland		From outside GB		Between neighbouring districts		Between neighbouring counties/Scottish Regions		Age
Males	Females	Males	Females	Males	Females	Males	Females	Males	Females	
k	l	m	n	o	p	q	r	s	t	a
										All migrants
470	**447**	**1,214**	**1,159**	**238**	**228**	**1,604**	**1,520**	**387**	**367**	**ALL AGES 1 AND OVER**
31	32	100	101	22	9	92	84	26	28	1 - 4
24	27	80	75	24	17	62	56	20	21	5 - 9
12	14	48	49	10	16	61	44	11	13	10 - 14
2	2	3	6	-	1	11	9	2	1	15
1	1	10	10	1	-	11	9	1	1	16
4	2	11	9	1	2	14	8	4	1	17
14	17	27	31	9	14	29	66	9	12	18 - 19
73	92	168	191	40	53	314	384	55	77	20 - 24
85	70	186	181	33	28	283	272	73	68	25 - 28
15	14	38	34	6	5	58	46	15	11	29
72	53	174	154	28	26	195	136	50	37	30 - 34
34	24	128	101	23	23	117	82	35	23	35 - 39
35	18	85	55	17	12	105	79	27	15	40 - 44
20	18	54	36	8	9	64	59	17	14	45 - 49
17	13	32	24	8	7	53	38	13	9	50 - 54
6	8	22	18	6	4	30	22	8	5	55 - 59
6	6	20	17	-	2	32	18	4	4	60 - 64
6	11	10	14	1	-	26	26	6	11	65 - 69
3	6	4	19	-	-	6	14	2	3	70 - 74
5	12	12	30	1	-	26	50	6	8	75 - 84
5	7	2	4	-	-	15	18	3	5	85 and over
										Migrants in households
433	**432**	**1,145**	**1,131**	**214**	**202**	**1,521**	**1,466**	**371**	**354**	**All ages 1 and over**
31	31	100	101	21	9	92	83	26	27	1 - 4
24	26	80	75	24	17	61	55	20	20	5 - 9
12	12	48	49	9	16	60	42	11	11	10 - 14
2	2	3	6	-	1	11	9	2	1	15
1	1	10	10	1	-	11	8	1	1	16
4	2	9	9	1	2	14	8	4	1	17
13	16	17	27	7	7	27	65	8	12	18 - 19
70	88	160	179	32	42	312	378	53	74	20 - 24
81	70	181	173	27	26	282	270	72	68	25 - 28
14	14	35	34	6	5	58	46	15	11	29
65	53	169	154	26	23	190	136	50	37	30 - 34
30	23	120	101	20	20	113	80	34	22	35 - 39
28	18	74	55	16	12	96	78	23	15	40 - 44
16	18	46	36	8	9	57	58	13	14	45 - 49
14	13	28	24	8	7	46	37	12	9	50 - 54
6	8	21	18	6	4	22	22	8	5	55 - 59
6	6	18	17	-	2	21	18	4	4	60 - 64
6	11	9	14	1	-	23	25	6	11	65 - 69
3	5	4	19	-	-	4	11	2	2	70 - 74
4	10	12	26	1	-	12	36	5	6	75 - 84
3	5	1	4	-	-	9	1	2	3	85 and over

Table 15 Migrants - continued

15. Residents with different address one year before census

Age	TOTAL PERSONS	Total males	Total females	Moved within wards		Between wards but within district		Between districts but within county	
				Males	Females	Males	Females	Males	Females
a	b	c	d	e	f	g	h	i	j
				Wansdyke					
All migrants									
ALL AGES 1 AND OVER	**6,444**	**3,110**	**3,334**	**544**	**613**	**870**	**923**	**757**	**821**
1 - 4	474	248	226	48	65	85	71	50	42
5 - 9	374	196	178	35	35	61	51	45	40
10 - 14	305	158	147	33	35	50	37	25	33
15	48	23	25	1	3	10	11	2	7
16	43	23	20	6	2	4	5	7	5
17	50	19	31	3	7	5	6	5	9
18 - 19	219	84	135	11	24	24	43	23	28
20 - 24	1,133	495	638	82	101	147	205	114	152
25 - 28	842	426	416	70	62	127	112	108	111
29	175	87	88	13	11	26	28	23	23
30 - 34	639	338	301	51	46	82	66	102	70
35 - 39	487	274	213	53	37	62	50	63	50
40 - 44	390	194	196	30	33	46	47	37	50
45 - 49	267	150	117	33	25	32	24	36	34
50 - 54	185	101	84	15	15	31	19	30	27
55 - 59	127	62	65	8	15	15	16	26	19
60 - 64	126	53	73	9	15	10	16	20	16
65 - 69	125	55	70	13	17	16	26	16	15
70 - 74	107	35	72	6	16	13	20	6	13
75 - 84	205	71	134	19	29	21	38	14	34
85 and over	123	18	105	5	20	3	32	5	43
Migrants in households									
All ages 1 and over	**6,190**	**3,044**	**3,146**	**536**	**593**	**858**	**873**	**737**	**753**
1 - 4	474	248	226	48	65	85	71	50	42
5 - 9	374	196	178	35	35	61	51	45	40
10 - 14	304	158	146	33	35	50	37	25	32
15	48	23	25	1	3	10	11	2	7
16	43	23	20	6	2	4	5	7	5
17	50	19	31	3	7	5	6	5	9
18 - 19	204	78	126	11	24	24	43	21	28
20 - 24	1,109	483	626	82	100	147	205	114	152
25 - 28	834	424	410	70	62	127	112	108	110
29	175	87	88	13	11	26	28	23	23
30 - 34	635	336	299	51	46	82	66	101	69
35 - 39	485	274	211	53	37	62	49	63	50
40 - 44	387	192	195	30	33	45	47	37	49
45 - 49	263	146	117	33	25	30	24	34	34
50 - 54	185	101	84	15	15	31	19	30	27
55 - 59	126	62	64	8	15	15	16	26	18
60 - 64	126	53	73	9	15	10	16	20	16
65 - 69	117	53	64	13	17	15	24	15	13
70 - 74	95	32	63	5	16	13	16	4	9
75 - 84	130	50	80	15	22	15	23	7	14
85 and over	26	6	20	2	8	1	4	-	6

Between counties but within region		Between regions or from Scotland		From outside GB		Between neighbouring districts		Between neighbouring counties/Scottish Regions		Age
Males	Females	Males	Females	Males	Females	Males	Females	Males	Females	
k	l	m	n	o	p	q	r	s	t	a
										All migrants
312	**328**	**527**	**529**	**100**	**120**	**937**	**1,013**	**257**	**278**	**ALL AGES 1 AND OVER**
23	20	35	27	7	1	63	49	22	14	1 - 4
14	17	38	30	3	5	53	48	11	14	5 - 9
9	6	35	31	6	5	30	39	7	6	10 - 14
3	-	6	4	1	-	5	7	3	-	15
1	1	3	5	2	2	8	6	1	1	16
3	1	3	6	-	2	7	10	4	1	17
10	18	10	11	6	11	26	38	9	15	18 - 19
55	66	79	80	18	34	142	197	38	60	20 - 24
50	45	57	69	14	17	138	143	44	39	25 - 28
9	10	15	16	1	-	29	27	8	11	29
37	40	61	67	5	12	127	91	33	34	30 - 34
30	20	56	48	10	8	77	60	23	16	35 - 39
28	20	43	40	10	6	53	62	18	14	40 - 44
13	13	29	17	7	4	44	42	13	10	45 - 49
8	8	15	13	2	2	37	30	10	8	50 - 54
2	4	9	10	2	1	27	19	1	3	55 - 59
5	10	7	13	2	3	22	21	4	6	60 - 64
3	4	6	6	1	2	17	18	1	3	65 - 69
3	6	5	14	2	3	7	15	1	5	70 - 74
5	13	12	18	-	2	19	45	5	13	75 - 84
1	6	3	4	1	-	6	46	1	5	85 and over
										Migrants in households
304	**307**	**510**	**512**	**99**	**108**	**916**	**931**	**252**	**260**	**All ages 1 and over**
23	20	35	27	7	1	63	49	22	14	1 - 4
14	17	38	30	3	5	53	48	11	14	5 - 9
9	6	35	31	6	5	30	38	7	6	10 - 14
3	-	6	4	1	-	5	7	3	-	15
1	1	3	5	2	2	8	6	1	1	16
3	1	3	6	-	2	7	10	4	1	17
7	15	9	8	6	8	24	37	6	12	18 - 19
53	63	70	76	17	30	142	196	37	59	20 - 24
49	45	56	67	14	14	138	142	44	39	25 - 28
9	10	15	16	1	-	29	27	8	11	29
36	39	61	67	5	12	125	90	32	33	30 - 34
30	20	56	48	10	7	77	60	23	16	35 - 39
27	20	43	40	10	6	53	61	18	14	40 - 44
13	13	29	17	7	4	42	42	13	10	45 - 49
8	8	15	13	2	2	37	30	10	8	50 - 54
2	4	9	10	2	1	27	18	1	3	55 - 59
5	10	7	13	2	3	22	21	4	6	60 - 64
3	2	6	6	1	2	16	14	1	1	65 - 69
3	6	5	13	2	3	5	11	1	5	70 - 74
5	6	8	14	-	1	12	18	5	6	75 - 84
1	1	1	1	1	-	1	6	1	1	85 and over

Table 15 Migrants - continued

15. Residents with different address one year before census

Age	TOTAL PERSONS	Total males	Total females	Moved within wards		Between wards but within district		Between districts but within county	
				Males	Females	Males	Females	Males	Females
a	b	c	d	e	f	g	h	i	j
				Woodspring					
All migrants									
ALL AGES 1 AND OVER	**17,727**	**8,792**	**8,935**	**1,810**	**1,887**	**3,293**	**3,495**	**864**	**884**
1 - 4	1,296	681	615	174	138	275	236	45	38
5 - 9	1,045	496	549	119	131	157	185	38	32
10 - 14	753	421	332	95	74	142	120	29	22
15	122	58	64	10	19	24	25	2	4
16	153	65	88	16	20	25	37	5	5
17	228	109	119	11	28	35	49	8	4
18 - 19	797	388	409	64	86	111	191	27	17
20 - 24	3,047	1,482	1,565	284	295	584	724	119	149
25 - 28	2,168	1,136	1,032	222	208	471	422	136	117
29	450	224	226	43	46	96	71	23	27
30 - 34	1,674	884	790	187	140	318	269	102	90
35 - 39	1,233	682	551	135	103	243	179	56	56
40 - 44	1,032	537	495	118	97	196	191	48	42
45 - 49	743	399	344	77	69	142	130	48	39
50 - 54	503	271	232	55	41	98	82	37	40
55 - 59	335	166	169	31	40	65	55	28	27
60 - 64	372	188	184	37	41	74	64	30	22
65 - 69	398	188	210	34	49	64	73	30	29
70 - 74	331	138	193	29	47	51	81	19	20
75 - 84	635	200	435	56	124	76	167	23	59
85 and over	412	79	333	13	91	46	144	11	45
Migrants in households									
All ages 1 and over	**16,284**	**8,093**	**8,191**	**1,726**	**1,707**	**3,132**	**3,215**	**797**	**764**
1 - 4	1,288	676	612	173	138	273	234	45	38
5 - 9	1,034	492	542	118	130	156	183	37	30
10 - 14	746	416	330	95	74	141	119	28	22
15	120	57	63	10	19	24	25	2	4
16	151	63	88	16	20	25	37	5	5
17	185	79	106	11	25	34	46	8	4
18 - 19	630	253	377	61	84	108	187	25	16
20 - 24	2,845	1,333	1,512	274	291	573	718	114	142
25 - 28	2,101	1,089	1,012	218	205	463	417	130	115
29	433	215	218	43	45	92	69	22	27
30 - 34	1,632	856	776	183	138	315	265	99	88
35 - 39	1,200	661	539	131	102	238	175	54	52
40 - 44	1,000	511	489	113	96	182	188	45	40
45 - 49	715	381	334	75	67	134	128	46	36
50 - 54	489	260	229	52	40	96	81	35	39
55 - 59	328	161	167	30	39	62	55	28	27
60 - 64	338	171	167	33	38	67	56	28	18
65 - 69	355	170	185	31	42	58	61	22	24
70 - 74	272	114	158	23	39	45	68	12	11
75 - 84	346	118	228	33	67	39	82	10	20
85 and over	76	17	59	3	8	7	21	2	6

Between counties but within region		Between regions or from Scotland		From outside GB		Between neighbouring districts		Between neighbouring counties/Scottish Regions		Age
Males	Females	Males	Females	Males	Females	Males	Females	Males	Females	
k	l	m	n	o	p	q	r	s	t	a
										All migrants
607	**586**	**1,797**	**1,685**	**421**	**398**	**310**	**340**	**412**	**398**	**ALL AGES 1 AND OVER**
35	37	117	137	35	29	20	20	25	31	1 - 4
28	31	127	139	27	31	5	21	14	20	5 - 9
21	23	102	68	32	25	9	10	13	13	10 - 14
1	2	17	10	4	4	1	1	-	2	15
4	7	13	11	2	8	3	4	3	6	16
17	12	35	23	3	3	3	4	12	7	17
34	31	144	72	8	12	17	17	27	20	18 - 19
117	98	305	230	73	69	56	63	74	68	20 - 24
79	72	170	170	58	43	53	46	57	49	25 - 28
12	20	38	46	12	16	5	5	9	10	29
62	48	173	194	42	49	27	19	41	29	30 - 34
44	33	161	137	43	43	19	17	24	24	35 - 39
34	36	111	111	30	18	22	20	32	26	40 - 44
33	25	80	64	19	17	13	16	20	18	45 - 49
15	16	58	48	8	5	13	12	12	8	50 - 54
9	13	28	27	5	7	10	15	7	10	55 - 59
12	13	26	37	9	7	9	7	8	10	60 - 64
20	17	36	38	4	4	10	9	13	11	65 - 69
14	14	24	31	1	-	5	5	8	12	70 - 74
12	22	27	55	6	8	8	13	10	15	75 - 84
4	16	5	37	-	-	2	16	3	9	85 and over
										Migrants in households
540	**544**	**1,503**	**1,573**	**395**	**388**	**291**	**314**	**372**	**371**	**All ages 1 and over**
34	37	116	136	35	29	20	20	25	31	1 - 4
27	31	127	137	27	31	5	21	14	20	5 - 9
20	23	100	67	32	25	8	10	12	13	10 - 14
1	1	16	10	4	4	1	-	-	1	15
3	7	12	11	2	8	3	4	3	6	16
11	12	14	17	1	2	3	4	10	7	17
21	27	35	51	3	12	15	16	21	19	18 - 19
100	91	204	204	68	66	53	61	63	62	20 - 24
76	70	148	163	54	42	51	46	55	47	25 - 28
11	18	36	46	11	13	5	5	9	9	29
58	45	163	192	38	48	26	18	38	28	30 - 34
43	31	155	136	40	43	18	16	23	22	35 - 39
32	36	109	111	30	18	20	20	30	26	40 - 44
29	25	78	62	19	16	10	16	17	18	45 - 49
14	16	55	48	8	5	13	12	12	8	50 - 54
9	13	27	26	5	7	10	15	7	10	55 - 59
11	13	24	35	8	7	9	7	7	10	60 - 64
19	17	36	37	4	4	10	9	12	11	65 - 69
11	12	22	28	1	-	4	4	7	10	70 - 74
7	14	24	37	5	8	6	5	5	9	75 - 84
3	5	2	19	-	-	1	5	2	4	85 and over

Note: * May include a small number of households with no adults

16. Wholly moving households; residents in such households

Household composition and number of residents	ALL TYPES OF MOVE	Moved within wards	Between wards but within district	Between districts but within county	Between counties but within region	Between regions or from Scotland	From outside GB	Between neigh-bouring districts	Between neigh-bouring counties/ Scottish Regions
a	b	c	d	e	f	g	h	i	j
				AVON					
TOTAL WHOLLY MOVING HOUSEHOLDS	**26,027**	**4,538**	**11,228**	**3,765**	**1,464**	**3,975**	**1,057**	**3,375**	**1,057**
TOTAL PERSONS IN WHOLLY MOVING HOUSEHOLDS	**56,704**	**10,349**	**24,555**	**7,799**	**2,948**	**8,563**	**2,490**	**7,060**	**2,122**
*Wholly moving households with dependent children**									
Persons	30,433	6,100	13,459	3,401	1,378	4,609	1,486	3,201	986
All households	8,494	1,698	3,843	940	390	1,229	394	890	284
Wholly moving households, no dependent children, no person aged 60 or over									
Persons	21,121	3,033	8,891	3,694	1,286	3,320	897	3,249	943
All households	14,111	1,988	5,899	2,395	890	2,345	594	2,108	651
Single person households	7,979	1,125	3,309	1,247	529	1,448	321	1,108	386
Wholly moving households, no dependent children, no person aged under 60									
Persons	3,816	933	1,679	458	215	446	85	404	147
All households	2,834	727	1,262	324	152	312	57	287	102
Single person households	1,863	524	848	192	90	180	29	171	58
Other wholly moving households									
Persons	1,334	283	526	246	69	188	22	206	46
All households	588	125	224	106	32	89	12	90	20
				Bath					
TOTAL WHOLLY MOVING HOUSEHOLDS	**2,605**	**370**	**1,179**	**208**	**224**	**458**	**166**	**121**	**169**
TOTAL PERSONS IN WHOLLY MOVING HOUSEHOLDS	**5,141**	**771**	**2,394**	**374**	**413**	**841**	**348**	**233**	**316**
*Wholly moving households with dependent children**									
Persons	2,431	388	1,170	140	173	385	175	98	141
All households	694	107	341	40	50	109	47	27	41
Wholly moving households, no dependent children, no person aged 60 or over									
Persons	2,163	267	947	197	197	398	157	113	141
All households	1,541	179	655	144	147	308	108	80	106
Single person households	999	110	402	96	103	222	66	51	75
Wholly moving households, no dependent children, no person aged under 60									
Persons	422	86	208	30	33	54	11	18	27
All households	315	71	155	20	23	38	8	12	19
Single person households	209	56	103	10	13	22	5	6	11
Other wholly moving households									
Persons	125	30	69	7	10	4	5	4	7
All households	55	13	28	4	4	3	3	2	3

Note: * May include a small number of households with no adults

16. Wholly moving households; residents in such households

Household composition and number of residents	ALL TYPES OF MOVE	Moved within wards	Between wards but within district	Between districts but within county	Between counties but within region	Between regions or from Scotland	From outside GB	Between neigh-bouring districts	Between neigh-bouring counties/ Scottish Regions
a	b	c	d	e	f	g	h	i	j
Bristol									
TOTAL WHOLLY MOVING HOUSEHOLDS	**10,794**	**2,016**	**5,344**	**1,041**	**413**	**1,447**	**533**	**986**	**258**
TOTAL PERSONS IN WHOLLY MOVING HOUSEHOLDS	**21,964**	**4,333**	**11,175**	**1,917**	**739**	**2,610**	**1,190**	**1,822**	**447**
*Wholly moving households with dependent children**									
Persons	11,391	2,510	5,974	788	305	1,135	679	756	177
All households	3,247	715	1,731	222	90	309	180	213	53
Wholly moving households, no dependent children, no person aged 60 or over									
Persons	9,010	1,394	4,392	1,001	384	1,370	469	940	245
All households	6,428	976	3,041	730	288	1,066	327	686	189
Single person households	4,131	619	1,845	491	196	784	196	463	136
Wholly moving households, no dependent children, no person aged under 60									
Persons	1,207	347	631	94	34	71	30	92	15
All households	953	286	492	72	27	57	19	70	12
Single person households	702	226	354	50	21	43	8	48	10
Other wholly moving households									
Persons	356	82	178	34	16	34	12	34	10
All households	166	39	80	17	8	15	7	17	4
Kingswood									
TOTAL WHOLLY MOVING HOUSEHOLDS	**2,038**	**262**	**809**	**711**	**69**	**160**	**27**	**656**	**48**
TOTAL PERSONS IN WHOLLY MOVING HOUSEHOLDS	**4,750**	**622**	**1,983**	**1,581**	**141**	**357**	**66**	**1,468**	**86**
*Wholly moving households with dependent children**									
Persons	2,645	359	1,226	761	71	189	39	719	31
All households	728	94	338	211	20	54	11	199	9
Wholly moving households, no dependent children, no person aged 60 or over									
Persons	1,647	179	547	684	60	154	23	625	50
All households	999	105	325	417	42	96	14	379	35
Single person households	434	44	137	177	25	45	6	160	20
Wholly moving households, no dependent children, no person aged under 60									
Persons	356	73	175	85	8	14	1	79	5
All households	270	58	131	64	6	10	1	60	4
Single person households	184	43	87	43	4	6	1	41	3
Other wholly moving households									
Persons	102	11	35	51	2	-	3	45	-
All households	41	5	15	19	1	-	1	18	-

Note: * May include a small number of households with no adults

16. Wholly moving households; residents in such households

Household composition and number of residents	ALL TYPES OF MOVE	Moved within wards	Between wards but within district	Between districts but within county	Between counties but within region	Between regions or from Scotland	From outside GB	Between neigh-bouring districts	Between neigh-bouring counties/ Scottish Regions
a	b	c	d	e	f	g	h	i	j
			Northavon						
TOTAL WHOLLY MOVING HOUSEHOLDS	**3,938**	**638**	**1,331**	**921**	**262**	**692**	**94**	**908**	**225**
TOTAL PERSONS IN WHOLLY MOVING HOUSEHOLDS	**9,328**	**1,637**	**3,241**	**1,934**	**574**	**1,680**	**262**	**1,944**	**499**
*Wholly moving households with dependent children**									
Persons	5,338	1,044	1,968	832	289	1,027	178	875	256
All households	1,449	278	541	231	80	273	46	243	72
Wholly moving households, no dependent children, no person aged 60 or over									
Persons	3,253	425	1,015	960	240	534	79	924	205
All households	2,015	249	621	604	149	347	45	575	125
Single person households	930	105	290	279	69	173	14	264	55
Wholly moving households, no dependent children, no person aged under 60									
Persons	517	128	190	92	30	74	3	97	27
All households	375	93	140	64	25	51	2	68	22
Single person households	234	58	91	36	20	28	1	39	17
Other wholly moving households									
Persons	220	40	68	50	15	45	2	48	11
All households	99	18	29	22	8	21	1	22	6
			Wansdyke						
TOTAL WHOLLY MOVING HOUSEHOLDS	**1,737**	**307**	**505**	**412**	**172**	**296**	**45**	**514**	**140**
TOTAL PERSONS IN WHOLLY MOVING HOUSEHOLDS	**4,227**	**779**	**1,250**	**979**	**377**	**729**	**113**	**1,203**	**312**
*Wholly moving households with dependent children**									
Persons	2,392	502	749	474	187	422	58	590	159
All households	650	139	205	126	53	112	15	159	45
Wholly moving households, no dependent children, no person aged 60 or over									
Persons	1,354	165	358	404	152	232	43	491	128
All households	788	93	210	228	97	138	22	287	82
Single person households	312	39	91	82	43	51	6	114	37
Wholly moving households, no dependent children, no person aged under 60									
Persons	342	81	104	64	29	52	12	78	16
All households	238	61	74	43	19	33	8	51	10
Single person households	135	41	44	23	9	14	4	25	4
Other wholly moving households									
Persons	139	31	39	37	9	23	-	44	9
All households	61	14	16	15	3	13	-	17	3

Note: * May include a small number of households with no adults

16. Wholly moving households; residents in such households

Household composition and number of residents	ALL TYPES OF MOVE	Moved within wards	Between wards but within district	Between districts but within county	Between counties but within region	Between regions or from Scotland	From outside GB	Between neigh-bouring districts	Between neigh-bouring counties/ Scottish Regions
a	b	c	d	e	f	g	h	i	j
			Woodspring						
TOTAL WHOLLY MOVING HOUSEHOLDS	**4,915**	**945**	**2,060**	**472**	**324**	**922**	**192**	**190**	**217**
TOTAL PERSONS IN WHOLLY MOVING HOUSEHOLDS	**11,294**	**2,207**	**4,512**	**1,014**	**704**	**2,346**	**511**	**390**	**462**
*Wholly moving households with dependent children**									
Persons	6,236	1,297	2,372	406	353	1,451	357	163	222
All households	1,726	365	687	110	97	372	95	49	64
Wholly moving households, no dependent children, no person aged 60 or over									
Persons	3,694	603	1,632	448	253	632	126	156	174
All households	2,340	386	1,047	272	167	390	78	101	114
Single person households	1,173	208	544	122	93	173	33	56	63
Wholly moving households, no dependent children, no person aged under 60									
Persons	972	218	371	93	81	181	28	40	57
All households	683	158	270	61	52	123	19	26	35
Single person households	399	100	169	30	23	67	10	12	13
Other wholly moving households									
Persons	392	89	137	67	17	82	-	31	9
All households	166	36	56	29	8	37	-	14	4

Table 17 Ethnic group of migrants

17. Residents aged 1 and over

	TOTAL PERSONS	Ethnic group										Persons born in Ireland
		White	Black Caribbean	Black African	Black other	Indian	Pakistani	Bangladeshi	Chinese	Other groups		
										Asian	Other	
a	b	c	d	e	f	g	h	i	j	k	l	m
AVON												
TOTAL PERSONS	**920,509**	**895,405**	**7,046**	**1,067**	**2,600**	**3,704**	**2,778**	**750**	**2,105**	**1,319**	**3,735**	**10,638**
With different address one year before census (migrants)	96,764	92,983	661	352	381	489	213	129	468	360	728	1,493
Bath												
TOTAL PERSONS	**77,855**	**75,829**	**542**	**79**	**232**	**202**	**29**	**72**	**299**	**158**	**413**	**1,075**
With different address one year before census (migrants)	9,636	9,164	45	37	46	25	11	31	110	71	96	167
Bristol												
TOTAL PERSONS	**370,813**	**351,994**	**5,888**	**798**	**2,017**	**2,716**	**2,649**	**543**	**1,125**	**759**	**2,324**	**5,571**
With different address one year before census (migrants)	41,822	39,193	538	277	275	354	186	82	264	185	468	835
Kingswood												
TOTAL PERSONS	**88,510**	**87,544**	**223**	**32**	**91**	**164**	**28**	**30**	**152**	**72**	**174**	**612**
With different address one year before census (migrants)	7,194	7,069	18	5	21	18	2	-	21	13	27	65
Northavon												
TOTAL PERSONS	**128,798**	**127,304**	**242**	**64**	**125**	**323**	**41**	**26**	**213**	**155**	**305**	**1,231**
With different address one year before census (migrants)	13,941	13,666	35	16	20	46	11	5	39	46	57	130
Wansdyke												
TOTAL PERSONS	**79,083**	**78,643**	**38**	**33**	**38**	**64**	**5**	**2**	**73**	**39**	**148**	**571**
With different address one year before census (migrants)	6,444	6,381	5	7	6	1	-	-	10	12	22	75
Woodspring												
TOTAL PERSONS	**175,450**	**174,091**	**113**	**61**	**97**	**235**	**26**	**77**	**243**	**136**	**371**	**1,578**
With different address one year before census (migrants)	17,727	17,510	20	10	13	45	3	11	24	33	58	221

18. Imputed residents of wholly absent households

Age, marital status, long-term illness, economic position and ethnic group	TOTAL PERSONS	Males	Females	Age, marital status, long-term illness, economic position and ethnic group	TOTAL PERSONS	Males	Females
a	b	c	d	a	b	c	d
	AVON				**Bristol**		
TOTAL PERSONS	**16,655**	**8,001**	**8,654**	**TOTAL PERSONS**	**10,580**	**5,149**	**5,431**
0 - 15	2,472	1,249	1,223	0 - 15	1,707	858	849
16 - 17	245	135	110	16 - 17	157	84	73
18 - 29	4,451	2,167	2,284	18 - 29	3,067	1,488	1,579
30 - 44	3,354	1,789	1,565	30 - 44	2,183	1,174	1,009
45 up to pensionable age	2,898	1,657	1,241	45 up to pensionable age	1,692	992	700
Pensionable age and over	3,235	1,004	2,231	Pensionable age and over	1,774	553	1,221
Single	7,864	4,064	3,800	Single	5,502	2,854	2,648
Married	6,078	3,035	3,043	Married	3,450	1,720	1,730
Widowed or divorced	2,713	902	1,811	Widowed or divorced	1,628	575	1,053
With limiting long-term illness	2,074	921	1,153	With limiting long-term illness	1,342	599	743
In employment	7,917	4,359	3,558	In employment	4,994	2,745	2,249
Unemployed	1,072	713	359	Unemployed	806	538	268
Economically inactive	5,194	1,680	3,514	Economically inactive	3,073	1,008	2,065
White	15,442	7,384	8,058	White	9,472	4,587	4,885
Other ethnic group	1,213	617	596	Other ethnic group	1,108	562	546
	Bath				**Kingswood**		
TOTAL PERSONS	**1,725**	**781**	**944**	**TOTAL PERSONS**	**711**	**340**	**371**
0 - 15	174	87	87	0 - 15	93	43	50
16 - 17	20	12	8	16 - 17	15	6	9
18 - 29	440	206	234	18 - 29	151	78	73
30 - 44	333	179	154	30 - 44	153	82	71
45 up to pensionable age	320	158	162	45 up to pensionable age	145	84	61
Pensionable age and over	438	139	299	Pensionable age and over	154	47	107
Single	770	369	401	Single	268	139	129
Married	652	328	324	Married	292	147	145
Widowed or divorced	303	84	219	Widowed or divorced	151	54	97
With limiting long-term illness	192	92	100	With limiting long-term illness	84	39	45
In employment	798	420	378	In employment	360	206	154
Unemployed	83	52	31	Unemployed	33	20	13
Economically inactive	670	222	448	Economically inactive	225	71	154
White	1,684	758	926	White	693	327	366
Other ethnic group	41	23	18	Other ethnic group	18	13	5

18. Imputed residents of wholly absent households

Age, marital status, long-term illness, economic position and ethnic group	TOTAL PERSONS	Males	Females
a	b	c	d
	Northavon		
TOTAL PERSONS	**1,083**	**524**	**559**
0 - 15	156	74	82
16 - 17	18	11	7
18 - 29	254	124	130
30 - 44	226	113	113
45 up to pensionable age	221	134	87
Pensionable age and over	208	68	140
Single	401	211	190
Married	540	266	274
Widowed or divorced	142	47	95
With limiting long-term illness	106	42	64
In employment	585	331	254
Unemployed	39	27	12
Economically inactive	303	92	211
White	1,064	516	548
Other ethnic group	19	8	11
	Wansdyke		
TOTAL PERSONS	**597**	**285**	**312**
0 - 15	94	52	42
16 - 17	8	5	3
18 - 29	111	58	53
30 - 44	105	56	49
45 up to pensionable age	133	68	65
Pensionable age and over	146	46	100
Single	213	117	96
Married	277	139	138
Widowed or divorced	107	29	78
With limiting long-term illness	58	25	33
In employment	268	156	112
Unemployed	19	11	8
Economically inactive	216	66	150
White	595	284	311
Other ethnic group	2	1	1

Age, marital status, long-term illness, economic position and ethnic group	TOTAL PERSONS	Males	Females
a	b	c	d
	Woodspring		
TOTAL PERSONS	**1,959**	**922**	**1,037**
0 - 15	248	135	113
16 - 17	27	17	10
18 - 29	428	213	215
30 - 44	354	185	169
45 up to pensionable age	387	221	166
Pensionable age and over	515	151	364
Single	710	374	336
Married	867	435	432
Widowed or divorced	382	113	269
With limiting long-term illness	292	124	168
In employment	912	501	411
Unemployed	92	65	27
Economically inactive	707	221	486
White	1,934	912	1,022
Other ethnic group	25	10	15

Table 19 Imputed households

19. Wholly absent households with imputed residents; imputed residents in such households

	TOTAL HOUSEHOLDS	Households with the following persons			TOTAL RESIDENTS
		1	2	3 or more	
a	b	c	d	e	f
	AVON				
ALL HOUSEHOLDS	**8,765**	**4,248**	**2,693**	**1,824**	**16,655**
Owner occupied	4,801	1,971	1,685	1,145	9,760
Rented privately	1,677	1,054	437	186	2,647
Rented from a housing association	530	356	107	67	838
Rented from a local authority or new town	1,584	783	421	380	3,055
Lacking or sharing use of a bath/shower and/or inside WC	416	368	35	13	487
No central heating	1,957	1,163	486	308	3,322
No car	3,366	2,294	691	381	5,134
1 person aged 16 and over with child(ren) aged 0 - 15	382		217	165	1,004
	Bath				
ALL HOUSEHOLDS	**996**	**511**	**342**	**143**	**1,725**
Owner occupied	515	247	193	75	915
Rented privately	256	154	75	27	393
Rented from a housing association	56	36	15	5	83
Rented from a local authority or new town	145	66	47	32	287
Lacking or sharing use of a bath/shower and/or inside WC	54	47	5	2	64
No central heating	192	137	43	12	263
No car	386	270	88	28	553
1 person aged 16 and over with child(ren) aged 0 - 15	32		21	11	80
	Bristol				
ALL HOUSEHOLDS	**5,452**	**2,628**	**1,614**	**1,210**	**10,580**
Owner occupied	2,594	1,018	890	686	5,488
Rented privately	1,146	723	291	132	1,836
Rented from a housing association	412	270	86	56	671
Rented from a local authority or new town	1,180	556	320	304	2,338
Lacking or sharing use of a bath/shower and/or inside WC	295	263	25	7	341
No central heating	1,402	792	357	253	2,496
No car	2,321	1,512	503	306	3,701
1 person aged 16 and over with child(ren) aged 0 - 15	298		163	135	799

19. Wholly absent households with imputed residents; imputed residents in such households

	TOTAL HOUSEHOLDS	Households with the following persons			TOTAL RESIDENTS
		1	2	3 or more	
a	b	c	d	e	f
	Kingswood				
ALL HOUSEHOLDS	**376**	**182**	**113**	**81**	**711**
Owner occupied	272	110	97	65	550
Rented privately	27	16	7	4	43
Rented from a housing association	11	9	-	2	16
Rented from a local authority or new town	64	46	9	9	97
Lacking or sharing use of a bath/shower and/or inside WC	7	7	-	-	7
No central heating	45	28	10	7	72
No car	110	86	11	13	154
1 person aged 16 and over with child(ren) aged 0 - 15	7		5	2	16
	Northavon				
ALL HOUSEHOLDS	**532**	**202**	**195**	**135**	**1,083**
Owner occupied	423	137	166	120	902
Rented privately	28	18	6	4	48
Rented from a housing association	16	12	3	1	22
Rented from a local authority or new town	56	30	19	7	94
Lacking or sharing use of a bath/shower and/or inside WC	7	7	-	-	7
No central heating	58	40	15	3	83
No car	112	75	28	9	162
1 person aged 16 and over with child(ren) aged 0 - 15	15		10	5	35
	Wansdyke				
ALL HOUSEHOLDS	**305**	**142**	**99**	**64**	**597**
Owner occupied	232	102	80	50	460
Rented privately	31	19	7	5	54
Rented from a housing association	3	1	1	1	8
Rented from a local authority or new town	36	18	11	7	69
Lacking or sharing use of a bath/shower and/or inside WC	8	5	1	2	13
No central heating	45	27	12	6	77
No car	70	62	5	3	90
1 person aged 16 and over with child(ren) aged 0 - 15	7		5	2	16

19. Wholly absent households with imputed residents; imputed residents in such households

	TOTAL HOUSEHOLDS	Households with the following persons			TOTAL RESIDENTS
		1	2	3 or more	
a	b	c	d	e	f
	Woodspring				
ALL HOUSEHOLDS	**1,104**	**583**	**330**	**191**	**1,959**
Owner occupied	765	357	259	149	1,445
Rented privately	189	124	51	14	273
Rented from a housing association	32	28	2	2	38
Rented from a local authority or new town	103	67	15	21	170
Lacking or sharing use of a bath/shower and/or inside WC	45	39	4	2	55
No central heating	215	139	49	27	331
No car	367	289	56	22	474
1 person aged 16 and over with child(ren) aged 0 - 15	23		13	10	58

20. Households with residents; residents in households

Amenities	All permanent	Tenure of households in permanent buildings: Owner occupied: Owned outright	Owner occupied: Buying	Rented privately: Furnished	Rented privately: Un-furnished	Rented with a job or business	Rented from a housing association	Rented from a local authority or new town	Non-permanent accommodation	No car
a	b	c	d	e	f	g	h	i	j	k
AVON										
TOTAL HOUSEHOLDS	**374,740**	**97,807**	**172,361**	**16,896**	**10,709**	**5,095**	**9,588**	**62,284**	**1,782**	**101,740**
Exclusive use of bath/shower	**371,040**	**97,280**	**172,190**	**14,791**	**10,264**	**5,053**	**9,362**	**62,100**	**1,646**	**99,144**
Exclusive use of inside WC	**370,400**	**97,016**	**172,098**	**14,698**	**10,174**	**5,033**	**9,350**	**62,031**	**1,612**	**98,750**
With central heating - all rooms	259,911	64,611	136,685	8,688	4,309	3,250	6,198	36,170	1,182	56,157
- some rooms	58,511	18,922	22,360	1,680	1,491	854	1,690	11,514	135	17,857
No central heating	51,978	13,483	13,053	4,330	4,374	929	1,462	14,347	295	24,736
Shared use of inside WC	**142**	**4**	**3**	**76**	**23**	**10**	**9**	**17**	**3**	**103**
With central heating - all rooms	68	2	3	30	3	8	6	16	1	50
- some rooms	8	-	-	3	3	2	-	-	-	5
No central heating	66	2	-	43	17	-	3	1	2	48
No inside WC	**498**	**260**	**89**	**17**	**67**	**10**	**3**	**52**	**31**	**291**
With central heating - all rooms	105	33	34	2	6	2	2	26	9	47
- some rooms	79	46	21	-	5	-	-	7	-	35
No central heating	314	181	34	15	56	8	1	19	22	209
Shared use of bath/shower	**2,881**	**105**	**92**	**2,063**	**237**	**27**	**216**	**141**	**16**	**1,917**
Exclusive use of inside WC	**250**	**27**	**8**	**45**	**26**	**-**	**86**	**58**	**1**	**193**
With central heating - all rooms	175	11	4	15	9	-	84	52	-	147
- some rooms	22	6	3	5	4	-	1	3	-	11
No central heating	53	10	1	25	13	-	1	3	1	35
Shared use of inside WC	**2,614**	**72**	**82**	**2,012**	**209**	**27**	**129**	**83**	**9**	**1,713**
With central heating - all rooms	952	30	59	606	74	20	92	71	5	563
- some rooms	149	16	11	91	13	1	13	4	-	87
No central heating	1,513	26	12	1,315	122	6	24	8	4	1,063
No inside WC	**17**	**6**	**2**	**6**	**2**	**-**	**1**	**-**	**6**	**11**
With central heating - all rooms	9	4	-	4	-	-	1	-	-	4
- some rooms	1	-	1	-	-	-	-	-	1	2
No central heating	7	2	1	2	2	-	-	-	5	5
No bath/shower	**819**	**422**	**79**	**42**	**208**	**15**	**10**	**43**	**120**	**679**
Exclusive use of inside WC	**383**	**185**	**49**	**23**	**74**	**8**	**6**	**38**	**28**	**303**
With central heating - all rooms	55	11	12	5	3	3	1	20	3	34
- some rooms	42	18	9	2	3	1	1	8	2	32
No central heating	286	156	28	16	68	4	4	10	23	237
Shared use of inside WC	**17**	**1**	**1**	**8**	**7**	**-**	**-**	**-**	**2**	**12**
With central heating - all rooms	-	-	-	-	-	-	-	-	-	-
- some rooms	-	-	-	-	-	-	-	-	-	-
No central heating	17	1	1	8	7	-	-	-	2	12
No inside WC	**419**	**236**	**29**	**11**	**127**	**7**	**4**	**5**	**90**	**364**
With central heating - all rooms	19	8	7	1	3	-	-	-	4	11
- some rooms	30	17	4	-	7	-	1	1	3	23
No central heating	370	211	18	10	117	7	3	4	83	330
No car	101,168	29,441	13,343	6,833	4,948	1,202	6,780	38,621	572	

20. Households with residents; residents in households

Amenities	All permanent	Tenure of households in permanent buildings							Non-permanent accomm-odation	No car
		Owner occupied		Rented privately		Rented with a job or business	Rented from a housing associa-tion	Rented from a local authority or new town		
		Owned outright	Buying	Furnished	Un-furnished					
a	b	c	d	e	f	g	h	i	j	k
				AVON - *continued*						
TOTAL PERSONS IN HOUSEHOLDS	**913,834**	**191,641**	**500,359**	**31,196**	**20,033**	**13,121**	**16,403**	**141,081**	**3,139**	**171,129**
Exclusive use of bath/shower	**909,051**	**190,897**	**499,972**	**28,791**	**19,411**	**13,060**	**16,155**	**140,765**	**2,851**	**167,996**
Exclusive use of inside WC	**907,927**	**190,465**	**499,737**	**28,675**	**19,273**	**13,027**	**16,139**	**140,611**	**2,790**	**167,411**
With central heating - all rooms	659,155	130,566	403,913	18,058	8,812	8,648	9,890	79,268	2,068	94,142
- some rooms	138,012	35,975	62,894	3,355	2,894	2,209	3,419	27,266	224	30,911
No central heating	110,760	23,924	32,930	7,262	7,567	2,170	2,830	34,077	498	42,358
Shared use of inside WC	**185**	**6**	**6**	**88**	**27**	**16**	**10**	**32**	**8**	**127**
With central heating - all rooms	98	2	6	35	5	13	7	30	1	67
- some rooms	11	-	-	4	4	3	-	-	-	6
No central heating	76	4	-	49	18	-	3	2	7	54
No inside WC	**939**	**426**	**229**	**28**	**111**	**17**	**6**	**122**	**53**	**458**
With central heating - all rooms	226	54	89	4	11	4	5	59	17	82
- some rooms	175	82	59	-	13	-	-	21	-	54
No central heating	538	290	81	24	87	13	1	42	36	322
Shared use of bath/shower	**3,595**	**175**	**227**	**2,350**	**335**	**33**	**238**	**237**	**28**	**2,245**
Exclusive use of inside WC	**322**	**40**	**29**	**56**	**38**	**-**	**90**	**69**	**3**	**214**
With central heating - all rooms	208	18	15	16	12	-	88	59	-	158
- some rooms	38	8	9	8	8	-	1	4	-	17
No central heating	76	14	5	32	18	-	1	6	3	39
Shared use of inside WC	**3,250**	**126**	**196**	**2,287**	**293**	**33**	**147**	**168**	**16**	**2,020**
With central heating - all rooms	1,315	55	139	732	124	25	102	138	9	750
- some rooms	218	29	33	108	20	1	13	14	-	109
No central heating	1,717	42	24	1,447	149	7	32	16	7	1,161
No inside WC	**23**	**9**	**2**	**7**	**4**	**-**	**1**	**-**	**9**	**11**
With central heating - all rooms	12	7	-	4	-	-	1	-	-	4
- some rooms	1	-	1	-	-	-	-	-	1	2
No central heating	10	2	1	3	4	-	-	-	8	5
No bath/shower	**1,188**	**569**	**160**	**55**	**287**	**28**	**10**	**79**	**260**	**888**
Exclusive use of inside WC	**560**	**241**	**97**	**31**	**104**	**13**	**6**	**68**	**70**	**390**
With central heating - all rooms	112	21	26	11	6	8	1	39	7	53
- some rooms	61	24	20	2	3	1	1	10	2	41
No central heating	387	196	51	18	95	4	4	19	61	296
Shared use of inside WC	**19**	**1**	**1**	**9**	**8**	**-**	**-**	**-**	**7**	**17**
With central heating - all rooms	-	-	-	-	-	-	-	-	-	-
- some rooms	-	-	-	-	-	-	-	-	-	-
No central heating	19	1	1	9	8	-	-	-	7	17
No inside WC	**609**	**327**	**62**	**15**	**175**	**15**	**4**	**11**	**183**	**481**
With central heating - all rooms	39	12	17	2	8	-	-	-	8	18
- some rooms	47	23	12	-	9	-	1	2	5	29
No central heating	523	292	33	13	158	15	3	9	170	434
No car	170,334	40,620	27,687	10,446	7,312	2,135	9,967	72,167	795	

20. Households with residents; residents in households

Amenities	All permanent	Tenure of households in permanent buildings: Owner occupied: Owned outright	Owner occupied: Buying	Rented privately: Furnished	Rented privately: Un-furnished	Rented with a job or business	Rented from a housing association	Rented from a local authority or new town	Non-permanent accomm-odation	No car
a	b	c	d	e	f	g	h	i	j	k
				Bath						
TOTAL HOUSEHOLDS	**34,039**	**9,623**	**12,369**	**2,530**	**1,665**	**476**	**1,167**	**6,209**	**89**	**12,148**
Exclusive use of bath/shower	**33,550**	**9,568**	**12,343**	**2,248**	**1,596**	**475**	**1,120**	**6,200**	**83**	**11,794**
Exclusive use of inside WC	**33,486**	**9,546**	**12,333**	**2,241**	**1,587**	**473**	**1,116**	**6,190**	**82**	**11,759**
With central heating - all rooms	22,695	6,258	9,575	1,403	667	324	789	3,679	64	6,720
- some rooms	6,362	2,074	1,854	238	227	71	178	1,720	9	2,585
No central heating	4,429	1,214	904	600	693	78	149	791	9	2,454
Shared use of inside WC	**21**	**-**	**-**	**6**	**7**	**1**	**2**	**5**	**-**	**11**
With central heating - all rooms	11	-	-	3	-	1	2	5	-	6
- some rooms	1	-	-	1	-	-	-	-	-	-
No central heating	9	-	-	2	7	-	-	-	-	5
No inside WC	**43**	**22**	**10**	**1**	**2**	**1**	**2**	**5**	**1**	**24**
With central heating - all rooms	12	4	4	-	-	-	1	3	-	5
- some rooms	6	3	1	-	-	-	-	2	-	5
No central heating	25	15	5	1	2	1	1	-	1	14
Shared use of bath/shower	**399**	**19**	**15**	**270**	**40**	**1**	**47**	**7**	**1**	**272**
Exclusive use of inside WC	**52**	**4**	**1**	**7**	**7**	**-**	**33**	**-**	**-**	**42**
With central heating - all rooms	39	1	1	3	1	-	33	-	-	32
- some rooms	2	-	-	1	1	-	-	-	-	1
No central heating	11	3	-	3	5	-	-	-	-	9
Shared use of inside WC	**345**	**14**	**14**	**263**	**32**	**1**	**14**	**7**	**1**	**229**
With central heating - all rooms	97	4	9	67	6	1	5	5	1	53
- some rooms	21	2	2	13	2	-	-	2	-	13
No central heating	227	8	3	183	24	-	9	-	-	163
No inside WC	**2**	**1**	**-**	**-**	**1**	**-**	**-**	**-**	**-**	**1**
With central heating - all rooms	1	1	-	-	-	-	-	-	-	-
- some rooms	-	-	-	-	-	-	-	-	-	-
No central heating	1	-	-	-	1	-	-	-	-	1
No bath/shower	**90**	**36**	**11**	**12**	**29**	**-**	**-**	**2**	**5**	**82**
Exclusive use of inside WC	**52**	**22**	**7**	**8**	**13**	**-**	**-**	**2**	**1**	**46**
With central heating - all rooms	5	1	4	-	-	-	-	-	-	3
- some rooms	5	1	1	1	2	-	-	-	1	6
No central heating	42	20	2	7	11	-	-	2	-	37
Shared use of inside WC	**4**	**-**	**-**	**2**	**2**	**-**	**-**	**-**	**-**	**3**
With central heating - all rooms	-	-	-	-	-	-	-	-	-	-
- some rooms	-	-	-	-	-	-	-	-	-	-
No central heating	4	-	-	2	2	-	-	-	-	3
No inside WC	**34**	**14**	**4**	**2**	**14**	**-**	**-**	**-**	**4**	**33**
With central heating - all rooms	1	-	-	1	-	-	-	-	-	-
- some rooms	-	-	-	-	-	-	-	-	-	-
No central heating	33	14	4	1	14	-	-	-	4	33
No car	12,112	3,345	1,520	1,114	873	160	885	4,215	36	

20. Households with residents; residents in households

Amenities	All permanent	Tenure of households in permanent buildings							Non-permanent accommodation	No car
		Owner occupied		Rented privately		Rented with a job or business	Rented from a housing association	Rented from a local authority or new town		
		Owned outright	Buying	Furnished	Unfurnished					
a	b	c	d	e	f	g	h	i	j	k
				Bath – *continued*						
TOTAL PERSONS IN HOUSEHOLDS	**76,745**	**18,021**	**34,404**	**4,672**	**2,856**	**1,144**	**1,856**	**13,792**	**131**	**19,883**
Exclusive use of bath/shower	**76,129**	**17,949**	**34,344**	**4,362**	**2,762**	**1,143**	**1,801**	**13,768**	**123**	**19,463**
Exclusive use of inside WC	**76,020**	**17,919**	**34,318**	**4,352**	**2,751**	**1,141**	**1,794**	**13,745**	**122**	**19,414**
With central heating - all rooms	53,233	12,031	27,063	2,894	1,219	811	1,220	7,995	92	11,068
- some rooms	14,506	3,773	5,118	472	418	163	330	4,232	13	4,606
No central heating	8,281	2,115	2,137	986	1,114	167	244	1,518	17	3,740
Shared use of inside WC	**33**	**-**	**-**	**9**	**7**	**1**	**3**	**13**	**-**	**11**
With central heating - all rooms	20	-	-	3	-	1	3	13	-	6
- some rooms	2	-	-	2	-	-	-	-	-	-
No central heating	11	-	-	4	7	-	-	-	-	5
No inside WC	**76**	**30**	**26**	**1**	**4**	**1**	**4**	**10**	**1**	**38**
With central heating - all rooms	27	6	12	-	-	-	3	6	-	9
- some rooms	12	7	1	-	-	-	-	4	-	8
No central heating	37	17	13	1	4	1	1	-	1	21
Shared use of bath/shower	**490**	**30**	**35**	**294**	**57**	**1**	**55**	**18**	**3**	**312**
Exclusive use of inside WC	**62**	**4**	**5**	**7**	**10**	**-**	**36**	**-**	**-**	**44**
With central heating - all rooms	46	1	5	3	1	-	36	-	-	34
- some rooms	3	-	-	1	2	-	-	-	-	1
No central heating	13	3	-	3	7	-	-	-	-	9
Shared use of inside WC	**425**	**24**	**30**	**287**	**46**	**1**	**19**	**18**	**3**	**267**
With central heating - all rooms	141	5	22	73	16	1	10	14	3	78
- some rooms	32	2	5	18	3	-	-	4	-	17
No central heating	252	17	3	196	27	-	9	-	-	172
No inside WC	**3**	**2**	**-**	**-**	**1**	**-**	**-**	**-**	**-**	**1**
With central heating - all rooms	2	2	-	-	-	-	-	-	-	-
- some rooms	-	-	-	-	-	-	-	-	-	-
No central heating	1	-	-	-	1	-	-	-	-	1
No bath/shower	**126**	**42**	**25**	**16**	**37**	**-**	**-**	**6**	**5**	**108**
Exclusive use of inside WC	**76**	**26**	**15**	**10**	**19**	**-**	**-**	**6**	**1**	**61**
With central heating - all rooms	11	1	10	-	-	-	-	-	-	7
- some rooms	8	2	3	1	2	-	-	-	1	9
No central heating	57	23	2	9	17	-	-	6	-	45
Shared use of inside WC	**5**	**-**	**-**	**3**	**2**	**-**	**-**	**-**	**-**	**4**
With central heating - all rooms	-	-	-	-	-	-	-	-	-	-
- some rooms	-	-	-	-	-	-	-	-	-	-
No central heating	5	-	-	3	2	-	-	-	-	4
No inside WC	**45**	**16**	**10**	**3**	**16**	**-**	**-**	**-**	**4**	**43**
With central heating - all rooms	2	-	-	2	-	-	-	-	-	-
- some rooms	-	-	-	-	-	-	-	-	-	-
No central heating	43	16	10	1	16	-	-	-	4	43
No car	19,841	4,632	2,899	1,697	1,245	268	1,236	7,864	42	

20. Households with residents; residents in households

Amenities	All permanent	Tenure of households in permanent buildings							Non-permanent accommodation	No car
		Owner occupied		Rented privately		Rented with a job or business	Rented from a housing association	Rented from a local authority or new town		
		Owned outright	Buying	Furnished	Unfurnished					
a	b	c	d	e	f	g	h	i	j	k
				Bristol						
TOTAL HOUSEHOLDS	**156,651**	**36,448**	**63,222**	**9,973**	**4,550**	**1,927**	**5,808**	**34,723**	**127**	**53,558**
Exclusive use of bath/shower	**154,380**	**36,166**	**63,146**	**8,513**	**4,324**	**1,904**	**5,655**	**34,672**	**104**	**51,995**
Exclusive use of inside WC	**154,003**	**35,995**	**63,101**	**8,450**	**4,278**	**1,897**	**5,648**	**34,634**	**100**	**51,736**
With central heating - all rooms	99,866	21,352	48,299	4,904	1,736	1,230	3,663	18,682	56	27,459
- some rooms	24,593	7,450	8,523	828	484	280	870	6,158	21	9,000
No central heating	29,544	7,193	6,279	2,718	2,058	387	1,115	9,794	23	15,277
Shared use of inside WC	**85**	**3**	**3**	**52**	**9**	**4**	**7**	**7**	**1**	**61**
With central heating - all rooms	35	1	3	16	1	3	4	7	-	24
- some rooms	5	-	-	2	2	1	-	-	-	3
No central heating	45	2	-	34	6	-	3	-	1	34
No inside WC	**292**	**168**	**42**	**11**	**37**	**3**	**-**	**31**	**3**	**198**
With central heating - all rooms	55	17	18	2	2	1	-	15	2	32
- some rooms	39	26	9	-	1	-	-	3	-	20
No central heating	198	125	15	9	34	2	-	13	1	146
Shared use of bath/shower	**1,880**	**55**	**49**	**1,443**	**152**	**18**	**143**	**20**	**1**	**1,233**
Exclusive use of inside WC	**103**	**15**	**3**	**18**	**11**	**-**	**49**	**7**	**-**	**77**
With central heating - all rooms	68	6	1	5	5	-	47	4	-	56
- some rooms	14	5	1	3	3	-	1	1	-	8
No central heating	21	4	1	10	3	-	1	2	-	13
Shared use of inside WC	**1,769**	**38**	**44**	**1,422**	**140**	**18**	**94**	**13**	**1**	**1,152**
With central heating - all rooms	624	16	31	437	54	11	69	6	-	372
- some rooms	105	11	7	63	9	1	13	1	-	60
No central heating	1,040	11	6	922	77	6	12	6	1	720
No inside WC	**8**	**2**	**2**	**3**	**1**	**-**	**-**	**-**	**-**	**4**
With central heating - all rooms	2	1	-	1	-	-	-	-	-	1
- some rooms	1	-	1	-	-	-	-	-	-	1
No central heating	5	1	1	2	1	-	-	-	-	2
No bath/shower	**391**	**227**	**27**	**17**	**74**	**5**	**10**	**31**	**22**	**330**
Exclusive use of inside WC	**194**	**102**	**23**	**8**	**26**	**3**	**6**	**26**	**4**	**151**
With central heating - all rooms	30	6	2	4	2	1	1	14	1	21
- some rooms	22	9	3	-	1	1	1	7	1	15
No central heating	142	87	18	4	23	1	4	5	2	115
Shared use of inside WC	**9**	**1**	**-**	**4**	**4**	**-**	**-**	**-**	**1**	**9**
With central heating - all rooms	-	-	-	-	-	-	-	-	-	-
- some rooms	-	-	-	-	-	-	-	-	-	-
No central heating	9	1	-	4	4	-	-	-	1	9
No inside WC	**188**	**124**	**4**	**5**	**44**	**2**	**4**	**5**	**17**	**170**
With central heating - all rooms	7	5	-	-	2	-	-	-	-	7
- some rooms	12	7	-	-	3	-	1	1	1	11
No central heating	169	112	4	5	39	2	3	4	16	152
No car	53,508	13,015	7,088	4,115	2,311	623	4,247	22,109	50	

20. Households with residents; residents in households

Amenities	All permanent	Tenure of households in permanent buildings							Non-permanent accomm-odation	No car
		Owner occupied		Rented privately		Rented with a job or business	Rented from a housing associa-tion	Rented from a local authority or new town		
		Owned outright	Buying	Furnished	Un-furnished					
a	b	c	d	e	f	g	h	i	j	k
				Bristol - continued						
TOTAL PERSONS IN HOUSEHOLDS	**369,899**	**71,192**	**177,505**	**18,197**	**8,233**	**4,649**	**9,902**	**80,221**	**232**	**93,883**
Exclusive use of bath/shower	**367,064**	**70,795**	**177,332**	**16,535**	**7,922**	**4,617**	**9,739**	**80,124**	**192**	**92,047**
Exclusive use of inside WC	**366,425**	**70,523**	**177,215**	**16,456**	**7,851**	**4,608**	**9,732**	**80,040**	**179**	**91,651**
With central heating - all rooms	245,533	43,617	137,576	10,163	3,456	3,053	5,861	41,807	105	48,338
- some rooms	56,843	14,059	23,540	1,692	894	654	1,677	14,327	34	15,929
No central heating	64,049	12,847	16,099	4,601	3,501	901	2,194	23,906	40	27,384
Shared use of inside WC	**105**	**5**	**6**	**58**	**12**	**6**	**7**	**11**	**4**	**74**
With central heating - all rooms	48	1	6	19	3	4	4	11	-	33
- some rooms	6	-	-	2	2	2	-	-	-	3
No central heating	51	4	-	37	7	-	3	-	4	38
No inside WC	**534**	**267**	**111**	**21**	**59**	**3**	**-**	**73**	**9**	**322**
With central heating - all rooms	113	26	46	4	2	1	-	34	6	57
- some rooms	83	43	27	-	3	-	-	10	-	28
No central heating	338	198	38	17	54	2	-	29	3	237
Shared use of bath/shower	**2,272**	**89**	**126**	**1,638**	**205**	**22**	**153**	**39**	**1**	**1,398**
Exclusive use of inside WC	**138**	**25**	**13**	**22**	**16**	**-**	**50**	**12**	**-**	**87**
With central heating - all rooms	81	11	4	5	7	-	48	6	-	59
- some rooms	25	6	4	6	6	-	1	2	-	14
No central heating	32	8	5	11	3	-	1	4	-	14
Shared use of inside WC	**2,122**	**61**	**111**	**1,612**	**186**	**22**	**103**	**27**	**1**	**1,307**
With central heating - all rooms	796	28	72	526	77	14	70	9	-	455
- some rooms	148	18	25	73	13	1	13	5	-	70
No central heating	1,178	15	14	1,013	96	7	20	13	1	782
No inside WC	**12**	**3**	**2**	**4**	**3**	**-**	**-**	**-**	**-**	**4**
With central heating - all rooms	3	2	-	1	-	-	-	-	-	1
- some rooms	1	-	1	-	-	-	-	-	-	1
No central heating	8	1	1	3	3	-	-	-	-	2
No bath/shower	**563**	**308**	**47**	**24**	**106**	**10**	**10**	**58**	**39**	**438**
Exclusive use of inside WC	**282**	**136**	**40**	**14**	**35**	**4**	**6**	**47**	**6**	**190**
With central heating - all rooms	58	10	3	10	2	2	1	30	2	30
- some rooms	35	14	9	-	1	1	1	9	1	20
No central heating	189	112	28	4	32	1	4	8	3	140
Shared use of inside WC	**10**	**1**	**-**	**4**	**5**	**-**	**-**	**-**	**4**	**13**
With central heating - all rooms	-	-	-	-	-	-	-	-	-	-
- some rooms	-	-	-	-	-	-	-	-	-	-
No central heating	10	1	-	4	5	-	-	-	4	13
No inside WC	**271**	**171**	**7**	**6**	**66**	**6**	**4**	**11**	**29**	**235**
With central heating - all rooms	13	7	-	-	6	-	-	-	-	13
- some rooms	19	11	-	-	5	-	1	2	2	17
No central heating	239	153	7	6	55	6	3	9	27	205
No car	93,809	18,627	14,934	6,290	3,493	1,132	6,421	42,912	74	

20. Households with residents; residents in households

Amenities	All permanent	Tenure of households in permanent buildings							Non-permanent accommodation	No car
		Owner occupied		Rented privately		Rented with a job or business	Rented from a housing association	Rented from a local authority or new town		
		Owned outright	Buying	Furnished	Unfurnished					
a	b	c	d	e	f	g	h	i	j	k
				Kingswood						
TOTAL HOUSEHOLDS	**34,535**	**9,920**	**18,210**	**547**	**499**	**240**	**619**	**4,500**	**122**	**7,045**
Exclusive use of bath/shower	**34,417**	**9,889**	**18,198**	**504**	**475**	**239**	**618**	**4,494**	**114**	**6,967**
Exclusive use of inside WC	**34,388**	**9,878**	**18,195**	**502**	**466**	**236**	**618**	**4,493**	**113**	**6,945**
With central heating - all rooms	27,810	7,156	15,351	347	231	187	382	4,156	75	5,183
- some rooms	4,190	1,698	1,892	59	61	25	207	248	4	872
No central heating	2,388	1,024	952	96	174	24	29	89	34	890
Shared use of inside WC	**9**	**1**	**-**	**2**	**3**	**3**	**-**	**-**	**-**	**8**
With central heating - all rooms	8	1	-	2	2	3	-	-	-	7
- some rooms	1	-	-	-	1	-	-	-	-	1
No central heating	-	-	-	-	-	-	-	-	-	-
No inside WC	**20**	**10**	**3**	**-**	**6**	**-**	**-**	**1**	**1**	**14**
With central heating - all rooms	5	1	2	-	1	-	-	1	-	2
- some rooms	3	2	1	-	-	-	-	-	-	3
No central heating	12	7	-	-	5	-	-	-	1	9
Shared use of bath/shower	**57**	**1**	**5**	**42**	**4**	**-**	**1**	**4**	**1**	**29**
Exclusive use of inside WC	**5**	**1**	**1**	**1**	**1**	**-**	**1**	**-**	**-**	**2**
With central heating - all rooms	4	1	-	1	1	-	1	-	-	2
- some rooms	1	-	1	-	-	-	-	-	-	-
No central heating	-	-	-	-	-	-	-	-	-	-
Shared use of inside WC	**52**	**-**	**4**	**41**	**3**	**-**	**-**	**4**	**1**	**27**
With central heating - all rooms	37	-	4	29	2	-	-	2	-	17
- some rooms	6	-	-	4	1	-	-	1	-	4
No central heating	9	-	-	8	-	-	-	1	1	6
No inside WC	**-**	**-**	**-**	**-**	**-**	**-**	**-**	**-**	**-**	**-**
With central heating - all rooms	-	-	-	-	-	-	-	-	-	-
- some rooms	-	-	-	-	-	-	-	-	-	-
No central heating	-	-	-	-	-	-	-	-	-	-
No bath/shower	**61**	**30**	**7**	**1**	**20**	**1**	**-**	**2**	**7**	**49**
Exclusive use of inside WC	**24**	**13**	**2**	**-**	**6**	**1**	**-**	**2**	**1**	**19**
With central heating - all rooms	5	-	1	-	1	1	-	2	-	2
- some rooms	2	2	-	-	-	-	-	-	-	2
No central heating	17	11	1	-	5	-	-	-	1	15
Shared use of inside WC	**1**	**-**	**-**	**1**	**-**	**-**	**-**	**-**	**-**	**-**
With central heating - all rooms	-	-	-	-	-	-	-	-	-	-
- some rooms	-	-	-	-	-	-	-	-	-	-
No central heating	1	-	-	1	-	-	-	-	-	-
No inside WC	**36**	**17**	**5**	**-**	**14**	**-**	**-**	**-**	**6**	**30**
With central heating - all rooms	3	-	2	-	1	-	-	-	-	-
- some rooms	3	1	1	-	1	-	-	-	1	2
No central heating	30	16	2	-	12	-	-	-	5	28
No car	7,007	2,566	949	164	221	59	362	2,686	38	

20. Households with residents; residents in households

Amenities	All permanent	Tenure of households in permanent buildings							Non-permanent accomm-odation	No car
		Owner occupied		Rented privately		Rented with a job or business	Rented from a housing associa-tion	Rented from a local authority or new town		
		Owned outright	Buying	Furnished	Un-furnished					
a	b	c	d	e	f	g	h	i	j	k
			Kingswood - *continued*							
TOTAL PERSONS IN HOUSEHOLDS	**88,703**	**20,328**	**54,875**	**1,127**	**1,038**	**602**	**1,214**	**9,519**	**213**	**11,280**
Exclusive use of bath/shower	**88,531**	**20,290**	**54,842**	**1,078**	**1,005**	**598**	**1,213**	**9,505**	**204**	**11,181**
Exclusive use of inside WC	**88,485**	**20,276**	**54,836**	**1,075**	**991**	**591**	**1,213**	**9,503**	**203**	**11,149**
With central heating - all rooms	73,364	15,137	47,104	785	539	484	612	8,703	132	8,434
- some rooms	10,281	3,405	5,402	119	128	63	558	606	12	1,424
No central heating	4,840	1,734	2,330	171	324	44	43	194	59	1,291
Shared use of inside WC	**15**	**1**	**-**	**3**	**4**	**7**	**-**	**-**	**-**	**14**
With central heating - all rooms	13	1	-	3	2	7	-	-	-	12
- some rooms	2	-	-	-	2	-	-	-	-	2
No central heating	-	-	-	-	-	-	-	-	-	-
No inside WC	**31**	**13**	**6**	**-**	**10**	**-**	**-**	**2**	**1**	**18**
With central heating - all rooms	9	2	4	-	1	-	-	2	-	2
- some rooms	4	2	2	-	-	-	-	-	-	4
No central heating	18	9	-	-	9	-	-	-	1	12
Shared use of bath/shower	**80**	**1**	**13**	**48**	**5**	**-**	**1**	**12**	**1**	**43**
Exclusive use of inside WC	**7**	**1**	**2**	**1**	**2**	**-**	**1**	**-**	**-**	**3**
With central heating - all rooms	5	1	-	1	2	-	1	-	-	3
- some rooms	2	-	2	-	-	-	-	-	-	-
No central heating	-	-	-	-	-	-	-	-	-	-
Shared use of inside WC	**73**	**-**	**11**	**47**	**3**	**-**	**-**	**12**	**1**	**40**
With central heating - all rooms	52	-	11	34	2	-	-	5	-	25
- some rooms	11	-	-	5	1	-	-	5	-	8
No central heating	10	-	-	8	-	-	-	2	1	7
No inside WC	**-**	**-**	**-**	**-**	**-**	**-**	**-**	**-**	**-**	**-**
With central heating - all rooms	-	-	-	-	-	-	-	-	-	-
- some rooms	-	-	-	-	-	-	-	-	-	-
No central heating	-	-	-	-	-	-	-	-	-	-
No bath/shower	**92**	**37**	**20**	**1**	**28**	**4**	**-**	**2**	**8**	**56**
Exclusive use of inside WC	**39**	**15**	**8**	**-**	**10**	**4**	**-**	**2**	**1**	**20**
With central heating - all rooms	12	-	2	-	4	4	-	2	-	2
- some rooms	2	2	-	-	-	-	-	-	-	2
No central heating	25	13	6	-	6	-	-	-	1	16
Shared use of inside WC	**1**	**-**	**-**	**1**	**-**	**-**	**-**	**-**	**-**	**-**
With central heating - all rooms	-	-	-	-	-	-	-	-	-	-
- some rooms	-	-	-	-	-	-	-	-	-	-
No central heating	1	-	-	1	-	-	-	-	-	-
No inside WC	**52**	**22**	**12**	**-**	**18**	**-**	**-**	**-**	**7**	**36**
With central heating - all rooms	6	-	4	-	2	-	-	-	-	-
- some rooms	5	1	3	-	1	-	-	-	2	2
No central heating	41	21	5	-	15	-	-	-	5	34
No car	11,231	3,449	2,051	280	340	109	528	4,474	49	

20. Households with residents; residents in households

Amenities	All permanent	Tenure of households in permanent buildings: Owner occupied: Owned outright	Owner occupied: Buying	Rented privately: Furnished	Rented privately: Un-furnished	Rented with a job or business	Rented from a housing associa-tion	Rented from a local authority or new town	Non-permanent accomm-odation	No car
a	b	c	d	e	f	g	h	i	j	k
					Northavon					
TOTAL HOUSEHOLDS	**49,086**	**11,522**	**29,323**	**824**	**1,077**	**760**	**596**	**4,984**	**540**	**7,332**
Exclusive use of bath/shower	**48,949**	**11,468**	**29,305**	**804**	**1,047**	**758**	**587**	**4,980**	**496**	**7,247**
Exclusive use of inside WC	**48,914**	**11,453**	**29,295**	**803**	**1,044**	**756**	**586**	**4,977**	**488**	**7,237**
With central heating - all rooms	36,607	8,117	23,866	537	468	464	402	2,753	366	4,289
- some rooms	8,255	2,236	3,908	151	205	149	114	1,492	39	1,660
No central heating	4,052	1,100	1,521	115	371	143	70	732	83	1,288
Shared use of inside WC	**2**	**-**	**-**	**1**	**-**	**-**	**-**	**1**	**1**	**2**
With central heating - all rooms	2	-	-	1	-	-	-	1	1	2
- some rooms	-	-	-	-	-	-	-	-	-	-
No central heating	-	-	-	-	-	-	-	-	-	-
No inside WC	**33**	**15**	**10**	**-**	**3**	**2**	**1**	**2**	**7**	**8**
With central heating - all rooms	9	4	3	-	-	-	1	1	1	-
- some rooms	10	4	5	-	-	-	-	1	-	2
No central heating	14	7	2	-	3	2	-	-	6	6
Shared use of bath/shower	**53**	**5**	**7**	**19**	**10**	**-**	**9**	**3**	**2**	**18**
Exclusive use of inside WC	**7**	**-**	**1**	**2**	**1**	**-**	**1**	**2**	**-**	**3**
With central heating - all rooms	3	-	-	1	-	-	1	1	-	2
- some rooms	2	-	1	-	-	-	-	1	-	-
No central heating	2	-	-	1	1	-	-	-	-	1
Shared use of inside WC	**44**	**3**	**6**	**17**	**9**	**-**	**8**	**1**	**2**	**14**
With central heating - all rooms	26	3	5	7	3	-	7	1	1	9
- some rooms	2	-	-	2	-	-	-	-	-	-
No central heating	16	-	1	8	6	-	1	-	1	5
No inside WC	**2**	**2**	**-**	**-**	**-**	**-**	**-**	**-**	**-**	**1**
With central heating - all rooms	2	2	-	-	-	-	-	-	-	1
- some rooms	-	-	-	-	-	-	-	-	-	-
No central heating	-	-	-	-	-	-	-	-	-	-
No bath/shower	**84**	**49**	**11**	**1**	**20**	**2**	**-**	**1**	**42**	**67**
Exclusive use of inside WC	**27**	**18**	**4**	**1**	**3**	**-**	**-**	**1**	**15**	**22**
With central heating - all rooms	3	2	1	-	-	-	-	-	1	-
- some rooms	4	2	2	-	-	-	-	-	-	3
No central heating	20	14	1	1	3	-	-	1	14	19
Shared use of inside WC	**-**	**-**	**-**	**-**	**-**	**-**	**-**	**-**	**1**	**-**
With central heating - all rooms	-	-	-	-	-	-	-	-	-	-
- some rooms	-	-	-	-	-	-	-	-	-	-
No central heating	-	-	-	-	-	-	-	-	1	-
No inside WC	**57**	**31**	**7**	**-**	**17**	**2**	**-**	**-**	**26**	**45**
With central heating - all rooms	2	-	2	-	-	-	-	-	2	1
- some rooms	5	2	2	-	1	-	-	-	1	2
No central heating	50	29	3	-	16	2	-	-	23	42
No car	7,190	2,432	1,154	159	345	82	335	2,683	142	

20. Households with residents; residents in households

Amenities	All permanent	Tenure of households in permanent buildings: Owner occupied: Owned outright	Owner occupied: Buying	Rented privately: Furnished	Rented privately: Unfurnished	Rented with a job or business	Rented from a housing association	Rented from a local authority or new town	Non-permanent accommodation	No car
a	b	c	d	e	f	g	h	i	j	k
Northavon - *continued*										
TOTAL PERSONS IN HOUSEHOLDS	**128,037**	**23,662**	**86,058**	**1,742**	**2,295**	**2,085**	**1,128**	**11,067**	**1,047**	**11,708**
Exclusive use of bath/shower	**127,819**	**23,579**	**86,021**	**1,717**	**2,246**	**2,079**	**1,115**	**11,062**	**915**	**11,580**
Exclusive use of inside WC	**127,740**	**23,549**	**85,997**	**1,716**	**2,241**	**2,074**	**1,113**	**11,050**	**898**	**11,562**
With central heating - all rooms	98,723	17,004	71,547	1,192	1,077	1,311	720	5,872	681	6,763
- some rooms	20,300	4,474	10,866	303	428	405	236	3,588	64	2,831
No central heating	8,717	2,071	3,584	221	736	358	157	1,590	153	1,968
Shared use of inside WC	**3**	**-**	**-**	**1**	**-**	**-**	**-**	**2**	**1**	**3**
With central heating - all rooms	3	-	-	1	-	-	-	2	1	3
- some rooms	-	-	-	-	-	-	-	-	-	-
No central heating	-	-	-	-	-	-	-	-	-	-
No inside WC	**76**	**30**	**24**	**-**	**5**	**5**	**2**	**10**	**16**	**15**
With central heating - all rooms	25	10	8	-	-	-	2	5	4	-
- some rooms	25	8	12	-	-	-	-	5	-	6
No central heating	26	12	4	-	5	5	-	-	12	9
Shared use of bath/shower	**84**	**10**	**13**	**24**	**21**	**-**	**13**	**3**	**3**	**28**
Exclusive use of inside WC	**12**	**-**	**3**	**4**	**2**	**-**	**1**	**2**	**-**	**4**
With central heating - all rooms	3	-	-	1	-	-	1	1	-	2
- some rooms	4	-	3	-	-	-	-	1	-	-
No central heating	5	-	-	3	2	-	-	-	-	2
Shared use of inside WC	**69**	**7**	**10**	**20**	**19**	**-**	**12**	**1**	**3**	**23**
With central heating - all rooms	51	7	9	10	13	-	11	1	2	18
- some rooms	2	-	-	2	-	-	-	-	-	-
No central heating	16	-	1	8	6	-	1	-	1	5
No inside WC	**3**	**3**	**-**	**-**	**-**	**-**	**-**	**-**	**-**	**1**
With central heating - all rooms	3	3	-	-	-	-	-	-	-	1
- some rooms	-	-	-	-	-	-	-	-	-	-
No central heating	-	-	-	-	-	-	-	-	-	-
No bath/shower	**134**	**73**	**24**	**1**	**28**	**6**	**-**	**2**	**129**	**100**
Exclusive use of inside WC	**38**	**26**	**6**	**1**	**3**	**-**	**-**	**2**	**50**	**37**
With central heating - all rooms	8	6	2	-	-	-	-	-	3	-
- some rooms	5	2	3	-	-	-	-	-	-	3
No central heating	25	18	1	1	3	-	-	2	47	34
Shared use of inside WC	**-**	**-**	**-**	**-**	**-**	**-**	**-**	**-**	**3**	**-**
With central heating - all rooms	-	-	-	-	-	-	-	-	-	-
- some rooms	-	-	-	-	-	-	-	-	-	-
No central heating	-	-	-	-	-	-	-	-	3	-
No inside WC	**96**	**47**	**18**	**-**	**25**	**6**	**-**	**-**	**76**	**63**
With central heating - all rooms	6	-	6	-	-	-	-	-	5	1
- some rooms	12	3	8	-	1	-	-	-	1	2
No central heating	78	44	4	-	24	6	-	-	70	60
No car	11,490	3,213	2,375	278	508	144	475	4,497	218	

20. Households with residents; residents in households

Amenities	All permanent	Tenure of households in permanent buildings: Owner occupied: Owned outright	Owner occupied: Buying	Rented privately: Furnished	Rented privately: Un-furnished	Rented with a job or business	Rented from a housing association	Rented from a local authority or new town	Non-permanent accommodation	No car
a	b	c	d	e	f	g	h	i	j	k
					Wansdyke					
TOTAL HOUSEHOLDS	**30,659**	**9,326**	**14,827**	**570**	**842**	**537**	**289**	**4,268**	**155**	**5,717**
Exclusive use of bath/shower	**30,510**	**9,285**	**14,813**	**553**	**806**	**532**	**289**	**4,232**	**131**	**5,606**
Exclusive use of inside WC	**30,458**	**9,267**	**14,802**	**551**	**791**	**532**	**289**	**4,226**	**116**	**5,587**
With central heating - all rooms	22,220	6,550	12,000	365	317	328	158	2,502	77	3,234
- some rooms	4,786	1,695	1,856	86	157	102	100	790	9	1,093
No central heating	3,452	1,022	946	100	317	102	31	934	30	1,260
Shared use of inside WC	**4**	**-**	**-**	**1**	**3**	**-**	**-**	**-**	**-**	**3**
With central heating - all rooms	-	-	-	-	-	-	-	-	-	-
- some rooms	-	-	-	-	-	-	-	-	-	-
No central heating	4	-	-	1	3	-	-	-	-	3
No inside WC	**48**	**18**	**11**	**1**	**12**	**-**	**-**	**6**	**15**	**16**
With central heating - all rooms	11	3	3	-	2	-	-	3	5	3
- some rooms	11	5	2	-	3	-	-	1	-	1
No central heating	26	10	6	1	7	-	-	2	10	12
Shared use of bath/shower	**57**	**2**	**4**	**13**	**3**	**1**	**-**	**34**	**4**	**41**
Exclusive use of inside WC	**36**	**1**	**-**	**2**	**-**	**-**	**-**	**33**	**-**	**35**
With central heating - all rooms	35	1	-	2	-	-	-	32	-	34
- some rooms	1	-	-	-	-	-	-	1	-	1
No central heating	-	-	-	-	-	-	-	-	-	-
Shared use of inside WC	**21**	**1**	**4**	**11**	**3**	**1**	**-**	**1**	**-**	**5**
With central heating - all rooms	19	1	4	9	3	1	-	1	-	5
- some rooms	-	-	-	-	-	-	-	-	-	-
No central heating	2	-	-	2	-	-	-	-	-	-
No inside WC	**-**	**-**	**-**	**-**	**-**	**-**	**-**	**-**	**4**	**1**
With central heating - all rooms	-	-	-	-	-	-	-	-	-	-
- some rooms	-	-	-	-	-	-	-	-	-	-
No central heating	-	-	-	-	-	-	-	-	4	1
No bath/shower	**92**	**39**	**10**	**4**	**33**	**4**	**-**	**2**	**20**	**70**
Exclusive use of inside WC	**33**	**13**	**3**	**2**	**11**	**2**	**-**	**2**	**1**	**22**
With central heating - all rooms	3	-	1	-	-	1	-	1	-	1
- some rooms	4	1	1	1	-	-	-	1	-	3
No central heating	26	12	1	1	11	1	-	-	1	18
Shared use of inside WC	**-**	**-**	**-**	**-**	**-**	**-**	**-**	**-**	**-**	**-**
With central heating - all rooms	-	-	-	-	-	-	-	-	-	-
- some rooms	-	-	-	-	-	-	-	-	-	-
No central heating	-	-	-	-	-	-	-	-	-	-
No inside WC	**59**	**26**	**7**	**2**	**22**	**2**	**-**	**-**	**19**	**48**
With central heating - all rooms	3	1	2	-	-	-	-	-	1	1
- some rooms	5	3	-	-	2	-	-	-	-	4
No central heating	51	22	5	2	20	2	-	-	18	43
No car	5,675	2,118	605	139	292	83	145	2,293	42	

20. Households with residents; residents in households

Amenities	All permanent	Tenure of households in permanent buildings: Owner occupied: Owned outright	Owner occupied: Buying	Rented privately: Furnished	Rented privately: Unfurnished	Rented with a job or business	Rented from a housing association	Rented from a local authority or new town	Non-permanent accommodation	No car
a	b	c	d	e	f	g	h	i	j	k
				Wansdyke – *continued*						
TOTAL PERSONS IN HOUSEHOLDS	**78,866**	**19,039**	**45,443**	**1,139**	**1,647**	**1,474**	**574**	**9,550**	**256**	**8,992**
Exclusive use of bath/shower	**78,671**	**18,989**	**45,418**	**1,120**	**1,596**	**1,468**	**574**	**9,506**	**218**	**8,860**
Exclusive use of inside WC	**78,567**	**18,952**	**45,393**	**1,118**	**1,571**	**1,468**	**574**	**9,491**	**196**	**8,837**
With central heating - all rooms	59,080	13,691	37,323	765	649	935	314	5,403	128	4,974
- some rooms	11,620	3,399	5,455	168	325	279	188	1,806	18	1,750
No central heating	7,867	1,862	2,615	185	597	254	72	2,282	50	2,113
Shared use of inside WC	**4**	**-**	**-**	**1**	**3**	**-**	**-**	**-**	**-**	**3**
With central heating - all rooms	-	-	-	-	-	-	-	-	-	-
- some rooms	-	-	-	-	-	-	-	-	-	-
No central heating	4	-	-	1	3	-	-	-	-	3
No inside WC	**100**	**37**	**25**	**1**	**22**	**-**	**-**	**15**	**22**	**20**
With central heating - all rooms	23	3	8	-	5	-	-	7	6	3
- some rooms	28	12	6	-	8	-	-	2	-	1
No central heating	49	22	11	1	9	-	-	6	16	16
Shared use of bath/shower	**71**	**3**	**7**	**14**	**6**	**1**	**-**	**40**	**5**	**49**
Exclusive use of inside WC	**42**	**2**	**-**	**2**	**-**	**-**	**-**	**38**	**-**	**40**
With central heating - all rooms	41	2	-	2	-	-	-	37	-	39
- some rooms	1	-	-	-	-	-	-	1	-	1
No central heating	-	-	-	-	-	-	-	-	-	-
Shared use of inside WC	**29**	**1**	**7**	**12**	**6**	**1**	**-**	**2**	**-**	**8**
With central heating - all rooms	27	1	7	10	6	1	-	2	-	8
- some rooms	-	-	-	-	-	-	-	-	-	-
No central heating	2	-	-	2	-	-	-	-	-	-
No inside WC	**-**	**-**	**-**	**-**	**-**	**-**	**-**	**-**	**5**	**1**
With central heating - all rooms	-	-	-	-	-	-	-	-	-	-
- some rooms	-	-	-	-	-	-	-	-	-	-
No central heating	-	-	-	-	-	-	-	-	5	1
No bath/shower	**124**	**47**	**18**	**5**	**45**	**5**	**-**	**4**	**33**	**83**
Exclusive use of inside WC	**46**	**14**	**6**	**2**	**17**	**3**	**-**	**4**	**1**	**27**
With central heating - all rooms	8	-	3	-	-	2	-	3	-	3
- some rooms	5	1	2	1	-	-	-	1	-	3
No central heating	33	13	1	1	17	1	-	-	1	21
Shared use of inside WC	**-**	**-**	**-**	**-**	**-**	**-**	**-**	**-**	**-**	**-**
With central heating - all rooms	-	-	-	-	-	-	-	-	-	-
- some rooms	-	-	-	-	-	-	-	-	-	-
No central heating	-	-	-	-	-	-	-	-	-	-
No inside WC	**78**	**33**	**12**	**3**	**28**	**2**	**-**	**-**	**32**	**56**
With central heating - all rooms	7	2	5	-	-	-	-	-	2	2
- some rooms	5	3	-	-	2	-	-	-	-	4
No central heating	66	28	7	3	26	2	-	-	30	50
No car	8,936	2,797	1,273	204	405	147	216	3,894	56	

Table 20 Tenure and amenities – continued

County, districts

20. Households with residents; residents in households

Amenities	All permanent	Tenure of households in permanent buildings: Owner occupied: Owned outright	Owner occupied: Buying	Rented privately: Furnished	Rented privately: Unfurnished	Rented with a job or business	Rented from a housing association	Rented from a local authority or new town	Non-permanent accommodation	No car
a	b	c	d	e	f	g	h	i	j	k
				Woodspring						
TOTAL HOUSEHOLDS	**69,770**	**20,968**	**34,410**	**2,452**	**2,076**	**1,155**	**1,109**	**7,600**	**749**	**15,940**
Exclusive use of bath/shower	**69,234**	**20,904**	**34,385**	**2,169**	**2,016**	**1,145**	**1,093**	**7,522**	**718**	**15,535**
Exclusive use of inside WC	**69,151**	**20,877**	**34,372**	**2,151**	**2,008**	**1,139**	**1,093**	**7,511**	**713**	**15,486**
With central heating - all rooms	50,713	15,178	27,594	1,132	890	717	804	4,398	544	9,272
- some rooms	10,325	3,769	4,327	318	357	227	221	1,106	53	2,647
No central heating	8,113	1,930	2,451	701	761	195	68	2,007	116	3,567
Shared use of inside WC	**21**	**-**	**-**	**14**	**1**	**2**	**-**	**4**	**1**	**18**
With central heating - all rooms	12	-	-	8	-	1	-	3	-	11
- some rooms	1	-	-	-	-	1	-	-	-	1
No central heating	8	-	-	6	1	-	-	1	1	6
No inside WC	**62**	**27**	**13**	**4**	**7**	**4**	**-**	**7**	**4**	**31**
With central heating - all rooms	13	4	4	-	1	1	-	3	1	5
- some rooms	10	6	3	-	1	-	-	-	-	4
No central heating	39	17	6	4	5	3	-	4	3	22
Shared use of bath/shower	**435**	**23**	**12**	**276**	**28**	**7**	**16**	**73**	**7**	**324**
Exclusive use of inside WC	**47**	**6**	**2**	**15**	**6**	**-**	**2**	**16**	**1**	**34**
With central heating - all rooms	26	2	2	3	2	-	2	15	-	21
- some rooms	2	1	-	1	-	-	-	-	-	1
No central heating	19	3	-	11	4	-	-	1	1	12
Shared use of inside WC	**383**	**16**	**10**	**258**	**22**	**7**	**13**	**57**	**4**	**286**
With central heating - all rooms	149	6	6	57	6	7	11	56	3	107
- some rooms	15	3	2	9	1	-	-	-	-	10
No central heating	219	7	2	192	15	-	2	1	1	169
No inside WC	**5**	**1**	**-**	**3**	**-**	**-**	**1**	**-**	**2**	**4**
With central heating - all rooms	4	-	-	3	-	-	1	-	-	2
- some rooms	-	-	-	-	-	-	-	-	1	1
No central heating	1	1	-	-	-	-	-	-	1	1
No bath/shower	**101**	**41**	**13**	**7**	**32**	**3**	**-**	**5**	**24**	**81**
Exclusive use of inside WC	**53**	**17**	**10**	**4**	**15**	**2**	**-**	**5**	**6**	**43**
With central heating - all rooms	9	2	3	1	-	-	-	3	1	7
- some rooms	5	3	2	-	-	-	-	-	-	3
No central heating	39	12	5	3	15	2	-	2	5	33
Shared use of inside WC	**3**	**-**	**1**	**1**	**1**	**-**	**-**	**-**	**-**	**-**
With central heating - all rooms	-	-	-	-	-	-	-	-	-	-
- some rooms	-	-	-	-	-	-	-	-	-	-
No central heating	3	-	1	1	1	-	-	-	-	-
No inside WC	**45**	**24**	**2**	**2**	**16**	**1**	**-**	**-**	**18**	**38**
With central heating - all rooms	3	2	1	-	-	-	-	-	1	2
- some rooms	5	4	1	-	-	-	-	-	-	4
No central heating	37	18	-	2	16	1	-	-	17	32
No car	15,676	5,965	2,027	1,142	906	195	806	4,635	264	

20. Households with residents; residents in households

Amenities	All permanent	Tenure of households in permanent buildings: Owner occupied: Owned outright	Owner occupied: Buying	Rented privately: Furnished	Rented privately: Un-furnished	Rented with a job or business	Rented from a housing association	Rented from a local authority or new town	Non-permanent accommodation	No car
a	b	c	d	e	f	g	h	i	j	k
				Woodspring – *continued*						
TOTAL PERSONS IN HOUSEHOLDS	**171,584**	**39,399**	**102,074**	**4,319**	**3,964**	**3,167**	**1,729**	**16,932**	**1,260**	**25,383**
Exclusive use of bath/shower	**170,837**	**39,295**	**102,015**	**3,979**	**3,880**	**3,155**	**1,713**	**16,800**	**1,199**	**24,865**
Exclusive use of inside WC	**170,690**	**39,246**	**101,978**	**3,958**	**3,868**	**3,145**	**1,713**	**16,782**	**1,192**	**24,798**
With central heating - all rooms	129,222	29,086	83,300	2,259	1,872	2,054	1,163	9,488	930	14,565
- some rooms	24,462	6,865	12,513	601	701	645	430	2,707	83	4,371
No central heating	17,006	3,295	6,165	1,098	1,295	446	120	4,587	179	5,862
Shared use of inside WC	**25**	**-**	**-**	**16**	**1**	**2**	**-**	**6**	**3**	**22**
With central heating - all rooms	14	-	-	9	-	1	-	4	-	13
- some rooms	1	-	-	-	-	1	-	-	-	1
No central heating	10	-	-	7	1	-	-	2	3	8
No inside WC	**122**	**49**	**37**	**5**	**11**	**8**	**-**	**12**	**4**	**45**
With central heating - all rooms	29	7	11	-	3	3	-	5	1	11
- some rooms	23	10	11	-	2	-	-	-	-	7
No central heating	70	32	15	5	6	5	-	7	3	27
Shared use of bath/shower	**598**	**42**	**33**	**332**	**41**	**9**	**16**	**125**	**15**	**415**
Exclusive use of inside WC	**61**	**8**	**6**	**20**	**8**	**-**	**2**	**17**	**3**	**36**
With central heating - all rooms	32	3	6	4	2	-	2	15	-	21
- some rooms	3	2	-	1	-	-	-	-	-	1
No central heating	26	3	-	15	6	-	-	2	3	14
Shared use of inside WC	**532**	**33**	**27**	**309**	**33**	**9**	**13**	**108**	**8**	**375**
With central heating - all rooms	248	14	18	79	10	9	11	107	4	166
- some rooms	25	9	3	10	3	-	-	-	-	14
No central heating	259	10	6	220	20	-	2	1	4	195
No inside WC	**5**	**1**	**-**	**3**	**-**	**-**	**1**	**-**	**4**	**4**
With central heating - all rooms	4	-	-	3	-	-	1	-	-	2
- some rooms	-	-	-	-	-	-	-	-	1	1
No central heating	1	1	-	-	-	-	-	-	3	1
No bath/shower	**149**	**62**	**26**	**8**	**43**	**3**	**-**	**7**	**46**	**103**
Exclusive use of inside WC	**79**	**24**	**22**	**4**	**20**	**2**	**-**	**7**	**11**	**55**
With central heating - all rooms	15	4	6	1	-	-	-	4	2	11
- some rooms	6	3	3	-	-	-	-	-	-	4
No central heating	58	17	13	3	20	2	-	3	9	40
Shared use of inside WC	**3**	**-**	**1**	**1**	**1**	**-**	**-**	**-**	**-**	**-**
With central heating - all rooms	-	-	-	-	-	-	-	-	-	-
- some rooms	-	-	-	-	-	-	-	-	-	-
No central heating	3	-	1	1	1	-	-	-	-	-
No inside WC	**67**	**38**	**3**	**3**	**22**	**1**	**-**	**-**	**35**	**48**
With central heating - all rooms	5	3	2	-	-	-	-	-	1	2
- some rooms	6	5	1	-	-	-	-	-	-	4
No central heating	56	30	-	3	22	1	-	-	34	42
No car	25,027	7,902	4,155	1,697	1,321	335	1,091	8,526	356	

Notes: (1) * Households with three or more cars are counted as having 3 cars
(2) ** May include a small number of households with no persons aged 17 and over

21. Households with residents; residents in households; cars in households

Number of persons aged 17 and over (with or without others)	TOTAL PERSONS (ALL AGES)	TOTAL HOUSEHOLDS	Households with: No car	1 car	2 cars	3 or more cars	TOTAL CARS*
a	b	c	d	e	f	g	h
		AVON					
ALL HOUSEHOLDS**	**916,973**	**376,522**	**101,740**	**171,813**	**84,684**	**18,285**	**396,036**
1 male aged 17 and over	41,269	39,350	15,758	21,662	1,581	349	25,871
1 female aged 17 and over	96,148	74,526	50,742	23,070	607	107	24,605
2 (1 male and 1 female) aged 17 and over	507,776	185,740	25,922	101,744	54,715	3,359	221,251
2 (same sex) aged 17 and over	27,500	12,379	3,870	5,376	2,851	282	11,924
3 or more aged 17 and over	244,175	64,458	5,404	19,942	24,926	14,186	112,352
TOTAL PERSONS (ALL AGES)		**916,973**	**171,129**	**414,474**	**264,276**	**67,094**	
Persons aged 17 and over		726,984	143,959	323,899	199,923	59,203	
		Bath					
ALL HOUSEHOLDS**	**76,876**	**34,128**	**12,148**	**15,274**	**5,669**	**1,037**	**29,723**
1 male aged 17 and over	4,191	4,032	1,903	1,946	159	24	2,336
1 female aged 17 and over	10,353	8,402	6,035	2,274	83	10	2,470
2 (1 male and 1 female) aged 17 and over	39,558	14,979	2,989	8,478	3,314	198	15,700
2 (same sex) aged 17 and over	3,080	1,428	567	574	264	23	1,171
3 or more aged 17 and over	19,691	5,284	652	2,001	1,849	782	8,045
TOTAL PERSONS (ALL AGES)		**76,876**	**19,883**	**35,756**	**17,493**	**3,744**	
Persons aged 17 and over		63,003	17,217	28,875	13,577	3,334	
		Bristol					
ALL HOUSEHOLDS**	**370,131**	**156,778**	**53,558**	**71,345**	**26,759**	**5,116**	**140,211**
1 male aged 17 and over	20,560	19,617	9,153	9,657	658	149	11,420
1 female aged 17 and over	46,938	35,118	25,020	9,790	242	66	10,472
2 (1 male and 1 female) aged 17 and over	192,497	70,573	13,879	40,012	15,814	868	74,244
2 (same sex) aged 17 and over	14,083	6,322	2,235	2,659	1,306	122	5,637
3 or more aged 17 and over	95,982	25,101	3,243	9,212	8,737	3,909	38,413
TOTAL PERSONS (ALL AGES)		**370,131**	**93,883**	**173,997**	**83,558**	**18,693**	
Persons aged 17 and over		293,325	77,194	135,074	64,473	16,584	
		Kingswood					
ALL HOUSEHOLDS**	**88,916**	**34,657**	**7,045**	**16,228**	**9,246**	**2,138**	**41,134**
1 male aged 17 and over	2,927	2,758	903	1,707	122	26	2,029
1 female aged 17 and over	7,280	5,633	3,825	1,772	30	6	1,850
2 (1 male and 1 female) aged 17 and over	51,857	18,744	1,786	10,598	6,022	338	23,656
2 (same sex) aged 17 and over	1,859	833	202	400	216	15	877
3 or more aged 17 and over	24,989	6,686	326	1,751	2,856	1,753	12,722
TOTAL PERSONS (ALL AGES)		**88,916**	**11,280**	**40,464**	**29,188**	**7,984**	
Persons aged 17 and over		70,029	9,768	31,114	22,017	7,130	
		Northavon					
ALL HOUSEHOLDS**	**129,084**	**49,626**	**7,332**	**23,404**	**15,256**	**3,634**	**64,818**
1 male aged 17 and over	4,507	4,278	973	2,995	251	59	3,674
1 female aged 17 and over	9,079	7,015	4,068	2,838	100	9	3,065
2 (1 male and 1 female) aged 17 and over	76,909	27,618	1,738	14,690	10,464	726	37,796
2 (same sex) aged 17 and over	2,855	1,276	243	581	400	52	1,537
3 or more aged 17 and over	35,726	9,435	309	2,298	4,040	2,788	18,742
TOTAL PERSONS (ALL AGES)		**129,084**	**11,708**	**57,011**	**47,102**	**13,263**	
Persons aged 17 and over		100,790	10,030	43,763	35,342	11,655	

Notes: (1) * Households with three or more cars are counted as having 3 cars
(2) ** May include a small number of households with no persons aged 17 and over

21. Households with residents; residents in households; cars in households

Number of persons aged 17 and over (with or without others)	TOTAL PERSONS (ALL AGES)	TOTAL HOUSEHOLDS	Households with: No car	1 car	2 cars	3 or more cars	TOTAL CARS*
a	b	c	d	e	f	g	h
		Wansdyke					
ALL HOUSEHOLDS**	**79,122**	**30,814**	**5,717**	**13,741**	**9,032**	**2,324**	**38,777**
1 male aged 17 and over	2,486	2,372	730	1,483	128	31	1,832
1 female aged 17 and over	5,959	4,950	3,106	1,783	57	4	1,909
2 (1 male and 1 female) aged 17 and over	45,709	16,570	1,474	8,648	6,014	434	21,978
2 (same sex) aged 17 and over	1,709	770	169	350	230	21	873
3 or more aged 17 and over	23,259	6,152	238	1,477	2,603	1,834	12,185
TOTAL PERSONS (ALL AGES)		**79,122**	**8,992**	**33,005**	**28,442**	**8,683**	
Persons aged 17 and over		62,697	7,901	26,016	21,196	7,584	
		Woodspring					
ALL HOUSEHOLDS**	**172,844**	**70,519**	**15,940**	**31,821**	**18,722**	**4,036**	**81,373**
1 male aged 17 and over	6,598	6,293	2,096	3,874	263	60	4,580
1 female aged 17 and over	16,539	13,408	8,688	4,613	95	12	4,839
2 (1 male and 1 female) aged 17 and over	101,246	37,256	4,056	19,318	13,087	795	47,877
2 (same sex) aged 17 and over	3,914	1,750	454	812	435	49	1,829
3 or more aged 17 and over	44,528	11,800	636	3,203	4,841	3,120	22,245
TOTAL PERSONS (ALL AGES)		**172,844**	**25,383**	**74,241**	**58,493**	**14,727**	
Persons aged 17 and over		137,140	21,849	59,057	43,318	12,916	

Table 22 Rooms and household size

22. Households with residents; residents in households; rooms in household spaces

Households with the following tenure and persons	TOTAL HOUSE-HOLDS	Households with the following rooms							TOTAL ROOMS
		1	2	3	4	5	6	7 or more	
a	b	c	d	e	f	g	h	i	j
				AVON					
ALL TENURES	**376,522**	**7,055**	**13,472**	**29,205**	**64,603**	**104,903**	**93,136**	**64,148**	**1,968,000**
1	100,534	6,131	9,828	17,215	23,496	21,322	16,425	6,117	424,103
2	132,374	704	3,257	9,683	27,794	39,192	33,672	18,072	686,281
3	58,265	138	274	1,570	8,014	18,991	17,198	12,080	329,725
4	58,966	35	85	558	4,102	17,987	18,457	17,742	358,383
5	19,668	31	19	144	936	5,594	5,633	7,311	124,975
6	5,133	15	6	24	200	1,406	1,360	2,122	33,827
7 or more	1,582	1	3	11	61	411	391	704	10,706
TOTAL PERSONS	**916,973**	**8,346**	**17,656**	**44,479**	**125,879**	**268,049**	**248,466**	**204,098**	
Owner occupied - owned outright	**99,184**	**169**	**960**	**3,716**	**16,613**	**29,394**	**31,332**	**17,000**	**548,748**
1	33,382	118	734	2,348	7,785	9,642	9,341	3,414	170,530
2	47,148	31	202	1,219	7,689	14,678	15,416	7,913	262,476
3	11,188	9	7	108	855	3,252	4,144	2,813	67,208
4	5,434	7	9	27	224	1,453	1,880	1,834	34,365
5	1,438	2	6	10	45	280	412	683	9,829
6	436	2	2	2	12	57	112	249	3,172
7 or more	158	-	-	2	3	32	27	94	1,168
Total persons	**194,007**	**257**	**1,237**	**5,297**	**26,943**	**56,552**	**63,068**	**40,653**	
Owner occupied - buying	**172,569**	**577**	**2,430**	**6,251**	**21,518**	**51,509**	**48,076**	**42,208**	**987,859**
1	23,981	407	1,526	3,047	6,205	6,614	4,282	1,900	110,736
2	53,290	127	817	2,565	9,559	17,201	14,038	8,983	287,597
3	33,907	20	58	420	3,281	11,183	10,561	8,384	198,850
4	43,683	7	23	164	1,968	12,431	14,196	14,894	272,439
5	13,734	10	5	41	392	3,262	4,016	6,008	90,502
6	3,160	6	-	8	91	661	815	1,579	21,870
7 or more	814	-	1	6	22	157	168	460	5,865
Total persons	**500,741**	**835**	**3,458**	**10,396**	**45,718**	**145,710**	**147,067**	**147,557**	
Rented privately - furnished	**16,987**	**3,924**	**2,143**	**2,831**	**2,921**	**2,267**	**1,669**	**1,232**	**59,638**
1	8,272	3,431	1,290	1,283	990	601	409	268	21,472
2	5,365	380	773	1,338	1,406	768	468	232	20,129
3	1,848	73	59	166	393	553	386	218	8,999
4	949	15	16	31	103	251	283	250	5,482
5	370	17	3	9	19	69	100	153	2,274
6	137	7	2	4	5	23	18	78	916
7 or more	46	1	-	-	5	2	5	33	366
Total persons	**31,359**	**4,605**	**3,104**	**4,650**	**5,554**	**5,297**	**4,281**	**3,868**	
Rented privately - unfurnished	**10,738**	**460**	**967**	**1,958**	**2,768**	**2,360**	**1,513**	**712**	**45,805**
1	4,812	374	647	1,081	1,208	867	465	170	18,197
2	3,834	70	288	730	1,106	889	540	211	16,610
3	1,154	14	23	119	308	322	224	144	5,732
4	639	2	8	20	120	185	195	109	3,490
5	215	-	-	5	22	71	68	49	1,252
6	69	-	-	3	4	21	16	25	427
7 or more	15	-	1	-	-	5	5	4	97
Total persons	**20,095**	**564**	**1,331**	**3,021**	**4,958**	**4,868**	**3,470**	**1,883**	

22. Households with residents; residents in households; rooms in household spaces

Households with the following tenure and persons	TOTAL HOUSE-HOLDS	Households with the following rooms							TOTAL ROOMS
		1	2	3	4	5	6	7 or more	
a	b	c	d	e	f	g	h	i	j
				AVON – *continued*					
Rented with a job or business	**5,116**	**107**	**213**	**489**	**981**	**1,249**	**1,036**	**1,041**	**27,083**
1	1,283	96	154	221	286	249	167	110	5,408
2	1,611	8	51	184	399	403	290	276	8,328
3	875	2	7	52	179	256	200	179	4,826
4	877	1	1	23	90	246	266	250	5,333
5	345	-	-	8	20	74	81	162	2,317
6	93	-	-	-	5	14	27	47	637
7 or more	32	-	-	1	2	7	5	17	234
Total persons	**13,167**	**122**	**281**	**884**	**2,126**	**3,311**	**3,013**	**3,430**	
Rented from a housing association	**9,598**	**1,027**	**2,229**	**2,511**	**1,889**	**1,211**	**527**	**204**	**31,492**
1	5,703	1,000	1,860	1,760	728	229	90	36	14,926
2	2,316	24	353	637	727	370	161	44	8,741
3	730	3	10	83	271	255	86	22	3,310
4	522	-	4	24	127	224	103	40	2,656
5	226	-	1	4	28	98	57	38	1,254
6	64	-	1	1	4	23	21	14	385
7 or more	37	-	-	2	4	12	9	10	220
Total persons	**16,413**	**1,057**	**2,623**	**3,423**	**3,699**	**3,351**	**1,561**	**699**	
Rented from a local authority or new town	**62,330**	**791**	**4,530**	**11,449**	**17,913**	**16,913**	**8,983**	**1,751**	**267,375**
1	23,101	705	3,617	7,475	6,294	3,120	1,671	219	82,834
2	18,810	64	773	3,010	6,908	4,883	2,759	413	82,400
3	8,563	17	110	622	2,727	3,170	1,597	320	40,800
4	6,862	3	24	269	1,470	3,197	1,534	365	34,618
5	3,340	2	4	67	410	1,740	899	218	17,547
6	1,174	-	1	6	79	607	351	130	6,420
7 or more	480	-	1	-	25	196	172	86	2,756
Total persons	**141,191**	**906**	**5,622**	**16,808**	**36,881**	**48,960**	**26,006**	**6,008**	
				Bath					
ALL TENURES	**34,128**	**987**	**1,867**	**3,949**	**6,564**	**7,727**	**7,482**	**5,552**	**171,000**
1	11,179	841	1,361	2,430	2,519	1,857	1,528	643	44,528
2	11,945	117	444	1,256	2,520	2,950	2,887	1,771	60,923
3	4,811	16	49	184	911	1,351	1,303	997	26,827
4	4,258	3	9	67	475	1,130	1,253	1,321	25,897
5	1,445	5	3	11	115	330	400	581	9,429
6	375	5	-	1	20	82	77	190	2,604
7 or more	115	-	1	-	4	27	34	49	792
TOTAL PERSONS	**76,876**	**1,190**	**2,454**	**5,823**	**12,920**	**18,667**	**18,945**	**16,877**	
Owner occupied - owned outright	**9,699**	**20**	**145**	**415**	**1,550**	**2,570**	**3,113**	**1,886**	**54,296**
1	3,655	14	113	310	849	970	994	405	18,575
2	4,461	3	28	99	625	1,205	1,567	934	25,603
3	986	2	2	5	64	250	370	293	6,080
4	451	1	1	1	7	124	155	162	2,945
5	102	-	1	-	5	19	21	56	726
6	36	-	-	-	-	1	4	31	302
7 or more	8	-	-	-	-	1	2	5	65
Total persons	**18,128**	**30**	**184**	**527**	**2,344**	**4,734**	**6,003**	**4,306**	

22. Households with residents; residents in households; rooms in household spaces

Households with the following tenure and persons	TOTAL HOUSE-HOLDS	Households with the following rooms							TOTAL ROOMS
		1	2	3	4	5	6	7 or more	
a	b	c	d	e	f	g	h	i	j
				Bath – *continued*					
Owner occupied - buying	**12,376**	**100**	**302**	**686**	**1,769**	**3,067**	**3,257**	**3,195**	**70,548**
1	2,167	69	205	353	579	476	325	160	9,446
2	3,836	24	89	270	668	1,066	987	732	20,738
3	2,391	4	4	39	316	695	713	620	14,121
4	2,816	-	3	18	170	657	906	1,062	17,961
5	911	1	-	6	29	136	279	460	6,360
6	213	2	-	-	7	31	38	135	1,600
7 or more	42	-	1	-	-	6	9	26	322
Total persons	**34,414**	**146**	**414**	**1,112**	**3,730**	**8,229**	**9,753**	**11,030**	
Rented privately - furnished	**2,535**	**551**	**346**	**501**	**436**	**299**	**235**	**167**	**8,747**
1	1,222	477	209	226	142	83	51	34	3,157
2	801	61	117	232	198	97	62	34	2,924
3	298	5	17	32	70	75	68	31	1,431
4	135	2	2	9	20	34	34	34	757
5	55	3	1	2	3	7	17	22	329
6	19	3	-	-	2	3	3	8	109
7 or more	5	-	-	-	1	-	-	4	40
Total persons	**4,683**	**655**	**507**	**832**	**863**	**691**	**618**	**517**	
Rented privately - unfurnished	**1,665**	**82**	**192**	**438**	**450**	**243**	**179**	**81**	**6,511**
1	834	64	133	259	208	95	58	17	2,910
2	595	17	55	155	178	100	65	25	2,384
3	143	1	4	21	46	30	26	15	680
4	68	-	-	2	17	13	24	12	373
5	19	-	-	1	1	4	4	9	124
6	6	-	-	-	-	1	2	3	40
7 or more	-	-	-	-	-	-	-	-	-
Total persons	**2,856**	**101**	**255**	**645**	**775**	**463**	**394**	**223**	
Rented with a job or business	**476**	**8**	**41**	**60**	**114**	**99**	**78**	**76**	**2,336**
1	140	6	30	29	36	20	11	8	529
2	157	1	9	22	47	35	23	20	755
3	77	1	1	5	19	20	19	12	410
4	70	-	1	4	10	19	19	17	399
5	23	-	-	-	1	3	5	14	169
6	7	-	-	-	1	2	1	3	45
7 or more	2	-	-	-	-	-	-	2	29
Total persons	**1,144**	**11**	**55**	**104**	**238**	**253**	**221**	**262**	
Rented from a housing association	**1,167**	**138**	**283**	**397**	**164**	**101**	**56**	**28**	**3,626**
1	758	135	241	285	72	12	9	4	1,922
2	253	2	39	96	64	28	19	5	914
3	73	1	3	14	19	20	11	5	326
4	54	-	-	2	8	26	11	7	290
5	24	-	-	-	-	13	5	6	146
6	2	-	-	-	-	1	1	-	11
7 or more	3	-	-	-	1	1	-	1	17
Total persons	**1,856**	**142**	**328**	**527**	**299**	**311**	**155**	**94**	

22. Households with residents; residents in households; rooms in household spaces

Households with the following tenure and persons	TOTAL HOUSE-HOLDS	Households with the following rooms							TOTAL ROOMS
		1	2	3	4	5	6	7 or more	
a	b	c	d	e	f	g	h	i	j
				Bath – *continued*					
Rented from a local authority or new town	**6,210**	**88**	**558**	**1,452**	**2,081**	**1,348**	**564**	**119**	**24,936**
1	2,403	76	430	968	633	201	80	15	7,989
2	1,842	9	107	382	740	419	164	21	7,605
3	843	2	18	68	377	261	96	21	3,779
4	664	-	2	31	243	257	104	27	3,172
5	311	1	1	2	76	148	69	14	1,575
6	92	-	-	1	10	43	28	10	497
7 or more	55	-	-	-	2	19	23	11	319
Total persons	**13,795**	**105**	**711**	**2,076**	**4,671**	**3,986**	**1,801**	**445**	
				Bristol					
ALL TENURES	**156,778**	**4,272**	**7,219**	**14,119**	**27,698**	**43,935**	**38,902**	**20,633**	**786,985**
1	47,600	3,761	5,306	8,201	9,999	9,539	8,095	2,699	196,050
2	53,411	398	1,721	4,564	11,391	15,488	14,002	5,847	270,022
3	23,261	73	134	901	3,699	7,855	6,870	3,729	127,320
4	21,290	19	47	336	1,955	7,262	6,717	4,954	124,585
5	7,939	15	9	93	485	2,711	2,336	2,290	48,350
6	2,383	5	2	16	126	810	660	764	14,864
7 or more	894	1	-	8	43	270	222	350	5,794
TOTAL PERSONS	**370,131**	**4,965**	**9,395**	**22,007**	**55,203**	**113,546**	**100,908**	**64,107**	
Owner occupied - owned outright	**36,517**	**62**	**284**	**1,182**	**4,739**	**10,810**	**13,530**	**5,910**	**204,360**
1	12,952	43	224	755	2,222	3,710	4,513	1,485	68,711
2	16,527	12	54	354	2,081	5,135	6,284	2,607	93,011
3	4,185	2	2	52	321	1,220	1,691	897	24,689
4	2,006	4	2	14	86	554	776	570	12,364
5	549	1	2	5	18	131	191	201	3,545
6	195	-	-	1	9	33	61	91	1,326
7 or more	103	-	-	1	2	27	14	59	714
Total persons	**71,311**	**94**	**356**	**1,716**	**7,850**	**20,918**	**26,693**	**13,684**	
Owner occupied - buying	**63,232**	**267**	**1,064**	**2,845**	**8,532**	**19,881**	**18,240**	**12,403**	**351,859**
1	10,876	200	702	1,504	2,701	2,966	1,995	808	49,889
2	19,842	50	326	1,047	3,596	6,535	5,571	2,717	105,500
3	11,933	9	21	185	1,211	4,136	3,930	2,441	68,731
4	14,043	2	12	77	778	4,459	4,772	3,943	85,406
5	4,868	3	3	22	180	1,359	1,524	1,777	31,198
6	1,265	3	-	5	51	330	361	515	8,335
7 or more	405	-	-	5	15	96	87	202	2,800
Total persons	**177,523**	**368**	**1,480**	**4,643**	**17,960**	**55,762**	**54,469**	**42,841**	
Rented privately - furnished	**9,983**	**2,607**	**1,276**	**1,698**	**1,622**	**1,144**	**934**	**702**	**33,711**
1	4,994	2,293	754	737	523	297	233	157	12,233
2	3,096	241	481	845	804	368	246	111	11,211
3	1,034	49	31	91	220	318	206	119	4,995
4	533	11	9	17	56	121	181	138	3,099
5	210	10	1	4	12	29	54	100	1,324
6	84	2	-	4	3	10	10	55	598
7 or more	32	1	-	-	4	1	4	22	251
Total persons	**18,215**	**3,036**	**1,850**	**2,812**	**3,121**	**2,683**	**2,428**	**2,285**	

22. Households with residents; residents in households; rooms in household spaces

Households with the following tenure and persons	TOTAL HOUSE-HOLDS	Households with the following rooms							TOTAL ROOMS
		1	2	3	4	5	6	7 or more	
a	b	c	d	e	f	g	h	i	j
				Bristol – *continued*					
Rented privately - unfurnished	**4,552**	**290**	**544**	**900**	**1,142**	**913**	**542**	**221**	**18,164**
1	2,170	238	365	496	474	335	192	70	7,719
2	1,568	41	163	328	464	338	176	58	6,405
3	477	10	10	60	139	136	74	48	2,259
4	226	1	6	12	51	72	58	26	1,155
5	80	-	-	3	11	20	31	15	454
6	25	-	-	1	3	10	7	4	138
7 or more	6	-	-	-	-	2	4	-	34
Total persons	**8,236**	**354**	**745**	**1,401**	**2,096**	**1,882**	**1,225**	**533**	
Rented with a job or business	**1,929**	**73**	**103**	**227**	**415**	**471**	**330**	**310**	**9,545**
1	590	68	80	100	130	109	70	33	2,307
2	624	5	19	89	160	157	101	93	3,142
3	286	-	4	22	69	87	61	43	1,495
4	263	-	-	10	45	77	64	67	1,528
5	113	-	-	6	5	31	20	51	729
6	38	-	-	-	4	5	11	18	254
7 or more	15	-	-	-	2	5	3	5	90
Total persons	**4,654**	**78**	**130**	**414**	**901**	**1,213**	**898**	**1,020**	
Rented from a housing association	**5,812**	**648**	**1,501**	**1,445**	**1,133**	**662**	**306**	**117**	**18,643**
1	3,497	626	1,254	1,016	397	128	54	22	8,915
2	1,352	20	234	355	438	201	82	22	5,012
3	463	2	7	52	183	150	57	12	2,084
4	305	-	4	18	87	122	57	17	1,504
5	121	-	1	1	22	37	35	25	678
6	48	-	1	1	4	16	14	12	293
7 or more	26	-	-	2	2	8	7	7	157
Total persons	**9,906**	**672**	**1,770**	**1,983**	**2,319**	**1,813**	**928**	**421**	
Rented from a local authority or new town	**34,753**	**325**	**2,447**	**5,822**	**10,115**	**10,054**	**5,020**	**970**	**150,703**
1	12,521	293	1,927	3,593	3,552	1,994	1,038	124	46,276
2	10,402	29	444	1,546	3,848	2,754	1,542	239	45,741
3	4,883	1	59	439	1,556	1,808	851	169	23,067
4	3,914	1	14	188	852	1,857	809	193	19,529
5	1,998	1	2	52	237	1,104	481	121	10,422
6	728	-	1	4	52	406	196	69	3,920
7 or more	307	-	-	-	18	131	103	55	1,748
Total persons	**80,286**	**363**	**3,064**	**9,038**	**20,956**	**29,275**	**14,267**	**3,323**	
				Kingswood					
ALL TENURES	**34,657**	**223**	**748**	**2,110**	**5,356**	**10,746**	**10,645**	**4,829**	**183,413**
1	7,364	196	549	1,318	1,738	1,669	1,559	335	32,375
2	12,352	19	183	662	2,409	4,103	3,741	1,235	64,278
3	5,976	5	13	83	733	2,124	2,091	927	33,307
4	6,537	2	1	33	390	2,148	2,437	1,526	38,482
5	1,929	1	1	10	75	576	656	610	11,753
6	407	-	1	2	9	106	130	159	2,609
7 or more	92	-	-	2	2	20	31	37	609
TOTAL PERSONS	**88,916**	**262**	**969**	**3,100**	**10,758**	**28,498**	**29,348**	**15,981**	

22. Households with residents; residents in households; rooms in household spaces

Households with the following tenure and persons	TOTAL HOUSE-HOLDS	Households with the following rooms							TOTAL ROOMS
		1	2	3	4	5	6	7 or more	
a	b	c	d	e	f	g	h	i	j
				Kingswood - *continued*					
Owner occupied - owned outright	**10,002**	**9**	**97**	**267**	**1,480**	**3,179**	**3,799**	**1,171**	**54,473**
1	2,835	8	73	162	595	854	962	181	14,412
2	4,947	-	22	92	750	1,640	1,903	540	27,059
3	1,361	-	-	9	102	451	611	188	7,749
4	672	1	-	2	29	196	269	175	4,045
5	154	-	1	1	4	33	45	70	992
6	30	-	1	-	-	5	9	15	195
7 or more	3	-	-	1	-	-	-	2	21
Total persons	**20,471**	**12**	**128**	**393**	**2,537**	**6,466**	**7,956**	**2,979**	
Owner occupied - buying	**18,233**	**26**	**155**	**422**	**2,196**	**6,155**	**5,848**	**3,431**	**102,062**
1	1,890	24	99	185	515	546	394	127	8,861
2	5,402	1	53	185	989	2,002	1,534	638	28,604
3	3,838	1	3	34	397	1,413	1,304	686	21,740
4	5,244	-	-	11	245	1,701	1,980	1,307	31,207
5	1,499	-	-	5	44	417	517	516	9,265
6	306	-	-	1	6	70	100	129	2,005
7 or more	54	-	-	1	-	6	19	28	380
Total persons	**54,915**	**29**	**214**	**740**	**4,920**	**18,142**	**18,616**	**12,254**	
Rented privately - furnished	**559**	**83**	**40**	**70**	**108**	**109**	**103**	**46**	**2,316**
1	221	66	23	37	39	25	25	6	702
2	185	11	16	28	47	40	32	11	788
3	87	4	1	4	17	27	24	10	436
4	42	1	-	-	4	10	16	11	245
5	19	1	-	1	1	5	6	5	110
6	2	-	-	-	-	1	-	1	13
7 or more	3	-	-	-	-	1	-	2	22
Total persons	**1,149**	**109**	**58**	**110**	**205**	**264**	**255**	**148**	
Rented privately - unfurnished	**500**	**13**	**22**	**68**	**122**	**129**	**114**	**32**	**2,316**
1	187	9	11	36	42	43	41	5	803
2	183	4	8	25	60	52	26	8	808
3	60	-	2	6	13	16	14	9	304
4	49	-	1	1	6	10	25	6	272
5	16	-	-	-	1	6	7	2	94
6	5	-	-	-	-	2	1	2	35
7 or more	-	-	-	-	-	-	-	-	-
Total persons	**1,039**	**17**	**37**	**108**	**230**	**277**	**276**	**94**	
Rented with a job or business	**241**	**2**	**8**	**26**	**45**	**71**	**55**	**34**	**1,220**
1	60	2	5	12	15	13	10	3	255
2	77	-	3	9	17	19	16	13	394
3	47	-	-	3	9	16	10	9	251
4	38	-	-	1	3	14	16	4	212
5	15	-	-	1	1	9	2	2	80
6	4	-	-	-	-	-	1	3	28
7 or more	-	-	-	-	-	-	-	-	-
Total persons	**606**	**2**	**11**	**48**	**93**	**200**	**152**	**100**	

22. Households with residents; residents in households; rooms in household spaces

Households with the following tenure and persons	TOTAL HOUSE-HOLDS	Households with the following rooms							TOTAL ROOMS
		1	2	3	4	5	6	7 or more	
a	b	c	d	e	f	g	h	i	j
				Kingswood – *continued*					
Rented from a housing association	**621**	**65**	**67**	**174**	**148**	**130**	**33**	**4**	**2,190**
1	319	65	52	127	59	11	5	-	871
2	156	-	15	43	57	33	6	2	602
3	53	-	-	2	20	25	6	-	247
4	55	-	-	2	10	33	9	1	273
5	28	-	-	-	1	23	4	-	143
6	6	-	-	-	-	3	2	1	34
7 or more	4	-	-	-	1	2	1	-	20
Total persons	**1,216**	**65**	**82**	**227**	**285**	**431**	**112**	**14**	
Rented from a local authority or new town	**4,501**	**25**	**359**	**1,083**	**1,257**	**973**	**693**	**111**	**18,836**
1	1,852	22	286	759	473	177	122	13	6,471
2	1,402	3	66	280	489	317	224	23	6,023
3	530	-	7	25	175	176	122	25	2,580
4	437	-	-	16	93	184	122	22	2,228
5	198	-	-	2	23	83	75	15	1,069
6	54	-	-	1	3	25	17	8	299
7 or more	28	-	-	-	1	11	11	5	166
Total persons	**9,520**	**28**	**439**	**1,474**	**2,488**	**2,718**	**1,981**	**392**	
				Northavon					
ALL TENURES	**49,626**	**289**	**1,034**	**2,372**	**7,180**	**15,435**	**12,971**	**10,345**	**273,608**
1	9,996	239	756	1,339	2,471	2,717	1,744	730	45,277
2	17,870	29	232	843	3,354	5,954	4,711	2,747	95,541
3	8,439	9	31	129	813	2,946	2,527	1,984	48,907
4	9,625	5	10	46	424	2,857	2,992	3,291	59,659
5	2,858	3	3	11	93	766	771	1,211	18,480
6	692	4	1	3	20	163	190	311	4,696
7 or more	146	-	1	1	5	32	36	71	1,048
TOTAL PERSONS	**129,084**	**383**	**1,381**	**3,676**	**13,940**	**39,929**	**35,978**	**33,797**	
Owner occupied - owned outright	**11,929**	**19**	**117**	**343**	**1,962**	**3,856**	**3,482**	**2,150**	**66,353**
1	3,426	7	77	189	863	1,120	831	339	17,352
2	5,933	7	31	137	960	1,995	1,851	952	32,872
3	1,513	2	2	11	101	496	505	396	9,064
4	773	-	4	3	26	207	227	306	5,046
5	215	1	2	2	9	29	54	118	1,518
6	60	2	1	1	2	6	10	38	450
7 or more	9	-	-	-	1	3	4	1	51
Total persons	**24,424**	**44**	**177**	**524**	**3,254**	**7,628**	**7,317**	**5,480**	
Owner occupied - buying	**29,399**	**60**	**317**	**820**	**3,331**	**9,346**	**7,973**	**7,552**	**169,317**
1	3,535	38	191	371	879	1,119	636	301	16,759
2	9,307	15	115	367	1,647	3,207	2,338	1,618	50,190
3	5,786	3	9	56	480	2,037	1,745	1,456	33,900
4	7,905	2	1	23	254	2,271	2,505	2,849	49,440
5	2,265	1	1	2	57	580	599	1,025	14,799
6	495	1	-	1	12	111	129	241	3,421
7 or more	106	-	-	-	2	21	21	62	808
Total persons	**86,218**	**96**	**457**	**1,381**	**7,006**	**26,445**	**24,496**	**26,337**	

22. Households with residents; residents in households; rooms in household spaces

Households with the following tenure and persons	TOTAL HOUSE-HOLDS	Households with the following rooms							TOTAL ROOMS
		1	2	3	4	5	6	7 or more	
a	b	c	d	e	f	g	h	i	j
				Northavon - *continued*					
Rented privately - furnished	**848**	**56**	**53**	**89**	**185**	**238**	**131**	**96**	**3,899**
1	311	45	38	39	65	66	31	27	1,227
2	307	6	13	41	95	87	45	20	1,392
3	120	3	2	8	19	46	23	19	631
4	69	-	-	1	6	25	18	19	401
5	28	1	-	-	-	9	12	6	165
6	11	1	-	-	-	5	2	3	68
7 or more	2	-	-	-	-	-	-	2	15
Total persons	**1,784**	**77**	**70**	**149**	**336**	**553**	**334**	**265**	
Rented privately - unfurnished	**1,092**	**10**	**32**	**99**	**277**	**350**	**194**	**130**	**5,404**
1	388	9	25	56	114	122	47	15	1,691
2	391	-	5	33	108	123	78	44	1,966
3	161	-	1	7	41	45	35	32	879
4	100	1	-	1	12	34	28	24	572
5	32	-	-	1	1	19	5	6	176
6	19	-	-	1	1	7	1	9	118
7 or more	1	-	1	-	-	-	-	-	2
Total persons	**2,334**	**13**	**45**	**158**	**512**	**776**	**451**	**379**	
Rented with a job or business	**767**	**4**	**14**	**53**	**111**	**196**	**174**	**215**	**4,429**
1	151	2	8	23	28	36	29	25	751
2	227	-	5	20	42	59	46	55	1,262
3	157	1	1	4	24	40	39	48	940
4	155	1	-	5	13	47	38	51	941
5	61	-	-	-	4	10	17	30	430
6	13	-	-	-	-	3	5	5	85
7 or more	3	-	-	1	-	1	-	1	20
Total persons	**2,100**	**9**	**21**	**102**	**256**	**537**	**505**	**670**	
Rented from a housing association	**598**	**30**	**114**	**128**	**141**	**102**	**62**	**21**	**2,257**
1	305	30	95	87	58	24	10	1	900
2	163	-	19	32	49	32	23	8	693
3	52	-	-	6	17	22	7	-	238
4	54	-	-	1	15	15	14	9	295
5	19	-	-	2	2	7	5	3	103
6	3	-	-	-	-	1	2	-	17
7 or more	2	-	-	-	-	1	1	-	11
Total persons	**1,130**	**30**	**133**	**183**	**277**	**262**	**177**	**68**	
Rented from a local authority or new town	**4,993**	**110**	**387**	**840**	**1,173**	**1,347**	**955**	**181**	**21,949**
1	1,880	108	322	574	464	230	160	22	6,597
2	1,542	1	44	213	453	451	330	50	7,166
3	650	-	16	37	131	260	173	33	3,255
4	569	1	5	12	98	258	162	33	2,964
5	238	-	-	4	20	112	79	23	1,289
6	91	-	-	-	5	30	41	15	537
7 or more	23	-	-	-	2	6	10	5	141
Total persons	**11,094**	**114**	**478**	**1,179**	**2,299**	**3,728**	**2,698**	**598**	

22. Households with residents; residents in households; rooms in household spaces

Households with the following tenure and persons	TOTAL HOUSE-HOLDS	Households with the following rooms							TOTAL ROOMS
		1	2	3	4	5	6	7 or more	
a	b	c	d	e	f	g	h	i	j
				Wansdyke					
ALL TENURES	**30,814**	**102**	**537**	**1,696**	**4,809**	**8,997**	**7,612**	**7,061**	**172,739**
1	6,663	84	402	1,077	1,726	1,678	1,176	520	30,565
2	11,055	13	124	532	2,154	3,441	2,726	2,065	60,349
3	5,068	3	8	60	579	1,651	1,433	1,334	30,042
4	5,680	1	2	22	290	1,688	1,655	2,022	35,725
5	1,817	1	1	5	48	437	496	829	12,201
6	423	-	-	-	11	81	99	232	3,064
7 or more	108	-	-	-	1	21	27	59	793
TOTAL PERSONS	**79,122**	**128**	**687**	**2,434**	**9,244**	**23,087**	**20,823**	**22,719**	
Owner occupied - owned outright	**9,440**	**22**	**67**	**283**	**1,704**	**2,850**	**2,536**	**1,978**	**53,315**
1	2,830	17	52	182	768	859	660	292	14,298
2	4,610	2	15	88	809	1,461	1,263	972	26,115
3	1,128	2	-	9	91	318	363	345	7,086
4	641	1	-	4	33	178	198	227	4,065
5	174	-	-	-	3	28	41	102	1,287
6	45	-	-	-	-	5	10	30	363
7 or more	12	-	-	-	-	1	1	10	101
Total persons	**19,226**	**31**	**82**	**401**	**2,806**	**5,624**	**5,339**	**4,943**	
Owner occupied - buying	**14,851**	**10**	**73**	**279**	**1,618**	**4,302**	**3,962**	**4,607**	**89,482**
1	1,453	5	41	114	399	454	294	146	7,200
2	4,344	4	30	132	737	1,381	1,083	977	24,478
3	3,026	-	1	21	265	968	870	901	18,240
4	4,344	-	1	11	185	1,183	1,274	1,690	27,779
5	1,325	1	-	1	23	264	364	672	9,099
6	291	-	-	-	8	42	61	180	2,175
7 or more	68	-	-	-	1	10	16	41	511
Total persons	**45,479**	**18**	**108**	**490**	**3,578**	**12,497**	**12,474**	**16,314**	
Rented privately - furnished	**576**	**39**	**38**	**80**	**134**	**129**	**86**	**70**	**2,595**
1	229	35	20	46	49	37	25	17	872
2	215	3	14	29	65	55	31	18	982
3	70	1	3	3	17	22	16	8	347
4	36	-	1	1	3	7	11	13	220
5	21	-	-	1	-	8	3	9	136
6	5	-	-	-	-	-	-	5	38
7 or more	-	-	-	-	-	-	-	-	-
Total persons	**1,148**	**44**	**61**	**122**	**242**	**281**	**194**	**204**	
Rented privately - unfurnished	**844**	**6**	**32**	**73**	**213**	**242**	**189**	**89**	**4,203**
1	340	5	22	40	100	97	52	24	1,558
2	313	1	9	28	79	88	82	26	1,559
3	108	-	1	4	23	31	31	18	599
4	61	-	-	1	9	20	14	17	356
5	18	-	-	-	2	5	8	3	104
6	2	-	-	-	-	-	2	-	12
7 or more	2	-	-	-	-	1	-	1	15
Total persons	**1,650**	**7**	**43**	**112**	**373**	**478**	**417**	**220**	

22. Households with residents; residents in households; rooms in household spaces

Households with the following tenure and persons	TOTAL HOUSE-HOLDS	Households with the following rooms							TOTAL ROOMS
		1	2	3	4	5	6	7 or more	
a	b	c	d	e	f	g	h	i	j
				Wansdyke - *continued*					
Rented with a job or business	**541**	**7**	**20**	**34**	**85**	**127**	**102**	**166**	**3,146**
1	104	5	14	13	24	18	13	17	485
2	168	2	6	12	35	40	36	37	906
3	107	-	-	7	19	25	22	34	636
4	106	-	-	2	6	34	20	44	700
5	43	-	-	-	1	8	9	25	313
6	10	-	-	-	-	2	1	7	79
7 or more	3	-	-	-	-	-	1	2	27
Total persons	**1,481**	**9**	**26**	**66**	**180**	**361**	**289**	**550**	
Rented from a housing association	**289**	**7**	**32**	**72**	**60**	**77**	**28**	**13**	**1,192**
1	133	6	23	56	25	14	6	3	460
2	89	1	9	15	27	22	13	2	374
3	27	-	-	1	4	19	1	2	137
4	22	-	-	-	2	13	5	2	119
5	14	-	-	-	2	7	2	3	78
6	4	-	-	-	-	2	1	1	24
7 or more	-	-	-	-	-	-	-	-	-
Total persons	**574**	**8**	**41**	**89**	**109**	**214**	**71**	**42**	
Rented from a local authority or new town	**4,273**	**11**	**275**	**875**	**995**	**1,270**	**709**	**138**	**18,806**
1	1,574	11	230	626	361	199	126	21	5,692
2	1,316	-	41	228	402	394	218	33	5,935
3	602	-	3	15	160	268	130	26	2,997
4	470	-	-	3	52	253	133	29	2,486
5	222	-	1	3	17	117	69	15	1,184
6	66	-	-	-	3	30	24	9	373
7 or more	23	-	-	-	-	9	9	5	139
Total persons	**9,564**	**11**	**326**	**1,154**	**1,956**	**3,632**	**2,039**	**446**	
				Woodspring					
ALL TENURES	**70,519**	**1,182**	**2,067**	**4,959**	**12,996**	**18,063**	**15,524**	**15,728**	**380,255**
1	17,732	1,010	1,454	2,850	5,043	3,862	2,323	1,190	75,308
2	25,741	128	553	1,826	5,966	7,256	5,605	4,407	135,168
3	10,710	32	39	213	1,279	3,064	2,974	3,109	63,322
4	11,576	5	16	54	568	2,902	3,403	4,628	74,035
5	3,680	6	2	14	120	774	974	1,790	24,762
6	853	1	2	2	14	164	204	466	5,990
7 or more	227	-	1	-	6	41	41	138	1,670
TOTAL PERSONS	**172,844**	**1,418**	**2,770**	**7,439**	**23,814**	**44,322**	**42,464**	**50,617**	
Owner occupied - owned outright	**21,597**	**37**	**250**	**1,226**	**5,178**	**6,129**	**4,872**	**3,905**	**115,951**
1	7,684	29	195	750	2,488	2,129	1,381	712	37,182
2	10,670	7	52	449	2,464	3,242	2,548	1,908	57,816
3	2,015	1	1	22	176	517	604	694	12,540
4	891	-	2	3	43	194	255	394	5,900
5	244	-	-	2	6	40	60	136	1,761
6	70	-	-	-	1	7	18	44	536
7 or more	23	-	-	-	-	-	6	17	216
Total persons	**40,447**	**46**	**310**	**1,736**	**8,152**	**11,182**	**9,760**	**9,261**	

22. Households with residents; residents in households; rooms in household spaces

Households with the following tenure and persons	TOTAL HOUSE-HOLDS	Households with the following rooms							TOTAL ROOMS
		1	2	3	4	5	6	7 or more	
a	b	c	d	e	f	g	h	i	j
Woodspring - *continued*									
Owner occupied - buying	**34,478**	**114**	**519**	**1,199**	**4,072**	**8,758**	**8,796**	**11,020**	**204,591**
1	4,060	71	288	520	1,132	1,053	638	358	18,581
2	10,559	33	204	564	1,922	3,010	2,525	2,301	58,087
3	6,933	3	20	85	612	1,934	1,999	2,280	42,118
4	9,331	3	6	24	336	2,160	2,759	4,043	60,646
5	2,866	4	1	5	59	506	733	1,558	19,781
6	590	-	-	1	7	77	126	379	4,334
7 or more	139	-	-	-	4	18	16	101	1,044
Total persons	**102,192**	**178**	**785**	**2,030**	**8,524**	**24,635**	**27,259**	**38,781**	
Rented privately - furnished	**2,486**	**588**	**390**	**393**	**436**	**348**	**180**	**151**	**8,370**
1	1,295	515	246	198	172	93	44	27	3,281
2	761	58	132	163	197	121	52	38	2,832
3	239	11	5	28	50	65	49	31	1,159
4	134	1	4	3	14	54	23	35	760
5	37	2	1	1	3	11	8	11	210
6	16	1	2	-	-	4	3	6	90
7 or more	4	-	-	-	-	-	1	3	38
Total persons	**4,380**	**684**	**558**	**625**	**787**	**825**	**452**	**449**	
Rented privately - unfurnished	**2,085**	**59**	**145**	**380**	**564**	**483**	**295**	**159**	**9,207**
1	893	49	91	194	270	175	75	39	3,516
2	784	7	48	161	217	188	113	50	3,488
3	205	3	5	21	46	64	44	22	1,011
4	135	-	1	3	25	36	46	24	762
5	50	-	-	-	6	17	13	14	300
6	12	-	-	1	-	1	3	7	84
7 or more	6	-	-	-	-	2	1	3	46
Total persons	**3,980**	**72**	**206**	**597**	**972**	**992**	**707**	**434**	
Rented with a job or business	**1,162**	**13**	**27**	**89**	**211**	**285**	**297**	**240**	**6,407**
1	238	13	17	44	53	53	34	24	1,081
2	358	-	9	32	98	93	68	58	1,869
3	201	-	1	11	39	68	49	33	1,094
4	245	-	-	1	13	55	109	67	1,553
5	90	-	-	1	8	13	28	40	596
6	21	-	-	-	-	2	8	11	146
7 or more	9	-	-	-	-	1	1	7	68
Total persons	**3,182**	**13**	**38**	**150**	**458**	**747**	**948**	**828**	
Rented from a housing association	**1,111**	**139**	**232**	**295**	**243**	**139**	**42**	**21**	**3,584**
1	691	138	195	189	117	40	6	6	1,858
2	303	1	37	96	92	54	18	5	1,146
3	62	-	-	8	28	19	4	3	278
4	32	-	-	1	5	15	7	4	175
5	20	-	-	1	1	11	6	1	106
6	1	-	-	-	-	-	1	-	6
7 or more	2	-	-	-	-	-	-	2	15
Total persons	**1,731**	**140**	**269**	**414**	**410**	**320**	**118**	**60**	

22. Households with residents; residents in households; rooms in household spaces

Households with the following tenure and persons	TOTAL HOUSE-HOLDS	Households with the following rooms							TOTAL ROOMS
		1	2	3	4	5	6	7 or more	
a	b	c	d	e	f	g	h	i	j
				Woodspring – *continued*					
Rented from a local authority or new town	**7,600**	**232**	**504**	**1,377**	**2,292**	**1,921**	**1,042**	**232**	**32,145**
1	2,871	195	422	955	811	319	145	24	9,809
2	2,306	22	71	361	976	548	281	47	9,930
3	1,055	14	7	38	328	397	225	46	5,122
4	808	1	3	19	132	388	204	61	4,239
5	373	-	-	4	37	176	126	30	2,008
6	143	-	-	-	6	73	45	19	794
7 or more	44	-	1	-	2	20	16	5	243
Total persons	**16,932**	**285**	**604**	**1,887**	**4,511**	**5,621**	**3,220**	**804**	

23. Households with residents; residents in households

Tenure	TOTAL HOUSEHOLDS	Up to 0.5 persons per room	Over 0.5 and up to 1 person per room	Over 1 and up to 1.5 persons per room	Over 1.5 persons per room
a	b	c	d	e	f
	AVON				
TOTAL HOUSEHOLDS	**376,522**	**251,342**	**119,606**	**4,177**	**1,397**
All permanent buildings	**374,740**	**250,148**	**119,110**	**4,158**	**1,324**
Owner occupied - owned outright	97,807	86,038	11,503	205	61
- buying	172,361	99,568	70,782	1,702	309
Rented privately - furnished	16,896	8,409	7,825	142	520
- unfurnished	10,709	7,580	2,931	97	101
Rented with a job or business	5,095	3,123	1,865	84	23
Rented from a housing association	9,588	6,131	3,301	106	50
Rented from a local authority or new town	62,284	39,299	20,903	1,822	260
Non - permanent accommodation	**1,782**	**1,194**	**496**	**19**	**73**
TOTAL PERSONS IN HOUSEHOLDS	**916,973**	**456,643**	**431,780**	**23,339**	**5,211**
All permanent buildings	**913,834**	**454,932**	**430,702**	**23,254**	**4,946**
Owner occupied - owned outright	191,641	148,663	41,434	1,231	313
- buying	500,359	210,338	278,792	9,819	1,410
Rented privately - furnished	31,196	12,890	16,351	609	1,346
- unfurnished	20,033	11,208	8,098	464	263
Rented with a job or business	13,121	5,869	6,706	449	97
Rented from a housing association	16,403	7,730	7,907	555	211
Rented from a local authority or new town	141,081	58,234	71,414	10,127	1,306
Non - permanent accommodation	**3,139**	**1,711**	**1,078**	**85**	**265**
	Bath				
TOTAL HOUSEHOLDS	**34,128**	**23,575**	**9,975**	**396**	**182**
All permanent buildings	**34,039**	**23,501**	**9,962**	**396**	**180**
Owner occupied - owned outright	9,623	8,684	918	13	8
- buying	12,369	7,530	4,693	104	42
Rented privately - furnished	2,530	1,251	1,166	34	79
- unfurnished	1,665	1,184	454	8	19
Rented with a job or business	476	301	162	10	3
Rented from a housing association	1,167	758	398	6	5
Rented from a local authority or new town	6,209	3,793	2,171	221	24
Non - permanent accommodation	**89**	**74**	**13**	**-**	**2**
TOTAL PERSONS IN HOUSEHOLDS	**76,876**	**40,872**	**33,364**	**2,081**	**559**
All permanent buildings	**76,745**	**40,775**	**33,339**	**2,081**	**550**
Owner occupied - owned outright	18,021	14,685	3,236	75	25
- buying	34,404	15,715	17,986	567	136
Rented privately - furnished	4,672	1,897	2,440	132	203
- unfurnished	2,856	1,650	1,133	31	42
Rented with a job or business	1,144	525	559	51	9
Rented from a housing association	1,856	916	892	23	25
Rented from a local authority or new town	13,792	5,387	7,093	1,202	110
Non - permanent accommodation	**131**	**97**	**25**	**-**	**9**

23. Households with residents; residents in households

Tenure		TOTAL HOUSEHOLDS	Up to 0.5 persons per room	Over 0.5 and up to 1 person per room	Over 1 and up to 1.5 persons per room	Over 1.5 persons per room
a		b	c	d	e	f
		Bristol				
TOTAL HOUSEHOLDS		**156,778**	**103,729**	**49,868**	**2,360**	**821**
All permanent buildings		**156,651**	**103,657**	**49,829**	**2,357**	**808**
Owner occupied	- owned outright	36,448	31,879	4,413	119	37
	- buying	63,222	37,542	24,681	839	160
Rented privately	- furnished	9,973	4,619	4,944	76	334
	- unfurnished	4,550	3,098	1,338	51	63
Rented with a job or business		1,927	1,193	683	37	14
Rented from a housing association		5,808	3,691	1,999	79	39
Rented from a local authority or new town		34,723	21,635	11,771	1,156	161
Non - permanent accommodation		**127**	**72**	**39**	**3**	**13**
TOTAL PERSONS IN HOUSEHOLDS		**370,131**	**179,744**	**173,881**	**13,263**	**3,243**
All permanent buildings		**369,899**	**179,642**	**173,798**	**13,251**	**3,208**
Owner occupied	- owned outright	71,192	54,128	16,096	737	231
	- buying	177,505	75,277	96,510	4,896	822
Rented privately	- furnished	18,197	7,001	10,003	324	869
	- unfurnished	8,233	4,408	3,408	248	169
Rented with a job or business		4,649	2,089	2,297	200	63
Rented from a housing association		9,902	4,613	4,716	413	160
Rented from a local authority or new town		80,221	32,126	40,768	6,433	894
Non - permanent accommodation		**232**	**102**	**83**	**12**	**35**
		Kingswood				
TOTAL HOUSEHOLDS		**34,657**	**22,169**	**12,149**	**290**	**49**
All permanent buildings		**34,535**	**22,111**	**12,090**	**288**	**46**
Owner occupied	- owned outright	9,920	8,487	1,420	10	3
	- buying	18,210	9,423	8,616	160	11
Rented privately	- furnished	547	319	208	3	17
	- unfurnished	499	348	140	6	5
Rented with a job or business		240	144	93	2	1
Rented from a housing association		619	359	250	9	1
Rented from a local authority or new town		4,500	3,031	1,363	98	8
Non - permanent accommodation		**122**	**58**	**59**	**2**	**3**
TOTAL PERSONS IN HOUSEHOLDS		**88,916**	**41,215**	**45,871**	**1,634**	**196**
All permanent buildings		**88,703**	**41,146**	**45,753**	**1,622**	**182**
Owner occupied	- owned outright	20,328	15,122	5,138	52	16
	- buying	54,875	19,835	34,060	920	60
Rented privately	- furnished	1,127	533	534	15	45
	- unfurnished	1,038	547	452	27	12
Rented with a job or business		602	253	335	9	5
Rented from a housing association		1,214	472	681	54	7
Rented from a local authority or new town		9,519	4,384	4,553	545	37
Non - permanent accommodation		**213**	**69**	**118**	**12**	**14**

23. Households with residents; residents in households

Tenure	TOTAL HOUSEHOLDS	Up to 0.5 persons per room	Over 0.5 and up to 1 person per room	Over 1 and up to 1.5 persons per room	Over 1.5 persons per room
a	b	c	d	e	f
	Northavon				
TOTAL HOUSEHOLDS	**49,626**	**32,524**	**16,585**	**425**	**92**
All permanent buildings	**49,086**	**32,178**	**16,432**	**417**	**59**
Owner occupied - owned outright	11,522	9,982	1,510	26	4
- buying	29,323	16,708	12,333	252	30
Rented privately - furnished	824	552	253	10	9
- unfurnished	1,077	800	266	10	1
Rented with a job or business	760	472	272	14	2
Rented from a housing association	596	397	191	6	2
Rented from a local authority or new town	4,984	3,267	1,607	99	11
Non - permanent accommodation	**540**	**346**	**153**	**8**	**33**
TOTAL PERSONS IN HOUSEHOLDS	**129,084**	**62,974**	**63,337**	**2,374**	**399**
All permanent buildings	**128,037**	**62,467**	**62,973**	**2,340**	**257**
Owner occupied - owned outright	23,662	17,974	5,522	151	15
- buying	86,058	35,780	48,688	1,451	139
Rented privately - furnished	1,742	912	750	57	23
- unfurnished	2,295	1,313	922	55	5
Rented with a job or business	2,085	965	1,041	68	11
Rented from a housing association	1,128	538	546	34	10
Rented from a local authority or new town	11,067	4,985	5,504	524	54
Non - permanent accommodation	**1,047**	**507**	**364**	**34**	**142**
	Wansdyke				
TOTAL HOUSEHOLDS	**30,814**	**20,877**	**9,683**	**223**	**31**
All permanent buildings	**30,659**	**20,792**	**9,623**	**223**	**21**
Owner occupied - owned outright	9,326	8,117	1,195	14	-
- buying	14,827	8,309	6,393	117	8
Rented privately - furnished	570	394	167	4	5
- unfurnished	842	664	172	5	1
Rented with a job or business	537	344	185	6	2
Rented from a housing association	289	196	88	4	1
Rented from a local authority or new town	4,268	2,768	1,423	73	4
Non - permanent accommodation	**155**	**85**	**60**	**-**	**10**
TOTAL PERSONS IN HOUSEHOLDS	**79,122**	**40,408**	**37,287**	**1,302**	**125**
All permanent buildings	**78,866**	**40,295**	**37,171**	**1,302**	**98**
Owner occupied - owned outright	19,039	14,533	4,431	75	-
- buying	45,443	18,919	25,763	710	51
Rented privately - furnished	1,139	640	470	13	16
- unfurnished	1,647	1,057	564	24	2
Rented with a job or business	1,474	739	699	32	4
Rented from a housing association	574	272	278	22	2
Rented from a local authority or new town	9,550	4,135	4,966	426	23
Non - permanent accommodation	**256**	**113**	**116**	**-**	**27**

23. Households with residents; residents in households

Tenure	TOTAL HOUSEHOLDS	Up to 0.5 persons per room	Over 0.5 and up to 1 person per room	Over 1 and up to 1.5 persons per room	Over 1.5 persons per room
a	b	c	d	e	f
	Woodspring				
TOTAL HOUSEHOLDS	**70,519**	**48,468**	**21,346**	**483**	**222**
All permanent buildings	**69,770**	**47,909**	**21,174**	**477**	**210**
Owner occupied - owned outright	20,968	18,889	2,047	23	9
- buying	34,410	20,056	14,066	230	58
Rented privately - furnished	2,452	1,274	1,087	15	76
- unfurnished	2,076	1,486	561	17	12
Rented with a job or business	1,155	669	470	15	1
Rented from a housing association	1,109	730	375	2	2
Rented from a local authority or new town	7,600	4,805	2,568	175	52
Non - permanent accommodation	**749**	**559**	**172**	**6**	**12**
TOTAL PERSONS IN HOUSEHOLDS	**172,844**	**91,430**	**78,040**	**2,685**	**689**
All permanent buildings	**171,584**	**90,607**	**77,668**	**2,658**	**651**
Owner occupied - owned outright	39,399	32,221	7,011	141	26
- buying	102,074	44,812	55,785	1,275	202
Rented privately - furnished	4,319	1,907	2,154	68	190
- unfurnished	3,964	2,233	1,619	79	33
Rented with a job or business	3,167	1,298	1,775	89	5
Rented from a housing association	1,729	919	794	9	7
Rented from a local authority or new town	16,932	7,217	8,530	997	188
Non - permanent accommodation	**1,260**	**823**	**372**	**27**	**38**

Note: * May include a small number of households with no persons aged 18 and over

24. Households with residents; residents in households

Households with the following persons	TOTAL HOUSEHOLDS*	Households with the following persons aged 18 and over				TOTAL PERSONS AGED 18 AND OVER
		1	2	3	4 or more	
a	b	c	d	e	f	g
AVON						
TOTAL HOUSEHOLDS	**376,522**	**115,012**	**202,677**	**42,571**	**16,101**	**715,701**
1	100,534	100,435				100,435
2	132,374	6,810	125,513			257,836
3	58,265	5,306	24,274	28,678		139,888
4 or more	85,349	2,461	52,890	13,893	16,101	217,542
TOTAL PERSONS	**916,973**	**140,700**	**554,870**	**147,847**	**73,318**	
Bath						
TOTAL HOUSEHOLDS	**34,128**	**12,558**	**16,696**	**3,571**	**1,293**	**62,109**
1	11,179	11,170				11,170
2	11,945	711	11,233			23,177
3	4,811	484	1,806	2,521		11,659
4 or more	6,193	193	3,657	1,050	1,293	16,103
TOTAL PERSONS	**76,876**	**14,879**	**43,920**	**12,226**	**5,840**	
Bristol						
TOTAL HOUSEHOLDS	**156,778**	**55,216**	**78,366**	**16,629**	**6,461**	**289,233**
1	47,600	47,542				47,542
2	53,411	3,643	49,729			103,101
3	23,261	2,572	9,259	11,423		55,359
4 or more	32,506	1,459	19,378	5,206	6,461	83,231
TOTAL PERSONS	**370,131**	**68,962**	**213,163**	**57,880**	**29,961**	
Kingswood						
TOTAL HOUSEHOLDS	**34,657**	**8,484**	**20,057**	**4,411**	**1,698**	**68,892**
1	7,364	7,359				7,359
2	12,352	466	11,884			24,234
3	5,976	500	2,489	2,987		14,439
4 or more	8,965	159	5,684	1,424	1,698	22,860
TOTAL PERSONS	**88,916**	**10,472**	**55,714**	**15,164**	**7,557**	
Northavon						
TOTAL HOUSEHOLDS	**49,626**	**11,438**	**29,682**	**6,129**	**2,371**	**99,031**
1	9,996	9,993				9,993
2	17,870	632	17,236			35,104
3	8,439	577	3,907	3,955		20,256
4 or more	13,321	236	8,539	2,174	2,371	33,678
TOTAL PERSONS	**129,084**	**13,986**	**83,045**	**21,396**	**10,646**	

Note: * May include a small number of households with no persons aged 18 and over

24. Households with residents; residents in households

Households with the following persons	TOTAL HOUSEHOLDS*	Households with the following persons aged 18 and over				TOTAL PERSONS AGED 18 AND OVER
		1	2	3	4 or more	
a	b	c	d	e	f	g
			Wansdyke			
TOTAL HOUSEHOLDS	**30,814**	**7,408**	**17,808**	**4,011**	**1,586**	**61,662**
1	6,663	6,662				6,662
2	11,055	345	10,710			21,765
3	5,068	307	2,093	2,668		12,497
4 or more	8,028	94	5,005	1,343	1,586	20,738
TOTAL PERSONS	**79,122**	**8,681**	**49,392**	**13,944**	**7,104**	
			Woodspring			
TOTAL HOUSEHOLDS	**70,519**	**19,908**	**40,068**	**7,820**	**2,692**	**134,774**
1	17,732	17,709				17,709
2	25,741	1,013	24,721			50,455
3	10,710	866	4,720	5,124		25,678
4 or more	16,336	320	10,627	2,696	2,692	40,932
TOTAL PERSONS	**172,844**	**23,720**	**109,636**	**27,237**	**12,210**	

Notes: (1) * Includes all students aged 18 and over, whether economically active or inactive
(2) ** Households with 3 or more cars are counted as having 3 cars

25. Households with persons present but no residents; persons present in such households; cars and rooms in such households

Households with no residents	TOTAL HOUSE-HOLDS	Lacking or sharing use of bath/ shower and/or inside WC	No central heating	Not self-contained accomm-odation	Tenure: Owner occupied	Tenure: Rented privately	Tenure: Rented from a housing assoc-iation	Tenure: Rented from a local authority or new town	TOTAL ROOMS	TOTAL CARS**	Total students* present
a	b	c	d	e	f	g	h	i	j	k	l
AVON											
TOTAL HOUSEHOLDS	**2,944**	**299**	**760**	**558**	**619**	**2,122**	**44**	**75**	**12,390**	**2,838**	**4,893**
Households with 1 or more students* aged 18 and over plus others	198	8	45	17	9	182	3	1	1,036	242	501
Households with student(s)* only	1,513	184	447	396	57	1,438	9	6	6,467	1,511	4,392
TOTAL PERSONS PRESENT	**7,186**	**372**	**1,729**	**843**	**1,117**	**5,716**	**72**	**142**			
Students* present	4,893	217	1,291	640	171	4,670	22	16			
Bath											
TOTAL HOUSEHOLDS	**575**	**51**	**128**	**102**	**89**	**462**	**11**	**8**	**2,319**	**551**	**1,130**
Households with 1 or more students* aged 18 and over plus others	40	1	8	2	4	34	-	-	183	50	97
Households with student(s)* only	347	33	89	73	6	335	3	3	1,437	355	1,033
TOTAL PERSONS PRESENT	**1,487**	**58**	**310**	**165**	**162**	**1,286**	**15**	**13**			
Students* present	1,130	39	262	123	15	1,098	5	8			
Bristol											
TOTAL HOUSEHOLDS	**1,810**	**208**	**495**	**431**	**251**	**1,452**	**24**	**41**	**7,670**	**1,713**	**3,594**
Households with 1 or more students* aged 18 and over plus others	148	6	36	14	5	139	3	-	798	178	388
Households with student(s)* only	1,103	148	345	320	48	1,046	4	2	4,739	1,069	3,206
TOTAL PERSONS PRESENT	**4,655**	**241**	**1,190**	**646**	**462**	**4,009**	**41**	**71**			
Students* present	3,594	173	997	512	152	3,415	13	4			
Kingswood											
TOTAL HOUSEHOLDS	**50**	**2**	**8**	**1**	**28**	**13**	**1**	**3**	**230**	**46**	**19**
Households with 1 or more students* aged 18 and over plus others	1	-	1	-	-	1	-	-	5	2	1
Households with student(s)* only	8	1	3	-	2	5	-	1	39	5	18
TOTAL PERSONS PRESENT	**89**	**2**	**17**	**1**	**43**	**30**	**1**	**9**			
Students* present	19	1	12	-	2	15	-	2			

Notes: (1) * Includes all students aged 18 and over, whether economically active or inactive
(2) ** Households with 3 or more cars are counted as having 3 cars

25. Households with persons present but no residents; persons present in such households; cars and rooms in such households

Households with no residents	TOTAL HOUSE-HOLDS	Lacking or sharing use of bath/ shower and/or inside WC	No central heating	Not self-contained accomm-odation	Tenure: Owner occupied	Tenure: Rented privately	Tenure: Rented from a housing assoc-iation	Tenure: Rented from a local authority or new town	TOTAL ROOMS	TOTAL CARS**	Total students* present
a	b	c	d	e	f	g	h	i	j	k	l
Northavon											
TOTAL HOUSEHOLDS	**133**	**9**	**31**	**2**	**63**	**60**	**-**	**4**	**610**	**144**	**60**
Households with 1 or more students* aged 18 and over plus others	3	-	-	-	-	2	-	1	15	3	5
Households with student(s)* only	24	1	5	1	1	23	-	-	115	32	55
TOTAL PERSONS PRESENT	**244**	**26**	**46**	**2**	**114**	**115**	**-**	**6**			
Students* present	60	2	11	1	2	56	-	2			
Wansdyke											
TOTAL HOUSEHOLDS	**109**	**7**	**16**	**5**	**43**	**44**	**3**	**12**	**502**	**119**	**49**
Households with 1 or more students* aged 18 and over plus others	1	-	-	-	-	1	-	-	6	2	1
Households with student(s)* only	15	-	2	-	-	13	2	-	74	23	48
TOTAL PERSONS PRESENT	**232**	**12**	**29**	**7**	**75**	**107**	**7**	**29**			
Students* present	49	-	6	-	-	45	4	-			
Woodspring											
TOTAL HOUSEHOLDS	**267**	**22**	**82**	**17**	**145**	**91**	**5**	**7**	**1,059**	**265**	**41**
Households with 1 or more students* aged 18 and over plus others	5	1	-	1	-	5	-	-	29	7	9
Households with student(s)* only	16	1	3	2	-	16	-	-	63	27	32
TOTAL PERSONS PRESENT	**479**	**33**	**137**	**22**	**261**	**169**	**8**	**14**			
Students* present	41	2	3	4	-	41	-	-			

Table 26 Students in households

Notes: (1) * Includes all students aged 18 and over whether economically active or inactive
(2) ** Households with 3 or more cars are counted as having 3 cars

26. Households with residents; residents in households; persons present in households; rooms in household spaces; cars in households

Households with residents enumerated with resident or visitor students aged 18 and over*	TOTAL HOUSE-HOLDS	Lacking or sharing use of bath/shower and/or inside WC	No central heating	Not self-contained accomm-odation	Tenure			
					Owner occupied	Rented privately	Rented from a housing association	Rented from a local authority or new town
a	b	c	d	e	f	g	h	i
			AVON					
TOTAL HOUSEHOLDS	**376,522**	**4,510**	**55,041**	**5,955**	**271,753**	**27,725**	**9,598**	**62,330**
Households with students* (resident or visitor) only	1,512	170	474	326	267	1,168	41	27
Households with students* (resident or visitor) and non-students	14,747	62	1,163	229	11,997	1,718	135	663
Number of students in household (included above)*								
1	13,247	209	1,250	430	10,526	1,726	150	650
2	2,046	20	208	60	1,490	471	18	33
3 or more	966	3	179	65	248	689	8	7
TOTAL PERSONS RESIDENT OR PRESENT	**932,120**	**6,327**	**116,499**	**8,862**	**705,824**	**53,955**	**16,597**	**142,262**
Students* resident or present	21,022	259	2,351	824	14,336	5,417	220	737
			Bath					
TOTAL HOUSEHOLDS	**34,128**	**560**	**4,795**	**975**	**22,075**	**4,200**	**1,167**	**6,210**
Households with students* (resident or visitor) only	315	25	82	63	40	265	5	4
Households with students* (resident or visitor) and non-students	1,753	10	152	40	1,288	344	14	75
Number of students in household (included above)*								
1	1,532	32	158	78	1,086	334	15	74
2	331	2	37	14	205	112	3	5
3 or more	205	1	39	11	37	163	1	-
TOTAL PERSONS RESIDENT OR PRESENT	**78,821**	**744**	**8,929**	**1,474**	**53,839**	**8,003**	**1,881**	**13,919**
Students* resident or present	2,973	39	379	150	1,625	1,190	25	84
			Bristol					
TOTAL HOUSEHOLDS	**156,778**	**2,675**	**31,218**	**3,833**	**99,749**	**14,535**	**5,812**	**34,753**
Households with students* (resident or visitor) only	1,073	138	359	250	183	832	33	19
Households with students* (resident or visitor) and non-students	5,878	45	730	166	4,153	1,162	102	375
Number of students in household (included above)*								
1	5,373	164	799	320	3,649	1,166	113	374
2	897	17	152	43	534	321	15	13
3 or more	681	2	138	53	153	507	7	7
TOTAL PERSONS RESIDENT OR PRESENT	**376,635**	**3,572**	**67,127**	**5,588**	**252,867**	**28,121**	**10,016**	**80,868**
Students* resident or present	9,804	205	1,635	633	5,233	3,852	173	421

TOTAL ROOMS	TOTAL CARS**	Total student* visitors	Total student* residents	Households with the following persons present or resident					Households with residents enumerated with resident or visitor students aged 18 and over*
				1	2	3	4	5 or more	
j	k	l	m	n	o	p	q	r	a
1,968,000	**396,036**	**3,075**	**17,947**	**97,289**	**131,303**	**59,135**	**59,972**	**28,823**	**TOTAL HOUSEHOLDS**
5,950	1,301	767	2,616	703	293	194	177	145	Households with students* (resident or visitor) only
95,912	24,528	2,308	15,331	-	1,929	3,878	5,440	3,500	Households with students* (resident or visitor) and non-students
									Number of students in household (included above)*
82,151	21,005	1,061	12,186	703	1,929	3,586	4,498	2,531	1
13,521	3,373	648	3,444	-	293	292	836	625	2
6,190	1,451	1,366	2,317	-	-	194	283	489	3 or more
									TOTAL PERSONS RESIDENT OR PRESENT
				703	2,515	4,752	7,196	5,856	Students* resident or present
171,000	**29,723**	**594**	**2,379**	**10,738**	**11,835**	**4,921**	**4,411**	**2,223**	**TOTAL HOUSEHOLDS**
1,138	271	155	573	129	69	48	44	25	Households with students* (resident or visitor) only
11,158	2,520	439	1,806	-	321	451	568	413	Households with students* (resident or visitor) and non-students
									Number of students in household (included above)*
8,979	2,034	166	1,366	129	321	390	436	256	1
2,066	460	133	529	-	69	61	109	92	2
1,251	297	295	484	-	-	48	67	90	3 or more
									TOTAL PERSONS RESIDENT OR PRESENT
				129	459	656	899	830	Students* resident or present
786,985	**140,211**	**1,922**	**7,882**	**45,992**	**53,156**	**23,735**	**21,718**	**12,177**	**TOTAL HOUSEHOLDS**
4,260	917	592	1,875	485	203	141	129	115	Households with students* (resident or visitor) only
36,043	8,414	1,330	6,007	-	1,105	1,519	1,785	1,469	Households with students* (resident or visitor) and non-students
									Number of students in household (included above)*
30,449	7,099	527	4,846	485	1,105	1,346	1,437	1,000	1
5,507	1,238	380	1,414	-	203	173	276	245	2
4,347	994	1,015	1,622	-	-	141	201	339	3 or more
									TOTAL PERSONS RESIDENT OR PRESENT
				485	1,511	2,115	2,721	2,972	Students* resident or present

Table 26 Students in households - continued

Notes: (1) * Includes all students aged 18 and over whether economically active or inactive
(2) ** Households with 3 or more cars are counted as having 3 cars

26. Households with residents; residents in households; persons present in households; rooms in household spaces; cars in households

Households with residents enumerated with resident or visitor students aged 18 and over*	TOTAL HOUSE-HOLDS	Lacking or sharing use of bath/shower and/or inside WC	No central heating	Not self-contained accomm-odation	Tenure			
					Owner occupied	Rented privately	Rented from a housing association	Rented from a local authority or new town
a	b	c	d	e	f	g	h	i
Kingswood								
TOTAL HOUSEHOLDS	**34,657**	**156**	**2,499**	**120**	**28,235**	**1,059**	**621**	**4,501**
Households with students* (resident or visitor) only	9	-	1	-	6	2	-	-
Households with students* (resident or visitor) and non-students	983	1	23	1	923	18	2	35
Number of students in household (included above)*								
1	903	1	22	1	846	17	2	33
2	81	-	2	-	76	2	-	2
3 or more	8	-	-	-	7	1	-	-
TOTAL PERSONS RESIDENT OR PRESENT	**89,711**	**230**	**5,046**	**177**	**76,075**	**2,219**	**1,229**	**9,575**
Students* resident or present	1,093	1	26	1	1,022	25	2	37
Northavon								
TOTAL HOUSEHOLDS	**49,626**	**224**	**4,282**	**102**	**41,328**	**1,940**	**598**	**4,993**
Households with students* (resident or visitor) only	44	1	6	2	20	21	-	3
Households with students* (resident or visitor) and non-students	1,943	-	67	5	1,797	56	6	57
Number of students in household (included above)*								
1	1,728	1	67	6	1,586	59	6	56
2	231	-	6	1	210	11	-	4
3 or more	28	-	-	-	21	7	-	-
TOTAL PERSONS RESIDENT OR PRESENT	**130,992**	**452**	**9,258**	**195**	**112,270**	**4,228**	**1,149**	**11,195**
Students* resident or present	2,283	1	79	8	2,074	106	6	64
Wansdyke								
TOTAL HOUSEHOLDS	**30,814**	**240**	**3,624**	**87**	**24,291**	**1,420**	**289**	**4,273**
Households with students* (resident or visitor) only	16	-	-	3	6	10	-	-
Households with students* (resident or visitor) and non-students	1,352	2	57	3	1,244	48	6	23
Number of students in household (included above)*								
1	1,177	2	55	5	1,078	45	6	22
2	171	-	2	-	157	9	-	1
3 or more	20	-	-	1	15	4	-	-
TOTAL PERSONS RESIDENT OR PRESENT	**80,353**	**360**	**8,202**	**152**	**65,754**	**2,877**	**580**	**9,622**
Students* resident or present	1,586	2	59	8	1,438	81	6	24

TOTAL ROOMS	TOTAL CARS**	Total student* visitors	Total student* residents	Households with the following persons present or resident					Households with residents enumerated with resident or visitor students aged 18 and over*
				1	2	3	4	5 or more	
j	k	l	m	n	o	p	q	r	a
183,413	**41,134**	**60**	**1,033**	**7,189**	**12,286**	**6,033**	**6,604**	**2,545**	**TOTAL HOUSEHOLDS**
49	12	4	16	4	3	-	1	1	Households with students* (resident or visitor) only
6,115	1,823	56	1,017	-	82	259	444	198	Households with students* (resident or visitor) and non-students
									Number of students in household (included above)*
5,572	1,649	49	854	4	82	252	392	173	1
538	167	7	155	-	3	7	48	23	2
54	19	4	24	-	-	-	5	3	3 or more
									TOTAL PERSONS RESIDENT OR PRESENT
				4	88	266	504	231	Students* resident or present
273,608	**64,818**	**185**	**2,098**	**9,668**	**17,653**	**8,519**	**9,731**	**4,055**	**TOTAL HOUSEHOLDS**
197	40	8	60	29	9	3	3	-	Households with students* (resident or visitor) only
13,070	3,769	177	2,038	-	146	498	865	434	Households with students* (resident or visitor) and non-students
									Number of students in household (included above)*
11,463	3,300	111	1,617	29	146	485	743	325	1
1,612	459	56	406	-	9	13	121	88	2
192	50	18	75	-	-	3	4	21	3 or more
									TOTAL PERSONS RESIDENT OR PRESENT
				29	164	520	1,000	570	Students* resident or present
172,739	**38,777**	**144**	**1,442**	**6,447**	**10,932**	**5,126**	**5,745**	**2,564**	**TOTAL HOUSEHOLDS**
86	23	7	26	9	3	1	-	3	Households with students* (resident or visitor) only
9,660	2,690	137	1,416	-	97	362	562	331	Households with students* (resident or visitor) and non-students
									Number of students in household (included above)*
8,270	2,299	83	1,094	9	97	354	465	252	1
1,317	371	33	309	-	3	8	95	65	2
159	43	28	39	-	-	1	2	17	3 or more
									TOTAL PERSONS RESIDENT OR PRESENT
				9	103	373	661	440	Students* resident or present

Table 26 Students in households – **continued**

Notes: (1) * Includes all students aged 18 and over whether economically active or inactive
(2) ** Households with 3 or more cars are counted as having 3 cars

26. Households with residents; residents in households; persons present in households; rooms in household spaces; cars in households

Households with residents enumerated with resident or visitor students aged 18 and over*	TOTAL HOUSE-HOLDS	Lacking or sharing use of bath/shower and/or inside WC	No central heating	Not self-contained accomm-odation	Tenure			
					Owner occupied	Rented privately	Rented from a housing association	Rented from a local authority or new town
a	b	c	d	e	f	g	h	i
			Woodspring					
TOTAL HOUSEHOLDS	**70,519**	**655**	**8,623**	**838**	**56,075**	**4,571**	**1,111**	**7,600**
Households with students* (resident or visitor) only	55	6	26	8	12	38	3	1
Households with students* (resident or visitor) and non-students	2,838	4	134	14	2,592	90	5	98
Number of students in household (included above)*								
1	2,534	9	149	20	2,281	105	8	91
2	335	1	9	2	308	16	-	8
3 or more	24	-	2	-	15	7	-	-
TOTAL PERSONS RESIDENT OR PRESENT	**175,608**	**969**	**17,937**	**1,276**	**145,019**	**8,507**	**1,742**	**17,083**
Students* resident or present	3,283	11	173	24	2,944	163	8	107

TOTAL ROOMS	TOTAL CARS**	Total student* visitors	Total student* residents	Households with the following persons present or resident: 1	2	3	4	5 or more	Households with residents enumerated with resident or visitor students aged 18 and over*
j	k	l	m	n	o	p	q	r	a
380,255	**81,373**	**170**	**3,113**	**17,255**	**25,441**	**10,801**	**11,763**	**5,259**	**TOTAL HOUSEHOLDS**
220	38	1	66	47	6	1	-	1	Households with students* (resident or visitor) only
19,866	5,312	169	3,047	-	178	789	1,216	655	Households with students* (resident or visitor) and non-students
									Number of students in household (included above)*
17,418	4,624	125	2,409	47	178	759	1,025	525	1
2,481	678	39	631	-	6	30	187	112	2
187	48	6	73	-	-	1	4	19	3 or more
									TOTAL PERSONS RESIDENT OR PRESENT
				47	190	822	1,411	813	Students* resident or present

Note: * Private households with a visitor or visitors present but no usual residents ie a household with '0 persons'

27. Line 1: 1991 households with persons present (1971 population base): present residents and visitors; rooms
Line 2: 1991 households (1981 population base): present and absent residents; rooms
Line 3: 1991 households enumerated or absent (1991 population base): present and absent residents and imputed members of wholly absent households; rooms

	Households with the following persons								TOTAL HOUSE-HOLDS	TOTAL PERSONS (1991)	TOTAL ROOMS (1991)
	0*	1	2	3	4	5	6	7 or more			
a	b	c	d	e	f	g	h	i	j	k	l
AVON											
1. 1971 population base		94,166	127,671	58,122	56,679	19,551	5,382	1,813	363,384	894,271	1,907,272
2. 1981 population base	2,944	92,499	126,972	56,984	58,042	19,376	5,031	1,536	363,384	888,169	1,907,272
3. 1991 population base	2,944	100,534	132,374	58,265	58,966	19,668	5,133	1,582	379,466	916,973	1,980,390
Bath											
1. 1971 population base		10,433	11,405	4,875	4,138	1,450	432	155	32,888	75,427	165,464
2. 1981 population base	575	10,205	11,316	4,699	4,189	1,422	370	112	32,888	73,865	165,464
3. 1991 population base	575	11,179	11,945	4,811	4,258	1,445	375	115	34,703	76,876	173,319
Bristol											
1. 1971 population base		43,905	50,951	22,992	20,748	7,964	2,489	976	150,025	359,935	757,671
2. 1981 population base	1,810	43,192	50,789	22,542	20,776	7,756	2,305	855	150,025	354,582	757,671
3. 1991 population base	1,810	47,600	53,411	23,261	21,290	7,939	2,383	894	158,588	370,131	794,655
Kingswood											
1. 1971 population base		7,087	12,064	6,010	6,243	1,887	425	96	33,812	86,916	179,231
2. 1981 population base	50	6,959	12,020	5,903	6,471	1,912	405	92	33,812	87,267	179,231
3. 1991 population base	50	7,364	12,352	5,976	6,537	1,929	407	92	34,707	88,916	183,643
Northavon											
1. 1971 population base		9,551	17,409	8,460	9,183	2,847	708	182	48,340	126,314	267,059
2. 1981 population base	133	9,368	17,321	8,317	9,522	2,845	688	146	48,340	126,491	267,059
3. 1991 population base	133	9,996	17,870	8,439	9,625	2,858	692	146	49,759	129,084	274,218
Wansdyke											
1. 1971 population base		6,401	10,800	5,092	5,420	1,773	431	141	30,058	77,456	168,697
2. 1981 population base	109	6,287	10,710	5,002	5,626	1,801	417	106	30,058	77,509	168,697
3. 1991 population base	109	6,663	11,055	5,068	5,680	1,817	423	108	30,923	79,122	173,241
Woodspring											
1. 1971 population base		16,789	25,042	10,693	10,947	3,630	897	263	68,261	168,223	369,150
2. 1981 population base	267	16,488	24,816	10,521	11,458	3,640	846	225	68,261	168,455	369,150
3. 1991 population base	267	17,732	25,741	10,710	11,576	3,680	853	227	70,786	172,844	381,314

Table 28 Dependants in households

28. Households with residents; residents in households

Household composition	TOTAL HOUSE-HOLDS	No non-dependants	1 male non-dependant		1 female non-dependant		1 male and 1 female non-dependants		
			Not in employment	In employment	Not in employment	In employment	Neither in employment	1 in employment	Both in employment
a	b	c	d	e	f	g	h	i	j
			AVON						
TOTAL HOUSEHOLDS	**376,522**	**28,544**	**15,410**	**24,839**	**49,530**	**24,221**	**29,618**	**48,022**	**88,861**
Households with no dependants	216,109		11,162	20,670	31,544	15,902	24,608	19,503	47,757
Households with 1 dependant									
Age of dependant									
0 - 4	16,195	18	45	50	1,786	638	852	5,970	5,273
5 - 15	18,426	14	109	251	1,223	1,553	398	2,066	5,270
16 - 18	6,045	42	19	119	148	348	85	502	1,305
19 up to pensionable age	12,167	3,188	534	1,217	2,485	1,581	323	613	512
Pensionable age and over	33,650	17,994	3,064	1,467	7,327	1,110	288	730	448
Households with at least 2 dependants									
Age of youngest dependant 0 - 4 and age of oldest									
0 - 4	9,367	2	16	17	708	114	694	4,666	2,750
5 - 15	18,318	5	53	54	1,732	468	1,347	7,108	6,289
16 - 18	586	2	3	3	49	19	36	163	130
19 up to pensionable age	726	42	35	113	253	65	14	40	15
Pensionable age and over	233	2	-	1	20	5	10	74	47
Age of youngest dependant 5 - 15 and age of oldest									
5 - 15	27,368	11	138	214	1,385	1,570	748	5,250	15,220
16 - 18	6,121	2	15	70	175	332	127	980	3,184
19 up to pensionable age	1,414	131	53	196	312	214	24	100	94
Pensionable age and over	525	14	6	10	43	33	15	77	152
Age of youngest dependant 16 - 18 and age of oldest									
16 - 18	608	2	2	12	20	33	17	89	321
19 up to pensionable age	254	31	11	31	37	30	10	22	17
Pensionable age and over	114	13	2	4	12	13	2	8	19
Age of youngest dependant 19 up to pensionable age and age of oldest									
19 up to pensionable age	695	437	20	40	58	50	8	19	15
Pensionable age and over	1,307	895	50	76	121	54	5	22	19
Age of youngest dependant pensionable age and over	6,294	5,699	73	224	92	89	7	20	24
TOTAL PERSONS	**916,973**	**36,208**	**20,294**	**30,403**	**75,449**	**36,621**	**69,457**	**151,176**	**255,197**
Persons in households with dependants									
Non-dependants	253,213		4,248	4,169	17,986	8,319	10,020	57,038	82,208
Dependants	260,034	36,208	4,884	5,564	25,919	12,400	10,221	55,132	77,475

2 same sex non-dependants			3 or more non-dependants			Household composition
Neither in employment	1 in employment	Both in employment	None in employment	1 in employment	2 or more in employment	
k	l	m	n	o	p	a
1,947	**4,022**	**5,934**	**1,835**	**6,555**	**47,184**	**TOTAL HOUSEHOLDS**
1,390	2,548	4,491	1,337	4,391	30,806	Households with no dependants
						Households with 1 dependant
						Age of dependant
60	115	80	79	224	1,005	0 - 4
80	185	308	82	461	6,426	5 - 15
24	85	105	44	291	2,928	16 - 18
93	297	396	40	158	730	19 up to pensionable age
104	360	148	30	97	483	Pensionable age and over
						Households with at least 2 dependants
						Age of youngest dependant 0 - 4 and age of oldest
27	26	12	13	99	223	0 - 4
55	97	44	65	232	769	5 - 15
3	6	3	10	32	127	16 - 18
22	24	6	5	32	60	19 up to pensionable age
11	10	2	3	16	32	Pensionable age and over
						Age of youngest dependant 5 - 15 and age of oldest
30	110	150	71	289	2,182	5 - 15
10	23	52	31	144	976	16 - 18
12	67	55	9	28	119	19 up to pensionable age
3	13	13	3	22	121	Pensionable age and over
						Age of youngest dependant 16 - 18 and age of oldest
2	3	2	6	17	82	16 - 18
4	14	16	1	6	24	19 up to pensionable age
2	2	2	1	4	30	Pensionable age and over
						Age of youngest dependant 19 up to pensionable age and age of oldest
3	16	9	1	5	14	19 up to pensionable age
6	13	19	3	5	19	Pensionable age and over
6	8	21	1	2	28	Age of youngest dependant pensionable age and over
4,757	**10,156**	**13,815**	**6,858**	**24,205**	**182,377**	**TOTAL PERSONS**
						Persons in households with dependants
1,114	2,948	2,886	1,602	6,832	53,843	Non-dependants
863	2,112	1,947	887	3,576	22,846	Dependants

Table 28 Dependants in households - **continued**

28. Households with residents; residents in households

Household composition	TOTAL HOUSE-HOLDS	No non-dependants	1 male non-dependant		1 female non-dependant		1 male and 1 female non-dependants		
			Not in employment	In employment	Not in employment	In employment	Neither in employment	1 in employment	Both in employment
a	b	c	d	e	f	g	h	i	j
			Bath						
TOTAL HOUSEHOLDS	**34,128**	**2,834**	**1,625**	**2,383**	**5,263**	**2,764**	**2,939**	**3,699**	**6,753**
Households with no dependants	21,181		1,274	2,028	3,706	1,945	2,542	1,734	3,781
Households with 1 dependant									
Age of dependant									
0 - 4	1,249	1	4	7	175	79	87	401	389
5 - 15	1,499	1	6	26	116	175	22	169	407
16 - 18	576	9	4	22	25	43	7	47	119
19 up to pensionable age	907	313	35	80	155	106	28	47	38
Pensionable age and over	3,334	1,902	262	129	691	131	26	57	26
Households with at least 2 dependants									
Age of youngest dependant 0 - 4 and age of oldest									
0 - 4	634	-	-	2	56	7	49	292	202
5 - 15	1,345	-	6	3	140	36	99	484	483
16 - 18	32	-	-	-	3	-	-	12	9
19 up to pensionable age	47	5	7	4	11	6	-	2	-
Pensionable age and over	15	1	-	-	-	-	1	5	3
Age of youngest dependant 5 - 15 and age of oldest									
5 - 15	1,928	-	9	21	128	157	59	352	1,010
16 - 18	477	-	1	4	16	35	8	69	242
19 up to pensionable age	91	7	3	17	15	17	1	8	3
Pensionable age and over	32	-	2	-	1	2	1	7	10
Age of youngest dependant 16 - 18 and age of oldest									
16 - 18	57	1	-	2	4	4	5	6	25
19 up to pensionable age	16	1	1	1	2	4	-	2	1
Pensionable age and over	8	-	1	-	-	2	1	1	-
Age of youngest dependant 19 up to pensionable age and age of oldest									
19 up to pensionable age	53	34	4	1	5	2	-	2	1
Pensionable age and over	110	81	1	8	6	3	1	1	2
Age of youngest dependant pensionable age and over	537	478	5	28	8	10	2	1	2
TOTAL PERSONS	**76,876**	**3,467**	**2,030**	**2,847**	**7,422**	**3,947**	**6,654**	**11,183**	**19,094**
Persons in households with dependants									
Non-dependants	18,960		351	355	1,557	819	794	3,930	5,944
Dependants	20,189	3,467	405	464	2,159	1,183	776	3,785	5,588

Household composition	2 same sex non-dependants: Neither in employment	2 same sex non-dependants: 1 in employment	2 same sex non-dependants: Both in employment	3 or more non-dependants: None in employment	3 or more non-dependants: 1 in employment	3 or more non-dependants: 2 or more in employment
a	k	l	m	n	o	p
TOTAL HOUSEHOLDS	**233**	**441**	**637**	**232**	**599**	**3,726**
Households with no dependants	187	320	523	191	424	2,526
Households with 1 dependant						
Age of dependant						
0 - 4	7	4	2	7	13	73
5 - 15	6	19	24	9	41	478
16 - 18	1	10	11	6	35	237
19 up to pensionable age	10	13	24	4	7	47
Pensionable age and over	5	42	14	1	7	41
Households with at least 2 dependants						
Age of youngest dependant 0 - 4 and age of oldest						
0 - 4	4	1	2	1	7	11
5 - 15	3	7	4	5	17	58
16 - 18	-	-	-	-	1	7
19 up to pensionable age	1	2	-	-	3	6
Pensionable age and over	1	-	-	-	-	4
Age of youngest dependant 5 - 15 and age of oldest						
5 - 15	3	9	17	3	26	134
16 - 18	3	-	6	2	15	76
19 up to pensionable age	-	7	2	1	1	9
Pensionable age and over	-	1	1	-	-	7
Age of youngest dependant 16 - 18 and age of oldest						
16 - 18	-	-	-	1	1	8
19 up to pensionable age	-	2	1	-	-	1
Pensionable age and over	1	-	-	-	1	1
Age of youngest dependant 19 up to pensionable age and age of oldest						
19 up to pensionable age	-	2	2	-	-	-
Pensionable age and over	1	2	2	1	-	1
Age of youngest dependant pensionable age and over	-	-	2	-	-	1
TOTAL PERSONS	**538**	**1,049**	**1,432**	**831**	**2,166**	**14,216**
Persons in households with dependants						
Non-dependants	92	242	228	129	558	3,961
Dependants	72	167	158	61	268	1,636

Table 28 Dependants in households - **continued**

28. Households with residents; residents in households

Household composition	TOTAL HOUSE-HOLDS	No non-dependants	1 male non-dependant		1 female non-dependant		1 male and 1 female non-dependants		
			Not in employment	In employment	Not in employment	In employment	Neither in employment	1 in employment	Both in employment
a	b	c	d	e	f	g	h	i	j
			Bristol						
TOTAL HOUSEHOLDS	**156,778**	**13,462**	**7,705**	**11,914**	**22,371**	**11,632**	**11,833**	**18,201**	**32,101**
Households with no dependants	90,473		5,778	10,097	13,671	7,835	9,039	7,568	17,980
Households with 1 dependant									
Age of dependant									
0 - 4	7,092	13	30	33	1,066	323	473	2,315	2,026
5 - 15	7,168	9	70	105	733	766	223	730	1,767
16 - 18	1,899	18	6	33	68	152	30	163	380
19 up to pensionable age	5,781	1,796	287	497	1,030	714	160	304	208
Pensionable age and over	14,987	8,383	1,284	705	2,943	510	126	318	202
Households with at least 2 dependants									
Age of youngest dependant 0 - 4 and age of oldest									
0 - 4	3,808	2	10	7	420	61	387	1,698	1,002
5 - 15	7,835	3	32	34	1,056	238	812	2,686	2,320
16 - 18	299	2	3	2	32	9	29	72	53
19 up to pensionable age	382	24	19	48	143	27	10	19	9
Pensionable age and over	109	1	-	1	14	-	7	31	21
Age of youngest dependant 5 - 15 and age of oldest									
5 - 15	10,001	8	72	80	754	654	429	1,835	4,975
16 - 18	2,014	1	9	22	99	118	63	313	941
19 up to pensionable age	702	80	24	70	173	98	15	55	39
Pensionable age and over	222	9	3	6	21	15	9	26	60
Age of youngest dependant 16 - 18 and age of oldest									
16 - 18	180	1	1	4	10	11	7	25	77
19 up to pensionable age	113	15	5	14	17	10	3	7	8
Pensionable age and over	39	7	1	1	4	6	-	3	7
Age of youngest dependant 19 up to pensionable age and age of oldest									
19 up to pensionable age	358	229	10	24	23	24	6	11	8
Pensionable age and over	650	458	27	30	59	22	3	12	9
Age of youngest dependant pensionable age and over	2,666	2,403	34	101	35	39	2	10	9
TOTAL PERSONS	**370,131**	**16,920**	**9,977**	**14,318**	**35,779**	**17,243**	**29,632**	**57,209**	**90,864**
Persons in households with dependants									
Non-dependants	99,032		1,927	1,817	8,700	3,797	5,588	21,266	28,242
Dependants	107,699	16,920	2,272	2,404	13,408	5,611	5,966	20,807	26,662

2 same sex non-dependants			3 or more non-dependants			Household composition
Neither in employment	1 in employment	Both in employment	None in employment	1 in employment	2 or more in employment	
k	l	m	n	o	p	a
1,019	**2,100**	**2,958**	**999**	**2,862**	**17,621**	**TOTAL HOUSEHOLDS**
698	1,355	2,326	683	1,860	11,583	Households with no dependants
						Households with 1 dependant
						Age of dependant
37	67	45	55	126	483	0 - 4
46	101	132	55	195	2,236	5 - 15
14	37	39	21	90	848	16 - 18
44	144	174	21	84	318	19 up to pensionable age
45	154	65	18	40	194	Pensionable age and over
						Households with at least 2 dependants
						Age of youngest dependant 0 - 4 and age of oldest
19	17	4	9	57	115	0 - 4
43	59	18	39	128	367	5 - 15
3	4	2	7	21	60	16 - 18
14	15	3	4	18	29	19 up to pensionable age
7	7	2	2	5	11	Pensionable age and over
						Age of youngest dependant 5 - 15 and age of oldest
16	58	63	52	135	870	5 - 15
6	10	16	20	62	334	16 - 18
10	37	24	6	18	53	19 up to pensionable age
3	6	8	1	6	49	Pensionable age and over
						Age of youngest dependant 16 - 18 and age of oldest
1	1	1	4	9	28	16 - 18
3	6	10	-	3	12	19 up to pensionable age
-	2	2	1	-	5	Pensionable age and over
						Age of youngest dependant 19 up to pensionable age and age of oldest
2	7	5	-	1	8	19 up to pensionable age
4	7	8	1	4	6	Pensionable age and over
4	6	11	-	-	12	Age of youngest dependant pensionable age and over
2,581	**5,313**	**6,776**	**3,889**	**10,852**	**68,778**	**TOTAL PERSONS**
						Persons in households with dependants
642	1,490	1,264	1,023	3,192	20,084	Non-dependants
543	1,113	860	581	1,745	8,807	Dependants

Table 28 Dependants in households - continued

28. Households with residents; residents in households

Household composition	TOTAL HOUSE-HOLDS	No non-dependants	1 male non-dependant		1 female non-dependant		1 male and 1 female non-dependants		
			Not in employment	In employment	Not in employment	In employment	Neither in employment	1 in employment	Both in employment
a	b	c	d	e	f	g	h	i	j
			Kingswood						
TOTAL HOUSEHOLDS	**34,657**	**2,307**	**1,076**	**1,825**	**3,866**	**1,780**	**2,589**	**4,851**	**9,653**
Households with no dependants	19,318		714	1,454	2,471	1,046	2,240	1,910	5,000
Households with 1 dependant									
Age of dependant									
0 - 4	1,537	-	4	1	120	33	56	652	556
5 - 15	1,944	1	4	16	76	119	31	210	579
16 - 18	537	1	1	15	10	20	8	43	114
19 up to pensionable age	1,068	188	45	113	236	145	26	68	70
Pensionable age and over	2,870	1,489	267	128	603	96	24	86	53
Households with at least 2 dependants									
Age of youngest dependant 0 - 4 and age of oldest									
0 - 4	988	-	-	1	49	11	51	522	334
5 - 15	1,832	1	3	4	127	47	82	730	744
16 - 18	50	-	-	-	3	4	2	10	16
19 up to pensionable age	48	4	1	6	14	6	1	5	1
Pensionable age and over	19	-	-	-	-	-	-	7	5
Age of youngest dependant 5 - 15 and age of oldest									
5 - 15	2,932	-	14	28	95	169	52	506	1,808
16 - 18	552	-	4	6	10	28	10	69	319
19 up to pensionable age	105	6	4	16	18	20	1	9	10
Pensionable age and over	37	-	-	1	2	2	2	7	8
Age of youngest dependant 16 - 18 and age of oldest									
16 - 18	42	-	-	1	3	1	-	5	28
19 up to pensionable age	22	1	-	3	2	4	1	3	2
Pensionable age and over	16	2	-	-	1	1	-	-	4
Age of youngest dependant 19 up to pensionable age and age of oldest									
19 up to pensionable age	51	32	2	3	4	7	-	2	-
Pensionable age and over	116	75	4	4	16	10	-	2	1
Age of youngest dependant pensionable age and over	573	507	9	25	6	11	2	5	1
TOTAL PERSONS	**88,916**	**2,958**	**1,488**	**2,316**	**5,761**	**2,914**	**5,844**	**15,226**	**28,038**
Persons in households with dependants									
Non-dependants	25,624		362	371	1,395	734	698	5,882	9,306
Dependants	24,802	2,958	412	491	1,895	1,134	666	5,524	8,732

2 same sex non-dependants: Neither in employment	2 same sex non-dependants: 1 in employment	2 same sex non-dependants: Both in employment	3 or more non-dependants: None in employment	3 or more non-dependants: 1 in employment	3 or more non-dependants: 2 or more in employment	Household composition
k	l	m	n	o	p	a
110	**288**	**437**	**89**	**547**	**5,239**	**TOTAL HOUSEHOLDS**
71	160	306	68	393	3,485	Households with no dependants
						Households with 1 dependant
						Age of dependant
3	6	7	1	16	82	0 - 4
9	19	32	5	41	802	5 - 15
1	10	5	1	17	291	16 - 18
11	23	42	3	14	84	19 up to pensionable age
7	38	13	3	10	53	Pensionable age and over
						Households with at least 2 dependants
						Age of youngest dependant 0 - 4 and age of oldest
1	1	-	1	4	13	0 - 4
2	7	6	3	14	62	5 - 15
-	1	-	-	1	13	16 - 18
3	2	-	-	-	5	19 up to pensionable age
-	1	-	-	1	5	Pensionable age and over
						Age of youngest dependant 5 - 15 and age of oldest
1	11	8	1	25	214	5 - 15
-	2	6	3	8	87	16 - 18
-	5	3	-	1	12	19 up to pensionable age
-	2	1	-	1	11	Pensionable age and over
						Age of youngest dependant 16 - 18 and age of oldest
-	-	-	-	-	4	16 - 18
-	-	3	-	-	3	19 up to pensionable age
-	-	-	-	1	7	Pensionable age and over
						Age of youngest dependant 19 up to pensionable age and age of oldest
-	-	-	-	-	1	19 up to pensionable age
-	-	3	-	-	1	Pensionable age and over
1	-	2	-	-	4	Age of youngest dependant pensionable age and over
273	**754**	**1,042**	**315**	**1,926**	**20,061**	**TOTAL PERSONS**
						Persons in households with dependants
78	256	262	66	478	5,736	Non-dependants
53	178	168	35	241	2,315	Dependants

Table 28 Dependants in households – **continued**

28. Households with residents; residents in households

Household composition	TOTAL HOUSE-HOLDS	No non-dependants	1 male non-dependant		1 female non-dependant		1 male and 1 female non-dependants		
			Not in employment	In employment	Not in employment	In employment	Neither in employment	1 in employment	Both in employment
a	b	c	d	e	f	g	h	i	j
			Northavon						
TOTAL HOUSEHOLDS	**49,626**	**2,457**	**1,321**	**3,253**	**4,616**	**2,633**	**3,245**	**7,174**	**15,317**
Households with no dependants	28,267		877	2,726	2,940	1,700	2,790	2,677	8,273
Households with 1 dependant									
Age of dependant									
0 - 4	2,421	1	2	4	117	68	66	1,014	931
5 - 15	2,772	1	8	36	100	161	30	317	890
16 - 18	983	-	1	20	11	42	11	78	223
19 up to pensionable age	1,256	217	53	169	267	185	32	66	61
Pensionable age and over	3,169	1,534	335	156	755	96	31	74	59
Households with at least 2 dependants									
Age of youngest dependant 0 - 4 and age of oldest									
0 - 4	1,513	-	2	3	66	14	62	807	505
5 - 15	2,549	-	5	5	135	41	115	1,075	1,029
16 - 18	59	-	-	-	1	1	-	23	12
19 up to pensionable age	79	5	1	24	24	7	2	2	1
Pensionable age and over	28	-	-	-	1	2	-	10	6
Age of youngest dependant 5 - 15 and age of oldest									
5 - 15	4,340	-	13	34	127	205	81	821	2,649
16 - 18	1,011	-	1	10	14	53	16	169	561
19 up to pensionable age	152	11	4	25	24	23	3	6	18
Pensionable age and over	68	-	-	1	3	6	1	9	24
Age of youngest dependant 16 - 18 and age of oldest									
16 - 18	101	-	1	1	-	6	3	14	59
19 up to pensionable age	34	5	2	5	4	3	1	4	3
Pensionable age and over	14	-	-	2	1	2	-	3	3
Age of youngest dependant 19 up to pensionable age and age of oldest									
19 up to pensionable age	70	43	1	2	7	4	1	-	5
Pensionable age and over	116	70	8	8	9	7	-	4	2
Age of youngest dependant pensionable age and over	624	570	7	22	10	7	-	1	3
TOTAL PERSONS	**129,084**	**3,196**	**1,821**	**3,968**	**6,927**	**4,069**	**7,399**	**22,896**	**43,815**
Persons in households with dependants									
Non-dependants	37,894		444	527	1,676	933	910	8,994	14,088
Dependants	35,378	3,196	500	715	2,311	1,436	909	8,548	13,181

Household composition	2 same sex non-dependants: Neither in employment	2 same sex non-dependants: 1 in employment	2 same sex non-dependants: Both in employment	3 or more non-dependants: None in employment	3 or more non-dependants: 1 in employment	3 or more non-dependants: 2 or more in employment
a	k	l	m	n	o	p
TOTAL HOUSEHOLDS	**158**	**388**	**710**	**155**	**761**	**7,438**
Households with no dependants	111	239	518	113	492	4,811
Households with 1 dependant						
Age of dependant						
0 - 4	6	12	14	6	32	148
5 - 15	8	15	43	4	60	1,099
16 - 18	3	5	20	4	42	523
19 up to pensionable age	11	35	48	6	16	90
Pensionable age and over	8	34	14	2	11	60
Households with at least 2 dependants						
Age of youngest dependant 0 - 4 and age of oldest						
0 - 4	-	4	2	2	14	32
5 - 15	4	10	5	6	22	97
16 - 18	-	-	-	-	-	22
19 up to pensionable age	1	2	2	1	2	5
Pensionable age and over	-	2	-	1	3	3
Age of youngest dependant 5 - 15 and age of oldest						
5 - 15	4	11	22	5	32	336
16 - 18	-	5	6	2	23	151
19 up to pensionable age	-	8	10	-	2	18
Pensionable age and over	-	-	1	1	6	16
Age of youngest dependant 16 - 18 and age of oldest						
16 - 18	1	-	1	1	-	14
19 up to pensionable age	-	2	1	1	2	1
Pensionable age and over	-	-	-	-	-	3
Age of youngest dependant 19 up to pensionable age and age of oldest						
19 up to pensionable age	-	3	1	-	-	3
Pensionable age and over	1	1	1	-	1	4
Age of youngest dependant pensionable age and over	-	-	1	-	1	2
TOTAL PERSONS	**377**	**990**	**1,677**	**563**	**2,829**	**28,557**
Persons in households with dependants						
Non-dependants	94	298	384	135	848	8,563
Dependants	61	214	257	75	435	3,540

Table 28 Dependants in households - continued

28. Households with residents; residents in households

Household composition	TOTAL HOUSE-HOLDS	No non-dependants	1 male non-dependant		1 female non-dependant		1 male and 1 female non-dependants		
			Not in employment	In employment	Not in employment	In employment	Neither in employment	1 in employment	Both in employment
a	b	c	d	e	f	g	h	i	j
			Wansdyke						
TOTAL HOUSEHOLDS	**30,814**	**1,881**	**1,013**	**1,472**	**3,663**	**1,531**	**2,719**	**4,489**	**7,936**
Households with no dependants	17,509		707	1,168	2,463	937	2,412	1,754	4,020
Households with 1 dependant									
Age of dependant									
0 - 4	1,215	-	-	1	64	40	50	529	430
5 - 15	1,576	-	4	24	43	92	29	214	478
16 - 18	633	2	3	10	7	29	12	62	135
19 up to pensionable age	844	128	22	90	215	117	24	42	46
Pensionable age and over	2,614	1,258	249	105	660	97	23	72	34
Households with at least 2 dependants									
Age of youngest dependant 0 - 4 and age of oldest									
0 - 4	778	-	2	-	19	7	47	457	219
5 - 15	1,486	-	2	1	57	30	69	677	552
16 - 18	54	-	-	1	2	1	2	20	22
19 up to pensionable age	40	1	2	7	15	2	-	2	1
Pensionable age and over	16	-	-	-	-	1	-	4	6
Age of youngest dependant 5 - 15 and age of oldest									
5 - 15	2,605	-	8	14	69	108	38	539	1,558
16 - 18	635	-	-	6	8	32	8	91	370
19 up to pensionable age	81	2	5	11	18	20	1	6	-
Pensionable age and over	52	-	1	1	1	3	1	6	16
Age of youngest dependant 16 - 18 and age of oldest									
16 - 18	74	-	-	2	-	3	1	11	42
19 up to pensionable age	15	3	2	1	2	1	1	-	1
Pensionable age and over	5	1	-	-	1	-	-	-	-
Age of youngest dependant 19 up to pensionable age and age of oldest									
19 up to pensionable age	36	18	-	4	3	5	-	1	-
Pensionable age and over	73	48	4	7	6	1	-	1	1
Age of youngest dependant pensionable age and over	473	420	2	19	10	5	1	1	5
TOTAL PERSONS	**79,122**	**2,387**	**1,355**	**1,875**	**5,177**	**2,412**	**6,002**	**14,235**	**23,391**
Persons in households with dependants									
Non-dependants	22,685		306	304	1,200	594	614	5,470	7,832
Dependants	21,754	2,387	342	403	1,514	881	564	5,257	7,519

2 same sex non-dependants			3 or more non-dependants			Household composition
Neither in employment	1 in employment	Both in employment	None in employment	1 in employment	2 or more in employment	
k	l	m	n	o	p	a
128	**254**	**387**	**100**	**600**	**4,641**	**TOTAL HOUSEHOLDS**
96	139	280	78	425	3,030	Households with no dependants
						Households with 1 dependant
						Age of dependant
2	6	4	4	10	75	0 - 4
-	8	19	2	32	631	5 - 15
3	8	7	1	33	321	16 - 18
2	30	30	1	15	82	19 up to pensionable age
15	29	16	1	8	47	Pensionable age and over
						Households with at least 2 dependants
						Age of youngest dependant 0 - 4 and age of oldest
1	-	-	-	3	23	0 - 4
-	6	1	6	17	68	5 - 15
-	1	-	1	1	3	16 - 18
3	2	-	-	4	1	19 up to pensionable age
-	-	-	-	2	3	Pensionable age and over
						Age of youngest dependant 5 - 15 and age of oldest
3	10	17	3	23	215	5 - 15
-	2	4	1	16	97	16 - 18
1	3	5	1	2	6	19 up to pensionable age
-	1	-	1	3	18	Pensionable age and over
						Age of youngest dependant 16 - 18 and age of oldest
-	-	-	-	4	11	16 - 18
-	3	-	-	-	1	19 up to pensionable age
-	-	-	-	-	3	Pensionable age and over
						Age of youngest dependant 19 up to pensionable age and age of oldest
1	2	-	-	2	-	19 up to pensionable age
-	2	2	-	-	1	Pensionable age and over
1	2	2	-	-	5	Age of youngest dependant pensionable age and over
301	**670**	**917**	**353**	**2,164**	**17,883**	**TOTAL PERSONS**
						Persons in households with dependants
64	230	214	68	543	5,246	Non-dependants
45	162	143	44	292	2,201	Dependants

Table 28 Dependants in households - continued

28. Households with residents; residents in households

Household composition	TOTAL HOUSE-HOLDS	No non-dependants	1 male non-dependant		1 female non-dependant		1 male and 1 female non-dependants		
			Not in employment	In employment	Not in employment	In employment	Neither in employment	1 in employment	Both in employment
a	b	c	d	e	f	g	h	i	j
			Woodspring						
TOTAL HOUSEHOLDS	**70,519**	**5,603**	**2,670**	**3,992**	**9,751**	**3,881**	**6,293**	**9,608**	**17,101**
Households with no dependants	39,361		1,812	3,197	6,293	2,439	5,585	3,860	8,703
Households with 1 dependant									
Age of dependant									
0 - 4	2,681	3	5	4	244	95	120	1,059	941
5 - 15	3,467	2	17	44	155	240	63	426	1,149
16 - 18	1,417	12	4	19	27	62	17	109	334
19 up to pensionable age	2,311	546	92	268	582	314	53	86	89
Pensionable age and over	6,676	3,428	667	244	1,675	180	58	123	74
Households with at least 2 dependants									
Age of youngest dependant 0 - 4 and age of oldest									
0 - 4	1,646	-	2	4	98	14	98	890	488
5 - 15	3,271	1	5	7	217	76	170	1,456	1,161
16 - 18	92	-	-	-	8	4	3	26	18
19 up to pensionable age	130	3	5	24	46	17	1	10	3
Pensionable age and over	46	-	-	-	5	2	2	17	6
Age of youngest dependant 5 - 15 and age of oldest									
5 - 15	5,562	3	22	37	212	277	89	1,197	3,220
16 - 18	1,432	1	-	22	28	66	22	269	751
19 up to pensionable age	283	25	13	57	64	36	3	16	24
Pensionable age and over	114	5	-	1	15	5	1	22	34
Age of youngest dependant 16 - 18 and age of oldest									
16 - 18	154	-	-	2	3	8	1	28	90
19 up to pensionable age	54	6	1	7	10	8	4	6	2
Pensionable age and over	32	3	-	1	5	2	1	1	5
Age of youngest dependant 19 up to pensionable age and age of oldest									
19 up to pensionable age	127	81	3	6	16	8	1	3	1
Pensionable age and over	242	163	6	19	25	11	1	2	4
Age of youngest dependant pensionable age and over	1,421	1,321	16	29	23	17	-	2	4
TOTAL PERSONS	**172,844**	**7,280**	**3,623**	**5,079**	**14,383**	**6,036**	**13,926**	**30,427**	**49,995**
Persons in households with dependants									
Non-dependants	49,018		858	795	3,458	1,442	1,416	11,496	16,796
Dependants	50,212	7,280	953	1,087	4,632	2,155	1,340	11,211	15,793

2 same sex non-dependants			3 or more non-dependants			Household composition
Neither in employment	1 in employment	Both in employment	None in employment	1 in employment	2 or more in employment	
k	l	m	n	o	p	a
299	**551**	**805**	**260**	**1,186**	**8,519**	**TOTAL HOUSEHOLDS**
227	335	538	204	797	5,371	Households with no dependants
						Households with 1 dependant
						Age of dependant
5	20	8	6	27	144	0 - 4
11	23	58	7	92	1,180	5 - 15
2	15	23	11	74	708	16 - 18
15	52	78	5	22	109	19 up to pensionable age
24	63	26	5	21	88	Pensionable age and over
						Households with at least 2 dependants
						Age of youngest dependant 0 - 4 and age of oldest
2	3	4	-	14	29	0 - 4
3	8	10	6	34	117	5 - 15
-	-	1	2	8	22	16 - 18
-	1	1	-	5	14	19 up to pensionable age
3	-	-	-	5	6	Pensionable age and over
						Age of youngest dependant 5 - 15 and age of oldest
3	11	23	7	48	413	5 - 15
1	4	14	3	20	231	16 - 18
1	7	11	1	4	21	19 up to pensionable age
-	3	2	-	6	20	Pensionable age and over
						Age of youngest dependant 16 - 18 and age of oldest
-	2	-	-	3	17	16 - 18
1	1	1	-	1	6	19 up to pensionable age
1	-	-	-	2	11	Pensionable age and over
						Age of youngest dependant 19 up to pensionable age and age of oldest
-	2	1	1	2	2	19 up to pensionable age
-	1	3	1	-	6	Pensionable age and over
-	-	3	1	1	4	Age of youngest dependant pensionable age and over
687	**1,380**	**1,971**	**907**	**4,268**	**32,882**	**TOTAL PERSONS**
						Persons in households with dependants
144	432	534	181	1,213	10,253	Non-dependants
89	278	361	91	595	4,347	Dependants

29. Households with residents; dependants in households

Household composition	TOTAL HOUSEHOLDS	TOTAL DEPENDANTS	Dependants: Aged 0 - 15: With long-term illness	Aged 0 - 15: With no long-term illness	Aged 16 - 18: Single, in full-time education and economically inactive	Aged 16 - 18: With long-term illness and permanently sick/retired	Aged 19 up to pensionable age with long-term illness and permanently sick/retired	Pensionable age and over with long-term illness and permanently sick/retired
a	b	c	d	e	f	g	h	i
AVON								
TOTAL HOUSEHOLDS	**376,522**	**260,034**	**3,750**	**175,111**	**14,903**	**86**	**17,538**	**48,646**
1 or more non-dependants, no dependants	216,109							
1 dependant, living alone	21,256	21,256	3	29	41	1	3,188	17,994
2 dependants, no non-dependants	7,003	14,006	11	121	36	1	1,736	12,101
3 or more dependants, no non-dependants	285	946	15	159	30	2	381	359
1 non-dependant with 1 or more dependant(s)	34,722	48,767	890	23,846	1,750	11	7,861	14,409
2 non-dependants with 1 or more dependant(s)	78,107	147,750	2,372	131,323	8,111	43	3,069	2,832
3 or more non-dependants with 1 or more dependant(s)	19,040	27,309	459	19,633	4,935	28	1,303	951
Bath								
TOTAL HOUSEHOLDS	**34,128**	**20,189**	**235**	**12,803**	**1,269**	**4**	**1,287**	**4,591**
1 or more non-dependants, no dependants	21,181							
1 dependant, living alone	2,226	2,226	-	2	9	-	313	1,902
2 dependants, no non-dependants	587	1,174	-	8	3	-	144	1,019
3 or more dependants, no non-dependants	21	67	-	10	1	-	25	31
1 non-dependant with 1 or more dependant(s)	3,082	4,211	60	2,106	193	1	508	1,343
2 non-dependants with 1 or more dependant(s)	5,615	10,546	153	9,290	656	1	216	230
3 or more non-dependants with 1 or more dependant(s)	1,416	1,965	22	1,387	407	2	81	66
Bristol								
TOTAL HOUSEHOLDS	**156,778**	**107,699**	**1,925**	**70,827**	**4,962**	**32**	**8,508**	**21,445**
1 or more non-dependants, no dependants	90,473							
1 dependant, living alone	10,219	10,219	1	21	18	-	1,796	8,383
2 dependants, no non-dependants	3,090	6,180	9	77	19	-	904	5,171
3 or more dependants, no non-dependants	153	521	11	94	16	1	216	183
1 non-dependant with 1 or more dependant(s)	16,241	23,695	570	12,775	750	5	3,509	6,086
2 non-dependants with 1 or more dependant(s)	29,246	55,951	1,101	49,548	2,558	16	1,477	1,251
3 or more non-dependants with 1 or more dependant(s)	7,356	11,133	233	8,312	1,601	10	606	371
Kingswood								
TOTAL HOUSEHOLDS	**34,657**	**24,802**	**286**	**17,510**	**1,297**	**10**	**1,472**	**4,227**
1 or more non-dependants, no dependants	19,318							
1 dependant, living alone	1,679	1,679	-	1	-	1	188	1,489
2 dependants, no non-dependants	613	1,226	-	9	2	-	139	1,076
3 or more dependants, no non-dependants	15	53	1	6	1	-	17	28
1 non-dependant with 1 or more dependant(s)	2,862	3,932	47	1,807	135	-	701	1,242
2 non-dependants with 1 or more dependant(s)	8,241	15,321	205	13,806	715	5	301	289
3 or more non-dependants with 1 or more dependant(s)	1,929	2,591	33	1,881	444	4	126	103
Northavon								
TOTAL HOUSEHOLDS	**49,626**	**35,378**	**424**	**26,100**	**2,368**	**17**	**1,809**	**4,660**
1 or more non-dependants, no dependants	28,267							
1 dependant, living alone	1,753	1,753	-	2	-	-	217	1,534
2 dependants, no non-dependants	676	1,352	-	5	4	-	151	1,192
3 or more dependants, no non-dependants	28	91	-	18	2	1	43	27
1 non-dependant with 1 or more dependant(s)	3,580	4,962	69	2,306	209	2	890	1,486
2 non-dependants with 1 or more dependant(s)	12,384	23,170	298	20,870	1,339	10	352	301
3 or more non-dependants with 1 or more dependant(s)	2,938	4,050	57	2,899	814	4	156	120

29. Households with residents; dependants in households

Household composition	TOTAL HOUSEHOLDS	Dependants						
		TOTAL DEPENDANTS	Aged 0 - 15		Aged 16 - 18		Aged 19 up to pensionable age with long-term illness and permanently sick/retired	Pensionable age and over with long-term illness and permanently sick/retired
			With long-term illness	With no long-term illness	Single, in full-time education and economically inactive	With long-term illness and permanently sick/retired		
a	b	c	d	e	f	g	h	i
		Wansdyke						
TOTAL HOUSEHOLDS	**30,814**	**21,754**	**246**	**15,094**	**1,547**	**8**	**1,136**	**3,723**
1 or more non-dependants, no dependants	17,509							
1 dependant, living alone	1,388	1,388	-	-	2	-	128	1,258
2 dependants, no non-dependants	482	964	-	2	4	-	80	878
3 or more dependants, no non-dependants	11	35	-	1	-	-	17	17
1 non-dependant with 1 or more dependant(s)	2,404	3,140	26	1,198	131	1	574	1,210
2 non-dependants with 1 or more dependant(s)	7,212	13,690	181	12,130	897	5	218	259
3 or more non-dependants with 1 or more dependant(s)	1,808	2,537	39	1,763	513	2	119	101
		Woodspring						
TOTAL HOUSEHOLDS	**70,519**	**50,212**	**634**	**32,777**	**3,460**	**15**	**3,326**	**10,000**
1 or more non-dependants, no dependants	39,361							
1 dependant, living alone	3,991	3,991	2	3	12	-	546	3,428
2 dependants, no non-dependants	1,555	3,110	2	20	4	1	318	2,765
3 or more dependants, no non-dependants	57	179	3	30	10	-	63	73
1 non-dependant with 1 or more dependant(s)	6,553	8,827	118	3,654	332	2	1,679	3,042
2 non-dependants with 1 or more dependant(s)	15,409	29,072	434	25,679	1,946	6	505	502
3 or more non-dependants with 1 or more dependant(s)	3,593	5,033	75	3,391	1,156	6	215	190

30. Households with residents; residents in households with dependants

Number, sex and age of non-dependants	TOTAL HOUSE-HOLDS	Households with no dependants	Households with 1 or more dependants: Age of youngest dependant 0 - 15 and age of oldest: 0 - 15	16 up to pension-able age	Pension-able age and over	Age of youngest dependant 16 up to pensionable age and age of oldest: 16 up to pension-able age	Pension-able age and over	Age of youngest dependant pension-able age and over	Persons in households with dependants: Non-depen-dants	Depen-dants
a	b	c	d	e	f	g	h	i	j	k
AVON										
TOTAL HOUSEHOLDS	**376,522**	**216,109**	**89,674**	**8,847**	**758**	**19,769**	**1,421**	**39,944**	**253,213**	**260,034**
No non-dependants	28,544		50	177	16	3,700	908	23,693		36,208
1 male	**40,249**	**31,832**	**947**	**488**	**17**	**2,005**	**132**	**4,828**	**8,417**	**10,448**
16 - 44	19,454	16,820	745	358	9	722	62	738	2,634	4,118
45 - 64	10,778	7,990	196	128	6	1,127	42	1,289	2,788	3,274
65 and over	10,017	7,022	6	2	2	156	28	2,801	2,995	3,056
1 female	**73,751**	**47,446**	**11,177**	**1,419**	**101**	**4,790**	**200**	**8,618**	**26,305**	**38,319**
16 - 44	23,287	10,419	10,518	1,168	71	750	30	331	12,868	23,794
45 - 59	10,428	6,280	606	235	23	2,362	73	849	4,148	4,959
60 and over	40,036	30,747	53	16	7	1,678	97	7,438	9,289	9,566
1 male and 1 female	**166,501**	**91,868**	**63,901**	**4,907**	**375**	**3,858**	**75**	**1,517**	**149,266**	**142,828**
Both of pensionable age	22,570	22,182	22	1	-	211	-	154	776	409
1 under, 1 of pensionable age	12,440	11,139	223	28	17	334	16	683	2,602	1,535
Both under pensionable age	131,491	58,547	63,656	4,878	358	3,313	59	680	145,888	140,884
2 of same sex	**11,903**	**8,429**	**1,379**	**283**	**52**	**1,069**	**44**	**647**	**6,948**	**4,922**
Both of pensionable age	844	778	2	-	-	20	2	42	132	68
1 under, 1 of pensionable age	2,237	1,515	138	25	30	152	14	363	1,444	877
Both under pensionable age	8,822	6,136	1,239	258	22	897	28	242	5,372	3,977
3 or more	**55,574**	**36,534**	**12,220**	**1,573**	**197**	**4,347**	**62**	**641**	**62,277**	**27,309**
All of pensionable age	252	238	-	-	-	2	-	12	44	15
1 or more under pensionable age	55,322	36,296	12,220	1,573	197	4,345	62	629	62,233	27,294
Bath										
TOTAL HOUSEHOLDS	**34,128**	**21,181**	**6,655**	**647**	**47**	**1,609**	**118**	**3,871**	**18,960**	**20,189**
No non-dependants	2,834		2	12	1	358	81	2,380		3,467
1 male	**4,008**	**3,302**	**84**	**36**	**2**	**150**	**10**	**424**	**706**	**869**
16 - 44	1,960	1,737	69	25	1	65	6	57	223	345
45 - 64	1,000	778	15	11	-	75	3	118	222	259
65 and over	1,048	787	-	-	1	10	1	249	261	265
1 female	**8,027**	**5,651**	**1,069**	**103**	**3**	**350**	**11**	**840**	**2,376**	**3,342**
16 - 44	2,573	1,370	1,005	78	2	83	1	34	1,203	2,078
45 - 59	1,054	714	59	25	1	160	7	88	340	414
60 and over	4,400	3,567	5	-	-	107	3	718	833	850
1 male and 1 female	**13,391**	**8,057**	**4,505**	**354**	**27**	**328**	**6**	**114**	**10,668**	**10,149**
Both of pensionable age	2,426	2,394	4	-	-	15	-	13	64	34
1 under, 1 of pensionable age	1,171	1,046	17	3	-	37	4	64	250	144
Both under pensionable age	9,794	4,617	4,484	351	27	276	2	37	10,354	9,971
2 of same sex	**1,311**	**1,030**	**112**	**21**	**3**	**76**	**6**	**63**	**562**	**397**
Both of pensionable age	108	105	-	-	-	-	1	2	6	4
1 under, 1 of pensionable age	254	183	14	1	2	11	2	41	142	84
Both under pensionable age	949	742	98	20	1	65	3	20	414	309
3 or more	**4,557**	**3,141**	**883**	**121**	**11**	**347**	**4**	**50**	**4,648**	**1,965**
All of pensionable age	30	30	-	-	-	-	-	-	-	-
1 or more under pensionable age	4,527	3,111	883	121	11	347	4	50	4,648	1,965

30. Households with residents; residents in households with dependants

Number, sex and age of non-dependants	TOTAL HOUSE-HOLDS	Households with no dependants	Households with 1 or more dependants: Age of youngest dependant 0 - 15 and age of oldest: 0 - 15	Age of youngest dependant 0 - 15 and age of oldest: 16 up to pension-able age	Age of youngest dependant 0 - 15 and age of oldest: Pension-able age and over	Age of youngest dependant 16 up to pensionable age and age of oldest: 16 up to pension-able age	Age of youngest dependant 16 up to pensionable age and age of oldest: Pension-able age and over	Age of youngest dependant pension-able age and over	Persons in households with dependants: Non-depen-dants	Persons in households with dependants: Depen-dants
a	b	c	d	e	f	g	h	i	j	k
Bristol										
TOTAL HOUSEHOLDS	**156,778**	**90,473**	**35,904**	**3,397**	**331**	**8,331**	**689**	**17,653**	**99,032**	**107,699**
No non-dependants	13,462		35	107	10	2,059	465	10,786		16,920
1 male	**19,619**	**15,875**	**473**	**197**	**10**	**881**	**59**	**2,124**	**3,744**	**4,676**
16 - 44	10,089	8,806	380	154	6	343	30	370	1,283	1,994
45 - 64	5,156	3,926	89	42	3	473	16	607	1,230	1,421
65 and over	4,374	3,143	4	1	1	65	13	1,147	1,231	1,261
1 female	**34,003**	**21,506**	**6,071**	**699**	**50**	**2,059**	**91**	**3,527**	**12,497**	**19,019**
16 - 44	12,689	5,771	5,734	584	40	370	20	170	6,918	12,967
45 - 59	4,524	2,756	306	106	7	977	24	348	1,768	2,119
60 and over	16,790	12,979	31	9	3	712	47	3,009	3,811	3,933
1 male and 1 female	**62,135**	**34,587**	**23,678**	**1,618**	**154**	**1,397**	**34**	**667**	**55,096**	**53,435**
Both of pensionable age	8,213	8,038	10	1	-	100	-	64	350	186
1 under, 1 of pensionable age	4,866	4,273	99	13	7	157	8	309	1,186	696
Both under pensionable age	49,056	22,276	23,569	1,604	147	1,140	26	294	53,560	52,553
2 of same sex	**6,077**	**4,379**	**725**	**144**	**33**	**488**	**23**	**285**	**3,396**	**2,516**
Both of pensionable age	357	329	2	-	-	10	1	15	56	29
1 under, 1 of pensionable age	1,069	739	74	13	18	61	9	155	660	418
Both under pensionable age	4,651	3,311	649	131	15	417	13	115	2,680	2,069
3 or more	**21,482**	**14,126**	**4,922**	**632**	**74**	**1,447**	**17**	**264**	**24,299**	**11,133**
All of pensionable age	102	94	-	-	-	1	-	7	24	8
1 or more under pensionable age	21,380	14,032	4,922	632	74	1,446	17	257	24,275	11,125
Kingswood										
TOTAL HOUSEHOLDS	**34,657**	**19,318**	**9,233**	**755**	**56**	**1,720**	**132**	**3,443**	**25,624**	**24,802**
No non-dependants	2,307		2	10	-	222	77	1,996		2,958
1 male	**2,901**	**2,168**	**75**	**37**	**1**	**183**	**8**	**429**	**733**	**903**
16 - 44	1,268	1,047	64	23	-	63	2	69	221	334
45 - 64	809	571	11	14	1	103	3	106	238	290
65 and over	824	550	-	-	-	17	3	254	274	279
1 female	**5,646**	**3,517**	**846**	**103**	**4**	**432**	**28**	**716**	**2,129**	**3,029**
16 - 44	1,543	570	809	87	2	49	3	23	973	1,794
45 - 59	855	486	36	15	-	230	8	80	369	419
60 and over	3,248	2,461	1	1	2	153	17	613	787	816
1 male and 1 female	**17,093**	**9,150**	**6,913**	**453**	**29**	**370**	**7**	**171**	**15,886**	**14,922**
Both of pensionable age	2,040	2,004	2	-	-	19	-	15	72	38
1 under, 1 of pensionable age	1,225	1,106	12	2	4	30	1	70	238	136
Both under pensionable age	13,828	6,040	6,899	451	25	321	6	86	15,576	14,748
2 of same sex	**835**	**537**	**113**	**22**	**4**	**95**	**3**	**61**	**596**	**399**
Both of pensionable age	47	41	-	-	-	4	-	2	12	6
1 under, 1 of pensionable age	180	107	11	2	3	15	-	42	146	84
Both under pensionable age	608	389	102	20	1	76	3	17	438	309
3 or more	**5,875**	**3,946**	**1,284**	**130**	**18**	**418**	**9**	**70**	**6,280**	**2,591**
All of pensionable age	21	20	-	-	-	-	-	1	3	1
1 or more under pensionable age	5,854	3,926	1,284	130	18	418	9	69	6,277	2,590

30. Households with residents; residents in households with dependants

Number, sex and age of non-dependants	TOTAL HOUSE-HOLDS	Households with no dependants	Households with 1 or more dependants: Age of youngest dependant 0 - 15 and age of oldest: 0 - 15	Age of youngest dependant 0 - 15 and age of oldest: 16 up to pension-able age	Age of youngest dependant 0 - 15 and age of oldest: Pension-able age and over	Age of youngest dependant 16 up to pensionable age and age of oldest: 16 up to pension-able age	Age of youngest dependant 16 up to pensionable age and age of oldest: Pension-able age and over	Age of youngest dependant pension-able age and over	Persons in households with dependants: Non-depen-dants	Persons in households with dependants: Depen-dants
a	b	c	d	e	f	g	h	i	j	k
				Northavon						
TOTAL HOUSEHOLDS	**49,626**	**28,267**	**13,595**	**1,301**	**96**	**2,444**	**130**	**3,793**	**37,894**	**35,378**
No non-dependants	2,457		2	16	-	265	70	2,104		3,196
1 male	**4,574**	**3,603**	**112**	**65**	**1**	**255**	**18**	**520**	**971**	**1,215**
16 - 44	2,348	2,062	85	46	1	78	7	69	286	467
45 - 64	1,220	871	27	19	-	154	6	143	349	406
65 and over	1,006	670	-	-	-	23	5	308	336	342
1 female	**7,249**	**4,640**	**1,034**	**147**	**12**	**529**	**19**	**868**	**2,609**	**3,747**
16 - 44	2,218	1,021	961	124	7	69	2	34	1,197	2,207
45 - 59	1,154	678	68	22	4	277	11	94	476	577
60 and over	3,877	2,941	5	1	1	183	6	740	936	963
1 male and 1 female	**25,736**	**13,740**	**10,392**	**813**	**50**	**561**	**12**	**168**	**23,992**	**22,638**
Both of pensionable age	2,499	2,456	2	-	-	26	-	15	86	45
1 under, 1 of pensionable age	1,533	1,408	21	2	1	30	2	69	250	146
Both under pensionable age	21,704	9,876	10,369	811	49	505	10	84	23,656	22,447
2 of same sex	**1,256**	**868**	**160**	**34**	**3**	**131**	**3**	**57**	**776**	**532**
Both of pensionable age	79	72	-	-	-	4	-	3	14	7
1 under, 1 of pensionable age	214	145	16	3	2	19	-	29	138	80
Both under pensionable age	963	651	144	31	1	108	3	25	624	445
3 or more	**8,354**	**5,416**	**1,895**	**226**	**30**	**703**	**8**	**76**	**9,546**	**4,050**
All of pensionable age	26	25	-	-	-	-	-	1	3	1
1 or more under pensionable age	8,328	5,391	1,895	226	30	703	8	75	9,543	4,049
				Wansdyke						
TOTAL HOUSEHOLDS	**30,814**	**17,509**	**7,660**	**810**	**68**	**1,602**	**78**	**3,087**	**22,685**	**21,754**
No non-dependants	1,881		-	3	-	151	49	1,678		2,387
1 male	**2,485**	**1,875**	**56**	**32**	**2**	**134**	**11**	**375**	**610**	**745**
16 - 44	924	749	41	26	1	42	6	59	175	276
45 - 64	732	540	15	6	1	84	3	83	192	221
65 and over	829	586	-	-	-	8	2	233	243	248
1 female	**5,194**	**3,400**	**529**	**98**	**5**	**382**	**8**	**772**	**1,794**	**2,395**
16 - 44	1,044	416	491	80	3	33	-	21	628	1,152
45 - 59	805	484	35	15	2	192	3	74	321	375
60 and over	3,345	2,500	3	3	-	157	5	677	845	868
1 male and 1 female	**15,144**	**8,186**	**5,886**	**523**	**33**	**378**	**2**	**136**	**13,916**	**13,340**
Both of pensionable age	2,298	2,260	1	-	-	20	-	17	76	40
1 under, 1 of pensionable age	1,203	1,078	29	3	2	26	-	65	250	148
Both under pensionable age	11,643	4,848	5,856	520	31	332	2	54	13,590	13,152
2 of same sex	**769**	**515**	**77**	**21**	**1**	**86**	**4**	**65**	**508**	**350**
Both of pensionable age	72	67	-	-	-	-	-	5	10	5
1 under, 1 of pensionable age	185	121	6	4	-	19	2	33	128	77
Both under pensionable age	512	327	71	17	1	67	2	27	370	268
3 or more	**5,341**	**3,533**	**1,112**	**133**	**27**	**471**	**4**	**61**	**5,857**	**2,537**
All of pensionable age	21	20	-	-	-	1	-	-	3	1
1 or more under pensionable age	5,320	3,513	1,112	133	27	470	4	61	5,854	2,536

30. Households with residents; residents in households with dependants

Number, sex and age of non-dependants	TOTAL HOUSE-HOLDS	Households with no dependants	Households with 1 or more dependants: Age of youngest dependant 0 - 15 and age of oldest: 0 - 15	16 up to pension-able age	Pension-able age and over	Age of youngest dependant 16 up to pensionable age and age of oldest: 16 up to pension-able age	Pension-able age and over	Age of youngest dependant pension-able age and over	Persons in households with dependants: Non-depen-dants	Depen-dants
a	b	c	d	e	f	g	h	i	j	k
				Woodspring						
TOTAL HOUSEHOLDS	**70,519**	**39,361**	**16,627**	**1,937**	**160**	**4,063**	**274**	**8,097**	**49,018**	**50,212**
No non-dependants	5,603		9	29	5	645	166	4,749		7,280
1 male	**6,662**	**5,009**	**147**	**121**	**1**	**402**	**26**	**956**	**1,653**	**2,040**
16 - 44	2,865	2,419	106	84	-	131	11	114	446	702
45 - 64	1,861	1,304	39	36	1	238	11	232	557	677
65 and over	1,936	1,286	2	1	-	33	4	610	650	661
1 female	**13,632**	**8,732**	**1,628**	**269**	**27**	**1,038**	**43**	**1,895**	**4,900**	**6,787**
16 - 44	3,220	1,271	1,518	215	17	146	4	49	1,949	3,596
45 - 59	2,036	1,162	102	52	9	526	20	165	874	1,055
60 and over	8,376	6,299	8	2	1	366	19	1,681	2,077	2,136
1 male and 1 female	**33,002**	**18,148**	**12,527**	**1,146**	**82**	**824**	**14**	**261**	**29,708**	**28,344**
Both of pensionable age	5,094	5,030	3	-	-	31	-	30	128	66
1 under, 1 of pensionable age	2,442	2,228	45	5	3	54	1	106	428	265
Both under pensionable age	25,466	10,890	12,479	1,141	79	739	13	125	29,152	28,013
2 of same sex	**1,655**	**1,100**	**192**	**41**	**8**	**193**	**5**	**116**	**1,110**	**728**
Both of pensionable age	181	164	-	-	-	2	-	15	34	17
1 under, 1 of pensionable age	335	220	17	2	5	27	1	63	230	134
Both under pensionable age	1,139	716	175	39	3	164	4	38	846	577
3 or more	**9,965**	**6,372**	**2,124**	**331**	**37**	**961**	**20**	**120**	**11,647**	**5,033**
All of pensionable age	52	49	-	-	-	-	-	3	11	4
1 or more under pensionable age	9,913	6,323	2,124	331	37	961	20	117	11,636	5,029

Table 31 Dependent children in households

Note: * May include a small number of households with no adults

31. Households with residents; residents in households

Households with the following adults	Households with no dependent children	Households with dependent children							Persons in households				
		All households	With 1 dependent child		With 2 or more dependent children			With no dependent child(ren)		With dependent child(ren)		
			Aged 0 - 4	Aged 5 and over	All aged 0 - 4	All aged 5 and over	1 or more aged 0 - 4 and 1 or more aged 5 and over	All persons	Persons economically active	Dependent children	Adults	Persons economically active
a	b	c	d	e	f	g	h	i	j	k	l	m
AVON												
ALL HOUSEHOLDS*	**270,266**	**106,256**	**16,610**	**25,788**	**9,507**	**35,043**	**19,308**	**500,734**	**295,879**	**193,764**	**222,475**	**171,919**
1 male	38,155	1,226	100	517	33	460	116	38,155	24,174	1,997	1,226	883
1 female	62,306	12,440	2,440	3,357	826	3,544	2,273	62,306	17,426	21,995	12,440	5,656
2 (1 male and 1 female)	115,427	72,192	12,257	10,051	8,188	26,402	15,294	230,854	126,963	140,099	144,384	114,020
2 (same sex)	10,514	1,803	271	839	69	407	217	21,028	13,835	2,767	3,606	2,521
3 or more (male(s) and female(s))	41,984	18,276	1,484	10,853	384	4,179	1,376	142,227	108,985	26,463	60,113	48,355
3 or more (same sex)	1,880	222	40	116	5	36	25	6,164	4,496	315	706	484
Bath												
ALL HOUSEHOLDS*	**26,123**	**8,005**	**1,275**	**2,167**	**646**	**2,516**	**1,401**	**46,143**	**25,682**	**14,307**	**16,426**	**12,669**
1 male	3,929	119	11	59	2	38	9	3,929	2,400	179	119	94
1 female	7,239	1,211	257	364	65	345	180	7,239	2,167	2,035	1,211	587
2 (1 male and 1 female)	9,995	5,138	885	803	549	1,803	1,098	19,990	10,280	9,918	10,276	8,188
2 (same sex)	1,258	151	13	76	8	40	14	2,516	1,615	236	302	213
3 or more (male(s) and female(s))	3,440	1,352	107	840	22	286	97	11,585	8,635	1,895	4,448	3,535
3 or more (same sex)	262	22	1	15	-	3	3	884	585	31	70	52
Bristol												
ALL HOUSEHOLDS*	**114,931**	**41,847**	**7,306**	**9,658**	**3,870**	**12,664**	**8,349**	**206,579**	**122,120**	**77,714**	**85,838**	**63,813**
1 male	19,029	579	67	227	17	194	74	19,029	12,303	949	579	371
1 female	28,531	6,646	1,399	1,769	481	1,661	1,336	28,531	8,765	11,910	6,646	2,723
2 (1 male and 1 female)	44,539	26,477	4,899	3,473	3,118	8,898	6,089	89,078	49,147	52,293	52,954	40,821
2 (same sex)	5,397	924	161	400	40	187	136	10,794	7,280	1,451	1,848	1,223
3 or more (male(s) and female(s))	16,337	7,045	736	3,710	209	1,695	695	55,523	41,964	10,862	23,426	18,434
3 or more (same sex)	1,098	119	31	52	3	19	14	3,624	2,661	170	385	241

Note: * May include a small number of households with no adults

31. Households with residents; residents in households

Households with the following adults	Households with no dependent children	Households with dependent children							Persons in households				
		All households	With 1 dependent child		With 2 or more dependent children				With no dependent child(ren)		With dependent child(ren)		
			Aged 0 - 4	Aged 5 and over	All aged 0 - 4	All aged 5 and over	1 or more aged 0 - 4 and 1 or more aged 5 and over		All persons	Persons economically active	Dependent children	Adults	Persons economically active
a	b	c	d	e	f	g	h		i	j	k	l	m
Kingswood													
ALL HOUSEHOLDS*	**24,001**	**10,656**	**1,567**	**2,592**	**997**	**3,590**	**1,910**		**47,206**	**29,277**	**19,093**	**22,617**	**18,227**
1 male	2,658	104	5	38	1	53	7		2,658	1,604	175	104	82
1 female	4,705	934	155	230	60	307	182		4,705	1,122	1,649	934	457
2 (1 male and 1 female)	11,228	7,633	1,273	1,019	911	2,833	1,597		22,456	12,918	14,567	15,266	12,388
2 (same sex)	695	139	16	76	2	28	17		1,390	918	206	278	212
3 or more (male(s) and female(s))	4,621	1,835	117	1,223	22	368	105		15,686	12,484	2,480	6,006	5,064
3 or more (same sex)	94	9	1	5	1	1	1		311	231	13	29	24
Northavon													
ALL HOUSEHOLDS*	**33,510**	**16,116**	**2,469**	**3,913**	**1,533**	**5,554**	**2,647**		**65,654**	**43,613**	**28,892**	**34,538**	**27,718**
1 male	4,137	147	7	65	5	60	10		4,137	2,909	240	147	125
1 female	5,857	1,175	185	321	82	407	180		5,857	1,792	2,087	1,175	631
2 (1 male and 1 female)	16,234	11,707	2,034	1,597	1,385	4,416	2,275		32,468	20,566	22,272	23,414	18,915
2 (same sex)	1,058	209	34	97	7	52	19		2,116	1,499	307	418	308
3 or more (male(s) and female(s))	6,087	2,848	206	1,815	53	613	161		20,646	16,499	3,943	9,296	7,668
3 or more (same sex)	137	28	2	17	1	6	2		430	348	41	88	71
Wansdyke													
ALL HOUSEHOLDS*	**21,553**	**9,261**	**1,237**	**2,295**	**788**	**3,377**	**1,564**		**42,254**	**24,490**	**16,887**	**19,981**	**15,800**
1 male	2,299	79	1	42	2	30	4		2,299	1,285	126	79	62
1 female	4,362	616	104	176	26	220	90		4,362	978	1,057	616	353
2 (1 male and 1 female)	10,075	6,746	1,013	959	730	2,686	1,358		20,150	10,581	13,114	13,492	10,691
2 (same sex)	657	106	12	45	2	39	8		1,314	818	171	212	161
3 or more (male(s) and female(s))	4,070	1,698	107	1,059	28	401	103		13,840	10,598	2,399	5,539	4,500
3 or more (same sex)	90	14	-	12	-	1	1		289	230	18	43	33

Table 31 Dependent children in households – continued

Note: * May include a small number of households with no adults

31. Households with residents; residents in households

Households with the following adults	Households with no dependent children	Households with dependent children						Persons in households				
		All households	With 1 dependent child		With 2 or more dependent children			With no dependent child(ren)		With dependent child(ren)		
			Aged 0 - 4	Aged 5 and over	All aged 0 - 4	All aged 5 and over	1 or more aged 0 - 4 and 1 or more aged 5 and over	All persons	Persons economically active	Dependent children	Adults	Persons economically active
a	b	c	d	e	f	g	h	i	j	k	l	m
Woodspring												
ALL HOUSEHOLDS*	**50,148**	**20,371**	**2,756**	**5,163**	**1,673**	**7,342**	**3,437**	**92,898**	**50,697**	**36,871**	**43,075**	**33,692**
1 male	6,103	198	9	86	6	85	12	6,103	3,673	328	198	149
1 female	11,612	1,858	340	497	112	604	305	11,612	2,602	3,257	1,858	905
2 (1 male and 1 female)	23,356	14,491	2,153	2,200	1,495	5,766	2,877	46,712	23,471	27,935	28,982	23,017
2 (same sex)	1,449	274	35	145	10	61	23	2,898	1,705	396	548	404
3 or more (male(s) and female(s))	7,429	3,498	211	2,206	50	816	215	24,947	18,805	4,884	11,398	9,154
3 or more (same sex)	199	30	5	15	-	6	4	626	441	42	91	63

Note: * May include a small number of households with no persons aged 16 and over

32. Households with residents; residents in households

Households with the following persons aged 16 and over	Households with no person aged 0 - 15	Households with persons aged 0 - 15						Persons in households				
		All households	With one person aged 0 - 15		With two or more persons aged 0 - 15			With no person aged 0 - 15		With person(s) aged 0 - 15		
			Aged 0 - 4	Aged 5 - 15	All aged 0 - 4	All aged 5 - 15	1 or more aged 0 - 4 and 1 or more aged 5 - 15	All persons	Persons economically active	Persons aged 0 - 15	Persons aged 16 and over	Persons economically active
a	b	c	d	e	f	g	h	i	j	k	l	m
AVON												
ALL HOUSEHOLDS*	**277,243**	**99,279**	**16,759**	**24,093**	**9,532**	**29,761**	**19,134**	**525,759**	**310,016**	**178,861**	**212,353**	**157,782**
1 male	38,175	979	100	375	34	360	110	38,175	24,174	1,622	979	666
1 female	62,327	11,287	2,440	2,840	826	2,975	2,206	62,327	17,426	19,895	11,287	4,846
2 (1 male and 1 female)	115,762	65,349	12,268	8,252	8,191	21,671	14,967	231,524	127,233	125,952	130,698	102,015
2 (same sex)	10,841	1,796	277	829	70	384	236	21,682	14,091	2,757	3,592	2,233
3 or more (male(s) and female(s))	48,091	19,562	1,611	11,646	404	4,319	1,582	165,355	122,345	28,200	64,989	47,511
3 or more (same sex)	2,047	256	45	137	5	41	28	6,696	4,747	364	808	511
Bath												
ALL HOUSEHOLDS*	**26,779**	**7,349**	**1,281**	**1,943**	**646**	**2,084**	**1,395**	**48,409**	**26,902**	**13,038**	**15,429**	**11,449**
1 male	3,932	86	11	33	2	31	9	3,932	2,400	137	86	65
1 female	7,245	1,079	257	295	65	285	177	7,245	2,167	1,818	1,079	497
2 (1 male and 1 female)	10,045	4,605	885	640	549	1,455	1,076	20,090	10,319	8,867	9,210	7,230
2 (same sex)	1,304	147	13	76	8	33	17	2,608	1,646	228	294	184
3 or more (male(s) and female(s))	3,977	1,402	113	878	22	276	113	13,608	9,765	1,948	4,672	3,412
3 or more (same sex)	276	28	1	20	-	4	3	926	605	38	88	61
Bristol												
ALL HOUSEHOLDS*	**117,146**	**39,632**	**7,389**	**9,079**	**3,883**	**11,028**	**8,253**	**214,421**	**126,469**	**72,752**	**82,958**	**59,464**
1 male	19,039	496	67	185	18	157	69	19,039	12,303	815	496	306
1 female	28,539	6,133	1,399	1,539	481	1,418	1,296	28,539	8,765	10,934	6,133	2,383
2 (1 male and 1 female)	44,686	24,360	4,906	2,934	3,120	7,460	5,940	89,372	49,265	47,679	48,720	37,161
2 (same sex)	5,524	926	166	381	41	194	144	11,048	7,384	1,473	1,852	1,095
3 or more (male(s) and female(s))	18,183	7,551	803	3,975	218	1,771	784	62,548	45,983	11,607	25,338	18,274
3 or more (same sex)	1,175	131	35	56	3	20	17	3,875	2,769	193	419	245

Table 32 Children aged 0 - 15 in households – continued

Note: * May include a small number of households with no persons aged 16 and over

32. Households with residents; residents in households

Households with the following persons aged 16 and over	Households with no person aged 0 - 15	Households with persons aged 0 - 15						Persons in households				
		All households	With one person aged 0 - 15		With two or more persons aged 0 - 15			With no person aged 0 - 15		With person(s) aged 0 - 15		
			Aged 0 - 4	Aged 5 - 15	All aged 0 - 4	All aged 5 - 15	1 or more aged 0 - 4 and 1 or more aged 5 - 15	All persons	Persons economically active	Persons aged 0 - 15	Persons aged 16 and over	Persons economically active
a	b	c	d	e	f	g	h	i	j	k	l	m
Delyn												
ALL HOUSEHOLDS*	**17,752**	**7,840**	**1,177**	**2,228**	**615**	**2,384**	**1,436**	**35,782**	**19,658**	**13,985**	**17,407**	**12,695**
1 male	2,084	48	5	29	-	13	1	2,084	1,143	69	48	34
1 female	3,544	777	124	213	55	224	161	3,544	657	1,419	777	342
2 (1 male and 1 female)	7,465	4,993	866	787	514	1,704	1,122	14,930	7,543	9,635	9,986	7,643
2 (same sex)	619	141	21	68	5	35	12	1,238	678	214	282	163
3 or more (male(s) and female(s))	3,957	1,842	151	1,111	40	406	134	13,718	9,454	2,597	6,207	4,450
3 or more (same sex)	83	35	9	20	-	2	4	268	183	43	107	63
Glyndŵr												
ALL HOUSEHOLDS*	**12,089**	**4,335**	**708**	**1,133**	**381**	**1,261**	**852**	**23,404**	**12,321**	**7,840**	**9,587**	**6,998**
1 male	1,489	40	7	13	-	19	1	1,489	825	63	40	31
1 female	2,853	369	81	88	33	104	63	2,853	596	626	369	172
2 (1 male and 1 female)	4,910	2,871	531	429	324	903	684	9,820	4,718	5,582	5,742	4,468
2 (same sex)	424	75	14	39	4	13	5	848	448	103	150	93
3 or more (male(s) and female(s))	2,360	969	72	559	20	221	97	8,223	5,627	1,451	3,251	2,215
3 or more (same sex)	53	11	3	5	-	1	2	171	107	15	35	19
Rhuddlan												
ALL HOUSEHOLDS*	**17,164**	**5,716**	**994**	**1,572**	**449**	**1,558**	**1,143**	**30,780**	**13,561**	**10,200**	**12,320**	**8,630**
1 male	2,433	74	8	37	1	20	8	2,433	1,304	121	74	52
1 female	4,660	802	183	194	60	197	168	4,660	887	1,425	802	345
2 (1 male and 1 female)	6,945	3,388	643	565	362	1,018	800	13,890	5,310	6,468	6,776	5,104
2 (same sex)	577	136	23	54	5	37	17	1,154	500	214	272	158
3 or more (male(s) and female(s))	2,491	1,289	133	713	21	281	141	8,460	5,455	1,921	4,324	2,924
3 or more (same sex)	58	23	2	9	-	3	9	183	105	44	72	47

Table 32 Children aged 0 - 15 in households – **continued**

Note: * May include a small number of households with no persons aged 16 and over

32. Households with residents; residents in households

Households with the following persons aged 16 and over	Households with no person aged 0 - 15	Households with persons aged 0 - 15							Persons in households				
		All households	With one person aged 0 - 15		With two or more persons aged 0 - 15			With no person aged 0 - 15		With person(s) aged 0 - 15		
			Aged 0 - 4	Aged 5 - 15	All aged 0 - 4	All aged 5 - 15	1 or more aged 0 - 4 and 1 or more aged 5 - 15	All persons	Persons economically active	Persons aged 0 - 15	Persons aged 16 and over	Persons economically active
a	b	c	d	e	f	g	h	i	j	k	l	m
Woodspring												
ALL HOUSEHOLDS*	**51,795**	**18,724**	**2,786**	**4,791**	**1,676**	**6,067**	**3,404**	**98,856**	**54,059**	**33,411**	**40,577**	**30,330**
1 male	6,108	151	9	63	6	61	12	6,108	3,673	254	151	105
1 female	11,619	1,647	340	406	112	496	293	11,619	2,602	2,872	1,647	756
2 (1 male and 1 female)	23,414	12,842	2,155	1,758	1,495	4,604	2,830	46,828	23,519	24,639	25,684	20,123
2 (same sex)	1,505	262	36	142	10	49	25	3,010	1,744	371	524	345
3 or more (male(s) and female(s))	8,922	3,776	237	2,400	53	846	240	30,580	22,040	5,212	12,457	8,927
3 or more (same sex)	227	37	6	20	-	8	3	711	481	50	114	74

33. Females resident in households of one male aged 16 or over and one female aged 16 or over with or without persons aged 0 - 15; number of persons aged 0 - 15 in such households

In households with:	TOTAL FEMALES	Economically active females					Economically inactive females
		Employees		Self-employed	Other	Economically active students	
		Full-time	Part-time				
a	b	c	d	e	f	g	h
AVON							
No persons aged 0 - 15	115,762	35,955	15,869	3,473	2,681	101	57,784
Person(s) aged 0 - 4 only	20,459	1,975	5,657	777	929	3	11,121
Person(s) aged 5 - 15 only	29,923	5,735	14,345	1,703	652	49	7,488
Persons aged 0 - 4 and 5 - 15	14,967	855	5,054	681	273	9	8,104
TOTAL PERSONS AGED 0 - 15	**125,952**	**14,550**	**48,572**	**6,025**	**3,049**	**114**	**53,756**
Persons aged 0 - 4	47,460	3,255	13,732	1,848	1,485	14	27,140
Bath							
No persons aged 0 - 15	10,045	2,682	1,476	360	243	13	5,284
Person(s) aged 0 - 4 only	1,434	117	409	89	64	-	755
Person(s) aged 5 - 15 only	2,095	369	1,019	145	48	3	514
Persons aged 0 - 4 and 5 - 15	1,076	53	394	59	22	-	548
TOTAL PERSONS AGED 0 - 15	**8,867**	**896**	**3,543**	**540**	**214**	**5**	**3,674**
Persons aged 0 - 4	3,365	192	1,034	191	102	-	1,846
Bristol							
No persons aged 0 - 15	44,686	14,183	5,901	1,107	1,332	57	22,163
Person(s) aged 0 - 4 only	8,026	825	2,117	282	397	2	4,405
Person(s) aged 5 - 15 only	10,394	2,034	4,781	519	264	21	2,796
Persons aged 0 - 4 and 5 - 15	5,940	372	1,843	253	149	5	3,323
TOTAL PERSONS AGED 0 - 15	**47,679**	**5,509**	**17,023**	**2,030**	**1,403**	**59**	**21,714**
Persons aged 0 - 4	18,781	1,382	5,093	667	685	9	10,954
Kingswood							
No persons aged 0 - 15	11,250	3,688	1,730	268	172	5	5,392
Person(s) aged 0 - 4 only	2,186	190	674	60	107	-	1,155
Person(s) aged 5 - 15 only	3,258	553	1,812	143	60	4	690
Persons aged 0 - 4 and 5 - 15	1,569	81	631	59	16	1	782
TOTAL PERSONS AGED 0 - 15	**13,322**	**1,403**	**5,994**	**496**	**282**	**9**	**5,147**
Persons aged 0 - 4	5,041	314	1,665	153	160	1	2,749
Northavon							
No persons aged 0 - 15	16,263	6,341	2,278	496	312	10	6,836
Person(s) aged 0 - 4 only	3,420	357	1,012	121	160	-	1,770
Person(s) aged 5 - 15 only	4,894	1,009	2,409	279	80	11	1,117
Persons aged 0 - 4 and 5 - 15	2,240	134	817	105	38	1	1,146
TOTAL PERSONS AGED 0 - 15	**19,952**	**2,526**	**8,128**	**977**	**435**	**18**	**7,886**
Persons aged 0 - 4	7,572	559	2,372	296	236	1	4,109
Wansdyke							
No persons aged 0 - 15	10,104	2,822	1,431	385	141	5	5,325
Person(s) aged 0 - 4 only	1,743	148	449	70	59	1	1,017
Person(s) aged 5 - 15 only	2,920	540	1,392	190	60	4	738
Persons aged 0 - 4 and 5 - 15	1,312	67	437	68	13	-	727
TOTAL PERSONS AGED 0 - 15	**11,493**	**1,312**	**4,435**	**641**	**212**	**7**	**4,893**
Persons aged 0 - 4	4,071	250	1,111	180	92	1	2,438

33. Females resident in households of one male aged 16 or over and one female aged 16 or over with or without persons aged 0 - 15; number of persons aged 0 - 15 in such households

In households with:	TOTAL FEMALES	Economically active females					Economically inactive females
		Employees		Self-employed	Other	Economically active students	
		Full-time	Part-time				
a	b	c	d	e	f	g	h
			Woodspring				
No persons aged 0 - 15	23,414	6,239	3,053	857	481	11	12,784
Person(s) aged 0 - 4 only	3,650	338	996	155	142	-	2,019
Person(s) aged 5 - 15 only	6,362	1,230	2,932	427	140	6	1,633
Persons aged 0 - 4 and 5 - 15	2,830	148	932	137	35	2	1,578
TOTAL PERSONS AGED 0 - 15	**24,639**	**2,904**	**9,449**	**1,341**	**503**	**16**	**10,442**
Persons aged 0 - 4	8,630	558	2,457	361	210	2	5,044

34. Residents aged 16 and over in households

Economic position	TOTAL PERSONS	Males: Single, widowed or divorced	Males: Married	Females: Single, widowed or divorced	Females: Married	Students (economically active or inactive)
a	b	c	d	e	f	g
AVON						
TOTAL PERSONS AGED 16 AND OVER	**738,112**	**136,700**	**217,340**	**164,909**	**219,163**	**32,095**
Economically active	**467,798**	**103,177**	**161,958**	**81,998**	**120,665**	**4,698**
Employees - full time	289,232	70,027	116,913	55,094	47,198	402
- part time	84,146	4,472	4,881	14,630	60,163	4,083
Self-employed - with employees	17,420	2,280	10,893	798	3,449	10
- without employees	36,183	9,286	18,855	2,614	5,428	27
On a Government scheme	4,782	2,194	492	1,701	395	
Unemployed	36,035	14,918	9,924	7,161	4,032	176
Economically active students (included above)	*4,698*	*2,042*	*67*	*2,504*	*85*	
Economically inactive	**270,314**	**33,523**	**55,382**	**82,911**	**98,498**	**27,397**
Students	27,397	13,244	571	12,908	674	27,397
Permanently sick	19,003	4,076	7,224	4,043	3,660	
Retired	137,597	15,206	46,386	42,846	33,159	
Other inactive	86,317	997	1,201	23,114	61,005	
Bath						
TOTAL PERSONS AGED 16 AND OVER	**63,838**	**12,669**	**17,133**	**16,687**	**17,349**	**3,544**
Economically active	**38,351**	**9,220**	**11,910**	**7,969**	**9,252**	**474**
Employees - full time	22,288	5,831	8,148	5,016	3,293	49
- part time	7,398	519	520	1,558	4,801	397
Self-employed - with employees	1,509	253	864	101	291	2
- without employees	3,525	979	1,637	374	535	3
On a Government scheme	437	182	52	154	49	
Unemployed	3,194	1,456	689	766	283	23
Economically active students (included above)	*474*	*203*	*9*	*252*	*10*	
Economically inactive	**25,487**	**3,449**	**5,223**	**8,718**	**8,097**	**3,070**
Students	3,070	1,422	76	1,489	83	3,070
Permanently sick	1,371	368	450	322	231	
Retired	14,116	1,574	4,591	4,752	3,199	
Other inactive	6,930	85	106	2,155	4,584	
Bristol						
TOTAL PERSONS AGED 16 AND OVER	**297,379**	**63,058**	**78,761**	**75,807**	**79,753**	**12,504**
Economically active	**185,933**	**48,034**	**57,040**	**38,276**	**42,583**	**1,559**
Employees - full time	115,185	31,990	40,626	25,670	16,899	155
- part time	31,194	1,897	1,910	6,306	21,081	1,300
Self-employed - with employees	5,392	906	3,219	302	965	3
- without employees	12,903	3,843	6,212	1,131	1,717	16
On a Government scheme	2,332	1,101	216	852	163	
Unemployed	18,927	8,297	4,857	4,015	1,758	85
Economically active students (included above)	*1,559*	*658*	*32*	*833*	*36*	
Economically inactive	**111,446**	**15,024**	**21,721**	**37,531**	**37,170**	**10,945**
Students	10,945	5,223	376	5,016	330	10,945
Permanently sick	9,332	2,190	3,350	2,123	1,669	
Retired	56,505	7,069	17,435	19,035	12,966	
Other inactive	34,664	542	560	11,357	22,205	

34. Residents aged 16 and over in households

Economic position	TOTAL PERSONS	Males		Females		Students (economically active or inactive)
		Single, widowed or divorced	Married	Single, widowed or divorced	Married	
a	b	c	d	e	f	g
		Kingswood				
TOTAL PERSONS AGED 16 AND OVER	**71,120**	**11,519**	**22,984**	**13,555**	**23,062**	**2,343**
Economically active	**47,504**	**8,980**	**17,945**	**7,132**	**13,447**	**437**
Employees - full time	30,058	6,513	13,445	5,143	4,957	34
- part time	9,352	341	460	1,181	7,370	389
Self-employed - with employees	1,549	184	1,049	46	270	1
- without employees	3,366	762	2,021	138	445	3
On a Government scheme	428	183	44	164	37	
Unemployed	2,751	997	926	460	368	10
Economically active students (included above)	*437*	*198*	*4*	*225*	*10*	
Economically inactive	**23,616**	**2,539**	**5,039**	**6,423**	**9,615**	**1,906**
Students	1,906	953	12	900	41	1,906
Permanently sick	1,568	306	659	276	327	
Retired	12,141	1,209	4,281	3,499	3,152	
Other inactive	8,001	71	87	1,748	6,095	
		Northavon				
TOTAL PERSONS AGED 16 AND OVER	**102,560**	**17,268**	**33,294**	**18,549**	**33,449**	**4,408**
Economically active	**71,331**	**13,561**	**27,148**	**10,314**	**20,308**	**753**
Employees - full time	46,632	10,034	20,635	7,384	8,579	60
- part time	12,514	553	581	1,736	9,644	672
Self-employed - with employees	2,682	279	1,763	94	546	1
- without employees	5,299	1,185	2,952	279	883	-
On a Government scheme	528	236	54	189	49	
Unemployed	3,676	1,274	1,163	632	607	20
Economically active students (included above)	*753*	*331*	*6*	*403*	*13*	
Economically inactive	**31,229**	**3,707**	**6,146**	**8,235**	**13,141**	**3,655**
Students	3,655	1,799	35	1,750	71	3,655
Permanently sick	1,889	347	755	354	433	
Retired	14,327	1,455	5,230	3,846	3,796	
Other inactive	11,358	106	126	2,285	8,841	
		Wansdyke				
TOTAL PERSONS AGED 16 AND OVER	**63,782**	**10,177**	**20,746**	**12,105**	**20,754**	**2,881**
Economically active	**40,290**	**7,495**	**15,627**	**5,791**	**11,377**	**441**
Employees - full time	24,294	5,143	10,975	3,855	4,321	41
- part time	7,661	335	476	1,110	5,740	380
Self-employed - with employees	2,163	218	1,426	84	435	2
- without employees	3,758	853	2,085	238	582	2
On a Government scheme	351	142	30	132	47	
Unemployed	2,063	804	635	372	252	16
Economically active students (included above)	*441*	*190*	*5*	*239*	*7*	
Economically inactive	**23,492**	**2,682**	**5,119**	**6,314**	**9,377**	**2,440**
Students	2,440	1,176	23	1,196	45	2,440
Permanently sick	1,229	230	541	224	234	
Retired	11,768	1,216	4,449	3,194	2,909	
Other inactive	8,055	60	106	1,700	6,189	

34. Residents aged 16 and over in households

Economic position	TOTAL PERSONS	Males		Females		Students (economically active or inactive)
		Single, widowed or divorced	Married	Single, widowed or divorced	Married	
a	b	c	d	e	f	g
		Woodspring				
TOTAL PERSONS AGED 16 AND OVER	**139,433**	**22,009**	**44,422**	**28,206**	**44,796**	**6,415**
Economically active	**84,389**	**15,887**	**32,288**	**12,516**	**23,698**	**1,034**
Employees - full time	50,775	10,516	23,084	8,026	9,149	63
- part time	16,027	827	934	2,739	11,527	945
Self-employed - with employees	4,125	440	2,572	171	942	1
- without employees	7,332	1,664	3,948	454	1,266	3
On a Government scheme	706	350	96	210	50	
Unemployed	5,424	2,090	1,654	916	764	22
Economically active students (included above)	*1,034*	*462*	*11*	*552*	*9*	
Economically inactive	**55,044**	**6,122**	**12,134**	**15,690**	**21,098**	**5,381**
Students	5,381	2,671	49	2,557	104	5,381
Permanently sick	3,614	635	1,469	744	766	
Retired	28,740	2,683	10,400	8,520	7,137	
Other inactive	17,309	133	216	3,869	13,091	

35. Residents in households

Age	TOTAL PERSONS	Males					Females				
		Total	Single	Married	Widowed	Divorced	Total	Single	Married	Widowed	Divorced
a	b	c	d	e	f	g	h	i	j	k	l
					AVON						
ALL AGES	**916,973**	**445,749**	**197,182**	**217,340**	**11,836**	**19,391**	**471,224**	**176,135**	**219,163**	**49,101**	**26,825**
0 - 4	59,829	30,727	30,727				29,102	29,102			
5 - 9	55,521	28,448	28,448				27,073	27,073			
10 - 14	53,015	27,161	27,161				25,854	25,854			
15	10,496	5,373	5,373				5,123	5,123			
16 - 17	22,411	11,502	11,476	23	1	2	10,909	10,861	39	3	6
18 - 19	24,475	12,380	12,287	80	-	13	12,095	11,798	282	4	11
20 - 24	69,509	34,623	31,074	3,375	7	167	34,886	27,034	7,334	39	479
25 - 29	74,925	37,111	20,561	15,421	19	1,110	37,814	15,008	20,629	75	2,102
30 - 34	67,078	33,232	9,401	21,505	41	2,285	33,846	6,450	23,925	130	3,341
35 - 39	61,547	30,573	5,253	22,519	63	2,738	30,974	3,317	23,784	210	3,663
40 - 44	67,910	33,748	3,904	26,520	135	3,189	34,162	2,156	27,159	440	4,407
45 - 49	58,252	29,153	2,529	23,612	233	2,779	29,099	1,400	23,474	727	3,498
50 - 54	49,972	25,017	1,853	20,604	309	2,251	24,955	1,142	20,092	1,134	2,587
55 - 59	47,097	23,331	1,713	19,413	495	1,710	23,766	1,146	18,343	2,161	2,116
60 - 64	47,001	22,788	1,729	18,746	1,013	1,300	24,213	1,432	17,094	4,087	1,600
65 - 69	46,542	21,366	1,488	17,328	1,659	891	25,176	1,626	15,348	6,916	1,286
70 - 74	38,361	16,518	982	12,908	2,084	544	21,843	1,564	10,827	8,613	839
75 - 79	31,029	12,445	657	9,185	2,341	262	18,584	1,663	6,676	9,704	541
80 - 84	19,919	6,933	383	4,451	1,982	117	12,986	1,361	3,062	8,326	237
85 - 89	9,190	2,665	146	1,417	1,072	30	6,525	762	927	4,743	93
90 and over	2,894	655	37	233	382	3	2,239	263	168	1,789	19
					Bath						
ALL AGES	**76,876**	**36,429**	**16,565**	**17,133**	**1,075**	**1,656**	**40,447**	**15,552**	**17,349**	**4,821**	**2,725**
0 - 4	4,359	2,223	2,223				2,136	2,136			
5 - 9	3,994	2,049	2,049				1,945	1,945			
10 - 14	3,844	1,947	1,947				1,897	1,897			
15	841	408	408				433	433			
16 - 17	1,729	920	916	4	-	-	809	804	5	-	-
18 - 19	2,045	973	963	8	-	2	1,072	1,050	19	2	1
20 - 24	6,288	3,094	2,888	192	-	14	3,194	2,723	423	5	43
25 - 29	6,009	2,992	2,029	890	1	72	3,017	1,574	1,282	8	153
30 - 34	5,273	2,611	966	1,472	3	170	2,662	669	1,678	15	300
35 - 39	4,879	2,372	524	1,628	2	218	2,507	375	1,736	20	376
40 - 44	5,330	2,622	410	1,916	7	289	2,708	236	2,021	21	430
45 - 49	4,576	2,248	266	1,745	9	228	2,328	157	1,758	57	356
50 - 54	4,063	2,006	195	1,586	27	198	2,057	146	1,577	87	247
55 - 59	3,972	1,877	163	1,534	41	139	2,095	133	1,568	178	216
60 - 64	4,338	2,006	183	1,621	78	124	2,332	185	1,582	351	214
65 - 69	4,549	2,064	185	1,649	141	89	2,485	218	1,430	662	175
70 - 74	3,885	1,631	113	1,266	195	57	2,254	265	1,078	809	102
75 - 79	3,339	1,314	78	953	250	33	2,025	266	726	967	66
80 - 84	2,208	740	43	485	193	19	1,468	208	330	893	37
85 - 89	1,021	261	13	151	94	3	760	95	112	545	8
90 and over	334	71	3	33	34	1	263	37	24	201	1

35. Residents in households

Age	TOTAL PERSONS	Males					Females				
		Total	Single	Married	Widowed	Divorced	Total	Single	Married	Widowed	Divorced
a	b	c	d	e	f	g	h	i	j	k	l
					Bristol						
ALL AGES	**370,131**	**179,039**	**86,140**	**78,761**	**5,099**	**9,039**	**191,092**	**77,762**	**79,753**	**21,214**	**12,363**
0 - 4	25,747	13,188	13,188				12,559	12,559			
5 - 9	22,783	11,648	11,648				11,135	11,135			
10 - 14	20,312	10,392	10,392				9,920	9,920			
15	3,910	1,992	1,992				1,918	1,918			
16 - 17	8,146	4,159	4,145	13	1	-	3,987	3,958	22	3	4
18 - 19	9,361	4,660	4,610	43	-	7	4,701	4,557	137	-	7
20 - 24	30,858	15,207	13,776	1,342	5	84	15,651	12,564	2,844	17	226
25 - 29	34,503	16,840	10,281	6,050	12	497	17,663	8,396	8,214	34	1,019
30 - 34	28,978	14,366	4,938	8,372	14	1,042	14,612	3,809	9,142	68	1,593
35 - 39	24,667	12,434	2,914	8,214	33	1,273	12,233	1,873	8,543	91	1,726
40 - 44	25,015	12,608	2,090	8,997	59	1,462	12,407	1,250	9,037	196	1,924
45 - 49	20,490	10,302	1,334	7,633	93	1,242	10,188	705	7,665	284	1,534
50 - 54	18,249	9,158	984	7,018	121	1,035	9,091	561	6,840	470	1,220
55 - 59	17,625	8,746	926	6,786	196	838	8,879	542	6,503	886	948
60 - 64	18,571	8,926	953	6,850	480	643	9,645	715	6,357	1,807	766
65 - 69	18,882	8,540	790	6,570	739	441	10,342	731	5,996	3,049	566
70 - 74	15,904	6,745	544	5,010	917	274	9,159	716	4,252	3,787	404
75 - 79	12,808	5,032	357	3,545	1,000	130	7,776	755	2,582	4,177	262
80 - 84	8,233	2,746	196	1,679	814	57	5,487	618	1,206	3,555	108
85 - 89	3,838	1,094	66	564	451	13	2,744	355	349	1,993	47
90 and over	1,251	256	16	75	164	1	995	125	64	797	9
					Kingswood						
ALL AGES	**88,916**	**43,562**	**17,849**	**22,984**	**1,056**	**1,673**	**45,354**	**15,690**	**23,062**	**4,387**	**2,215**
0 - 4	5,928	3,061	3,061				2,867	2,867			
5 - 9	5,495	2,782	2,782				2,713	2,713			
10 - 14	5,315	2,685	2,685				2,630	2,630			
15	1,058	531	531				527	527			
16 - 17	2,228	1,128	1,127	-	-	1	1,100	1,099	1	-	-
18 - 19	2,389	1,245	1,241	3	-	1	1,144	1,125	19	-	-
20 - 24	6,183	3,133	2,838	282	-	13	3,050	2,296	710	2	42
25 - 29	7,003	3,464	1,584	1,746	1	133	3,539	1,030	2,308	9	192
30 - 34	6,788	3,379	677	2,455	5	242	3,409	428	2,660	7	314
35 - 39	6,276	3,103	316	2,529	8	250	3,173	214	2,614	18	327
40 - 44	6,602	3,325	281	2,771	12	261	3,277	111	2,762	38	366
45 - 49	5,917	2,927	177	2,493	29	228	2,990	92	2,544	61	293
50 - 54	5,240	2,639	120	2,316	32	171	2,601	63	2,237	116	185
55 - 59	5,234	2,558	112	2,249	54	143	2,676	72	2,181	250	173
60 - 64	4,740	2,311	98	2,049	80	84	2,429	70	1,798	430	131
65 - 69	4,290	2,062	107	1,747	136	72	2,228	92	1,440	608	88
70 - 74	3,173	1,389	47	1,095	209	38	1,784	75	918	742	49
75 - 79	2,458	991	32	750	186	23	1,467	61	526	853	27
80 - 84	1,626	594	22	374	188	10	1,032	68	254	691	19
85 - 89	753	215	8	112	93	2	538	41	79	412	6
90 and over	220	40	3	13	23	1	180	16	11	150	3

35. Residents in households

Age	TOTAL PERSONS	Males					Females				
		Total	Single	Married	Widowed	Divorced	Total	Single	Married	Widowed	Divorced
a	b	c	d	e	f	g	h	i	j	k	l
					Northavon						
ALL AGES	**129,084**	**64,277**	**27,324**	**33,294**	**1,339**	**2,320**	**64,807**	**23,366**	**33,449**	**5,038**	**2,954**
0 - 4	8,795	4,541	4,541				4,254	4,254			
5 - 9	7,992	4,145	4,145				3,847	3,847			
10 - 14	8,098	4,146	4,146				3,952	3,952			
15	1,639	883	883				756	756			
16 - 17	3,529	1,832	1,829	3	-	-	1,697	1,695	1	-	1
18 - 19	3,746	1,915	1,907	8	-	-	1,831	1,786	42	1	2
20 - 24	10,142	5,044	4,333	686	2	23	5,098	3,585	1,458	5	50
25 - 29	11,270	5,663	2,552	2,938	3	170	5,607	1,583	3,745	4	275
30 - 34	9,889	5,069	1,088	3,668	8	305	4,820	566	3,855	11	388
35 - 39	8,852	4,348	487	3,531	3	327	4,504	255	3,810	28	411
40 - 44	10,501	5,185	382	4,393	18	392	5,316	162	4,547	57	550
45 - 49	9,501	4,796	246	4,142	35	373	4,705	146	4,029	105	425
50 - 54	7,719	3,938	187	3,434	54	263	3,781	97	3,257	148	279
55 - 59	6,563	3,330	160	2,915	72	183	3,233	118	2,637	266	212
60 - 64	5,759	2,992	152	2,566	137	137	2,767	104	2,128	415	120
65 - 69	5,044	2,412	107	2,029	200	76	2,632	122	1,660	739	111
70 - 74	3,916	1,683	79	1,360	203	41	2,233	92	1,190	893	58
75 - 79	3,134	1,328	57	999	251	21	1,806	103	658	994	51
80 - 84	1,921	718	20	479	212	7	1,203	81	327	781	14
85 - 89	831	251	18	133	98	2	580	51	92	432	5
90 and over	243	58	5	10	43	-	185	11	13	159	2
					Wansdyke						
ALL AGES	**79,122**	**38,854**	**15,806**	**20,746**	**1,030**	**1,272**	**40,268**	**13,691**	**20,754**	**4,106**	**1,717**
0 - 4	4,706	2,413	2,413				2,293	2,293			
5 - 9	4,742	2,479	2,479				2,263	2,263			
10 - 14	4,881	2,533	2,533				2,348	2,348			
15	1,011	506	506				505	505			
16 - 17	2,120	1,070	1,067	2	-	1	1,050	1,047	3	-	-
18 - 19	2,230	1,157	1,151	6	-	-	1,073	1,057	15	-	1
20 - 24	5,105	2,624	2,353	262	-	9	2,481	1,866	584	2	29
25 - 29	5,103	2,584	1,307	1,200	1	76	2,519	779	1,593	9	138
30 - 34	5,173	2,521	607	1,771	1	142	2,652	315	2,153	8	176
35 - 39	5,401	2,695	341	2,164	3	187	2,706	196	2,260	15	235
40 - 44	6,455	3,170	237	2,719	13	201	3,285	134	2,807	34	310
45 - 49	5,517	2,738	162	2,361	22	193	2,779	93	2,389	69	228
50 - 54	4,723	2,346	134	2,030	20	162	2,377	95	1,997	102	183
55 - 59	4,533	2,277	137	1,981	41	118	2,256	86	1,803	208	159
60 - 64	4,412	2,118	118	1,854	80	66	2,294	98	1,755	353	88
65 - 69	4,241	2,017	95	1,699	154	69	2,224	113	1,447	582	82
70 - 74	3,377	1,492	63	1,241	159	29	1,885	126	1,000	716	43
75 - 79	2,688	1,153	42	879	221	11	1,535	125	587	798	25
80 - 84	1,713	649	44	425	174	6	1,064	88	280	681	15
85 - 89	742	251	13	129	107	2	491	52	65	370	4
90 and over	249	61	4	23	34	-	188	12	16	159	1

35. Residents in households

Age	TOTAL PERSONS	Males					Females				
		Total	Single	Married	Widowed	Divorced	Total	Single	Married	Widowed	Divorced
a	b	c	d	e	f	g	h	i	j	k	l
					Woodspring						
ALL AGES	**172,844**	**83,588**	**33,498**	**44,422**	**2,237**	**3,431**	**89,256**	**30,074**	**44,796**	**9,535**	**4,851**
0 - 4	10,294	5,301	5,301				4,993	4,993			
5 - 9	10,515	5,345	5,345				5,170	5,170			
10 - 14	10,565	5,458	5,458				5,107	5,107			
15	2,037	1,053	1,053				984	984			
16 - 17	4,659	2,393	2,392	1	-	-	2,266	2,258	7	-	1
18 - 19	4,704	2,430	2,415	12	-	3	2,274	2,223	50	1	-
20 - 24	10,933	5,521	4,886	611	-	24	5,412	4,000	1,315	8	89
25 - 29	11,037	5,568	2,808	2,597	1	162	5,469	1,646	3,487	11	325
30 - 34	10,977	5,286	1,125	3,767	10	384	5,691	663	4,437	21	570
35 - 39	11,472	5,621	671	4,453	14	483	5,851	404	4,821	38	588
40 - 44	14,007	6,838	504	5,724	26	584	7,169	263	5,985	94	827
45 - 49	12,251	6,142	344	5,238	45	515	6,109	207	5,089	151	662
50 - 54	9,978	4,930	233	4,220	55	422	5,048	180	4,184	211	473
55 - 59	9,170	4,543	215	3,948	91	289	4,627	195	3,651	373	408
60 - 64	9,181	4,435	225	3,806	158	246	4,746	260	3,474	731	281
65 - 69	9,536	4,271	204	3,634	289	144	5,265	350	3,375	1,276	264
70 - 74	8,106	3,578	136	2,936	401	105	4,528	290	2,389	1,666	183
75 - 79	6,602	2,627	91	2,059	433	44	3,975	353	1,597	1,915	110
80 - 84	4,218	1,486	58	1,009	401	18	2,732	298	665	1,725	44
85 - 89	2,005	593	28	328	229	8	1,412	168	230	991	23
90 and over	597	169	6	79	84	-	428	62	40	323	3

36. Households with residents; resident adults; dependent children

Households with the following adults: Number	Economically active	In employment	TOTAL HOUSEHOLDS	Households with the following dependent children: 0	1	2	3 or more	TOTAL DEPENDENT CHILDREN
a	b	c	d	e	f	g	h	i
AVON								
None	None	None	97		73	19	5	128
One	None	None	65,988	58,861	3,057	2,509	1,561	13,393
One	One	None	5,703	5,028	399	201	75	1,048
One	One	One	42,436	36,572	2,958	2,251	655	9,551
Two or more	None	None	46,217	44,734	693	458	332	2,786
Two or more	One	None	6,920	3,121	1,161	1,407	1,231	8,317
Two or more	One	One	54,403	27,908	8,596	12,014	5,885	52,134
Two or more	Two or more	None	1,959	1,265	295	238	161	1,348
Two or more	Two or more	One	10,820	6,818	1,963	1,461	578	6,794
Two or more	Two or more	Two or more	141,979	85,959	23,203	25,041	7,776	98,265
TOTAL HOUSEHOLDS			**376,522**	**270,266**	**42,398**	**45,599**	**18,259**	**193,764**
TOTAL ADULTS			**723,209**	**500,734**	**94,446**	**91,707**	**36,322**	
Economically active			467,798	295,879	74,033	72,158	25,728	
In employment			431,763	272,191	68,230	68,059	23,283	
Bath								
None	None	None	12		11	1	-	13
One	None	None	7,250	6,601	303	218	128	1,172
One	One	None	652	594	36	19	3	83
One	One	One	4,596	3,973	352	215	56	959
Two or more	None	None	4,485	4,380	45	35	25	209
Two or more	One	None	557	267	105	100	85	599
Two or more	One	One	4,386	2,561	641	759	425	3,556
Two or more	Two or more	None	170	118	26	17	9	89
Two or more	Two or more	One	904	596	154	109	45	514
Two or more	Two or more	Two or more	11,116	7,033	1,769	1,737	577	7,113
TOTAL HOUSEHOLDS			**34,128**	**26,123**	**3,442**	**3,210**	**1,353**	**14,307**
TOTAL ADULTS			**62,569**	**46,143**	**7,423**	**6,351**	**2,652**	
Economically active			38,351	25,682	5,773	5,002	1,894	
In employment			35,157	23,445	5,287	4,691	1,734	
Bristol								
None	None	None	57		40	13	4	79
One	None	None	30,623	26,492	1,781	1,369	981	7,884
One	One	None	3,578	3,136	269	116	57	693
One	One	One	20,584	17,932	1,412	925	315	4,282
Two or more	None	None	18,233	17,397	370	256	210	1,634
Two or more	One	None	3,713	1,532	643	781	757	4,929
Two or more	One	One	21,006	11,252	3,223	4,181	2,350	19,553
Two or more	Two or more	None	1,185	755	172	146	112	877
Two or more	Two or more	One	5,119	3,302	889	615	313	3,172
Two or more	Two or more	Two or more	52,680	33,133	8,165	8,410	2,972	34,611
TOTAL HOUSEHOLDS			**156,778**	**114,931**	**16,964**	**16,812**	**8,071**	**77,714**
TOTAL ADULTS			**292,417**	**206,579**	**36,451**	**33,505**	**15,882**	
Economically active			185,933	122,120	27,638	25,489	10,686	
In employment			167,006	109,669	24,735	23,414	9,188	

36. Households with residents; resident adults; dependent children

Households with the following adults			TOTAL HOUSEHOLDS	Households with the following dependent children				TOTAL DEPENDENT CHILDREN
Number	Economically active	In employment		0	1	2	3 or more	
a	b	c	d	e	f	g	h	i
				Kingswood				
None	None	None	2		1	1	-	3
One	None	None	5,136	4,637	206	202	91	908
One	One	None	261	226	18	16	1	53
One	One	One	3,004	2,500	204	250	50	863
Two or more	None	None	4,021	3,940	40	23	18	152
Two or more	One	None	500	251	75	102	72	518
Two or more	One	One	5,351	2,698	869	1,247	537	5,114
Two or more	Two or more	None	117	71	25	12	9	81
Two or more	Two or more	One	936	557	199	135	45	617
Two or more	Two or more	Two or more	15,329	9,121	2,522	2,915	771	10,784
TOTAL HOUSEHOLDS			**34,657**	**24,001**	**4,159**	**4,903**	**1,594**	**19,093**
TOTAL ADULTS			**69,823**	**47,206**	**9,621**	**9,800**	**3,196**	
Economically active			47,504	29,277	7,834	8,019	2,374	
In employment			44,753	27,507	7,327	7,691	2,228	
				Northavon				
None	None	None	2		2	-	-	2
One	None	None	5,859	5,293	218	227	121	1,070
One	One	None	327	275	29	18	5	80
One	One	One	5,130	4,426	331	284	89	1,177
Two or more	None	None	4,940	4,816	59	45	20	220
Two or more	One	None	668	333	98	130	107	724
Two or more	One	One	7,750	3,517	1,385	2,004	844	8,154
Two or more	Two or more	None	156	94	22	23	17	122
Two or more	Two or more	One	1,329	796	273	200	60	871
Two or more	Two or more	Two or more	23,465	13,960	3,965	4,345	1,195	16,472
TOTAL HOUSEHOLDS			**49,626**	**33,510**	**6,382**	**7,276**	**2,458**	**28,892**
TOTAL ADULTS			**100,192**	**65,654**	**14,792**	**14,788**	**4,958**	
Economically active			71,331	43,613	12,035	11,974	3,709	
In employment			67,655	41,284	11,364	11,523	3,484	
				Wansdyke				
None	None	None	2		2	-	-	2
One	None	None	4,678	4,398	120	117	43	506
One	One	None	172	158	7	6	1	22
One	One	One	2,506	2,105	196	161	44	655
Two or more	None	None	4,145	4,058	48	19	20	151
Two or more	One	None	429	205	69	93	62	465
Two or more	One	One	5,160	2,562	824	1,218	556	5,084
Two or more	Two or more	None	78	49	13	14	2	47
Two or more	Two or more	One	680	415	119	110	36	453
Two or more	Two or more	Two or more	12,964	7,603	2,134	2,462	765	9,502
TOTAL HOUSEHOLDS			**30,814**	**21,553**	**3,532**	**4,200**	**1,529**	**16,887**
TOTAL ADULTS			**62,235**	**42,254**	**8,204**	**8,644**	**3,133**	
Economically active			40,290	24,490	6,543	6,930	2,327	
In employment			38,227	23,169	6,207	6,649	2,202	

36. Households with residents; resident adults; dependent children

Households with the following adults			TOTAL HOUSEHOLDS	Households with the following dependent children				TOTAL DEPENDENT CHILDREN
Number	Economically active	In employment		0	1	2	3 or more	
a	b	c	d	e	f	g	h	i
				Woodspring				
None	None	None	22		17	4	1	29
One	None	None	12,442	11,440	429	376	197	1,853
One	One	None	713	639	40	26	8	117
One	One	One	6,616	5,636	463	416	101	1,615
Two or more	None	None	10,393	10,143	131	80	39	420
Two or more	One	None	1,053	533	171	201	148	1,082
Two or more	One	One	10,750	5,318	1,654	2,605	1,173	10,673
Two or more	Two or more	None	253	178	37	26	12	132
Two or more	Two or more	One	1,852	1,152	329	292	79	1,167
Two or more	Two or more	Two or more	26,425	15,109	4,648	5,172	1,496	19,783
TOTAL HOUSEHOLDS			**70,519**	**50,148**	**7,919**	**9,198**	**3,254**	**36,871**
TOTAL ADULTS			**135,973**	**92,898**	**17,955**	**18,619**	**6,501**	
Economically active			84,389	50,697	14,210	14,744	4,738	
In employment			78,965	47,117	13,310	14,091	4,447	

37. Residents aged 16 - 24 in households

Age	TOTAL PERSONS		Married		Lone 'parent' aged 16 - 24 with child(ren) aged 0 - 15		Economically active		On a Government scheme		Unemployed		Students (including those economically active)	
	Males	Females	Males	Females	Males	Females	Males	Females	Males	Females	Males	Females	Males	Females
a	b	c	d	e	f	g	h	i	j	k	l	m	n	o
AVON														
ALL AGES 16 - 24	**58,505**	**57,890**	**3,478**	**7,655**	**44**	**1,915**	**45,431**	**39,640**	**1,608**	**1,244**	**6,840**	**3,689**	**14,346**	**14,479**
16	5,653	5,475	10	16	3	4	1,836	1,759	259	216	307	216	4,276	4,340
17	5,849	5,434	13	23	2	23	3,723	3,096	547	430	510	333	2,646	2,886
18	6,052	5,835	18	80	3	71	4,480	3,941	311	255	747	473	1,917	2,097
19	6,328	6,260	62	202	1	144	5,030	4,584	124	82	936	510	1,376	1,345
20	6,735	6,687	125	429	6	200	5,457	4,891	75	54	897	490	1,325	1,316
21	6,583	6,558	268	835	3	244	5,425	4,842	62	44	842	407	1,164	1,022
22	6,838	6,997	540	1,356	5	354	5,965	5,254	73	60	832	431	865	780
23	7,010	7,144	959	2,020	10	408	6,459	5,504	64	56	890	413	474	418
24	7,457	7,500	1,483	2,694	11	467	7,056	5,769	93	47	879	416	303	275
Bath														
ALL AGES 16 - 24	**4,987**	**5,075**	**204**	**447**	**-**	**204**	**3,617**	**3,240**	**130**	**101**	**598**	**331**	**1,499**	**1,589**
16	434	401	2	3	-	-	143	119	23	12	36	17	337	332
17	486	408	2	2	-	-	278	207	51	27	42	28	255	241
18	470	482	3	3	-	7	321	300	15	18	79	36	171	209
19	503	590	5	16	-	15	381	398	12	15	77	50	126	169
20	614	631	9	30	-	19	450	396	9	3	80	54	177	205
21	613	619	15	47	-	30	451	404	-	8	84	30	170	171
22	641	672	30	69	-	41	502	455	8	3	70	42	142	154
23	602	636	57	110	-	45	522	479	7	5	73	48	78	71
24	624	636	81	167	-	47	569	482	5	10	57	26	43	37
Bristol														
ALL AGES 16 - 24	**24,026**	**24,339**	**1,398**	**3,003**	**33**	**1,114**	**19,014**	**16,602**	**737**	**568**	**3,502**	**1,926**	**5,271**	**5,265**
16	2,042	2,012	5	9	2	2	741	707	119	93	164	118	1,422	1,480
17	2,117	1,975	8	13	2	20	1,410	1,208	224	186	248	177	854	866
18	2,206	2,242	6	43	3	50	1,712	1,539	133	112	366	234	570	678
19	2,454	2,459	37	94	1	92	1,968	1,776	51	34	436	252	499	476
20	2,690	2,778	59	184	4	129	2,166	1,945	38	24	443	234	525	521
21	2,793	2,837	123	328	3	134	2,248	2,014	42	21	409	210	534	452
22	2,997	3,212	218	496	4	211	2,571	2,338	41	40	459	244	423	377
23	3,225	3,288	358	762	5	221	2,933	2,417	34	29	483	218	258	246
24	3,502	3,536	584	1,074	9	255	3,265	2,658	55	29	494	239	186	169
Kingswood														
ALL AGES 16 - 24	**5,506**	**5,294**	**285**	**730**	**1**	**117**	**4,539**	**3,945**	**141**	**132**	**556**	**261**	**1,112**	**1,101**
16	541	550	-	1	-	-	177	206	23	23	22	25	407	425
17	587	550	-	-	-	1	420	360	56	46	45	17	224	254
18	600	560	-	5	-	3	473	423	29	36	62	30	169	170
19	645	584	3	14	-	10	550	496	8	6	95	36	105	59
20	680	582	6	29	-	13	605	478	9	5	85	38	84	76
21	590	590	20	69	-	16	528	475	4	4	67	33	61	53
22	608	617	45	129	1	18	566	498	2	4	59	32	40	44
23	628	592	95	202	-	21	609	490	2	5	59	24	14	11
24	627	669	116	281	-	35	611	519	8	3	62	26	8	9

37. Residents aged 16 - 24 in households

Age	TOTAL PERSONS		Married		Lone 'parent' aged 16 - 24 with child(ren) aged 0 - 15		Economically active		On a Government scheme		Unemployed		Students (including those economically active)	
	Males	Females	Males	Females	Males	Females	Males	Females	Males	Females	Males	Females	Males	Females
a	b	c	d	e	f	g	h	i	j	k	l	m	n	o
Northavon														
ALL AGES 16 - 24	**8,791**	**8,626**	**697**	**1,501**	**3**	**150**	**6,954**	**6,206**	**207**	**161**	**701**	**398**	**2,085**	**2,108**
16	912	858	2	1	1	1	295	268	36	30	31	19	703	707
17	920	839	1	-	-	-	601	477	76	66	63	39	416	484
18	1,011	923	3	12	-	2	763	626	56	33	91	56	312	348
19	904	908	5	30	-	10	723	683	17	13	107	60	192	189
20	974	996	22	81	-	13	809	793	3	4	89	54	168	162
21	986	986	49	180	-	23	851	798	4	7	84	47	139	102
22	965	1,023	109	284	-	18	883	838	4	2	75	44	85	62
23	1,010	1,045	197	414	1	41	949	860	2	6	83	36	50	33
24	1,109	1,048	309	499	1	42	1,080	863	9	-	78	43	20	21
Wansdyke														
ALL AGES 16 - 24	**4,851**	**4,604**	**270**	**602**	**4**	**70**	**3,650**	**3,070**	**119**	**105**	**423**	**217**	**1,336**	**1,388**
16	558	527	1	1	-	-	173	137	22	25	17	7	443	455
17	512	523	1	2	-	-	310	273	48	35	24	26	235	306
18	566	521	2	4	-	3	402	337	24	22	39	27	211	220
19	591	552	4	11	-	8	471	394	9	5	69	39	129	141
20	584	527	10	25	-	5	461	402	3	8	48	31	127	112
21	529	488	16	56	-	5	430	375	2	1	61	25	102	80
22	512	461	39	117	-	15	451	364	8	5	45	21	54	42
23	487	486	74	154	3	15	459	383	2	4	61	24	19	21
24	512	519	123	232	1	19	493	405	1	-	59	17	16	11
Woodspring														
ALL AGES 16 - 24	**10,344**	**9,952**	**624**	**1,372**	**3**	**260**	**7,657**	**6,577**	**274**	**177**	**1,060**	**556**	**3,043**	**3,028**
16	1,166	1,127	-	1	-	1	307	322	36	33	37	30	964	941
17	1,227	1,139	1	6	-	2	704	571	92	70	88	46	662	735
18	1,199	1,107	4	13	-	6	809	716	54	34	110	90	484	472
19	1,231	1,167	8	37	-	9	937	837	27	9	152	73	325	311
20	1,193	1,173	19	80	2	21	966	877	13	10	152	79	244	240
21	1,072	1,038	45	155	-	36	917	776	10	3	137	62	158	164
22	1,115	1,012	99	261	-	51	992	761	10	6	124	48	121	101
23	1,058	1,097	178	378	1	65	987	875	17	7	131	63	55	36
24	1,083	1,092	270	441	-	69	1,038	842	15	5	129	65	30	28

38. Residents in households

Age	TOTAL PERSONS	Males	Females	Age	TOTAL PERSONS	Males	Females
a	b	c	d	a	b	c	d
	AVON				**AVON** - *continued*		
ALL AGES	**916,973**	**445,749**	**471,224**				
0	12,097	6,151	5,946	45	11,863	5,901	5,962
1	12,168	6,323	5,845	46	12,616	6,332	6,284
2	12,047	6,166	5,881	47	11,985	5,946	6,039
3	11,860	6,150	5,710	48	11,656	5,858	5,798
4	11,657	5,937	5,720	49	10,132	5,116	5,016
5	11,732	6,066	5,666	50	9,582	4,811	4,771
6	11,257	5,726	5,531	51	10,439	5,158	5,281
7	10,855	5,506	5,349	52	10,290	5,182	5,108
8	10,672	5,513	5,159	53	10,086	5,111	4,975
9	11,005	5,637	5,368	54	9,575	4,755	4,820
10	10,959	5,596	5,363	55	9,596	4,838	4,758
11	11,127	5,650	5,477	56	9,397	4,636	4,761
12	10,701	5,568	5,133	57	9,069	4,499	4,570
13	10,126	5,165	4,961	58	9,488	4,733	4,755
14	10,102	5,182	4,920	59	9,547	4,625	4,922
15	10,496	5,373	5,123	60	9,912	4,851	5,061
16	11,128	5,653	5,475	61	9,429	4,532	4,897
17	11,283	5,849	5,434	62	9,387	4,554	4,833
18	11,887	6,052	5,835	63	9,037	4,408	4,629
19	12,588	6,328	6,260	64	9,236	4,443	4,793
20	13,422	6,735	6,687	65	9,333	4,407	4,926
21	13,141	6,583	6,558	66	9,168	4,251	4,917
22	13,835	6,838	6,997	67	9,134	4,137	4,997
23	14,154	7,010	7,144	68	9,086	4,124	4,962
24	14,957	7,457	7,500	69	9,821	4,447	5,374
25	15,339	7,473	7,866	70	10,115	4,451	5,664
26	15,195	7,603	7,592	71	9,282	4,086	5,196
27	15,060	7,395	7,665	72	6,316	2,623	3,693
28	14,766	7,336	7,430	73	5,845	2,542	3,303
29	14,565	7,304	7,261	74	6,803	2,816	3,987
30	14,182	7,012	7,170	75	6,579	2,712	3,867
31	13,542	6,680	6,862	76	6,673	2,778	3,895
32	13,392	6,657	6,735	77	6,524	2,580	3,944
33	13,373	6,576	6,797	78	5,937	2,292	3,645
34	12,589	6,307	6,282	79	5,316	2,083	3,233
35	12,539	6,239	6,300	80	4,878	1,783	3,095
36	12,097	6,085	6,012	81	4,541	1,682	2,859
37	12,596	6,196	6,400	82	3,987	1,338	2,649
38	12,252	6,089	6,163	83	3,516	1,148	2,368
39	12,063	5,964	6,099	84	2,997	982	2,015
40	12,161	6,046	6,115	85	2,623	826	1,797
41	12,894	6,424	6,470	86	2,164	634	1,530
42	13,296	6,521	6,775	87	1,872	534	1,338
43	14,564	7,234	7,330	88	1,436	386	1,050
44	14,995	7,523	7,472	89	1,095	285	810
				90 and over	2,894	655	2,239

38. Residents in households

Age	TOTAL PERSONS	Males	Females	Age	TOTAL PERSONS	Males	Females
a	b	c	d	a	b	c	d
	Bath				**Bath** – *continued*		
ALL AGES	**76,876**	**36,429**	**40,447**				
0	827	433	394	45	894	433	461
1	889	455	434	46	1,019	489	530
2	895	455	440	47	943	469	474
3	846	433	413	48	895	435	460
4	902	447	455	49	825	422	403
5	807	420	387	50	782	372	410
6	819	429	390	51	830	388	442
7	790	390	400	52	824	421	403
8	743	393	350	53	809	406	403
9	835	417	418	54	818	419	399
10	760	354	406	55	805	410	395
11	836	429	407	56	783	365	418
12	763	397	366	57	741	351	390
13	755	392	363	58	794	370	424
14	730	375	355	59	849	381	468
15	841	408	433	60	885	419	466
16	835	434	401	61	868	408	460
17	894	486	408	62	863	396	467
18	952	470	482	63	877	407	470
19	1,093	503	590	64	845	376	469
20	1,245	614	631	65	938	418	520
21	1,232	613	619	66	901	455	446
22	1,313	641	672	67	885	384	501
23	1,238	602	636	68	864	367	497
24	1,260	624	636	69	961	440	521
25	1,240	649	591	70	995	442	553
26	1,185	597	588	71	928	397	531
27	1,250	621	629	72	641	259	382
28	1,155	550	605	73	594	246	348
29	1,179	575	604	74	727	287	440
30	1,148	567	581	75	665	271	394
31	1,107	577	530	76	696	294	402
32	1,006	492	514	77	719	283	436
33	1,025	497	528	78	661	243	418
34	987	478	509	79	598	223	375
35	1,012	515	497	80	537	189	348
36	941	473	468	81	503	190	313
37	966	463	503	82	425	132	293
38	988	462	526	83	388	129	259
39	972	459	513	84	355	100	255
40	981	492	489	85	273	81	192
41	984	461	523	86	230	49	181
42	1,048	523	525	87	243	65	178
43	1,150	570	580	88	161	39	122
44	1,167	576	591	89	114	27	87
				90 and over	334	71	263

38. Residents in households

Age	TOTAL PERSONS	Males	Females	Age	TOTAL PERSONS	Males	Females
a	b	c	d	a	b	c	d
	Bristol				**Bristol** – *continued*		
ALL AGES	**370,131**	**179,039**	**191,092**				
0	5,290	2,656	2,634	45	4,126	2,093	2,033
1	5,364	2,823	2,541	46	4,340	2,141	2,199
2	5,030	2,565	2,465	47	4,241	2,126	2,115
3	5,060	2,618	2,442	48	4,190	2,121	2,069
4	5,003	2,526	2,477	49	3,593	1,821	1,772
5	5,020	2,622	2,398	50	3,460	1,712	1,748
6	4,726	2,389	2,337	51	3,870	1,963	1,907
7	4,323	2,215	2,108	52	3,764	1,877	1,887
8	4,284	2,163	2,121	53	3,681	1,878	1,803
9	4,430	2,259	2,171	54	3,474	1,728	1,746
10	4,300	2,212	2,088	55	3,535	1,729	1,806
11	4,317	2,153	2,164	56	3,498	1,732	1,766
12	4,073	2,124	1,949	57	3,392	1,695	1,697
13	3,869	1,990	1,879	58	3,610	1,830	1,780
14	3,753	1,913	1,840	59	3,590	1,760	1,830
15	3,910	1,992	1,918	60	3,875	1,853	2,022
16	4,054	2,042	2,012	61	3,643	1,746	1,897
17	4,092	2,117	1,975	62	3,808	1,854	1,954
18	4,448	2,206	2,242	63	3,564	1,737	1,827
19	4,913	2,454	2,459	64	3,681	1,736	1,945
20	5,468	2,690	2,778	65	3,704	1,735	1,969
21	5,630	2,793	2,837	66	3,705	1,638	2,067
22	6,209	2,997	3,212	67	3,675	1,639	2,036
23	6,513	3,225	3,288	68	3,711	1,683	2,028
24	7,038	3,502	3,536	69	4,087	1,845	2,242
25	7,156	3,426	3,730	70	4,224	1,819	2,405
26	7,181	3,532	3,649	71	3,944	1,712	2,232
27	6,844	3,347	3,497	72	2,628	1,083	1,545
28	6,777	3,285	3,492	73	2,328	1,009	1,319
29	6,545	3,250	3,295	74	2,780	1,122	1,658
30	6,252	3,047	3,205	75	2,685	1,094	1,591
31	5,899	2,908	2,991	76	2,725	1,086	1,639
32	5,847	2,950	2,897	77	2,702	1,017	1,685
33	5,755	2,818	2,937	78	2,497	984	1,513
34	5,225	2,643	2,582	79	2,199	851	1,348
35	5,148	2,637	2,511	80	1,979	718	1,261
36	4,920	2,517	2,403	81	1,860	669	1,191
37	5,114	2,519	2,595	82	1,656	518	1,138
38	4,843	2,406	2,437	83	1,460	466	994
39	4,642	2,355	2,287	84	1,278	375	903
40	4,702	2,386	2,316	85	1,096	346	750
41	4,834	2,448	2,386	86	948	274	674
42	4,914	2,436	2,478	87	771	208	563
43	5,298	2,656	2,642	88	583	152	431
44	5,267	2,682	2,585	89	440	114	326
				90 and over	1,251	256	995

38. Residents in households

Age	TOTAL PERSONS	Males	Females	Age	TOTAL PERSONS	Males	Females
a	b	c	d	a	b	c	d
	Kingswood				**Kingswood** – *continued*		
ALL AGES	**88,916**	**43,562**	**45,354**				
0	1,204	618	586	45	1,214	596	618
1	1,151	600	551	46	1,252	637	615
2	1,185	616	569	47	1,170	592	578
3	1,181	621	560	48	1,197	587	610
4	1,207	606	601	49	1,084	515	569
5	1,153	575	578	50	1,005	514	491
6	1,178	585	593	51	1,042	505	537
7	1,068	552	516	52	1,055	533	522
8	1,021	519	502	53	1,083	561	522
9	1,075	551	524	54	1,055	526	529
10	1,075	530	545	55	1,058	522	536
11	1,126	549	577	56	1,082	539	543
12	1,128	603	525	57	997	486	511
13	971	482	489	58	1,056	513	543
14	1,015	521	494	59	1,041	498	543
15	1,058	531	527	60	1,004	473	531
16	1,091	541	550	61	996	493	503
17	1,137	587	550	62	916	428	488
18	1,160	600	560	63	924	479	445
19	1,229	645	584	64	900	438	462
20	1,262	680	582	65	914	453	461
21	1,180	590	590	66	849	418	431
22	1,225	608	617	67	821	391	430
23	1,220	628	592	68	874	409	465
24	1,296	627	669	69	832	391	441
25	1,339	641	698	70	878	400	478
26	1,311	636	675	71	732	336	396
27	1,464	729	735	72	524	204	320
28	1,469	715	754	73	485	226	259
29	1,420	743	677	74	554	223	331
30	1,408	714	694	75	557	214	343
31	1,427	704	723	76	513	233	280
32	1,359	655	704	77	533	214	319
33	1,314	652	662	78	447	159	288
34	1,280	654	626	79	408	171	237
35	1,302	625	677	80	406	144	262
36	1,220	605	615	81	375	152	223
37	1,263	622	641	82	345	129	216
38	1,285	654	631	83	252	83	169
39	1,206	597	609	84	248	86	162
40	1,187	594	593	85	223	65	158
41	1,304	679	625	86	178	56	122
42	1,255	587	668	87	143	45	98
43	1,416	716	700	88	118	28	90
44	1,440	749	691	89	91	21	70
				90 and over	220	40	180

38. Residents in households

Age	TOTAL PERSONS	Males	Females	Age	TOTAL PERSONS	Males	Females
a	b	c	d	a	b	c	d
	Northavon				**Northavon** – *continued*		
ALL AGES	**129,084**	**64,277**	**64,807**				
0	1,848	943	905	45	1,919	949	970
1	1,777	933	844	46	2,116	1,109	1,007
2	1,797	914	883	47	1,989	952	1,037
3	1,730	899	831	48	1,891	958	933
4	1,643	852	791	49	1,586	828	758
5	1,621	821	800	50	1,536	767	769
6	1,583	819	764	51	1,649	833	816
7	1,611	811	800	52	1,594	835	759
8	1,638	884	754	53	1,533	789	744
9	1,539	810	729	54	1,407	714	693
10	1,633	819	814	55	1,413	754	659
11	1,666	892	774	56	1,289	627	662
12	1,609	834	775	57	1,313	667	646
13	1,546	746	800	58	1,272	639	633
14	1,644	855	789	59	1,276	643	633
15	1,639	883	756	60	1,263	679	584
16	1,770	912	858	61	1,205	606	599
17	1,759	920	839	62	1,175	609	566
18	1,934	1,011	923	63	1,047	545	502
19	1,812	904	908	64	1,069	553	516
20	1,970	974	996	65	1,071	559	512
21	1,972	986	986	66	1,010	486	524
22	1,988	965	1,023	67	957	423	534
23	2,055	1,010	1,045	68	960	474	486
24	2,157	1,109	1,048	69	1,046	470	576
25	2,400	1,173	1,227	70	1,039	457	582
26	2,293	1,179	1,114	71	965	431	534
27	2,286	1,097	1,189	72	648	272	376
28	2,167	1,123	1,044	73	582	230	352
29	2,124	1,091	1,033	74	682	293	389
30	2,115	1,067	1,048	75	688	297	391
31	1,959	995	964	76	694	323	371
32	1,953	1,022	931	77	652	279	373
33	1,972	1,028	944	78	578	218	360
34	1,890	957	933	79	522	211	311
35	1,719	852	867	80	480	198	282
36	1,764	875	889	81	434	168	266
37	1,816	900	916	82	377	136	241
38	1,784	872	912	83	357	109	248
39	1,769	849	920	84	273	107	166
40	1,809	883	926	85	234	75	159
41	1,977	996	981	86	180	53	127
42	1,969	997	972	87	177	56	121
43	2,307	1,124	1,183	88	135	33	102
44	2,439	1,185	1,254	89	105	34	71
				90 and over	243	58	185

38. Residents in households

Age	TOTAL PERSONS	Males	Females	Age	TOTAL PERSONS	Males	Females
a	b	c	d	a	b	c	d
	Wansdyke				**Wansdyke** – *continued*		
ALL AGES	**79,122**	**38,854**	**40,268**				
0	920	469	451	45	1,118	550	568
1	981	491	490	46	1,229	632	597
2	998	519	479	47	1,130	532	598
3	915	487	428	48	1,090	539	551
4	892	447	445	49	950	485	465
5	969	507	462	50	857	455	402
6	946	504	442	51	952	454	498
7	945	495	450	52	1,021	501	520
8	944	478	466	53	990	502	488
9	938	495	443	54	903	434	469
10	1,034	555	479	55	923	466	457
11	1,001	510	491	56	909	462	447
12	1,000	520	480	57	880	427	453
13	903	459	444	58	868	460	408
14	943	489	454	59	953	462	491
15	1,011	506	505	60	927	451	476
16	1,085	558	527	61	851	399	452
17	1,035	512	523	62	877	422	455
18	1,087	566	521	63	835	399	436
19	1,143	591	552	64	922	447	475
20	1,111	584	527	65	844	398	446
21	1,017	529	488	66	854	411	443
22	973	512	461	67	859	414	445
23	973	487	486	68	797	366	431
24	1,031	512	519	69	887	428	459
25	1,018	509	509	70	890	409	481
26	1,022	544	478	71	793	353	440
27	987	482	505	72	568	251	317
28	1,024	532	492	73	544	245	299
29	1,052	517	535	74	582	234	348
30	1,068	534	534	75	563	251	312
31	1,023	479	544	76	575	260	315
32	1,011	492	519	77	560	243	317
33	1,055	529	526	78	510	212	298
34	1,016	487	529	79	480	187	293
35	1,130	555	575	80	410	152	258
36	1,042	538	504	81	398	151	247
37	1,069	523	546	82	333	140	193
38	1,068	544	524	83	324	117	207
39	1,092	535	557	84	248	89	159
40	1,128	561	567	85	205	75	130
41	1,233	588	645	86	173	54	119
42	1,267	614	653	87	151	50	101
43	1,373	674	699	88	114	41	73
44	1,454	733	721	89	99	31	68
				90 and over	249	61	188

38. Residents in households

Age	TOTAL PERSONS	Males	Females	Age	TOTAL PERSONS	Males	Females
a	b	c	d	a	b	c	d
	Woodspring				**Woodspring** – *continued*		
ALL AGES	**172,844**	**83,588**	**89,256**				
0	2,008	1,032	976	45	2,592	1,280	1,312
1	2,006	1,021	985	46	2,660	1,324	1,336
2	2,142	1,097	1,045	47	2,512	1,275	1,237
3	2,128	1,092	1,036	48	2,393	1,218	1,175
4	2,010	1,059	951	49	2,094	1,045	1,049
5	2,162	1,121	1,041	50	1,942	991	951
6	2,005	1,000	1,005	51	2,096	1,015	1,081
7	2,118	1,043	1,075	52	2,032	1,015	1,017
8	2,042	1,076	966	53	1,990	975	1,015
9	2,188	1,105	1,083	54	1,918	934	984
10	2,157	1,126	1,031	55	1,862	957	905
11	2,181	1,117	1,064	56	1,836	911	925
12	2,128	1,090	1,038	57	1,746	873	873
13	2,082	1,096	986	58	1,888	921	967
14	2,017	1,029	988	59	1,838	881	957
15	2,037	1,053	984	60	1,958	976	982
16	2,293	1,166	1,127	61	1,866	880	986
17	2,366	1,227	1,139	62	1,748	845	903
18	2,306	1,199	1,107	63	1,790	841	949
19	2,398	1,231	1,167	64	1,819	893	926
20	2,366	1,193	1,173	65	1,862	844	1,018
21	2,110	1,072	1,038	66	1,849	843	1,006
22	2,127	1,115	1,012	67	1,937	886	1,051
23	2,155	1,058	1,097	68	1,880	825	1,055
24	2,175	1,083	1,092	69	2,008	873	1,135
25	2,186	1,075	1,111	70	2,089	924	1,165
26	2,203	1,115	1,088	71	1,920	857	1,063
27	2,229	1,119	1,110	72	1,307	554	753
28	2,174	1,131	1,043	73	1,312	586	726
29	2,245	1,128	1,117	74	1,478	657	821
30	2,191	1,083	1,108	75	1,421	585	836
31	2,127	1,017	1,110	76	1,470	582	888
32	2,216	1,046	1,170	77	1,358	544	814
33	2,252	1,052	1,200	78	1,244	476	768
34	2,191	1,088	1,103	79	1,109	440	669
35	2,228	1,055	1,173	80	1,066	382	684
36	2,210	1,077	1,133	81	971	352	619
37	2,368	1,169	1,199	82	851	283	568
38	2,284	1,151	1,133	83	735	244	491
39	2,382	1,169	1,213	84	595	225	370
40	2,354	1,130	1,224	85	592	184	408
41	2,562	1,252	1,310	86	455	148	307
42	2,843	1,364	1,479	87	387	110	277
43	3,020	1,494	1,526	88	325	93	232
44	3,228	1,598	1,630	89	246	58	188
				90 and over	597	169	428

Notes: (1) * May include a small number of heads aged under 16
(2) ** May include a small number of persons in households with heads aged under 16

39. Residents in households

AVON

Heads of households

Age	TOTAL PERSONS	Males				Females			
		Total	Single	Married	Widowed or divorced	Total	Single	Married	Widowed or divorced
a	b	c	d	e	f	g	h	i	j
All ages 16 and over*	**376,522**	**263,286**	**36,127**	**202,263**	**24,896**	**113,236**	**29,343**	**18,405**	**65,488**
16 - 19*	1,667	618	573	41	4	1,049	1,005	37	7
20 - 24	17,050	9,874	7,100	2,703	71	7,176	5,863	989	324
25 - 29	34,086	23,792	9,791	13,362	639	10,294	6,343	2,564	1,387
30 - 44	104,769	80,989	10,596	64,370	6,023	23,780	6,823	7,632	9,325
45 - 59	87,075	70,194	3,902	60,185	6,107	16,881	2,365	4,004	10,512
60 - 64	28,366	21,300	1,286	18,016	1,998	7,066	1,098	740	5,228
65 - 74	55,719	35,575	1,928	29,071	4,576	20,144	2,512	1,318	16,314
75 - 84	38,338	18,028	802	12,982	4,244	20,310	2,479	887	16,944
85 and over	9,452	2,916	149	1,533	1,234	6,536	855	234	5,447

All persons in households by head's age, sex and marital status

Age	TOTAL PERSONS	Males Total	Males Single	Males Married	Males Widowed or divorced	Females Total	Females Single	Females Married	Females Widowed or divorced
All ages 16 and over**	**916,973**	**713,429**	**60,925**	**612,751**	**39,753**	**203,544**	**50,202**	**51,087**	**102,255**
16 - 19**	3,417	1,240	1,119	116	5	2,177	2,055	108	14
20 - 24	36,927	21,231	13,879	7,206	146	15,696	12,129	2,706	861
25 - 29	82,472	59,098	17,906	39,905	1,287	23,374	12,322	7,387	3,665
30 - 44	334,751	271,761	17,380	241,956	12,425	62,990	12,356	25,547	25,087
45 - 59	235,900	203,113	5,397	186,806	10,910	32,787	3,194	9,959	19,634
60 - 64	57,356	47,337	1,629	42,898	2,810	10,019	1,328	1,430	7,261
65 - 74	96,942	71,801	2,420	63,631	5,750	25,141	2,922	2,313	19,906
75 - 84	56,786	33,066	1,005	27,087	4,974	23,720	2,901	1,322	19,497
85 and over	12,422	4,782	190	3,146	1,446	7,640	995	315	6,330

Bath

Heads of households

Age	TOTAL PERSONS	Males Total	Males Single	Males Married	Males Widowed or divorced	Females Total	Females Single	Females Married	Females Widowed or divorced
All ages 16 and over*	**34,128**	**21,763**	**3,791**	**15,780**	**2,192**	**12,365**	**3,863**	**1,786**	**6,716**
16 - 19*	207	76	71	5	-	131	126	5	-
20 - 24	1,767	863	711	148	4	904	791	75	38
25 - 29	2,802	1,741	983	722	36	1,061	753	195	113
30 - 44	8,531	6,039	1,128	4,441	470	2,492	817	734	941
45 - 59	7,183	5,462	399	4,553	510	1,721	312	410	999
60 - 64	2,659	1,889	142	1,567	180	770	152	83	535
65 - 74	5,649	3,457	242	2,792	423	2,192	394	151	1,647
75 - 84	4,233	1,927	99	1,377	451	2,306	403	102	1,801
85 and over	1,097	309	16	175	118	788	115	31	642

All persons in households by head's age, sex and marital status

Age	TOTAL PERSONS	Males Total	Males Single	Males Married	Males Widowed or divorced	Females Total	Females Single	Females Married	Females Widowed or divorced
All ages 16 and over**	**76,876**	**55,664**	**6,241**	**46,085**	**3,338**	**21,212**	**6,218**	**4,813**	**10,181**
16 - 19**	406	156	145	11	-	250	239	11	-
20 - 24	3,796	1,887	1,450	432	5	1,909	1,607	206	96
25 - 29	6,260	4,028	1,764	2,193	71	2,232	1,375	548	309
30 - 44	25,280	19,052	1,724	16,356	972	6,228	1,387	2,404	2,437
45 - 59	18,710	15,448	543	14,043	862	3,262	398	1,035	1,829
60 - 64	5,203	4,175	165	3,749	261	1,028	177	147	704
65 - 74	9,626	6,891	311	6,075	505	2,735	451	270	2,014
75 - 84	6,165	3,521	119	2,875	527	2,644	453	149	2,042
85 and over	1,430	506	20	351	135	924	131	43	750

Notes: (1) * May include a small number of heads aged under 16
(2) ** May include a small number of persons in households with heads aged under 16

39. Residents in households

Age	TOTAL PERSONS	Males				Females			
		Total	Single	Married	Widowed or divorced	Total	Single	Married	Widowed or divorced
a	b	c	d	e	f	g	h	i	j
Bristol									
Heads of households									
All ages 16 and over*	**156,778**	**102,720**	**19,414**	**72,170**	**11,136**	**54,058**	**16,656**	**8,152**	**29,250**
16 - 19*	979	366	338	25	3	613	587	21	5
20 - 24	8,997	4,862	3,807	1,016	39	4,135	3,516	460	159
25 - 29	16,385	10,475	5,096	5,090	289	5,910	3,941	1,263	706
30 - 44	43,310	31,271	5,794	22,795	2,682	12,039	4,218	3,418	4,403
45 - 59	32,317	24,859	2,125	20,016	2,718	7,458	1,186	1,652	4,620
60 - 64	11,385	8,184	702	6,535	947	3,201	538	322	2,341
65 - 74	23,192	14,275	1,055	11,124	2,096	8,917	1,135	558	7,224
75 - 84	16,101	7,222	430	4,971	1,821	8,879	1,127	355	7,397
85 and over	4,112	1,206	67	598	541	2,906	408	103	2,395
All persons in households by head's age, sex and marital status									
All ages 16 and over**	**370,131**	**270,370**	**33,206**	**219,553**	**17,611**	**99,761**	**30,011**	**22,931**	**46,819**
16 - 19**	2,020	733	659	71	3	1,287	1,215	63	9
20 - 24	19,598	10,445	7,540	2,817	88	9,153	7,427	1,302	424
25 - 29	39,351	25,688	9,507	15,586	595	13,663	7,969	3,788	1,906
30 - 44	133,018	101,709	9,715	86,572	5,422	31,309	8,002	11,394	11,913
45 - 59	84,473	70,027	2,922	62,432	4,673	14,446	1,642	4,110	8,694
60 - 64	22,725	18,067	915	15,803	1,349	4,658	646	621	3,391
65 - 74	39,935	28,632	1,328	24,624	2,680	11,303	1,320	970	9,013
75 - 84	23,606	13,096	535	10,403	2,158	10,510	1,312	540	8,658
85 and over	5,405	1,973	85	1,245	643	3,432	478	143	2,811
Kingswood									
Heads of households									
All ages 16 and over*	**34,657**	**26,136**	**2,215**	**21,711**	**2,210**	**8,521**	**1,404**	**1,482**	**5,635**
16 - 19*	71	19	19	-	-	52	48	4	-
20 - 24	1,028	665	435	226	4	363	259	81	23
25 - 29	2,910	2,257	635	1,551	71	653	306	215	132
30 - 44	10,280	8,478	644	7,258	576	1,802	350	646	806
45 - 59	8,877	7,537	241	6,758	538	1,340	115	310	915
60 - 64	2,828	2,217	78	1,992	147	611	49	55	507
65 - 74	4,867	3,275	115	2,746	414	1,592	129	93	1,370
75 - 84	3,059	1,474	40	1,069	365	1,585	99	62	1,424
85 and over	737	214	8	111	95	523	49	16	458
All persons in households by head's age, sex and marital status									
All ages 16 and over**	**88,916**	**73,670**	**3,788**	**66,299**	**3,583**	**15,246**	**2,395**	**4,183**	**8,668**
16 - 19**	155	42	42	-	-	113	99	14	-
20 - 24	2,290	1,458	848	600	10	832	554	217	61
25 - 29	7,477	5,924	1,173	4,613	138	1,553	597	618	338
30 - 44	34,277	29,393	1,073	27,129	1,191	4,884	580	2,139	2,165
45 - 59	24,761	22,146	349	20,787	1,010	2,615	168	787	1,660
60 - 64	5,824	4,978	97	4,673	208	846	65	119	662
65 - 74	8,630	6,676	145	6,020	511	1,954	150	168	1,636
75 - 84	4,557	2,704	49	2,248	407	1,853	127	99	1,627
85 and over	945	349	12	229	108	596	55	22	519

Notes: (1) * May include a small number of heads aged under 16
(2) ** May include a small number of persons in households with heads aged under 16

39. Residents in households

Age	TOTAL PERSONS	Males				Females			
		Total	Single	Married	Widowed or divorced	Total	Single	Married	Widowed or divorced
a	b	c	d	e	f	g	h	i	j
Northavon									
Heads of households									
All ages 16 and over*	**49,626**	**38,400**	**4,205**	**31,277**	**2,918**	**11,226**	**2,256**	**2,340**	**6,630**
16 - 19*	103	41	37	4	-	62	61	1	-
20 - 24	2,215	1,534	943	581	10	681	488	159	34
25 - 29	5,160	4,086	1,360	2,630	96	1,074	542	374	158
30 - 44	15,237	12,733	1,179	10,770	784	2,504	502	975	1,027
45 - 59	13,124	11,184	361	10,038	785	1,940	226	511	1,203
60 - 64	3,482	2,824	110	2,472	242	658	82	73	503
65 - 74	5,806	3,858	137	3,259	462	1,948	169	126	1,653
75 - 84	3,721	1,887	61	1,396	430	1,834	134	100	1,600
85 and over	778	253	17	127	109	525	52	21	452
All persons in households by head's age, sex and marital status									
All ages 16 and over**	**129,084**	**108,292**	**6,992**	**96,351**	**4,949**	**20,792**	**3,648**	**6,492**	**10,652**
16 - 19**	229	96	84	12	-	133	130	3	-
20 - 24	4,669	3,243	1,795	1,429	19	1,426	954	388	84
25 - 29	12,381	10,081	2,382	7,518	181	2,300	927	966	407
30 - 44	50,541	43,634	1,833	40,143	1,658	6,907	818	3,321	2,768
45 - 59	37,015	33,101	498	31,077	1,526	3,914	306	1,276	2,332
60 - 64	7,286	6,335	144	5,862	329	951	102	153	696
65 - 74	10,293	7,860	157	7,124	579	2,433	197	222	2,014
75 - 84	5,638	3,526	81	2,916	529	2,112	155	139	1,818
85 and over	1,032	416	18	270	128	616	59	24	533
Wansdyke									
Heads of households									
All ages 16 and over*	**30,814**	**23,174**	**1,862**	**19,486**	**1,826**	**7,640**	**1,347**	**1,330**	**4,963**
16 - 19*	50	15	14	1	-	35	33	1	1
20 - 24	763	496	271	223	2	267	194	59	14
25 - 29	2,001	1,562	473	1,047	42	439	208	153	78
30 - 44	8,479	7,070	541	6,151	378	1,409	274	579	556
45 - 59	8,078	6,771	276	6,071	424	1,307	165	309	833
60 - 64	2,539	2,005	83	1,794	128	534	74	54	406
65 - 74	4,900	3,318	126	2,831	361	1,582	176	102	1,304
75 - 84	3,250	1,666	61	1,229	376	1,584	173	62	1,349
85 and over	754	271	17	139	115	483	50	11	422
All persons in households by head's age, sex and marital status									
All ages 16 and over**	**79,122**	**65,696**	**3,172**	**59,550**	**2,974**	**13,426**	**2,103**	**3,803**	**7,520**
16 - 19**	117	32	30	2	-	85	78	4	3
20 - 24	1,752	1,138	548	586	4	614	402	174	38
25 - 29	5,139	4,102	894	3,131	77	1,037	377	454	206
30 - 44	29,036	25,121	947	23,355	819	3,915	464	1,943	1,508
45 - 59	22,912	20,321	391	19,101	829	2,591	213	808	1,570
60 - 64	5,353	4,588	99	4,301	188	765	90	106	569
65 - 74	8,860	6,867	161	6,226	480	1,993	210	197	1,586
75 - 84	4,943	3,080	79	2,556	445	1,863	210	102	1,551
85 and over	1,010	447	23	292	132	563	59	15	489

Notes: (1) * May include a small number of heads aged under 16
(2) ** May include a small number of persons in households with heads aged under 16

39. Residents in households

Age	TOTAL PERSONS	Males				Females			
		Total	Single	Married	Widowed or divorced	Total	Single	Married	Widowed or divorced
a	b	c	d	e	f	g	h	i	j
				Woodspring					
				Heads of households					
All ages 16 and over*	**70,519**	**51,093**	**4,640**	**41,839**	**4,614**	**19,426**	**3,817**	**3,315**	**12,294**
16 - 19*	257	101	94	6	1	156	150	5	1
20 - 24	2,280	1,454	933	509	12	826	615	155	56
25 - 29	4,828	3,671	1,244	2,322	105	1,157	593	364	200
30 - 44	18,932	15,398	1,310	12,955	1,133	3,534	662	1,280	1,592
45 - 59	17,496	14,381	500	12,749	1,132	3,115	361	812	1,942
60 - 64	5,473	4,181	171	3,656	354	1,292	203	153	936
65 - 74	11,305	7,392	253	6,319	820	3,913	509	288	3,116
75 - 84	7,974	3,852	111	2,940	801	4,122	543	206	3,373
85 and over	1,974	663	24	383	256	1,311	181	52	1,078
				All persons in households by head's age, sex and marital status					
All ages 16 and over**	**172,844**	**139,737**	**7,526**	**124,913**	**7,298**	**33,107**	**5,827**	**8,865**	**18,415**
16 - 19**	490	181	159	20	2	309	294	13	2
20 - 24	4,822	3,060	1,698	1,342	20	1,762	1,185	419	158
25 - 29	11,864	9,275	2,186	6,864	225	2,589	1,077	1,013	499
30 - 44	62,599	52,852	2,088	48,401	2,363	9,747	1,105	4,346	4,296
45 - 59	48,029	42,070	694	39,366	2,010	5,959	467	1,943	3,549
60 - 64	10,965	9,194	209	8,510	475	1,771	248	284	1,239
65 - 74	19,598	14,875	318	13,562	995	4,723	594	486	3,643
75 - 84	11,877	7,139	142	6,089	908	4,738	644	293	3,801
85 and over	2,600	1,091	32	759	300	1,509	213	68	1,228

40. Lone 'parents' aged 16 and over in households of one person aged 16 and over with person(s) aged 0 - 15; persons aged 0 - 15 in such households

Age of child(ren)	TOTAL LONE 'PARENTS'	Male lone 'parents'								Female lone 'parents'						
		Total male lone 'parents'	Economically active					Econom-ically inactive	Total female lone 'parents'	Economically active					Econom-ically inactive
			Employees		Self-employed	Other	Econom-ically active students			Employees		Self-employed	Other	Econom-ically active students	
			Full-time	Part-time						Full-time	Part-time				
a	b	c	d	e	f	g	h	i	j	k	l	m	n	o	p
AVON															
Total households	**12,266**	**979**	**380**	**51**	**133**	**102**	**3**	**313**	**11,287**	**1,488**	**2,394**	**296**	**668**	**22**	**6,441**
Child(ren) aged 0 - 4 only	3,400	134	42	11	13	13	1	55	3,266	251	398	46	202	4	2,369
Child(ren) aged 5 - 15 only	6,550	735	312	37	110	67	2	209	5,815	1,147	1,671	217	380	17	2,400
Child(ren) aged 0 - 4 and 5 - 15	2,316	110	26	3	10	22	-	49	2,206	90	325	33	86	1	1,672
TOTAL CHILDREN AGED 0 - 15	**21,517**	**1,622**	**603**	**86**	**202**	**164**	**4**	**567**	**19,895**	**2,236**	**4,086**	**489**	**1,055**	**33**	**12,029**
Children aged 0 - 4	7,187	296	84	17	29	38	1	128	6,891	377	835	97	341	7	5,241
Bath															
Total households	**1,165**	**86**	**33**	**7**	**19**	**6**	**-**	**21**	**1,079**	**133**	**252**	**52**	**60**	**2**	**582**
Child(ren) aged 0 - 4 only	335	13	5	2	2	1	-	3	322	14	59	7	16	-	226
Child(ren) aged 5 - 15 only	644	64	25	5	17	5	-	12	580	112	172	38	37	2	221
Child(ren) aged 0 - 4 and 5 - 15	186	9	3	-	-	-	-	6	177	7	21	7	7	-	135
TOTAL CHILDREN AGED 0 - 15	**1,955**	**137**	**54**	**10**	**27**	**8**	**-**	**38**	**1,818**	**203**	**383**	**87**	**89**	**2**	**1,056**
Children aged 0 - 4	648	26	12	2	2	1	-	9	622	23	90	18	25	-	466
Bristol															
Total households	**6,629**	**496**	**158**	**26**	**55**	**67**	**3**	**190**	**6,133**	**765**	**1,047**	**126**	**445**	**13**	**3,750**
Child(ren) aged 0 - 4 only	1,965	85	25	6	8	9	1	37	1,880	147	173	24	149	2	1,387
Child(ren) aged 5 - 15 only	3,299	342	122	17	42	37	2	124	2,957	560	720	88	238	11	1,351
Child(ren) aged 0 - 4 and 5 - 15	1,365	69	11	3	5	21	-	29	1,296	58	154	14	58	-	1,012
TOTAL CHILDREN AGED 0 - 15	**11,749**	**815**	**241**	**44**	**85**	**113**	**4**	**332**	**10,934**	**1,136**	**1,790**	**204**	**702**	**19**	**7,102**
Children aged 0 - 4	4,216	183	40	11	18	33	1	81	4,033	235	375	44	247	2	3,132

Table 40 Lone 'parents' – **continued**

40. Lone 'parents' aged 16 and over in households of one person aged 16 and over with person(s) aged 0 - 15; persons aged 0 - 15 in such households

Age of child(ren)	TOTAL LONE 'PARENTS'	Male lone 'parents'								Female lone 'parents'						
		Total male lone 'parents'	Economically active					Econom-ically inactive	Total female lone 'parents'	Economically active					Econom-ically inactive
			Employees		Self-employed	Other	Econom-ically active students			Employees		Self-employed	Other	Econom-ically active students	
			Full-time	Part-time						Full-time	Part-time				
a	b	c	d	e	f	g	h	i	j	k	l	m	n	o	p
Kingswood															
Total households	**930**	**76**	**32**	**8**	**10**	**7**	**-**	**19**	**854**	**108**	**241**	**17**	**35**	**2**	**453**
Child(ren) aged 0 - 4 only	221	6	1	-	1	2	-	2	215	13	28	1	9	-	164
Child(ren) aged 5 - 15 only	527	63	28	8	8	5	-	14	464	87	177	15	21	1	164
Child(ren) aged 0 - 4 and 5 - 15	182	7	3	-	1	-	-	3	175	8	36	1	5	1	125
TOTAL CHILDREN AGED 0 - 15	**1,640**	**134**	**53**	**15**	**18**	**10**	**-**	**38**	**1,506**	**174**	**426**	**26**	**60**	**3**	**820**
Children aged 0 - 4	508	14	4	-	3	2	-	5	494	23	76	2	17	1	376
Northavon															
Total households	**1,157**	**113**	**63**	**3**	**15**	**10**	**-**	**22**	**1,044**	**184**	**263**	**31**	**46**	**-**	**520**
Child(ren) aged 0 - 4 only	279	12	6	1	-	-	-	5	267	32	43	3	8	-	181
Child(ren) aged 5 - 15 only	690	91	53	2	14	10	-	12	599	144	192	24	34	-	205
Child(ren) aged 0 - 4 and 5 - 15	188	10	4	-	1	-	-	5	178	8	28	4	4	-	134
TOTAL CHILDREN AGED 0 - 15	**2,043**	**191**	**105**	**6**	**22**	**16**	**-**	**42**	**1,852**	**287**	**459**	**56**	**72**	**-**	**978**
Children aged 0 - 4	606	31	15	1	1	-	-	14	575	41	90	11	15	-	418
Wansdyke															
Total households	**587**	**57**	**28**	**3**	**9**	**2**	**-**	**15**	**530**	**83**	**157**	**27**	**18**	**-**	**245**
Child(ren) aged 0 - 4 only	133	3	-	1	-	-	-	2	130	10	30	4	4	-	82
Child(ren) aged 5 - 15 only	364	51	27	2	9	2	-	11	313	70	104	21	10	-	108
Child(ren) aged 0 - 4 and 5 - 15	90	3	1	-	-	-	-	2	87	3	23	2	4	-	55
TOTAL CHILDREN AGED 0 - 15	**1,004**	**91**	**40**	**6**	**12**	**3**	**-**	**30**	**913**	**134**	**261**	**46**	**29**	**-**	**443**
Children aged 0 - 4	263	8	1	1	-	-	-	6	255	13	60	8	8	-	166

40. Lone 'parents' aged 16 and over in households of one person aged 16 and over with person(s) aged 0 - 15; persons aged 0 - 15 in such households

Age of child(ren)	TOTAL LONE 'PARENTS'	Male lone 'parents'								Female lone 'parents'						
		Total male lone 'parents'	Economically active					Econom-ically inactive	Total female lone 'parents'	Economically active					Econom-ically inactive
			Employees		Self-employed	Other	Econom-ically active students			Employees		Self-employed	Other	Econom-ically active students	
			Full-time	Part-time						Full-time	Part-time				
a	b	c	d	e	f	g	h	i	j	k	l	m	n	o	p
Woodspring															
Total households	**1,798**	**151**	**66**	**4**	**25**	**10**	**-**	**46**	**1,647**	**215**	**434**	**43**	**64**	**5**	**891**
Child(ren) aged 0 - 4 only	467	15	5	1	2	1	-	6	452	35	65	7	16	2	329
Child(ren) aged 5 - 15 only	1,026	124	57	3	20	8	-	36	902	174	306	31	40	3	351
Child(ren) aged 0 - 4 and 5 - 15	305	12	4	-	3	1	-	4	293	6	63	5	8	-	211
TOTAL CHILDREN AGED 0 - 15	**3,126**	**254**	**110**	**5**	**38**	**14**	**-**	**87**	**2,872**	**302**	**767**	**70**	**103**	**9**	**1,630**
Children aged 0 - 4	946	34	12	2	5	2	-	13	912	42	144	14	29	4	683

Table 41 Shared accommodation

41. Households with residents not in self-contained accommodation; rooms in such households

Households with the following persons	TOTAL HOUSE-HOLDS	Over one person per room	Exclusive use of bath/shower			Shared use of bath/shower			No bath/shower			Central heating			No car	TOTAL ROOMS
			Exclusive use of inside WC	Shared use of inside WC	No inside WC	Exclusive use of inside WC	Shared use of inside WC	No inside WC	Exclusive use of inside WC	Shared use of inside WC	No inside WC	All rooms	Some rooms	No rooms		
a	b	c	d	e	f	g	h	i	j	k	l	m	n	o	p	q
AVON																
TOTAL HOUSEHOLDS	**5,955**	**414**	**3,271**	**100**	**14**	**98**	**2,398**	**15**	**26**	**16**	**17**	**2,404**	**465**	**3,086**	**3,406**	**13,506**
1 person	4,360		2,090	86	8	74	2,042	11	25	14	10	1,600	262	2,498	2,875	7,399
2 persons	1,063	291	744	11	6	14	276	3	1	2	6	484	130	449	418	3,302
3 or more persons	532	123	437	3	-	10	80	1	-	-	1	320	73	139	113	2,805
Bath																
TOTAL HOUSEHOLDS	**975**	**63**	**599**	**12**	**3**	**19**	**326**	**2**	**8**	**4**	**2**	**355**	**91**	**529**	**574**	**2,356**
1 person	702		378	10	2	16	283	1	8	3	1	220	44	438	474	1,286
2 persons	182	43	145	-	1	1	32	1	-	1	1	79	37	66	78	597
3 or more persons	91	20	76	2	-	2	11	-	-	-	-	56	10	25	22	473
Bristol																
TOTAL HOUSEHOLDS	**3,833**	**267**	**2,021**	**65**	**7**	**44**	**1,661**	**7**	**10**	**9**	**9**	**1,537**	**285**	**2,011**	**2,221**	**8,229**
1 person	2,897		1,334	55	3	34	1,441	5	10	8	7	1,077	178	1,642	1,910	4,722
2 persons	626	193	426	9	4	5	178	1	-	1	2	281	65	280	244	1,840
3 or more persons	310	74	261	1	-	5	42	1	-	-	-	179	42	89	67	1,667
Kingswood																
TOTAL HOUSEHOLDS	**120**	**13**	**68**	**4**	**-**	**4**	**44**	**-**	**-**	**-**	**-**	**92**	**7**	**21**	**57**	**242**
1 person	82		39	4	-	2	37	-	-	-	-	61	5	16	45	120
2 persons	26	11	17	-	-	2	7	-	-	-	-	20	2	4	11	63
3 or more persons	12	2	12	-	-	-	-	-	-	-	-	11	-	1	1	59
Northavon																
TOTAL HOUSEHOLDS	**102**	**4**	**57**	**-**	**1**	**3**	**37**	**2**	**-**	**-**	**2**	**55**	**12**	**35**	**19**	**322**
1 person	58		26	-	-	2	29	1	-	-	-	27	3	28	16	107
2 persons	22	3	15	-	1	-	4	1	-	-	1	16	2	4	2	88
3 or more persons	22	1	16	-	-	1	4	-	-	-	1	12	7	3	1	127

Table 41 Shared accommodation - **continued**

41. Households with residents not in self-contained accommodation; rooms in such households

Households with the following persons	TOTAL HOUSE-HOLDS	Over one person per room	Exclusive use of bath/shower			Shared use of bath/shower			No bath/shower			Central heating			No car	TOTAL ROOMS
			Exclusive use of inside WC	Shared use of inside WC	No inside WC	Exclusive use of inside WC	Shared use of inside WC	No inside WC	Exclusive use of inside WC	Shared use of inside WC	No inside WC	All rooms	Some rooms	No rooms		
a	b	c	d	e	f	g	h	i	j	k	l	m	n	o	p	q
Wansdyke																
TOTAL HOUSEHOLDS	**87**	**4**	**61**	**4**	**1**	**2**	**18**	**-**	**-**	**-**	**1**	**60**	**11**	**16**	**31**	**272**
1 person	53		31	4	1	2	14	-	-	-	1	36	4	13	25	100
2 persons	19	2	15	-	-	-	4	-	-	-	-	13	4	2	5	73
3 or more persons	15	2	15	-	-	-	-	-	-	-	-	11	3	1	1	99
Woodspring																
TOTAL HOUSEHOLDS	**838**	**63**	**465**	**15**	**2**	**26**	**312**	**4**	**8**	**3**	**3**	**305**	**59**	**474**	**504**	**2,085**
1 person	568		282	13	2	18	238	4	7	3	1	179	28	361	405	1,064
2 persons	188	39	126	2	-	6	51	-	1	-	2	75	20	93	78	641
3 or more persons	82	24	57	-	-	2	23	-	-	-	-	51	11	20	21	380

Table 42 Household composition and housing

Note: * May include a small number of households with no resident adults

42. Households with residents; dependent children in households

TOTAL HOUSE-HOLDS	Over 1 and up to 1.5 persons per room	Over 1.5 persons per room	Lacking or sharing use of bath/shower and/or inside WC	No central heating	Lacking or sharing use of bath/shower and/or inside WC and/or no central heating	Not self-contained accomm-odation	Household composition	
							Adults	Dependent children
a	b	c	d	e	f	g	h	i
					AVON			
376,522	**4,177**	**1,397**	**4,510**	**55,041**	**56,783**	**5,955**	**ALL HOUSEHOLDS***	
55,763	-	-	1,054	11,633	12,005	635	1 adult of pensionable age	0
44,698	-	-	2,325	10,276	11,116	3,707	1 adult under pensionable age	0
13,666	197	120	97	2,396	2,455	138	1 adult any age	1 or more
115,427	-	551	597	15,216	15,464	792	2 adults (1 male and 1 female)	0
72,192	2,436	346	141	5,991	6,079	208		1 or more
10,514	-	74	109	2,073	2,116	171	2 adults (same sex)	0
1,803	51	5	3	296	298	8		1 or more
41,984	199	93	125	5,025	5,084	186	3 or more adults (male(s) and female(s))	0
18,276	1,270	185	44	1,725	1,751	53		1 or more
1,880	10	19	6	338	341	38	3 or more adults (same sex)	0
222	14	4	1	45	46	1		1 or more
193,764	**12,335**	**1,876**	**480**	**19,433**	**19,709**	**671**	**TOTAL DEPENDENT CHILDREN AGED 0 - 18**	
59,829	4,267	775	199	6,596	6,711	277	Dependent children aged 0 - 4	
119,032	7,610	1,017	249	11,763	11,908	320	Dependent children aged 5 - 15	
11,771	401	71	21	881	890	46	Dependent children aged 16 - 17	
					Bath			
34,128	**396**	**182**	**560**	**4,795**	**4,998**	**975**	**ALL HOUSEHOLDS***	
6,256	-	-	144	1,163	1,214	129	1 adult of pensionable age	0
4,912	-	-	307	1,195	1,286	571	1 adult under pensionable age	0
1,330	21	17	16	122	133	26	1 adult any age	1 or more
9,995	-	91	48	1,251	1,274	126	2 adults (1 male and 1 female)	0
5,138	234	31	10	303	309	29		1 or more
1,258	-	14	13	210	217	38	2 adults (same sex)	0
151	7	-	2	20	21	1		1 or more
3,440	30	10	11	372	379	31	3 or more adults (male(s) and female(s))	0
1,352	100	14	8	103	109	14		1 or more
262	4	4	-	51	51	8	3 or more adults (same sex)	0
22	-	1	-	4	4	-		1 or more
14,307	**1,053**	**150**	**58**	**898**	**939**	**103**	**TOTAL DEPENDENT CHILDREN AGED 0 - 18**	
4,359	428	73	18	322	333	48	Dependent children aged 0 - 4	
8,679	591	74	35	495	522	47	Dependent children aged 5 - 15	
965	29	1	3	62	64	3	Dependent children aged 16 - 17	
					Bristol			
156,778	**2,360**	**821**	**2,675**	**31,218**	**32,242**	**3,833**	**ALL HOUSEHOLDS***	
24,505	-	-	546	6,438	6,621	364	1 adult of pensionable age	0
23,055	-	-	1,555	6,093	6,674	2,521	1 adult under pensionable age	0
7,225	135	59	36	1,669	1,688	78	1 adult any age	1 or more
44,539	-	311	318	8,065	8,196	466	2 adults (1 male and 1 female)	0
26,477	1,374	200	60	3,527	3,564	104		1 or more
5,397	-	50	66	1,203	1,229	107	2 adults (same sex)	0
924	33	5	-	204	204	7		1 or more
16,337	105	57	62	2,701	2,734	114	3 or more adults (male(s) and female(s))	0
7,045	704	123	22	1,049	1,060	29		1 or more
1,098	1	13	3	219	220	30	3 or more adults (same sex)	0
119	8	3	1	33	34	1		1 or more
77,714	**7,126**	**1,223**	**200**	**12,474**	**12,580**	**381**	**TOTAL DEPENDENT CHILDREN AGED 0 - 18**	
25,747	2,455	488	73	4,213	4,252	143	Dependent children aged 0 - 4	
47,005	4,418	674	111	7,654	7,716	195	Dependent children aged 5 - 15	
3,952	220	52	10	496	498	29	Dependent children aged 16 - 17	

Tenure								
Owner occupied		Rented privately		Rented with a job or business	Rented from a housing association	Rented from a local authority or new town	No car	2 or more cars
Owned outright	Buying	Furnished	Unfurnished					
j	k	l	m	n	o	p	q	r
99,184	**172,569**	**16,987**	**10,738**	**5,116**	**9,598**	**62,330**	**101,740**	**102,969**
27,582	3,174	912	2,659	442	4,047	16,947	43,194	242
5,795	20,792	7,325	2,149	840	1,652	6,145	15,933	2,121
789	4,620	531	460	117	858	6,291	7,348	347
43,731	47,507	3,708	3,139	1,419	1,643	14,280	20,489	29,289
3,228	55,609	1,070	1,042	1,204	699	9,340	5,473	30,310
2,993	3,822	1,300	417	134	199	1,649	3,287	2,733
215	887	64	44	27	45	521	582	422
12,300	22,439	1,203	581	601	284	4,576	3,589	25,740
2,251	12,968	158	170	287	119	2,323	1,302	10,824
259	637	660	68	39	46	171	413	863
32	93	21	4	4	1	67	66	71
10,619	**134,886**	**2,956**	**2,833**	**3,020**	**3,100**	**36,350**	**27,177**	**75,169**
1,712	39,832	1,440	1,141	939	1,204	13,561	10,080	19,663
6,951	84,222	1,311	1,510	1,838	1,781	21,419	15,775	47,296
1,471	8,537	135	139	197	97	1,195	1,127	6,212
9,699	**12,376**	**2,535**	**1,665**	**476**	**1,167**	**6,210**	**12,148**	**6,706**
3,040	356	129	429	45	590	1,667	4,956	28
614	1,806	1,089	405	95	167	736	2,227	220
90	369	51	63	12	64	681	769	37
4,070	3,291	528	465	136	186	1,319	2,408	1,808
285	3,522	143	109	85	78	916	582	1,817
334	373	238	85	15	31	182	499	263
17	77	9	6	2	3	37	56	29
1,037	1,638	181	70	53	31	430	441	1,723
176	862	24	19	28	14	229	135	663
30	66	138	14	5	2	7	65	115
4	11	1	-	-	-	6	4	3
915	**8,709**	**359**	**297**	**212**	**262**	**3,553**	**2,687**	**4,571**
121	2,439	190	121	59	88	1,341	979	1,225
582	5,436	140	141	133	164	2,083	1,561	2,800
161	634	19	17	17	7	110	116	401
36,517	**63,232**	**9,983**	**4,552**	**1,929**	**5,812**	**34,753**	**53,558**	**31,875**
10,584	1,412	388	1,050	195	2,257	8,619	20,035	86
2,367	9,459	4,585	1,120	394	1,237	3,893	9,698	908
301	1,924	264	211	58	610	3,857	4,411	140
15,072	17,013	2,067	1,245	529	887	7,726	10,684	8,619
1,155	18,410	431	386	333	371	5,391	3,220	8,413
1,289	1,931	843	190	65	132	947	1,862	1,287
100	372	32	16	15	38	351	375	151
4,632	7,845	803	240	220	168	2,429	2,090	8,422
881	4,489	74	55	104	76	1,366	835	3,349
116	333	458	37	12	32	110	266	466
16	34	17	1	2	1	48	46	29
4,115	**46,364**	**1,286**	**1,082**	**967**	**1,968**	**21,932**	**16,662**	**21,911**
726	14,560	641	482	289	763	8,286	6,244	6,232
2,719	28,569	546	543	600	1,129	12,899	9,656	13,547
505	2,570	53	52	59	64	649	652	1,595

Table 42 Household composition and housing - continued

Note: * May include a small number of households with no resident adults

42. Households with residents; dependent children in households

TOTAL HOUSE-HOLDS	Over 1 and up to 1.5 persons per room	Over 1.5 persons per room	Lacking or sharing use of bath/shower and/or inside WC	No central heating	Lacking or sharing use of bath/shower and/or inside WC and/or no central heating	Not self-contained accomm-odation	Household composition	
							Adults	Dependent children
a	b	c	d	e	f	g	h	i
					Kingswood			
34,657	**290**	**49**	**156**	**2,499**	**2,578**	**120**	**ALL HOUSEHOLDS***	
4,500	-	-	46	600	610	4	1 adult of pensionable age	0
2,863	-	-	60	379	418	78	1 adult under pensionable age	0
1,038	9	5	5	56	61	4	1 adult any age	1 or more
11,228	-	10	25	799	811	18	2 adults (1 male and 1 female)	0
7,633	160	15	4	226	230	9		1 or more
695	-	5	8	98	102	4	2 adults (same sex)	0
139	3	-	-	6	6	-		1 or more
4,621	14	6	5	255	258	3	3 or more adults (male(s) and female(s))	0
1,835	104	8	3	69	71	-		1 or more
94	-	-	-	8	8	-	3 or more adults (same sex)	0
9	-	-	-	2	2	-		1 or more
19,093	**838**	**68**	**17**	**601**	**617**	**17**	**TOTAL DEPENDENT CHILDREN AGED 0 - 18**	
5,928	297	37	12	224	235	12	Dependent children aged 0 - 4	
11,868	507	31	5	344	349	5	Dependent children aged 5 - 15	
1,054	31	-	-	27	27	-	Dependent children aged 16 - 17	
					Northavon			
49,626	**425**	**92**	**224**	**4,282**	**4,359**	**102**	**ALL HOUSEHOLDS***	
5,145	-	-	53	819	831	6	1 adult of pensionable age	0
4,849	-	-	64	673	696	52	1 adult under pensionable age	0
1,322	7	4	7	81	82	-	1 adult any age	1 or more
16,234	-	29	42	1,432	1,448	20	2 adults (1 male and 1 female)	0
11,707	245	37	29	450	467	18		1 or more
1,058	-	-	8	148	150	2	2 adults (same sex)	0
209	4	-	1	16	17	-		1 or more
6,087	20	7	14	500	502	3	3 or more adults (male(s) and female(s))	0
2,848	147	13	5	146	149	1		1 or more
137	1	2	1	14	14	-	3 or more adults (same sex)	0
28	1	-	-	2	2	-		1 or more
28,892	**1,214**	**167**	**89**	**1,227**	**1,266**	**35**	**TOTAL DEPENDENT CHILDREN AGED 0 - 18**	
8,795	397	61	33	395	410	12	Dependent children aged 0 - 4	
17,729	762	101	53	750	772	18	Dependent children aged 5 - 15	
1,863	48	5	3	69	71	2	Dependent children aged 16 - 17	
					Wansdyke			
30,814	**223**	**31**	**240**	**3,624**	**3,722**	**87**	**ALL HOUSEHOLDS***	
4,344	-	-	92	796	839	6	1 adult of pensionable age	0
2,317	-	-	61	370	388	47	1 adult under pensionable age	0
695	5	3	6	98	100	2	1 adult any age	1 or more
10,075	-	11	53	1,123	1,144	15	2 adults (1 male and 1 female)	0
6,746	126	8	8	461	465	7		1 or more
657	-	1	7	137	139	2	2 adults (same sex)	0
106	1	-	-	17	17	-		1 or more
4,070	9	1	11	475	481	8	3 or more adults (male(s) and female(s))	0
1,698	81	7	1	126	127	-		1 or more
90	-	-	1	20	21	-	3 or more adults (same sex)	0
14	1	-	-	1	1	-		1 or more
16,887	**686**	**54**	**23**	**1,287**	**1,297**	**15**	**TOTAL DEPENDENT CHILDREN AGED 0 - 18**	
4,706	200	18	13	389	394	7	Dependent children aged 0 - 4	
10,634	461	36	9	817	821	7	Dependent children aged 5 - 15	
1,213	22	-	-	67	67	1	Dependent children aged 16 - 17	

Owner occupied: Owned outright	Owner occupied: Buying	Rented privately: Furnished	Rented privately: Unfurnished	Rented with a job or business	Rented from a housing association	Rented from a local authority or new town	No car	2 or more cars
j	k	l	m	n	o	p	q	r
10,002	**18,233**	**559**	**500**	**241**	**621**	**4,501**	**7,045**	**11,384**
2,312	244	45	124	19	254	1,502	3,573	6
523	1,646	176	62	41	65	350	716	156
65	499	31	27	6	63	347	436	25
4,674	4,967	131	145	71	120	1,120	1,493	3,080
317	6,476	71	71	57	79	562	301	3,371
243	265	36	24	5	10	112	177	191
19	83	3	3	1	2	28	30	44
1,605	2,582	42	28	29	15	320	231	3,238
219	1,424	10	13	11	11	147	71	1,220
22	44	12	2	1	1	12	13	48
3	3	2	-	-	-	1	2	5
966	**15,249**	**186**	**197**	**140**	**318**	**2,037**	**1,507**	**8,193**
123	4,688	108	79	48	104	778	569	2,224
646	9,579	68	107	84	204	1,180	867	5,221
151	798	8	11	8	10	68	59	582
11,929	**29,399**	**848**	**1,092**	**767**	**598**	**4,993**	**7,332**	**18,890**
2,743	295	50	248	47	217	1,545	3,696	33
683	3,238	261	140	104	88	335	840	340
114	678	40	49	10	47	384	502	53
5,572	8,527	234	337	212	120	1,232	1,404	5,716
470	10,006	125	154	213	67	672	339	5,761
302	516	52	33	13	7	135	210	376
28	133	5	7	-	-	36	34	73
1,675	3,690	48	89	111	34	440	218	4,445
318	2,234	14	33	47	9	193	69	1,994
21	63	18	1	10	9	15	16	83
3	17	1	1	-	-	6	4	15
1,499	**23,489**	**327**	**420**	**486**	**210**	**2,461**	**1,672**	**13,885**
241	7,099	130	157	163	100	905	620	3,620
979	14,504	181	243	285	105	1,432	961	8,727
202	1,482	16	16	35	4	108	80	1,166
9,440	**14,851**	**576**	**844**	**541**	**289**	**4,273**	**5,717**	**11,356**
2,336	234	63	225	41	96	1,349	3,109	33
493	1,219	165	115	63	37	225	479	160
77	292	21	21	10	22	252	250	39
4,297	4,009	169	276	149	72	1,103	1,221	3,149
404	5,368	56	92	142	42	642	251	3,512
276	208	34	23	12	1	103	147	207
14	65	2	2	4	-	19	21	47
1,270	2,175	38	71	81	13	422	168	2,924
251	1,234	14	16	35	5	143	56	1,226
19	37	13	2	4	1	14	12	52
2	10	-	1	-	-	1	2	7
1,229	**12,796**	**152**	**209**	**343**	**125**	**2,033**	**1,094**	**8,731**
197	3,480	59	86	106	60	718	371	2,112
808	8,135	84	113	203	61	1,230	664	5,563
173	919	7	6	27	3	78	51	803

Table 42 Household composition and housing – continued

Note: * May include a small number of households with no resident adults

42. Households with residents; dependent children in households

TOTAL HOUSE-HOLDS	Over 1 and up to 1.5 persons per room	Over 1.5 persons per room	Lacking or sharing use of bath/shower and/or inside WC	No central heating	Lacking or sharing use of bath/shower and/or inside WC and/or no central heating	Not self-contained accomm-odation	Household composition: Adults	Household composition: Dependent children
a	b	c	d	e	f	g	h	i
				Woodspring				
70,519	**483**	**222**	**655**	**8,623**	**8,884**	**838**	**ALL HOUSEHOLDS***	
11,013	-	-	173	1,817	1,890	126	1 adult of pensionable age	0
6,702	-	-	278	1,566	1,654	438	1 adult under pensionable age	0
2,056	20	32	27	370	391	28	1 adult any age	1 or more
23,356	-	99	111	2,546	2,591	147	2 adults (1 male and 1 female)	0
14,491	297	55	30	1,024	1,044	41		1 or more
1,449	-	4	7	277	279	18	2 adults (same sex)	0
274	3	-	-	33	33	-		1 or more
7,429	21	12	22	722	730	27	3 or more adults (male(s) and female(s))	0
3,498	134	20	5	232	235	9		1 or more
199	4	-	1	26	27	-	3 or more adults (same sex)	0
30	4	-	-	3	3	-		1 or more
36,871	**1,418**	**214**	**93**	**2,946**	**3,010**	**120**	**TOTAL DEPENDENT CHILDREN AGED 0 - 18**	
10,294	490	98	50	1,053	1,087	55	Dependent children aged 0 - 4	
23,117	871	101	36	1,703	1,728	48	Dependent children aged 5 - 15	
2,724	51	13	5	160	163	11	Dependent children aged 16 - 17	

Tenure								
Owner occupied		Rented privately		Rented with a job or business	Rented from a housing association	Rented from a local authority or new town	No car	2 or more cars
Owned outright	Buying	Furnished	Unfurnished					
j	k	l	m	n	o	p	q	r
21,597	**34,478**	**2,486**	**2,085**	**1,162**	**1,111**	**7,600**	**15,940**	**22,758**
6,567	633	237	583	95	633	2,265	7,825	56
1,115	3,424	1,049	307	143	58	606	1,973	337
142	858	124	89	21	52	770	980	53
10,046	9,700	579	671	322	258	1,780	3,279	6,917
597	11,827	244	230	374	62	1,157	780	7,436
549	529	97	62	24	18	170	392	409
37	157	13	10	5	2	50	66	78
2,081	4,509	91	83	107	23	535	441	4,988
406	2,725	22	34	62	4	245	136	2,372
51	94	21	12	7	1	13	41	99
4	18	-	1	2	-	5	8	12
1,895	**28,279**	**646**	**628**	**872**	**217**	**4,334**	**3,555**	**17,878**
304	7,566	312	216	274	89	1,533	1,297	4,250
1,217	17,999	292	363	533	118	2,595	2,066	11,438
279	2,134	32	37	51	9	182	169	1,665

Table 43 Household composition and ethnic group

Note: * May include a small number of households with no resident adults

43. Households with residents; residents in households

Household composition: Adults	Dependent children	TOTAL HOUSE-HOLDS	White	Black Caribbean	Black African	Black other	Indian	Pakistani	Bangladeshi	Chinese	Other groups: Asian	Other groups: Other	Household head born in Ireland
a	b	c	d	e	f	g	h	i	j	k	l	m	n
AVON													
ALL HOUSEHOLDS*		**376,522**	**368,457**	**3,227**	**352**	**534**	**1,100**	**628**	**177**	**664**	**384**	**999**	**5,667**
1 adult of pensionable age	0	55,763	55,428	222	5	9	21	5	-	23	8	42	903
1 adult under pensionable age	0	44,698	43,108	732	100	151	135	42	10	130	69	221	862
1 adult any age	1 or more	13,666	12,782	477	47	119	45	28	7	33	30	98	178
2 adults (1 male and 1 female)	0	115,427	114,131	614	34	86	144	48	9	111	53	197	1,609
	1 or more	72,192	70,196	470	105	89	413	245	96	169	138	271	812
2 adults (same sex)	0	10,514	10,244	125	12	11	29	10	4	30	13	36	212
	1 or more	1,803	1,688	56	5	14	10	11	-	6	3	10	37
3 or more adults (male(s) and female(s))	0	41,984	41,272	315	14	34	121	62	15	60	24	67	699
	1 or more	18,276	17,526	178	23	15	169	170	28	88	39	40	302
3 or more adults (same sex)	0	1,880	1,794	25	7	6	11	4	7	10	6	10	48
	1 or more	222	210	4	-	-	1	3	1	-	-	3	4
Households containing persons of pensionable age only (any number)		95,107	94,637	302	6	13	46	6	-	28	13	56	1,483
TOTAL PERSONS IN HOUSEHOLDS		**916,973**	**893,373**	**7,925**	**1,004**	**1,298**	**3,882**	**2,929**	**794**	**1,980**	**1,186**	**2,602**	**13,351**
All dependent children 0 - 18		193,764	185,881	2,182	382	433	1,383	1,308	374	603	418	800	2,475
Dependent children aged 0 - 4		59,829	57,330	689	135	193	398	360	125	155	120	324	615
Dependent children aged 5 - 15		119,032	114,283	1,330	221	231	879	825	216	353	263	431	1,587
Dependent children 0 - 17 included above		*190,632*	*182,908*	*2,149*	*373*	*432*	*1,357*	*1,279*	*365*	*572*	*409*	*788*	*2,419*
Persons pensionable age - 74		109,116	108,082	626	13	20	144	43	5	68	25	90	2,035
Persons aged 75 - 84		50,948	50,775	77	3	10	28	11	1	17	6	20	665
Persons aged 85 and over		12,084	12,059	10	-	-	3	4	-	2	3	3	88

Table 43 Household composition and ethnic group – **continued**

Note: * May include a small number of households with no resident adults

43. Households with residents; residents in households

Household composition: Adults	Dependent children	TOTAL HOUSE-HOLDS	Ethnic group of head of household: White	Black Caribbean	Black African	Black other	Indian	Pakistani	Bangladeshi	Chinese	Other groups: Asian	Other groups: Other	Household head born in Ireland
a	b	c	d	e	f	g	h	i	j	k	l	m	n
Bath													
ALL HOUSEHOLDS*		**34,128**	**33,479**	**234**	**24**	**34**	**70**	**9**	**18**	**97**	**38**	**125**	**606**
1 adult of pensionable age	0	6,256	6,230	12	-	-	2	-	-	2	1	9	124
1 adult under pensionable age	0	4,912	4,778	43	9	5	11	1	-	26	8	31	80
1 adult any age	1 or more	1,330	1,267	33	6	4	1	1	-	9	3	6	23
2 adults (1 male and 1 female)	0	9,995	9,886	43	3	8	16	-	1	16	1	21	180
	1 or more	5,138	4,985	34	2	7	23	3	13	16	16	39	76
2 adults (same sex)	0	1,258	1,227	10	1	4	3	1	-	6	2	4	30
	1 or more	151	145	1	-	1	1	-	-	1	-	2	3
3 or more adults (male(s) and female(s))	0	3,440	3,369	42	1	4	4	1	3	10	-	6	64
	1 or more	1,352	1,313	13	1	1	8	2	-	7	5	2	20
3 or more adults (same sex)	0	262	249	3	1	-	1	-	1	4	1	2	6
	1 or more	22	20	-	-	-	-	-	-	-	-	2	-
Households containing persons of pensionable age only (any number)		10,245	10,208	22	-	-	3	-	-	2	1	9	199
TOTAL PERSONS IN HOUSEHOLDS		**76,876**	**75,120**	**601**	**49**	**90**	**212**	**33**	**74**	**257**	**115**	**325**	**1,342**
All dependent children 0 - 18		14,307	13,818	129	13	25	63	9	31	65	46	108	220
Dependent children aged 0 - 4		4,359	4,211	37	5	10	12	2	13	12	14	43	64
Dependent children aged 5 - 15		8,679	8,394	76	6	13	42	5	15	47	23	58	147
Dependent children 0 - 17 included above		*14,003*	*13,530*	*126*	*12*	*25*	*62*	*8*	*31*	*64*	*39*	*106*	*220*
Persons pensionable age - 74		10,766	10,673	58	-	1	9	-	-	10	2	13	227
Persons aged 75 - 84		5,547	5,537	4	-	2	-	-	-	2	-	2	115
Persons aged 85 and over		1,355	1,352	2	-	-	-	-	-	-	-	1	14

Table 43 Household composition and ethnic group – **continued**

Note: * May include a small number of households with no resident adults

43. Households with residents; residents in households

Household composition: Adults	Household composition: Dependent children	TOTAL HOUSE-HOLDS	Ethnic group of head of household: White	Black Caribbean	Black African	Black other	Indian	Pakistani	Bangladeshi	Chinese	Other groups: Asian	Other groups: Other	Household head born in Ireland
a	b	c	d	e	f	g	h	i	j	k	l	m	n
Bristol													
ALL HOUSEHOLDS*		**156,778**	**150,637**	**2,743**	**278**	**434**	**781**	**583**	**124**	**363**	**233**	**602**	**3,065**
1 adult of pensionable age	0	24,505	24,227	203	4	8	17	5	-	18	5	18	484
1 adult under pensionable age	0	23,055	21,783	643	81	133	102	37	7	76	48	145	566
1 adult any age	1 or more	7,225	6,469	428	37	113	36	26	7	18	16	75	102
2 adults (1 male and 1 female)	0	44,539	43,585	526	26	60	86	39	6	59	32	120	827
	1 or more	26,477	25,088	354	80	62	290	229	68	91	78	137	362
2 adults (same sex)	0	5,397	5,181	110	11	5	25	9	2	21	8	25	124
	1 or more	924	823	52	4	13	9	11	-	3	3	6	27
3 or more adults (male(s) and female(s))	0	16,337	15,811	258	8	25	82	56	9	28	15	45	388
	1 or more	7,045	6,481	136	21	10	125	165	21	42	24	20	148
3 or more adults (same sex)	0	1,098	1,037	20	6	5	7	3	3	5	4	8	34
	1 or more	119	109	4	-	-	1	3	1	-	-	1	3
Households containing persons of pensionable age only (any number)		39,611	39,227	271	4	11	38	6	-	19	9	26	752
TOTAL PERSONS IN HOUSEHOLDS		**370,131**	**352,224**	**6,596**	**802**	**1,035**	**2,834**	**2,786**	**573**	**1,042**	**718**	**1,521**	**6,971**
All dependent children 0 - 18		77,714	71,598	1,813	309	363	1,066	1,268	283	316	248	450	1,179
Dependent children aged 0 - 4		25,747	23,810	575	113	158	295	347	93	81	77	198	301
Dependent children aged 5 - 15		47,005	43,276	1,116	179	199	696	804	166	183	160	226	737
Dependent children 0 - 17 included above		*76,704*	*70,697*	*1,787*	*302*	*362*	*1,050*	*1,241*	*276*	*298*	*247*	*444*	*1,151*
Persons pensionable age - 74		44,431	43,590	551	10	15	115	42	5	37	20	46	1,087
Persons aged 75 - 84		21,041	20,904	73	2	7	19	11	1	12	4	8	308
Persons aged 85 and over		5,089	5,069	8	-	-	2	4	-	2	3	1	35

Note: * May include a small number of households with no resident adults

43. Households with residents; residents in households

Household composition: Adults	Dependent children	TOTAL HOUSE-HOLDS	White	Black Caribbean	Black African	Black other	Indian	Pakistani	Bangladeshi	Chinese	Other groups: Asian	Other groups: Other	Household head born in Ireland
a	b	c	d	e	f	g	h	i	j	k	l	m	n
Kingswood													
ALL HOUSEHOLDS*		**34,657**	**34,368**	**93**	**8**	**18**	**47**	**11**	**7**	**36**	**27**	**42**	**295**
1 adult of pensionable age	0	4,500	4,497	-	-	-	-	-	-	1	-	2	33
1 adult under pensionable age	0	2,863	2,836	11	-	2	3	-	1	4	2	4	37
1 adult any age	1 or more	1,038	1,018	6	-	1	5	-	-	1	4	3	6
2 adults (1 male and 1 female)	0	11,228	11,180	20	2	3	6	5	-	2	3	7	90
	1 or more	7,633	7,520	33	5	9	20	2	3	10	12	19	63
2 adults (same sex)	0	695	687	3	-	1	-	-	1	-	1	2	5
	1 or more	139	138	1	-	-	-	-	-	-	-	-	1
3 or more adults (male(s) and female(s))	0	4,621	4,593	7	1	1	6	3	-	2	5	3	44
	1 or more	1,835	1,795	12	-	1	7	1	2	15	-	2	14
3 or more adults (same sex)	0	94	94	-	-	-	-	-	-	-	-	-	2
	1 or more	9	9	-	-	-	-	-	-	-	-	-	-
Households containing persons of pensionable age only (any number)		7,957	7,951	-	1	-	-	-	-	2	-	3	71
TOTAL PERSONS IN HOUSEHOLDS		**88,916**	**87,956**	**286**	**29**	**54**	**162**	**36**	**31**	**149**	**86**	**127**	**768**
All dependent children 0 - 18		19,093	18,751	95	12	19	56	8	16	60	32	44	166
Dependent children aged 0 - 4		5,928	5,807	27	5	16	25	2	3	19	7	17	38
Dependent children aged 5 - 15		11,868	11,678	56	6	3	25	5	10	34	25	26	115
Dependent children 0 - 17 included above		*18,850*	*18,518*	*93*	*12*	*19*	*54*	*7*	*14*	*58*	*32*	*43*	*166*
Persons pensionable age - 74		9,892	9,874	4	2	-	3	-	-	3	1	5	108
Persons aged 75 - 84		4,084	4,081	-	1	-	-	-	-	1	-	1	27
Persons aged 85 and over		973	973	-	-	-	-	-	-	-	-	-	6

Table 43 Household composition and ethnic group – **continued**

Note: * May include a small number of households with no resident adults

43. Households with residents; residents in households

Household composition: Adults	Dependent children	TOTAL HOUSE-HOLDS	White	Black Caribbean	Black African	Black other	Indian	Pakistani	Bangladeshi	Chinese	Other groups: Asian	Other groups: Other	Household head born in Ireland
a	b	c	d	e	f	g	h	i	j	k	l	m	n
Northavon													
ALL HOUSEHOLDS*		**49,626**	**49,174**	**101**	**16**	**22**	**101**	**15**	**8**	**65**	**39**	**85**	**633**
1 adult of pensionable age	0	5,145	5,134	2	-	1	1	-	-	1	1	5	82
1 adult under pensionable age	0	4,849	4,777	24	4	3	11	2	-	7	3	18	64
1 adult any age	1 or more	1,322	1,305	6	1	-	2	1	-	1	2	4	21
2 adults (1 male and 1 female)	0	16,234	16,150	17	1	8	16	3	1	13	7	18	183
	1 or more	11,707	11,546	32	6	6	43	5	3	23	15	28	125
2 adults (same sex)	0	1,058	1,052	1	-	-	1	-	-	-	1	3	20
	1 or more	209	205	1	1	-	-	-	-	2	-	-	3
3 or more adults (male(s) and female(s))	0	6,087	6,049	4	2	1	11	2	2	11	3	2	78
	1 or more	2,848	2,796	12	1	2	15	1	1	7	6	7	53
3 or more adults (same sex)	0	137	130	2	-	1	1	1	1	-	1	-	3
	1 or more	28	28	-	-	-	-	-	-	-	-	-	1
Households containing persons of pensionable age only (any number)		9,335	9,320	2	-	1	3	-	-	2	1	6	143
TOTAL PERSONS IN HOUSEHOLDS		**129,084**	**127,709**	**288**	**49**	**59**	**339**	**43**	**30**	**210**	**128**	**229**	**1,665**
All dependent children 0 - 18		28,892	28,458	96	18	13	109	11	5	67	41	74	388
Dependent children aged 0 - 4		8,795	8,654	31	4	3	33	3	3	21	12	31	92
Dependent children aged 5 - 15		17,729	17,481	55	11	10	66	7	1	35	23	40	254
Dependent children 0 - 17 included above		*28,387*	*27,963*	*95*	*18*	*13*	*105*	*11*	*5*	*63*	*41*	*73*	*376*
Persons pensionable age - 74		11,727	11,702	2	-	1	7	1	-	5	1	8	205
Persons aged 75 - 84		5,055	5,045	-	-	1	6	-	-	-	-	3	68
Persons aged 85 and over		1,074	1,073	-	-	-	1	-	-	-	-	-	12

Table 43 Household composition and ethnic group – **continued**

Note: * May include a small number of households with no resident adults

43. Households with residents; residents in households

Household composition		TOTAL HOUSE-HOLDS	Ethnic group of head of household										Household head born in Ireland
Adults	Dependent children		White	Black Caribbean	Black African	Black other	Indian	Pakistani	Bangladeshi	Chinese	Other groups: Asian	Other groups: Other	
a	b	c	d	e	f	g	h	i	j	k	l	m	n
Wansdyke													
ALL HOUSEHOLDS*		**30,814**	**30,690**	**12**	**9**	**9**	**19**	**2**	**-**	**26**	**7**	**40**	**259**
1 adult of pensionable age	0	4,344	4,340	-	1	-	-	-	-	-	-	3	42
1 adult under pensionable age	0	2,317	2,299	2	3	4	1	-	-	2	3	3	25
1 adult any age	1 or more	695	688	-	1	-	-	-	-	3	-	3	5
2 adults (1 male and 1 female)	0	10,075	10,043	1	-	4	5	1	-	7	3	11	72
	1 or more	6,746	6,711	3	3	1	6	1	-	9	-	12	51
2 adults (same sex)	0	657	655	-	-	-	-	-	-	1	-	1	8
	1 or more	106	105	1	-	-	-	-	-	-	-	-	1
3 or more adults (male(s) and female(s))	0	4,070	4,059	2	1	-	4	-	-	-	-	4	37
	1 or more	1,698	1,685	3	-	-	3	-	-	3	1	3	16
3 or more adults (same sex)	0	90	90	-	-	-	-	-	-	-	-	-	2
	1 or more	14	14	-	-	-	-	-	-	-	-	-	-
Households containing persons of pensionable age only (any number)		8,043	8,036	-	1	1	1	-	-	-	-	4	69
TOTAL PERSONS IN HOUSEHOLDS		**79,122**	**78,769**	**40**	**24**	**16**	**62**	**6**	**-**	**82**	**13**	**110**	**665**
All dependent children 0 - 18		16,887	16,788	10	9	2	15	2	-	31	1	29	142
Dependent children aged 0 - 4		4,706	4,676	4	3	1	5	-	-	7	-	10	43
Dependent children aged 5 - 15		10,634	10,575	5	6	1	8	1	-	18	1	19	79
Dependent children 0 - 17 included above		*16,553*	*16,457*	*10*	*9*	*2*	*14*	*2*	-	*29*	*1*	*29*	*132*
Persons pensionable age - 74		9,912	9,898	1	1	2	4	-	-	1	-	5	99
Persons aged 75 - 84		4,401	4,400	-	-	-	-	-	-	-	-	1	26
Persons aged 85 and over		991	991	-	-	-	-	-	-	-	-	-	3

Table 43 Household composition and ethnic group – **continued**

Note: * May include a small number of households with no resident adults

43. Households with residents; residents in households

Household composition: Adults	Dependent children	TOTAL HOUSE-HOLDS	White	Black Caribbean	Black African	Black other	Indian	Pakistani	Bangladeshi	Chinese	Other groups: Asian	Other groups: Other	Household head born in Ireland
a	b	c	d	e	f	g	h	i	j	k	l	m	n
Woodspring													
ALL HOUSEHOLDS*		**70,519**	**70,109**	**44**	**17**	**17**	**82**	**8**	**20**	**77**	**40**	**105**	**809**
1 adult of pensionable age	0	11,013	11,000	5	-	-	1	-	-	1	1	5	138
1 adult under pensionable age	0	6,702	6,635	9	3	4	7	2	2	15	5	20	90
1 adult any age	1 or more	2,056	2,035	4	2	1	1	-	-	1	5	7	21
2 adults (1 male and 1 female)	0	23,356	23,287	7	2	3	15	-	1	14	7	20	257
	1 or more	14,491	14,346	14	9	4	31	5	9	20	17	36	135
2 adults (same sex)	0	1,449	1,442	1	-	1	-	-	1	2	1	1	25
	1 or more	274	272	-	-	-	-	-	-	-	-	2	2
3 or more adults (male(s) and female(s))	0	7,429	7,391	2	1	3	14	-	1	9	1	7	88
	1 or more	3,498	3,456	2	-	1	11	1	4	14	3	6	51
3 or more adults (same sex)	0	199	194	-	-	-	2	-	2	1	-	-	1
	1 or more	30	30	-	-	-	-	-	-	-	-	-	-
Households containing persons of pensionable age only (any number)		19,916	19,895	7	-	-	1	-	-	3	2	8	249
TOTAL PERSONS IN HOUSEHOLDS		**172,844**	**171,595**	**114**	**51**	**44**	**273**	**25**	**86**	**240**	**126**	**290**	**1,940**
All dependent children 0 - 18		36,871	36,468	39	21	11	74	10	39	64	50	95	380
Dependent children aged 0 - 4		10,294	10,172	15	5	5	28	6	13	15	10	25	77
Dependent children aged 5 - 15		23,117	22,879	22	13	5	42	3	24	36	31	62	255
Dependent children 0 - 17 included above		*36,135*	*35,743*	*38*	*20*	*11*	*72*	*10*	*39*	*60*	*49*	*93*	*374*
Persons pensionable age - 74		22,388	22,345	10	-	1	6	-	-	12	1	13	309
Persons aged 75 - 84		10,820	10,808	-	-	-	3	-	-	2	2	5	121
Persons aged 85 and over		2,602	2,601	-	-	-	-	-	-	-	-	1	18

Table 44 Household composition and long-term illness

Note: * May include a small number of households with no resident adults

44. Households containing persons with limiting long-term illness; residents in such households

TOTAL HOUSE-HOLDS	TOTAL PERSONS		Total with limiting long-term illness		Persons with limiting long-term illness aged:				Household composition	
					0 - 4		5 - 15		Adults	Dependent children
	Males	Females	Males	Females	Males	Females	Males	Females		
a	b	c	d	e	f	g	h	i	j	k
						AVON				
81,974	**81,617**	**92,881**	**45,867**	**54,257**	**641**	**423**	**1,528**	**1,158**	**ALL HOUSEHOLDS***	
27,291	8,063	19,228	8,063	19,228					1 adult	0
1,324	1,417	2,363	583	1,061	148	88	306	251		1 or more
30,388	30,388	30,388	21,759	19,272					2 adults (1 male and 1 female)	0
5,859	12,151	11,421	4,173	3,112	430	268	954	694		1 or more
2,773	1,900	3,646	1,166	2,316					2 adults (same sex)	0
264	278	688	84	251	9	10	37	19		1 or more
10,482	18,795	16,508	7,582	6,660					3 or more adults (male(s) and female(s))	0
3,165	7,930	7,880	2,152	2,013	53	52	225	191		1 or more
384	626	635	279	296					3 or more adults (same sex)	0
41	69	121	26	45	1	3	6	2		1 or more
									Households with:	
48,327	30,886	45,149	24,668	34,428	139	91	230	204	0 persons economically active	
18,272	22,926	22,378	10,937	11,034	318	202	595	439	1 person economically active	
15,480	19,277	19,250	9,080	9,464	249	152	478	372	- in employment	
2,792	3,649	3,128	1,857	1,570	69	50	117	67	- unemployed	
15,375	27,805	25,354	10,262	8,795	184	130	703	515	2 or more persons economically active	
14,947	26,980	24,747	9,950	8,535	171	123	681	501	- 1 or more in employment	
428	825	607	312	260	13	7	22	14	- all unemployed	
	32,544	22,316	11,039	6,620					Persons economically active	
	27,465	20,462	8,834	5,807					Persons in employment	
						Bath				
7,251	**6,535**	**7,813**	**3,772**	**4,867**	**52**	**32**	**94**	**57**	**ALL HOUSEHOLDS***	
2,868	810	2,058	810	2,058					1 adult	0
116	111	203	42	86	8	10	21	14		1 or more
2,477	2,477	2,477	1,762	1,548					2 adults (1 male and 1 female)	0
406	847	757	284	210	38	18	54	37		1 or more
303	200	406	128	251					2 adults (same sex)	0
26	37	61	10	23	1	2	5	2		1 or more
801	1,462	1,230	566	533					3 or more adults (male(s) and female(s))	0
225	564	548	160	133	5	2	14	4		1 or more
25	23	58	9	22					3 or more adults (same sex)	0
4	4	15	1	3	-	-	-	-		1 or more
									Households with:	
4,571	2,654	4,185	2,129	3,284	8	10	8	9	0 persons economically active	
1,527	1,822	1,746	927	891	29	14	42	22	1 person economically active	
1,283	1,527	1,500	769	755	24	9	34	19	- in employment	
244	295	246	158	136	5	5	8	3	- unemployed	
1,153	2,059	1,882	716	692	15	8	44	26	2 or more persons economically active	
1,119	2,004	1,836	695	673	14	8	44	26	- 1 or more in employment	
34	55	46	21	19	1	-	-	-	- all unemployed	
	2,479	1,777	860	606					Persons economically active	
	2,080	1,624	689	526					Persons in employment	

Persons with limiting long-term illness aged:															
16 - 29		30 - 44		45 - 54		55 - 59		60 - 64		65 - 74		75 - 84		85 and over	
Males	Females	Males	Females	Males	Females	Males	Females	Males	Females	Males	Females	Males	Females	Males	Females
l	m	n	o	p	q	r	s	t	u	v	w	x	y	z	aa
3,014	**2,685**	**4,713**	**4,502**	**4,839**	**4,828**	**3,858**	**3,533**	**5,836**	**4,567**	**11,613**	**13,103**	**7,993**	**13,978**	**1,832**	**5,480**
346	239	852	509	814	770	612	720	850	1,092	1,944	4,695	1,971	7,773	674	3,430
43	215	50	380	22	103	5	16	5	3	2	4	2	1	-	-
525	476	842	801	1,467	1,772	1,800	1,804	3,450	2,589	7,785	6,702	5,038	4,332	852	796
436	509	1,511	1,302	538	269	140	34	94	15	54	18	13	3	3	-
146	127	127	197	159	209	89	119	143	148	241	373	195	648	66	495
13	40	16	69	6	29	1	15	1	13	1	32	-	17	-	7
1,045	688	827	718	1,334	1,319	1,021	728	1,124	602	1,372	1,008	658	938	201	659
386	320	423	478	462	309	156	78	135	86	178	225	103	212	31	62
68	59	61	41	33	41	32	19	33	16	36	43	12	48	4	29
6	12	4	7	4	7	2	-	1	3	-	3	1	6	1	2
376	436	1,095	936	1,106	1,120	1,162	1,287	2,878	2,774	9,088	10,843	7,009	12,079	1,585	4,658
880	834	1,699	1,772	1,512	1,672	1,385	1,322	1,833	1,282	1,832	1,666	728	1,298	155	547
640	658	1,316	1,476	1,201	1,389	1,085	1,129	1,604	1,130	1,702	1,499	663	1,168	142	491
240	176	383	296	311	283	300	193	229	152	130	167	65	130	13	56
1,758	1,415	1,919	1,794	2,221	2,036	1,311	924	1,125	511	693	594	256	601	92	275
1,674	1,364	1,859	1,734	2,174	1,985	1,280	895	1,091	494	676	578	252	591	92	270
84	51	60	60	47	51	31	29	34	17	17	16	4	10	-	5
1,873	1,275	2,877	1,860	2,592	1,766	1,567	873	1,394	441	574	283	139	100	23	22
1,345	1,044	2,312	1,613	2,112	1,561	1,203	765	1,139	433	562	279	138	90	23	22
256	**228**	**388**	**379**	**392**	**355**	**248**	**257**	**424**	**325**	**958**	**1,176**	**764**	**1,438**	**196**	**620**
41	23	110	54	90	73	55	63	80	107	169	486	193	844	72	408
5	25	6	29	2	6	-	1	-	-	-	1	-	-	-	-
43	37	61	75	103	123	107	121	233	155	632	550	483	404	100	83
31	34	98	93	46	23	11	2	4	2	2	1	-	-	-	-
14	17	11	21	26	22	9	11	11	12	30	39	20	69	7	60
1	6	3	6	-	4	-	-	-	-	-	-	-	2	-	1
87	50	63	57	84	84	56	55	87	44	113	83	61	101	15	59
29	28	33	39	40	18	10	4	8	5	12	14	7	12	2	7
4	7	3	5	1	2	-	-	1	-	-	2	-	4	-	2
1	1	-	-	-	-	-	-	-	-	-	-	-	2	-	-
41	43	74	80	103	81	71	96	222	202	746	982	679	1,250	177	531
80	57	166	153	140	126	95	84	124	88	166	152	69	131	16	64
55	40	126	124	113	100	74	69	107	75	159	143	63	119	14	57
25	17	40	29	27	26	21	15	17	13	7	9	6	12	2	7
135	128	148	146	149	148	82	77	78	35	46	42	16	57	3	25
127	123	145	140	145	145	80	75	75	35	46	41	16	56	3	24
8	5	3	6	4	3	2	2	3	-	-	1	-	1	-	1
149	122	251	166	202	163	116	73	94	38	38	30	9	13	1	1
100	101	200	142	169	139	95	64	77	37	38	30	9	12	1	1

Table 44 Household composition and long-term illness – **continued**

Note: * May include a small number of households with no resident adults

44. Households containing persons with limiting long-term illness; residents in such households

TOTAL HOUSE-HOLDS	TOTAL PERSONS		Total with limiting long-term illness		Persons with limiting long-term illness aged:				Household composition	
					0 - 4		5 - 15		Adults	Dependent children
	Males	Females	Males	Females	Males	Females	Males	Females		
a	b	c	d	e	f	g	h	i	j	k
					Bristol					
36,912	**36,683**	**41,511**	**20,808**	**24,438**	**353**	**220**	**773**	**579**	**ALL HOUSEHOLDS***	
13,124	4,132	8,992	4,132	8,992					1 adult	0
791	898	1,401	384	624	108	54	194	160		1 or more
12,622	12,622	12,622	9,079	8,105					2 adults (1 male and 1 female)	0
2,571	5,444	5,114	1,914	1,375	208	129	447	303		1 or more
1,382	998	1,766	613	1,125					2 adults (same sex)	0
154	169	393	56	145	7	5	24	9		1 or more
4,626	8,379	7,200	3,455	2,943					3 or more adults (male(s) and female(s))	0
1,411	3,662	3,600	1,007	942	29	29	106	106		1 or more
204	337	339	156	158					3 or more adults (same sex)	0
26	42	83	12	28	1	2	2	1		1 or more
									Households with:	
21,786	13,906	20,272	11,094	15,490	104	54	159	140	0 persons economically active	
8,546	10,712	10,348	5,216	5,142	160	108	318	215	1 person economically active	
6,916	8,528	8,535	4,123	4,240	106	73	238	166	- in employment	
1,630	2,184	1,813	1,093	902	54	35	80	49	- unemployed	
6,580	12,065	10,891	4,498	3,806	89	58	296	224	2 or more persons economically active	
6,308	11,522	10,484	4,295	3,632	81	55	281	211	- 1 or more in employment	
272	543	407	203	174	8	3	15	13	- all unemployed	
	14,409	9,865	5,011	3,021					Persons economically active	
	11,543	8,862	3,764	2,582					Persons in employment	
					Kingswood					
7,047	**7,231**	**8,181**	**3,988**	**4,632**	**46**	**32**	**107**	**101**	**ALL HOUSEHOLDS***	
2,131	596	1,535	596	1,535					1 adult	0
75	72	132	29	66	6	6	17	11		1 or more
2,702	2,702	2,702	1,935	1,719					2 adults (1 male and 1 female)	0
507	1,028	1,004	351	257	39	23	71	71		1 or more
192	114	270	67	171					2 adults (same sex)	0
12	17	35	4	9	1	-	1	2		1 or more
1,116	1,972	1,769	817	673					3 or more adults (male(s) and female(s))	0
282	669	688	170	174	-	3	18	17		1 or more
29	58	44	18	28					3 or more adults (same sex)	0
1	3	2	1	-	-	-	-	-		1 or more
									Households with:	
3,966	2,511	3,694	2,028	2,852	5	6	11	4	0 persons economically active	
1,552	1,979	1,982	940	938	29	11	35	49	1 person economically active	
1,386	1,773	1,782	830	845	26	9	34	47	- in employment	
166	206	200	110	93	3	2	1	2	- unemployed	
1,529	2,741	2,505	1,020	842	12	15	61	48	2 or more persons economically active	
1,504	2,694	2,476	1,001	828	11	14	60	48	- 1 or more in employment	
25	47	29	19	14	1	1	1	-	- all unemployed	
	3,091	2,144	1,004	543					Persons economically active	
	2,707	2,017	828	500					Persons in employment	

Persons with limiting long-term illness aged:															
16 - 29		30 - 44		45 - 54		55 - 59		60 - 64		65 - 74		75 - 84		85 and over	
Males	Females	Males	Females	Males	Females	Males	Females	Males	Females	Males	Females	Males	Females	Males	Females
l	m	n	o	p	q	r	s	t	u	v	w	x	y	z	aa
1,468	**1,360**	**2,367**	**2,173**	**2,238**	**2,181**	**1,761**	**1,591**	**2,661**	**2,091**	**5,103**	**5,752**	**3,333**	**6,099**	**751**	**2,392**
192	147	493	318	460	425	345	358	467	543	985	2,138	896	3,503	294	1,560
27	135	32	206	16	52	3	12	3	1	1	3	-	1	-	-
265	228	414	373	621	735	748	746	1,441	1,091	3,235	2,801	2,026	1,800	329	331
205	259	667	532	247	112	62	20	46	8	25	10	6	2	1	-
85	71	81	107	84	107	50	53	70	77	119	181	95	309	29	220
11	27	8	40	3	17	1	11	1	11	1	16	-	5	-	4
463	303	419	346	590	551	463	331	535	295	636	482	263	383	86	252
180	143	212	218	202	159	70	47	79	54	78	100	41	71	10	15
38	42	39	27	13	18	18	13	18	9	23	19	5	22	2	8
2	5	2	6	2	5	1	-	1	2	-	2	1	3	-	2
205	270	635	529	600	584	568	607	1,308	1,256	3,949	4,710	2,917	5,274	649	2,066
448	460	871	860	723	755	632	561	845	590	848	764	305	601	66	228
299	341	629	685	541	585	480	470	725	510	771	676	272	532	62	202
149	119	242	175	182	170	152	91	120	80	77	88	33	69	4	26
815	630	861	784	915	842	561	423	508	245	306	278	111	224	36	98
761	597	827	745	879	808	545	405	487	235	291	266	107	215	36	95
54	33	34	39	36	34	16	18	21	10	15	12	4	9	-	3
955	626	1,358	863	1,118	747	677	403	599	207	236	124	59	42	9	9
651	499	1,017	729	844	639	491	346	465	205	229	121	58	34	9	9
261	**197**	**403**	**338**	**391**	**410**	**378**	**349**	**541**	**454**	**1,049**	**1,133**	**661**	**1,136**	**151**	**482**
17	11	59	22	34	42	47	51	53	86	158	384	169	641	59	298
2	11	2	30	1	7	-	1	-	-	-	-	1	-	-	-
44	34	64	68	121	159	184	193	352	269	715	598	392	330	63	68
45	37	139	104	39	18	6	1	5	-	5	3	2	-	-	-
5	6	13	18	6	11	3	13	7	16	16	26	13	36	4	45
-	2	1	-	1	3	-	-	-	-	-	1	-	1	-	-
117	67	95	49	143	141	116	81	114	70	135	102	77	100	20	63
28	29	27	46	42	24	20	6	6	8	20	15	5	20	4	6
3	-	3	1	4	5	2	3	4	5	-	4	2	8	-	2
-	-	-	-	-	-	-	-	-	-	-	-	-	-	1	-
22	20	69	59	60	76	104	113	249	250	812	954	570	969	126	401
69	60	153	125	112	130	123	133	166	137	171	129	68	106	14	58
56	54	130	116	98	122	95	110	148	121	165	118	64	98	14	50
13	6	23	9	14	8	28	23	18	16	6	11	4	8	-	8
170	117	181	154	219	204	151	103	126	67	66	50	23	61	11	23
165	113	178	152	217	202	148	101	123	65	65	49	23	61	11	23
5	4	3	2	2	2	3	2	3	2	1	1	-	-	-	-
163	95	259	147	225	153	158	81	147	45	37	16	14	4	1	2
124	80	216	133	193	146	122	74	121	45	37	16	14	4	1	2

Table 44 Household composition and long-term illness – **continued**

Note: * May include a small number of households with no resident adults

44. Households containing persons with limiting long-term illness; residents in such households

TOTAL HOUSE-HOLDS	TOTAL PERSONS		Total with limiting long-term illness		Persons with limiting long-term illness aged:				Household composition	
					0 - 4		5 - 15			
	Males	Females	Males	Females	Males	Females	Males	Females	Adults	Dependent children
a	b	c	d	e	f	g	h	i	j	k
									Northavon	
8,626	**9,393**	**10,151**	**4,930**	**5,601**	**63**	**50**	**184**	**127**	**ALL HOUSEHOLDS***	
2,325	694	1,631	694	1,631					1 adult	0
102	98	187	33	92	6	6	22	21		1 or more
3,431	3,431	3,431	2,381	2,181					2 adults (1 male and 1 female)	0
748	1,562	1,417	513	405	50	36	127	85		1 or more
261	212	310	129	195					2 adults (same sex)	0
23	16	63	6	22	-	3	4	-		1 or more
1,281	2,268	2,061	859	804					3 or more adults (male(s) and female(s))	0
418	1,029	1,015	272	255	7	5	30	21		1 or more
34	73	33	39	14					3 or more adults (same sex)	0
3	10	3	4	2	-	-	1	-		1 or more
									Households with:	
4,497	3,023	4,203	2,392	3,171	6	10	15	15	0 persons economically active	
2,048	2,635	2,530	1,185	1,247	30	20	62	45	1 person economically active	
1,830	2,351	2,273	1,043	1,118	29	19	56	41	- in employment	
218	284	257	142	129	1	1	6	4	- unemployed	
2,081	3,735	3,418	1,353	1,183	27	20	107	67	2 or more persons economically active	
2,055	3,690	3,385	1,338	1,169	27	20	106	67	- 1 or more in employment	
26	45	33	15	14	-	-	1	-	- all unemployed	
	4,209	2,800	1,407	802					Persons economically active	
	3,755	2,631	1,214	731					Persons in employment	
									Wansdyke	
6,177	**6,370**	**7,134**	**3,508**	**3,989**	**24**	**29**	**117**	**76**	**ALL HOUSEHOLDS***	
1,790	502	1,288	502	1,288					1 adult	0
52	50	92	20	41	2	1	14	7		1 or more
2,515	2,515	2,515	1,807	1,528					2 adults (1 male and 1 female)	0
450	924	875	292	242	20	24	78	57		1 or more
190	118	262	71	165					2 adults (same sex)	0
14	13	41	3	12	-	-	2	-		1 or more
901	1,619	1,442	631	561					3 or more adults (male(s) and female(s))	0
233	562	583	153	136	2	4	22	11		1 or more
29	63	28	25	10					3 or more adults (same sex)	0
3	4	8	4	6	-	-	1	1		1 or more
									Households with:	
3,561	2,346	3,331	1,867	2,469	1	1	10	4	0 persons economically active	
1,317	1,681	1,670	793	785	14	17	43	24	1 person economically active	
1,187	1,506	1,515	704	712	13	16	35	23	- in employment	
130	175	155	89	73	1	1	8	1	- unemployed	
1,299	2,343	2,133	848	735	9	11	64	48	2 or more persons economically active	
1,280	2,311	2,106	833	726	9	10	61	48	- 1 or more in employment	
19	32	27	15	9	-	1	3	-	- all unemployed	
	2,603	1,778	821	503					Persons economically active	
	2,342	1,675	700	463					Persons in employment	

Persons with limiting long-term illness aged:															
16 - 29		30 - 44		45 - 54		55 - 59		60 - 64		65 - 74		75 - 84		85 and over	
Males	Females	Males	Females	Males	Females	Males	Females	Males	Females	Males	Females	Males	Females	Males	Females
l	m	n	o	p	q	r	s	t	u	v	w	x	y	z	aa
339	**327**	**493**	**519**	**570**	**579**	**450**	**404**	**683**	**466**	**1,142**	**1,338**	**846**	**1,322**	**160**	**469**
33	18	55	32	59	46	52	71	78	79	175	438	189	682	53	265
2	10	2	39	-	15	-	-	1	1	-	-	-	-	-	-
57	75	93	87	192	231	220	227	419	313	793	735	542	440	65	73
53	53	189	192	52	34	23	2	12	1	6	2	1	-	-	-
15	13	10	16	18	18	10	12	24	12	19	34	25	59	8	31
1	1	-	7	1	3	-	-	-	1	-	3	-	3	-	1
114	107	81	79	186	194	128	86	124	53	128	91	72	111	26	83
50	44	57	65	59	36	13	5	17	5	16	34	16	26	7	14
13	4	5	2	3	2	3	1	8	1	5	1	1	1	1	2
1	2	1	-	-	-	1	-	-	-	-	-	-	-	-	-
33	29	75	64	87	86	104	133	317	269	902	1,083	725	1,111	128	371
92	90	156	210	168	200	175	174	226	134	167	180	93	134	16	60
79	81	134	188	149	181	138	153	203	118	153	161	89	122	13	54
13	9	22	22	19	19	37	21	23	16	14	19	4	12	3	6
214	208	262	245	315	293	171	97	140	63	73	75	28	77	16	38
211	205	258	242	314	289	167	96	138	61	73	74	28	77	16	38
3	3	4	3	1	4	4	1	2	2	-	1	-	-	-	-
207	164	346	236	361	224	214	88	192	45	65	34	21	8	1	3
176	148	305	215	320	204	163	78	166	43	62	33	21	7	1	3
197	**158**	**269**	**289**	**327**	**321**	**312**	**275**	**457**	**366**	**944**	**1,008**	**691**	**1,058**	**170**	**409**
6	8	19	14	34	35	29	35	51	60	141	345	160	553	62	238
1	8	1	19	1	5	-	-	-	1	1	-	-	-	-	-
28	21	62	56	104	127	162	151	280	238	645	528	446	355	80	52
25	34	110	102	39	18	6	3	11	3	1	-	2	1	-	-
7	6	2	12	9	10	6	11	13	11	16	30	13	54	5	31
-	-	1	6	-	1	-	1	-	-	-	2	-	2	-	-
102	54	47	48	102	104	93	71	94	50	118	88	55	67	20	79
24	22	22	31	33	17	10	3	8	2	17	14	13	24	2	8
3	2	4	1	4	3	6	-	-	-	5	1	2	2	1	1
1	3	1	-	1	1	-	-	-	1	-	-	-	-	-	-
15	14	53	48	50	57	81	79	204	213	706	813	597	912	150	328
44	42	91	105	102	109	109	108	156	113	166	139	57	89	11	39
41	38	77	92	83	96	95	96	138	107	160	126	52	81	10	37
3	4	14	13	19	13	14	12	18	6	6	13	5	8	1	2
138	102	125	136	175	155	122	88	97	40	72	56	37	57	9	42
137	100	119	134	175	153	118	86	97	40	71	56	37	57	9	42
1	2	6	2	-	2	4	2	-	-	1	-	-	-	-	-
107	85	181	130	189	128	133	81	123	43	73	24	13	9	2	3
84	73	151	122	162	119	108	71	107	42	73	24	13	9	2	3

Table 44 Household composition and long-term illness – continued

Note: * May include a small number of households with no resident adults

44. Households containing persons with limiting long-term illness; residents in such households

TOTAL HOUSE-HOLDS	TOTAL PERSONS		Total with limiting long-term illness		Persons with limiting long-term illness aged:				Household composition	
					0 - 4		5 - 15		Adults	Dependent children
	Males	Females	Males	Females	Males	Females	Males	Females		
a	b	c	d	e	f	g	h	i	j	k
						Woodspring				
15,961	**15,405**	**18,091**	**8,861**	**10,730**	**103**	**60**	**253**	**218**	**ALL HOUSEHOLDS***	
5,053	1,329	3,724	1,329	3,724					1 adult	0
188	188	348	75	152	18	11	38	38		1 or more
6,641	6,641	6,641	4,795	4,191					2 adults (1 male and 1 female)	0
1,177	2,346	2,254	819	623	75	38	177	141		1 or more
445	258	632	158	409					2 adults (same sex)	0
35	26	95	5	40	-	-	1	6		1 or more
1,757	3,095	2,806	1,254	1,146					3 or more adults (male(s) and female(s))	0
596	1,444	1,446	390	373	10	9	35	32		1 or more
63	72	133	32	64					3 or more adults (same sex)	0
4	6	10	4	6	-	1	2	-		1 or more
									Households with:	
9,946	6,446	9,464	5,158	7,162	15	10	27	32	0 persons economically active	
3,282	4,097	4,102	1,876	2,031	56	32	95	84	1 person economically active	
2,878	3,592	3,645	1,611	1,794	51	26	81	76	- in employment	
404	505	457	265	237	5	6	14	8	- unemployed	
2,733	4,862	4,525	1,827	1,537	32	18	131	102	2 or more persons economically active	
2,681	4,759	4,460	1,788	1,507	29	16	129	101	- 1 or more in employment	
52	103	65	39	30	3	2	2	1	- all unemployed	
	5,753	3,952	1,936	1,145					Persons economically active	
	5,038	3,653	1,639	1,005					Persons in employment	

Persons with limiting long-term illness aged:															
16 - 29		30 - 44		45 - 54		55 - 59		60 - 64		65 - 74		75 - 84		85 and over	
Males	Females	Males	Females	Males	Females	Males	Females	Males	Females	Males	Females	Males	Females	Males	Females
l	m	n	o	p	q	r	s	t	u	v	w	x	y	z	aa
493	**415**	**793**	**804**	**921**	**982**	**709**	**657**	**1,070**	**865**	**2,417**	**2,696**	**1,698**	**2,925**	**404**	**1,108**
57	32	116	69	137	149	84	142	121	217	316	904	364	1,550	134	661
6	26	7	57	2	18	2	2	1	-	-	-	1	-	-	-
88	81	148	142	326	397	379	366	725	523	1,765	1,490	1,149	1,003	215	189
77	92	308	279	115	64	32	6	16	1	15	2	2	-	2	-
20	14	10	23	16	41	11	19	18	20	41	63	29	121	13	108
-	4	3	10	1	1	-	3	-	1	-	10	-	4	-	1
162	107	122	139	229	245	165	104	170	90	242	162	130	176	34	123
75	54	72	79	86	55	33	13	17	12	35	48	21	59	6	12
7	4	7	5	8	11	3	2	2	1	3	16	2	11	-	14
1	1	-	1	1	1	-	-	-	-	-	1	-	1	-	-
60	60	189	156	206	236	234	259	578	584	1,973	2,301	1,521	2,563	355	961
147	125	262	319	267	352	251	262	316	220	314	302	136	237	32	98
110	104	220	271	217	305	203	231	283	199	294	275	123	216	29	91
37	21	42	48	50	47	48	31	33	21	20	27	13	21	3	7
286	230	342	329	448	394	224	136	176	61	130	93	41	125	17	49
273	226	332	321	444	388	222	132	171	58	130	92	41	125	17	48
13	4	10	8	4	6	2	4	5	3	-	1	-	-	-	1
292	183	482	318	497	351	269	147	239	63	125	55	23	24	9	4
210	143	423	272	424	314	224	132	203	61	123	55	23	24	9	4

Table 45 Migrant household heads

Note: * May include a small number of heads aged under 16

45. Households with residents

Tenure of household and economic activity of head	Households with head with different address one year before census: age and sex of head									
	Total migrant heads*		16 - 29*		30 - 44		45 up to pensionable age		Pensionable age and over	
	Males	Females	Males	Females	Males	Females	Males	Females	Males	Females
a	b	c	d	e	f	g	h	i	j	k
					AVON					
TOTAL HEADS	**24,277**	**12,475**	**11,224**	**6,740**	**8,306**	**3,014**	**3,415**	**1,005**	**1,332**	**1,716**
Owner occupied	**13,666**	**4,592**	**5,754**	**1,939**	**5,199**	**1,555**	**2,127**	**517**	**586**	**581**
Economically active	12,762	3,589	5,692	1,787	5,144	1,338	1,867	414	59	50
Unemployed	504	153	186	54	199	58	119	40	-	1
Economically active students (included above)	*16*	*7*	*9*	*5*	*4*	*2*	*3*	-	-	-
Economically inactive	904	1,003	62	152	55	217	260	103	527	531
Rented privately or with a job or business	**7,580**	**4,361**	**4,403**	**3,220**	**2,302**	**781**	**761**	**230**	**114**	**130**
Economically active	6,684	3,431	3,846	2,566	2,143	644	674	193	21	28
Unemployed	981	378	581	266	289	73	110	37	1	2
Economically active students (included above)	*67*	*74*	*62*	*70*	*5*	*4*	-	-	-	-
Economically inactive	896	930	557	654	159	137	87	37	93	102
Rented from a housing association	**562**	**700**	**178**	**269**	**132**	**128**	**110**	**42**	**142**	**261**
Economically active	347	251	163	152	106	63	73	27	5	9
Unemployed	131	66	69	43	33	16	29	7	-	-
Economically active students (included above)	-	*2*	-	*2*	-	-	-	-	-	-
Economically inactive	215	449	15	117	26	65	37	15	137	252
Rented from a local authority or new town	**2,469**	**2,822**	**889**	**1,312**	**673**	**550**	**417**	**216**	**490**	**744**
Economically active	1,686	789	822	390	593	245	249	133	22	21
Unemployed	598	206	297	117	220	48	81	40	-	1
Economically active students (included above)	*2*	*3*	*2*	*2*	-	*1*	-	-	-	-
Economically inactive	783	2,033	67	922	80	305	168	83	468	723
					Bath					
TOTAL HEADS	**2,278**	**1,551**	**1,042**	**884**	**750**	**345**	**349**	**115**	**137**	**207**
Owner occupied	**938**	**454**	**315**	**150**	**384**	**169**	**178**	**61**	**61**	**74**
Economically active	856	327	309	137	383	140	152	44	12	6
Unemployed	34	16	10	4	13	6	11	6	-	-
Economically active students (included above)	*3*	-	*2*	-	-	-	*1*	-	-	-
Economically inactive	82	127	6	13	1	29	26	17	49	68
Rented privately or with a job or business	**1,039**	**744**	**637**	**573**	**276**	**125**	**116**	**28**	**10**	**18**
Economically active	890	588	522	454	256	110	111	23	1	1
Unemployed	108	59	57	36	35	17	16	6	-	-
Economically active students (included above)	*7*	*16*	*6*	*16*	*1*	-	-	-	-	-
Economically inactive	149	156	115	119	20	15	5	5	9	17
Rented from a housing association	**66**	**85**	**17**	**28**	**10**	**10**	**15**	**3**	**24**	**44**
Economically active	36	30	15	20	10	6	11	2	-	2
Unemployed	12	5	3	3	5	1	4	1	-	-
Economically active students (included above)	-	*1*	-	*1*	-	-	-	-	-	-
Economically inactive	30	55	2	8	-	4	4	1	24	42
Rented from a local authority or new town	**235**	**268**	**73**	**133**	**80**	**41**	**40**	**23**	**42**	**71**
Economically active	176	88	70	47	73	22	30	18	3	1
Unemployed	60	30	26	19	26	5	8	6	-	-
Economically active students (included above)	*1*	*1*	*1*	*1*	-	-	-	-	-	-
Economically inactive	59	180	3	86	7	19	10	5	39	70

All households: age and sex of head										
TOTAL HOUSEHOLD HEADS*		16 - 29*		30 - 44		45 up to pensionable age		Pensionable age and over		Tenure of household and economic activity of head
Males	Females	Males	Females	Males	Females	Males	Females	Males	Females	
l	m	n	o	p	q	r	s	t	u	a
263,286	**113,236**	**34,284**	**18,519**	**80,989**	**23,780**	**91,494**	**16,881**	**56,519**	**54,056**	**TOTAL HEADS**
206,460	**65,293**	**22,659**	**7,048**	**67,241**	**15,377**	**76,603**	**11,694**	**39,957**	**31,174**	**Owner occupied**
158,464	30,221	22,361	6,013	66,443	12,929	66,170	8,985	3,490	2,294	Economically active
7,125	1,229	957	232	2,508	500	3,632	471	28	26	Unemployed
88	*70*	*31*	*30*	*43*	*34*	*13*	*6*	*1*	-	*Economically active students (included above)*
47,996	35,072	298	1,035	798	2,448	10,433	2,709	36,467	28,880	Economically inactive
20,581	**12,260**	**7,625**	**5,542**	**5,852**	**2,165**	**4,319**	**1,139**	**2,785**	**3,414**	**Rented privately or with a job or business**
16,417	7,334	6,719	4,415	5,503	1,770	3,838	904	357	245	Economically active
2,259	790	1,010	451	726	201	519	135	4	3	Unemployed
111	*117*	*97*	*104*	*14*	*13*	-	-	-	-	*Economically active students (included above)*
4,164	4,926	906	1,127	349	395	481	235	2,428	3,169	Economically inactive
3,930	**5,668**	**513**	**797**	**848**	**899**	**846**	**458**	**1,723**	**3,514**	**Rented from a housing association**
1,845	1,386	466	433	718	549	585	301	76	103	Economically active
550	282	160	118	225	107	161	57	4	-	Unemployed
5	*4*	*1*	*2*	*3*	*2*	*1*	-	-	-	*Economically active students (included above)*
2,085	4,282	47	364	130	350	261	157	1,647	3,411	Economically inactive
32,315	**30,015**	**3,487**	**5,132**	**7,048**	**5,339**	**9,726**	**3,590**	**12,054**	**15,954**	**Rented from a local authority or new town**
17,089	7,160	3,264	1,642	6,329	2,810	6,881	2,141	615	567	Economically active
4,445	1,277	1,078	387	1,721	451	1,627	416	19	23	Unemployed
8	*19*	*6*	*11*	*2*	*8*	-	-	-	-	*Economically active students (included above)*
15,226	22,855	223	3,490	719	2,529	2,845	1,449	11,439	15,387	Economically inactive

l	m	n	o	p	q	r	s	t	u	a
21,763	**12,365**	**2,680**	**2,096**	**6,039**	**2,492**	**7,351**	**1,721**	**5,693**	**6,056**	**TOTAL HEADS**
15,508	**6,567**	**1,187**	**522**	**4,451**	**1,489**	**5,871**	**1,119**	**3,999**	**3,437**	**Owner occupied**
10,898	2,910	1,155	455	4,400	1,263	4,989	898	354	294	Economically active
446	137	60	30	156	50	227	51	3	6	Unemployed
12	*11*	*6*	*5*	*4*	*4*	*2*	*2*	-	-	*Economically active students (included above)*
4,610	3,657	32	67	51	226	882	221	3,645	3,143	Economically inactive
2,692	**1,984**	**1,107**	**946**	**737**	**330**	**481**	**175**	**367**	**533**	**Rented privately or with a job or business**
2,106	1,222	933	750	698	286	432	146	43	40	Economically active
251	125	105	65	95	38	51	22	-	-	Unemployed
16	*27*	*15*	*26*	*1*	*1*	-	-	-	-	*Economically active students (included above)*
586	762	174	196	39	44	49	29	324	493	Economically inactive
463	**704**	**56**	**57**	**99**	**91**	**86**	**41**	**222**	**515**	**Rented from a housing association**
217	144	49	39	94	59	65	30	9	16	Economically active
44	20	10	6	23	9	11	5	-	-	Unemployed
1	*1*	-	*1*	-	-	*1*	-	-	-	*Economically active students (included above)*
246	560	7	18	5	32	21	11	213	499	Economically inactive
3,100	**3,110**	**330**	**571**	**752**	**582**	**913**	**386**	**1,105**	**1,571**	**Rented from a local authority or new town**
1,743	873	305	222	676	328	689	259	73	64	Economically active
418	161	85	49	190	51	142	60	1	1	Unemployed
2	*1*	*2*	*1*	-	-	-	-	-	-	*Economically active students (included above)*
1,357	2,237	25	349	76	254	224	127	1,032	1,507	Economically inactive

Table 45 Migrant household heads - continued

Note: * May include a small number of heads aged under 16

45. Households with residents

Tenure of household and economic activity of head	Households with head with different address one year before census: age and sex of head									
	Total migrant heads*		16 - 29*		30 - 44		45 up to pensionable age		Pensionable age and over	
	Males	Females	Males	Females	Males	Females	Males	Females	Males	Females
a	b	c	d	e	f	g	h	i	j	k
					Bristol					
TOTAL HEADS	**10,075**	**6,338**	**5,378**	**3,788**	**3,195**	**1,507**	**1,086**	**424**	**416**	**619**
Owner occupied	**4,370**	**1,944**	**2,088**	**911**	**1,637**	**689**	**528**	**187**	**117**	**157**
Economically active	4,136	1,599	2,048	822	1,607	609	466	151	15	17
Unemployed	188	71	72	30	77	27	39	14	-	-
Economically active students (included above)	*7*	*6*	*5*	*5*	*1*	*1*	*1*	-	-	-
Economically inactive	234	345	40	89	30	80	62	36	102	140
Rented privately or with a job or business	**4,021**	**2,475**	**2,640**	**1,926**	**1,085**	**394**	**258**	**106**	**38**	**49**
Economically active	3,453	1,989	2,235	1,545	989	330	220	95	9	19
Unemployed	525	225	355	166	130	36	39	21	1	2
Economically active students (included above)	*52*	*45*	*48*	*43*	*4*	*2*	-	-	-	-
Economically inactive	568	486	405	381	96	64	38	11	29	30
Rented from a housing association	**363**	**446**	**125**	**196**	**92**	**89**	**69**	**26**	**77**	**135**
Economically active	237	176	114	112	73	45	46	16	4	3
Unemployed	103	54	60	37	23	13	20	4	-	-
Economically active students (included above)	-	*1*	-	*1*	-	-	-	-	-	-
Economically inactive	126	270	11	84	19	44	23	10	73	132
Rented from a local authority or new town	**1,321**	**1,473**	**525**	**755**	**381**	**335**	**231**	**105**	**184**	**278**
Economically active	947	427	475	224	328	136	138	60	6	7
Unemployed	365	129	178	77	133	32	54	20	-	-
Economically active students (included above)	-	*2*	-	*1*	-	*1*	-	-	-	-
Economically inactive	374	1,046	50	531	53	199	93	45	178	271
					Kingswood					
TOTAL HEADS	**1,939**	**763**	**874**	**339**	**665**	**199**	**274**	**63**	**126**	**162**
Owner occupied	**1,448**	**351**	**684**	**148**	**530**	**132**	**195**	**34**	**39**	**37**
Economically active	1,385	285	679	140	527	113	177	28	2	4
Unemployed	46	8	19	2	21	5	6	1	-	-
Economically active students (included above)	*1*	-	*1*	-	-	-	-	-	-	-
Economically inactive	63	66	5	8	3	19	18	6	37	33
Rented privately or with a job or business	**297**	**134**	**138**	**96**	**105**	**23**	**49**	**9**	**5**	**6**
Economically active	283	108	136	80	101	19	45	7	1	2
Unemployed	45	13	21	9	13	4	11	-	-	-
Economically active students (included above)	*1*	*1*	*1*	*1*	-	-	-	-	-	-
Economically inactive	14	26	2	16	4	4	4	2	4	4
Rented from a housing association	**45**	**52**	**13**	**11**	**9**	**12**	**8**	**5**	**15**	**24**
Economically active	24	11	11	2	8	4	5	3	-	2
Unemployed	7	2	2	-	2	1	3	1	-	-
Economically active students (included above)	-	-	-	-	-	-	-	-	-	-
Economically inactive	21	41	2	9	1	8	3	2	15	22
Rented from a local authority or new town	**149**	**226**	**39**	**84**	**21**	**32**	**22**	**15**	**67**	**95**
Economically active	73	44	37	16	20	17	14	10	2	1
Unemployed	22	6	16	2	6	2	-	2	-	-
Economically active students (included above)	-	-	-	-	-	-	-	-	-	-
Economically inactive	76	182	2	68	1	15	8	5	65	94

Tenure of household and economic activity of head	All households: age and sex of head									
	TOTAL HOUSEHOLD HEADS*		16 - 29*		30 - 44		45 up to pensionable age		Pensionable age and over	
	Males	Females	Males	Females	Males	Females	Males	Females	Males	Females
a	l	m	n	o	p	q	r	s	t	u
TOTAL HEADS	**102,720**	**54,058**	**15,703**	**10,658**	**31,271**	**12,039**	**33,043**	**7,458**	**22,703**	**23,903**
Owner occupied	**72,188**	**27,561**	**8,698**	**3,466**	**23,809**	**7,046**	**25,203**	**4,637**	**14,478**	**12,412**
Economically active	54,653	13,491	8,517	2,952	23,416	6,026	21,488	3,574	1,232	939
Unemployed	3,125	626	428	133	1,161	259	1,519	219	17	15
Economically active students (included above)	*45*	*44*	*15*	*20*	*25*	*21*	*5*	*3*	-	-
Economically inactive	17,535	14,070	181	514	393	1,020	3,715	1,063	13,246	11,473
Rented privately or with a job or business	**10,085**	**6,379**	**4,478**	**3,374**	**2,720**	**1,144**	**1,835**	**510**	**1,052**	**1,351**
Economically active	8,061	4,162	3,819	2,696	2,496	947	1,610	412	136	107
Unemployed	1,278	476	616	289	372	114	287	70	3	3
Economically active students (included above)	*85*	*74*	*72*	*65*	*13*	*9*	-	-	-	-
Economically inactive	2,024	2,217	659	678	224	197	225	98	916	1,244
Rented from a housing association	**2,348**	**3,464**	**341**	**587**	**543**	**642**	**542**	**305**	**922**	**1,930**
Economically active	1,153	956	306	323	441	386	365	189	41	58
Unemployed	411	231	132	104	157	85	120	42	2	-
Economically active students (included above)	*4*	*3*	*1*	*1*	*3*	*2*	-	-	-	-
Economically inactive	1,195	2,508	35	264	102	256	177	116	881	1,872
Rented from a local authority or new town	**18,099**	**16,654**	**2,186**	**3,231**	**4,199**	**3,207**	**5,463**	**2,006**	**6,251**	**8,210**
Economically active	9,894	4,055	2,039	991	3,765	1,601	3,774	1,164	316	299
Unemployed	2,888	850	727	276	1,130	310	1,018	244	13	20
Economically active students (included above)	*5*	*13*	*3*	*6*	*2*	*7*	-	-	-	-
Economically inactive	8,205	12,599	147	2,240	434	1,606	1,689	842	5,935	7,911
TOTAL HEADS	**26,136**	**8,521**	**2,941**	**1,068**	**8,478**	**1,802**	**9,754**	**1,340**	**4,963**	**4,311**
Owner occupied	**22,684**	**5,551**	**2,483**	**581**	**7,696**	**1,375**	**8,851**	**1,047**	**3,654**	**2,548**
Economically active	18,155	2,631	2,467	496	7,625	1,144	7,755	808	308	183
Unemployed	766	95	71	14	257	43	437	37	1	1
Economically active students (included above)	*4*	*3*	*1*	*1*	*2*	*2*	*1*	-	-	-
Economically inactive	4,529	2,920	16	85	71	231	1,096	239	3,346	2,365
Rented privately or with a job or business	**845**	**455**	**249**	**165**	**260**	**75**	**188**	**46**	**148**	**169**
Economically active	667	230	246	128	249	58	163	33	9	11
Unemployed	99	24	43	14	32	7	24	3	-	-
Economically active students (included above)	*1*	*1*	*1*	*1*	-	-	-	-	-	-
Economically inactive	178	225	3	37	11	17	25	13	139	158
Rented from a housing association	**274**	**347**	**23**	**35**	**80**	**54**	**58**	**38**	**113**	**220**
Economically active	147	74	21	8	75	29	45	30	6	7
Unemployed	41	9	4	1	24	3	12	5	1	-
Economically active students (included above)	-	-	-	-	-	-	-	-	-	-
Economically inactive	127	273	2	27	5	25	13	8	107	213
Rented from a local authority or new town	**2,333**	**2,168**	**186**	**287**	**442**	**298**	**657**	**209**	**1,048**	**1,374**
Economically active	1,109	413	175	87	402	165	490	130	42	31
Unemployed	218	52	51	15	84	15	82	22	1	-
Economically active students (included above)	-	-	-	-	-	-	-	-	-	-
Economically inactive	1,224	1,755	11	200	40	133	167	79	1,006	1,343

Table 45 Migrant household heads – **continued**

Note: * May include a small number of heads aged under 16

45. Households with residents

Tenure of household and economic activity of head	Households with head with different address one year before census: age and sex of head									
	Total migrant heads*		16 - 29*		30 - 44		45 up to pensionable age		Pensionable age and over	
	Males	Females	Males	Females	Males	Females	Males	Females	Males	Females
a	b	c	d	e	f	g	h	i	j	k
					Northavon					
TOTAL HEADS	**3,835**	**1,340**	**1,653**	**628**	**1,431**	**342**	**576**	**135**	**175**	**235**
Owner occupied	**2,995**	**737**	**1,333**	**371**	**1,136**	**207**	**439**	**80**	**87**	**79**
Economically active	2,865	609	1,329	355	1,125	179	404	69	7	6
Unemployed	92	27	45	10	29	8	18	8	-	1
Economically active students (included above)	*2*	-	*1*	-	*1*	-	-	-	-	-
Economically inactive	130	128	4	16	11	28	35	11	80	73
Rented privately or with a job or business	**562**	**222**	**231**	**123**	**225**	**67**	**87**	**19**	**19**	**13**
Economically active	526	172	222	99	219	55	82	16	3	2
Unemployed	45	12	14	7	20	2	11	3	-	-
Economically active students (included above)	*6*	*1*	*6*	*1*	-	-	-	-	-	-
Economically inactive	36	50	9	24	6	12	5	3	16	11
Rented from a housing association	**33**	**36**	**13**	**10**	**9**	**8**	**7**	**3**	**4**	**15**
Economically active	27	16	13	9	8	4	6	3	-	-
Unemployed	3	2	2	1	-	-	1	1	-	-
Economically active students (included above)	-	-	-	-	-	-	-	-	-	-
Economically inactive	6	20	-	1	1	4	1	-	4	15
Rented from a local authority or new town	**245**	**345**	**76**	**124**	**61**	**60**	**43**	**33**	**65**	**128**
Economically active	155	89	71	35	55	29	27	21	2	4
Unemployed	40	13	17	6	16	4	7	3	-	-
Economically active students (included above)	-	-	-	-	-	-	-	-	-	-
Economically inactive	90	256	5	89	6	31	16	12	63	124
					Wansdyke					
TOTAL HEADS	**1,649**	**609**	**593**	**254**	**625**	**156**	**313**	**65**	**118**	**134**
Owner occupied	**1,151**	**312**	**387**	**104**	**472**	**102**	**230**	**42**	**62**	**64**
Economically active	1,063	227	384	98	469	85	199	39	11	5
Unemployed	41	6	10	2	21	3	10	1	-	-
Economically active students (included above)	*1*	-	-	-	*1*	-	-	-	-	-
Economically inactive	88	85	3	6	3	17	31	3	51	59
Rented privately or with a job or business	**327**	**134**	**143**	**83**	**111**	**31**	**66**	**12**	**7**	**8**
Economically active	307	109	135	72	110	26	61	11	1	-
Unemployed	31	9	15	7	7	1	9	1	-	-
Economically active students (included above)	*1*	*3*	*1*	*3*	-	-	-	-	-	-
Economically inactive	20	25	8	11	1	5	5	1	6	8
Rented from a housing association	**11**	**12**	**3**	**6**	**-**	**1**	**3**	**1**	**5**	**4**
Economically active	4	3	3	3	-	-	1	-	-	-
Unemployed	-	1	-	1	-	-	-	-	-	-
Economically active students (included above)	-	-	-	-	-	-	-	-	-	-
Economically inactive	7	9	-	3	-	1	2	1	5	4
Rented from a local authority or new town	**160**	**151**	**60**	**61**	**42**	**22**	**14**	**10**	**44**	**58**
Economically active	113	43	59	21	41	13	10	7	3	2
Unemployed	26	6	14	2	12	-	-	4	-	-
Economically active students (included above)	*1*	-	*1*	-	-	-	-	-	-	-
Economically inactive	47	108	1	40	1	9	4	3	41	56

TOTAL HOUSEHOLD HEADS*		16 - 29*		30 - 44		45 up to pensionable age		Pensionable age and over		Tenure of household and economic activity of head
All households: age and sex of head										
Males	Females	Males	Females	Males	Females	Males	Females	Males	Females	
l	m	n	o	p	q	r	s	t	u	a
38,400	**11,226**	**5,661**	**1,817**	**12,733**	**2,504**	**14,008**	**1,940**	**5,998**	**4,965**	**TOTAL HEADS**
33,611	**7,717**	**4,938**	**1,215**	**11,639**	**1,968**	**12,546**	**1,509**	**4,488**	**3,025**	**Owner occupied**
28,042	4,126	4,916	1,063	11,542	1,631	11,176	1,186	408	246	Economically active
1,009	151	190	29	304	59	511	61	4	2	Unemployed
10	*3*	*3*	-	*5*	*2*	*1*	*1*	*1*	-	*Economically active students (included above)*
5,569	3,591	22	152	97	337	1,370	323	4,080	2,779	Economically inactive
1,919	**788**	**451**	**229**	**593**	**162**	**553**	**96**	**322**	**301**	**Rented privately or with a job or business**
1,580	411	433	187	581	128	505	79	61	17	Economically active
114	32	31	16	48	6	35	10	-	-	Unemployed
7	*1*	*7*	*1*	-	-	-	-	-	-	*Economically active students (included above)*
339	377	18	42	12	34	48	17	261	284	Economically inactive
271	**327**	**51**	**62**	**49**	**37**	**69**	**29**	**102**	**199**	**Rented from a housing association**
150	94	51	41	46	29	49	21	4	3	Economically active
20	8	7	2	8	5	5	1	-	-	Unemployed
-	-	-	-	-	-	-	-	-	-	*Economically active students (included above)*
121	233	-	21	3	8	20	8	98	196	Economically inactive
2,599	**2,394**	**221**	**311**	**452**	**337**	**840**	**306**	**1,086**	**1,440**	**Rented from a local authority or new town**
1,335	521	210	90	413	201	652	190	60	40	Economically active
255	59	53	13	84	20	118	26	-	-	Unemployed
-	*2*	-	*1*	-	*1*	-	-	-	-	*Economically active students (included above)*
1,264	1,873	11	221	39	136	188	116	1,026	1,400	Economically inactive
23,174	**7,640**	**2,073**	**741**	**7,070**	**1,409**	**8,776**	**1,307**	**5,255**	**4,183**	**TOTAL HEADS**
19,328	**4,963**	**1,594**	**373**	**6,219**	**1,018**	**7,623**	**1,012**	**3,892**	**2,560**	**Owner occupied**
14,837	2,147	1,584	309	6,173	864	6,666	768	414	206	Economically active
470	48	60	8	178	16	232	23	-	1	Unemployed
3	*1*	*1*	-	*2*	*1*	-	-	-	-	*Economically active students (included above)*
4,491	2,816	10	64	46	154	957	244	3,478	2,354	Economically inactive
1,337	**624**	**266**	**143**	**384**	**117**	**408**	**83**	**279**	**281**	**Rented privately or with a job or business**
1,045	300	255	124	379	96	374	65	37	15	Economically active
80	21	27	10	28	3	24	8	1	-	Unemployed
2	*3*	*2*	*3*	-	-	-	-	-	-	*Economically active students (included above)*
292	324	11	19	5	21	34	18	242	266	Economically inactive
148	**141**	**20**	**19**	**29**	**26**	**31**	**16**	**68**	**80**	**Rented from a housing association**
69	35	19	6	29	18	19	11	2	-	Economically active
11	4	4	2	3	-	4	2	-	-	Unemployed
-	-	-	-	-	-	-	-	-	-	*Economically active students (included above)*
79	106	1	13	-	8	12	5	66	80	Economically inactive
2,361	**1,912**	**193**	**206**	**438**	**248**	**714**	**196**	**1,016**	**1,262**	**Rented from a local authority or new town**
1,180	397	185	78	403	144	536	120	56	55	Economically active
211	43	48	6	66	15	96	22	1	-	Unemployed
1	-	*1*	-	-	-	-	-	-	-	*Economically active students (included above)*
1,181	1,515	8	128	35	104	178	76	960	1,207	Economically inactive

Note: * May include a small number of heads aged under 16

45. Households with residents

Tenure of household and economic activity of head	Households with head with different address one year before census: age and sex of head									
	Total migrant heads*		16 - 29*		30 - 44		45 up to pensionable age		Pensionable age and over	
	Males	Females	Males	Females	Males	Females	Males	Females	Males	Females
a	b	c	d	e	f	g	h	i	j	k
				Woodspring						
TOTAL HEADS	**4,501**	**1,874**	**1,684**	**847**	**1,640**	**465**	**817**	**203**	**360**	**359**
Owner occupied	**2,764**	**794**	**947**	**255**	**1,040**	**256**	**557**	**113**	**220**	**170**
Economically active	2,457	542	943	235	1,033	212	469	83	12	12
Unemployed	103	25	30	6	38	9	35	10	-	-
Economically active students (included above)	*2*	*1*	-	-	*1*	*1*	*1*	-	-	-
Economically inactive	307	252	4	20	7	44	88	30	208	158
Rented privately or with a job or business	**1,334**	**652**	**614**	**419**	**500**	**141**	**185**	**56**	**35**	**36**
Economically active	1,225	465	596	316	468	104	155	41	6	4
Unemployed	227	60	119	41	84	13	24	6	-	-
Economically active students (included above)	-	*8*	-	*6*	-	*2*	-	-	-	-
Economically inactive	109	187	18	103	32	37	30	15	29	32
Rented from a housing association	**44**	**69**	**7**	**18**	**12**	**8**	**8**	**4**	**17**	**39**
Economically active	19	15	7	6	7	4	4	3	1	2
Unemployed	6	2	2	1	3	1	1	-	-	-
Economically active students (included above)	-	-	-	-	-	-	-	-	-	-
Economically inactive	25	54	-	12	5	4	4	1	16	37
Rented from a local authority or new town	**359**	**359**	**116**	**155**	**88**	**60**	**67**	**30**	**88**	**114**
Economically active	222	98	110	47	76	28	30	17	6	6
Unemployed	85	22	46	11	27	5	12	5	-	1
Economically active students (included above)	-	-	-	-	-	-	-	-	-	-
Economically inactive	137	261	6	108	12	32	37	13	82	108

All households: age and sex of head										Tenure of household and economic activity of head
TOTAL HOUSEHOLD HEADS*		16 - 29*		30 - 44		45 up to pensionable age		Pensionable age and over		
Males	Females	Males	Females	Males	Females	Males	Females	Males	Females	
l	m	n	o	p	q	r	s	t	u	a
51,093	**19,426**	**5,226**	**2,139**	**15,398**	**3,534**	**18,562**	**3,115**	**11,907**	**10,638**	**TOTAL HEADS**
43,141	**12,934**	**3,759**	**891**	**13,427**	**2,481**	**16,509**	**2,370**	**9,446**	**7,192**	**Owner occupied**
31,879	4,916	3,722	738	13,287	2,001	14,096	1,751	774	426	Economically active
1,309	172	148	18	452	73	706	80	3	1	Unemployed
14	*8*	*5*	*4*	*5*	*4*	*4*	-	-	-	*Economically active students (included above)*
11,262	8,018	37	153	140	480	2,413	619	8,672	6,766	Economically inactive
3,703	**2,030**	**1,074**	**685**	**1,158**	**337**	**854**	**229**	**617**	**779**	**Rented privately or with a job or business**
2,958	1,009	1,033	530	1,100	255	754	169	71	55	Economically active
437	112	188	57	151	33	98	22	-	-	Unemployed
-	*11*	-	*8*	-	*3*	-	-	-	-	*Economically active students (included above)*
745	1,021	41	155	58	82	100	60	546	724	Economically inactive
426	**685**	**22**	**37**	**48**	**49**	**60**	**29**	**296**	**570**	**Rented from a housing association**
109	83	20	16	33	28	42	20	14	19	Economically active
23	10	3	3	10	5	9	2	1	-	Unemployed
-	-	-	-	-	-	-	-	-	-	*Economically active students (included above)*
317	602	2	21	15	21	18	9	282	551	Economically inactive
3,823	**3,777**	**371**	**526**	**765**	**667**	**1,139**	**487**	**1,548**	**2,097**	**Rented from a local authority or new town**
1,828	901	350	174	670	371	740	278	68	78	Economically active
455	112	114	28	167	40	171	42	3	2	Unemployed
-	*3*	-	*3*	-	-	-	-	-	-	*Economically active students (included above)*
1,995	2,876	21	352	95	296	399	209	1,480	2,019	Economically inactive

Table 46 Households with dependent children: housing

46. Households with dependent children; residents in such households

Household composition	TOTAL HOUSE-HOLDS	Over 1 and up to 1.5 persons per room	Over 1.5 persons per room	Lacking or sharing use of bath/ shower and/or inside WC	No central heating	Not self-contained accomm-odation	Tenure: Owner occupied	Tenure: Rented privately	Tenure: Rented from a housing association	Tenure: Rented from a local authority or new town	No car	TOTAL PERSONS IN HOUSE-HOLDS
a	b	c	d	e	f	g	h	i	j	k	l	m
AVON												
ALL HOUSEHOLDS WITH DEPENDENT CHILDREN	**106,256**	**3,968**	**660**	**294**	**10,480**	**426**	**80,722**	**3,604**	**1,727**	**18,562**	**14,835**	**416,239**
Households of 1 adult with 1 or more dependent children	**13,666**	**197**	**120**	**97**	**2,396**	**138**	**5,409**	**991**	**858**	**6,291**	**7,348**	**37,658**
Dependent child(ren) aged 0 - 4 only	3,399	20	60	49	643	68	770	378	281	1,943	2,263	7,765
Dependent child(ren) aged 5 and over only	7,878	32	42	34	1,288	53	3,978	492	418	2,919	3,588	20,911
Dependent children aged 0 - 4 and 5 and over	2,389	145	18	14	465	17	661	121	159	1,429	1,497	8,982
Dependent children in households of 1 adult with 1 or more dependent children												
All dependent children	23,992	817	221	145	4,252	190	9,361	1,461	1,434	11,533	13,043	
Dependent children aged 0 - 4	7,269	293	100	74	1,407	95	1,708	590	543	4,367	4,787	
Dependent children aged 5 - 15	15,214	509	111	65	2,619	80	6,727	750	844	6,767	7,727	
Dependent children aged 0 - 17	23,703	815	216	142	4,209	185	9,174	1,425	1,428	11,475	12,987	
Other households with dependent children	**92,590**	**3,771**	**540**	**197**	**8,084**	**288**	**75,313**	**2,613**	**869**	**12,271**	**7,487**	**378,581**
Dependent child(ren) aged 0 - 4 only	22,718	680	167	69	2,232	112	17,665	1,148	282	3,239	2,197	80,468
Dependent child(ren) aged 5 and over only	52,953	1,265	130	95	4,134	133	44,943	1,047	370	5,734	3,621	216,787
Dependent children aged 0 - 4 and 5 and over	16,919	1,826	243	33	1,718	43	12,705	418	217	3,298	1,669	81,326
Persons in other households with dependent children												
All adults	208,809	9,806	1,495	448	18,539	638	170,089	5,650	1,901	27,731	16,686	
All dependent children	169,772	11,518	1,655	335	15,181	481	136,144	4,328	1,666	24,817	14,134	
Dependent children aged 0 - 4	52,560	3,974	675	125	5,189	182	39,836	1,991	661	9,194	5,293	
Dependent children aged 5 - 15	103,818	7,101	906	184	9,144	240	84,446	2,071	937	14,652	8,048	
Dependent children aged 0 - 17	166,929	11,463	1,647	327	15,031	458	133,551	4,251	1,654	24,700	13,995	
Households with 3 or more dependent children	18,259	2,636	337	42	2,146	50	12,611	461	339	4,553	3,022	96,490
Households with 3 or more persons aged 0 - 15	16,457	2,506	319	40	1,992	44	11,115	425	325	4,330	2,841	87,206
Households with 4 or more dependent children	4,155	1,587	178	14	680	19	2,452	105	94	1,433	966	26,203
Households with 4 or more persons aged 0 - 15	3,676	1,469	169	13	617	14	2,103	88	84	1,347	892	23,273

46. Households with dependent children; residents in such households

Household composition	TOTAL HOUSE-HOLDS	Over 1 and up to 1.5 persons per room	Over 1.5 persons per room	Lacking or sharing use of bath/ shower and/or inside WC	No central heating	Not self-contained accomm-odation	Tenure: Owner occupied	Tenure: Rented privately	Tenure: Rented from a housing association	Tenure: Rented from a local authority or new town	No car	TOTAL PERSONS IN HOUSE-HOLDS
a	b	c	d	e	f	g	h	i	j	k	l	m
				Bath								
ALL HOUSEHOLDS WITH DEPENDENT CHILDREN	**8,005**	**362**	**63**	**37**	**553**	**72**	**5,420**	**429**	**160**	**1,869**	**1,552**	**30,733**
Households of 1 adult with 1 or more dependent children	**1,330**	**21**	**17**	**16**	**122**	**26**	**459**	**114**	**64**	**681**	**769**	**3,544**
Dependent child(ren) aged 0 - 4 only	335	2	8	6	35	15	53	39	21	220	244	747
Dependent child(ren) aged 5 and over only	806	2	7	7	79	7	372	66	33	329	402	2,089
Dependent children aged 0 - 4 and 5 and over	189	17	2	3	8	4	34	9	10	132	123	708
Dependent children in households of 1 adult with 1 or more dependent children												
All dependent children	2,214	80	31	25	195	35	758	157	102	1,176	1,277	
Dependent children aged 0 - 4	651	30	12	9	56	20	104	55	34	451	452	
Dependent children aged 5 - 15	1,384	50	17	13	118	13	558	76	63	675	759	
Dependent children aged 0 - 17	2,169	80	30	24	188	34	740	141	100	1,167	1,267	
Other households with dependent children	**6,675**	**341**	**46**	**21**	**431**	**46**	**4,961**	**315**	**96**	**1,188**	**783**	**27,189**
Dependent child(ren) aged 0 - 4 only	1,586	77	21	6	141	20	1,066	159	32	308	229	5,608
Dependent child(ren) aged 5 and over only	3,877	86	7	13	221	23	3,088	109	48	557	397	15,723
Dependent children aged 0 - 4 and 5 and over	1,212	178	18	2	69	3	807	47	16	323	157	5,858
Persons in other households with dependent children												
All adults	15,096	854	120	53	1,008	112	11,239	683	213	2,687	1,750	
All dependent children	12,093	973	119	33	703	68	8,866	499	160	2,377	1,410	
Dependent children aged 0 - 4	3,708	398	61	9	266	28	2,456	256	54	890	527	
Dependent children aged 5 - 15	7,295	541	57	22	377	34	5,460	205	101	1,408	802	
Dependent children aged 0 - 17	11,834	968	118	32	691	64	8,633	487	159	2,367	1,389	
Households with 3 or more dependent children	1,353	220	26	4	76	6	834	55	25	424	270	7,097
Households with 3 or more persons aged 0 - 15	1,212	210	25	4	70	6	721	47	25	406	259	6,376
Households with 4 or more dependent children	285	106	14	-	16	1	151	8	2	121	68	1,801
Households with 4 or more persons aged 0 - 15	257	98	14	-	15	1	133	7	2	112	63	1,631

Table 46 Households with dependent children: housing – continued

46. Households with dependent children; residents in such households

Household composition	TOTAL HOUSE-HOLDS	Over 1 and up to 1.5 persons per room	Over 1.5 persons per room	Lacking or sharing use of bath/ shower and/or inside WC	No central heating	Not self-contained accomm-odation	Tenure: Owner occupied	Tenure: Rented privately	Tenure: Rented from a housing association	Tenure: Rented from a local authority or new town	No car	TOTAL PERSONS IN HOUSE-HOLDS
a	b	c	d	e	f	g	h	i	j	k	l	m
Bristol												
ALL HOUSEHOLDS WITH DEPENDENT CHILDREN	**41,847**	**2,254**	**390**	**125**	**6,499**	**231**	**27,696**	**1,509**	**1,099**	**11,029**	**8,923**	**163,552**
Households of 1 adult with 1 or more dependent children	**7,225**	**135**	**59**	**36**	**1,669**	**78**	**2,225**	**475**	**610**	**3,857**	**4,411**	**20,084**
Dependent child(ren) aged 0 - 4 only	1,964	11	22	17	420	29	357	183	193	1,214	1,391	4,500
Dependent child(ren) aged 5 and over only	3,851	24	25	13	884	38	1,561	242	300	1,717	2,065	10,178
Dependent children aged 0 - 4 and 5 and over	1,410	100	12	6	365	11	307	50	117	926	955	5,406
Dependent children in households of 1 adult with 1 or more dependent children												
All dependent children	12,859	564	125	52	3,027	113	3,827	680	1,037	7,216	7,943	
Dependent children aged 0 - 4	4,267	200	46	26	1,000	46	784	277	391	2,780	2,998	
Dependent children aged 5 - 15	7,948	351	72	23	1,884	55	2,708	350	615	4,216	4,654	
Dependent children aged 0 - 17	12,750	562	122	50	3,004	110	3,764	666	1,034	7,189	7,913	
Other households with dependent children	**34,622**	**2,119**	**331**	**89**	**4,830**	**153**	**25,471**	**1,034**	**489**	**7,172**	**4,512**	**143,468**
Dependent child(ren) aged 0 - 4 only	9,212	383	95	27	1,273	55	6,510	493	152	1,944	1,318	32,816
Dependent child(ren) aged 5 and over only	18,471	686	73	48	2,417	74	14,371	382	205	3,257	2,134	76,497
Dependent children aged 0 - 4 and 5 and over	6,939	1,050	163	14	1,140	24	4,590	159	132	1,971	1,060	34,155
Persons in other households with dependent children												
All adults	78,613	5,492	959	204	11,120	345	58,021	2,243	1,086	16,214	10,133	
All dependent children	64,855	6,562	1,098	148	9,447	268	46,652	1,688	931	14,716	8,719	
Dependent children aged 0 - 4	21,480	2,255	442	47	3,213	97	14,502	846	372	5,506	3,246	
Dependent children aged 5 - 15	39,057	4,067	602	88	5,770	140	28,580	739	514	8,683	5,002	
Dependent children aged 0 - 17	63,954	6,531	1,092	144	9,359	257	45,885	1,651	922	14,645	8,639	
Households with 3 or more dependent children	8,071	1,518	230	16	1,502	31	4,723	189	213	2,846	1,974	43,008
Households with 3 or more persons aged 0 - 15	7,385	1,450	217	15	1,408	28	4,196	178	205	2,718	1,856	39,477
Households with 4 or more dependent children	2,149	950	123	6	508	14	1,072	41	72	934	663	13,668
Households with 4 or more persons aged 0 - 15	1,940	886	115	5	469	11	935	38	66	878	611	12,389

Table 46 Households with dependent children: housing – **continued**

46. Households with dependent children; residents in such households

Household composition	TOTAL HOUSE-HOLDS	Over 1 and up to 1.5 persons per room	Over 1.5 persons per room	Lacking or sharing use of bath/shower and/or inside WC	No central heating	Not self-contained accomm-odation	Tenure: Owner occupied	Tenure: Rented privately	Tenure: Rented from a housing association	Tenure: Rented from a local authority or new town	No car	TOTAL PERSONS IN HOUSE-HOLDS
a	b	c	d	e	f	g	h	i	j	k	l	m
Kingswood												
ALL HOUSEHOLDS WITH DEPENDENT CHILDREN	**10,656**	**276**	**28**	**12**	**360**	**13**	**9,108**	**232**	**156**	**1,085**	**842**	**41,710**
Households of 1 adult with 1 or more dependent children	**1,038**	**9**	**5**	**5**	**56**	**4**	**564**	**58**	**63**	**347**	**436**	**2,862**
Dependent child(ren) aged 0 - 4 only	221	1	4	3	22	4	69	21	20	111	124	507
Dependent child(ren) aged 5 and over only	628	2	1	1	30	-	414	23	29	157	212	1,684
Dependent children aged 0 - 4 and 5 and over	189	6	-	1	4	-	81	14	14	79	100	671
Dependent children in households of 1 adult with 1 or more dependent children												
All dependent children	1,824	36	8	8	85	4	1,000	93	118	601	782	
Dependent children aged 0 - 4	517	15	4	5	33	4	186	44	42	243	293	
Dependent children aged 5 - 15	1,192	21	4	3	48	-	732	44	73	334	452	
Dependent children aged 0 - 17	1,806	36	8	8	84	4	986	92	118	598	781	
Other households with dependent children	**9,618**	**267**	**23**	**7**	**304**	**9**	**8,544**	**174**	**93**	**738**	**406**	**38,848**
Dependent child(ren) aged 0 - 4 only	2,343	41	9	5	102	6	2,047	83	19	176	117	8,251
Dependent child(ren) aged 5 and over only	5,554	99	5	2	154	2	5,035	66	46	372	208	22,521
Dependent children aged 0 - 4 and 5 and over	1,721	127	9	-	48	1	1,462	25	28	190	81	8,076
Persons in other households with dependent children												
All adults	21,579	723	61	19	697	18	19,163	375	200	1,691	911	
All dependent children	17,269	802	60	9	516	13	15,215	290	200	1,436	725	
Dependent children aged 0 - 4	5,411	282	33	7	191	8	4,625	143	62	535	276	
Dependent children aged 5 - 15	10,676	486	27	2	296	5	9,493	131	131	846	415	
Dependent children aged 0 - 17	17,044	799	60	9	511	13	14,999	289	200	1,428	714	
Households with 3 or more dependent children	1,594	179	11	1	46	-	1,279	32	42	226	148	8,324
Households with 3 or more persons aged 0 - 15	1,454	170	11	1	41	-	1,158	30	40	211	135	7,601
Households with 4 or more dependent children	279	101	7	1	11	-	196	10	10	61	33	1,746
Households with 4 or more persons aged 0 - 15	251	92	7	1	10	-	175	5	9	60	31	1,576

Table 46 Households with dependent children: housing – **continued**

46. Households with dependent children; residents in such households

Household composition	TOTAL HOUSE-HOLDS	Over 1 and up to 1.5 persons per room	Over 1.5 persons per room	Lacking or sharing use of bath/ shower and/or inside WC	No central heating	Not self-contained accomm-odation	Tenure				No car	TOTAL PERSONS IN HOUSE-HOLDS
							Owner occupied	Rented privately	Rented from a housing association	Rented from a local authority or new town		
a	b	c	d	e	f	g	h	i	j	k	l	m
Northavon												
ALL HOUSEHOLDS WITH DEPENDENT CHILDREN	**16,116**	**404**	**54**	**42**	**696**	**19**	**14,003**	**429**	**123**	**1,291**	**948**	**63,430**
Households of 1 adult with 1 or more dependent children	**1,322**	**7**	**4**	**7**	**81**	**-**	**792**	**89**	**47**	**384**	**502**	**3,649**
Dependent child(ren) aged 0 - 4 only	279	2	-	2	19	-	118	21	21	116	147	657
Dependent child(ren) aged 5 and over only	853	-	2	3	44	-	583	55	21	187	260	2,303
Dependent children aged 0 - 4 and 5 and over	190	5	2	2	18	-	91	13	5	81	95	689
Dependent children in households of 1 adult with 1 or more dependent children												
All dependent children	2,327	27	11	15	151	-	1,397	155	61	691	870	
Dependent children aged 0 - 4	608	14	2	4	47	-	257	41	31	272	325	
Dependent children aged 5 - 15	1,542	13	9	11	97	-	1,005	105	27	392	508	
Dependent children aged 0 - 17	2,288	27	11	15	148	-	1,366	154	60	685	865	
Other households with dependent children	**14,794**	**397**	**50**	**35**	**615**	**19**	**13,211**	**340**	**76**	**907**	**446**	**59,781**
Dependent child(ren) aged 0 - 4 only	3,723	81	11	8	180	6	3,253	129	30	236	129	13,128
Dependent child(ren) aged 5 and over only	8,614	153	12	15	338	8	7,842	147	28	456	228	35,088
Dependent children aged 0 - 4 and 5 and over	2,457	163	27	12	97	5	2,116	64	18	215	89	11,565
Persons in other households with dependent children												
All adults	33,216	1,048	129	77	1,428	39	29,623	747	163	2,093	1,000	
All dependent children	26,565	1,187	156	74	1,076	35	23,591	592	149	1,770	802	
Dependent children aged 0 - 4	8,187	383	59	29	348	12	7,083	246	69	633	295	
Dependent children aged 5 - 15	16,187	749	92	42	653	18	14,478	319	78	1,040	453	
Dependent children aged 0 - 17	26,099	1,180	156	74	1,066	32	23,141	589	149	1,760	796	
Households with 3 or more dependent children	2,458	263	33	14	122	4	2,038	68	19	285	163	12,916
Households with 3 or more persons aged 0 - 15	2,208	248	31	13	114	1	1,812	65	19	270	155	11,630
Households with 4 or more dependent children	491	163	15	4	35	-	381	18	4	79	44	3,060
Households with 4 or more persons aged 0 - 15	426	143	14	4	26	-	325	14	3	77	42	2,657

46. Households with dependent children; residents in such households

Household composition	TOTAL HOUSE-HOLDS	Over 1 and up to 1.5 persons per room	Over 1.5 persons per room	Lacking or sharing use of bath/ shower and/or inside WC	No central heating	Not self-contained accomm-odation	Tenure: Owner occupied	Tenure: Rented privately	Tenure: Rented from a housing association	Tenure: Rented from a local authority or new town	No car	TOTAL PERSONS IN HOUSE-HOLDS
a	b	c	d	e	f	g	h	i	j	k	l	m
Wansdyke												
ALL HOUSEHOLDS WITH DEPENDENT CHILDREN	**9,261**	**214**	**18**	**15**	**703**	**9**	**7,718**	**226**	**69**	**1,057**	**581**	**36,868**
Households of 1 adult with 1 or more dependent children	**695**	**5**	**3**	**6**	**98**	**2**	**369**	**42**	**22**	**252**	**250**	**1,878**
Dependent child(ren) aged 0 - 4 only	133	2	3	3	24	2	41	15	10	65	62	296
Dependent child(ren) aged 5 and over only	468	-	-	3	60	-	298	23	9	130	139	1,244
Dependent children aged 0 - 4 and 5 and over	94	3	-	-	14	-	30	4	3	57	49	338
Dependent children in households of 1 adult with 1 or more dependent children												
All dependent children	1,183	22	5	8	167	2	624	62	30	454	442	
Dependent children aged 0 - 4	267	9	5	5	48	2	82	23	14	146	130	
Dependent children aged 5 - 15	801	13	-	3	109	-	452	33	15	292	283	
Dependent children aged 0 - 17	1,160	22	5	8	164	2	605	60	30	452	439	
Other households with dependent children	**8,566**	**209**	**15**	**9**	**605**	**7**	**7,349**	**184**	**47**	**805**	**331**	**34,990**
Dependent child(ren) aged 0 - 4 only	1,892	22	2	4	142	3	1,547	69	22	212	90	6,687
Dependent child(ren) aged 5 and over only	5,204	87	5	3	337	2	4,628	82	15	378	155	21,324
Dependent children aged 0 - 4 and 5 and over	1,470	100	8	2	126	2	1,174	33	10	215	86	6,979
Persons in other households with dependent children												
All adults	19,286	565	40	20	1,392	14	16,564	414	99	1,801	737	
All dependent children	15,704	664	49	15	1,120	13	13,401	299	95	1,579	652	
Dependent children aged 0 - 4	4,439	191	13	8	341	5	3,595	122	46	572	241	
Dependent children aged 5 - 15	9,833	448	36	6	708	7	8,491	164	46	938	381	
Dependent children aged 0 - 17	15,393	661	49	14	1,109	13	13,107	295	94	1,574	647	
Households with 3 or more dependent children	1,529	149	9	1	126	2	1,218	25	15	239	121	8,088
Households with 3 or more persons aged 0 - 15	1,335	140	9	1	110	2	1,044	23	13	227	114	7,080
Households with 4 or more dependent children	303	87	5	-	34	-	223	5	2	67	46	1,908
Households with 4 or more persons aged 0 - 15	241	83	5	-	29	-	171	3	1	63	42	1,530

Table 46 Households with dependent children: housing – **continued**

46. Households with dependent children; residents in such households

Household composition	TOTAL HOUSE-HOLDS	Over 1 and up to 1.5 persons per room	Over 1.5 persons per room	Lacking or sharing use of bath/ shower and/or inside WC	No central heating	Not self-contained accomm-odation	Tenure: Owner occupied	Tenure: Rented privately	Tenure: Rented from a housing association	Tenure: Rented from a local authority or new town	No car	TOTAL PERSONS IN HOUSE-HOLDS
a	b	c	d	e	f	g	h	i	j	k	l	m
Woodspring												
ALL HOUSEHOLDS WITH DEPENDENT CHILDREN	**20,371**	**458**	**107**	**63**	**1,669**	**82**	**16,777**	**779**	**120**	**2,231**	**1,989**	**79,946**
Households of 1 adult with 1 or more dependent children	**2,056**	**20**	**32**	**27**	**370**	**28**	**1,000**	**213**	**52**	**770**	**980**	**5,641**
Dependent child(ren) aged 0 - 4 only	467	2	23	18	123	18	132	99	16	217	295	1,058
Dependent child(ren) aged 5 and over only	1,272	4	7	7	191	8	750	83	26	399	510	3,413
Dependent children aged 0 - 4 and 5 and over	317	14	2	2	56	2	118	31	10	154	175	1,170
Dependent children in households of 1 adult with 1 or more dependent children												
All dependent children	3,585	88	41	37	627	36	1,755	314	86	1,395	1,729	
Dependent children aged 0 - 4	959	25	31	25	223	23	295	150	31	475	589	
Dependent children aged 5 - 15	2,347	61	9	12	363	12	1,272	142	51	858	1,071	
Dependent children aged 0 - 17	3,530	88	40	37	621	35	1,713	312	86	1,384	1,722	
Other households with dependent children	**18,315**	**438**	**75**	**36**	**1,299**	**54**	**15,777**	**566**	**68**	**1,461**	**1,009**	**74,305**
Dependent child(ren) aged 0 - 4 only	3,962	76	29	19	394	22	3,242	215	27	363	314	13,978
Dependent child(ren) aged 5 and over only	11,233	154	28	14	667	24	9,979	261	28	714	499	45,634
Dependent children aged 0 - 4 and 5 and over	3,120	208	18	3	238	8	2,556	90	13	384	196	14,693
Persons in other households with dependent children												
All adults	41,019	1,124	186	75	2,894	110	35,479	1,188	140	3,245	2,155	
All dependent children	33,286	1,330	173	56	2,319	84	28,419	960	131	2,939	1,826	
Dependent children aged 0 - 4	9,335	465	67	25	830	32	7,575	378	58	1,058	708	
Dependent children aged 5 - 15	20,770	810	92	24	1,340	36	17,944	513	67	1,737	995	
Dependent children aged 0 - 17	32,605	1,324	172	54	2,295	79	27,786	940	130	2,926	1,810	
Households with 3 or more dependent children	3,254	307	28	6	274	7	2,519	92	25	533	346	17,057
Households with 3 or more persons aged 0 - 15	2,863	288	26	6	249	7	2,184	82	23	498	322	15,042
Households with 4 or more dependent children	648	180	14	3	76	4	429	23	4	171	112	4,020
Households with 4 or more persons aged 0 - 15	561	167	14	3	68	2	364	21	3	157	103	3,490

Table 47 Households with pensioners: housing

47. Households with one or more residents of pensionable age; residents in such households

Household composition	TOTAL HOUSE-HOLDS	Up to 0.5 persons per room	Lacking or sharing use of bath/shower and/or inside WC	No central heating	Lacking or sharing use of bath/shower and/or inside WC and/or no central heating	Not self-contained accommodation
a	b	c	d	e	f	g
AVON						
TOTAL HOUSEHOLDS WITH 1 OR MORE PENSIONER(S)	**126,696**	**112,288**	**1,459**	**22,907**	**23,404**	**895**
Lone male 65 - 74	5,555	5,294	192	1,444	1,488	135
Lone male 75 - 84	4,627	4,455	120	1,222	1,254	66
Lone male 85 and over	1,273	1,221	36	387	396	8
Lone female 60 - 74	21,099	20,822	186	3,592	3,666	177
Lone female 75 - 84	17,569	17,050	331	3,620	3,772	169
Lone female 85 and over	5,640	5,370	189	1,368	1,429	80
2 or more, all pensioners, under 75	22,778	21,122	81	2,962	2,993	65
2 or more, all pensioners, any aged 75 and over	16,566	14,321	157	3,138	3,180	79
1 or more pensioner(s) with 1 non-pensioner	22,223	19,322	119	3,772	3,807	80
1 or more pensioner(s) with 2 or more non-pensioners	9,366	3,311	48	1,402	1,419	36
TOTAL PERSONS IN HOUSEHOLDS WITH PENSIONERS	**219,727**	**177,071**	**1,979**	**37,615**	**38,275**	**1,256**
Total persons of pensionable age	**172,148**	**150,449**	**1,737**	**30,196**	**30,779**	**1,075**
Pensionable age - 74	109,116	95,304	729	16,927	17,167	578
75 - 84	50,948	44,660	707	10,355	10,610	369
85 and over	12,084	10,485	301	2,914	3,002	128
Persons with limiting long-term illness						
Pensionable age - 74	29,283	24,880	243	4,900	4,982	154
75 - 84	21,971	19,019	320	4,305	4,424	171
85 and over	7,312	6,289	201	1,662	1,734	79
Bath						
TOTAL HOUSEHOLDS WITH 1 OR MORE PENSIONER(S)	**13,078**	**11,670**	**181**	**2,137**	**2,204**	**189**
Lone male 65 - 74	572	537	23	122	127	26
Lone male 75 - 84	515	492	19	120	125	16
Lone male 85 and over	124	120	3	43	45	-
Lone female 60 - 74	2,339	2,299	34	349	360	46
Lone female 75 - 84	2,023	1,971	35	369	386	27
Lone female 85 and over	683	653	30	160	171	14
2 or more, all pensioners, under 75	2,180	2,002	7	249	252	16
2 or more, all pensioners, any aged 75 and over	1,809	1,522	15	320	328	22
1 or more pensioner(s) with 1 non-pensioner	2,088	1,772	10	305	307	13
1 or more pensioner(s) with 2 or more non-pensioners	745	302	5	100	103	9
TOTAL PERSONS IN HOUSEHOLDS WITH PENSIONERS	**21,728**	**17,922**	**228**	**3,379**	**3,467**	**268**
Total persons of pensionable age	**17,668**	**15,468**	**205**	**2,823**	**2,901**	**231**
Pensionable age - 74	10,766	9,403	85	1,437	1,464	124
75 - 84	5,547	4,873	79	1,062	1,098	83
85 and over	1,355	1,192	41	324	339	24
Persons with limiting long-term illness						
Pensionable age - 74	2,459	2,089	24	379	387	23
75 - 84	2,202	1,898	27	410	427	32
85 and over	816	716	33	178	192	14

Tenure: Owner occupied	Tenure: Rented privately: Furnished	Tenure: Rented privately: Unfurnished	Tenure: Rented with a job or business	Tenure: Rented from a housing association	Tenure: Rented from a local authority or new town	No car	Persons with limiting long-term illness	Household composition
h	i	j	k	l	m	n	o	a
84,604	**1,292**	**4,398**	**1,084**	**5,385**	**29,933**	**61,862**	**65,106**	**TOTAL HOUSEHOLDS WITH 1 OR MORE PENSIONER(S)**
2,935	191	238	83	307	1,801	2,686	1,944	Lone male 65 - 74
2,562	116	222	61	322	1,344	2,895	1,971	Lone male 75 - 84
699	30	73	12	93	366	1,054	674	Lone male 85 and over
12,486	227	807	155	1,181	6,243	15,408	5,787	Lone female 60 - 74
9,334	247	970	102	1,553	5,363	15,719	7,773	Lone female 75 - 84
2,740	101	349	29	591	1,830	5,432	3,430	Lone female 85 and over
17,476	84	458	153	414	4,193	5,075	12,459	2 or more, all pensioners, under 75
11,796	102	676	111	574	3,307	7,603	13,489	2 or more, all pensioners, any aged 75 and over
17,092	116	477	239	264	4,035	4,807	11,814	1 or more pensioner(s) with 1 non-pensioner
7,484	78	128	139	86	1,451	1,183	5,765	1 or more pensioner(s) with 2 or more non-pensioners
156,253	**1,865**	**6,428**	**2,071**	**6,950**	**46,160**	**83,470**	**65,106**	**TOTAL PERSONS IN HOUSEHOLDS WITH PENSIONERS**
118,724	**1,509**	**5,642**	**1,439**	**6,446**	**38,388**	**75,657**	**58,566**	**Total persons of pensionable age**
78,560	775	2,731	959	2,881	23,210	36,419		Pensionable age - 74
32,850	550	2,283	388	2,737	12,140	30,296		75 - 84
7,314	184	628	92	828	3,038	8,942		85 and over
								Persons with limiting long-term illness
18,576	219	792	273	1,039	8,384	12,316		Pensionable age - 74
13,287	241	935	158	1,259	6,091	14,299		75 - 84
4,338	105	361	48	505	1,955	5,426		85 and over
8,502	**172**	**692**	**98**	**754**	**2,860**	**7,121**	**5,963**	**TOTAL HOUSEHOLDS WITH 1 OR MORE PENSIONER(S)**
283	25	35	6	45	178	309	169	Lone male 65 - 74
285	13	29	7	48	133	338	193	Lone male 75 - 84
61	5	10	-	13	35	108	72	Lone male 85 and over
1,392	33	147	17	159	591	1,705	593	Lone female 60 - 74
1,055	35	151	12	214	556	1,829	844	Lone female 75 - 84
320	18	57	3	111	174	667	408	Lone female 85 and over
1,698	18	53	14	43	354	556	936	2 or more, all pensioners, under 75
1,264	8	122	12	75	328	893	1,344	2 or more, all pensioners, any aged 75 and over
1,566	14	74	13	35	386	596	984	1 or more pensioner(s) with 1 non-pensioner
578	3	14	14	11	125	120	420	1 or more pensioner(s) with 2 or more non-pensioners
15,045	**222**	**989**	**196**	**947**	**4,329**	**9,587**	**5,963**	**TOTAL PERSONS IN HOUSEHOLDS WITH PENSIONERS**
11,943	**198**	**885**	**137**	**882**	**3,623**	**8,704**	**5,477**	**Total persons of pensionable age**
7,690	112	413	85	369	2,097	4,091		Pensionable age - 74
3,479	58	371	45	362	1,232	3,526		75 - 84
774	28	101	7	151	294	1,087		85 and over
								Persons with limiting long-term illness
1,518	15	84	26	101	715	1,231		Pensionable age - 74
1,296	21	123	22	164	576	1,507		75 - 84
460	17	60	3	94	182	656		85 and over

47. Households with one or more residents of pensionable age; residents in such households

Household composition	TOTAL HOUSE-HOLDS	Up to 0.5 persons per room	Lacking or sharing use of bath/shower and/or inside WC	No central heating	Lacking or sharing use of bath/shower and/or inside WC and/or no central heating	Not self-contained accommodation
a	b	c	d	e	f	g
	Bristol					
TOTAL HOUSEHOLDS WITH 1 OR MORE PENSIONER(S)	**52,842**	**46,617**	**749**	**12,510**	**12,753**	**484**
Lone male 65 - 74	2,647	2,490	114	822	854	80
Lone male 75 - 84	2,039	1,951	62	654	667	41
Lone male 85 and over	545	522	18	204	206	6
Lone female 60 - 74	9,245	9,109	90	2,031	2,073	87
Lone female 75 - 84	7,560	7,324	175	1,980	2,051	98
Lone female 85 and over	2,469	2,357	87	747	770	52
2 or more, all pensioners, under 75	8,686	8,003	36	1,592	1,607	26
2 or more, all pensioners, any aged 75 and over	6,420	5,594	86	1,653	1,667	28
1 or more pensioner(s) with 1 non-pensioner	9,288	8,020	61	2,065	2,087	48
1 or more pensioner(s) with 2 or more non-pensioners	3,943	1,247	20	762	771	18
TOTAL PERSONS IN HOUSEHOLDS WITH PENSIONERS	**90,561**	**72,089**	**1,009**	**20,437**	**20,761**	**649**
Total persons of pensionable age	**70,561**	**61,371**	**895**	**16,368**	**16,650**	**554**
Pensionable age - 74	44,431	38,390	378	9,281	9,421	291
75 - 84	21,041	18,511	377	5,500	5,613	191
85 and over	5,089	4,470	140	1,587	1,616	72
Persons with limiting long-term illness						
Pensionable age - 74	12,946	10,882	125	2,730	2,782	76
75 - 84	9,432	8,244	174	2,346	2,391	91
85 and over	3,143	2,740	90	929	951	41
	Kingswood					
TOTAL HOUSEHOLDS WITH 1 OR MORE PENSIONER(S)	**10,904**	**9,648**	**65**	**1,166**	**1,180**	**8**
Lone male 65 - 74	444	436	4	68	68	-
Lone male 75 - 84	387	376	6	79	80	1
Lone male 85 and over	96	93	-	16	16	-
Lone female 60 - 74	1,725	1,714	6	168	169	1
Lone female 75 - 84	1,384	1,350	18	186	189	1
Lone female 85 and over	464	439	12	83	88	1
2 or more, all pensioners, under 75	2,149	1,988	4	148	149	3
2 or more, all pensioners, any aged 75 and over	1,308	1,088	7	154	156	1
1 or more pensioner(s) with 1 non-pensioner	2,103	1,849	8	209	210	-
1 or more pensioner(s) with 2 or more non-pensioners	844	315	-	55	55	-
TOTAL PERSONS IN HOUSEHOLDS WITH PENSIONERS	**19,285**	**15,505**	**85**	**1,881**	**1,899**	**12**
Total persons of pensionable age	**14,949**	**12,986**	**77**	**1,536**	**1,553**	**12**
Pensionable age - 74	9,892	8,642	24	817	822	7
75 - 84	4,084	3,524	34	559	565	4
85 and over	973	820	19	160	166	1
Persons with limiting long-term illness						
Pensionable age - 74	2,636	2,220	8	245	247	2
75 - 84	1,797	1,516	13	214	218	2
85 and over	633	527	15	99	103	1

Tenure						No car	Persons with limiting long-term illness	Household composition
Owner occupied	Rented privately		Rented with a job or business	Rented from a housing association	Rented from a local authority or new town			
	Furnished	Unfurnished						
h	i	j	k	l	m	n	o	a
31,739	**534**	**1,645**	**449**	**2,932**	**15,543**	**29,497**	**28,557**	**TOTAL HOUSEHOLDS WITH 1 OR MORE PENSIONER(S)**
1,194	96	102	39	194	1,022	1,479	985	Lone male 65 - 74
1,000	58	96	25	181	679	1,414	896	Lone male 75 - 84
284	11	25	6	53	166	483	294	Lone male 85 and over
4,772	92	337	78	663	3,303	7,303	2,681	Lone female 60 - 74
3,625	89	377	39	871	2,559	6,968	3,503	Lone female 75 - 84
1,121	42	113	8	295	890	2,388	1,560	Lone female 85 and over
6,023	24	152	55	200	2,232	2,638	5,179	2 or more, all pensioners, under 75
4,233	28	223	45	278	1,613	3,466	5,438	2 or more, all pensioners, any aged 75 and over
6,556	47	176	105	147	2,257	2,647	5,443	1 or more pensioner(s) with 1 non-pensioner
2,931	47	44	49	50	822	711	2,578	1 or more pensioner(s) with 2 or more non-pensioners
58,559	**795**	**2,340**	**815**	**3,744**	**24,308**	**40,716**	**28,557**	**TOTAL PERSONS IN HOUSEHOLDS WITH PENSIONERS**
43,967	**597**	**2,057**	**575**	**3,454**	**19,911**	**36,213**	**25,521**	**Total persons of pensionable age**
28,692	321	1,016	383	1,541	12,478	18,397		Pensionable age - 74
12,402	211	839	154	1,495	5,940	13,843		75 - 84
2,873	65	202	38	418	1,493	3,973		85 and over
								Persons with limiting long-term illness
7,266	88	310	107	598	4,577	6,354		Pensionable age - 74
5,128	92	371	62	706	3,073	6,676		75 - 84
1,718	38	112	20	252	1,003	2,459		85 and over
7,660	**73**	**215**	**59**	**338**	**2,559**	**5,005**	**5,652**	**TOTAL HOUSEHOLDS WITH 1 OR MORE PENSIONER(S)**
259	7	11	3	14	150	199	158	Lone male 65 - 74
224	7	15	2	26	113	239	169	Lone male 75 - 84
55	2	2	-	7	30	81	59	Lone male 85 and over
1,067	8	32	5	70	543	1,301	470	Lone female 60 - 74
737	12	45	7	97	486	1,299	641	Lone female 75 - 84
214	9	19	2	40	180	454	298	Lone female 85 and over
1,719	9	20	8	30	363	404	1,143	2 or more, all pensioners, under 75
919	6	34	8	38	303	611	1,076	2 or more, all pensioners, any aged 75 and over
1,743	3	27	16	15	299	347	1,106	1 or more pensioner(s) with 1 non-pensioner
723	10	10	8	1	92	70	532	1 or more pensioner(s) with 2 or more non-pensioners
14,467	**119**	**325**	**110**	**431**	**3,833**	**6,637**	**5,652**	**TOTAL PERSONS IN HOUSEHOLDS WITH PENSIONERS**
10,784	**90**	**276**	**77**	**413**	**3,309**	**6,117**	**5,066**	**Total persons of pensionable age**
7,539	45	123	52	184	1,949	2,934		Pensionable age - 74
2,678	26	120	19	178	1,063	2,450		75 - 84
567	19	33	6	51	297	733		85 and over
								Persons with limiting long-term illness
1,763	16	40	17	67	733	999		Pensionable age - 74
1,109	18	42	6	73	549	1,173		75 - 84
362	12	22	4	34	199	479		85 and over

Table 47 Households with pensioners: housing – continued

47. Households with one or more residents of pensionable age; residents in such households

Household composition	TOTAL HOUSE-HOLDS	Up to 0.5 persons per room	Lacking or sharing use of bath/shower and/or inside WC	No central heating	Lacking or sharing use of bath/shower and/or inside WC and/or no central heating	Not self-contained accommodation
a	b	c	d	e	f	g
	Northavon					
TOTAL HOUSEHOLDS WITH 1 OR MORE PENSIONER(S)	**13,037**	**11,543**	**89**	**1,785**	**1,803**	**12**
Lone male 65 - 74	533	518	11	105	107	1
Lone male 75 - 84	431	417	6	113	114	1
Lone male 85 and over	112	107	-	25	25	-
Lone female 60 - 74	2,000	1,978	7	264	265	1
Lone female 75 - 84	1,613	1,568	20	234	241	3
Lone female 85 and over	456	429	9	78	79	-
2 or more, all pensioners, under 75	2,534	2,406	10	230	232	1
2 or more, all pensioners, any aged 75 and over	1,656	1,456	9	264	267	3
1 or more pensioner(s) with 1 non-pensioner	2,537	2,255	9	322	323	1
1 or more pensioner(s) with 2 or more non-pensioners	1,165	409	8	150	150	1
TOTAL PERSONS IN HOUSEHOLDS WITH PENSIONERS	**23,574**	**18,868**	**140**	**3,087**	**3,111**	**19**
Total persons of pensionable age	**17,856**	**15,675**	**111**	**2,378**	**2,401**	**16**
Pensionable age - 74	11,727	10,369	54	1,330	1,339	7
75 - 84	5,055	4,422	44	852	864	8
85 and over	1,074	884	13	196	198	1
Persons with limiting long-term illness						
Pensionable age - 74	2,946	2,555	16	355	360	2
75 - 84	2,168	1,878	18	355	359	3
85 and over	629	511	7	107	109	1
	Wansdyke					
TOTAL HOUSEHOLDS WITH 1 OR MORE PENSIONER(S)	**11,001**	**9,815**	**134**	**1,746**	**1,805**	**14**
Lone male 65 - 74	412	412	9	108	108	-
Lone male 75 - 84	402	399	12	95	100	-
Lone male 85 and over	121	116	4	31	33	-
Lone female 60 - 74	1,627	1,623	15	220	229	2
Lone female 75 - 84	1,362	1,356	29	246	264	4
Lone female 85 and over	420	412	23	96	105	-
2 or more, all pensioners, under 75	2,173	2,037	10	256	259	1
2 or more, all pensioners, any aged 75 and over	1,526	1,335	15	248	253	2
1 or more pensioner(s) with 1 non-pensioner	2,012	1,781	11	302	308	3
1 or more pensioner(s) with 2 or more non-pensioners	946	344	6	144	146	2
TOTAL PERSONS IN HOUSEHOLDS WITH PENSIONERS	**19,879**	**16,008**	**187**	**3,031**	**3,112**	**26**
Total persons of pensionable age	**15,304**	**13,467**	**162**	**2,357**	**2,426**	**18**
Pensionable age - 74	9,912	8,717	59	1,392	1,414	10
75 - 84	4,401	3,897	68	759	792	5
85 and over	991	853	35	206	220	3
Persons with limiting long-term illness						
Pensionable age - 74	2,318	2,008	15	359	362	4
75 - 84	1,749	1,519	31	306	323	2
85 and over	579	489	23	118	130	2

Owner occupied	Rented privately: Furnished	Rented privately: Unfurnished	Rented with a job or business	Rented from a housing association	Rented from a local authority or new town	No car	Persons with limiting long-term illness	Household composition
h	i	j	k	l	m	n	o	a
9,327	**93**	**460**	**143**	**328**	**2,686**	**5,017**	**6,432**	**TOTAL HOUSEHOLDS WITH 1 OR MORE PENSIONER(S)**
336	9	22	11	16	139	192	175	Lone male 65 - 74
259	6	20	10	14	122	242	189	Lone male 75 - 84
57	1	6	3	4	41	88	53	Lone male 85 and over
1,297	16	70	11	78	528	1,344	517	Lone female 60 - 74
879	16	95	9	77	537	1,393	682	Lone female 75 - 84
210	2	35	3	28	178	437	265	Lone female 85 and over
2,028	9	59	30	35	373	342	1,319	2 or more, all pensioners, under 75
1,223	13	67	16	32	305	595	1,333	2 or more, all pensioners, any aged 75 and over
2,063	16	66	28	33	331	304	1,235	1 or more pensioner(s) with 1 non-pensioner
975	5	20	22	11	132	80	664	1 or more pensioner(s) with 2 or more non-pensioners
17,846	**151**	**723**	**289**	**466**	**4,099**	**6,504**	**6,432**	**TOTAL PERSONS IN HOUSEHOLDS WITH PENSIONERS**
13,090	**119**	**603**	**203**	**403**	**3,438**	**6,007**	**5,743**	**Total persons of pensionable age**
9,011	60	307	140	225	1,984	2,753		Pensionable age - 74
3,409	48	234	51	139	1,174	2,570		75 - 84
670	11	62	12	39	280	684		85 and over
								Persons with limiting long-term illness
2,059	18	91	38	74	666	889		Pensionable age - 74
1,406	15	103	23	70	551	1,213		75 - 84
398	5	34	8	24	160	391		85 and over
7,805	**91**	**411**	**120**	**154**	**2,420**	**4,350**	**5,184**	**TOTAL HOUSEHOLDS WITH 1 OR MORE PENSIONER(S)**
246	3	22	5	15	121	162	141	Lone male 65 - 74
243	8	19	8	5	119	218	160	Lone male 75 - 84
66	4	11	2	1	37	93	62	Lone male 85 and over
1,063	13	57	14	32	448	1,075	405	Lone female 60 - 74
747	28	68	9	33	477	1,163	553	Lone female 75 - 84
205	7	48	3	10	147	398	238	Lone female 85 and over
1,729	7	58	20	15	344	335	1,037	2 or more, all pensioners, under 75
1,100	11	70	10	29	306	570	1,152	2 or more, all pensioners, any aged 75 and over
1,623	8	41	31	9	300	272	923	1 or more pensioner(s) with 1 non-pensioner
783	2	17	18	5	121	64	513	1 or more pensioner(s) with 2 or more non-pensioners
14,877	**129**	**632**	**250**	**221**	**3,770**	**5,749**	**5,184**	**TOTAL PERSONS IN HOUSEHOLDS WITH PENSIONERS**
11,120	**112**	**552**	**165**	**198**	**3,157**	**5,317**	**4,646**	**Total persons of pensionable age**
7,560	42	278	114	100	1,818	2,415		Pensionable age - 74
2,947	57	198	39	76	1,084	2,244		75 - 84
613	13	76	12	22	255	658		85 and over
								Persons with limiting long-term illness
1,578	17	73	26	32	592	767		Pensionable age - 74
1,100	22	80	10	23	514	1,013		75 - 84
363	6	42	5	13	150	375		85 and over

Table 47 Households with pensioners: housing - **continued**

47. Households with one or more residents of pensionable age; residents in such households

Household composition	TOTAL HOUSE-HOLDS	Up to 0.5 persons per room	Lacking or sharing use of bath/shower and/or inside WC	No central heating	Lacking or sharing use of bath/shower and/or inside WC and/or no central heating	Not self-contained accommodation
a	b	c	d	e	f	g
	Woodspring					
TOTAL HOUSEHOLDS WITH 1 OR MORE PENSIONER(S)	**25,834**	**22,995**	**241**	**3,563**	**3,659**	**188**
Lone male 65 - 74	947	901	31	219	224	28
Lone male 75 - 84	853	820	15	161	168	7
Lone male 85 and over	275	263	11	68	71	2
Lone female 60 - 74	4,163	4,099	34	560	570	40
Lone female 75 - 84	3,627	3,481	54	605	641	36
Lone female 85 and over	1,148	1,080	28	204	216	13
2 or more, all pensioners, under 75	5,056	4,686	14	487	494	18
2 or more, all pensioners, any aged 75 and over	3,847	3,326	25	499	509	23
1 or more pensioner(s) with 1 non-pensioner	4,195	3,645	20	569	572	15
1 or more pensioner(s) with 2 or more non-pensioners	1,723	694	9	191	194	6
TOTAL PERSONS IN HOUSEHOLDS WITH PENSIONERS	**44,700**	**36,679**	**330**	**5,800**	**5,925**	**282**
Total persons of pensionable age	**35,810**	**31,482**	**287**	**4,734**	**4,848**	**244**
Pensionable age - 74	22,388	19,783	129	2,670	2,707	139
75 - 84	10,820	9,433	105	1,623	1,678	78
85 and over	2,602	2,266	53	441	463	27
Persons with limiting long-term illness						
Pensionable age - 74	5,978	5,126	55	832	844	47
75 - 84	4,623	3,964	57	674	706	41
85 and over	1,512	1,306	33	231	249	20

Tenure						No car	Persons with limiting long-term illness	Household composition
Owner occupied	Rented privately		Rented with a job or business	Rented from a housing association	Rented from a local authority or new town			
	Furnished	Unfurnished						
h	i	j	k	l	m	n	o	a
19,571	**329**	**975**	**215**	**879**	**3,865**	**10,872**	**13,318**	**TOTAL HOUSEHOLDS WITH 1 OR MORE PENSIONER(S)**
617	51	46	19	23	191	345	316	Lone male 65 - 74
551	24	43	9	48	178	444	364	Lone male 75 - 84
176	7	19	1	15	57	201	134	Lone male 85 and over
2,895	65	164	30	179	830	2,680	1,121	Lone female 60 - 74
2,291	67	234	26	261	748	3,067	1,550	Lone female 75 - 84
670	23	77	10	107	261	1,088	661	Lone female 85 and over
4,279	17	116	26	91	527	800	2,845	2 or more, all pensioners, under 75
3,057	36	160	20	122	452	1,468	3,146	2 or more, all pensioners, any aged 75 and over
3,541	28	93	46	25	462	641	2,123	1 or more pensioner(s) with 1 non-pensioner
1,494	11	23	28	8	159	138	1,058	1 or more pensioner(s) with 2 or more non-pensioners
35,459	**449**	**1,419**	**411**	**1,141**	**5,821**	**14,277**	**13,318**	**TOTAL PERSONS IN HOUSEHOLDS WITH PENSIONERS**
27,820	**393**	**1,269**	**282**	**1,096**	**4,950**	**13,299**	**12,113**	**Total persons of pensionable age**
18,068	195	594	185	462	2,884	5,829		Pensionable age - 74
7,935	150	521	80	487	1,647	5,663		75 - 84
1,817	48	154	17	147	419	1,807		85 and over
								Persons with limiting long-term illness
4,392	65	194	59	167	1,101	2,076		Pensionable age - 74
3,248	73	216	35	223	828	2,717		75 - 84
1,037	27	91	8	88	261	1,066		85 and over

48. Households with residents

Non-dependants, dependants and age of youngest or only dependant	Age of oldest dependant	ALL HOUSE-HOLDS	Over 1 person per room	Lacking or sharing use of bath/shower and/or inside WC	No central heating	Not self-contained accomm-odation	No car
a	b	c	d	e	f	g	h
		AVON					
TOTAL HOUSEHOLDS		**376,522**	**5,574**	**4,510**	**55,041**	**5,955**	**101,740**
1 or more non-dependants, no dependants		216,109	845	3,422	34,363	5,007	58,456
1 dependent male living alone							
0 up to pensionable age		1,928		102	587	130	1,296
Pensionable age - 74		1,840		66	463	42	1,074
75 - 84		1,934		48	484	28	1,383
85 and over		663		20	191	3	584
1 dependent female living alone							
0 up to pensionable age		1,335		42	309	68	1,006
Pensionable age - 74		4,719		49	836	34	3,905
75 - 84		6,154		130	1,174	55	5,778
85 and over		2,683		106	602	39	2,616
2 or more persons dependant, no non-dependants							
0 up to pensionable age	0 up to pensionable age	728	9	5	131	5	352
	Pensionable age - 74	480	3	3	92	1	191
	75 - 84	178	-	5	46	1	92
	85 and over	58	-	-	16	-	32
Pensionable age - 74	Pensionable age - 74	2,572	2	12	374	6	906
	75 - 84	1,083	1	8	181	5	572
	85 and over	238	-	3	37	1	95
75 - 84	75 - 84	1,418	2	16	278	9	835
	85 and over	347	-	9	76	3	261
85 and over	85 and over	186	-	5	47	1	140
1 male non-dependant with 1 or more dependant(s)							
0 - 4	0 - 4	128	5	6	26	10	46
	5 - 15	107	3	-	17	-	41
	16 up to pensionable age	154	11	2	13	-	27
	Pensionable age and over	1	-	-	1	-	-
5 - 15	5 - 15	712	6	2	126	4	199
	16 up to pensionable age	334	4	1	40	-	54
	Pensionable age and over	16	-	-	1	-	6
16 up to pensionable age	16 up to pensionable age	2,010	14	19	328	15	441
	Pensionable age and over	119	-	2	19	-	23
Pensionable age and over	Pensionable age and over	4,836	7	48	952	15	1,468
1 female non-dependant with 1 or more dependant(s)							
0 - 4	0 - 4	3,246	74	42	608	56	2,202
	5 - 15	2,200	151	14	428	16	1,410
	16 up to pensionable age	386	62	2	79	3	151
	Pensionable age and over	25	2	-	8	1	10
5 - 15	5 - 15	5,731	54	26	959	36	2,870
	16 up to pensionable age	1,034	33	4	169	4	311
	Pensionable age and over	75	1	-	7	-	28
16 up to pensionable age	16 up to pensionable age	4,791	16	18	742	29	1,320
	Pensionable age and over	192	2	-	29	1	52
Pensionable age and over	Pensionable age and over	8,625	5	56	1,359	39	3,496
2 or more non-dependants with 1 or more dependant(s)							
0 - 4	0 - 4	22,168	801	66	2,141	105	2,049
	5 - 15	16,006	1,823	31	1,583	34	1,502
	16 up to pensionable age	728	191	-	106	10	117
	Pensionable age and over	205	34	1	25	-	28
5 - 15	5 - 15	39,326	963	63	3,156	81	2,619
	16 up to pensionable age	6,035	320	9	394	16	345
	Pensionable age and over	419	31	2	49	-	35
16 up to pensionable age	16 up to pensionable age	9,274	78	27	879	27	855
	Pensionable age and over	174	7	1	29	2	22
Pensionable age and over	Pensionable age and over	2,812	14	17	481	13	439

48. Households with residents

Non-dependants, dependants and age of youngest or only dependant	Age of oldest dependant	ALL HOUSE-HOLDS	Over 1 person per room	Lacking or sharing use of bath/ shower and/or inside WC	No central heating	Not self-contained accomm-odation	No car
a	b	c	d	e	f	g	h
		Bath					
TOTAL HOUSEHOLDS		**34,128**	**578**	**560**	**4,795**	**975**	**12,148**
1 or more non-dependants, no dependants		21,181	147	438	3,366	832	7,557
1 dependent male living alone							
0 up to pensionable age		207		6	59	13	148
Pensionable age - 74		162		6	35	5	112
75 - 84		191		5	44	6	136
85 and over		72		3	20	-	65
1 dependent female living alone							
0 up to pensionable age		117		3	24	9	100
Pensionable age - 74		487		9	76	4	407
75 - 84		677		11	115	6	637
85 and over		313		23	72	6	311
2 or more persons dependant, no non-dependants							
0 up to pensionable age	0 up to pensionable age	53	-	-	7	1	27
	Pensionable age - 74	37	-	-	5	1	10
	75 - 84	20	-	1	3	-	11
	85 and over	8	-	-	3	-	6
Pensionable age - 74	Pensionable age - 74	180	-	1	20	3	71
	75 - 84	104	-	1	17	1	65
	85 and over	26	-	-	5	-	13
75 - 84	75 - 84	126	-	3	24	4	76
	85 and over	35	-	1	7	2	25
85 and over	85 and over	19	-	-	4	-	14
1 male non-dependant with 1 or more dependant(s)							
0 - 4	0 - 4	13	-	1	2	1	6
	5 - 15	9	1	-	1	-	4
	16 up to pensionable age	11	2	-	1	-	4
	Pensionable age and over	-	-	-	-	-	-
5 - 15	5 - 15	62	1	-	10	-	19
	16 up to pensionable age	25	1	-	3	-	7
	Pensionable age and over	2	-	-	-	-	2
16 up to pensionable age	16 up to pensionable age	150	3	-	20	3	40
	Pensionable age and over	9	-	-	3	-	5
Pensionable age and over	Pensionable age and over	425	-	5	88	1	164
1 female non-dependant with 1 or more dependant(s)							
0 - 4	0 - 4	317	10	5	31	13	235
	5 - 15	176	18	3	7	4	116
	16 up to pensionable age	20	3	-	1	-	9
	Pensionable age and over	-	-	-	-	-	-
5 - 15	5 - 15	576	6	4	49	5	321
	16 up to pensionable age	83	-	2	11	1	25
	Pensionable age and over	3	-	-	-	-	1
16 up to pensionable age	16 up to pensionable age	350	2	2	39	1	134
	Pensionable age and over	11	-	-	1	-	4
Pensionable age and over	Pensionable age and over	840	-	5	126	7	405
2 or more non-dependants with 1 or more dependant(s)							
0 - 4	0 - 4	1,552	91	6	139	20	217
	5 - 15	1,160	181	2	66	3	152
	16 up to pensionable age	43	12	-	2	-	5
	Pensionable age and over	14	5	-	1	-	1
5 - 15	5 - 15	2,788	55	11	158	18	302
	16 up to pensionable age	453	30	-	18	-	31
	Pensionable age and over	27	2	-	2	-	3
16 up to pensionable age	16 up to pensionable age	751	5	3	63	3	88
	Pensionable age and over	16	1	-	4	-	3
Pensionable age and over	Pensionable age and over	227	2	-	43	2	54

48. Households with residents

Non-dependants, dependants and age of youngest or only dependant	Age of oldest dependant	ALL HOUSE-HOLDS	Over 1 person per room	Lacking or sharing use of bath/ shower and/or inside WC	No central heating	Not self-contained accomm-odation	No car
a	b	c	d	e	f	g	h
		Bristol					
TOTAL HOUSEHOLDS		**156,778**	**3,181**	**2,675**	**31,218**	**3,833**	**53,558**
1 or more non-dependants, no dependants		90,473	481	2,136	18,938	3,294	30,270
1 dependent male living alone							
0 up to pensionable age		1,092		60	346	81	815
Pensionable age - 74		923		41	272	27	590
75 - 84		876		24	260	16	665
85 and over		289		8	98	2	270
1 dependent female living alone							
0 up to pensionable age		745		30	198	42	581
Pensionable age - 74		2,211		21	486	18	1,924
75 - 84		2,836		68	689	37	2,700
85 and over		1,247		45	343	25	1,219
2 or more persons dependant, no non-dependants							
0 up to pensionable age	0 up to pensionable age	390	6	4	79	3	217
	Pensionable age - 74	257	2	2	60	-	114
	75 - 84	92	-	3	28	-	59
	85 and over	28	-	-	10	-	17
Pensionable age - 74	Pensionable age - 74	1,120	2	5	203	2	468
	75 - 84	439	1	5	87	3	273
	85 and over	113	-	2	16	-	50
75 - 84	75 - 84	592	-	8	152	1	394
	85 and over	141	-	4	43	-	112
85 and over	85 and over	71	-	3	28	1	52
1 male non-dependant with 1 or more dependant(s)							
0 - 4	0 - 4	80	1	3	17	7	32
	5 - 15	66	2	-	13	-	28
	16 up to pensionable age	72	9	1	9	-	15
	Pensionable age and over	1	-	-	1	-	-
5 - 15	5 - 15	327	3	-	75	3	123
	16 up to pensionable age	125	2	1	25	-	27
	Pensionable age and over	9	-	-	1	-	3
16 up to pensionable age	16 up to pensionable age	884	7	10	183	10	264
	Pensionable age and over	53	-	-	7	-	11
Pensionable age and over	Pensionable age and over	2,127	4	28	524	10	759
1 female non-dependant with 1 or more dependant(s)							
0 - 4	0 - 4	1,870	32	13	398	22	1,349
	5 - 15	1,294	102	6	334	10	897
	16 up to pensionable age	211	37	1	53	1	96
	Pensionable age and over	14	-	-	7	1	6
5 - 15	5 - 15	2,907	36	10	684	25	1,653
	16 up to pensionable age	489	25	1	107	2	193
	Pensionable age and over	35	1	-	4	-	20
16 up to pensionable age	16 up to pensionable age	2,060	9	6	430	19	731
	Pensionable age and over	86	1	-	23	-	28
Pensionable age and over	Pensionable age and over	3,531	3	27	753	19	1,707
2 or more non-dependants with 1 or more dependant(s)							
0 - 4	0 - 4	8,935	450	25	1,214	49	1,229
	5 - 15	6,472	1,061	13	1,044	20	939
	16 up to pensionable age	372	121	-	76	6	87
	Pensionable age and over	93	20	1	17	-	19
5 - 15	5 - 15	13,918	520	30	1,875	44	1,523
	16 up to pensionable age	2,022	174	4	212	9	215
	Pensionable age and over	168	16	2	29	-	22
16 up to pensionable age	16 up to pensionable age	3,332	42	15	502	17	525
	Pensionable age and over	68	4	-	9	-	15
Pensionable age and over	Pensionable age and over	1,222	7	9	256	7	252

Table 48 Households with dependants: housing – **continued**

48. Households with residents

Non-dependants, dependants and age of youngest or only dependant	Age of oldest dependant	ALL HOUSE-HOLDS	Over 1 person per room	Lacking or sharing use of bath/ shower and/or inside WC	No central heating	Not self-contained accomm-odation	No car
a	b	c	d	e	f	g	h
		Kingswood					
TOTAL HOUSEHOLDS		**34,657**	**339**	**156**	**2,499**	**120**	**7,045**
1 or more non-dependants, no dependants		19,318	30	117	1,645	103	3,993
1 dependent male living alone							
0 up to pensionable age		113		1	19	-	59
Pensionable age - 74		154		2	19	-	91
75 - 84		166		2	26	-	118
85 and over		58		-	11	-	51
1 dependent female living alone							
0 up to pensionable age		77		-	8	-	49
Pensionable age - 74		385		-	35	-	328
75 - 84		506		4	50	-	492
85 and over		220		6	33	1	217
2 or more persons dependant, no non-dependants							
0 up to pensionable age	0 up to pensionable age	52	1	-	4	-	17
	Pensionable age - 74	42	-	-	3	-	16
	75 - 84	7	-	-	2	-	3
	85 and over	5	-	-	1	-	3
Pensionable age - 74	Pensionable age - 74	244	-	1	17	-	77
	75 - 84	107	-	-	11	-	55
	85 and over	21	-	-	1	-	7
75 - 84	75 - 84	103	-	-	12	1	61
	85 and over	26	-	2	1	-	22
85 and over	85 and over	21	-	-	3	-	20
1 male non-dependant with 1 or more dependant(s)							
0 - 4	0 - 4	6	2	-	-	2	1
	5 - 15	7	-	-	-	-	2
	16 up to pensionable age	7	-	-	-	-	1
	Pensionable age and over	-	-	-	-	-	-
5 - 15	5 - 15	62	1	1	10	-	12
	16 up to pensionable age	30	-	-	2	-	4
	Pensionable age and over	1	-	-	-	-	-
16 up to pensionable age	16 up to pensionable age	183	-	2	20	-	31
	Pensionable age and over	8	-	-	-	-	-
Pensionable age and over	Pensionable age and over	429	-	2	47	-	98
1 female non-dependant with 1 or more dependant(s)							
0 - 4	0 - 4	213	3	3	21	2	123
	5 - 15	174	6	1	3	-	94
	16 up to pensionable age	27	3	-	2	1	8
	Pensionable age and over	-	-	-	-	-	-
5 - 15	5 - 15	459	2	-	17	-	167
	16 up to pensionable age	76	1	-	3	-	17
	Pensionable age and over	4	-	-	-	-	1
16 up to pensionable age	16 up to pensionable age	432	-	1	44	1	88
	Pensionable age and over	27	-	-	2	-	7
Pensionable age and over	Pensionable age and over	717	-	3	71	1	261
2 or more non-dependants with 1 or more dependant(s)							
0 - 4	0 - 4	2,306	48	5	100	5	107
	5 - 15	1,650	122	-	46	1	76
	16 up to pensionable age	60	11	-	3	-	6
	Pensionable age and over	19	2	-	-	-	2
5 - 15	5 - 15	4,354	80	2	121	2	166
	16 up to pensionable age	545	18	-	13	-	15
	Pensionable age and over	32	1	-	2	-	2
16 up to pensionable age	16 up to pensionable age	883	5	-	35	-	39
	Pensionable age and over	18	-	-	2	-	1
Pensionable age and over	Pensionable age and over	303	3	1	34	-	37

48. Households with residents

Non-dependants, dependants and age of youngest or only dependant	Age of oldest dependant	ALL HOUSE-HOLDS	Over 1 person per room	Lacking or sharing use of bath/ shower and/or inside WC	No central heating	Not self-contained accomm-odation	No car
a	b	c	d	e	f	g	h
		Northavon					
TOTAL HOUSEHOLDS		**49,626**	**517**	**224**	**4,282**	**102**	**7,332**
1 or more non-dependants, no dependants		28,267	53	142	2,884	80	4,289
1 dependent male living alone							
0 up to pensionable age		129		6	31	-	62
Pensionable age - 74		169		2	30	-	75
75 - 84		184		2	51	-	128
85 and over		53		-	13	-	45
1 dependent female living alone							
0 up to pensionable age		90		1	9	-	62
Pensionable age - 74		415		1	61	-	309
75 - 84		510		6	58	1	473
85 and over		203		3	30	-	200
2 or more persons dependant, no non-dependants							
0 up to pensionable age	0 up to pensionable age	72	-	-	6	-	23
	Pensionable age - 74	33	-	-	7	-	8
	75 - 84	12	-	-	3	-	3
	85 and over	3	-	-	-	-	-
Pensionable age - 74	Pensionable age - 74	263	-	2	21	-	67
	75 - 84	109	-	-	20	-	38
	85 and over	19	-	-	-	-	2
75 - 84	75 - 84	153	-	2	28	-	70
	85 and over	28	-	-	6	-	19
85 and over	85 and over	12	-	-	3	-	8
1 male non-dependant with 1 or more dependant(s)							
0 - 4	0 - 4	11	-	-	1	-	2
	5 - 15	10	-	-	-	-	5
	16 up to pensionable age	25	-	-	-	-	-
	Pensionable age and over	-	-	-	-	-	-
5 - 15	5 - 15	91	-	-	4	-	11
	16 up to pensionable age	40	1	-	3	-	3
	Pensionable age and over	1	-	-	-	-	-
16 up to pensionable age	16 up to pensionable age	255	-	4	25	-	37
	Pensionable age and over	18	-	1	3	-	2
Pensionable age and over	Pensionable age and over	520	-	3	75	1	124
1 female non-dependant with 1 or more dependant(s)							
0 - 4	0 - 4	265	2	2	18	-	144
	5 - 15	176	7	2	18	-	87
	16 up to pensionable age	33	3	-	2	-	10
	Pensionable age and over	3	1	-	1	-	2
5 - 15	5 - 15	593	2	3	33	-	210
	16 up to pensionable age	114	-	-	3	-	18
	Pensionable age and over	9	-	-	-	-	1
16 up to pensionable age	16 up to pensionable age	529	-	1	36	-	77
	Pensionable age and over	19	-	-	3	-	4
Pensionable age and over	Pensionable age and over	868	1	5	106	1	249
2 or more non-dependants with 1 or more dependant(s)							
0 - 4	0 - 4	3,657	90	8	173	6	124
	5 - 15	2,363	166	12	93	4	80
	16 up to pensionable age	75	20	-	5	1	2
	Pensionable age and over	25	2	-	2	-	1
5 - 15	5 - 15	6,427	117	12	256	5	167
	16 up to pensionable age	998	42	2	41	2	25
	Pensionable age and over	58	2	-	5	-	1
16 up to pensionable age	16 up to pensionable age	1,395	7	1	71	1	48
	Pensionable age and over	23	1	-	3	-	1
Pensionable age and over	Pensionable age and over	301	-	1	41	-	16

48. Households with residents

Non-dependants, dependants and age of youngest or only dependant	Age of oldest dependant	ALL HOUSE-HOLDS	Over 1 person per room	Lacking or sharing use of bath/ shower and/or inside WC	No central heating	Not self-contained accomm-odation	No car
a	b	c	d	e	f	g	h
		Wansdyke					
TOTAL HOUSEHOLDS		**30,814**	**254**	**240**	**3,624**	**87**	**5,717**
1 or more non-dependants, no dependants		17,509	21	161	2,235	72	3,373
1 dependent male living alone							
0 up to pensionable age		77		4	24	1	37
Pensionable age - 74		132		3	30	-	63
75 - 84		158		6	37	-	111
85 and over		61		4	18	-	48
1 dependent female living alone							
0 up to pensionable age		53		-	9	-	34
Pensionable age - 74		320		2	35	-	255
75 - 84		412		14	63	1	375
85 and over		175		12	39	-	168
2 or more persons dependant, no non-dependants							
0 up to pensionable age	0 up to pensionable age	28	-	1	3	-	12
	Pensionable age - 74	25	-	-	4	-	11
	75 - 84	8	-	-	3	-	2
	85 and over	2	-	-	-	-	1
Pensionable age - 74	Pensionable age - 74	179	-	-	27	-	48
	75 - 84	82	-	2	18	-	36
	85 and over	18	-	-	5	-	6
75 - 84	75 - 84	110	-	-	17	-	59
	85 and over	27	-	1	4	-	22
85 and over	85 and over	14	-	-	3	-	7
1 male non-dependant with 1 or more dependant(s)							
0 - 4	0 - 4	3	2	2	2	-	-
	5 - 15	3	-	-	1	-	-
	16 up to pensionable age	10	-	1	2	-	1
	Pensionable age and over	-	-	-	-	-	-
5 - 15	5 - 15	50	-	-	13	-	10
	16 up to pensionable age	22	-	-	2	-	1
	Pensionable age and over	2	-	-	-	-	1
16 up to pensionable age	16 up to pensionable age	134	-	-	27	-	20
	Pensionable age and over	10	-	-	1	-	1
Pensionable age and over	Pensionable age and over	376	-	4	72	1	84
1 female non-dependant with 1 or more dependant(s)							
0 - 4	0 - 4	130	3	1	22	2	62
	5 - 15	87	3	-	13	-	48
	16 up to pensionable age	20	5	-	3	-	4
	Pensionable age and over	1	-	-	-	-	-
5 - 15	5 - 15	312	-	3	37	-	102
	16 up to pensionable age	78	1	-	10	-	16
	Pensionable age and over	4	-	-	-	-	-
16 up to pensionable age	16 up to pensionable age	382	-	1	48	-	69
	Pensionable age and over	8	-	-	-	-	2
Pensionable age and over	Pensionable age and over	772	-	6	107	1	261
2 or more non-dependants with 1 or more dependant(s)							
0 - 4	0 - 4	1,860	24	4	137	3	85
	5 - 15	1,396	97	1	116	1	79
	16 up to pensionable age	63	5	-	8	1	7
	Pensionable age and over	15	1	-	2	-	-
5 - 15	5 - 15	3,819	72	2	257	2	120
	16 up to pensionable age	614	18	-	38	-	11
	Pensionable age and over	46	1	-	4	-	2
16 up to pensionable age	16 up to pensionable age	935	-	1	76	1	35
	Pensionable age and over	10	-	-	5	-	1
Pensionable age and over	Pensionable age and over	262	1	4	47	1	27

48. Households with residents

Non-dependants, dependants and age of youngest or only dependant	Age of oldest dependant	ALL HOUSE-HOLDS	Over 1 person per room	Lacking or sharing use of bath/ shower and/or inside WC	No central heating	Not self-contained accomm-odation	No car
a	b	c	d	e	f	g	h
		Woodspring					
TOTAL HOUSEHOLDS		**70,519**	**705**	**655**	**8,623**	**838**	**15,940**
1 or more non-dependants, no dependants		39,361	113	428	5,295	626	8,974
1 dependent male living alone							
0 up to pensionable age		310		25	108	35	175
Pensionable age - 74		300		12	77	10	143
75 - 84		359		9	66	6	225
85 and over		130		5	31	1	105
1 dependent female living alone							
0 up to pensionable age		253		8	61	17	180
Pensionable age - 74		901		16	143	12	682
75 - 84		1,213		27	199	10	1,101
85 and over		525		17	85	7	501
2 or more persons dependant, no non-dependants							
0 up to pensionable age	0 up to pensionable age	133	2	-	32	1	56
	Pensionable age - 74	86	1	1	13	-	32
	75 - 84	39	-	1	7	1	14
	85 and over	12	-	-	2	-	5
Pensionable age - 74	Pensionable age - 74	586	-	3	86	1	175
	75 - 84	242	-	-	28	1	105
	85 and over	41	-	1	10	1	17
75 - 84	75 - 84	334	2	3	45	3	175
	85 and over	90	-	1	15	1	61
85 and over	85 and over	49	-	2	6	-	39
1 male non-dependant with 1 or more dependant(s)							
0 - 4	0 - 4	15	-	-	4	-	5
	5 - 15	12	-	-	2	-	2
	16 up to pensionable age	29	-	-	1	-	6
	Pensionable age and over	-	-	-	-	-	-
5 - 15	5 - 15	120	1	1	14	1	24
	16 up to pensionable age	92	-	-	5	-	12
	Pensionable age and over	1	-	-	-	-	-
16 up to pensionable age	16 up to pensionable age	404	4	3	53	2	49
	Pensionable age and over	21	-	1	5	-	4
Pensionable age and over	Pensionable age and over	959	3	6	146	2	239
1 female non-dependant with 1 or more dependant(s)							
0 - 4	0 - 4	451	24	18	118	17	289
	5 - 15	293	15	2	53	2	168
	16 up to pensionable age	75	11	1	18	1	24
	Pensionable age and over	7	1	-	-	-	2
5 - 15	5 - 15	884	8	6	139	6	417
	16 up to pensionable age	194	6	1	35	1	42
	Pensionable age and over	20	-	-	3	-	5
16 up to pensionable age	16 up to pensionable age	1,038	5	7	145	8	221
	Pensionable age and over	41	1	-	-	1	7
Pensionable age and over	Pensionable age and over	1,897	1	10	196	10	613
2 or more non-dependants with 1 or more dependant(s)							
0 - 4	0 - 4	3,858	98	18	378	22	287
	5 - 15	2,965	196	3	218	5	176
	16 up to pensionable age	115	22	-	12	2	10
	Pensionable age and over	39	4	-	3	-	5
5 - 15	5 - 15	8,020	119	6	489	10	341
	16 up to pensionable age	1,403	38	3	72	5	48
	Pensionable age and over	88	9	-	7	-	5
16 up to pensionable age	16 up to pensionable age	1,978	19	7	132	5	120
	Pensionable age and over	39	1	1	6	2	1
Pensionable age and over	Pensionable age and over	497	1	2	60	3	53

49. Households with residents; residents in households

	TOTAL HOUSE-HOLDS	Ethnic group of household head										Household head born in:	
		White	Black Caribbean	Black African	Black other	Indian	Pakistani	Bangladeshi	Chinese	Other groups		New Common-wealth	Ireland
										Asian	Other		
a	b	c	d	e	f	g	h	i	j	k	l	m	n
AVON													
ALL HOUSEHOLDS	**376,522**	**368,457**	**3,227**	**352**	**534**	**1,100**	**628**	**177**	**664**	**384**	**999**	**7,971**	**5,667**
Over 1 and up to 1.5 persons per room	4,177	3,710	85	26	19	92	115	36	41	21	32	378	69
Over 1.5 persons per room	1,397	1,225	21	15	7	23	41	18	18	11	18	134	41
Owner occupied - owned outright	99,184	98,200	392	11	27	157	152	7	102	26	110	1,429	1,302
- buying	172,569	168,779	1,411	138	170	669	344	96	321	195	446	4,217	2,184
Rented privately	27,725	26,728	186	100	77	148	43	17	135	88	203	807	612
Rented from a housing association	9,598	9,067	301	28	79	17	8	2	11	22	63	274	216
Rented from local authority or new town	62,330	60,745	907	64	173	79	74	40	49	44	155	1,086	1,225
Lacking or sharing use of bath/shower and/or inside WC	4,510	4,333	39	19	13	16	15	6	28	13	28	113	120
No central heating	55,041	53,458	640	77	112	154	195	38	134	51	182	1,350	1,017
Not self-contained accommodation	5,955	5,702	51	34	20	25	12	5	40	23	43	168	159
No car	101,740	98,653	1,611	154	271	232	184	71	139	100	325	2,379	2,208
Containing person(s) with limiting long-term illness	81,974	80,471	752	47	77	187	154	39	61	45	141	1,583	1,446
ALL RESIDENTS IN HOUSEHOLDS	**916,973**	**893,373**	**7,925**	**1,004**	**1,298**	**3,882**	**2,929**	**794**	**1,980**	**1,186**	**2,602**	**23,017**	**13,351**
Over 1 and up to 1.5 persons per room	23,339	20,597	470	135	92	566	757	230	216	109	167	2,282	417
Over 1.5 persons per room	5,211	4,233	94	61	18	146	316	115	92	54	82	803	159
Lacking or sharing use of bath/shower and/or inside WC	6,256	5,960	48	23	18	31	48	23	52	18	35	205	190
No central heating	114,903	110,486	1,420	174	230	553	937	159	393	120	431	3,822	2,136
Not self-contained accommodation	8,544	8,108	75	51	27	55	39	25	61	35	68	306	226
No car	171,129	163,912	3,417	372	580	653	748	311	246	210	680	5,381	3,827

Table 49 Ethnic group: housing – continued

49. Households with residents; residents in households

	TOTAL HOUSE-HOLDS	Ethnic group of household head											Household head born in:	
		White	Black Caribbean	Black African	Black other	Indian	Pakistani	Bangladeshi	Chinese	Other groups			New Common-wealth	Ireland
										Asian	Other			
a	b	c	d	e	f	g	h	i	j	k	l		m	n

a	b	c	d	e	f	g	h	i	j	k	l	m	n
Bath													
ALL HOUSEHOLDS	**34,128**	**33,479**	**234**	**24**	**34**	**70**	**9**	**18**	**97**	**38**	**125**	**800**	**606**
Over 1 and up to 1.5 persons per room	396	368	5	1	1	3	1	2	6	2	7	17	4
Over 1.5 persons per room	182	164	1	1	-	1	1	1	3	3	7	10	3
Owner occupied - owned outright	9,699	9,625	37	-	3	5	1	-	12	1	15	186	143
- buying	12,376	12,114	94	2	7	44	1	10	41	12	51	354	211
Rented privately	4,200	4,059	13	20	8	9	4	3	27	19	38	122	74
Rented from a housing association	1,167	1,150	4	-	5	2	1	-	2	1	2	22	27
Rented from local authority or new town	6,210	6,073	84	2	11	9	2	5	3	5	16	101	130
Lacking or sharing use of bath/shower and/or inside WC	560	535	2	3	-	1	1	-	11	3	4	16	12
No central heating	4,795	4,707	25	5	4	6	4	1	18	4	21	89	89
Not self-contained accommodation	975	939	6	5	1	3	1	-	10	4	6	26	16
No car	12,148	11,894	109	13	12	16	5	8	33	14	44	266	284
Containing person(s) with limiting long-term illness	7,251	7,154	48	2	6	10	2	6	8	2	13	124	138
ALL RESIDENTS IN HOUSEHOLDS	**76,876**	**75,120**	**601**	**49**	**90**	**212**	**33**	**74**	**257**	**115**	**325**	**2,006**	**1,342**
Over 1 and up to 1.5 persons per room	2,081	1,939	26	4	6	20	5	10	28	9	34	93	20
Over 1.5 persons per room	559	481	6	2	-	5	3	5	12	12	33	42	12
Lacking or sharing use of bath/shower and/or inside WC	734	696	2	3	-	1	1	-	23	4	4	21	18
No central heating	8,722	8,520	50	9	6	13	15	5	45	13	46	196	164
Not self-contained accommodation	1,420	1,359	15	5	2	4	1	-	19	4	11	40	29
No car	19,883	19,328	230	28	25	37	12	31	69	32	91	507	499

49. Households with residents; residents in households

	TOTAL HOUSE-HOLDS	Ethnic group of household head										Household head born in:	
		White	Black Caribbean	Black African	Black other	Indian	Pakistani	Bangladeshi	Chinese	Other groups		New Common-wealth	Ireland
										Asian	Other		
a	b	c	d	e	f	g	h	i	j	k	l	m	n
					Bristol								
ALL HOUSEHOLDS	**156,778**	**150,637**	**2,743**	**278**	**434**	**781**	**583**	**124**	**363**	**233**	**602**	**5,172**	**3,065**
Over 1 and up to 1.5 persons per room	2,360	1,964	75	19	16	80	114	28	27	18	19	321	43
Over 1.5 persons per room	821	680	17	14	7	21	40	15	12	6	9	114	26
Owner occupied - owned outright	36,517	35,725	340	9	18	134	148	6	63	20	54	880	630
- buying	63,232	60,605	1,123	105	124	434	314	62	143	97	225	2,546	1,035
Rented privately	14,535	13,784	157	70	64	119	36	12	93	59	141	554	397
Rented from a housing association	5,812	5,315	293	28	70	15	7	2	7	18	57	225	147
Rented from local authority or new town	34,753	33,390	807	57	150	59	71	33	36	36	114	874	808
Lacking or sharing use of bath/shower and/or inside WC	2,675	2,537	33	16	12	13	13	6	14	10	21	84	80
No central heating	31,218	29,837	597	68	100	138	185	33	88	42	130	1,104	703
Not self-contained accommodation	3,833	3,634	40	28	18	21	11	5	25	17	34	120	117
No car	53,558	50,905	1,462	130	242	201	178	51	80	71	238	1,861	1,382
Containing person(s) with limiting long-term illness	36,912	35,666	683	36	61	147	150	29	28	32	80	1,169	859
ALL RESIDENTS IN HOUSEHOLDS	**370,131**	**352,224**	**6,596**	**802**	**1,035**	**2,834**	**2,786**	**573**	**1,042**	**718**	**1,521**	**15,272**	**6,971**
Over 1 and up to 1.5 persons per room	13,263	10,901	417	101	77	499	752	179	143	94	100	1,960	257
Over 1.5 persons per room	3,243	2,421	72	59	18	136	313	95	62	26	41	706	87
Lacking or sharing use of bath/shower and/or inside WC	3,527	3,295	42	20	17	26	44	23	20	14	26	159	114
No central heating	66,176	62,250	1,339	158	207	510	905	141	255	101	310	3,263	1,477
Not self-contained accommodation	5,357	5,005	55	45	24	50	38	25	34	27	54	231	153
No car	93,883	87,610	3,103	322	515	578	735	245	125	140	510	4,402	2,394

Table 49 Ethnic group: housing – continued

49. Households with residents; residents in households

	TOTAL HOUSE-HOLDS	Ethnic group of household head										Household head born in:	
		White	Black Caribbean	Black African	Black other	Indian	Pakistani	Bangladeshi	Chinese	Other groups		New Common-wealth	Ireland
										Asian	Other		
a	b	c	d	e	f	g	h	i	j	k	l	m	n
Kingswood													
ALL HOUSEHOLDS	**34,657**	**34,368**	**93**	**8**	**18**	**47**	**11**	**7**	**36**	**27**	**42**	**347**	**295**
Over 1 and up to 1.5 persons per room	290	276	2	3	2	2	-	2	3	-	-	11	3
Over 1.5 persons per room	49	44	-	-	-	1	-	-	2	1	1	4	1
Owner occupied - owned outright	10,002	9,981	7	1	-	1	-	-	4	1	7	44	64
- buying	18,233	18,007	79	4	14	39	11	5	25	23	26	256	153
Rented privately	1,059	1,042	3	-	-	3	-	1	4	1	5	17	17
Rented from a housing association	621	620	-	-	1	-	-	-	-	-	-	4	8
Rented from local authority or new town	4,501	4,483	3	3	3	1	-	-	2	2	4	21	48
Lacking or sharing use of bath/shower and/or inside WC	156	151	-	-	-	2	1	-	2	-	-	5	1
No central heating	2,499	2,481	3	1	2	3	3	-	5	1	-	24	17
Not self-contained accommodation	120	118	1	-	-	1	-	-	-	-	-	2	1
No car	7,045	7,010	11	-	5	3	-	1	5	4	6	41	75
Containing person(s) with limiting long-term illness	7,047	7,015	7	1	2	6	1	1	6	2	6	57	66
ALL RESIDENTS IN HOUSEHOLDS	**88,916**	**87,956**	**286**	**29**	**54**	**162**	**36**	**31**	**149**	**86**	**127**	**1,051**	**768**
Over 1 and up to 1.5 persons per room	1,634	1,558	10	15	9	12	-	14	16	-	-	63	21
Over 1.5 persons per room	196	168	-	-	-	5	-	-	13	5	5	23	4
Lacking or sharing use of bath/shower and/or inside WC	228	213	-	-	-	4	3	-	8	-	-	15	1
No central heating	5,002	4,953	4	2	5	6	7	-	24	1	-	61	28
Not self-contained accommodation	176	174	1	-	-	1	-	-	-	-	-	2	1
No car	11,280	11,194	29	-	12	9	-	2	12	11	11	86	129

49. Households with residents; residents in households

	TOTAL HOUSE-HOLDS	Ethnic group of household head										Household head born in:	
		White	Black Caribbean	Black African	Black other	Indian	Pakistani	Bangladeshi	Chinese	Other groups		New Common-wealth	Ireland
										Asian	Other		
a	b	c	d	e	f	g	h	i	j	k	l	m	n
Northavon													
ALL HOUSEHOLDS	**49,626**	**49,174**	**101**	**16**	**22**	**101**	**15**	**8**	**65**	**39**	**85**	**609**	**633**
Over 1 and up to 1.5 persons per room	425	413	2	2	-	3	-	-	1	-	4	9	10
Over 1.5 persons per room	92	89	1	-	-	-	-	1	-	1	-	1	7
Owner occupied - owned outright	11,929	11,888	3	1	3	13	3	-	7	1	10	88	170
- buying	29,399	29,060	83	12	12	75	10	5	48	36	58	433	328
Rented privately	1,940	1,913	7	2	2	6	1	1	3	1	4	38	32
Rented from a housing association	598	593	1	-	1	-	-	-	1	1	1	9	14
Rented from local authority or new town	4,993	4,966	5	1	4	6	1	-	3	-	7	32	73
Lacking or sharing use of bath/shower and/or inside WC	224	223	-	-	1	-	-	-	-	-	-	2	9
No central heating	4,282	4,253	5	-	3	2	1	2	5	2	9	38	69
Not self-contained accommodation	102	101	-	-	-	-	-	-	-	1	-	1	4
No car	7,332	7,277	13	2	5	9	-	3	5	2	16	59	140
Containing person(s) with limiting long-term illness	8,626	8,571	6	3	3	17	1	1	6	4	14	71	140
ALL RESIDENTS IN HOUSEHOLDS	**129,084**	**127,709**	**288**	**49**	**59**	**339**	**43**	**30**	**210**	**128**	**229**	**1,754**	**1,665**
Over 1 and up to 1.5 persons per room	2,374	2,316	11	10	-	11	-	-	6	-	20	49	65
Over 1.5 persons per room	399	374	7	-	-	-	-	7	-	11	-	7	38
Lacking or sharing use of bath/shower and/or inside WC	446	445	-	-	1	-	-	-	-	-	-	2	33
No central heating	9,153	9,081	10	-	6	6	5	7	13	3	22	83	172
Not self-contained accommodation	186	183	-	-	-	-	-	-	-	3	-	1	5
No car	11,708	11,585	25	4	13	20	-	10	13	2	36	114	235

Table 49 Ethnic group: housing – continued

49. Households with residents; residents in households

	TOTAL HOUSE-HOLDS	Ethnic group of household head										Household head born in:	
		White	Black Caribbean	Black African	Black other	Indian	Pakistani	Bangladeshi	Chinese	Other groups		New Common-wealth	Ireland
										Asian	Other		
a	b	c	d	e	f	g	h	i	j	k	l	m	n
Wansdyke													
ALL HOUSEHOLDS	**30,814**	**30,690**	**12**	**9**	**9**	**19**	**2**	**-**	**26**	**7**	**40**	**271**	**259**
Over 1 and up to 1.5 persons per room	223	220	1	-	-	-	-	-	2	-	-	4	2
Over 1.5 persons per room	31	31	-	-	-	-	-	-	-	-	-	1	1
Owner occupied - owned outright	9,440	9,424	1	-	3	1	-	-	2	1	8	65	74
- buying	14,851	14,775	7	1	3	16	2	-	19	5	23	157	115
Rented privately	1,420	1,405	1	5	1	2	-	-	2	1	3	21	20
Rented from a housing association	289	288	-	-	1	-	-	-	-	-	-	1	-
Rented from local authority or new town	4,273	4,262	2	1	1	-	-	-	2	-	5	20	45
Lacking or sharing use of bath/shower and/or inside WC	240	239	-	-	-	-	-	-	-	-	1	-	3
No central heating	3,624	3,614	2	-	1	1	-	-	3	-	3	16	28
Not self-contained accommodation	87	83	1	1	1	-	-	-	-	-	1	2	1
No car	5,717	5,703	2	4	2	1	-	-	1	-	4	31	58
Containing person(s) with limiting long-term illness	6,177	6,162	3	1	2	-	-	-	2	-	7	34	50
ALL RESIDENTS IN HOUSEHOLDS	**79,122**	**78,769**	**40**	**24**	**16**	**62**	**6**	**-**	**82**	**13**	**110**	**750**	**665**
Over 1 and up to 1.5 persons per room	1,302	1,285	6	-	-	-	-	-	11	-	-	23	14
Over 1.5 persons per room	125	125	-	-	-	-	-	-	-	-	-	4	8
Lacking or sharing use of bath/shower and/or inside WC	359	358	-	-	-	-	-	-	-	-	1	-	3
No central heating	8,123	8,091	5	-	2	1	-	-	10	-	14	36	68
Not self-contained accommodation	148	144	1	1	1	-	-	-	-	-	1	2	1
No car	8,992	8,967	4	5	3	2	-	-	1	-	10	58	95

49. Households with residents; residents in households

	TOTAL HOUSE-HOLDS	Ethnic group of household head										Household head born in:	
		White	Black Caribbean	Black African	Black other	Indian	Pakistani	Bangladeshi	Chinese	Other groups		New Common-wealth	Ireland
										Asian	Other		
a	b	c	d	e	f	g	h	i	j	k	l	m	n
Woodspring													
ALL HOUSEHOLDS	**70,519**	**70,109**	**44**	**17**	**17**	**82**	**8**	**20**	**77**	**40**	**105**	**772**	**809**
Over 1 and up to 1.5 persons per room	483	469	-	1	-	4	-	4	2	1	2	16	7
Over 1.5 persons per room	222	217	2	-	-	-	-	1	1	-	1	4	3
Owner occupied - owned outright	21,597	21,557	4	-	-	3	-	1	14	2	16	166	221
- buying	34,478	34,218	25	14	10	61	6	14	45	22	63	471	342
Rented privately	4,571	4,525	5	3	2	9	2	-	6	7	12	55	72
Rented from a housing association	1,111	1,101	3	-	1	-	-	-	1	2	3	13	20
Rented from local authority or new town	7,600	7,571	6	-	4	4	-	2	3	1	9	38	121
Lacking or sharing use of bath/shower and/or inside WC	655	648	4	-	-	-	-	-	1	-	2	6	15
No central heating	8,623	8,566	8	3	2	4	2	2	15	2	19	79	111
Not self-contained accommodation	838	827	3	-	-	-	-	-	5	1	2	17	20
No car	15,940	15,864	14	5	5	2	1	8	15	9	17	121	269
Containing person(s) with limiting long-term illness	15,961	15,903	5	4	3	7	-	2	11	5	21	128	193
ALL RESIDENTS IN HOUSEHOLDS	**172,844**	**171,595**	**114**	**51**	**44**	**273**	**25**	**86**	**240**	**126**	**290**	**2,184**	**1,940**
Over 1 and up to 1.5 persons per room	2,685	2,598	-	5	-	24	-	27	12	6	13	94	40
Over 1.5 persons per room	689	664	9	-	-	-	-	8	5	-	3	21	10
Lacking or sharing use of bath/shower and/or inside WC	962	953	4	-	-	-	-	-	1	-	4	8	21
No central heating	17,727	17,591	12	5	4	17	5	6	46	2	39	183	227
Not self-contained accommodation	1,257	1,243	3	-	-	-	-	-	8	1	2	30	37
No car	25,383	25,228	26	13	12	7	1	23	26	25	22	214	475

Table 50 Country of birth: household heads and residents

Notes: (1) * Includes Channel Islands, the Isle of Man and United Kingdom (part not stated)
(2) ** Includes Ireland (part not stated)

50. Residents in households; household heads

Country of birth of household head	TOTAL PERSONS	Age and birthplace of persons							
		Total born		0 - 4		5 - 15		16 - 29	
		Inside UK	Outside UK	Inside UK	Outside UK	Inside UK	Outside UK	Inside UK	Outside UK
a	b	c	d	e	f	g	h	i	j
AVON									
ALL COUNTRIES OF BIRTH	**916,973**	**875,130**	**41,843**	**59,100**	**729**	**116,204**	**2,828**	**183,171**	**8,149**
United Kingdom*	**865,885**	**852,332**	**13,553**	**55,845**	**375**	**109,526**	**1,664**	**176,739**	**3,707**
England	811,412	799,285	12,127	53,212	334	103,835	1,490	167,124	3,358
Scotland	14,793	14,402	391	858	14	1,885	68	2,791	111
Wales	34,650	34,110	540	1,454	15	3,184	71	5,874	144
Northern Ireland	4,336	4,164	172	280	10	531	23	861	41
Irish Republic**	9,015	3,985	5,030	295	30	840	193	1,261	453
Old Commonwealth	2,748	1,159	1,589	176	25	221	99	264	332
New Commonwealth	**23,017**	**10,669**	**12,348**	**1,835**	**119**	**3,873**	**438**	**3,071**	**2,118**
Eastern Africa	2,193	1,026	1,167	249	10	357	31	230	303
Other Africa	1,044	487	557	102	15	158	43	106	129
Caribbean	6,544	2,890	3,654	383	8	977	40	1,117	192
Bangladesh	771	281	490	93	17	137	81	35	158
India	4,039	1,893	2,146	217	21	664	65	518	250
Pakistan	2,907	1,485	1,422	327	15	716	81	357	354
South East Asia	2,764	1,207	1,557	234	22	401	59	335	510
Cyprus	1,064	528	536	88	4	180	7	167	93
Other New Commonwealth	1,691	872	819	142	7	283	31	206	129
Other European Community	6,646	3,174	3,472	422	33	823	97	972	594
Other Europe	2,610	1,046	1,564	69	13	147	11	263	97
United States of America	1,163	446	717	53	22	98	57	107	126
China	429	118	311	15	3	40	13	30	64
Vietnam	257	61	196	22	1	29	39	8	57
Rest of the world	5,203	2,140	3,063	368	108	607	217	456	601
Bath									
ALL COUNTRIES OF BIRTH	**76,876**	**71,758**	**5,118**	**4,266**	**93**	**8,359**	**320**	**14,999**	**1,072**
United Kingdom*	**71,237**	**69,530**	**1,707**	**3,984**	**41**	**7,821**	**187**	**14,328**	**492**
England	66,309	64,762	1,547	3,769	40	7,417	168	13,424	460
Scotland	1,605	1,558	47	79	-	155	3	297	9
Wales	2,704	2,658	46	99	-	173	9	487	10
Northern Ireland	555	523	32	36	1	66	6	117	7
Irish Republic**	787	333	454	26	1	70	5	88	37
Old Commonwealth	423	140	283	14	5	26	17	37	54
New Commonwealth	**2,006**	**824**	**1,182**	**103**	**16**	**213**	**61**	**277**	**210**
Eastern Africa	205	93	112	20	3	24	5	22	33
Other Africa	113	49	64	5	-	19	4	13	22
Caribbean	528	222	306	12	1	44	5	119	26
Bangladesh	66	20	46	10	2	7	8	3	12
India	427	165	262	11	-	48	15	35	15
Pakistan	64	26	38	4	1	3	3	8	6
South East Asia	340	123	217	15	6	42	14	41	74
Cyprus	71	38	33	10	-	6	-	15	11
Other New Commonwealth	192	88	104	16	3	20	7	21	11
Other European Community	1,017	429	588	62	9	112	4	147	98
Other Europe	360	143	217	12	2	28	1	35	29
United States of America	216	72	144	6	2	18	8	16	28
China	77	12	65	2	1	-	3	5	18
Vietnam	14	1	13	1	-	-	1	-	7
Rest of the world	739	274	465	56	16	71	33	66	99

30 - 44		45 up to pensionable age		Pensionable age - 74		75 and over		TOTAL HOUSEHOLD HEADS	Country of birth of household head
Age and birthplace of persons									
Inside UK	Outside UK	Inside UK	Outside UK	Inside UK	Outside UK	Inside UK	Outside UK		
k	l	m	n	o	p	q	r	s	a
184,490	**12,045**	**168,121**	**9,988**	**103,004**	**6,112**	**61,040**	**1,992**	**376,522**	**ALL COUNTRIES OF BIRTH**
181,421	**3,578**	**166,297**	**2,136**	**101,749**	**1,725**	**60,755**	**368**	**356,658**	**United Kingdom***
170,828	3,254	155,363	1,864	93,051	1,531	55,872	296	332,410	England
3,498	89	2,962	56	1,727	42	681	11	6,105	Scotland
6,000	125	7,095	77	6,478	95	4,025	13	16,073	Wales
1,031	34	825	39	466	20	170	5	1,779	Northern Ireland
608	971	529	1,708	372	1,177	80	498	3,888	Irish Republic**
216	476	108	244	137	237	37	176	1,248	Old Commonwealth
1,024	**4,369**	**549**	**3,690**	**244**	**1,255**	**73**	**359**	**7,971**	**New Commonwealth**
140	600	37	172	11	36	2	15	745	Eastern Africa
89	285	19	67	8	10	5	8	401	Other Africa
247	1,017	116	1,702	43	609	7	86	2,613	Caribbean
7	135	8	93	1	5	-	1	173	Bangladesh
157	626	191	693	107	342	39	149	1,389	India
30	509	39	372	13	68	3	23	666	Pakistan
159	649	50	224	21	69	7	24	997	South East Asia
70	191	14	176	8	52	1	13	364	Cyprus
125	357	75	191	32	64	9	40	623	Other New Commonwealth
563	1,050	228	937	139	604	27	157	2,716	Other European Community
171	181	158	457	206	610	32	195	1,215	Other Europe
93	218	45	147	41	99	9	48	510	United States of America
5	80	12	91	13	39	3	21	175	China
1	56	1	30	-	7	-	6	65	Vietnam
388	1,066	194	548	103	359	24	164	2,076	Rest of the world
14,167	**1,315**	**13,499**	**1,118**	**9,920**	**846**	**6,548**	**354**	**34,128**	**ALL COUNTRIES OF BIRTH**
13,855	**410**	**13,276**	**264**	**9,765**	**252**	**6,501**	**61**	**31,662**	**United Kingdom***
12,942	380	12,308	229	8,897	221	6,005	49	29,309	England
354	16	320	10	244	7	109	2	739	Scotland
429	2	553	10	561	13	356	2	1,355	Wales
125	6	89	6	60	5	30	1	226	Northern Ireland
42	68	52	138	38	124	17	81	380	Irish Republic**
23	82	17	34	14	43	9	48	214	Old Commonwealth
100	**355**	**76**	**333**	**45**	**145**	**10**	**62**	**800**	**New Commonwealth**
19	50	5	14	3	6	-	1	78	Eastern Africa
10	28	2	10	-	-	-	-	46	Other Africa
20	57	17	154	9	52	1	11	207	Caribbean
-	17	-	7	-	-	-	-	16	Bangladesh
23	52	25	84	18	63	5	33	189	India
2	11	4	11	4	2	1	4	26	Pakistan
9	82	13	33	2	6	1	2	129	South East Asia
4	14	-	3	2	2	1	3	30	Cyprus
13	44	10	17	7	14	1	8	79	Other New Commonwealth
68	156	28	181	8	103	4	37	448	Other European Community
19	30	21	51	24	75	4	29	172	Other Europe
18	40	4	28	8	26	2	12	100	United States of America
1	17	1	14	3	11	-	1	36	China
-	2	-	2	-	1	-	-	4	Vietnam
41	155	24	73	15	66	1	23	312	Rest of the world

Table 50 Country of birth: household heads and residents – **continued**

Notes: (1) * Includes Channel Islands, the Isle of Man and United Kingdom (part not stated)
(2) ** Includes Ireland (part not stated)

50. Residents in households; household heads

Country of birth of household head	TOTAL PERSONS	Age and birthplace of persons: Total born		0 - 4		5 - 15		16 - 29	
		Inside UK	Outside UK	Inside UK	Outside UK	Inside UK	Outside UK	Inside UK	Outside UK
a	b	c	d	e	f	g	h	i	j
				Bristol					
ALL COUNTRIES OF BIRTH	**370,131**	**347,669**	**22,462**	**25,401**	**346**	**45,758**	**1,247**	**78,312**	**4,556**
United Kingdom*	**340,318**	**334,747**	**5,571**	**23,425**	**134**	**41,692**	**555**	**74,358**	**1,714**
England	319,918	314,940	4,978	22,389	120	39,794	492	70,333	1,556
Scotland	5,537	5,380	157	348	5	636	26	1,171	48
Wales	12,755	12,524	231	553	4	1,059	22	2,412	69
Northern Ireland	1,836	1,766	70	114	4	173	11	405	18
Irish Republic**	5,135	2,135	3,000	167	16	430	123	731	310
Old Commonwealth	1,237	529	708	99	13	90	48	140	177
New Commonwealth	**15,272**	**6,955**	**8,317**	**1,246**	**79**	**2,755**	**291**	**2,110**	**1,448**
Eastern Africa	1,226	541	685	135	5	203	21	132	184
Other Africa	534	235	299	52	10	78	23	59	77
Caribbean	5,275	2,275	3,000	313	5	793	31	888	133
Bangladesh	582	218	364	73	13	111	64	24	121
India	2,445	1,176	1,269	172	18	474	38	346	192
Pakistan	2,613	1,358	1,255	309	12	688	70	322	331
South East Asia	1,376	572	804	106	11	200	29	174	304
Cyprus	493	216	277	33	4	77	5	74	38
Other New Commonwealth	728	364	364	53	1	131	10	91	68
Other European Community	3,263	1,467	1,796	196	13	361	50	512	345
Other Europe	1,376	531	845	35	8	72	5	142	47
United States of America	496	191	305	20	9	45	22	58	65
China	205	59	146	6	-	26	6	15	29
Vietnam	157	45	112	19	1	17	23	7	28
Rest of the world	2,672	1,010	1,662	188	73	270	124	239	393
				Kingswood					
ALL COUNTRIES OF BIRTH	**88,916**	**86,782**	**2,134**	**5,896**	**32**	**11,724**	**144**	**17,455**	**348**
United Kingdom*	**86,396**	**85,545**	**851**	**5,721**	**25**	**11,377**	**96**	**17,150**	**195**
England	82,242	81,472	770	5,501	19	10,978	90	16,497	180
Scotland	1,004	985	19	68	5	139	3	169	2
Wales	2,810	2,776	34	127	1	207	2	416	8
Northern Ireland	284	278	6	22	-	45	-	58	2
Irish Republic**	484	243	241	16	-	56	14	65	13
Old Commonwealth	112	50	62	6	1	12	1	2	10
New Commonwealth	**1,051**	**512**	**539**	**88**	**1**	**179**	**17**	**145**	**89**
Eastern Africa	126	53	73	17	-	12	-	16	17
Other Africa	53	32	21	6	-	15	-	4	7
Caribbean	253	134	119	17	-	51	2	43	3
Bangladesh	24	8	16	2	-	5	3	1	5
India	163	68	95	8	-	22	-	21	11
Pakistan	51	21	30	2	1	4	3	11	5
South East Asia	203	94	109	24	-	34	7	17	25
Cyprus	39	23	16	2	-	8	1	9	3
Other New Commonwealth	139	79	60	10	-	28	1	23	13
Other European Community	354	197	157	30	1	49	2	48	17
Other Europe	203	81	122	8	-	10	1	22	3
United States of America	56	21	35	3	2	3	5	1	-
China	9	2	7	-	2	1	-	1	3
Vietnam	8	2	6	1	-	-	-	1	3
Rest of the world	243	129	114	23	-	37	8	20	15

Age and birthplace of persons								TOTAL HOUSEHOLD HEADS	Country of birth of household head
30 - 44		45 up to pensionable age		Pensionable age - 74		75 and over			
Inside UK	Outside UK	Inside UK	Outside UK	Inside UK	Outside UK	Inside UK	Outside UK		
k	l	m	n	o	p	q	r	s	a
72,014	**6,646**	**59,670**	**5,620**	**41,304**	**3,127**	**25,210**	**920**	**156,778**	**ALL COUNTRIES OF BIRTH**
70,531	**1,562**	**58,856**	**789**	**40,782**	**666**	**25,103**	**151**	**145,386**	**United Kingdom***
66,452	1,407	55,202	695	37,551	594	23,219	114	135,807	England
1,345	39	1,019	18	627	15	234	6	2,421	Scotland
2,271	65	2,259	32	2,390	32	1,580	7	6,222	Wales
438	14	366	15	201	7	69	1	815	Northern Ireland
324	597	262	1,023	188	691	33	240	2,250	Irish Republic**
102	228	39	93	46	79	13	70	555	Old Commonwealth
494	**2,869**	**243**	**2,588**	**82**	**860**	**25**	**182**	**5,172**	**New Commonwealth**
55	362	13	88	2	19	1	6	419	Eastern Africa
36	147	7	34	-	4	3	4	210	Other Africa
167	803	84	1,423	25	536	5	69	2,160	Caribbean
5	95	5	65	-	5	-	1	125	Bangladesh
74	431	63	374	35	161	12	55	739	India
16	466	18	310	4	50	1	16	556	Pakistan
72	318	14	103	5	31	1	8	517	South East Asia
24	90	7	105	1	27	-	8	172	Cyprus
45	157	32	86	10	27	2	15	274	Other New Commonwealth
246	530	84	483	64	304	4	71	1,346	Other European Community
96	101	78	256	91	323	17	105	650	Other Europe
40	100	14	56	10	38	4	15	226	United States of America
1	42	5	45	5	16	1	8	79	China
1	37	1	13	-	4	-	6	41	Vietnam
179	580	88	274	36	146	10	72	1,073	Rest of the world

k	l	m	n	o	p	q	r	s	a
18,998	**668**	**18,187**	**515**	**9,561**	**331**	**4,961**	**96**	**34,657**	**ALL COUNTRIES OF BIRTH**
18,786	**234**	**18,084**	**148**	**9,481**	**127**	**4,946**	**26**	**33,726**	**United Kingdom***
18,007	215	17,195	133	8,717	110	4,577	23	31,954	England
235	5	217	2	108	2	49	-	377	Scotland
466	10	616	2	629	10	315	1	1,268	Wales
75	1	47	1	26	2	5	-	107	Northern Ireland
46	56	30	80	26	54	4	24	188	Irish Republic**
8	15	7	17	12	15	3	3	55	Old Commonwealth
63	**228**	**26**	**161**	**9**	**30**	**2**	**13**	**347**	**New Commonwealth**
5	33	1	20	2	2	-	1	44	Eastern Africa
7	13	-	1	-	-	-	-	19	Other Africa
19	55	2	54	2	3	-	2	81	Caribbean
-	5	-	3	-	-	-	-	6	Bangladesh
4	28	10	32	2	19	1	5	64	India
-	7	4	14	-	-	-	-	15	Pakistan
14	54	3	15	1	5	1	3	59	South East Asia
3	7	-	4	1	1	-	-	11	Cyprus
11	26	6	18	1	-	-	2	48	Other New Commonwealth
46	60	16	41	5	32	3	4	133	Other European Community
12	12	10	39	17	50	2	17	86	Other Europe
5	13	4	7	4	5	1	3	23	United States of America
-	-	-	2	-	-	-	-	2	China
-	1	-	2	-	-	-	-	3	Vietnam
32	49	10	18	7	18	-	6	94	Rest of the world

Table 50 Country of birth: household heads and residents – **continued**

Notes: (1) * Includes Channel Islands, the Isle of Man and United Kingdom (part not stated)
(2) ** Includes Ireland (part not stated)

50. Residents in households; household heads

Country of birth of household head	TOTAL PERSONS	Age and birthplace of persons							
		Total born		0 - 4		5 - 15		16 - 29	
		Inside UK	Outside UK	Inside UK	Outside UK	Inside UK	Outside UK	Inside UK	Outside UK
a	b	c	d	e	f	g	h	i	j
				Northavon					
ALL COUNTRIES OF BIRTH	**129,084**	**124,900**	**4,184**	**8,712**	**83**	**17,367**	**362**	**27,853**	**834**
United Kingdom*	**124,326**	**122,586**	**1,740**	**8,402**	**50**	**16,733**	**231**	**27,276**	**464**
England	115,326	113,757	1,569	7,927	46	15,625	212	25,657	422
Scotland	2,185	2,145	40	122	-	323	4	410	12
Wales	6,128	6,048	80	295	3	683	14	1,085	25
Northern Ireland	614	594	20	50	1	91	1	116	3
Irish Republic**	1,051	518	533	34	7	133	29	153	52
Old Commonwealth	280	134	146	19	-	26	9	32	27
New Commonwealth	**1,754**	**870**	**884**	**157**	**8**	**265**	**27**	**208**	**160**
Eastern Africa	291	146	145	40	-	50	5	28	35
Other Africa	134	68	66	11	1	20	6	12	8
Caribbean	264	141	123	21	-	51	1	44	15
Bangladesh	21	6	15	1	-	-	-	4	5
India	360	170	190	7	3	45	6	44	12
Pakistan	75	33	42	4	-	9	1	8	6
South East Asia	316	157	159	40	1	40	1	38	53
Cyprus	75	48	27	14	-	15	-	9	6
Other New Commonwealth	218	101	117	19	3	35	7	21	20
Other European Community	739	399	340	57	1	99	17	104	61
Other Europe	169	62	107	3	2	7	2	16	4
United States of America	163	63	100	5	6	17	14	13	15
China	38	9	29	-	-	1	2	3	7
Vietnam	34	11	23	1	-	10	7	-	3
Rest of the world	530	248	282	34	9	76	24	48	41
				Wansdyke					
ALL COUNTRIES OF BIRTH	**79,122**	**76,910**	**2,212**	**4,659**	**47**	**10,442**	**192**	**14,192**	**366**
United Kingdom*	**76,789**	**75,742**	**1,047**	**4,524**	**35**	**10,144**	**149**	**13,928**	**247**
England	73,131	72,185	946	4,363	32	9,728	136	13,394	222
Scotland	1,088	1,055	33	53	2	127	10	155	12
Wales	2,237	2,208	29	82	1	242	2	317	7
Northern Ireland	268	258	10	23	-	41	-	48	3
Irish Republic**	397	198	199	19	1	31	7	72	13
Old Commonwealth	222	101	121	12	2	30	6	13	15
New Commonwealth	**750**	**405**	**345**	**62**	**5**	**122**	**7**	**83**	**45**
Eastern Africa	104	60	44	7	-	21	-	13	11
Other Africa	70	36	34	17	1	7	3	1	5
Caribbean	61	31	30	4	2	8	-	9	8
Bangladesh	4	2	2	-	-	-	-	-	-
India	174	87	87	4	-	20	1	24	2
Pakistan	37	22	15	2	-	7	-	5	1
South East Asia	155	83	72	15	2	28	1	19	14
Cyprus	29	18	11	1	-	11	1	1	2
Other New Commonwealth	116	66	50	12	-	20	1	11	2
Other European Community	372	204	168	18	1	55	6	46	10
Other Europe	199	94	105	2	-	7	-	23	9
United States of America	74	23	51	1	2	4	3	5	5
China	28	9	19	1	-	6	1	1	2
Vietnam	6	-	6	-	-	-	1	-	3
Rest of the world	285	134	151	20	1	43	12	21	17

Age and birthplace of persons								TOTAL HOUSEHOLD HEADS	Country of birth of household head
30 - 44		45 up to pensionable age		Pensionable age - 74		75 and over			
Inside UK	Outside UK	Inside UK	Outside UK	Inside UK	Outside UK	Inside UK	Outside UK		
k	l	m	n	o	p	q	r	s	a
27,962	**1,280**	**25,825**	**950**	**11,212**	**515**	**5,969**	**160**	**49,626**	**ALL COUNTRIES OF BIRTH**
27,579	**459**	**25,592**	**309**	**11,067**	**195**	**5,937**	**32**	**47,860**	**United Kingdom***
25,715	426	23,629	264	9,908	172	5,296	27	44,148	England
549	6	467	11	202	6	72	1	833	Scotland
1,163	11	1,376	13	899	13	547	1	2,622	Wales
146	5	114	7	57	2	20	1	229	Northern Ireland
81	104	67	186	41	105	9	50	404	Irish Republic**
25	50	13	28	18	21	1	11	120	Old Commonwealth
129	**394**	**71**	**216**	**30**	**53**	**10**	**26**	**609**	**New Commonwealth**
17	80	10	20	1	4	-	1	90	Eastern Africa
19	37	4	10	1	1	1	3	51	Other Africa
19	62	5	40	1	4	-	1	89	Caribbean
1	4	-	6	-	-	-	-	5	Bangladesh
19	50	33	76	16	26	6	17	134	India
6	8	5	23	1	4	-	-	28	Pakistan
24	76	6	18	7	9	2	1	111	South East Asia
8	16	-	4	2	1	-	-	25	Cyprus
16	61	8	19	1	4	1	3	76	Other New Commonwealth
71	110	43	88	20	52	5	11	283	Other European Community
6	15	11	29	17	44	2	11	78	Other Europe
15	32	7	23	5	6	1	4	59	United States of America
2	4	1	12	2	2	-	2	15	China
-	10	-	2	-	1	-	-	6	Vietnam
54	102	20	57	12	36	4	13	192	Rest of the world

k	l	m	n	o	p	q	r	s	a
16,422	**607**	**16,377**	**514**	**9,546**	**366**	**5,272**	**120**	**30,814**	**ALL COUNTRIES OF BIRTH**
16,217	**273**	**16,245**	**188**	**9,429**	**126**	**5,255**	**29**	**29,893**	**United Kingdom***
15,555	254	15,390	162	8,783	116	4,972	24	28,358	England
251	3	252	3	161	3	56	-	431	Scotland
342	9	550	6	454	3	221	1	980	Wales
63	2	50	3	28	1	5	1	100	Northern Ireland
28	40	26	67	20	50	2	21	159	Irish Republic**
23	39	8	23	14	25	1	11	95	Old Commonwealth
62	**131**	**44**	**97**	**25**	**39**	**7**	**21**	**271**	**New Commonwealth**
14	21	4	9	1	1	-	2	36	Eastern Africa
9	22	1	2	1	1	-	-	24	Other Africa
7	8	3	10	-	1	-	1	19	Caribbean
-	-	1	2	1	-	-	-	2	Bangladesh
7	15	17	37	11	22	4	10	73	India
3	5	4	5	1	4	-	-	13	Pakistan
11	35	7	15	3	1	-	4	54	South East Asia
4	7	-	-	1	1	-	-	8	Cyprus
7	18	7	17	6	8	3	4	42	Other New Commonwealth
41	56	19	50	21	35	4	10	148	Other European Community
20	5	14	29	27	52	1	10	89	Other Europe
5	15	6	15	2	7	-	4	38	United States of America
-	6	-	2	1	4	-	4	11	China
-	-	-	2	-	-	-	-	1	Vietnam
26	42	15	41	7	28	2	10	109	Rest of the world

Table 50 Country of birth: household heads and residents - **continued**

Notes: (1) * Includes Channel Islands, the Isle of Man and United Kingdom (part not stated)
(2) ** Includes Ireland (part not stated)

50. Residents in households; household heads

Country of birth of household head	TOTAL PERSONS	Age and birthplace of persons							
		Total born		0 - 4		5 - 15		16 - 29	
		Inside UK	Outside UK	Inside UK	Outside UK	Inside UK	Outside UK	Inside UK	Outside UK
a	b	c	d	e	f	g	h	i	j
				Woodspring					
ALL COUNTRIES OF BIRTH	**172,844**	**167,111**	**5,733**	**10,166**	**128**	**22,554**	**563**	**30,360**	**973**
United Kingdom*	**166,819**	**164,182**	**2,637**	**9,789**	**90**	**21,759**	**446**	**29,699**	**595**
England	154,486	152,169	2,317	9,263	77	20,293	392	27,819	518
Scotland	3,374	3,279	95	188	2	505	22	589	28
Wales	8,016	7,896	120	298	6	820	22	1,157	25
Northern Ireland	779	745	34	35	4	115	5	117	8
Irish Republic**	1,161	558	603	33	5	120	15	152	28
Old Commonwealth	474	205	269	26	4	37	18	40	49
New Commonwealth	**2,184**	**1,103**	**1,081**	**179**	**10**	**339**	**35**	**248**	**166**
Eastern Africa	241	133	108	30	2	47	-	19	23
Other Africa	140	67	73	11	3	19	7	17	10
Caribbean	163	87	76	16	-	30	1	14	7
Bangladesh	74	27	47	7	2	14	6	3	15
India	470	227	243	15	-	55	5	48	18
Pakistan	67	25	42	6	1	5	4	3	5
South East Asia	374	178	196	34	2	57	7	46	40
Cyprus	357	185	172	28	-	63	-	59	33
Other New Commonwealth	298	174	124	32	-	49	5	39	15
Other European Community	901	478	423	59	8	147	18	115	63
Other Europe	303	135	168	9	1	23	2	25	5
United States of America	158	76	82	18	1	11	5	14	13
China	72	27	45	6	-	6	1	5	5
Vietnam	38	2	36	-	-	2	7	-	13
Rest of the world	734	345	389	47	9	110	16	62	36

Age and birthplace of persons								TOTAL HOUSEHOLD HEADS	Country of birth of household head
30 - 44		45 up to pensionable age		Pensionable age - 74		75 and over			
Inside UK	Outside UK	Inside UK	Outside UK	Inside UK	Outside UK	Inside UK	Outside UK		
k	l	m	n	o	p	q	r	s	a
34,927	**1,529**	**34,563**	**1,271**	**21,461**	**927**	**13,080**	**342**	**70,519**	**ALL COUNTRIES OF BIRTH**
34,453	**640**	**34,244**	**438**	**21,225**	**359**	**13,013**	**69**	**68,131**	**United Kingdom***
32,157	572	31,639	381	19,195	318	11,803	59	62,834	England
764	20	687	12	385	9	161	2	1,304	Scotland
1,329	28	1,741	14	1,545	24	1,006	1	3,626	Wales
184	6	159	7	94	3	41	1	302	Northern Ireland
87	106	92	214	59	153	15	82	507	Irish Republic**
35	62	24	49	33	54	10	33	209	Old Commonwealth
176	**392**	**89**	**295**	**53**	**128**	**19**	**55**	**772**	**New Commonwealth**
30	54	4	21	2	4	1	4	78	Eastern Africa
8	38	5	10	6	4	1	1	51	Other Africa
15	32	5	21	6	13	1	2	57	Caribbean
1	14	2	10	-	-	-	-	19	Bangladesh
30	50	43	90	25	51	11	29	190	India
3	12	4	9	3	8	1	3	28	Pakistan
29	84	7	40	3	17	2	6	127	South East Asia
27	57	7	60	1	20	-	2	118	Cyprus
33	51	12	34	7	11	2	8	104	Other New Commonwealth
91	138	38	94	21	78	7	24	358	Other European Community
18	18	24	53	30	66	6	23	140	Other Europe
10	18	10	18	12	17	1	10	64	United States of America
1	11	5	16	2	6	2	6	32	China
-	6	-	9	-	1	-	-	10	Vietnam
56	138	37	85	26	65	7	40	296	Rest of the world

Table 51 Country of birth and ethnic group

Notes: (1) * Includes Channel Islands, the Isle of Man and United Kingdom (part not stated)
(2) ** Includes Ireland (part not stated)

51. Residents in households; household heads

Country of birth	TOTAL PERSONS	Ethnic group								Other groups	
		White	Black Caribbean	Black African	Black other	Indian	Pakistani	Bangla-deshi	Chinese	Asian	Other
a	b	c	d	e	f	g	h	i	j	k	l
AVON											
TOTAL PERSONS	**916,973**	**891,872**	**7,044**	**942**	**2,705**	**3,713**	**2,825**	**764**	**2,013**	**1,286**	**3,809**
United Kingdom*	**875,697**	**862,567**	**3,499**	**344**	**2,481**	**1,692**	**1,466**	**286**	**601**	**245**	**2,516**
England	831,585	818,723	3,459	336	2,439	1,658	1,440	278	577	242	2,433
Scotland	11,585	11,505	12	1	8	7	11	8	6	-	27
Wales	28,608	28,448	25	4	30	17	15	-	16	2	51
Northern Ireland	3,308	3,290	3	3	4	2	-	-	2	1	3
Irish Republic**	6,946	6,924	5	4	-	2	-	-	5	-	6
Old Commonwealth	3,033	2,986	3	14	1	4	-	-	4	-	21
New Commonwealth	**15,526**	**5,792**	**3,499**	**354**	**138**	**1,960**	**1,339**	**475**	**1,032**	**484**	**453**
Eastern Africa	1,709	874	-	94	16	582	25	-	4	71	43
Other Africa	838	567	3	220	19	10	-	1	-	1	17
Caribbean	4,038	357	3,483	21	53	23	9	-	6	9	77
Bangladesh	502	30	2	-	3	7	2	450	-	4	4
India	2,530	1,028	-	4	4	1,236	80	1	1	36	140
Pakistan	1,504	168	8	1	7	34	1,219	19	-	20	28
South East Asia	2,322	1,058	3	1	4	25	2	3	1,013	120	93
Cyprus	775	745	-	-	9	3	-	-	1	2	15
Other New Commonwealth	1,308	965	-	13	23	40	2	1	7	221	36
Other European Community	6,941	6,845	12	9	27	3	3	2	4	2	34
Other Europe	2,175	2,159	3	3	1	2	1	-	-	-	6
United States of America	1,330	1,280	1	6	21	1	-	1	1	2	17
China	360	101	-	-	-	1	2	-	246	8	2
Vietnam	204	19	-	3	-	-	-	-	68	110	4
Rest of the world	4,761	3,199	22	205	36	48	14	-	52	435	750
Total household heads	**376,522**	**368,457**	**3,227**	**352**	**534**	**1,100**	**628**	**177**	**664**	**384**	**999**
United Kingdom*	**356,658**	**354,606**	**859**	**64**	**444**	**146**	**43**	**14**	**52**	**20**	**410**
England	332,410	330,432	842	64	425	139	41	10	48	20	389
Scotland	6,105	6,087	1	-	4	-	1	4	3	-	5
Wales	16,073	16,023	16	-	13	4	1	-	1	-	15
Northern Ireland	1,779	1,776	-	-	2	1	-	-	-	-	-
Irish Republic**	3,888	3,881	1	-	-	2	-	-	1	-	3
Old Commonwealth	1,248	1,235	1	6	-	1	-	-	3	-	2
New Commonwealth	**7,971**	**2,830**	**2,343**	**183**	**63**	**927**	**579**	**162**	**457**	**214**	**213**
Eastern Africa	745	369	-	41	6	262	10	-	3	38	16
Other Africa	401	271	1	117	2	5	-	-	-	-	5
Caribbean	2,613	174	2,335	15	31	12	4	-	4	2	36
Bangladesh	173	14	1	-	-	4	1	150	-	2	1
India	1,389	642	-	4	3	591	44	1	-	16	88
Pakistan	666	95	4	-	3	19	518	9	-	7	11
South East Asia	997	461	2	-	2	11	1	1	444	43	32
Cyprus	364	347	-	-	5	1	-	-	-	2	9
Other New Commonwealth	623	457	-	6	11	22	1	1	6	104	15
Other European Community	2,716	2,683	9	4	6	-	2	1	-	-	11
Other Europe	1,215	1,206	2	1	-	1	1	-	-	-	4
United States of America	510	494	-	2	7	1	-	-	-	1	5
China	175	61	-	-	-	-	-	-	111	2	1
Vietnam	65	7	-	3	-	-	-	-	23	31	1
Rest of the world	2,076	1,454	12	89	14	22	3	-	17	116	349

Notes: (1) * Includes Channel Islands, the Isle of Man and United Kingdom (part not stated)
(2) ** Includes Ireland (part not stated)

51. Residents in households; household heads

Country of birth	TOTAL PERSONS	Ethnic group									
		White	Black Caribbean	Black African	Black other	Indian	Pakistani	Bangla-deshi	Chinese	Other groups	
										Asian	Other
a	b	c	d	e	f	g	h	i	j	k	l
					AVON – *continued*						
TOTAL PERSONS	**916,973**	**891,872**	**7,044**	**942**	**2,705**	**3,713**	**2,825**	**764**	**2,013**	**1,286**	**3,809**
Country of birth of household head											
United Kingdom*	**865,885**	**857,844**	**2,198**	**295**	**1,847**	**597**	**202**	**42**	**313**	**372**	**2,175**
England	811,412	803,770	2,131	279	1,743	573	197	38	289	353	2,039
Scotland	14,793	14,702	6	5	23	1	2	4	11	5	34
Wales	34,650	34,386	50	6	75	19	3	-	13	10	88
Northern Ireland	4,336	4,298	10	4	6	2	-	-	-	3	13
Irish Republic**	9,015	8,961	5	1	12	4	-	-	5	2	25
Old Commonwealth	2,748	2,700	4	16	-	5	-	-	8	2	13
New Commonwealth	**23,017**	**8,110**	**4,777**	**380**	**759**	**3,051**	**2,601**	**718**	**1,275**	**542**	**804**
Eastern Africa	2,193	1,038	4	86	17	867	34	-	5	73	69
Other Africa	1,044	712	16	229	39	10	2	-	-	6	30
Caribbean	6,544	824	4,730	37	606	26	21	1	7	13	279
Bangladesh	771	55	2	5	4	15	2	674	-	9	5
India	4,039	1,646	-	8	13	1,943	173	1	1	65	189
Pakistan	2,907	295	11	1	21	97	2,360	30	1	37	54
South East Asia	2,764	1,287	3	2	7	25	1	8	1,253	93	85
Cyprus	1,064	1,014	-	-	10	1	-	-	1	8	30
Other New Commonwealth	1,691	1,239	11	12	42	67	8	4	7	238	63
Other European Community	6,646	6,542	23	10	24	3	6	4	6	3	25
Other Europe	2,610	2,575	3	4	7	1	5	-	-	3	12
United States of America	1,163	1,131	-	7	9	1	-	-	1	2	12
China	429	132	-	1	-	-	-	-	289	4	3
Vietnam	257	45	1	5	-	-	-	-	81	119	6
Rest of the world	5,203	3,832	33	223	47	51	11	-	35	237	734
					Bath						
TOTAL PERSONS	**76,876**	**74,952**	**533**	**56**	**236**	**189**	**26**	**72**	**260**	**147**	**405**
United Kingdom*	**71,815**	**70,952**	**261**	**19**	**209**	**51**	**5**	**22**	**49**	**18**	**229**
England	67,726	66,875	260	19	208	48	4	21	48	18	225
Scotland	1,372	1,369	-	-	-	-	-	1	-	-	2
Wales	2,282	2,277	1	-	1	-	1	-	1	-	1
Northern Ireland	372	371	-	-	-	1	-	-	-	-	-
Irish Republic**	669	669	-	-	-	-	-	-	-	-	-
Old Commonwealth	504	501	-	1	-	-	-	-	1	-	1
New Commonwealth	**1,556**	**815**	**269**	**22**	**17**	**133**	**21**	**48**	**135**	**51**	**45**
Eastern Africa	180	119	-	8	1	44	2	-	-	2	4
Other Africa	92	74	-	9	5	3	-	-	-	-	1
Caribbean	334	48	269	1	6	4	-	-	-	-	6
Bangladesh	48	2	-	-	-	-	-	46	-	-	-
India	311	204	-	-	1	76	1	1	-	5	23
Pakistan	55	31	-	-	1	1	17	1	-	-	4
South East Asia	315	149	-	-	1	2	1	-	133	25	4
Cyprus	60	58	-	-	1	1	-	-	-	-	-
Other New Commonwealth	161	130	-	4	1	2	-	-	2	19	3
Other European Community	998	990	1	-	4	-	-	2	-	1	-
Other Europe	289	287	-	-	-	1	-	-	-	-	1
United States of America	268	263	1	-	3	-	-	-	1	-	-
China	80	21	-	-	-	-	-	-	57	1	1
Vietnam	14	-	-	1	-	-	-	-	-	13	-
Rest of the world	683	454	1	13	3	4	-	-	17	63	128

Notes: (1) * Includes Channel Islands, the Isle of Man and United Kingdom (part not stated)
(2) ** Includes Ireland (part not stated)

51. Residents in households; household heads

Country of birth	TOTAL PERSONS	Ethnic group									
		White	Black Caribbean	Black African	Black other	Indian	Pakistani	Bangla-deshi	Chinese	Other groups	
										Asian	Other
a	b	c	d	e	f	g	h	i	j	k	l
				Bath - *continued*							
Total household heads	**34,128**	**33,479**	**234**	**24**	**34**	**70**	**9**	**18**	**97**	**38**	**125**
United Kingdom*	**31,662**	**31,514**	**62**	**5**	**27**	**3**	**-**	**-**	**4**	**1**	**46**
England	29,309	29,163	62	5	26	3	-	-	4	1	45
Scotland	739	739	-	-	-	-	-	-	-	-	-
Wales	1,355	1,354	-	-	1	-	-	-	-	-	-
Northern Ireland	226	226	-	-	-	-	-	-	-	-	-
Irish Republic**	380	380	-	-	-	-	-	-	-	-	-
Old Commonwealth	214	212	-	1	-	-	-	-	1	-	-
New Commonwealth	**800**	**417**	**172**	**10**	**5**	**65**	**9**	**17**	**64**	**20**	**21**
Eastern Africa	78	51	-	4	-	20	1	-	-	2	-
Other Africa	46	39	-	4	-	2	-	-	-	-	1
Caribbean	207	27	172	1	2	1	-	-	-	-	4
Bangladesh	16	1	-	-	-	-	-	15	-	-	-
India	189	134	-	-	1	38	-	1	-	1	14
Pakistan	26	16	-	-	1	1	7	1	-	-	-
South East Asia	129	56	-	-	-	1	1	-	62	9	-
Cyprus	30	29	-	-	-	1	-	-	-	-	-
Other New Commonwealth	79	64	-	1	1	1	-	-	2	8	2
Other European Community	448	445	-	-	2	-	-	1	-	-	-
Other Europe	172	172	-	-	-	-	-	-	-	-	-
United States of America	100	100	-	-	-	-	-	-	-	-	-
China	36	12	-	-	-	-	-	-	24	-	-
Vietnam	4	-	-	1	-	-	-	-	-	3	-
Rest of the world	312	227	-	7	-	2	-	-	4	14	58
TOTAL PERSONS	**76,876**	**74,952**	**533**	**56**	**236**	**189**	**26**	**72**	**260**	**147**	**405**
Country of birth of household head											
United Kingdom*	**71,237**	**70,569**	**166**	**20**	**172**	**30**	**4**	**3**	**35**	**43**	**195**
England	66,309	65,668	163	19	169	27	4	3	31	41	184
Scotland	1,605	1,596	-	1	-	-	-	-	3	2	3
Wales	2,704	2,694	2	-	3	3	-	-	1	-	1
Northern Ireland	555	548	1	-	-	-	-	-	-	-	6
Irish Republic**	787	783	-	-	2	-	-	-	1	-	1
Old Commonwealth	423	420	-	1	-	-	-	-	2	-	-
New Commonwealth	**2,006**	**1,032**	**367**	**19**	**55**	**157**	**22**	**65**	**165**	**55**	**69**
Eastern Africa	205	137	-	6	-	55	2	-	-	3	2
Other Africa	113	101	1	6	-	3	-	-	-	-	2
Caribbean	528	97	365	3	46	1	-	-	3	1	12
Bangladesh	66	5	-	-	-	-	-	61	-	-	-
India	427	293	-	-	1	92	-	1	1	5	34
Pakistan	64	38	-	-	1	1	18	3	-	-	3
South East Asia	340	148	1	-	1	1	1	-	159	22	7
Cyprus	71	68	-	-	-	1	-	-	-	-	2
Other New Commonwealth	192	145	-	4	6	3	1	-	2	24	7
Other European Community	1,017	1,005	-	-	5	-	-	4	-	-	3
Other Europe	360	356	-	2	2	-	-	-	-	-	-
United States of America	216	215	-	-	-	-	-	-	-	1	-
China	77	24	-	1	-	-	-	-	52	-	-
Vietnam	14	-	-	1	-	-	-	-	-	13	-
Rest of the world	739	548	-	12	-	2	-	-	5	35	137

Notes: (1) * Includes Channel Islands, the Isle of Man and United Kingdom (part not stated)
(2) ** Includes Ireland (part not stated)

51. Residents in households; household heads

Country of birth	TOTAL PERSONS	Ethnic group									
		White	Black Caribbean	Black African	Black other	Indian	Pakistani	Bangla-deshi	Chinese	Other groups	
										Asian	Other
a	b	c	d	e	f	g	h	i	j	k	l
					Bristol						
TOTAL PERSONS	**370,131**	**351,160**	**5,917**	**712**	**2,114**	**2,744**	**2,706**	**556**	**1,076**	**750**	**2,396**
United Kingdom*	**347,892**	**337,591**	**2,931**	**250**	**1,957**	**1,346**	**1,431**	**222**	**348**	**166**	**1,650**
England	331,377	321,266	2,902	243	1,929	1,324	1,406	215	332	163	1,597
Scotland	4,350	4,292	9	1	4	6	11	7	5	-	15
Wales	10,463	10,347	19	3	22	12	14	-	9	2	35
Northern Ireland	1,466	1,453	1	3	2	1	-	-	2	1	3
Irish Republic**	3,898	3,880	5	3	-	2	-	-	2	-	6
Old Commonwealth	1,224	1,196	1	8	-	4	-	-	3	-	12
New Commonwealth	**9,620**	**2,285**	**2,947**	**274**	**101**	**1,356**	**1,255**	**333**	**537**	**285**	**247**
Eastern Africa	904	369	-	68	13	356	19	-	1	51	27
Other Africa	401	200	2	174	12	3	-	1	-	1	8
Caribbean	3,263	192	2,932	18	44	13	8	-	5	7	44
Bangladesh	363	21	2	-	2	6	2	322	-	4	4
India	1,421	342	-	4	3	908	75	-	1	24	64
Pakistan	1,303	62	8	1	6	29	1,148	10	-	19	20
South East Asia	1,099	421	3	1	2	12	1	-	527	81	51
Cyprus	330	309	-	-	7	1	-	-	1	2	10
Other New Commonwealth	536	369	-	8	12	28	2	-	2	96	19
Other European Community	3,209	3,146	10	6	16	2	3	-	2	-	24
Other Europe	1,085	1,074	3	2	1	1	1	-	-	-	3
United States of America	539	509	-	4	14	1	-	1	-	-	10
China	166	30	-	-	-	1	2	-	126	6	1
Vietnam	118	10	-	2	-	-	-	-	40	63	3
Rest of the world	2,380	1,439	20	163	25	31	14	-	18	230	440
Total household heads	**156,778**	**150,637**	**2,743**	**278**	**434**	**781**	**583**	**124**	**363**	**233**	**602**
United Kingdom*	**145,386**	**143,782**	**726**	**49**	**360**	**115**	**42**	**11**	**32**	**13**	**256**
England	135,807	134,264	711	49	345	109	40	7	28	13	241
Scotland	2,421	2,404	1	-	3	-	1	4	3	-	5
Wales	6,222	6,181	14	-	11	4	1	-	1	-	10
Northern Ireland	815	813	-	-	1	1	-	-	-	-	-
Irish Republic**	2,250	2,243	1	-	-	2	-	-	1	-	3
Old Commonwealth	555	548	-	3	-	1	-	-	2	-	1
New Commonwealth	**5,172**	**1,192**	**1,993**	**145**	**52**	**646**	**535**	**113**	**246**	**124**	**126**
Eastern Africa	419	177	-	29	4	163	7	-	1	27	11
Other Africa	210	106	1	95	2	2	-	-	-	-	4
Caribbean	2,160	97	1,985	12	27	9	4	-	4	1	21
Bangladesh	125	10	1	-	-	3	1	107	-	2	1
India	739	209	-	4	2	431	40	-	-	11	42
Pakistan	556	33	4	-	2	15	482	6	-	6	8
South East Asia	517	214	2	-	2	8	-	-	240	27	24
Cyprus	172	158	-	-	5	-	-	-	-	2	7
Other New Commonwealth	274	188	-	5	8	15	1	-	1	48	8
Other European Community	1,346	1,319	9	3	4	-	2	-	-	-	9
Other Europe	650	642	2	1	-	1	1	-	-	-	3
United States of America	226	216	-	2	6	1	-	-	-	-	1
China	79	18	-	-	-	-	-	-	59	1	1
Vietnam	41	4	-	2	-	-	-	-	15	19	1
Rest of the world	1,073	673	12	73	12	15	3	-	8	76	201

Notes: (1) * Includes Channel Islands, the Isle of Man and United Kingdom (part not stated)
(2) ** Includes Ireland (part not stated)

51. Residents in households; household heads

Country of birth	TOTAL PERSONS	Ethnic group								Other groups	
		White	Black Caribbean	Black African	Black other	Indian	Pakistani	Bangla-deshi	Chinese	Asian	Other
a	b	c	d	e	f	g	h	i	j	k	l
					Bristol – *continued*						
TOTAL PERSONS	**370,131**	**351,160**	**5,917**	**712**	**2,114**	**2,744**	**2,706**	**556**	**1,076**	**750**	**2,396**
Country of birth of household head											
United Kingdom*	**340,318**	**334,499**	**1,812**	**182**	**1,408**	**430**	**191**	**34**	**168**	**185**	**1,409**
England	319,918	314,393	1,756	171	1,324	415	186	30	156	177	1,310
Scotland	5,537	5,473	6	4	18	1	2	4	3	1	25
Wales	12,755	12,550	42	3	61	11	3	-	9	7	69
Northern Ireland	1,836	1,812	8	4	5	2	-	-	-	-	5
Irish Republic**	5,135	5,093	5	1	10	4	-	-	2	2	18
Old Commonwealth	1,237	1,206	2	8	-	5	-	-	6	2	8
New Commonwealth	**15,272**	**3,522**	**4,039**	**309**	**625**	**2,259**	**2,494**	**522**	**670**	**332**	**500**
Eastern Africa	1,226	474	4	68	13	548	23	-	1	57	38
Other Africa	534	266	14	188	37	3	2	-	-	1	23
Caribbean	5,275	505	3,997	30	499	21	20	1	4	5	193
Bangladesh	582	36	2	5	4	13	2	509	-	8	3
India	2,445	592	-	8	12	1,520	168	-	-	52	93
Pakistan	2,613	130	11	1	20	89	2,272	12	-	32	46
South East Asia	1,376	568	2	1	6	22	-	-	662	64	51
Cyprus	493	451	-	-	10	-	-	-	1	8	23
Other New Commonwealth	728	500	9	8	24	43	7	-	2	105	30
Other European Community	3,263	3,183	22	9	18	3	6	-	4	3	15
Other Europe	1,376	1,347	3	2	5	1	5	-	-	3	10
United States of America	496	477	-	6	8	1	-	-	1	-	3
China	205	44	-	-	-	-	-	-	159	1	1
Vietnam	157	32	1	4	-	-	-	-	46	69	5
Rest of the world	2,672	1,757	33	191	40	41	10	-	20	153	427
					Kingswood						
TOTAL PERSONS	**88,916**	**87,944**	**220**	**31**	**95**	**162**	**28**	**30**	**154**	**73**	**179**
United Kingdom*	**86,820**	**86,354**	**98**	**9**	**88**	**63**	**10**	**8**	**48**	**12**	**130**
England	83,564	83,112	97	8	85	61	10	8	47	12	124
Scotland	700	697	-	-	2	-	-	-	-	-	1
Wales	2,319	2,311	-	1	-	1	-	-	1	-	5
Northern Ireland	198	196	1	-	1	-	-	-	-	-	-
Irish Republic**	404	401	-	-	-	-	-	-	3	-	-
Old Commonwealth	171	169	-	1	1	-	-	-	-	-	-
New Commonwealth	**711**	**300**	**121**	**8**	**1**	**99**	**18**	**22**	**93**	**31**	**18**
Eastern Africa	102	37	-	2	1	53	-	-	-	7	2
Other Africa	46	39	-	5	-	2	-	-	-	-	-
Caribbean	138	13	121	-	-	-	1	-	-	1	2
Bangladesh	15	-	-	-	-	-	-	15	-	-	-
India	115	60	-	-	-	44	-	-	-	2	9
Pakistan	29	4	-	-	-	-	17	7	-	-	1
South East Asia	149	53	-	-	-	-	-	-	93	1	2
Cyprus	32	32	-	-	-	-	-	-	-	-	-
Other New Commonwealth	85	62	-	1	-	-	-	-	-	20	2
Other European Community	366	358	-	-	4	-	-	-	2	1	1
Other Europe	145	144	-	-	-	-	-	-	-	-	1
United States of America	68	65	-	1	1	-	-	-	-	-	1
China	8	1	-	-	-	-	-	-	7	-	-
Vietnam	6	-	-	-	-	-	-	-	-	6	-
Rest of the world	217	152	1	12	-	-	-	-	1	23	28

Notes: (1) * Includes Channel Islands, the Isle of Man and United Kingdom (part not stated)
(2) ** Includes Ireland (part not stated)

51. Residents in households; household heads

Country of birth	TOTAL PERSONS	Ethnic group									
		White	Black Caribbean	Black African	Black other	Indian	Pakistani	Bangla-deshi	Chinese	Other groups: Asian	Other groups: Other
a	b	c	d	e	f	g	h	i	j	k	l
					Kingswood – *continued*						
Total household heads	**34,657**	**34,368**	**93**	**8**	**18**	**47**	**11**	**7**	**36**	**27**	**42**
United Kingdom*	**33,726**	**33,668**	**19**	**-**	**17**	**4**	**-**	**-**	**1**	**1**	**16**
England	31,954	31,898	19	-	16	3	-	-	1	1	16
Scotland	377	377	-	-	-	-	-	-	-	-	-
Wales	1,268	1,268	-	-	-	-	-	-	-	-	-
Northern Ireland	107	106	-	-	1	-	-	-	-	-	-
Irish Republic**	188	188	-	-	-	-	-	-	-	-	-
Old Commonwealth	55	55	-	-	-	-	-	-	-	-	-
New Commonwealth	**347**	**145**	**74**	**3**	**1**	**43**	**11**	**7**	**33**	**18**	**12**
Eastern Africa	44	15	-	1	1	22	-	-	-	3	2
Other Africa	19	16	-	2	-	1	-	-	-	-	-
Caribbean	81	5	74	-	-	-	-	-	-	1	1
Bangladesh	6	-	-	-	-	-	-	6	-	-	-
India	64	36	-	-	-	20	-	-	-	1	7
Pakistan	15	2	-	-	-	-	11	1	-	-	1
South East Asia	59	25	-	-	-	-	-	-	33	1	-
Cyprus	11	11	-	-	-	-	-	-	-	-	-
Other New Commonwealth	48	35	-	-	-	-	-	-	-	12	1
Other European Community	133	132	-	-	-	-	-	-	-	-	1
Other Europe	86	86	-	-	-	-	-	-	-	-	-
United States of America	23	22	-	-	-	-	-	-	-	-	1
China	2	-	-	-	-	-	-	-	2	-	-
Vietnam	3	-	-	-	-	-	-	-	-	3	-
Rest of the world	94	72	-	5	-	-	-	-	-	5	12
TOTAL PERSONS	**88,916**	**87,944**	**220**	**31**	**95**	**162**	**28**	**30**	**154**	**73**	**179**
Country of birth of household head											
United Kingdom*	**86,396**	**86,094**	**50**	**14**	**59**	**23**	**1**	**-**	**18**	**23**	**114**
England	82,242	81,954	49	14	56	21	1	-	16	23	108
Scotland	1,004	1,000	-	-	-	-	-	-	2	-	2
Wales	2,810	2,802	1	-	2	1	-	-	-	-	4
Northern Ireland	284	283	-	-	1	-	-	-	-	-	-
Irish Republic**	484	484	-	-	-	-	-	-	-	-	-
Old Commonwealth	112	112	-	-	-	-	-	-	-	-	-
New Commonwealth	**1,051**	**443**	**170**	**7**	**32**	**139**	**27**	**30**	**126**	**39**	**38**
Eastern Africa	126	40	-	4	1	68	-	-	-	7	6
Other Africa	53	46	-	3	-	4	-	-	-	-	-
Caribbean	253	39	170	-	31	-	1	-	-	1	11
Bangladesh	24	-	-	-	-	-	-	23	-	1	-
India	163	83	-	-	-	67	-	-	-	3	10
Pakistan	51	17	-	-	-	-	26	7	-	-	1
South East Asia	203	72	-	-	-	-	-	-	126	1	4
Cyprus	39	39	-	-	-	-	-	-	-	-	-
Other New Commonwealth	139	107	-	-	-	-	-	-	-	26	6
Other European Community	354	350	-	-	-	-	-	-	1	-	3
Other Europe	203	203	-	-	-	-	-	-	-	-	-
United States of America	56	54	-	-	-	-	-	-	-	-	2
China	9	-	-	-	-	-	-	-	9	-	-
Vietnam	8	1	-	-	-	-	-	-	-	6	1
Rest of the world	243	203	-	10	4	-	-	-	-	5	21

Notes: (1) * Includes Channel Islands, the Isle of Man and United Kingdom (part not stated)
(2) ** Includes Ireland (part not stated)

51. Residents in households; household heads

Country of birth	TOTAL PERSONS	Ethnic group									
		White	Black Caribbean	Black African	Black other	Indian	Pakistani	Bangla-deshi	Chinese	Other groups	
										Asian	Other
a	b	c	d	e	f	g	h	i	j	k	l
					Northavon						
TOTAL PERSONS	**129,084**	**127,633**	**235**	**51**	**127**	**319**	**37**	**26**	**203**	**149**	**304**
United Kingdom*	**124,959**	**124,310**	**123**	**20**	**107**	**123**	**9**	**9**	**60**	**26**	**172**
England	117,946	117,315	117	20	103	122	9	9	59	26	166
Scotland	1,572	1,569	1	-	-	-	-	-	-	-	2
Wales	4,908	4,895	4	-	4	-	-	-	1	-	4
Northern Ireland	467	466	1	-	-	-	-	-	-	-	-
Irish Republic**	748	747	-	1	-	-	-	-	-	-	-
Old Commonwealth	336	330	1	1	-	-	-	-	-	-	4
New Commonwealth	**1,306**	**707**	**110**	**25**	**14**	**190**	**28**	**17**	**108**	**61**	**46**
Eastern Africa	197	99	-	6	1	82	2	-	1	4	2
Other Africa	113	90	-	17	-	-	-	-	-	-	6
Caribbean	153	28	110	2	2	3	-	-	1	1	6
Bangladesh	18	1	-	-	1	-	-	16	-	-	-
India	236	127	-	-	-	95	3	-	-	1	10
Pakistan	51	24	-	-	-	3	23	-	-	-	1
South East Asia	281	154	-	-	-	1	-	-	105	5	16
Cyprus	64	63	-	-	1	-	-	-	-	-	-
Other New Commonwealth	193	121	-	-	9	6	-	1	1	50	5
Other European Community	821	813	1	1	2	-	-	-	-	-	4
Other Europe	181	181	-	-	-	-	-	-	-	-	-
United States of America	173	170	-	-	1	-	-	-	-	-	2
China	29	11	-	-	-	-	-	-	18	-	-
Vietnam	22	4	-	-	-	-	-	-	10	8	-
Rest of the world	509	360	-	3	3	6	-	-	7	54	76
Total household heads	**49,626**	**49,174**	**101**	**16**	**22**	**101**	**15**	**8**	**65**	**39**	**85**
United Kingdom*	**47,860**	**47,755**	**31**	**3**	**16**	**11**	**-**	**2**	**6**	**3**	**33**
England	44,148	44,049	29	3	15	11	-	2	6	3	30
Scotland	833	833	-	-	-	-	-	-	-	-	-
Wales	2,622	2,616	2	-	1	-	-	-	-	-	3
Northern Ireland	229	229	-	-	-	-	-	-	-	-	-
Irish Republic**	404	404	-	-	-	-	-	-	-	-	-
Old Commonwealth	120	119	1	-	-	-	-	-	-	-	-
New Commonwealth	**609**	**326**	**69**	**12**	**5**	**89**	**15**	**6**	**46**	**26**	**15**
Eastern Africa	90	42	-	3	1	39	1	-	1	3	-
Other Africa	51	44	-	7	-	-	-	-	-	-	-
Caribbean	89	13	69	2	2	1	-	-	-	-	2
Bangladesh	5	-	-	-	-	-	-	5	-	-	-
India	134	77	-	-	-	44	3	-	-	1	9
Pakistan	28	15	-	-	-	2	11	-	-	-	-
South East Asia	111	60	-	-	-	-	-	-	44	3	4
Cyprus	25	25	-	-	-	-	-	-	-	-	-
Other New Commonwealth	76	50	-	-	2	3	-	1	1	19	-
Other European Community	283	282	-	-	-	-	-	-	-	-	1
Other Europe	78	78	-	-	-	-	-	-	-	-	-
United States of America	59	58	-	-	1	-	-	-	-	-	-
China	15	8	-	-	-	-	-	-	7	-	-
Vietnam	6	1	-	-	-	-	-	-	3	2	-
Rest of the world	192	143	-	1	-	1	-	-	3	8	36

Notes: (1) * Includes Channel Islands, the Isle of Man and United Kingdom (part not stated)
(2) ** Includes Ireland (part not stated)

51. Residents in households; household heads

Country of birth	TOTAL PERSONS	Ethnic group									
		White	Black Caribbean	Black African	Black other	Indian	Pakistani	Bangla-deshi	Chinese	Other groups	
										Asian	Other
a	b	c	d	e	f	g	h	i	j	k	l
					Northavon – *continued*						
TOTAL PERSONS	**129,084**	**127,633**	**235**	**51**	**127**	**319**	**37**	**26**	**203**	**149**	**304**
Country of birth of household head											
United Kingdom*	**124,326**	**123,835**	**85**	**24**	**88**	**42**	**3**	**4**	**35**	**54**	**156**
England	115,326	114,864	80	22	79	41	3	4	32	51	150
Scotland	2,185	2,182	-	-	2	-	-	-	1	-	-
Wales	6,128	6,107	3	1	7	1	-	-	2	1	6
Northern Ireland	614	611	1	-	-	-	-	-	-	2	-
Irish Republic**	1,051	1,050	-	-	-	-	-	-	-	-	1
Old Commonwealth	280	278	1	-	-	-	-	-	-	-	1
New Commonwealth	**1,754**	**957**	**149**	**24**	**38**	**273**	**33**	**22**	**130**	**62**	**66**
Eastern Africa	291	143	-	3	1	132	3	-	2	3	4
Other Africa	134	110	1	18	2	-	-	-	-	-	3
Caribbean	264	59	148	2	24	2	-	-	-	4	25
Bangladesh	21	2	-	-	-	1	-	18	-	-	-
India	360	216	-	-	-	124	4	-	-	1	15
Pakistan	75	40	-	-	-	5	26	-	-	2	2
South East Asia	316	176	-	1	-	-	-	-	127	3	9
Cyprus	75	75	-	-	-	-	-	-	-	-	-
Other New Commonwealth	218	136	-	-	11	9	-	4	1	49	8
Other European Community	739	734	-	-	-	-	-	-	1	-	4
Other Europe	169	169	-	-	-	-	-	-	-	-	-
United States of America	163	159	-	-	1	-	-	-	-	-	3
China	38	20	-	-	-	-	-	-	18	-	-
Vietnam	34	6	-	-	-	-	-	-	15	13	-
Rest of the world	530	425	-	3	-	4	1	-	4	20	73
					Wansdyke						
TOTAL PERSONS	**79,122**	**78,688**	**37**	**36**	**38**	**62**	**5**	**-**	**75**	**30**	**151**
United Kingdom*	**76,964**	**76,761**	**21**	**14**	**36**	**26**	**1**	**-**	**26**	**4**	**75**
England	73,951	73,749	21	14	35	26	1	-	26	4	75
Scotland	925	924	-	-	1	-	-	-	-	-	-
Wales	1,828	1,828	-	-	-	-	-	-	-	-	-
Northern Ireland	204	204	-	-	-	-	-	-	-	-	-
Irish Republic**	316	316	-	-	-	-	-	-	-	-	-
Old Commonwealth	256	255	-	-	-	-	-	-	-	-	1
New Commonwealth	**619**	**465**	**16**	**12**	**-**	**34**	**4**	**-**	**37**	**10**	**41**
Eastern Africa	102	89	-	3	-	4	-	-	-	3	3
Other Africa	66	57	-	9	-	-	-	-	-	-	-
Caribbean	51	25	16	-	-	1	-	-	-	-	9
Bangladesh	2	1	-	-	-	1	-	-	-	-	-
India	136	93	-	-	-	25	1	-	-	-	17
Pakistan	22	18	-	-	-	-	3	-	-	-	1
South East Asia	130	84	-	-	-	3	-	-	36	1	6
Cyprus	27	25	-	-	-	-	-	-	-	-	2
Other New Commonwealth	83	73	-	-	-	-	-	-	1	6	3
Other European Community	405	402	-	-	1	-	-	-	-	-	2
Other Europe	161	161	-	-	-	-	-	-	-	-	-
United States of America	101	97	-	-	-	-	-	-	-	2	2
China	18	13	-	-	-	-	-	-	5	-	-
Vietnam	8	-	-	-	-	-	-	-	6	1	1
Rest of the world	274	218	-	10	1	2	-	-	1	13	29

Notes: (1) * Includes Channel Islands, the Isle of Man and United Kingdom (part not stated)
(2) ** Includes Ireland (part not stated)

51. Residents in households; household heads

Country of birth	TOTAL PERSONS	Ethnic group									
		White	Black Caribbean	Black African	Black other	Indian	Pakistani	Bangla-deshi	Chinese	Other groups	
										Asian	Other
a	b	c	d	e	f	g	h	i	j	k	l
					Wansdyke – *continued*						
Total household heads	**30,814**	**30,690**	**12**	**9**	**9**	**19**	**2**	**-**	**26**	**7**	**40**
United Kingdom*	**29,893**	**29,862**	**3**	**1**	**8**	**4**	**-**	**-**	**3**	**-**	**12**
England	28,358	28,327	3	1	8	4	-	-	3	-	12
Scotland	431	431	-	-	-	-	-	-	-	-	-
Wales	980	980	-	-	-	-	-	-	-	-	-
Northern Ireland	100	100	-	-	-	-	-	-	-	-	-
Irish Republic**	159	159	-	-	-	-	-	-	-	-	-
Old Commonwealth	95	95	-	-	-	-	-	-	-	-	-
New Commonwealth	**271**	**202**	**9**	**7**	**-**	**14**	**2**	**-**	**18**	**4**	**15**
Eastern Africa	36	32	-	2	-	1	-	-	-	1	-
Other Africa	24	19	-	5	-	-	-	-	-	-	-
Caribbean	19	6	9	-	-	-	-	-	-	-	4
Bangladesh	2	1	-	-	-	1	-	-	-	-	-
India	73	54	-	-	-	11	1	-	-	-	7
Pakistan	13	11	-	-	-	-	1	-	-	-	1
South East Asia	54	35	-	-	-	1	-	-	17	1	-
Cyprus	8	7	-	-	-	-	-	-	-	-	1
Other New Commonwealth	42	37	-	-	-	-	-	-	1	2	2
Other European Community	148	148	-	-	-	-	-	-	-	-	-
Other Europe	89	89	-	-	-	-	-	-	-	-	-
United States of America	38	35	-	-	-	-	-	-	-	1	2
China	11	7	-	-	-	-	-	-	4	-	-
Vietnam	1	-	-	-	-	-	-	-	1	-	-
Rest of the world	109	93	-	1	1	1	-	-	-	2	11
TOTAL PERSONS	**79,122**	**78,688**	**37**	**36**	**38**	**62**	**5**	**-**	**75**	**30**	**151**
Country of birth of household head											
United Kingdom*	**76,789**	**76,572**	**17**	**21**	**34**	**24**	**2**	**-**	**15**	**15**	**89**
England	73,131	72,919	17	21	33	22	2	-	15	15	87
Scotland	1,088	1,087	-	-	1	-	-	-	-	-	-
Wales	2,237	2,234	-	-	-	2	-	-	-	-	1
Northern Ireland	268	267	-	-	-	-	-	-	-	-	1
Irish Republic**	397	397	-	-	-	-	-	-	-	-	-
Old Commonwealth	222	221	-	-	-	-	-	-	-	-	1
New Commonwealth	**750**	**587**	**20**	**10**	**3**	**37**	**3**	**-**	**43**	**10**	**37**
Eastern Africa	104	96	-	2	1	1	-	-	-	1	3
Other Africa	70	58	-	8	-	-	-	-	-	2	2
Caribbean	61	26	18	-	2	-	-	-	-	-	15
Bangladesh	4	3	-	-	-	1	-	-	-	-	-
India	174	127	-	-	-	34	1	-	-	-	12
Pakistan	37	31	-	-	-	-	2	-	1	2	1
South East Asia	155	111	-	-	-	1	-	-	41	1	1
Cyprus	29	28	-	-	-	-	-	-	-	-	1
Other New Commonwealth	116	107	2	-	-	-	-	-	1	4	2
Other European Community	372	372	-	-	-	-	-	-	-	-	-
Other Europe	199	199	-	-	-	-	-	-	-	-	-
United States of America	74	70	-	-	-	-	-	-	-	1	3
China	28	15	-	-	-	-	-	-	11	-	2
Vietnam	6	-	-	-	-	-	-	-	6	-	-
Rest of the world	285	255	-	5	1	1	-	-	-	4	19

Table 51 Country of birth and ethnic group – **continued**

Notes: (1) * Includes Channel Islands, the Isle of Man and United Kingdom (part not stated)
(2) ** Includes Ireland (part not stated)

51. Residents in households; household heads

Country of birth	TOTAL PERSONS	Ethnic group									
		White	Black Caribbean	Black African	Black other	Indian	Pakistani	Bangla-deshi	Chinese	Other groups	
										Asian	Other
a	b	c	d	e	f	g	h	i	j	k	l
					Woodspring						
TOTAL PERSONS	**172,844**	**171,495**	**102**	**56**	**95**	**237**	**23**	**80**	**245**	**137**	**374**
United Kingdom*	**167,247**	**166,599**	**65**	**32**	**84**	**83**	**10**	**25**	**70**	**19**	**260**
England	157,021	156,406	62	32	79	77	10	25	65	19	246
Scotland	2,666	2,654	2	-	1	1	-	-	1	-	7
Wales	6,808	6,790	1	-	3	4	-	-	4	-	6
Northern Ireland	601	600	-	-	1	-	-	-	-	-	-
Irish Republic**	911	911	-	-	-	-	-	-	-	-	-
Old Commonwealth	542	535	1	3	-	-	-	-	-	-	3
New Commonwealth	**1,714**	**1,220**	**36**	**13**	**5**	**148**	**13**	**55**	**122**	**46**	**56**
Eastern Africa	224	161	-	7	-	43	2	-	2	4	5
Other Africa	120	107	1	6	2	2	-	-	-	-	2
Caribbean	99	51	35	-	1	2	-	-	-	-	10
Bangladesh	56	5	-	-	-	-	-	51	-	-	-
India	311	202	-	-	-	88	-	-	-	4	17
Pakistan	44	29	-	-	-	1	11	1	-	1	1
South East Asia	348	197	-	-	1	7	-	3	119	7	14
Cyprus	262	258	-	-	-	1	-	-	-	-	3
Other New Commonwealth	250	210	-	-	1	4	-	-	1	30	4
Other European Community	1,142	1,136	-	2	-	1	-	-	-	-	3
Other Europe	314	312	-	1	-	-	-	-	-	-	1
United States of America	181	176	-	1	2	-	-	-	-	-	2
China	59	25	-	-	-	-	-	-	33	1	-
Vietnam	36	5	-	-	-	-	-	-	12	19	-
Rest of the world	698	576	-	4	4	5	-	-	8	52	49
Total household heads	**70,519**	**70,109**	**44**	**17**	**17**	**82**	**8**	**20**	**77**	**40**	**105**
United Kingdom*	**68,131**	**68,025**	**18**	**6**	**16**	**9**	**1**	**1**	**6**	**2**	**47**
England	62,834	62,731	18	6	15	9	1	1	6	2	45
Scotland	1,304	1,303	-	-	1	-	-	-	-	-	-
Wales	3,626	3,624	-	-	-	-	-	-	-	-	2
Northern Ireland	302	302	-	-	-	-	-	-	-	-	-
Irish Republic**	507	507	-	-	-	-	-	-	-	-	-
Old Commonwealth	209	206	-	2	-	-	-	-	-	-	1
New Commonwealth	**772**	**548**	**26**	**6**	**-**	**70**	**7**	**19**	**50**	**22**	**24**
Eastern Africa	78	52	-	2	-	17	1	-	1	2	3
Other Africa	51	47	-	4	-	-	-	-	-	-	-
Caribbean	57	26	26	-	-	1	-	-	-	-	4
Bangladesh	19	2	-	-	-	-	-	17	-	-	-
India	190	132	-	-	-	47	-	-	-	2	9
Pakistan	28	18	-	-	-	1	6	1	-	1	1
South East Asia	127	71	-	-	-	1	-	1	48	2	4
Cyprus	118	117	-	-	-	-	-	-	-	-	1
Other New Commonwealth	104	83	-	-	-	3	-	-	1	15	2
Other European Community	358	357	-	1	-	-	-	-	-	-	-
Other Europe	140	139	-	-	-	-	-	-	-	-	1
United States of America	64	63	-	-	-	-	-	-	-	-	1
China	32	16	-	-	-	-	-	-	15	1	-
Vietnam	10	2	-	-	-	-	-	-	4	4	-
Rest of the world	296	246	-	2	1	3	-	-	2	11	31

Notes: (1) * Includes Channel Islands, the Isle of Man and United Kingdom (part not stated)
(2) ** Includes Ireland (part not stated)

51. Residents in households; household heads

Country of birth	TOTAL PERSONS	Ethnic group									
		White	Black Caribbean	Black African	Black other	Indian	Pakistani	Bangla-deshi	Chinese	Other groups	
										Asian	Other
a	b	c	d	e	f	g	h	i	j	k	l
				Woodspring - *continued*							
TOTAL PERSONS	**172,844**	**171,495**	**102**	**56**	**95**	**237**	**23**	**80**	**245**	**137**	**374**
Country of birth of household head											
United Kingdom*	**166,819**	**166,275**	**68**	**34**	**86**	**48**	**1**	**1**	**42**	**52**	**212**
England	154,486	153,972	66	32	82	47	1	1	39	46	200
Scotland	3,374	3,364	-	-	2	-	-	-	2	2	4
Wales	8,016	7,999	2	2	2	1	-	-	1	2	7
Northern Ireland	779	777	-	-	-	-	-	-	-	1	1
Irish Republic**	1,161	1,154	-	-	-	-	-	-	2	-	5
Old Commonwealth	474	463	1	7	-	-	-	-	-	-	3
New Commonwealth	**2,184**	**1,569**	**32**	**11**	**6**	**186**	**22**	**79**	**141**	**44**	**94**
Eastern Africa	241	148	-	3	1	63	6	-	2	2	16
Other Africa	140	131	-	6	-	-	-	-	-	3	-
Caribbean	163	98	32	2	4	2	-	-	-	2	23
Bangladesh	74	9	-	-	-	-	-	63	-	-	2
India	470	335	-	-	-	106	-	-	-	4	25
Pakistan	67	39	-	-	-	2	16	8	-	1	1
South East Asia	374	212	-	-	-	1	-	8	138	2	13
Cyprus	357	353	-	-	-	-	-	-	-	-	4
Other New Commonwealth	298	244	-	-	1	12	-	-	1	30	10
Other European Community	901	898	1	1	1	-	-	-	-	-	-
Other Europe	303	301	-	-	-	-	-	-	-	-	2
United States of America	158	156	-	1	-	-	-	-	-	-	1
China	72	29	-	-	-	-	-	-	40	3	-
Vietnam	38	6	-	-	-	-	-	-	14	18	-
Rest of the world	734	644	-	2	2	3	-	-	6	20	57

Table 52 Language indicators

52. Residents

Age	Country of birth: New Commonwealth	Country of birth: Outside of United Kingdom, Ireland, Old Commonwealth and United States of America
a	b	c
AVON		
TOTAL PERSONS	**15,953**	**30,886**
0 - 17	1,137	3,070
18 - 44	8,680	15,549
45 up to pensionable age	4,174	7,059
Pensionable age and over	1,962	5,208
Persons in households	**15,526**	**29,967**
0 - 17	1,121	3,026
18 - 44	8,359	14,917
45 up to pensionable age	4,140	6,995
Pensionable age and over	1,906	5,029
Persons in households by country of birth of head	**23,017**	**38,162**
0 - 17	6,980	10,419
18 - 44	9,867	16,208
45 up to pensionable age	4,239	6,895
Pensionable age and over	1,931	4,640
Bath		
TOTAL PERSONS	**1,657**	**3,831**
0 - 17	120	353
18 - 44	866	1,911
45 up to pensionable age	399	815
Pensionable age and over	272	752
Persons in households	**1,556**	**3,620**
0 - 17	118	347
18 - 44	778	1,734
45 up to pensionable age	393	802
Pensionable age and over	267	737
Persons in households by country of birth of head	**2,006**	**4,213**
0 - 17	449	922
18 - 44	886	1,820
45 up to pensionable age	409	804
Pensionable age and over	262	667
Bristol		
TOTAL PERSONS	**9,843**	**17,017**
0 - 17	600	1,394
18 - 44	5,281	8,797
45 up to pensionable age	2,779	4,132
Pensionable age and over	1,183	2,694
Persons in households	**9,620**	**16,578**
0 - 17	591	1,374
18 - 44	5,114	8,504
45 up to pensionable age	2,766	4,106
Pensionable age and over	1,149	2,594
Persons in households by country of birth of head	**15,272**	**22,945**
0 - 17	4,856	6,511
18 - 44	6,436	9,844
45 up to pensionable age	2,831	4,158
Pensionable age and over	1,149	2,432
Kingswood		
TOTAL PERSONS	**712**	**1,457**
0 - 17	40	128
18 - 44	430	747
45 up to pensionable age	186	330
Pensionable age and over	56	252
Persons in households	**711**	**1,453**
0 - 17	40	128
18 - 44	429	745
45 up to pensionable age	186	330
Pensionable age and over	56	250
Persons in households by country of birth of head	**1,051**	**1,868**
0 - 17	320	515
18 - 44	490	813
45 up to pensionable age	187	325
Pensionable age and over	54	215

52. Residents

Age	Country of birth: New Commonwealth	Country of birth: Outside of United Kingdom, Ireland, Old Commonwealth and United States of America	Age	Country of birth: New Commonwealth	Country of birth: Outside of United Kingdom, Ireland, Old Commonwealth and United States of America
a	b	c	a	b	c
Northavon			**Woodspring**		
TOTAL PERSONS	**1,353**	**3,001**	**TOTAL PERSONS**	**1,761**	**4,070**
0 - 17	104	375	0 - 17	210	634
18 - 44	845	1,614	18 - 44	929	1,812
45 up to pensionable age	291	604	45 up to pensionable age	379	833
Pensionable age and over	113	408	Pensionable age and over	243	791
Persons in households	**1,306**	**2,868**	**Persons in households**	**1,714**	**3,963**
0 - 17	104	364	0 - 17	206	628
18 - 44	808	1,511	18 - 44	903	1,766
45 up to pensionable age	285	594	45 up to pensionable age	373	822
Pensionable age and over	109	399	Pensionable age and over	232	747
Persons in households by country of birth of head	**1,754**	**3,264**	**Persons in households by country of birth of head**	**2,184**	**4,232**
0 - 17	514	905	0 - 17	628	1,159
18 - 44	834	1,456	18 - 44	917	1,663
45 up to pensionable age	287	550	45 up to pensionable age	384	745
Pensionable age and over	119	353	Pensionable age and over	255	665
Wansdyke					
TOTAL PERSONS	**627**	**1,510**			
0 - 17	63	186			
18 - 44	329	668			
45 up to pensionable age	140	345			
Pensionable age and over	95	311			
Persons in households	**619**	**1,485**			
0 - 17	62	185			
18 - 44	327	657			
45 up to pensionable age	137	341			
Pensionable age and over	93	302			
Persons in households by country of birth of head	**750**	**1,640**			
0 - 17	213	407			
18 - 44	304	612			
45 up to pensionable age	141	313			
Pensionable age and over	92	308			

53. Residents aged 16 and over in households

Lifestage category		ALL PERSONS: In a 'couple' household	ALL PERSONS: Not in a 'couple' household	All household heads: In a 'couple' household	All household heads: Not in a 'couple' household
a		b	c	d	e
AVON					
Aged 16 - 24	No children aged 0 - 15 in household	17,632	65,198	6,140	7,869
	Child(ren) aged 0 - 15 in household	7,568	25,997	2,442	2,216
Aged 25 - 34	No children aged 0 - 15 in household	36,177	36,459	17,936	17,706
	Child(ren) aged 0 - 4 in household	44,823	6,545	20,857	4,130
	Child(ren) in household, youngest aged 5 - 10	11,788	3,746	4,584	2,690
	Child(ren) in household, youngest aged 11 - 15	1,300	1,165	488	500
Aged 35 - 54	No children 0 - 15 in household	49,497	84,695	23,592	48,258
	Child(ren) aged 0 - 4 in household	19,399	5,474	12,048	3,083
	Child(ren) in household, youngest aged 5 - 10	28,741	10,596	15,713	6,282
	Child(ren) in household, youngest aged 11 - 15	15,627	23,652	8,111	12,822
Aged 55 - pensionable age	Working or retired	29,628	22,289	20,985	17,491
	Unemployed or economically inactive (but not retired)	9,656	8,312	4,779	5,175
Pensionable age - 74		65,169	43,947	28,401	34,384
Aged 75 and over		25,217	37,815	15,035	32,755
Bath					
Aged 16 - 24	No children aged 0 - 15 in household	1,365	6,134	471	1,096
	Child(ren) aged 0 - 15 in household	559	2,004	184	221
Aged 25 - 34	No children aged 0 - 15 in household	2,848	3,839	1,385	1,997
	Child(ren) aged 0 - 4 in household	2,930	462	1,337	317
	Child(ren) in household, youngest aged 5 - 10	670	310	257	239
	Child(ren) in household, youngest aged 11 - 15	112	111	43	45
Aged 35 - 54	No children 0 - 15 in household	3,865	7,161	1,847	4,335
	Child(ren) aged 0 - 4 in household	1,598	415	979	247
	Child(ren) in household, youngest aged 5 - 10	2,073	800	1,114	499
	Child(ren) in household, youngest aged 11 - 15	1,135	1,801	596	1,009
Aged 55 - pensionable age	Working or retired	2,619	2,072	1,816	1,626
	Unemployed or economically inactive (but not retired)	648	639	304	413
Pensionable age - 74		6,193	4,573	2,732	3,687
Aged 75 and over		2,685	4,217	1,585	3,745
Bristol					
Aged 16 - 24	No children aged 0 - 15 in household	7,534	26,680	2,693	4,757
	Child(ren) aged 0 - 15 in household	3,512	10,639	1,172	1,319
Aged 25 - 34	No children aged 0 - 15 in household	15,424	18,758	7,595	9,738
	Child(ren) aged 0 - 4 in household	17,579	3,752	8,275	2,404
	Child(ren) in household, youngest aged 5 - 10	4,753	2,027	1,922	1,485
	Child(ren) in household, youngest aged 11 - 15	606	582	244	275
Aged 35 - 54	No children 0 - 15 in household	18,295	33,255	8,819	19,889
	Child(ren) aged 0 - 4 in household	7,280	2,689	4,487	1,540
	Child(ren) in household, youngest aged 5 - 10	9,462	4,319	5,220	2,609
	Child(ren) in household, youngest aged 11 - 15	4,924	8,197	2,583	4,558
Aged 55 - pensionable age	Working or retired	10,063	8,786	7,020	6,837
	Unemployed or economically inactive (but not retired)	3,810	3,892	2,056	2,640
Pensionable age - 74		24,965	19,466	11,022	15,371
Aged 75 and over		9,885	16,245	5,938	14,275

53. Residents aged 16 and over in households

Lifestage category		ALL PERSONS		All household heads	
		In a 'couple' household	Not in a 'couple' household	In a 'couple' household	Not in a 'couple' household
a		b	c	d	e
Kingswood					
Aged 16 - 24	No children aged 0 - 15 in household	1,506	6,167	490	288
	Child(ren) aged 0 - 15 in household	628	2,499	188	131
Aged 25 - 34	No children aged 0 - 15 in household	3,581	2,752	1,788	1,041
	Child(ren) aged 0 - 4 in household	5,165	477	2,409	309
	Child(ren) in household, youngest aged 5 - 10	1,312	295	490	217
	Child(ren) in household, youngest aged 11 - 15	117	92	38	39
Aged 35 - 54	No children 0 - 15 in household	4,928	8,488	2,328	4,533
	Child(ren) aged 0 - 4 in household	1,804	417	1,160	228
	Child(ren) in household, youngest aged 5 - 10	3,174	880	1,756	533
	Child(ren) in household, youngest aged 11 - 15	1,702	2,642	875	1,406
Aged 55 - pensionable age	Working or retired	3,442	2,288	2,441	1,754
	Unemployed or economically inactive (but not retired)	1,029	786	483	456
Pensionable age - 74		6,135	3,757	2,628	2,850
Aged 75 and over		2,003	3,054	1,189	2,607
Northavon					
Aged 16 - 24	No children aged 0 - 15 in household	3,197	9,361	1,156	666
	Child(ren) aged 0 - 15 in household	1,039	3,820	322	172
Aged 25 - 34	No children aged 0 - 15 in household	6,190	4,228	3,176	2,110
	Child(ren) aged 0 - 4 in household	7,538	639	3,551	390
	Child(ren) in household, youngest aged 5 - 10	1,885	387	720	257
	Child(ren) in household, youngest aged 11 - 15	152	140	53	60
Aged 35 - 54	No children 0 - 15 in household	7,724	12,417	3,678	6,753
	Child(ren) aged 0 - 4 in household	2,879	688	1,787	361
	Child(ren) in household, youngest aged 5 - 10	4,576	1,544	2,514	878
	Child(ren) in household, youngest aged 11 - 15	2,855	3,890	1,466	2,057
Aged 55 - pensionable age	Working or retired	4,421	2,953	3,149	2,324
	Unemployed or economically inactive (but not retired)	1,259	922	569	492
Pensionable age - 74		7,377	4,350	3,133	3,331
Aged 75 and over		2,542	3,587	1,543	2,956
Wansdyke					
Aged 16 - 24	No children aged 0 - 15 in household	1,102	5,508	350	192
	Child(ren) aged 0 - 15 in household	586	2,259	185	86
Aged 25 - 34	No children aged 0 - 15 in household	2,549	2,254	1,234	714
	Child(ren) aged 0 - 4 in household	3,718	356	1,699	178
	Child(ren) in household, youngest aged 5 - 10	1,024	203	377	124
	Child(ren) in household, youngest aged 11 - 15	96	76	33	23
Aged 35 - 54	No children 0 - 15 in household	4,400	7,610	2,057	3,963
	Child(ren) aged 0 - 4 in household	1,864	409	1,156	228
	Child(ren) in household, youngest aged 5 - 10	2,987	961	1,625	542
	Child(ren) in household, youngest aged 11 - 15	1,546	2,319	800	1,220
Aged 55 - pensionable age	Working or retired	2,957	2,175	2,134	1,720
	Unemployed or economically inactive (but not retired)	822	697	372	364
Pensionable age - 74		6,219	3,693	2,675	2,759
Aged 75 and over		2,288	3,104	1,382	2,622

53. Residents aged 16 and over in households

Lifestage category		ALL PERSONS		All household heads	
		In a 'couple' household	Not in a 'couple' household	In a 'couple' household	Not in a 'couple' household
a		b	c	d	e
	Woodspring				
Aged 16 - 24	No children aged 0 - 15 in household	2,928	11,348	980	870
	Child(ren) aged 0 - 15 in household	1,244	4,776	391	287
Aged 25 - 34	No children aged 0 - 15 in household	5,585	4,628	2,758	2,106
	Child(ren) aged 0 - 4 in household	7,893	859	3,586	532
	Child(ren) in household, youngest aged 5 - 10	2,144	524	818	368
	Child(ren) in household, youngest aged 11 - 15	217	164	77	58
Aged 35 - 54	No children 0 - 15 in household	10,285	15,764	4,863	8,785
	Child(ren) aged 0 - 4 in household	3,974	856	2,479	479
	Child(ren) in household, youngest aged 5 - 10	6,469	2,092	3,484	1,221
	Child(ren) in household, youngest aged 11 - 15	3,465	4,803	1,791	2,572
Aged 55 - pensionable age	Working or retired	6,126	4,015	4,425	3,230
	Unemployed or economically inactive (but not retired)	2,088	1,376	995	810
Pensionable age - 74		14,280	8,108	6,211	6,386
Aged 75 and over		5,814	7,608	3,398	6,550

54. Household spaces; rooms in household spaces; rooms in hotels and boarding houses

Occupancy type	TOTAL HOUSEHOLD SPACES	TOTAL ROOMS
a	b	c
AVON		
ALL TYPES OF OCCUPANCY	**397,118**	**2,060,275**
Households with residents	**376,522**	**1,968,000**
Enumerated with person(s) present	360,440	1,894,882
Absent households (enumerated)	7,317	35,382
Absent households (imputed)	8,765	37,736
Vacant accommodation	**15,991**	**73,193**
New, never occupied	1,683	8,230
Under improvement	2,583	12,361
Other	11,725	52,602
Accommodation not used as main residence	**4,605**	**19,082**
No persons present	1,661	6,692
Second residences	1,242	5,279
Holiday accommodation	342	1,154
Student accommodation	77	259
Persons enumerated but no residents	2,944	12,390
Owner occupied	619	2,864
Not owner occupied	2,325	9,526
Hotels and boarding houses		9,281

Occupancy type	TOTAL HOUSEHOLD SPACES	TOTAL ROOMS
a	b	c
Bristol		
ALL TYPES OF OCCUPANCY	**166,039**	**827,443**
Households with residents	**156,778**	**786,985**
Enumerated with person(s) present	148,215	750,001
Absent households (enumerated)	3,111	14,158
Absent households (imputed)	5,452	22,826
Vacant accommodation	**7,112**	**31,358**
New, never occupied	372	1,708
Under improvement	1,311	6,060
Other	5,429	23,590
Accommodation not used as main residence	**2,149**	**9,100**
No persons present	339	1,430
Second residences	278	1,202
Holiday accommodation	14	66
Student accommodation	47	162
Persons enumerated but no residents	1,810	7,670
Owner occupied	251	1,225
Not owner occupied	1,559	6,445
Hotels and boarding houses		3,222

Occupancy type	TOTAL HOUSEHOLD SPACES	TOTAL ROOMS
a	b	c
Bath		
ALL TYPES OF OCCUPANCY	**36,838**	**181,953**
Households with residents	**34,128**	**171,000**
Enumerated with person(s) present	32,313	163,145
Absent households (enumerated)	819	3,818
Absent households (imputed)	996	4,037
Vacant accommodation	**1,499**	**6,257**
New, never occupied	67	266
Under improvement	294	1,314
Other	1,138	4,677
Accommodation not used as main residence	**1,211**	**4,696**
No persons present	636	2,377
Second residences	529	2,016
Holiday accommodation	90	310
Student accommodation	17	51
Persons enumerated but no residents	575	2,319
Owner occupied	89	398
Not owner occupied	486	1,921
Hotels and boarding houses		2,277

Occupancy type	TOTAL HOUSEHOLD SPACES	TOTAL ROOMS
a	b	c
Kingswood		
ALL TYPES OF OCCUPANCY	**35,817**	**188,904**
Households with residents	**34,657**	**183,413**
Enumerated with person(s) present	33,762	179,001
Absent households (enumerated)	519	2,631
Absent households (imputed)	376	1,781
Vacant accommodation	**1,081**	**5,121**
New, never occupied	164	739
Under improvement	154	794
Other	763	3,588
Accommodation not used as main residence	**79**	**370**
No persons present	29	140
Second residences	24	116
Holiday accommodation	4	18
Student accommodation	1	6
Persons enumerated but no residents	50	230
Owner occupied	28	128
Not owner occupied	22	102
Hotels and boarding houses		43

54. Household spaces; rooms in household spaces; rooms in hotels and boarding houses

Occupancy type	TOTAL HOUSEHOLD SPACES	TOTAL ROOMS
a	b	c
Northavon		
ALL TYPES OF OCCUPANCY	**51,700**	**284,241**
Households with residents	**49,626**	**273,608**
Enumerated with person(s) present	48,207	266,449
Absent households (enumerated)	887	4,537
Absent households (imputed)	532	2,622
Vacant accommodation	**1,874**	**9,676**
New, never occupied	451	2,488
Under improvement	220	1,164
Other	1,203	6,024
Accommodation not used as main residence	**200**	**957**
No persons present	67	347
Second residences	55	297
Holiday accommodation	10	41
Student accommodation	2	9
Persons enumerated but no residents	133	610
Owner occupied	63	280
Not owner occupied	70	330
Hotels and boarding houses		954
Wansdyke		
ALL TYPES OF OCCUPANCY	**32,133**	**179,416**
Households with residents	**30,814**	**172,739**
Enumerated with person(s) present	29,949	168,195
Absent households (enumerated)	560	3,034
Absent households (imputed)	305	1,510
Vacant accommodation	**1,103**	**5,630**
New, never occupied	175	942
Under improvement	200	1,039
Other	728	3,649
Accommodation not used as main residence	**216**	**1,047**
No persons present	107	545
Second residences	74	406
Holiday accommodation	32	134
Student accommodation	1	5
Persons enumerated but no residents	109	502
Owner occupied	43	221
Not owner occupied	66	281
Hotels and boarding houses		285

Occupancy type	TOTAL HOUSEHOLD SPACES	TOTAL ROOMS
a	b	c
Woodspring		
ALL TYPES OF OCCUPANCY	**74,591**	**398,318**
Households with residents	**70,519**	**380,255**
Enumerated with person(s) present	67,994	368,091
Absent households (enumerated)	1,421	7,204
Absent households (imputed)	1,104	4,960
Vacant accommodation	**3,322**	**15,151**
New, never occupied	454	2,087
Under improvement	404	1,990
Other	2,464	11,074
Accommodation not used as main residence	**750**	**2,912**
No persons present	483	1,853
Second residences	282	1,242
Holiday accommodation	192	585
Student accommodation	9	26
Persons enumerated but no residents	267	1,059
Owner occupied	145	612
Not owner occupied	122	447
Hotels and boarding houses		2,500

55. Household spaces in permanent buildings: dwellings

Occupancy type	TOTAL HOUSEHOLD SPACES	Household spaces in dwellings with the following number of household spaces			Unattached household spaces (not in a dwelling)
		1	2	3 or more	
a	b	c	d	e	f
	AVON				
ALL TYPES OF OCCUPANCY	**395,242**	**388,418**	**1,624**	**4,254**	**946**
Households with residents	**374,740**	**369,193**	**1,411**	**3,340**	**796**
Enumerated with person(s) present	358,756	354,041	1,258	2,720	737
Absent households (enumerated)	7,271	7,046	39	158	28
Absent households (imputed)	8,713	8,106	114	462	31
Vacant accommodation	**15,991**	**15,299**	**104**	**499**	**89**
New, never occupied	1,683	1,676	4	2	1
Under improvement	2,583	2,510	13	50	10
Other	11,725	11,113	87	447	78
Accommodation not used as main residence	**4,511**	**3,926**	**109**	**415**	**61**
No persons present	1,661	1,601	6	40	14
Second residences	1,242	1,214	3	15	10
Holiday accommodation	342	329	-	12	1
Student accommodation	77	58	3	13	3
Persons enumerated but no residents	2,850	2,325	103	375	47
Owner occupied	553	543	4	1	5
Not owner occupied	2,297	1,782	99	374	42
TOTAL DWELLINGS	**390,113**	**388,418**	**812**	**883**	
	Bath				
ALL TYPES OF OCCUPANCY	**36,749**	**35,638**	**286**	**626**	**199**
Households with residents	**34,039**	**33,122**	**241**	**507**	**169**
Enumerated with person(s) present	32,226	31,442	215	410	159
Absent households (enumerated)	818	777	9	26	6
Absent households (imputed)	995	903	17	71	4
Vacant accommodation	**1,499**	**1,421**	**22**	**43**	**13**
New, never occupied	67	66	1	-	-
Under improvement	294	289	3	2	-
Other	1,138	1,066	18	41	13
Accommodation not used as main residence	**1,211**	**1,095**	**23**	**76**	**17**
No persons present	636	617	1	12	6
Second residences	529	518	-	7	4
Holiday accommodation	90	87	-	2	1
Student accommodation	17	12	1	3	1
Persons enumerated but no residents	575	478	22	64	11
Owner occupied	89	89	-	-	-
Not owner occupied	486	389	22	64	11
TOTAL DWELLINGS	**35,901**	**35,638**	**143**	**120**	

55. Household spaces in permanent buildings: dwellings

Occupancy type	TOTAL HOUSEHOLD SPACES	Household spaces in dwellings with the following number of household spaces			Unattached household spaces (not in a dwelling)
		1	2	3 or more	
a	b	c	d	e	f
	Bristol				
ALL TYPES OF OCCUPANCY	**165,909**	**161,392**	**1,022**	**2,912**	**583**
Households with residents	**156,651**	**153,030**	**883**	**2,255**	**483**
Enumerated with person(s) present	148,113	145,096	771	1,806	440
Absent households (enumerated)	3,107	2,952	24	111	20
Absent households (imputed)	5,431	4,982	88	338	23
Vacant accommodation	**7,112**	**6,644**	**61**	**347**	**60**
New, never occupied	372	367	3	2	-
Under improvement	1,311	1,253	6	44	8
Other	5,429	5,024	52	301	52
Accommodation not used as main residence	**2,146**	**1,718**	**78**	**310**	**40**
No persons present	339	318	2	13	6
Second residences	278	270	-	4	4
Holiday accommodation	14	13	-	1	-
Student accommodation	47	35	2	8	2
Persons enumerated but no residents	1,807	1,400	76	297	34
Owner occupied	251	241	4	1	5
Not owner occupied	1,556	1,159	72	296	29
TOTAL DWELLINGS	**162,501**	**161,392**	**511**	**598**	
	Kingswood				
ALL TYPES OF OCCUPANCY	**35,693**	**35,558**	**28**	**96**	**11**
Households with residents	**34,535**	**34,425**	**28**	**73**	**9**
Enumerated with person(s) present	33,649	33,547	28	66	8
Absent households (enumerated)	517	515	-	2	-
Absent households (imputed)	369	363	-	5	1
Vacant accommodation	**1,081**	**1,059**	**-**	**20**	**2**
New, never occupied	164	164	-	-	-
Under improvement	154	154	-	-	-
Other	763	741	-	20	2
Accommodation not used as main residence	**77**	**74**	**-**	**3**	**-**
No persons present	29	27	-	2	-
Second residences	24	22	-	2	-
Holiday accommodation	4	4	-	-	-
Student accommodation	1	1	-	-	-
Persons enumerated but no residents	48	47	-	1	-
Owner occupied	26	26	-	-	-
Not owner occupied	22	21	-	1	-
TOTAL DWELLINGS	**35,595**	**35,558**	**14**	**23**	

55. Household spaces in permanent buildings: dwellings

Occupancy type	TOTAL HOUSEHOLD SPACES	Household spaces in dwellings with the following number of household spaces			Unattached household spaces (not in a dwelling)
		1	2	3 or more	
a	b	c	d	e	f
	Northavon				
ALL TYPES OF OCCUPANCY	**51,149**	**51,052**	**50**	**35**	**12**
Households with residents	**49,086**	**48,999**	**46**	**30**	**11**
Enumerated with person(s) present	47,688	47,609	42	26	11
Absent households (enumerated)	872	870	1	1	-
Absent households (imputed)	526	520	3	3	-
Vacant accommodation	**1,874**	**1,866**	**3**	**4**	**1**
New, never occupied	451	451	-	-	-
Under improvement	220	220	-	-	-
Other	1,203	1,195	3	4	1
Accommodation not used as main residence	**189**	**187**	**1**	**1**	**-**
No persons present	67	67	-	-	-
Second residences	55	55	-	-	-
Holiday accommodation	10	10	-	-	-
Student accommodation	2	2	-	-	-
Persons enumerated but no residents	122	120	1	1	-
Owner occupied	54	54	-	-	-
Not owner occupied	68	66	1	1	-
TOTAL DWELLINGS	**51,086**	**51,052**	**25**	**9**	
	Wansdyke				
ALL TYPES OF OCCUPANCY	**31,966**	**31,891**	**26**	**40**	**9**
Households with residents	**30,659**	**30,593**	**25**	**33**	**8**
Enumerated with person(s) present	29,810	29,753	21	28	8
Absent households (enumerated)	552	547	3	2	-
Absent households (imputed)	297	293	1	3	-
Vacant accommodation	**1,103**	**1,099**	**-**	**4**	**-**
New, never occupied	175	175	-	-	-
Under improvement	200	200	-	-	-
Other	728	724	-	4	-
Accommodation not used as main residence	**204**	**199**	**1**	**3**	**1**
No persons present	107	107	-	-	-
Second residences	74	74	-	-	-
Holiday accommodation	32	32	-	-	-
Student accommodation	1	1	-	-	-
Persons enumerated but no residents	97	92	1	3	1
Owner occupied	36	36	-	-	-
Not owner occupied	61	56	1	3	1
TOTAL DWELLINGS	**31,914**	**31,891**	**13**	**10**	

55. Household spaces in permanent buildings: dwellings

Occupancy type	TOTAL HOUSEHOLD SPACES	Household spaces in dwellings with the following number of household spaces			Unattached household spaces (not in a dwelling)
		1	2	3 or more	
a	b	c	d	e	f
	Woodspring				
ALL TYPES OF OCCUPANCY	**73,776**	**72,887**	**212**	**545**	**132**
Households with residents	**69,770**	**69,024**	**188**	**442**	**116**
Enumerated with person(s) present	67,270	66,594	181	384	111
Absent households (enumerated)	1,405	1,385	2	16	2
Absent households (imputed)	1,095	1,045	5	42	3
Vacant accommodation	**3,322**	**3,210**	**18**	**81**	**13**
New, never occupied	454	453	-	-	1
Under improvement	404	394	4	4	2
Other	2,464	2,363	14	77	10
Accommodation not used as main residence	**684**	**653**	**6**	**22**	**3**
No persons present	483	465	3	13	2
Second residences	282	275	3	2	2
Holiday accommodation	192	183	-	9	-
Student accommodation	9	7	-	2	-
Persons enumerated but no residents	201	188	3	9	1
Owner occupied	97	97	-	-	-
Not owner occupied	104	91	3	9	1
TOTAL DWELLINGS	**73,116**	**72,887**	**106**	**123**	

Table 56 Household space type and occupancy

56. Household spaces

Occupancy type	TOTAL HOUSEHOLD SPACES	Household space type in permanent buildings													Non-permanent accomm-odation
		Unshared dwellings - purpose-built					Unshared dwellings - converted		Unshared dwellings - not self-contained			Other household spaces - not self-contained			
		Detached	Semi-detached	Terraced	Purpose-built flat in: Residential building	Purpose-built flat in: Commercial building	Converted flat	Converted flatlet	Not self-contained flat	Not self-contained 'rooms'	Bedsit	Not self-contained flat	Not self-contained 'rooms'	Bedsit	
a	b	c	d	e	f	g	h	i	j	k	l	m	n	o	p
AVON															
ALL TYPES OF OCCUPANCY	**397,118**	**67,344**	**114,642**	**127,182**	**43,947**	**5,338**	**27,788**	**1,705**	**332**		**140**	**2,614**		**4,210**	**1,876**
Households with residents	**376,522**	**64,744**	**111,716**	**121,678**	**40,801**	**4,437**	**23,973**	**1,436**	**236**	**70**	**102**	**1,552**	**659**	**3,336**	**1,782**
Enumerated with person(s) present	360,440	62,789	108,767	117,164	38,139	4,052	21,516	1,244	217	67	86	1,410	607	2,698	1,684
Absent households	16,082	1,955	2,949	4,514	2,662	385	2,457	192	19	3	16	142	52	638	98
Vacant accommodation	**15,991**	**2,281**	**2,532**	**4,586**	**2,514**	**749**	**2,411**	**195**	**12**		**19**	**247**		**445**	
New, never occupied	1,683	588	100	312	615	8	49	4	-		-	3		4	
Other	14,308	1,693	2,432	4,274	1,899	741	2,362	191	12		19	244		441	
Accommodation not used as main residence	**4,605**	**319**	**394**	**918**	**632**	**152**	**1,404**	**74**	**14**		**19**	**156**		**429**	
No persons present	1,661	168	153	261	326	48	621	24	-		-	17		43	
Persons enumerated but no residents	2,944	151	241	657	306	104	783	50	14	-	19	101	38	386	94
Bath															
ALL TYPES OF OCCUPANCY	**36,838**	**3,578**	**7,851**	**12,836**	**4,512**	**524**	**5,930**	**338**	**47**		**22**	**491**		**620**	**89**
Households with residents	**34,128**	**3,444**	**7,630**	**12,239**	**4,116**	**427**	**4,912**	**296**	**33**	**11**	**14**	**330**	**94**	**493**	**89**
Enumerated with person(s) present	32,313	3,297	7,387	11,799	3,858	389	4,393	270	29	10	10	299	87	398	87
Absent households	1,815	147	243	440	258	38	519	26	4	1	4	31	7	95	2
Vacant accommodation	**1,499**	**100**	**163**	**369**	**260**	**62**	**441**	**20**	**2**		**4**	**37**		**41**	
New, never occupied	67	15	3	9	39	-	-	-	-		-	1		-	
Other	1,432	85	160	360	221	62	441	20	2		4	36		41	
Accommodation not used as main residence	**1,211**	**34**	**58**	**228**	**136**	**35**	**577**	**22**	**1**		**4**	**30**		**86**	
No persons present	636	16	24	77	92	21	374	13	-		-	1		18	
Persons enumerated but no residents	575	18	34	151	44	14	203	9	1	-	4	24	5	68	-

56. Household spaces

Occupancy type	TOTAL HOUSEHOLD SPACES	Household space type in permanent buildings														Non-permanent accomm-odation
		Unshared dwellings - purpose-built					Unshared dwellings - converted		Unshared dwellings - not self-contained			Other household spaces - not self-contained			
		Detached	Semi-detached	Terraced	Purpose-built flat in: Residential building	Purpose-built flat in: Commercial building	Converted flat	Converted flatlet	Not self-contained flat	Not self-contained 'rooms'	Bedsit	Not self-contained flat	Not self-contained 'rooms'	Bedsit	
a	b	c	d	e	f	g	h	i	j	k	l	m	n	o	p
					Bristol										
ALL TYPES OF OCCUPANCY	**166,039**	**8,538**	**42,761**	**66,852**	**24,480**	**2,966**	**14,605**	**940**	**163**		**87**	**1,592**		**2,925**	**130**
Households with residents	**156,778**	**8,224**	**41,765**	**63,867**	**22,921**	**2,456**	**12,775**	**810**	**111**	**32**	**69**	**912**	**416**	**2,293**	**127**
Enumerated with person(s) present	148,215	7,906	40,598	61,039	21,210	2,192	11,277	682	105	30	57	815	381	1,821	102
Absent households	8,563	318	1,167	2,828	1,711	264	1,498	128	6	2	12	97	35	472	25
Vacant accommodation	**7,112**	**283**	**852**	**2,497**	**1,261**	**421**	**1,219**	**97**	**9**		**5**	**152**		**316**	
New, never occupied	372	63	22	48	198	8	26	2	-		-	1		4	
Other	6,740	220	830	2,449	1,063	413	1,193	95	9		5	151		312	
Accommodation not used as main residence	**2,149**	**31**	**144**	**488**	**298**	**89**	**611**	**33**	**11**		**13**	**112**		**316**	
No persons present	339	7	33	75	103	15	82	3	-		-	6		15	
Persons enumerated but no residents	1,810	24	111	413	195	74	529	30	11	-	13	74	32	301	3
					Kingswood										
ALL TYPES OF OCCUPANCY	**35,817**	**5,516**	**13,867**	**12,577**	**2,894**	**387**	**288**	**19**	**8**		**2**	**41**		**94**	**124**
Households with residents	**34,657**	**5,326**	**13,603**	**12,184**	**2,743**	**290**	**254**	**15**	**7**	**1**	**2**	**26**	**7**	**77**	**122**
Enumerated with person(s) present	33,762	5,202	13,300	11,873	2,631	279	238	14	7	1	2	25	7	70	113
Absent households	895	124	303	311	112	11	16	1	-	-	-	1	-	7	9
Vacant accommodation	**1,081**	**181**	**247**	**362**	**143**	**92**	**30**	**4**	**-**		**-**	**6**		**16**	
New, never occupied	164	52	14	49	49	-	-	-	-		-	-		-	
Other	917	129	233	313	94	92	30	4	-		-	6		16	
Accommodation not used as main residence	**79**	**9**	**17**	**31**	**8**	**5**	**4**	**-**	**-**		**-**	**2**		**1**	
No persons present	29	3	6	13	2	3	-	-	-		-	2		-	
Persons enumerated but no residents	50	6	11	18	6	2	4	-	-	-	-	-	-	1	2

Table 56 Household space type and occupancy – **continued**

56. Household spaces

Occupancy type	TOTAL HOUSEHOLD SPACES	Household space type in permanent buildings														Non-permanent accomm-odation
		Unshared dwellings - purpose-built					Unshared dwellings - converted		Unshared dwellings - not self-contained			Other household spaces - not self-contained			
		Detached	Semi-detached	Terraced	Purpose-built flat in: Residential building	Purpose-built flat in: Commercial building	Converted flat	Converted flatlet	Not self-contained flat	Not self-contained 'rooms'	Bedsit	Not self-contained flat	Not self-contained 'rooms'	Bedsit	
a	b	c	d	e	f	g	h	i	j	k	l	m	n	o	p
					Northavon										
ALL TYPES OF OCCUPANCY	**51,700**	**14,761**	**17,261**	**14,756**	**3,583**	**367**	**299**	**10**	**13**		**2**	**50**		**47**	**551**
Households with residents	**49,626**	**14,119**	**16,792**	**14,105**	**3,373**	**312**	**273**	**10**	**8**	**5**	**2**	**30**	**16**	**41**	**540**
Enumerated with person(s) present	48,207	13,772	16,366	13,702	3,183	301	261	10	7	5	2	29	14	36	519
Absent households	1,419	347	426	403	190	11	12	-	1	-	-	1	2	5	21
Vacant accommodation	**1,874**	**588**	**424**	**592**	**192**	**50**	**20**	**-**	**-**		**-**	**4**		**4**	
New, never occupied	451	247	25	154	25	-	-	-	-		-	-		-	
Other	1,423	341	399	438	167	50	20	-	-		-	4		4	
Accommodation not used as main residence	**200**	**54**	**45**	**59**	**18**	**5**	**6**	**-**	**-**		**-**	**-**		**2**	
No persons present	67	28	15	17	3	-	4	-	-		-	-		-	
Persons enumerated but no residents	133	26	30	42	15	5	2	-	-	-	-	-	-	2	11
					Wansdyke										
ALL TYPES OF OCCUPANCY	**32,133**	**10,139**	**10,442**	**8,292**	**2,193**	**263**	**518**	**23**	**19**		**2**	**42**		**33**	**167**
Households with residents	**30,814**	**9,712**	**10,180**	**7,890**	**2,058**	**237**	**478**	**17**	**16**	**3**	**2**	**22**	**14**	**30**	**155**
Enumerated with person(s) present	29,949	9,430	9,941	7,697	1,980	226	442	16	16	3	2	19	13	25	139
Absent households	865	282	239	193	78	11	36	1	-	-	-	3	1	5	16
Vacant accommodation	**1,103**	**355**	**225**	**350**	**120**	**21**	**24**	**4**	**-**		**-**	**4**		**-**	
New, never occupied	175	86	8	12	65	-	4	-	-		-	-		-	
Other	928	269	217	338	55	21	20	4	-		-	4		-	
Accommodation not used as main residence	**216**	**72**	**37**	**52**	**15**	**5**	**16**	**2**	**-**		**-**	**2**		**3**	
No persons present	107	41	18	36	6	2	4	-	-		-	-		-	
Persons enumerated but no residents	109	31	19	16	9	3	12	2	-	-	-	2	-	3	12

56. Household spaces

Occupancy type	TOTAL HOUSEHOLD SPACES	Household space type in permanent buildings													Non-permanent accomm-odation
		Unshared dwellings - purpose-built					Unshared dwellings - converted		Unshared dwellings - not self-contained			Other household spaces - not self-contained			
		Detached	Semi-detached	Terraced	Purpose-built flat in:										
					Residential building	Commercial building	Converted flat	Converted flatlet	Not self-contained flat	Not self-contained 'rooms'	Bedsit	Not self-contained flat	Not self-contained 'rooms'	Bedsit	
a	b	c	d	e	f	g	h	i	j	k	l	m	n	o	p
					Woodspring										
ALL TYPES OF OCCUPANCY	**74,591**	**24,812**	**22,460**	**11,869**	**6,285**	**831**	**6,148**	**375**	**82**		**25**	**398**		**491**	**815**
Households with residents	**70,519**	**23,919**	**21,746**	**11,393**	**5,590**	**715**	**5,281**	**288**	**61**	**18**	**13**	**232**	**112**	**402**	**749**
Enumerated with person(s) present	67,994	23,182	21,175	11,054	5,277	665	4,905	252	53	18	13	223	105	348	724
Absent households	2,525	737	571	339	313	50	376	36	8	-	-	9	7	54	25
Vacant accommodation	**3,322**	**774**	**621**	**416**	**538**	**103**	**677**	**70**	**1**		**10**	**44**		**68**	
New, never occupied	454	125	28	40	239	-	19	2	-		-	1		-	
Other	2,868	649	593	376	299	103	658	68	1		10	43		68	
Accommodation not used as main residence	**750**	**119**	**93**	**60**	**157**	**13**	**190**	**17**	**2**		**2**	**10**		**21**	
No persons present	483	73	57	43	120	7	157	8	-		-	8		10	
Persons enumerated but no residents	267	46	36	17	37	6	33	9	2	-	2	1	1	11	66

Table 57 Household space type: rooms and household size

Note: Maximum number of rooms in non-permanent accommodation is 5

57. Households with residents; residents in households; rooms in household spaces

	TOTAL HOUSE-HOLDS	Household space type in permanent buildings														Non-permanent accomm-odation	With migrant head
		Unshared dwellings - purpose-built					Unshared dwellings - converted		Unshared dwellings - not self-contained			Other household spaces - not self-contained				
		Detached	Semi-detached	Terraced	Purpose-built flat in: Residential building	Purpose-built flat in: Commercial building	Converted flat	Converted flatlet	Not self-contained flat	Not self-contained 'rooms'	Bedsit	Not self-contained flat	Not self-contained 'rooms'	Bedsit		
a	b	c	d	e	f	g	h	i	j	k	l	m	n	o	p	q
AVON																
Households with the following rooms																
TOTAL	**376,522**	**64,744**	**111,716**	**121,678**	**40,801**	**4,437**	**23,973**	**1,436**	**236**	**70**	**102**	**1,552**	**659**	**3,336**	**1,782**	**36,752**
1	7,055	20	39	154	1,710	137	-	1,436			102			3,336	121	2,549
2	13,472	94	445	1,325	6,258	333	4,157		26	22		281	307		224	2,759
3	29,205	580	2,064	4,663	12,486	831	7,411		45	21		404	189		511	5,104
4	64,603	5,445	12,270	21,132	16,065	1,251	7,248		43	17		362	80		690	7,925
5	104,903	12,685	39,026	45,154	3,532	1,006	2,995		45	3		188	33		236	7,896
6	93,136	16,000	39,933	34,793	579	515	1,149		19	1		125	22			5,800
7 or more	64,148	29,920	17,939	14,457	171	364	1,013		58	6		192	28			4,719
TOTAL ROOMS	**1,968,000**	**421,296**	**630,784**	**646,677**	**138,612**	**19,283**	**90,364**	**1,436**	**1,200**	**249**	**102**	**6,591**	**2,028**	**3,336**	**6,042**	**166,514**
Households with the following persons																
TOTAL	**376,522**	**64,744**	**111,716**	**121,678**	**40,801**	**4,437**	**23,973**	**1,436**	**236**	**70**	**102**	**1,552**	**659**	**3,336**	**1,782**	**36,752**
1	100,534	9,065	20,327	28,320	23,177	1,339	12,039	1,160	76	39	72	723	453	2,997	747	11,123
2	132,374	24,466	39,371	43,533	12,378	1,620	8,858	234	80	22	15	524	146	276	851	14,021
3	58,265	11,142	19,770	21,076	3,316	693	1,873	31	30	6	8	141	29	49	101	5,444
4	58,966	14,292	22,227	19,416	1,480	493	848	5	34	2	3	93	23	6	44	4,206
5	19,668	4,485	7,554	6,701	376	199	261	5	9	1	3	37	7	5	25	1,418
6	5,133	1,056	1,896	1,941	62	58	79	1	5	-	1	18	1	3	12	417
7 or more	1,582	238	571	691	12	35	15	-	2	-	-	16	-	-	2	123
TOTAL PERSONS	**916,973**	**179,140**	**300,707**	**306,629**	**66,140**	**10,245**	**40,657**	**1,772**	**554**	**114**	**159**	**2,989**	**965**	**3,763**	**3,139**	**82,837**
Households with the following persons per room																
TOTAL	**376,522**	**64,744**	**111,716**	**121,678**	**40,801**	**4,437**	**23,973**	**1,436**	**236**	**70**	**102**	**1,552**	**659**	**3,336**	**1,782**	**36,752**
Over 1.5	1,397	32	107	192	235	58	39	276	3	-	30	10	3	339	73	505
Over 1 and up to 1.5	4,177	164	1,286	1,786	546	125	222	-	-	1	-	21	7	-	19	385
Over 0.5 and up to 1	119,606	17,624	38,530	39,601	10,575	1,669	6,209	1,160	76	19	72	435	143	2,997	496	13,466
Up to 0.5	251,342	46,924	71,793	80,099	29,445	2,585	17,503	-	157	50	-	1,086	506	-	1,194	22,396

Note: Maximum number of rooms in non-permanent accommodation is 5

57. Households with residents; residents in households; rooms in household spaces

	TOTAL HOUSE-HOLDS	Household space type in permanent buildings													Non-permanent accomm-odation	With migrant head
		Unshared dwellings - purpose-built					Unshared dwellings - converted		Unshared dwellings - not self-contained			Other household spaces - not self-contained				
		Detached	Semi-detached	Terraced	Purpose-built flat in: Residential building	Purpose-built flat in: Commercial building	Converted flat	Converted flatlet	Not self-contained flat	Not self-contained 'rooms'	Bedsit	Not self-contained flat	Not self-contained 'rooms'	Bedsit		
a	b	c	d	e	f	g	h	i	j	k	l	m	n	o	p	q
Bath																
Households with the following rooms																
TOTAL	**34,128**	**3,444**	**7,630**	**12,239**	**4,116**	**427**	**4,912**	**296**	**33**	**11**	**14**	**330**	**94**	**493**	**89**	**3,829**
1	987	-	3	18	147	10	-	296			14			493	6	381
2	1,867	7	42	122	594	32	961		5	1		58	34		11	369
3	3,949	25	145	539	1,245	88	1,746		10	4		92	37		18	742
4	6,564	201	823	2,410	1,531	137	1,317		3	5		83	10		44	812
5	7,727	531	2,131	3,908	524	78	500		3	-		35	7		10	630
6	7,482	950	2,903	3,288	52	50	205		3	-		28	3			496
7 or more	5,552	1,730	1,583	1,954	23	32	183		9	1		34	3			399
TOTAL ROOMS	**171,000**	**23,268**	**44,711**	**66,195**	**14,302**	**1,835**	**17,729**	**296**	**163**	**42**	**14**	**1,347**	**297**	**493**	**308**	**15,928**
Households with the following persons																
TOTAL	**34,128**	**3,444**	**7,630**	**12,239**	**4,116**	**427**	**4,912**	**296**	**33**	**11**	**14**	**330**	**94**	**493**	**89**	**3,829**
1	11,179	564	1,498	3,063	2,345	133	2,594	225	11	6	7	167	66	445	55	1,364
2	11,945	1,468	2,845	4,241	1,217	169	1,733	60	12	4	2	109	14	41	30	1,405
3	4,811	560	1,242	2,190	329	72	362	9	2	-	1	30	8	4	2	527
4	4,258	567	1,351	1,956	172	36	150	1	6	1	2	12	3	-	1	363
5	1,445	217	487	611	43	12	61	1	1	-	1	8	2	1	-	123
6	375	51	154	138	10	4	9	-	1	-	1	3	1	2	1	33
7 or more	115	17	53	40	-	1	3	-	-	-	-	1	-	-	-	14
TOTAL PERSONS	**76,876**	**8,972**	**20,072**	**30,120**	**6,729**	**924**	**8,127**	**381**	**76**	**18**	**33**	**591**	**146**	**556**	**131**	**8,130**
Households with the following persons per room																
TOTAL	**34,128**	**3,444**	**7,630**	**12,239**	**4,116**	**427**	**4,912**	**296**	**33**	**11**	**14**	**330**	**94**	**493**	**89**	**3,829**
Over 1.5	182	2	11	12	16	3	8	71	-	-	7	2	-	48	2	71
Over 1 and up to 1.5	396	6	121	133	64	9	57	-	-	-	-	2	4	-	-	52
Over 0.5 and up to 1	9,975	697	2,207	3,768	1,031	142	1,330	225	13	3	7	76	18	445	13	1,497
Up to 0.5	23,575	2,739	5,291	8,326	3,005	273	3,517	-	20	8	-	250	72	-	74	2,209

Table 57 Household space type: rooms and household size – continued

Note: Maximum number of rooms in non-permanent accommodation is 5

57. Households with residents; residents in households; rooms in household spaces

	TOTAL HOUSE-HOLDS	Household space type in permanent buildings													Non-permanent accomm-odation	With migrant head
		Unshared dwellings - purpose-built					Unshared dwellings - converted		Unshared dwellings - not self-contained			Other household spaces - not self-contained				
		Detached	Semi-detached	Terraced	Purpose-built flat in: Residential building	Purpose-built flat in: Commercial building	Converted flat	Converted flatlet	Not self-contained flat	Not self-contained 'rooms'	Bedsit	Not self-contained flat	Not self-contained 'rooms'	Bedsit		
a	b	c	d	e	f	g	h	i	j	k	l	m	n	o	p	q
Bristol																
Households with the following rooms																
TOTAL	**156,778**	**8,224**	**41,765**	**63,867**	**22,921**	**2,456**	**12,775**	**810**	**111**	**32**	**69**	**912**	**416**	**2,293**	**127**	**16,413**
1	4,272	5	24	97	857	93	-	810			69			2,293	24	1,586
2	7,219	15	141	379	3,714	210	2,348		12	12		169	203		16	1,407
3	14,119	139	506	1,479	7,199	484	3,910		22	8		234	109		29	2,535
4	27,698	1,103	3,240	9,610	8,895	673	3,842		24	6		211	47		47	3,629
5	43,935	1,440	15,306	23,073	1,826	552	1,576		18	3		109	21		11	3,254
6	38,902	1,858	15,376	20,385	319	267	605		9	-		69	14			2,337
7 or more	20,633	3,664	7,172	8,844	111	177	494		26	3		120	22			1,665
TOTAL ROOMS	**786,985**	**52,611**	**240,313**	**348,969**	**77,512**	**10,404**	**47,751**	**810**	**566**	**109**	**69**	**3,908**	**1,284**	**2,293**	**386**	**70,064**
Households with the following persons																
TOTAL	**156,778**	**8,224**	**41,765**	**63,867**	**22,921**	**2,456**	**12,775**	**810**	**111**	**32**	**69**	**912**	**416**	**2,293**	**127**	**16,413**
1	47,600	1,429	7,508	15,027	12,807	779	6,436	663	35	20	54	422	295	2,071	54	5,647
2	53,411	3,180	14,278	22,698	6,862	894	4,696	124	37	10	6	297	89	187	53	5,966
3	23,261	1,318	7,355	10,987	2,041	357	1,019	17	16	1	6	89	16	28	11	2,357
4	21,290	1,535	8,177	9,843	936	264	437	4	12	-	1	58	12	5	6	1,579
5	7,939	534	3,251	3,652	234	104	124	2	5	1	2	22	4	1	3	606
6	2,383	166	903	1,179	33	32	53	-	4	-	-	12	-	1	-	191
7 or more	894	62	293	481	8	26	10	-	2	-	-	12	-	-	-	67
TOTAL PERSONS	**370,131**	**22,024**	**114,722**	**161,730**	**37,824**	**5,608**	**21,646**	**988**	**271**	**48**	**98**	**1,791**	**589**	**2,560**	**232**	**35,645**
Households with the following persons per room																
TOTAL	**156,778**	**8,224**	**41,765**	**63,867**	**22,921**	**2,456**	**12,775**	**810**	**111**	**32**	**69**	**912**	**416**	**2,293**	**127**	**16,413**
Over 1.5	821	11	68	142	136	38	19	147	3	-	15	6	1	222	13	285
Over 1 and up to 1.5	2,360	42	680	1,071	356	82	106	-	-	-	-	17	3	-	3	179
Over 0.5 and up to 1	49,868	2,050	14,470	19,652	6,194	920	3,360	663	37	8	54	268	82	2,071	39	6,445
Up to 0.5	103,729	6,121	26,547	43,002	16,235	1,416	9,290	-	71	24	-	621	330	-	72	9,504

Table 57 Household space type: rooms and household size – continued

Note: Maximum number of rooms in non-permanent accommodation is 5

57. Households with residents; residents in households; rooms in household spaces

	TOTAL HOUSE-HOLDS	Household space type in permanent buildings														Non-permanent accomm-odation	With migrant head
		Unshared dwellings - purpose-built					Unshared dwellings - converted		Unshared dwellings - not self-contained			Other household spaces - not self-contained					
		Detached	Semi-detached	Terraced	Purpose-built flat in: Residential building	Purpose-built flat in: Commercial building	Converted flat	Converted flatlet	Not self-contained flat	Not self-contained 'rooms'	Bedsit	Not self-contained flat	Not self-contained 'rooms'	Bedsit			
a	b	c	d	e	f	g	h	i	j	k	l	m	n	o		p	q
Kingswood																	
Households with the following rooms																	
TOTAL	**34,657**	**5,326**	**13,603**	**12,184**	**2,743**	**290**	**254**	**15**	**7**	**1**	**2**	**26**	**7**	**77**		**122**	**2,702**
1	223	-	1	5	101	10	-	15			2			77		12	74
2	748	9	32	183	421	20	37		1	-		5	3			37	153
3	2,110	33	252	664	962	49	90		-	-		6	3			51	311
4	5,356	359	1,646	2,118	1,053	91	62		1	1		7	1			17	551
5	10,746	1,249	4,519	4,697	167	72	34		1	-		2	-			5	722
6	10,645	1,450	5,426	3,685	34	30	13		2	-		5	-				563
7 or more	4,829	2,226	1,727	832	5	18	18		2	-		1	-				328
TOTAL ROOMS	**183,413**	**33,541**	**75,392**	**62,552**	**9,115**	**1,234**	**990**	**15**	**37**	**4**	**2**	**103**	**19**	**77**		**332**	**12,951**
Households with the following persons																	
TOTAL	**34,657**	**5,326**	**13,603**	**12,184**	**2,743**	**290**	**254**	**15**	**7**	**1**	**2**	**26**	**7**	**77**		**122**	**2,702**
1	7,364	591	2,166	2,588	1,657	85	127	10	1	-	-	12	3	66		58	662
2	12,352	1,906	4,989	4,400	780	110	87	4	2	1	2	8	4	9		50	1,146
3	5,976	970	2,531	2,200	195	45	20	1	2	-	-	2	-	2		8	403
4	6,537	1,352	2,883	2,161	85	33	15	-	2	-	-	4	-	-		2	348
5	1,929	416	836	637	24	10	5	-	-	-	-	-	-	-		1	107
6	407	74	164	158	2	6	-	-	-	-	-	-	-	-		3	28
7 or more	92	17	34	40	-	1	-	-	-	-	-	-	-	-		-	8
TOTAL PERSONS	**88,916**	**15,371**	**36,690**	**31,059**	**4,274**	**666**	**446**	**21**	**19**	**2**	**4**	**50**	**11**	**90**		**213**	**6,317**
Households with the following persons per room																	
TOTAL	**34,657**	**5,326**	**13,603**	**12,184**	**2,743**	**290**	**254**	**15**	**7**	**1**	**2**	**26**	**7**	**77**		**122**	**2,702**
Over 1.5	49	3	5	8	5	7	-	5	-	-	2	-	-	11		3	15
Over 1 and up to 1.5	290	14	88	143	35	5	3	-	-	-	-	-	-	-		2	26
Over 0.5 and up to 1	12,149	1,808	4,965	4,388	660	105	72	10	3	-	-	9	4	66		59	867
Up to 0.5	22,169	3,501	8,545	7,645	2,043	173	179	-	4	1	-	17	3	-		58	1,794

Table 57 Household space type: rooms and household size – continued

Note: Maximum number of rooms in non-permanent accommodation is 5

57. Households with residents; residents in households; rooms in household spaces

	TOTAL HOUSE-HOLDS	Household space type in permanent buildings													Non-permanent accomm-odation	With migrant head
		Unshared dwellings - purpose-built					Unshared dwellings - converted		Unshared dwellings - not self-contained			Other household spaces - not self-contained				
		Detached	Semi-detached	Terraced	Purpose-built flat in: Residential building	Purpose-built flat in: Commercial building	Converted flat	Converted flatlet	Not self-contained flat	Not self-contained 'rooms'	Bedsit	Not self-contained flat	Not self-contained 'rooms'	Bedsit		
a	b	c	d	e	f	g	h	i	j	k	l	m	n	o	p	q
Northavon																
Households with the following rooms																
TOTAL	**49,626**	**14,119**	**16,792**	**14,105**	**3,373**	**312**	**273**	**10**	**8**	**5**	**2**	**30**	**16**	**41**	**540**	**5,175**
1	289	3	2	5	194	7	-	10			2			41	25	62
2	1,034	22	123	232	523	13	37		-	1		4	7		72	248
3	2,372	96	385	745	884	60	44		1	2		2	3		150	491
4	7,180	843	1,967	2,589	1,366	96	97		1	2		6	1		212	1,037
5	15,435	2,593	6,192	6,122	338	65	30		4	-		7	3		81	1,424
6	12,971	3,505	5,918	3,417	62	42	21		-	-		4	2			988
7 or more	10,345	7,057	2,205	995	6	29	44		2	-		7	-			925
TOTAL ROOMS	**273,608**	**93,004**	**92,522**	**71,706**	**11,462**	**1,400**	**1,310**	**10**	**44**	**16**	**2**	**165**	**54**	**41**	**1,872**	**26,351**
Households with the following persons																
TOTAL	**49,626**	**14,119**	**16,792**	**14,105**	**3,373**	**312**	**273**	**10**	**8**	**5**	**2**	**30**	**16**	**41**	**540**	**5,175**
1	9,996	1,628	3,006	3,011	1,900	76	116	8	1	1	1	8	9	38	193	1,225
2	17,870	4,941	6,057	5,313	1,054	114	101	2	2	2	1	11	4	2	266	2,129
3	8,439	2,641	2,990	2,416	263	54	30	-	1	2	-	4	1	1	36	802
4	9,625	3,567	3,453	2,394	122	42	17	-	3	-	-	4	2	-	21	738
5	2,858	1,047	1,006	735	27	18	6	-	1	-	-	2	-	-	16	210
6	692	251	219	199	7	6	3	-	-	-	-	1	-	-	6	58
7 or more	146	44	61	37	-	2	-	-	-	-	-	-	-	-	2	13
TOTAL PERSONS	**129,084**	**40,770**	**44,702**	**35,603**	**5,462**	**778**	**524**	**12**	**25**	**11**	**3**	**74**	**28**	**45**	**1,047**	**12,337**
Households with the following persons per room																
TOTAL	**49,626**	**14,119**	**16,792**	**14,105**	**3,373**	**312**	**273**	**10**	**8**	**5**	**2**	**30**	**16**	**41**	**540**	**5,175**
Over 1.5	92	5	8	10	27	3	-	2	-	-	1	-	-	3	33	24
Over 1 and up to 1.5	425	42	148	169	44	11	3	-	-	-	-	-	-	-	8	63
Over 0.5 and up to 1	16,585	4,317	5,958	5,027	870	137	53	8	4	4	1	10	5	38	153	1,536
Up to 0.5	32,524	9,755	10,678	8,899	2,432	161	217	-	4	1	-	20	11	-	346	3,552

Note: Maximum number of rooms in non-permanent accommodation is 5

57. Households with residents; residents in households; rooms in household spaces

	TOTAL HOUSE-HOLDS	Household space type in permanent buildings														Non-permanent accomm-odation	With migrant head
		Unshared dwellings - purpose-built					Unshared dwellings - converted		Unshared dwellings - not self-contained			Other household spaces - not self-contained				
		Detached	Semi-detached	Terraced	Purpose-built flat in: Residential building	Purpose-built flat in: Commercial building	Converted flat	Converted flatlet	Not self-contained flat	Not self-contained 'rooms'	Bedsit	Not self-contained flat	Not self-contained 'rooms'	Bedsit		
a	b	c	d	e	f	g	h	i	j	k	l	m	n	o	p	q
Wansdyke																
Households with the following rooms																
TOTAL	**30,814**	**9,712**	**10,180**	**7,890**	**2,058**	**237**	**478**	**17**	**16**	**3**	**2**	**22**	**14**	**30**	**155**	**2,258**
1	102	1	4	10	9	3	-	17			2			30	26	41
2	537	15	45	142	216	15	62		-	1		4	6		31	85
3	1,696	66	260	444	699	35	127		3	1		7	8		46	205
4	4,809	716	1,347	1,648	874	52	133		2	1		2	-		34	464
5	8,997	1,915	3,545	3,166	219	60	69		1	-		4	-		18	553
6	7,612	2,244	3,452	1,808	35	36	34		2	-		1	-			435
7 or more	7,061	4,755	1,527	672	6	36	53		8	-		4	-			475
TOTAL ROOMS	**172,739**	**64,927**	**56,441**	**40,051**	**7,396**	**1,142**	**2,041**	**17**	**101**	**9**	**2**	**94**	**36**	**30**	**452**	**11,779**
Households with the following persons																
TOTAL	**30,814**	**9,712**	**10,180**	**7,890**	**2,058**	**237**	**478**	**17**	**16**	**3**	**2**	**22**	**14**	**30**	**155**	**2,258**
1	6,663	1,291	1,893	1,902	1,168	58	209	15	1	2	2	9	12	27	74	482
2	11,055	3,715	3,469	2,866	654	79	184	2	7	1	-	7	2	2	67	919
3	5,068	1,668	1,843	1,306	153	42	41	-	4	-	-	1	-	1	9	393
4	5,680	2,125	2,146	1,271	57	39	32	-	4	-	-	2	-	-	4	328
5	1,817	698	657	413	20	15	10	-	-	-	-	3	-	-	1	98
6	423	176	137	98	6	4	2	-	-	-	-	-	-	-	-	33
7 or more	108	39	35	34	-	-	-	-	-	-	-	-	-	-	-	5
TOTAL PERSONS	**79,122**	**27,063**	**27,309**	**19,541**	**3,299**	**597**	**890**	**19**	**43**	**4**	**2**	**49**	**16**	**34**	**256**	**5,534**
Households with the following persons per room																
TOTAL	**30,814**	**9,712**	**10,180**	**7,890**	**2,058**	**237**	**478**	**17**	**16**	**3**	**2**	**22**	**14**	**30**	**155**	**2,258**
Over 1.5	31	2	7	3	1	2	1	2	-	-	-	-	-	3	10	14
Over 1 and up to 1.5	223	28	74	97	13	4	6	-	-	-	-	1	-	-	-	14
Over 0.5 and up to 1	9,683	2,522	3,686	2,680	454	96	127	15	4	-	2	8	2	27	60	717
Up to 0.5	20,877	7,160	6,413	5,110	1,590	135	344	-	12	3	-	13	12	-	85	1,513

Table 57 Household space type: rooms and household size – continued

Note: Maximum number of rooms in non-permanent accommodation is 5

57. Households with residents; residents in households; rooms in household spaces

	TOTAL HOUSE-HOLDS	Household space type in permanent buildings													Non-permanent accomm-odation	With migrant head
		Unshared dwellings - purpose-built					Unshared dwellings - converted		Unshared dwellings - not self-contained			Other household spaces - not self-contained				
		Detached	Semi-detached	Terraced	Purpose-built flat in: Residential building	Purpose-built flat in: Commercial building	Converted flat	Converted flatlet	Not self-contained flat	Not self-contained 'rooms'	Bedsit	Not self-contained flat	Not self-contained 'rooms'	Bedsit		
a	b	c	d	e	f	g	h	i	j	k	l	m	n	o	p	q
Woodspring																
Households with the following rooms																
TOTAL	**70,519**	**23,919**	**21,746**	**11,393**	**5,590**	**715**	**5,281**	**288**	**61**	**18**	**13**	**232**	**112**	**402**	**749**	**6,375**
1	1,182	11	5	19	402	14	-	288			13			402	28	405
2	2,067	26	62	267	790	43	712		8	7		41	54		57	497
3	4,959	221	516	792	1,497	115	1,494		9	6		63	29		217	820
4	12,996	2,223	3,247	2,757	2,346	202	1,797		12	2		53	21		336	1,432
5	18,063	4,957	7,333	4,188	458	179	786		18	-		31	2		111	1,313
6	15,524	5,993	6,858	2,210	77	90	271		3	1		18	3			981
7 or more	15,728	10,488	3,725	1,160	20	72	221		11	2		26	3			927
TOTAL ROOMS	**380,255**	**153,945**	**121,405**	**57,204**	**18,825**	**3,268**	**20,543**	**288**	**289**	**69**	**13**	**974**	**338**	**402**	**2,692**	**29,441**
Households with the following persons																
TOTAL	**70,519**	**23,919**	**21,746**	**11,393**	**5,590**	**715**	**5,281**	**288**	**61**	**18**	**13**	**232**	**112**	**402**	**749**	**6,375**
1	17,732	3,562	4,256	2,729	3,300	208	2,557	239	27	10	8	105	68	350	313	1,743
2	25,741	9,256	7,733	4,015	1,811	254	2,057	42	20	4	4	92	33	35	385	2,456
3	10,710	3,985	3,809	1,977	335	123	401	4	5	3	1	15	4	13	35	962
4	11,576	5,146	4,217	1,791	108	79	197	-	7	1	-	13	6	1	10	850
5	3,680	1,573	1,317	653	28	40	55	2	2	-	-	2	1	3	4	274
6	853	338	319	169	4	6	12	1	-	-	-	2	-	-	2	74
7 or more	227	59	95	59	4	5	2	-	-	-	-	3	-	-	-	16
TOTAL PERSONS	**172,844**	**64,940**	**57,212**	**28,576**	**8,552**	**1,672**	**9,024**	**351**	**120**	**31**	**19**	**434**	**175**	**478**	**1,260**	**14,874**
Households with the following persons per room																
TOTAL	**70,519**	**23,919**	**21,746**	**11,393**	**5,590**	**715**	**5,281**	**288**	**61**	**18**	**13**	**232**	**112**	**402**	**749**	**6,375**
Over 1.5	222	9	8	17	50	5	11	49	-	-	5	2	2	52	12	96
Over 1 and up to 1.5	483	32	175	173	34	14	47	-	-	1	-	1	-	-	6	51
Over 0.5 and up to 1	21,346	6,230	7,244	4,086	1,366	269	1,267	239	15	4	8	64	32	350	172	2,404
Up to 0.5	48,468	17,648	14,319	7,117	4,140	427	3,956	-	46	13	-	165	78	-	559	3,824

58. Households with residents

Tenure and amenities	TOTAL HOUSE-HOLDS	Household space type in permanent buildings														Non-permanent accomm-odation
		Unshared dwellings - purpose-built					Unshared dwellings - converted		Unshared dwellings - not self-contained			Other household spaces - not self-contained			
		Detached	Semi-detached	Terraced	Purpose-built flat in: Residential building	Purpose-built flat in: Commercial building	Converted flat	Converted flatlet	Not self-contained flat	Not self-contained 'rooms'	Bedsit	Not self-contained flat	Not self-contained 'rooms'	Bedsit	
a	b	c	d	e	f	g	h	i	j	k	l	m	n	o	p
AVON															
TOTAL HOUSEHOLDS	**376,522**	**64,744**	**111,716**	**121,678**	**40,801**	**4,437**	**23,973**	**1,436**	**236**	**70**	**102**	**1,552**	**659**	**3,336**	**1,782**
Owner occupied - owned outright	99,184	23,002	33,364	31,884	4,510	512	4,020	47	46	13	3	298	93	15	1,377
- buying	172,569	37,625	56,373	63,545	5,390	972	7,797	206	66	10	3	285	59	30	208
Rented privately - furnished	16,987	752	1,400	3,273	1,161	857	4,864	651	58	31	75	570	346	2,858	91
- unfurnished	10,738	976	1,535	2,346	1,018	895	3,116	164	30	11	14	291	118	195	29
Rented with a job or business	5,116	1,178	1,182	682	567	1,002	355	22	7	2	-	29	6	63	21
Rented from a housing association	9,598	146	767	1,605	5,053	34	1,554	226	12	2	2	26	27	134	10
Rented from a local authority or new town	62,330	1,065	17,095	18,343	23,102	165	2,267	120	17	1	5	53	10	41	46
Exclusive use of bath/shower and inside WC	**372,012**	**64,588**	**111,469**	**120,873**	**40,463**	**4,327**	**23,973**	**1,436**	**236**		**61**	**1,552**		**1,422**	**1,612**
With central heating - all rooms	261,093	56,755	79,864	75,235	27,918	2,326	15,587	727	140		32	700		627	1,182
- some rooms	58,646	5,719	18,340	23,728	7,068	591	2,661	89	40		4	202		69	135
No central heating	52,273	2,114	13,265	21,910	5,477	1,410	5,725	620	56		25	650		726	295
Exclusive use of bath/shower, shared or no inside WC	**674**	**60**	**113**	**302**	**30**	**21**	**-**	**-**		**5**	**1**		**51**	**57**	**34**
With central heating - all rooms	183	15	37	44	26	11	-	-		3	1		11	25	10
- some rooms	87	12	21	45	-	4	-	-		-	-		5	-	-
No central heating	404	33	55	213	4	6	-	-		2	-		35	32	24
Exclusive use of inside WC, shared or no bath/shower	**662**	**25**	**64**	**230**	**171**	**19**	**-**	**-**		**18**	**1**		**76**	**29**	**29**
With central heating - all rooms	233	5	8	18	153	5	-	-		9	1		19	12	3
- some rooms	66	3	7	25	10	1	-	-		3	-		15	-	2
No central heating	363	17	49	187	8	13	-	-		6	-		42	17	24
Lacking or sharing use of bath/shower and inside WC	**3,174**	**71**	**70**	**273**	**137**	**70**	**-**	**-**		**47**	**39**		**532**	**1,828**	**107**
With central heating - all rooms	989	11	12	15	93	25	-	-		20	16		170	618	9
- some rooms	184	6	7	16	18	6	-	-		5	2		46	74	4
No central heating	2,001	54	51	242	26	39	-	-		22	21		316	1,136	94

58. Households with residents

Tenure and amenities	TOTAL HOUSE-HOLDS	Household space type in permanent buildings													Non-permanent accomm-odation
		Unshared dwellings - purpose-built					Unshared dwellings - converted		Unshared dwellings - not self-contained			Other household spaces - not self-contained			
		Detached	Semi-detached	Terraced	Purpose-built flat in: Residential building	Purpose-built flat in: Commercial building	Converted flat	Converted flatlet	Not self-contained flat	Not self-contained 'rooms'	Bedsit	Not self-contained flat	Not self-contained 'rooms'	Bedsit	
a	b	c	d	e	f	g	h	i	j	k	l	m	n	o	p
					Bath										
TOTAL HOUSEHOLDS	**34,128**	**3,444**	**7,630**	**12,239**	**4,116**	**427**	**4,912**	**296**	**33**	**11**	**14**	**330**	**94**	**493**	**89**
Owner occupied - owned outright	9,699	1,608	2,763	3,688	633	44	779	12	4	3	-	70	15	4	76
- buying	12,376	1,626	3,189	5,581	464	96	1,282	62	10	3	1	43	7	5	7
Rented privately - furnished	2,535	53	126	485	174	61	964	83	12	2	10	99	35	426	5
- unfurnished	1,665	53	107	305	152	72	789	39	5	3	2	81	23	34	-
Rented with a job or business	476	62	86	65	49	124	77	4	1	-	-	4	1	3	-
Rented from a housing association	1,167	15	48	180	493	4	344	54	1	-	-	6	7	15	-
Rented from a local authority or new town	6,210	27	1,311	1,935	2,151	26	677	42	-	-	1	27	6	6	1
Exclusive use of bath/shower and inside WC	**33,568**	**3,440**	**7,615**	**12,142**	**4,062**	**420**	**4,912**	**296**	**33**		**11**	**330**		**225**	**82**
With central heating - all rooms	22,759	3,003	5,352	7,622	2,828	254	3,208	173	19		6	137		93	64
- some rooms	6,371	351	1,662	2,742	911	51	560	19	7		1	46		12	9
No central heating	4,438	86	601	1,778	323	115	1,144	104	7		4	147		120	9
Exclusive use of bath/shower, shared or no inside WC	**65**	**2**	**7**	**29**	**7**	**4**	**-**	**-**		**-**	**-**		**11**	**4**	**1**
With central heating - all rooms	23	2	3	5	7	1	-	-		-	-		3	2	-
- some rooms	7	-	2	3	-	1	-	-		-	-		1	-	-
No central heating	35	-	2	21	-	2	-	-		-	-		7	2	1
Exclusive use of inside WC, shared or no bath/shower	**105**	**-**	**4**	**39**	**34**	**-**	**-**	**-**		**4**	**-**		**18**	**5**	**1**
With central heating - all rooms	44	-	1	3	33	-	-	-		1	-		4	2	-
- some rooms	8	-	-	3	-	-	-	-		-	-		4	-	1
No central heating	53	-	3	33	1	-	-	-		3	-		10	3	-
Lacking or sharing use of bath/shower and inside WC	**390**	**2**	**4**	**29**	**13**	**3**	**-**	**-**		**7**	**3**		**65**	**259**	**5**
With central heating - all rooms	100	2	-	1	6	2	-	-		3	1		19	65	1
- some rooms	21	-	-	-	1	-	-	-		2	-		11	7	-
No central heating	269	-	4	28	6	1	-	-		2	2		35	187	4

58. Households with residents

Tenure and amenities	TOTAL HOUSE-HOLDS	Household space type in permanent buildings													Non-permanent accomm-odation
		Unshared dwellings - purpose-built					Unshared dwellings - converted		Unshared dwellings - not self-contained			Other household spaces - not self-contained			
		Detached	Semi-detached	Terraced	Purpose-built flat in: Residential building	Purpose-built flat in: Commercial building	Converted flat	Converted flatlet	Not self-contained flat	Not self-contained 'rooms'	Bedsit	Not self-contained flat	Not self-contained 'rooms'	Bedsit	
a	b	c	d	e	f	g	h	i	j	k	l	m	n	o	p
					Bristol										
TOTAL HOUSEHOLDS	**156,778**	**8,224**	**41,765**	**63,867**	**22,921**	**2,456**	**12,775**	**810**	**111**	**32**	**69**	**912**	**416**	**2,293**	**127**
Owner occupied - owned outright	36,517	2,704	11,978	18,212	1,524	291	1,482	14	18	5	2	160	50	8	69
- buying	63,232	4,222	19,239	31,951	2,441	513	4,499	115	21	3	2	163	36	17	10
Rented privately - furnished	9,983	106	477	2,022	713	570	3,015	377	32	18	54	387	242	1,960	10
- unfurnished	4,552	81	346	1,111	503	524	1,522	91	14	4	8	148	66	132	2
Rented with a job or business	1,929	210	334	311	344	464	177	14	3	-	-	16	4	50	2
Rented from a housing association	5,812	66	400	921	3,000	24	1,086	154	10	2	1	19	16	109	4
Rented from a local authority or new town	34,753	835	8,991	9,339	14,396	70	994	45	13	-	2	19	2	17	30
Exclusive use of bath/shower and inside WC	**154,103**	**8,211**	**41,675**	**63,355**	**22,775**	**2,381**	**12,775**	**810**	**111**		**40**	**912**		**958**	**100**
With central heating - all rooms	99,922	7,001	28,683	38,039	15,159	1,174	8,495	395	59		20	411		430	56
- some rooms	24,614	934	6,532	11,486	4,005	300	1,113	37	15		2	118		51	21
No central heating	29,567	276	6,460	13,830	3,611	907	3,167	378	37		18	383		477	23
Exclusive use of bath/shower, shared or no inside WC	**381**	**5**	**55**	**219**	**14**	**12**	**-**	**-**		**3**	**1**		**28**	**40**	**4**
With central heating - all rooms	92	4	20	24	13	7	-	-		2	1		4	15	2
- some rooms	44	-	8	31	-	1	-	-		-	-		4	-	-
No central heating	245	1	27	164	1	4	-	-		1	-		20	25	2
Exclusive use of inside WC, shared or no bath/shower	**301**	**4**	**19**	**130**	**76**	**14**	**-**	**-**		**7**	**1**		**31**	**15**	**4**
With central heating - all rooms	99	1	1	10	64	3	-	-		5	1		6	7	1
- some rooms	37	1	2	14	8	1	-	-		-	-		10	-	1
No central heating	165	2	16	106	4	10	-	-		2	-		15	8	2
Lacking or sharing use of bath/shower and inside WC	**1,993**	**4**	**16**	**163**	**56**	**49**	**-**	**-**		**22**	**27**		**357**	**1,280**	**19**
With central heating - all rooms	633	2	5	10	22	18	-	-		9	11		112	444	-
- some rooms	119	1	4	6	16	6	-	-		2	1		27	55	1
No central heating	1,241	1	7	147	18	25	-	-		11	15		218	781	18

Table 58 Household space type: tenure and amenities – **continued**

58. Households with residents

Tenure and amenities	TOTAL HOUSE-HOLDS	Household space type in permanent buildings													Non-permanent accomm-odation
		Unshared dwellings - purpose-built					Unshared dwellings - converted		Unshared dwellings - not self-contained			Other household spaces - not self-contained			
		Detached	Semi-detached	Terraced	Purpose-built flat in: Residential building	Purpose-built flat in: Commercial building	Converted flat	Converted flatlet	Not self-contained flat	Not self-contained 'rooms'	Bedsit	Not self-contained flat	Not self-contained 'rooms'	Bedsit	
a	b	c	d	e	f	g	h	i	j	k	l	m	n	o	p
Kingswood															
TOTAL HOUSEHOLDS	**34,657**	**5,326**	**13,603**	**12,184**	**2,743**	**290**	**254**	**15**	**7**	**1**	**2**	**26**	**7**	**77**	**122**
Owner occupied - owned outright	10,002	1,668	4,624	3,242	318	17	41	2	3	-	-	4	1	-	82
- buying	18,233	3,484	7,602	6,559	403	71	76	2	2	1	-	7	1	2	23
Rented privately - furnished	559	45	135	150	43	60	33	3	-	-	1	10	2	65	12
- unfurnished	500	52	121	152	53	75	28	4	1	-	1	4	3	5	1
Rented with a job or business	241	48	48	50	35	54	3	-	-	-	-	-	-	2	1
Rented from a housing association	621	4	42	192	341	1	37	2	-	-	-	-	-	-	2
Rented from a local authority or new town	4,501	25	1,031	1,839	1,550	12	36	2	1	-	-	1	-	3	1
Exclusive use of bath/shower and inside WC	**34,501**	**5,319**	**13,584**	**12,130**	**2,737**	**281**	**254**	**15**	**7**		**2**	**26**		**33**	**113**
With central heating - all rooms	27,885	4,915	11,183	9,029	2,271	156	194	8	6		2	24		22	75
- some rooms	4,194	297	1,650	1,823	346	44	28	1	-		-	-		1	4
No central heating	2,422	107	751	1,278	120	81	32	6	1		-	2		10	34
Exclusive use of bath/shower, shared or no inside WC	**30**	**3**	**6**	**11**	**1**	**4**	-	-		-	-		**1**	**3**	**1**
With central heating - all rooms	13	1	1	3	1	3	-	-		-	-		1	3	-
- some rooms	4	-	1	2	-	1	-	-		-	-		-	-	-
No central heating	13	2	4	6	-	-	-	-		-	-		-	-	1
Exclusive use of inside WC, shared or no bath/shower	**30**	**2**	**7**	**13**	**2**	**1**	-	-		**1**	-		**2**	**1**	**1**
With central heating - all rooms	9	-	2	1	2	1	-	-		-	-		2	1	-
- some rooms	3	1	-	1	-	-	-	-		1	-		-	-	-
No central heating	18	1	5	11	-	-	-	-		-	-		-	-	1
Lacking or sharing use of bath/shower and inside WC	**96**	**2**	**6**	**30**	**3**	**4**	-	-		-	-		**4**	**40**	**7**
With central heating - all rooms	40	-	2	2	2	3	-	-		-	-		2	29	-
- some rooms	10	-	1	2	1	-	-	-		-	-		2	3	1
No central heating	46	2	3	26	-	1	-	-		-	-		-	8	6

Table 58 Household space type: tenure and amenities – continued

58. Households with residents

Tenure and amenities	TOTAL HOUSE-HOLDS	Household space type in permanent buildings													Non-permanent accomm-odation
		Unshared dwellings - purpose-built					Unshared dwellings - converted		Unshared dwellings - not self-contained			Other household spaces - not self-contained			
		Detached	Semi-detached	Terraced	Purpose-built flat in:										
					Residential building	Commercial building	Converted flat	Converted flatlet	Not self-contained flat	Not self-contained 'rooms'	Bedsit	Not self-contained flat	Not self-contained 'rooms'	Bedsit	
a	b	c	d	e	f	g	h	i	j	k	l	m	n	o	p
					Northavon										
TOTAL HOUSEHOLDS	**49,626**	**14,119**	**16,792**	**14,105**	**3,373**	**312**	**273**	**10**	**8**	**5**	**2**	**30**	**16**	**41**	**540**
Owner occupied - owned outright	11,929	3,954	4,423	2,645	378	31	75	1	3	2	-	5	4	1	407
- buying	29,399	9,330	9,622	9,325	900	61	66	-	4	1	-	10	3	1	76
Rented privately - furnished	848	159	213	257	66	38	39	8	-	1	2	10	3	28	24
- unfurnished	1,092	273	343	248	117	56	30	-	1	-	-	2	2	5	15
Rented with a job or business	767	309	208	63	40	116	20	-	-	1	-	2	-	1	7
Rented from a housing association	598	20	109	88	356	3	12	-	-	-	-	-	3	5	2
Rented from a local authority or new town	4,993	74	1,874	1,479	1,516	7	31	1	-	-	-	1	1	-	9
Exclusive use of bath/shower and inside WC	**49,402**	**14,070**	**16,752**	**14,079**	**3,363**	**310**	**273**	**10**	**8**		**-**	**30**		**19**	**488**
With central heating - all rooms	36,973	12,480	12,147	9,156	2,402	197	188	7	5		-	17		8	366
- some rooms	8,294	1,093	3,098	3,331	615	52	56	1	3		-	6		-	39
No central heating	4,135	497	1,507	1,592	346	61	29	2	-		-	7		11	83
Exclusive use of bath/shower, shared or no inside WC	**43**	**13**	**10**	**9**	**2**	**-**	**-**	**-**		**-**	**-**		**1**	**-**	**8**
With central heating - all rooms	13	2	3	3	2	-	-	-		-	-		1	-	2
- some rooms	10	5	2	3	-	-	-	-		-	-		-	-	-
No central heating	20	6	5	3	-	-	-	-		-	-		-	-	6
Exclusive use of inside WC, shared or no bath/shower	**49**	**5**	**13**	**9**	**3**	**1**	**-**	**-**		**2**	**-**		**-**	**1**	**15**
With central heating - all rooms	7	1	1	1	1	-	-	-		1	-		-	1	1
- some rooms	6	-	2	2	1	-	-	-		1	-		-	-	-
No central heating	36	4	10	6	1	1	-	-		-	-		-	-	14
Lacking or sharing use of bath/shower and inside WC	**132**	**31**	**17**	**8**	**5**	**1**	**-**	**-**		**3**	**2**		**15**	**21**	**29**
With central heating - all rooms	33	4	-	1	3	-	-	-		1	2		11	8	3
- some rooms	8	2	1	2	-	-	-	-		-	-		1	1	1
No central heating	91	25	16	5	2	1	-	-		2	-		3	12	25

Table 58 Household space type: tenure and amenities – continued

58. Households with residents

Tenure and amenities	TOTAL HOUSE-HOLDS	Household space type in permanent buildings														Non-permanent accomm-odation
		Unshared dwellings - purpose-built					Unshared dwellings - converted		Unshared dwellings - not self-contained			Other household spaces - not self-contained			
		Detached	Semi-detached	Terraced	Purpose-built flat in: Residential building	Purpose-built flat in: Commercial building	Converted flat	Converted flatlet	Not self-contained flat	Not self-contained 'rooms'	Bedsit	Not self-contained flat	Not self-contained 'rooms'	Bedsit	
a	b	c	d	e	f	g	h	i	j	k	l	m	n	o	p
					Wansdyke										
TOTAL HOUSEHOLDS	**30,814**	**9,712**	**10,180**	**7,890**	**2,058**	**237**	**478**	**17**	**16**	**3**	**2**	**22**	**14**	**30**	**155**
Owner occupied - owned outright	9,440	3,946	2,962	1,849	422	29	108	5	2	-	-	2	1	-	114
- buying	14,851	5,218	5,211	3,922	280	61	120	2	6	1	-	4	2	-	24
Rented privately - furnished	576	121	126	136	33	28	80	7	2	2	1	7	4	23	6
- unfurnished	844	186	224	278	35	35	67	1	3	-	1	4	6	2	2
Rented with a job or business	541	204	132	71	26	75	20	1	2	-	-	3	1	2	4
Rented from a housing association	289	10	60	78	122	-	16	1	-	-	-	-	-	2	-
Rented from a local authority or new town	4,273	27	1,465	1,556	1,140	9	67	-	1	-	-	2	-	1	5
Exclusive use of bath/shower and inside WC	**30,574**	**9,673**	**10,141**	**7,829**	**2,022**	**237**	**478**	**17**	**16**		**-**	**22**		**23**	**116**
With central heating - all rooms	22,297	8,346	7,221	4,737	1,409	142	307	16	13		-	14		15	77
- some rooms	4,795	939	1,681	1,666	354	46	88	1	1		-	8		2	9
No central heating	3,482	388	1,239	1,426	259	49	83	-	2		-	-		6	30
Exclusive use of bath/shower, shared or no inside WC	**67**	**17**	**17**	**13**	**-**	**-**	**-**	**-**		**-**	**-**		**5**	**-**	**15**
With central heating - all rooms	16	3	4	4	-	-	-	-		-	-		-	-	5
- some rooms	11	4	5	2	-	-	-	-		-	-		-	-	-
No central heating	40	10	8	7	-	-	-	-		-	-		5	-	10
Exclusive use of inside WC, shared or no bath/shower	**70**	**5**	**9**	**19**	**34**	**-**	**-**	**-**		**2**	**-**		**-**	**-**	**1**
With central heating - all rooms	38	1	1	1	33	-	-	-		2	-		-	-	-
- some rooms	5	-	1	3	1	-	-	-		-	-		-	-	-
No central heating	27	4	7	15	-	-	-	-		-	-		-	-	1
Lacking or sharing use of bath/shower and inside WC	**103**	**17**	**13**	**29**	**2**	**-**	**-**	**-**		**1**	**2**		**9**	**7**	**23**
With central heating - all rooms	23	2	2	-	2	-	-	-		1	1		7	7	1
- some rooms	5	-	1	4	-	-	-	-		-	-		-	-	-
No central heating	75	15	10	25	-	-	-	-		-	1		2	-	22

58. Households with residents

Tenure and amenities	TOTAL HOUSE-HOLDS	Household space type in permanent buildings														Non-permanent accomm-odation
		Unshared dwellings - purpose-built					Unshared dwellings - converted		Unshared dwellings - not self-contained			Other household spaces - not self-contained			
		Detached	Semi-detached	Terraced	Purpose-built flat in: Residential building	Purpose-built flat in: Commercial building	Converted flat	Converted flatlet	Not self-contained flat	Not self-contained 'rooms'	Bedsit	Not self-contained flat	Not self-contained 'rooms'	Bedsit	
a	b	c	d	e	f	g	h	i	j	k	l	m	n	o	p
					Woodspring										
TOTAL HOUSEHOLDS	**70,519**	**23,919**	**21,746**	**11,393**	**5,590**	**715**	**5,281**	**288**	**61**	**18**	**13**	**232**	**112**	**402**	**749**
Owner occupied - owned outright	21,597	9,122	6,614	2,248	1,235	100	1,535	13	16	3	1	57	22	2	629
- buying	34,478	13,745	11,510	6,207	902	170	1,754	25	23	1	-	58	10	5	68
Rented privately - furnished	2,486	268	323	223	132	100	733	173	12	8	7	57	60	356	34
- unfurnished	2,085	331	394	252	158	133	680	29	6	4	2	52	18	17	9
Rented with a job or business	1,162	345	374	122	73	169	58	3	1	1	-	4	-	5	7
Rented from a housing association	1,111	31	108	146	741	2	59	15	1	-	1	1	1	3	2
Rented from a local authority or new town	7,600	77	2,423	2,195	2,349	41	462	30	2	1	2	3	1	14	-
Exclusive use of bath/shower and inside WC	**69,864**	**23,875**	**21,702**	**11,338**	**5,504**	**698**	**5,281**	**288**	**61**		**8**	**232**		**164**	**713**
With central heating - all rooms	51,257	21,010	15,278	6,652	3,849	403	3,195	128	38		4	97		59	544
- some rooms	10,378	2,105	3,717	2,680	837	98	816	30	14		1	24		3	53
No central heating	8,229	760	2,707	2,006	818	197	1,270	130	9		3	111		102	116
Exclusive use of bath/shower, shared or no inside WC	**88**	**20**	**18**	**21**	**6**	**1**	**-**	**-**		**2**	**-**		**5**	**10**	**5**
With central heating - all rooms	26	3	6	5	3	-	-	-		1	-		2	5	1
- some rooms	11	3	3	4	-	1	-	-		-	-		-	-	-
No central heating	51	14	9	12	3	-	-	-		1	-		3	5	4
Exclusive use of inside WC, shared or no bath/shower	**107**	**9**	**12**	**20**	**22**	**3**	**-**	**-**		**2**	**-**		**25**	**7**	**7**
With central heating - all rooms	36	2	2	2	20	1	-	-		-	-		7	1	1
- some rooms	7	1	2	2	-	-	-	-		1	-		1	-	-
No central heating	64	6	8	16	2	2	-	-		1	-		17	6	6
Lacking or sharing use of bath/shower and inside WC	**460**	**15**	**14**	**14**	**58**	**13**	**-**	**-**		**14**	**5**		**82**	**221**	**24**
With central heating - all rooms	160	1	3	1	58	2	-	-		6	1		19	65	4
- some rooms	21	3	-	2	-	-	-	-		1	1		5	8	1
No central heating	279	11	11	11	-	11	-	-		7	3		58	148	19

Table 59 Household space type: household composition

Note: * May include a small number of households with no resident adults

59. Households with residents; residents in households

Household composition: Adults	Dependent children	TOTAL HOUSE-HOLDS	Household space type in permanent buildings: Unshared dwellings - purpose-built: Detached	Semi-detached	Terraced	Purpose-built flat in: Residential building	Commercial building	Unshared dwellings - converted: Converted flat	Converted flatlet
a	b	c	d	e	f	g	h	i	j
			AVON						
All households*		**376,522**	**64,744**	**111,716**	**121,678**	**40,801**	**4,437**	**23,973**	**1,436**
1 adult of pensionable age	0	55,763	5,806	13,334	15,611	14,915	287	4,503	268
1 adult under pensionable age	0	44,698	3,256	6,986	12,703	8,252	1,046	7,518	888
1 adult any age	1 or more	13,666	859	3,411	5,225	3,017	141	825	15
2 adults (1 male and 1 female)	0	115,427	23,031	35,683	37,433	9,180	1,327	6,989	203
	1 or more	72,192	16,153	26,036	24,568	2,999	656	1,449	30
2 adults (same sex)	0	10,514	1,102	2,607	3,996	1,121	200	1,262	17
	1 or more	1,803	232	571	776	138	16	60	-
3 or more adults (male(s) and female(s))	0	41,984	9,449	15,727	14,303	896	476	882	6
	1 or more	18,276	4,621	6,870	6,084	189	220	218	4
3 or more adults (same sex)	0	1,880	193	408	867	71	56	245	1
	1 or more	222	37	72	96	8	5	3	-
Households containing persons of pensionable age only (any number)		95,107	13,860	26,663	27,286	19,017	443	6,020	279
Households containing persons aged 75 and over only (any number)		37,768	4,475	9,158	10,652	9,787	152	2,811	165
All dependent children		193,764	40,228	69,853	67,736	9,349	1,764	3,837	66
Dependent children aged 0 - 4		59,829	8,909	19,784	22,746	5,706	575	1,705	33
Dependent children aged 5 - 15		119,032	26,496	44,875	40,926	3,403	1,025	1,804	27
Persons pensionable age - 74		109,116	20,426	36,219	32,962	12,708	577	4,550	124
Persons aged 75 - 84		50,948	7,779	14,369	15,060	9,660	230	3,060	125
Persons aged 85 and over		12,084	1,816	3,107	3,390	2,712	54	798	47
			Bath						
All households*		**34,128**	**3,444**	**7,630**	**12,239**	**4,116**	**427**	**4,912**	**296**
1 adult of pensionable age	0	6,256	403	1,085	1,863	1,573	36	1,064	65
1 adult under pensionable age	0	4,912	161	412	1,199	769	96	1,528	159
1 adult any age	1 or more	1,330	49	255	531	285	16	166	2
2 adults (1 male and 1 female)	0	9,995	1,367	2,525	3,564	877	129	1,326	52
	1 or more	5,138	652	1,488	2,347	292	50	271	7
2 adults (same sex)	0	1,258	75	228	452	145	28	285	6
	1 or more	151	14	32	77	15	1	11	-
3 or more adults (male(s) and female(s))	0	3,440	483	1,084	1,500	125	48	165	2
	1 or more	1,352	224	479	553	23	13	45	1
3 or more adults (same sex)	0	262	14	35	140	8	9	47	1
	1 or more	22	2	6	12	1	-	1	-
Households containing persons of pensionable age only (any number)		10,245	1,031	2,267	3,205	2,011	52	1,392	66
Households containing persons aged 75 and over only (any number)		4,281	320	785	1,320	1,044	21	657	36
All dependent children		14,307	1,729	4,385	6,270	939	123	744	11
Dependent children aged 0 - 4		4,359	310	1,151	1,991	499	40	312	7
Dependent children aged 5 - 15		8,679	1,142	2,854	3,803	403	72	354	2
Persons pensionable age - 74		10,766	1,544	3,043	3,554	1,349	58	1,018	32
Persons aged 75 - 84		5,547	543	1,276	1,825	1,039	36	690	25
Persons aged 85 and over		1,355	120	248	436	305	5	202	11

Household space type in permanent buildings: Unshared dwellings - not self-contained: Not self-contained flat	Not self-contained 'rooms'	Bedsit	Other household spaces - not self-contained: Not self-contained flat	Not self-contained 'rooms'	Bedsit	Non-permanent accommodation	Households with migrant head	Persons in households with migrant head	Household composition: Adults	Dependent children
k	l	m	n	o	p	q	r	s	a	b
236	**70**	**102**	**1,552**	**659**	**3,336**	**1,782**	**36,752**	**82,837**	**All households***	
27	15	6	264	118	205	404	1,880	1,880	1 adult of pensionable age	0
49	24	66	458	335	2,775	342	9,213	9,213	1 adult under pensionable age	0
15	1	5	50	24	43	35	2,320	6,028	1 adult any age	1 or more
54	17	8	403	109	201	789	11,138	22,276	2 adults (1 male and 1 female)	0
31	3	2	115	27	30	93	7,134	27,107		1 or more
16	5	2	87	22	39	38	1,566	3,132	2 adults (same sex)	0
1	1	-	6	-	-	2	190	663		1 or more
30	4	8	107	17	20	59	1,907	6,621	3 or more adults (male(s) and female(s))	0
8	-	1	36	7	1	17	801	3,881		1 or more
5	-	4	24	-	5	1	541	1,856	3 or more adults (same sex)	0
-	-	-	1	-	-	-	29	144		1 or more
39	19	9	362	142	208	760	2,753	3,634	Households containing persons of pensionable age only (any number)	
21	12	4	181	76	82	192	993	1,154	Households containing persons aged 75 and over only (any number)	
92	9	8	368	86	108	260	18,135		All dependent children	
38	6	8	125	38	62	94	8,736		Dependent children aged 0 - 4	
46	3	-	199	44	28	156	8,632		Dependent children aged 5 - 15	
38	11	7	298	87	137	972	2,951		Persons pensionable age - 74	
20	11	5	186	71	76	296	1,353		Persons aged 75 - 84	
17	3	1	69	26	12	32	240		Persons aged 85 and over	
33	**11**	**14**	**330**	**94**	**493**	**89**	**3,829**	**8,130**	**All households***	
5	4	-	65	27	28	38	209	209	1 adult of pensionable age	0
6	2	7	102	39	415	17	1,150	1,150	1 adult under pensionable age	0
-	-	1	10	7	8	-	223	559	1 adult any age	1 or more
8	2	1	80	7	28	29	1,016	2,032	2 adults (1 male and 1 female)	0
3	-	1	20	4	1	2	566	2,157		1 or more
4	2	-	22	4	6	1	256	512	2 adults (same sex)	0
-	1	-	-	-	-	-	14	47		1 or more
5	-	2	19	3	2	2	221	785	3 or more adults (male(s) and female(s))	0
1	-	1	8	3	1	-	59	280		1 or more
1	-	1	4	-	2	-	108	384	3 or more adults (same sex)	0
-	-	-	-	-	-	-	1	8		1 or more
7	5	-	98	29	28	54	307	405	Households containing persons of pensionable age only (any number)	
2	3	-	45	15	9	24	98	110	Households containing persons aged 75 and over only (any number)	
6	2	3	54	22	16	3	1,476		All dependent children	
1	-	3	25	11	8	1	735		Dependent children aged 0 - 4	
3	2	-	27	10	5	2	657		Dependent children aged 5 - 15	
8	2	-	79	16	19	44	338		Persons pensionable age - 74	
3	2	-	56	15	7	30	134		Persons aged 75 - 84	
3	2	-	13	4	2	4	33		Persons aged 85 and over	

Table 59 Household space type: household composition - continued

Note: * May include a small number of households with no resident adults

59. Households with residents; residents in households

Household composition: Adults	Dependent children	TOTAL HOUSE-HOLDS	Household space type in permanent buildings: Unshared dwellings - purpose-built: Detached	Semi-detached	Terraced	Purpose-built flat in: Residential building	Commercial building	Unshared dwellings - converted: Converted flat	Converted flatlet
a	b	c	d	e	f	g	h	i	j
Bristol									
All households*		**156,778**	**8,224**	**41,765**	**63,867**	**22,921**	**2,456**	**12,775**	**810**
1 adult of pensionable age	0	24,505	929	5,107	8,284	7,776	146	1,762	118
1 adult under pensionable age	0	23,055	499	2,399	6,738	5,024	632	4,664	543
1 adult any age	1 or more	7,225	127	1,569	2,882	1,980	71	504	8
2 adults (1 male and 1 female)	0	44,539	2,948	12,735	19,155	4,817	729	3,535	108
	1 or more	26,477	1,732	9,389	12,320	1,857	330	714	18
2 adults (same sex)	0	5,397	179	1,112	2,395	688	118	788	8
	1 or more	924	34	282	462	91	12	36	-
3 or more adults (male(s) and female(s))	0	16,337	1,169	6,073	7,738	506	251	478	4
	1 or more	7,045	568	2,838	3,255	120	126	107	1
3 or more adults (same sex)	0	1,098	33	210	568	46	34	177	-
	1 or more	119	3	46	59	5	5	-	-
Households containing persons of pensionable age only (any number)		39,611	2,065	10,112	14,621	9,752	230	2,252	124
Households containing persons aged 75 and over only (any number)		16,008	665	3,440	5,654	4,882	69	1,011	68
All dependent children		77,714	4,706	27,804	35,828	5,962	939	2,023	36
Dependent children aged 0 - 4		25,747	1,008	7,636	12,004	3,681	324	920	19
Dependent children aged 5 - 15		47,005	3,145	18,187	21,814	2,147	529	951	14
Persons pensionable age - 74		44,431	2,933	14,197	18,143	6,725	303	1,722	61
Persons aged 75 - 84		21,041	1,174	5,502	8,186	4,723	109	1,088	59
Persons aged 85 and over		5,089	227	1,211	1,882	1,379	24	279	14
Kingswood									
All households*		**34,657**	**5,326**	**13,603**	**12,184**	**2,743**	**290**	**254**	**15**
1 adult of pensionable age	0	4,500	335	1,347	1,553	1,163	18	59	4
1 adult under pensionable age	0	2,863	256	819	1,035	494	66	68	6
1 adult any age	1 or more	1,038	90	299	459	163	14	6	-
2 adults (1 male and 1 female)	0	11,228	1,810	4,646	3,945	597	86	77	4
	1 or more	7,633	1,461	3,309	2,588	191	47	18	1
2 adults (same sex)	0	695	71	255	280	61	14	8	-
	1 or more	139	18	54	57	10	-	-	-
3 or more adults (male(s) and female(s))	0	4,621	859	2,080	1,571	55	34	16	-
	1 or more	1,835	405	765	644	7	10	2	-
3 or more adults (same sex)	0	94	19	28	45	2	-	-	-
	1 or more	9	2	1	6	-	-	-	-
Households containing persons of pensionable age only (any number)		7,957	823	2,882	2,684	1,418	24	83	4
Households containing persons aged 75 and over only (any number)		3,006	247	887	1,031	775	12	40	3
All dependent children		19,093	3,604	8,053	6,698	535	120	42	1
Dependent children aged 0 - 4		5,928	901	2,343	2,226	376	39	19	1
Dependent children aged 5 - 15		11,868	2,385	5,158	4,074	147	66	21	-
Persons pensionable age - 74		9,892	1,351	4,230	3,329	839	29	69	1
Persons aged 75 - 84		4,084	464	1,426	1,381	737	12	44	2
Persons aged 85 and over		973	110	307	330	207	5	12	1

Household space type in permanent buildings: Unshared dwellings - not self-contained: Not self-contained flat	Not self-contained 'rooms'	Bedsit	Other household spaces - not self-contained: Not self-contained flat	Not self-contained 'rooms'	Bedsit	Non-permanent accommodation	Households with migrant head	Persons in households with migrant head	Household composition: Adults	Dependent children
k	l	m	n	o	p	q	r	s	a	b
111	**32**	**69**	**912**	**416**	**2,293**	**127**	**16,413**	**35,645**	**All households***	
10	8	4	138	67	137	19	709	709	1 adult of pensionable age	0
25	12	50	283	228	1,923	35	4,922	4,922	1 adult under pensionable age	0
12	-	-	33	12	21	6	1,200	3,121	1 adult any age	1 or more
19	8	4	227	66	142	46	4,367	8,734	2 adults (1 male and 1 female)	0
13	2	-	60	16	13	13	2,594	9,830		1 or more
11	2	2	49	15	28	2	901	1,802	2 adults (same sex)	0
1	-	-	6	-	-	-	106	379		1 or more
12	-	6	72	9	15	4	904	3,227	3 or more adults (male(s) and female(s))	0
4	-	-	22	3	-	1	328	1,626		1 or more
4	-	3	20	-	3	-	345	1,177	3 or more adults (same sex)	0
-	-	-	1	-	-	-	20	100		1 or more
12	9	6	172	80	139	37	946	1,186	Households containing persons of pensionable age only (any number)	
8	5	3	94	44	62	3	364	410	Households containing persons aged 75 and over only (any number)	
54	4	-	226	46	51	35	7,303		All dependent children	
19	3	-	73	20	28	12	3,725		Dependent children aged 0 - 4	
32	1	-	125	25	12	23	3,290		Dependent children aged 5 - 15	
11	5	5	139	49	82	56	929		Persons pensionable age - 74	
6	4	3	81	42	55	9	449		Persons aged 75 - 84	
5	1	1	43	12	10	1	79		Persons aged 85 and over	
7	**1**	**2**	**26**	**7**	**77**	**122**	**2,702**	**6,317**	**All households***	
1	-	-	1	1	1	17	189	189	1 adult of pensionable age	0
-	-	-	11	2	65	41	473	473	1 adult under pensionable age	0
-	-	2	1	-	1	3	155	410	1 adult any age	1 or more
2	1	-	7	4	4	45	986	1,972	2 adults (1 male and 1 female)	0
3	-	-	4	-	2	9	622	2,355		1 or more
-	-	-	-	-	4	2	72	144	2 adults (same sex)	0
-	-	-	-	-	-	-	11	35		1 or more
1	-	-	2	-	-	3	114	386	3 or more adults (male(s) and female(s))	0
-	-	-	-	-	-	2	58	271		1 or more
-	-	-	-	-	-	-	20	70	3 or more adults (same sex)	0
-	-	-	-	-	-	-	2	12		1 or more
2	-	-	4	1	1	31	269	349	Households containing persons of pensionable age only (any number)	
2	-	-	1	-	1	7	102	118	Households containing persons aged 75 and over only (any number)	
5	-	2	7	-	3	23	1,470		All dependent children	
2	-	2	5	-	3	11	733		Dependent children aged 0 - 4	
3	-	-	2	-	-	12	680		Dependent children aged 5 - 15	
-	-	-	6	1	-	37	258		Persons pensionable age - 74	
2	-	-	1	-	1	14	128		Persons aged 75 - 84	
1	-	-	-	-	-	-	22		Persons aged 85 and over	

Table 59 Household space type: household composition – continued

Note: * May include a small number of households with no resident adults

59. Households with residents; residents in households

Household composition		TOTAL HOUSE-HOLDS	Household space type in permanent buildings						
			Unshared dwellings - purpose-built					Unshared dwellings - converted	
						Purpose-built flat in:			
Adults	Dependent children		Detached	Semi-detached	Terraced	Residential building	Commercial building	Converted flat	Converted flatlet
a	b	c	d	e	f	g	h	i	j
Northavon									
All households*		**49,626**	**14,119**	**16,792**	**14,105**	**3,373**	**312**	**273**	**10**
1 adult of pensionable age	0	5,145	844	1,743	1,251	1,123	10	66	2
1 adult under pensionable age	0	4,849	783	1,263	1,760	777	66	50	6
1 adult any age	1 or more	1,322	200	407	453	227	11	7	-
2 adults (1 male and 1 female)	0	16,234	4,636	5,573	4,747	822	101	91	2
	1 or more	11,707	4,058	4,081	3,187	237	57	27	-
2 adults (same sex)	0	1,058	224	343	382	78	10	4	-
	1 or more	209	49	66	83	9	-	1	-
3 or more adults (male(s) and female(s))	0	6,087	2,174	2,272	1,483	79	39	16	-
	1 or more	2,848	1,107	998	696	14	14	10	-
3 or more adults (same sex)	0	137	32	38	54	7	4	1	-
	1 or more	28	11	8	9	-	-	-	-
Households containing persons of pensionable age only (any number)		9,335	2,005	3,341	2,232	1,421	23	106	3
Households containing persons aged 75 and over only (any number)		3,466	629	1,126	843	752	8	42	2
All dependent children		28,892	9,769	10,102	7,904	722	157	70	-
Dependent children aged 0 - 4		8,795	2,417	2,993	2,819	434	46	31	-
Dependent children aged 5 - 15		17,729	6,274	6,366	4,583	271	98	34	-
Persons pensionable age - 74		11,727	3,169	4,518	2,709	953	37	94	2
Persons aged 75 - 84		5,055	1,213	1,727	1,215	718	14	63	2
Persons aged 85 and over		1,074	278	345	231	202	1	9	-
Wansdyke									
All households*		**30,814**	**9,712**	**10,180**	**7,890**	**2,058**	**237**	**478**	**17**
1 adult of pensionable age	0	4,344	848	1,256	1,187	891	10	110	11
1 adult under pensionable age	0	2,317	443	636	715	277	47	99	4
1 adult any age	1 or more	695	104	224	235	110	2	12	1
2 adults (1 male and 1 female)	0	10,075	3,487	3,182	2,562	538	69	160	1
	1 or more	6,746	2,342	2,553	1,594	147	49	47	-
2 adults (same sex)	0	657	176	201	210	40	9	16	-
	1 or more	106	37	35	27	5	-	1	-
3 or more adults (male(s) and female(s))	0	4,070	1,539	1,482	937	41	35	24	-
	1 or more	1,698	704	571	394	8	12	9	-
3 or more adults (same sex)	0	90	25	36	25	1	3	-	-
	1 or more	14	7	3	4	-	-	-	-
Households containing persons of pensionable age only (any number)		8,043	2,144	2,451	2,029	1,183	18	156	11
Households containing persons aged 75 and over only (any number)		3,077	690	880	799	605	6	70	11
All dependent children		16,887	5,913	6,231	4,085	397	112	113	1
Dependent children aged 0 - 4		4,706	1,236	1,755	1,410	218	32	36	1
Dependent children aged 5 - 15		10,634	3,892	3,984	2,434	168	74	66	-
Persons pensionable age - 74		9,912	3,282	3,232	2,389	785	36	124	-
Persons aged 75 - 84		4,401	1,226	1,340	1,066	652	11	84	2
Persons aged 85 and over		991	301	263	247	146	6	15	9

Household space type in permanent buildings						Non-permanent accommodation	Households with migrant head	Persons in households with migrant head	Household composition	
Unshared dwellings - not self-contained			Other household spaces - not self-contained							
Not self-contained flat	Not self-contained 'rooms'	Bedsit	Not self-contained flat	Not self-contained 'rooms'	Bedsit				Adults	Dependent children
k	l	m	n	o	p	q	r	s	a	b
8	**5**	**2**	**30**	**16**	**41**	**540**	**5,175**	**12,337**	**All households***	
1	-	-	2	1	2	100	241	241	1 adult of pensionable age	0
-	1	1	6	8	36	92	984	984	1 adult under pensionable age	0
-	-	-	-	-	-	17	258	690	1 adult any age	1 or more
2	1	1	11	3	2	242	1,861	3,722	2 adults (1 male and 1 female)	0
5	1	-	9	2	1	42	1,266	4,814		1 or more
-	1	-	-	1	-	15	140	280	2 adults (same sex)	0
-	-	-	-	-	-	1	20	68		1 or more
-	1	-	1	1	-	21	238	780	3 or more adults (male(s) and female(s))	0
-	-	-	1	-	-	8	139	667		1 or more
-	-	-	-	-	-	1	27	87	3 or more adults (same sex)	0
-	-	-	-	-	-	-	1	4		1 or more
1	-	-	4	3	2	194	364	487	Households containing persons of pensionable age only (any number)	
-	-	-	3	2	1	58	147	175	Households containing persons aged 75 and over only (any number)	
10	1	-	20	3	1	133	2,945		All dependent children	
6	1	-	2	2	1	43	1,354		Dependent children aged 0 - 4	
3	-	-	14	1	-	85	1,475		Dependent children aged 5 - 15	
1	1	-	3	1	1	238	395		Persons pensionable age - 74	
-	-	-	4	3	1	95	202		Persons aged 75 - 84	
-	-	-	-	1	-	7	35		Persons aged 85 and over	
16	**3**	**2**	**22**	**14**	**30**	**155**	**2,258**	**5,534**	**All households***	
-	2	-	4	-	-	25	138	138	1 adult of pensionable age	0
1	-	2	5	12	27	49	343	343	1 adult under pensionable age	0
1	-	-	-	1	-	5	104	272	1 adult any age	1 or more
6	1	-	6	1	1	61	806	1,612	2 adults (1 male and 1 female)	0
2	-	-	4	-	1	7	595	2,253		1 or more
-	-	-	1	-	1	3	60	120	2 adults (same sex)	0
-	-	-	-	-	-	1	10	34		1 or more
6	-	-	2	-	-	4	120	398	3 or more adults (male(s) and female(s))	0
-	-	-	-	-	-	-	63	301		1 or more
-	-	-	-	-	-	-	15	50	3 or more adults (same sex)	0
-	-	-	-	-	-	-	3	12		1 or more
2	2	-	5	-	-	42	225	314	Households containing persons of pensionable age only (any number)	
1	2	-	2	-	-	11	71	92	Households containing persons aged 75 and over only (any number)	
4	-	-	9	1	1	20	1,343		All dependent children	
3	-	-	2	1	1	11	600		Dependent children aged 0 - 4	
-	-	-	7	-	-	9	695		Dependent children aged 5 - 15	
5	-	-	4	-	1	54	274		Persons pensionable age - 74	
1	2	-	2	-	-	15	115		Persons aged 75 - 84	
3	-	-	-	-	-	1	18		Persons aged 85 and over	

Table 59 Household space type: household composition – continued

Note: * May include a small number of households with no resident adults

59. Households with residents; residents in households

Household composition: Adults	Dependent children	TOTAL HOUSEHOLDS	Unshared dwellings - purpose-built: Detached	Semi-detached	Terraced	Purpose-built flat in: Residential building	Commercial building	Unshared dwellings - converted: Converted flat	Converted flatlet
a	b	c	d	e	f	g	h	i	j
			Woodspring						
All households*		**70,519**	**23,919**	**21,746**	**11,393**	**5,590**	**715**	**5,281**	**288**
1 adult of pensionable age	0	11,013	2,447	2,796	1,473	2,389	67	1,442	68
1 adult under pensionable age	0	6,702	1,114	1,457	1,256	911	139	1,109	170
1 adult any age	1 or more	2,056	289	657	665	252	27	130	4
2 adults (1 male and 1 female)	0	23,356	8,783	7,022	3,460	1,529	213	1,800	36
	1 or more	14,491	5,908	5,216	2,532	275	123	372	4
2 adults (same sex)	0	1,449	377	468	277	109	21	161	3
	1 or more	274	80	102	70	8	3	11	-
3 or more adults (male(s) and female(s))	0	7,429	3,225	2,736	1,074	90	69	183	-
	1 or more	3,498	1,613	1,219	542	17	45	45	2
3 or more adults (same sex)	0	199	70	61	35	7	6	20	-
	1 or more	30	12	8	6	2	-	2	-
Households containing persons of pensionable age only (any number)		19,916	5,792	5,610	2,515	3,232	96	2,031	71
Households containing persons aged 75 and over only (any number)		7,930	1,924	2,040	1,005	1,729	36	991	45
All dependent children		36,871	14,507	13,278	6,951	794	313	845	17
Dependent children aged 0 - 4		10,294	3,037	3,906	2,296	498	94	387	5
Dependent children aged 5 - 15		23,117	9,658	8,326	4,218	267	186	378	11
Persons pensionable age - 74		22,388	8,147	6,999	2,838	2,057	114	1,523	28
Persons aged 75 - 84		10,820	3,159	3,098	1,387	1,791	48	1,091	35
Persons aged 85 and over		2,602	780	733	264	473	13	281	12

Household space type in permanent buildings						Non-permanent accommodation	Households with migrant head	Persons in households with migrant head	Household composition	
Unshared dwellings - not self-contained			Other household spaces - not self-contained						Adults	Dependent children
Not self-contained flat	Not self-contained 'rooms'	Bedsit	Not self-contained flat	Not self-contained 'rooms'	Bedsit					
k	l	m	n	o	p	q	r	s	a	b
61	**18**	**13**	**232**	**112**	**402**	**749**	**6,375**	**14,874**	**All households***	
10	1	2	54	22	37	205	394	394	1 adult of pensionable age	0
17	9	6	51	46	309	108	1,341	1,341	1 adult under pensionable age	0
2	1	2	6	4	13	4	380	976	1 adult any age	1 or more
17	4	2	72	28	24	366	2,102	4,204	2 adults (1 male and 1 female)	0
5	-	1	18	5	12	20	1,491	5,698		1 or more
1	-	-	15	2	-	15	137	274	2 adults (same sex)	0
-	-	-	-	-	-	-	29	100		1 or more
6	3	-	11	4	3	25	310	1,045	3 or more adults (male(s) and female(s))	0
3	-	-	5	1	-	6	154	736		1 or more
-	-	-	-	-	-	-	26	88	3 or more adults (same sex)	0
-	-	-	-	-	-	-	2	8		1 or more
15	3	3	79	29	38	402	642	893	Households containing persons of pensionable age only (any number)	
8	2	1	36	15	9	89	211	249	Households containing persons aged 75 and over only (any number)	
13	2	3	52	14	36	46	3,598		All dependent children	
7	2	3	18	4	21	16	1,589		Dependent children aged 0 - 4	
5	-	-	24	8	11	25	1,835		Dependent children aged 5 - 15	
13	3	2	67	20	34	543	757		Persons pensionable age - 74	
8	3	2	42	11	12	133	325		Persons aged 75 - 84	
5	-	-	13	9	-	19	53		Persons aged 85 and over	

Table 60 Dwellings and household spaces

Note: * Includes unshared dwelling(s) plus an unattached household space (not in a dwelling)

60. Converted or shared accommodation; dwellings; household spaces; rooms in such accommodation

Type of dwelling(s) in converted or shared accommodation	TOTAL CONVERTED OR SHARED ACCOMMODATION	TOTAL DWELLINGS	Total shared dwellings	Shared dwellings with the following household spaces				Un-attached spaces	TOTAL HOUSEHOLD SPACES	Household space type						TOTAL ROOMS
				2	3	4	5 or more			Converted flat	Converted flatlet	Not self-contained flat	Not self-contained 'rooms'	Bedsit	Not self-contained unoccupied	
a	b	c	d	e	f	g	h	i	j	k	l	m	n	o	p	q
AVON																
TOTAL CONVERTED OR SHARED ACCOMMODATION	**11,189**	**31,660**	**1,695**	**812**	**297**	**211**	**375**	**946**	**36,789**	**27,788**	**1,705**	**1,903**	**767**	**4,350**	**276**	**122,012**
Unconverted accommodation																
1 shared dwelling	1,001	1,001	1,001	507	164	124	206		3,376			690	378	2,215	93	7,048
Partly converted accommodation																
1 shared, 1 unshared dwelling*	807	1,188	381	150	71	50	110	426	2,695	678	111	496	182	1,150	78	6,944
1 shared, 2 unshared dwellings*	394	965	177	85	34	19	39	209	1,589	680	90	230	93	463	33	4,305
1 shared, 3 or more unshared dwellings*	449	2,040	136	70	28	18	20	311	2,663	1,578	300	250	50	423	62	7,311
Converted accommodation																
2 unshared dwellings	4,360	8,720							8,720	8,189	245	184	45	53	4	35,090
3 unshared dwellings	1,583	4,749							4,749	4,475	205	21	13	30	5	17,615
4 or more unshared dwellings	2,595	12,997							12,997	12,188	754	32	6	16	1	43,699
Bath																
TOTAL CONVERTED OR SHARED ACCOMMODATION	**1,985**	**6,600**	**263**	**143**	**38**	**27**	**55**	**199**	**7,448**	**5,930**	**338**	**388**	**110**	**642**	**40**	**24,240**
Unconverted accommodation																
1 shared dwelling	158	158	158	86	22	21	29		540			134	60	325	21	1,189
Partly converted accommodation																
1 shared, 1 unshared dwelling*	131	192	61	29	12	3	17	70	440	113	16	100	19	185	7	1,170
1 shared, 2 unshared dwellings*	67	152	18	11	-	1	6	49	244	122	10	48	9	50	5	742
1 shared, 3 or more unshared dwellings*	106	517	26	17	4	2	3	80	643	440	47	75	12	64	5	1,926
Converted accommodation																
2 unshared dwellings	517	1,034							1,034	951	35	25	9	14	-	4,310
3 unshared dwellings	310	930							930	885	41	2	-	1	1	3,223
4 or more unshared dwellings	696	3,617							3,617	3,419	189	4	1	3	1	11,680

Table 60 Dwellings and household spaces – **continued**

Note: * Includes unshared dwelling(s) plus an unattached household space (not in a dwelling)

60. Converted or shared accommodation; dwellings; household spaces; rooms in such accommodation

Type of dwelling(s) in converted or shared accommodation	TOTAL CONVERTED OR SHARED ACCOMM-ODATION	TOTAL DWELLINGS	Total shared dwellings	Shared dwellings with the following household spaces				Un-attached spaces	TOTAL HOUSE-HOLD SPACES	Household space type						TOTAL ROOMS
				2	3	4	5 or more			Converted flat	Converted flatlet	Not self-contained flat	Not self-contained 'rooms'	Bedsit	Not self-contained unocc-upied	
a	b	c	d	e	f	g	h	i	j	k	l	m	n	o	p	q
Bristol																
TOTAL CONVERTED OR SHARED ACCOMMODATION	**6,170**	**16,904**	**1,109**	**511**	**185**	**143**	**270**	**583**	**20,312**	**14,605**	**940**	**1,108**	**480**	**3,012**	**167**	**65,785**
Unconverted accommodation																
1 shared dwelling	664	664	664	315	106	83	160		2,327			404	239	1,637	47	4,533
Partly converted accommodation																
1 shared, 1 unshared dwelling*	536	788	252	102	41	36	73	284	1,776	448	75	316	123	759	55	4,593
1 shared, 2 unshared dwellings*	259	642	124	59	24	15	26	129	1,058	443	62	145	61	327	20	2,826
1 shared, 3 or more unshared dwellings*	241	984	69	35	14	9	11	170	1,325	753	145	130	29	230	38	3,678
Converted accommodation																
2 unshared dwellings	2,160	4,320							4,320	4,030	145	90	19	32	4	16,858
3 unshared dwellings	916	2,748							2,748	2,584	127	10	6	18	3	10,244
4 or more unshared dwellings	1,394	6,758							6,758	6,347	386	13	3	9	-	23,053
Kingswood																
TOTAL CONVERTED OR SHARED ACCOMMODATION	**170**	**354**	**37**	**14**	**14**	**5**	**4**	**11**	**452**	**288**	**19**	**33**	**8**	**96**	**8**	**1,423**
Unconverted accommodation																
1 shared dwelling	28	28	28	11	13	3	1		78			16	4	56	2	142
Partly converted accommodation																
1 shared, 1 unshared dwelling*	13	18	5	1	1	1	2	8	53	10	3	7	2	29	2	107
1 shared, 2 unshared dwellings*	6	15	3	2	-	-	1	2	24	10	2	2	1	9	-	54
1 shared, 3 or more unshared dwellings*	2	15	1	-	-	1	-	1	19	14	-	1	-	-	4	60
Converted accommodation																
2 unshared dwellings	106	212							212	195	7	7	1	2	-	807
3 unshared dwellings	8	24							24	19	5	-	-	-	-	72
4 or more unshared dwellings	7	42							42	40	2	-	-	-	-	181

Table 60 Dwellings and household spaces – **continued**

Note: * Includes unshared dwelling(s) plus an unattached household space (not in a dwelling)

60. Converted or shared accommodation; dwellings; household spaces; rooms in such accommodation

Type of dwelling(s) in converted or shared accommodation	TOTAL CONVERTED OR SHARED ACCOMMODATION	TOTAL DWELLINGS	Total shared dwellings	Shared dwellings with the following household spaces				Un-attached spaces	TOTAL HOUSEHOLD SPACES	Household space type						TOTAL ROOMS
				2	3	4	5 or more			Converted flat	Converted flatlet	Not self-contained flat	Not self-contained 'rooms'	Bedsit	Not self-contained unoccupied	
a	b	c	d	e	f	g	h	i	j	k	l	m	n	o	p	q
Northavon																
TOTAL CONVERTED OR SHARED ACCOMMODATION	**169**	**358**	**34**	**25**	**5**	**2**	**2**	**12**	**421**	**299**	**10**	**38**	**21**	**49**	**4**	**1,755**
Unconverted accommodation																
1 shared dwelling	30	30	30	23	3	2	2		75			18	13	41	3	197
Partly converted accommodation																
1 shared, 1 unshared dwelling*	11	13	2	-	2	-	-	9	26	7	3	6	2	7	1	83
1 shared, 2 unshared dwellings*	4	10	2	2	-	-	-	2	14	6	2	5	1	-	-	48
1 shared, 3 or more unshared dwellings*	1	7	-	-	-	-	-	1	8	7	-	1	-	-	-	35
Converted accommodation																
2 unshared dwellings	95	190							190	173	4	8	5	-	-	921
3 unshared dwellings	10	30							30	29	-	-	-	1	-	162
4 or more unshared dwellings	18	78							78	77	1	-	-	-	-	309
Wansdyke																
TOTAL CONVERTED OR SHARED ACCOMMODATION	**228**	**585**	**23**	**13**	**6**	**2**	**2**	**9**	**637**	**518**	**23**	**40**	**17**	**35**	**4**	**2,514**
Unconverted accommodation																
1 shared dwelling	12	12	12	9	2	1	-		28			13	8	7	-	86
Partly converted accommodation																
1 shared, 1 unshared dwelling*	11	18	7	2	2	1	2	4	43	11	-	6	4	18	4	121
1 shared, 2 unshared dwellings*	6	15	3	1	2	-	-	3	23	7	5	3	2	6	-	61
1 shared, 3 or more unshared dwellings*	3	15	1	1	-	-	-	2	18	13	1	2	-	2	-	56
Converted accommodation																
2 unshared dwellings	142	284							284	263	3	15	3	-	-	1,297
3 unshared dwellings	21	63							63	61	-	-	-	2	-	258
4 or more unshared dwellings	33	178							178	163	14	1	-	-	-	635

Note: * Includes unshared dwelling(s) plus an unattached household space (not in a dwelling)

60. Converted or shared accommodation; dwellings; household spaces; rooms in such accommodation

Type of dwelling(s) in converted or shared accommodation	TOTAL CONVERTED OR SHARED ACCOMM-ODATION	TOTAL DWELLINGS	Total shared dwellings	Shared dwellings with the following household spaces				Un-attached spaces	TOTAL HOUSE-HOLD SPACES	Household space type						TOTAL ROOMS
				2	3	4	5 or more			Converted flat	Converted flatlet	Not self-contained flat	Not self-contained 'rooms'	Bedsit	Not self-contained unocc-upied	
a	b	c	d	e	f	g	h	i	j	k	l	m	n	o	p	q
Woodspring																
TOTAL CONVERTED OR SHARED ACCOMMODATION	**2,467**	**6,859**	**229**	**106**	**49**	**32**	**42**	**132**	**7,519**	**6,148**	**375**	**296**	**131**	**516**	**53**	**26,295**
Unconverted accommodation																
1 shared dwelling	109	109	109	63	18	14	14		328			105	54	149	20	901
Partly converted accommodation																
1 shared, 1 unshared dwelling*	105	159	54	16	13	9	16	51	357	89	14	61	32	152	9	870
1 shared, 2 unshared dwellings*	52	131	27	10	8	3	6	24	226	92	9	27	19	71	8	574
1 shared, 3 or more unshared dwellings*	96	502	39	17	10	6	6	57	650	351	107	41	9	127	15	1,556
Converted accommodation																
2 unshared dwellings	1,340	2,680							2,680	2,577	51	39	8	5	-	10,897
3 unshared dwellings	318	954							954	897	32	9	7	8	1	3,656
4 or more unshared dwellings	447	2,324							2,324	2,142	162	14	2	4	-	7,841

Table 61 Dwelling type and occupancy

61. Dwellings; non-permanent accommodation

Occupancy type	TOTAL DWELLINGS	Unshared dwellings											Shared dwellings	TOTAL NON-PERM-ANENT ACCOMM-ODATION
		Total unshared dwellings	Unshared dwellings - purpose-built					Unshared dwellings - converted		Unshared dwellings - not self-contained				
			Detached	Semi-detached	Terraced	Purpose-built flat in: Residential building	Purpose-built flat in: Commercial building	Converted flat	Converted flatlet	Not self-contained flat	Not self-contained 'rooms'	Bedsit		
a	b	c	d	e	f	g	h	i	j	k	l	m	n	o
					AVON									
ALL TYPES OF OCCUPANCY	**390,113**	**388,418**	**67,344**	**114,642**	**127,182**	**43,947**	**5,338**	**27,788**	**1,705**	**332**		**140**	**1,695**	**1,876**
Dwellings with residents	**370,793**	**369,193**	**64,744**	**111,716**	**121,678**	**40,801**	**4,437**	**23,973**	**1,436**	**236**	**70**	**102**	**1,600**	**1,782**
Dwellings with person(s) present	355,602	354,041	62,789	108,767	117,164	38,139	4,052	21,516	1,244	217	67	86	1,561	1,684
Dwellings with no person(s) present	15,191	15,152	1,955	2,949	4,514	2,662	385	2,457	192	19	3	16	39	98
Vacant accommodation	**15,361**	**15,299**	**2,281**	**2,532**	**4,586**	**2,514**	**749**	**2,411**	**195**	**12**		**19**	**62**	
New, never occupied	1,677	1,676	588	100	312	615	8	49	4	-		-	1	
Under improvement	2,524	2,510	275	436	891	304	80	481	37	4		2	14	
Other	11,160	11,113	1,418	1,996	3,383	1,595	661	1,881	154	8		17	47	
Accommodation not used as main residence	**3,959**	**3,926**	**319**	**394**	**918**	**632**	**152**	**1,404**	**74**	**14**		**19**	**33**	**94**
No persons present	1,603	1,601	168	153	261	326	48	621	24	-		-	2	
Second residences	1,214	1,214	120	113	207	258	39	463	14	-		-	-	
Holiday accommodation	330	329	43	34	39	64	7	133	9	-		-	1	
Student accommodation	59	58	5	6	15	4	2	25	1	-		-	1	
Persons enumerated but no residents	2,356	2,325	151	241	657	306	104	783	50	14	-	19	31	94
Owner occupied	543	543	86	86	136	91	8	124	9	2	-	1	-	66
Not owner occupied	1,813	1,782	65	155	521	215	96	659	41	12	-	18	31	28
					Bath									
ALL TYPES OF OCCUPANCY	**35,901**	**35,638**	**3,578**	**7,851**	**12,836**	**4,512**	**524**	**5,930**	**338**	**47**		**22**	**263**	**89**
Dwellings with residents	**33,370**	**33,122**	**3,444**	**7,630**	**12,239**	**4,116**	**427**	**4,912**	**296**	**33**	**11**	**14**	**248**	**89**
Dwellings with person(s) present	31,688	31,442	3,297	7,387	11,799	3,858	389	4,393	270	29	10	10	246	87
Dwellings with no person(s) present	1,682	1,680	147	243	440	258	38	519	26	4	1	4	2	2
Vacant accommodation	**1,428**	**1,421**	**100**	**163**	**369**	**260**	**62**	**441**	**20**	**2**		**4**	**7**	
New, never occupied	66	66	15	3	9	39	-	-	-	-		-	-	
Under improvement	290	289	16	32	85	70	15	68	2	1		-	1	
Other	1,072	1,066	69	128	275	151	47	373	18	1		4	6	
Accommodation not used as main residence	**1,103**	**1,095**	**34**	**58**	**228**	**136**	**35**	**577**	**22**	**1**		**4**	**8**	-
No persons present	617	617	16	24	77	92	21	374	13	-		-	-	
Second residences	518	518	13	21	65	70	18	319	12	-		-	-	
Holiday accommodation	87	87	2	1	10	19	3	51	1	-		-	-	
Student accommodation	12	12	1	2	2	3	-	4	-	-		-	-	
Persons enumerated but no residents	486	478	18	34	151	44	14	203	9	1	-	4	8	-
Owner occupied	89	89	10	7	18	15	2	35	1	1	-	-	-	-
Not owner occupied	397	389	8	27	133	29	12	168	8	-	-	4	8	-

61. Dwellings; non-permanent accommodation

Occupancy type	TOTAL DWELLINGS	Unshared dwellings											Shared dwellings	TOTAL NON-PERM-ANENT ACCOMM-ODATION
		Total unshared dwellings	Unshared dwellings - purpose-built					Unshared dwellings - converted		Unshared dwellings - not self-contained				
			Detached	Semi-detached	Terraced	Purpose-built flat in:								
						Residential building	Commercial building	Converted flat	Converted flatlet	Not self-contained flat	Not self-contained 'rooms'	Bedsit		
a	b	c	d	e	f	g	h	i	j	k	l	m	n	o
Bristol														
ALL TYPES OF OCCUPANCY	**162,501**	**161,392**	**8,538**	**42,761**	**66,852**	**24,480**	**2,966**	**14,605**	**940**	**163**		**87**	**1,109**	**130**
Dwellings with residents	**154,078**	**153,030**	**8,224**	**41,765**	**63,867**	**22,921**	**2,456**	**12,775**	**810**	**111**	**32**	**69**	**1,048**	**127**
Dwellings with person(s) present	146,109	145,096	7,906	40,598	61,039	21,210	2,192	11,277	682	105	30	57	1,013	102
Dwellings with no person(s) present	7,969	7,934	318	1,167	2,828	1,711	264	1,498	128	6	2	12	35	25
Vacant accommodation	**6,682**	**6,644**	**283**	**852**	**2,497**	**1,261**	**421**	**1,219**	**97**	**9**		**5**	**38**	
New, never occupied	368	367	63	22	48	198	8	26	2	-		-	1	
Under improvement	1,263	1,253	44	165	531	173	37	283	16	3		1	10	
Other	5,051	5,024	176	665	1,918	890	376	910	79	6		4	27	
Accommodation not used as main residence	**1,741**	**1,718**	**31**	**144**	**488**	**298**	**89**	**611**	**33**	**11**		**13**	**23**	**3**
No persons present	319	318	7	33	75	103	15	82	3	-		-	1	
Second residences	270	270	5	25	64	98	13	63	2	-		-	-	
Holiday accommodation	13	13	-	5	1	4	-	3	-	-		-	-	
Student accommodation	36	35	2	3	10	1	2	16	1	-		-	1	
Persons enumerated but no residents	1,422	1,400	24	111	413	195	74	529	30	11	-	13	22	3
Owner occupied	241	241	13	39	74	41	2	64	8	-	-	-	-	-
Not owner occupied	1,181	1,159	11	72	339	154	72	465	22	11	-	13	22	3
Kingswood														
ALL TYPES OF OCCUPANCY	**35,595**	**35,558**	**5,516**	**13,867**	**12,577**	**2,894**	**387**	**288**	**19**	**8**		**2**	**37**	**124**
Dwellings with residents	**34,461**	**34,425**	**5,326**	**13,603**	**12,184**	**2,743**	**290**	**254**	**15**	**7**	**1**	**2**	**36**	**122**
Dwellings with person(s) present	33,583	33,547	5,202	13,300	11,873	2,631	279	238	14	7	1	2	36	113
Dwellings with no person(s) present	878	878	124	303	311	112	11	16	1	-	-	-	-	9
Vacant accommodation	**1,060**	**1,059**	**181**	**247**	**362**	**143**	**92**	**30**	**4**	**-**		**-**	**1**	
New, never occupied	164	164	52	14	49	49	-	-	-	-		-	-	
Under improvement	154	154	25	41	75	-	6	7	-	-		-	-	
Other	742	741	104	192	238	94	86	23	4	-		-	1	
Accommodation not used as main residence	**74**	**74**	**9**	**17**	**31**	**8**	**5**	**4**	**-**	**-**		**-**	**-**	**2**
No persons present	27	27	3	6	13	2	3	-	-	-		-	-	
Second residences	22	22	3	5	10	2	2	-	-	-		-	-	
Holiday accommodation	4	4	-	1	2	-	1	-	-	-		-	-	
Student accommodation	1	1	-	-	1	-	-	-	-	-		-	-	
Persons enumerated but no residents	47	47	6	11	18	6	2	4	-	-	-	-	-	2
Owner occupied	26	26	4	4	12	3	1	2	-	-	-	-	-	2
Not owner occupied	21	21	2	7	6	3	1	2	-	-	-	-	-	-

Table 61 Dwelling type and occupancy – **continued**

61. Dwellings; non-permanent accommodation

Occupancy type	TOTAL DWELLINGS	Unshared dwellings											Shared dwellings	TOTAL NON-PERM-ANENT ACCOMM-ODATION
		Total unshared dwellings	Unshared dwellings - purpose-built					Unshared dwellings - converted		Unshared dwellings - not self-contained				
			Detached	Semi-detached	Terraced	Purpose-built flat in: Residential building	Purpose-built flat in: Commercial building	Converted flat	Converted flatlet	Not self-contained flat	Not self-contained 'rooms'	Bedsit		
a	b	c	d	e	f	g	h	i	j	k	l	m	n	o
Northavon														
ALL TYPES OF OCCUPANCY	**51,086**	**51,052**	**14,761**	**17,261**	**14,756**	**3,583**	**367**	**299**	**10**	**13**		**2**	**34**	**551**
Dwellings with residents	**49,032**	**48,999**	**14,119**	**16,792**	**14,105**	**3,373**	**312**	**273**	**10**	**8**	**5**	**2**	**33**	**540**
Dwellings with person(s) present	47,641	47,609	13,772	16,366	13,702	3,183	301	261	10	7	5	2	32	519
Dwellings with no person(s) present	1,391	1,390	347	426	403	190	11	12	-	1	-	-	1	21
Vacant accommodation	**1,867**	**1,866**	**588**	**424**	**592**	**192**	**50**	**20**	**-**	**-**		**-**	**1**	
New, never occupied	451	451	247	25	154	25	-	-	-	-		-	-	
Under improvement	220	220	56	72	58	26	6	2	-	-		-	-	
Other	1,196	1,195	285	327	380	141	44	18	-	-		-	1	
Accommodation not used as main residence	**187**	**187**	**54**	**45**	**59**	**18**	**5**	**6**	**-**	**-**		**-**	**-**	**11**
No persons present	67	67	28	15	17	3	-	4	-	-		-	-	
Second residences	55	55	20	14	16	3	-	2	-	-		-	-	
Holiday accommodation	10	10	7	1	-	-	-	2	-	-		-	-	
Student accommodation	2	2	1	-	1	-	-	-	-	-		-	-	
Persons enumerated but no residents	120	120	26	30	42	15	5	2	-	-	-	-	-	11
Owner occupied	54	54	15	12	18	8	1	-	-	-	-	-	-	9
Not owner occupied	66	66	11	18	24	7	4	2	-	-	-	-	-	2
Wansdyke														
ALL TYPES OF OCCUPANCY	**31,914**	**31,891**	**10,139**	**10,442**	**8,292**	**2,193**	**263**	**518**	**23**	**19**		**2**	**23**	**167**
Dwellings with residents	**30,615**	**30,593**	**9,712**	**10,180**	**7,890**	**2,058**	**237**	**478**	**17**	**16**	**3**	**2**	**22**	**155**
Dwellings with person(s) present	29,775	29,753	9,430	9,941	7,697	1,980	226	442	16	16	3	2	22	139
Dwellings with no person(s) present	840	840	282	239	193	78	11	36	1	-	-	-	-	16
Vacant accommodation	**1,100**	**1,099**	**355**	**225**	**350**	**120**	**21**	**24**	**4**	**-**		**-**	**1**	
New, never occupied	175	175	86	8	12	65	-	4	-	-		-	-	
Under improvement	200	200	56	50	80	4	4	5	1	-		-	-	
Other	725	724	213	167	258	51	17	15	3	-		-	1	
Accommodation not used as main residence	**199**	**199**	**72**	**37**	**52**	**15**	**5**	**16**	**2**	**-**		**-**	**-**	**12**
No persons present	107	107	41	18	36	6	2	4	-	-		-	-	
Second residences	74	74	24	12	27	5	2	4	-	-		-	-	
Holiday accommodation	32	32	17	6	8	1	-	-	-	-		-	-	
Student accommodation	1	1	-	-	1	-	-	-	-	-		-	-	
Persons enumerated but no residents	92	92	31	19	16	9	3	12	2	-	-	-	-	12
Owner occupied	36	36	15	9	5	3	1	3	-	-	-	-	-	7
Not owner occupied	56	56	16	10	11	6	2	9	2	-	-	-	-	5

61. Dwellings; non-permanent accommodation

Occupancy type	TOTAL DWELLINGS	Unshared dwellings											Shared dwellings	TOTAL NON-PERM-ANENT ACCOMM-ODATION
		Total unshared dwellings	Unshared dwellings - purpose-built					Unshared dwellings - converted		Unshared dwellings - not self-contained				
			Detached	Semi-detached	Terraced	Purpose-built flat in:								
						Residential building	Commercial building	Converted flat	Converted flatlet	Not self-contained flat	Not self-contained 'rooms'	Bedsit		
a	b	c	d	e	f	g	h	i	j	k	l	m	n	o
						Woodspring								
ALL TYPES OF OCCUPANCY	**73,116**	**72,887**	**24,812**	**22,460**	**11,869**	**6,285**	**831**	**6,148**	**375**		**82**	**25**	**229**	**815**
Dwellings with residents	**69,237**	**69,024**	**23,919**	**21,746**	**11,393**	**5,590**	**715**	**5,281**	**288**	**61**	**18**	**13**	**213**	**749**
Dwellings with person(s) present	66,806	66,594	23,182	21,175	11,054	5,277	665	4,905	252	53	18	13	212	724
Dwellings with no person(s) present	2,431	2,430	737	571	339	313	50	376	36	8	-	-	1	25
Vacant accommodation	**3,224**	**3,210**	**774**	**621**	**416**	**538**	**103**	**677**	**70**		**1**	**10**	**14**	
New, never occupied	453	453	125	28	40	239	-	19	2		-	-	-	
Under improvement	397	394	78	76	62	31	12	116	18		-	1	3	
Other	2,374	2,363	571	517	314	268	91	542	50		1	9	11	
Accommodation not used as main residence	**655**	**653**	**119**	**93**	**60**	**157**	**13**	**190**	**17**		**2**	**2**	**2**	**66**
No persons present	466	465	73	57	43	120	7	157	8		-	-	1	
Second residences	275	275	55	36	25	80	4	75	-		-	-	-	
Holiday accommodation	184	183	17	20	18	40	3	77	8		-	-	1	
Student accommodation	7	7	1	1	-	-	-	5	-		-	-	-	
Persons enumerated but no residents	189	188	46	36	17	37	6	33	9	2	-	2	1	66
Owner occupied	97	97	29	15	9	21	1	20	-	1	-	1	-	48
Not owner occupied	92	91	17	21	8	16	5	13	9	1	-	1	1	18

Table 62 Occupancy and tenure of dwellings

62. Dwellings with persons present or resident

Occupancy type	TOTAL DWELLINGS	Owner occupied		Rented privately		Rented with a job or business	Rented from a housing association	Rented from a local authority or new town
		Owned outright	Buying	Furnished	Unfurnished			
a	b	c	d	e	f	g	h	i
AVON								
ALL TYPES OF OCCUPANCY	**373,149**	**97,916**	**172,472**	**15,481**	**10,421**	**5,088**	**9,491**	**62,280**
Dwellings with residents	**370,793**	**97,667**	**172,178**	**13,931**	**10,339**	**5,010**	**9,452**	**62,216**
Dwellings with person(s) present	355,602	93,605	166,261	12,716	9,677	4,742	8,727	59,874
Dwellings with no person(s) present	15,191	4,062	5,917	1,215	662	268	725	2,342
Dwellings with persons enumerated but no residents	**2,356**	**249**	**294**	**1,550**	**82**	**78**	**39**	**64**
Bath								
ALL TYPES OF OCCUPANCY	**33,856**	**9,650**	**12,376**	**2,428**	**1,585**	**474**	**1,158**	**6,185**
Dwellings with residents	**33,370**	**9,597**	**12,340**	**2,063**	**1,573**	**469**	**1,150**	**6,178**
Dwellings with person(s) present	31,688	9,111	11,785	1,890	1,447	434	1,065	5,956
Dwellings with no person(s) present	1,682	486	555	173	126	35	85	222
Dwellings with persons enumerated but no residents	**486**	**53**	**36**	**365**	**12**	**5**	**8**	**7**
Bristol								
ALL TYPES OF OCCUPANCY	**155,500**	**36,472**	**63,257**	**9,002**	**4,401**	**1,906**	**5,720**	**34,742**
Dwellings with residents	**154,078**	**36,371**	**63,117**	**7,973**	**4,348**	**1,867**	**5,697**	**34,705**
Dwellings with person(s) present	146,109	34,677	60,257	7,167	4,008	1,717	5,167	33,116
Dwellings with no person(s) present	7,969	1,694	2,860	806	340	150	530	1,589
Dwellings with persons enumerated but no residents	**1,422**	**101**	**140**	**1,029**	**53**	**39**	**23**	**37**
Kingswood								
ALL TYPES OF OCCUPANCY	**34,508**	**9,925**	**18,226**	**494**	**499**	**243**	**620**	**4,501**
Dwellings with residents	**34,461**	**9,918**	**18,207**	**484**	**497**	**238**	**619**	**4,498**
Dwellings with person(s) present	33,583	9,626	17,800	466	474	233	606	4,378
Dwellings with no person(s) present	878	292	407	18	23	5	13	120
Dwellings with persons enumerated but no residents	**47**	**7**	**19**	**10**	**2**	**5**	**1**	**3**
Northavon								
ALL TYPES OF OCCUPANCY	**49,152**	**11,536**	**29,353**	**844**	**1,076**	**764**	**592**	**4,987**
Dwellings with residents	**49,032**	**11,518**	**29,317**	**793**	**1,071**	**758**	**592**	**4,983**
Dwellings with person(s) present	47,641	11,142	28,569	746	1,029	732	563	4,860
Dwellings with no person(s) present	1,391	376	748	47	42	26	29	123
Dwellings with persons enumerated but no residents	**120**	**18**	**36**	**51**	**5**	**6**	**-**	**4**
Wansdyke								
ALL TYPES OF OCCUPANCY	**30,707**	**9,346**	**14,841**	**582**	**837**	**536**	**291**	**4,274**
Dwellings with residents	**30,615**	**9,326**	**14,825**	**544**	**834**	**531**	**288**	**4,267**
Dwellings with person(s) present	29,775	9,002	14,479	514	793	522	280	4,185
Dwellings with no person(s) present	840	324	346	30	41	9	8	82
Dwellings with persons enumerated but no residents	**92**	**20**	**16**	**38**	**3**	**5**	**3**	**7**

62. Dwellings with persons present or resident

Occupancy type	TOTAL DWELLINGS	Owner occupied		Rented privately		Rented with a job or business	Rented from a housing association	Rented from a local authority or new town
		Owned outright	Buying	Furnished	Unfurnished			
a	b	c	d	e	f	g	h	i
		Woodspring						
ALL TYPES OF OCCUPANCY	**69,426**	**20,987**	**34,419**	**2,131**	**2,023**	**1,165**	**1,110**	**7,591**
Dwellings with residents	**69,237**	**20,937**	**34,372**	**2,074**	**2,016**	**1,147**	**1,106**	**7,585**
Dwellings with person(s) present	66,806	20,047	33,371	1,933	1,926	1,104	1,046	7,379
Dwellings with no person(s) present	2,431	890	1,001	141	90	43	60	206
Dwellings with persons enumerated but no residents	**189**	**50**	**47**	**57**	**7**	**18**	**4**	**6**

Table 63 Dwelling type and tenure

63. Dwellings with residents; non-permanent accommodation

Tenure	TOTAL DWELLINGS	Unshared dwellings												Shared dwellings	TOTAL NON-PERMANENT ACCOMMODATION
		Total unshared dwellings	Unshared dwellings - purpose-built					Unshared dwellings - converted		Unshared dwellings - not self-contained					
			Detached	Semi-detached	Terraced	Purpose-built flat in: Residential building	Purpose-built flat in: Commercial building	Converted flat	Converted flatlet	Not self-contained flat	Not self-contained 'rooms'	Bedsit			
a	b	c	d	e	f	g	h	i	j	k	l	m		n	o
AVON															
ALL TENURES	**370,793**	**369,193**	**64,744**	**111,716**	**121,678**	**40,801**	**4,437**	**23,973**	**1,436**	**236**	**70**	**102**		**1,600**	**1,782**
Owner occupied - owned outright	97,667	97,401	23,002	33,364	31,884	4,510	512	4,020	47	46	13	3		266	1,377
- buying	172,178	171,987	37,625	56,373	63,545	5,390	972	7,797	206	66	10	3		191	208
Rented privately - furnished	13,931	13,122	752	1,400	3,273	1,161	857	4,864	651	58	31	75		809	91
- unfurnished	10,339	10,105	976	1,535	2,346	1,018	895	3,116	164	30	11	14		234	29
Rented with a job or business	5,010	4,997	1,178	1,182	682	567	1,002	355	22	7	2	-		13	21
Rented from a housing association	9,452	9,401	146	767	1,605	5,053	34	1,554	226	12	2	2		51	10
Rented from a local authority or new town	62,216	62,180	1,065	17,095	18,343	23,102	165	2,267	120	17	1	5		36	46
Bath															
ALL TENURES	**33,370**	**33,122**	**3,444**	**7,630**	**12,239**	**4,116**	**427**	**4,912**	**296**	**33**	**11**	**14**		**248**	**89**
Owner occupied - owned outright	9,597	9,534	1,608	2,763	3,688	633	44	779	12	4	3	-		63	76
- buying	12,340	12,314	1,626	3,189	5,581	464	96	1,282	62	10	3	1		26	7
Rented privately - furnished	2,063	1,970	53	126	485	174	61	964	83	12	2	10		93	5
- unfurnished	1,573	1,527	53	107	305	152	72	789	39	5	3	2		46	-
Rented with a job or business	469	468	62	86	65	49	124	77	4	1	-	-		1	-
Rented from a housing association	1,150	1,139	15	48	180	493	4	344	54	1	-	-		11	-
Rented from a local authority or new town	6,178	6,170	27	1,311	1,935	2,151	26	677	42	-	-	1		8	1
Bristol															
ALL TENURES	**154,078**	**153,030**	**8,224**	**41,765**	**63,867**	**22,921**	**2,456**	**12,775**	**810**	**111**	**32**	**69**		**1,048**	**127**
Owner occupied - owned outright	36,371	36,230	2,704	11,978	18,212	1,524	291	1,482	14	18	5	2		141	69
- buying	63,117	63,006	4,222	19,239	31,951	2,441	513	4,499	115	21	3	2		111	10
Rented privately - furnished	7,973	7,384	106	477	2,022	713	570	3,015	377	32	18	54		589	10
- unfurnished	4,348	4,204	81	346	1,111	503	524	1,522	91	14	4	8		144	2
Rented with a job or business	1,867	1,857	210	334	311	344	464	177	14	3	-	-		10	2
Rented from a housing association	5,697	5,664	66	400	921	3,000	24	1,086	154	10	2	1		33	4
Rented from a local authority or new town	34,705	34,685	835	8,991	9,339	14,396	70	994	45	13	-	2		20	30

Table 63 Dwelling type and tenure – **continued**

63. Dwellings with residents; non-permanent accommodation

Tenure	TOTAL DWELLINGS	Unshared dwellings											Shared dwellings	TOTAL NON-PERMANENT ACCOMMODATION
		Total unshared dwellings	Unshared dwellings - purpose-built					Unshared dwellings - converted		Unshared dwellings - not self-contained				
			Detached	Semi-detached	Terraced	Purpose-built flat in:								
						Residential building	Commercial building	Converted flat	Converted flatlet	Not self-contained flat	Not self-contained 'rooms'	Bedsit		
a	b	c	d	e	f	g	h	i	j	k	l	m	n	o
Kingswood														
ALL TENURES	**34,461**	**34,425**	**5,326**	**13,603**	**12,184**	**2,743**	**290**	**254**	**15**	**7**	**1**	**2**	**36**	**122**
Owner occupied - owned outright	9,918	9,915	1,668	4,624	3,242	318	17	41	2	3	-	-	3	82
- buying	18,207	18,200	3,484	7,602	6,559	403	71	76	2	2	1	-	7	23
Rented privately - furnished	484	470	45	135	150	43	60	33	3	-	-	1	14	12
- unfurnished	497	487	52	121	152	53	75	28	4	1	-	1	10	1
Rented with a job or business	238	238	48	48	50	35	54	3	-	-	-	-	-	1
Rented from a housing association	619	619	4	42	192	341	1	37	2	-	-	-	-	2
Rented from a local authority or new town	4,498	4,496	25	1,031	1,839	1,550	12	36	2	1	-	-	2	1
Northavon														
ALL TENURES	**49,032**	**48,999**	**14,119**	**16,792**	**14,105**	**3,373**	**312**	**273**	**10**	**8**	**5**	**2**	**33**	**540**
Owner occupied - owned outright	11,518	11,512	3,954	4,423	2,645	378	31	75	1	3	2	-	6	407
- buying	29,317	29,309	9,330	9,622	9,325	900	61	66	-	4	1	-	8	76
Rented privately - furnished	793	783	159	213	257	66	38	39	8	-	1	2	10	24
- unfurnished	1,071	1,068	273	343	248	117	56	30	-	1	-	-	3	15
Rented with a job or business	758	757	309	208	63	40	116	20	-	-	1	-	1	7
Rented from a housing association	592	588	20	109	88	356	3	12	-	-	-	-	4	2
Rented from a local authority or new town	4,983	4,982	74	1,874	1,479	1,516	7	31	1	-	-	-	1	9
Wansdyke														
ALL TENURES	**30,615**	**30,593**	**9,712**	**10,180**	**7,890**	**2,058**	**237**	**478**	**17**	**16**	**3**	**2**	**22**	**155**
Owner occupied - owned outright	9,326	9,323	3,946	2,962	1,849	422	29	108	5	2	-	-	3	114
- buying	14,825	14,821	5,218	5,211	3,922	280	61	120	2	6	1	-	4	24
Rented privately - furnished	544	536	121	126	136	33	28	80	7	2	2	1	8	6
- unfurnished	834	830	186	224	278	35	35	67	1	3	-	1	4	2
Rented with a job or business	531	531	204	132	71	26	75	20	1	2	-	-	-	4
Rented from a housing association	288	287	10	60	78	122	-	16	1	-	-	-	1	-
Rented from a local authority or new town	4,267	4,265	27	1,465	1,556	1,140	9	67	-	1	-	-	2	5

Table 63 Dwelling type and tenure – continued

63. Dwellings with residents; non-permanent accommodation

Tenure	TOTAL DWELLINGS	Unshared dwellings											Shared dwellings	TOTAL NON-PERM-ANENT ACCOMM-ODATION
		Total unshared dwellings	Unshared dwellings - purpose-built					Unshared dwellings - converted		Unshared dwellings - not self-contained				
			Detached	Semi-detached	Terraced	Purpose-built flat in: Residential building	Purpose-built flat in: Commercial building	Converted flat	Converted flatlet	Not self-contained flat	Not self-contained 'rooms'	Bedsit		
a	b	c	d	e	f	g	h	i	j	k	l	m	n	o
Woodspring														
ALL TENURES	**69,237**	**69,024**	**23,919**	**21,746**	**11,393**	**5,590**	**715**	**5,281**	**288**	**61**	**18**	**13**	**213**	**749**
Owner occupied - owned outright	20,937	20,887	9,122	6,614	2,248	1,235	100	1,535	13	16	3	1	50	629
- buying	34,372	34,337	13,745	11,510	6,207	902	170	1,754	25	23	1	-	35	68
Rented privately - furnished	2,074	1,979	268	323	223	132	100	733	173	12	8	7	95	34
- unfurnished	2,016	1,989	331	394	252	158	133	680	29	6	4	2	27	9
Rented with a job or business	1,147	1,146	345	374	122	73	169	58	3	1	1	-	1	7
Rented from a housing association	1,106	1,104	31	108	146	741	2	59	15	1	-	1	2	2
Rented from a local authority or new town	7,585	7,582	77	2,423	2,195	2,349	41	462	30	2	1	2	3	-

Table 64 Tenure of dwellings and household spaces

64. Dwellings; household spaces in dwellings

Tenure or occupancy type of dwelling	TOTAL DWELLINGS	Unshared dwellings	Shared dwellings	TOTAL HOUSE-HOLD SPACES	Tenure or occupancy type of household spaces										
					Owner occupied		Rented privately		Rented with a job or business	Rented from a housing assoc-iation	Rented from a local authority or new town	Vacant accomm-odation	Accommodation not used as main residence - no persons present		
					Owned outright	Buying	Furnished	Un-furnished					Second residences	Holiday accomm-odation	Student accomm-odation
a	b	c	d	e	f	g	h	i	j	k	l	m	n	o	p
AVON															
ALL TENURES OR OCCUPANCY TYPES	**390,113**	**388,418**	**1,695**	**394,296**	**97,962**	**172,523**	**18,536**	**10,648**	**5,163**	**9,599**	**62,316**	**15,902**	**1,232**	**341**	**74**
Dwellings with residents	**370,793**	**369,193**	**1,600**	**374,781**	**97,713**	**172,229**	**16,911**	**10,565**	**5,085**	**9,560**	**62,251**	**432**	**14**	**9**	**12**
Owner occupied - owned outright	97,667	97,401	266	98,039	97,713	21	211	66	5	-	1	20	1	-	1
- buying	172,178	171,987	191	172,467		172,208	211	30	2	1	5	9	-	-	1
Rented privately - furnished	13,931	13,122	809	16,337			15,965		33			318	5	6	10
- unfurnished	10,339	10,105	234	10,948			425	10,447	7			61	5	3	-
Rented with a job or business	5,010	4,997	13	5,030					5,027			3	-	-	-
Rented from a housing association	9,452	9,401	51	9,654			54	16	8	9,559	1	13	3	-	-
Rented from a local authority or new town	62,216	62,180	36	62,306			45	6	3		62,244	8	-	-	-
Persons enumerated but no residents	**2,356**	**2,325**	**31**	**2,425**	**249**	**294**	**1,615**	**83**	**78**	**39**	**65**		**-**	**-**	**2**
Owner occupied	543	543	-	543	249	294	-	-	-	-	-		-	-	-
Not owner occupied	1,813	1,782	31	1,882			1,615	83	78	39	65			-	2
Vacant accommodation	15,361	15,299	62	15,484	-	-	10	-	-	-	-	15,470	4	-	-
Other unoccupied accommodation	1,603	1,601	2	1,606			-	-	-	-	-		1,214	332	60
Bath															
ALL TENURES OR OCCUPANCY TYPES	**35,901**	**35,638**	**263**	**36,550**	**9,657**	**12,389**	**2,906**	**1,634**	**479**	**1,172**	**6,197**	**1,486**	**525**	**89**	**16**
Dwellings with residents	**33,370**	**33,122**	**248**	**33,995**	**9,604**	**12,353**	**2,526**	**1,622**	**474**	**1,164**	**6,190**	**51**	**7**	**2**	**2**
Owner occupied - owned outright	9,597	9,534	63	9,695	9,604	7	60	17	1	-	1	3	1	-	1
- buying	12,340	12,314	26	12,376		12,346	23	5	-	-	2	-	-	-	-
Rented privately - furnished	2,063	1,970	93	2,371			2,330		2			38	-	-	1
- unfurnished	1,573	1,527	46	1,711			102	1,596	1			7	3	2	-
Rented with a job or business	469	468	1	470					469			1	-	-	-
Rented from a housing association	1,150	1,139	11	1,179			9	-	1	1,164	1	1	3	-	-
Rented from a local authority or new town	6,178	6,170	8	6,193			2	4	-		6,186	1	-	-	-
Persons enumerated but no residents	**486**	**478**	**8**	**502**	**53**	**36**	**379**	**12**	**5**	**8**	**7**		**-**	**-**	**2**
Owner occupied	89	89	-	89	53	36	-	-	-	-	-		-	-	-
Not owner occupied	397	389	8	413			379	12	5	8	7			-	2
Vacant accommodation	1,428	1,421	7	1,436	-	-	1	-	-	-	-	1,435	-	-	-
Other unoccupied accommodation	617	617	-	617			-	-	-	-	-		518	87	12

Table 64 Tenure of dwellings and household spaces – **continued**

64. Dwellings; household spaces in dwellings

Tenure or occupancy type of dwelling	TOTAL DWELLINGS	Unshared dwellings	Shared dwellings	TOTAL HOUSE-HOLD SPACES	Tenure or occupancy type of household spaces: Owner occupied		Rented privately		Rented with a job or business	Rented from a housing association	Rented from a local authority or new town	Vacant accomm-odation	Accommodation not used as main residence - no persons present		
					Owned outright	Buying	Furnished	Un-furnished					Second residences	Holiday accomm-odation	Student accomm-odation
a	b	c	d	e	f	g	h	i	j	k	l	m	n	o	p
Bristol															
ALL TENURES OR OCCUPANCY TYPES	**162,501**	**161,392**	**1,109**	**165,326**	**36,493**	**63,281**	**11,121**	**4,528**	**1,960**	**5,807**	**34,751**	**7,052**	**274**	**14**	**45**
Dwellings with residents	**154,078**	**153,030**	**1,048**	**156,766**	**36,392**	**63,141**	**10,034**	**4,474**	**1,921**	**5,784**	**34,713**	**294**	**4**	**1**	**8**
Owner occupied - owned outright	36,371	36,230	141	36,563	36,392	9	117	32	3	-	-	10	-	-	-
- buying	63,117	63,006	111	63,291		63,132	132	18	1	1	1	5	-	-	1
Rented privately - furnished	7,973	7,384	589	9,722			9,458		25			229	3	-	7
- unfurnished	4,348	4,204	144	4,696			250	4,410	4			30	1	1	-
Rented with a job or business	1,867	1,857	10	1,882					1,880			2	-	-	-
Rented from a housing association	5,697	5,664	33	5,856			43	13	5	5,783	-	12	-	-	-
Rented from a local authority or new town	34,705	34,685	20	34,756			34	1	3		34,712	6	-	-	-
Persons enumerated but no residents	**1,422**	**1,400**	**22**	**1,473**	**101**	**140**	**1,078**	**54**	**39**	**23**	**38**		**-**	**-**	**-**
Owner occupied	241	241	-	241	101	140	-	-	-	-	-		-	-	-
Not owner occupied	1,181	1,159	22	1,232			1,078	54	39	23	38			-	-
Vacant accommodation	6,682	6,644	38	6,767	-	-	9	-	-	-	-	6,758	-	-	-
Other unoccupied accommodation	319	318	1	320			-	-	-	-	-		270	13	37
Kingswood															
ALL TENURES OR OCCUPANCY TYPES	**35,595**	**35,558**	**37**	**35,682**	**9,925**	**18,227**	**554**	**501**	**245**	**620**	**4,502**	**1,079**	**24**	**4**	**1**
Dwellings with residents	**34,461**	**34,425**	**36**	**34,545**	**9,918**	**18,208**	**544**	**499**	**240**	**619**	**4,499**	**18**	**-**	**-**	**-**
Owner occupied - owned outright	9,918	9,915	3	9,921	9,918	-	3	-	-	-	-	-	-	-	-
- buying	18,207	18,200	7	18,216		18,208	7	-	-	-	-	1	-	-	-
Rented privately - furnished	484	470	14	517			515		-			2	-	-	-
- unfurnished	497	487	10	532			16	499	2			15	-	-	-
Rented with a job or business	238	238	-	238					238			-	-	-	-
Rented from a housing association	619	619	-	619			-	-	-	619	-	-	-	-	-
Rented from a local authority or new town	4,498	4,496	2	4,502			3	-	-		4,499	-	-	-	-
Persons enumerated but no residents	**47**	**47**	**-**	**47**	**7**	**19**	**10**	**2**	**5**	**1**	**3**		**-**	**-**	**-**
Owner occupied	26	26	-	26	7	19	-	-	-	-	-		-	-	-
Not owner occupied	21	21	-	21			10	2	5	1	3			-	-
Vacant accommodation	1,060	1,059	1	1,063	-	-	-	-	-	-	-	1,061	2	-	-
Other unoccupied accommodation	27	27	-	27			-	-	-	-	-		22	4	1

64. Dwellings; household spaces in dwellings

Tenure or occupancy type of dwelling	TOTAL DWELLINGS	Unshared dwellings	Shared dwellings	TOTAL HOUSE-HOLD SPACES	Tenure or occupancy type of household spaces										
					Owner occupied		Rented privately		Rented with a job or business	Rented from a housing assoc-iation	Rented from a local authority or new town	Vacant accomm-odation	Accommodation not used as main residence - no persons present		
					Owned outright	Buying	Furnished	Un-furnished					Second residences	Holiday accomm-odation	Student accomm-odation
a	b	c	d	e	f	g	h	i	j	k	l	m	n	o	p
Northavon															
ALL TENURES OR OCCUPANCY TYPES	**51,086**	**51,052**	**34**	**51,137**	**11,538**	**29,356**	**871**	**1,082**	**766**	**596**	**4,988**	**1,873**	**55**	**10**	**2**
Dwellings with residents	**49,032**	**48,999**	**33**	**49,082**	**11,520**	**29,320**	**820**	**1,077**	**760**	**596**	**4,984**	**5**	-	-	-
Owner occupied - owned outright	11,518	11,512	6	11,524	11,520	1	2	1	-	-	-	-	-	-	-
- buying	29,317	29,309	8	29,327		29,319	7	-	-	-	-	1	-	-	-
Rented privately - furnished	793	783	10	809			805		1			3	-	-	-
- unfurnished	1,071	1,068	3	1,082			6	1,075	-			1	-	-	-
Rented with a job or business	758	757	1	759					759			-	-	-	-
Rented from a housing association	592	588	4	597			-	1	-	596	-	-	-	-	-
Rented from a local authority or new town	4,983	4,982	1	4,984			-	-	-		4,984	-	-	-	-
Persons enumerated but no residents	**120**	**120**	-	**120**	**18**	**36**	**51**	**5**	**6**	-	**4**		-	-	-
Owner occupied	54	54	-	54	18	36	-	-	-	-	-		-	-	-
Not owner occupied	66	66	-	66			51	5	6	-	4			-	-
Vacant accommodation	1,867	1,866	1	1,868	-	-	-	-	-	-	-	1,868	-	-	-
Other unoccupied accommodation	67	67	-	67			-	-	-	-	-		55	10	2
Wansdyke															
ALL TENURES OR OCCUPANCY TYPES	**31,914**	**31,891**	**23**	**31,957**	**9,346**	**14,841**	**610**	**843**	**541**	**291**	**4,275**	**1,103**	**74**	**32**	**1**
Dwellings with residents	**30,615**	**30,593**	**22**	**30,656**	**9,326**	**14,825**	**572**	**840**	**536**	**288**	**4,268**	**1**	-	-	-
Owner occupied - owned outright	9,326	9,323	3	9,329	9,326	-	3	-	-	-	-	-	-	-	-
- buying	14,825	14,821	4	14,831		14,825	4	2	-	-	-	-	-	-	-
Rented privately - furnished	544	536	8	561			557		4			-	-	-	-
- unfurnished	834	830	4	844			6	837	-			1	-	-	-
Rented with a job or business	531	531	-	531					531			-	-	-	-
Rented from a housing association	288	287	1	290			1	-	1	288	-	-	-	-	-
Rented from a local authority or new town	4,267	4,265	2	4,270			1	1	-		4,268	-	-	-	-
Persons enumerated but no residents	**92**	**92**	-	**92**	**20**	**16**	**38**	**3**	**5**	**3**	**7**		-	-	-
Owner occupied	36	36	-	36	20	16	-	-	-	-	-		-	-	-
Not owner occupied	56	56	-	56			38	3	5	3	7			-	-
Vacant accommodation	1,100	1,099	1	1,102	-	-	-	-	-	-	-	1,102	-	-	-
Other unoccupied accommodation	107	107	-	107			-	-	-	-	-		74	32	1

Table 64 Tenure of dwellings and household spaces – **continued**

64. Dwellings; household spaces in dwellings

Tenure or occupancy type of dwelling	TOTAL DWELLINGS	Unshared dwellings	Shared dwellings	TOTAL HOUSE-HOLD SPACES	Tenure or occupancy type of household spaces										
					Owner occupied		Rented privately		Rented with a job or business	Rented from a housing assoc-iation	Rented from a local authority or new town	Vacant accomm-odation	Accommodation not used as main residence - no persons present		
					Owned outright	Buying	Furnished	Un-furnished					Second residences	Holiday accomm-odation	Student accomm-odation
a	b	c	d	e	f	g	h	i	j	k	l	m	n	o	p
					Woodspring										
ALL TENURES OR OCCUPANCY TYPES	**73,116**	**72,887**	**229**	**73,644**	**21,003**	**34,429**	**2,474**	**2,060**	**1,172**	**1,113**	**7,603**	**3,309**	**280**	**192**	**9**
Dwellings with residents	**69,237**	**69,024**	**213**	**69,737**	**20,953**	**34,382**	**2,415**	**2,053**	**1,154**	**1,109**	**7,597**	**63**	**3**	**6**	**2**
Owner occupied - owned outright	20,937	20,887	50	21,007	20,953	4	26	16	1	-	-	7	-	-	-
- buying	34,372	34,337	35	34,426		34,378	38	5	1	-	2	2	-	-	-
Rented privately - furnished	2,074	1,979	95	2,357			2,300		1			46	2	6	2
- unfurnished	2,016	1,989	27	2,083			45	2,030	-			7	1	-	-
Rented with a job or business	1,147	1,146	1	1,150					1,150			-	-	-	-
Rented from a housing association	1,106	1,104	2	1,113			1	2	1	1,109	-	-	-	-	-
Rented from a local authority or new town	7,585	7,582	3	7,601			5	-	-		7,595	1	-	-	-
Persons enumerated but no residents	**189**	**188**	**1**	**191**	**50**	**47**	**59**	**7**	**18**	**4**	**6**		**-**	**-**	**-**
Owner occupied	97	97	-	97	50	47	-	-	-	-	-		-	-	-
Not owner occupied	92	91	1	94			59	7	18	4	6			-	-
Vacant accommodation	3,224	3,210	14	3,248	-	-	-	-	-	-	-	3,246	2	-	-
Other unoccupied accommodation	466	465	1	468			-	-	-	-	-		275	186	7

65. Dwellings; household spaces in dwellings

Occupancy type of dwelling	TOTAL DWELLINGS	Unshared dwellings	Shared dwellings	TOTAL HOUSE-HOLD SPACES	Occupancy type of household spaces									
					Households with residents		Vacant accommodation			Accommodation not used as main residence				
										No persons present			Persons enumerated but no residents	
					Persons present	Absent household	New	Under improve-ment	Other	Second residences	Holiday accomm-odation	Student accomm-odation	Owner occupied	Not owner occupied
a	b	c	d	e	f	g	h	i	j	k	l	m	n	o
AVON														
ALL TYPES OF OCCUPANCY	**390,113**	**388,418**	**1,695**	**394,296**	**358,019**	**15,925**	**1,682**	**2,573**	**11,647**	**1,232**	**341**	**74**	**548**	**2,255**
Dwellings with residents	**370,793**	**369,193**	**1,600**	**374,781**	**358,019**	**15,925**	**4**	**13**	**415**	**14**	**9**	**12**	**5**	**365**
Dwellings with person(s) present	355,602	354,041	1,561	359,526	358,019	697	2	13	392	14	9	10	5	365
Dwellings with no person(s) present	15,191	15,152	39	15,255		15,228	2	-	23	-	-	2	-	-
Vacant accommodation	**15,361**	**15,299**	**62**	**15,484**			**1,678**	**2,560**	**11,232**	**4**	**-**	**-**	**-**	**10**
New, never occupied	1,677	1,676	1	1,678			1,678							
Under improvement	2,524	2,510	14	2,566			-	2,560	5	-	-	-	-	1
Other	11,160	11,113	47	11,240			-		11,227	4	-	-	-	9
Accommodation not used as main residence	**3,959**	**3,926**	**33**	**4,031**			**-**			**1,214**	**332**	**62**	**543**	**1,880**
No persons present	1,603	1,601	2	1,606			-			1,214	332	60		-
Second residences	1,214	1,214	-	1,214			-			1,214	-	-		-
Holiday accommodation	330	329	1	332			-				332	-		
Student accommodation	59	58	1	60			-					60		
Persons enumerated but no residents	2,356	2,325	31	2,425			-			-	-	2	543	1,880
Owner occupied	543	543	-	543			-			-	-	-	543	-
Not owner occupied	1,813	1,782	31	1,882			-				-	2		1,880

65. Dwellings; household spaces in dwellings

Occupancy type of dwelling	TOTAL DWELLINGS	Unshared dwellings	Shared dwellings	TOTAL HOUSE-HOLD SPACES	Occupancy type of household spaces									
					Households with residents		Vacant accommodation			Accommodation not used as main residence				
										No persons present			Persons enumerated but no residents	
					Persons present	Absent household	New	Under improve-ment	Other	Second residences	Holiday accomm-odation	Student accomm-odation	Owner occupied	Not owner occupied
a	b	c	d	e	f	g	h	i	j	k	l	m	n	o
					Bath									
ALL TYPES OF OCCUPANCY	**35,901**	**35,638**	**263**	**36,550**	**32,067**	**1,803**	**67**	**294**	**1,125**	**525**	**89**	**16**	**89**	**475**
Dwellings with residents	**33,370**	**33,122**	**248**	**33,995**	**32,067**	**1,803**	**1**	**4**	**46**	**7**	**2**	**2**	**-**	**63**
Dwellings with person(s) present	31,688	31,442	246	32,311	32,067	120	1	4	45	7	2	2	-	63
Dwellings with no person(s) present	1,682	1,680	2	1,684		1,683	-	-	1	-	-	-	-	-
Vacant accommodation	**1,428**	**1,421**	**7**	**1,436**			**66**	**290**	**1,079**	**-**	**-**	**-**	**-**	**1**
New, never occupied	66	66	-	66			66							
Under improvement	290	289	1	291			-	290	1	-	-	-	-	-
Other	1,072	1,066	6	1,079			-		1,078	-	-	-	-	1
Accommodation not used as main residence	**1,103**	**1,095**	**8**	**1,119**			**-**			**518**	**87**	**14**	**89**	**411**
No persons present	617	617	-	617			-			518	87	12		-
Second residences	518	518	-	518			-			518	-	-		-
Holiday accommodation	87	87	-	87			-				87	-		
Student accommodation	12	12	-	12			-					12		
Persons enumerated but no residents	486	478	8	502			-			-	-	2	89	411
Owner occupied	89	89	-	89			-			-	-	-	89	-
Not owner occupied	397	389	8	413			-				-	2		411

65. Dwellings; household spaces in dwellings

Occupancy type of dwelling	TOTAL DWELLINGS	Unshared dwellings	Shared dwellings	TOTAL HOUSE-HOLD SPACES	Occupancy type of household spaces									
					Households with residents		Vacant accommodation			Accommodation not used as main residence				
										No persons present			Persons enumerated but no residents	
					Persons present	Absent household	New	Under improve-ment	Other	Second residences	Holiday accomm-odation	Student accomm-odation	Owner occupied	Not owner occupied
a	b	c	d	e	f	g	h	i	j	k	l	m	n	o
					Bristol									
ALL TYPES OF OCCUPANCY	**162,501**	**161,392**	**1,109**	**165,326**	**147,673**	**8,495**	**372**	**1,303**	**5,377**	**274**	**14**	**45**	**246**	**1,527**
Dwellings with residents	**154,078**	**153,030**	**1,048**	**156,766**	**147,673**	**8,495**	**3**	**4**	**287**	**4**	**1**	**8**	**5**	**286**
Dwellings with person(s) present	146,109	145,096	1,013	148,738	147,673	491	1	4	267	4	1	6	5	286
Dwellings with no person(s) present	7,969	7,934	35	8,028		8,004	2	-	20	-	-	2	-	-
Vacant accommodation	**6,682**	**6,644**	**38**	**6,767**			**369**	**1,299**	**5,090**	**-**	**-**	**-**	**-**	**9**
New, never occupied	368	367	1	369			369							
Under improvement	1,263	1,253	10	1,301			-	1,299	1	-	-	-	-	1
Other	5,051	5,024	27	5,097			-		5,089	-	-	-	-	8
Accommodation not used as main residence	**1,741**	**1,718**	**23**	**1,793**			**-**			**270**	**13**	**37**	**241**	**1,232**
No persons present	319	318	1	320			-			270	13	37		-
Second residences	270	270	-	270			-			270	-	-		-
Holiday accommodation	13	13	-	13			-				13	-		
Student accommodation	36	35	1	37			-					37		
Persons enumerated but no residents	1,422	1,400	22	1,473			-			-	-	-	241	1,232
Owner occupied	241	241	-	241			-			-	-	-	241	-
Not owner occupied	1,181	1,159	22	1,232			-				-	-		1,232

65. Dwellings; household spaces in dwellings

Occupancy type of dwelling	TOTAL DWELLINGS	Unshared dwellings	Shared dwellings	TOTAL HOUSE-HOLD SPACES	Occupancy type of household spaces									
					Households with residents		Vacant accommodation			Accommodation not used as main residence				
										No persons present			Persons enumerated but no residents	
					Persons present	Absent household	New	Under improve-ment	Other	Second residences	Holiday accomm-odation	Student accomm-odation	Owner occupied	Not owner occupied
a	b	c	d	e	f	g	h	i	j	k	l	m	n	o
					Kingswood									
ALL TYPES OF OCCUPANCY	**35,595**	**35,558**	**37**	**35,682**	**33,641**	**885**	**164**	**154**	**761**	**24**	**4**	**1**	**26**	**22**
Dwellings with residents	**34,461**	**34,425**	**36**	**34,545**	**33,641**	**885**	**-**	**-**	**18**	**-**	**-**	**-**	**-**	**1**
Dwellings with person(s) present	33,583	33,547	36	33,667	33,641	7	-	-	18	-	-	-	-	1
Dwellings with no person(s) present	878	878	-	878		878	-	-	-	-	-	-	-	-
Vacant accommodation	**1,060**	**1,059**	**1**	**1,063**			**164**	**154**	**743**	**2**	**-**	**-**	**-**	**-**
New, never occupied	164	164	-	164			164							
Under improvement	154	154	-	154			-	154	-	-	-	-	-	-
Other	742	741	1	745			-		743	2	-	-	-	-
Accommodation not used as main residence	**74**	**74**	**-**	**74**			**-**			**22**	**4**	**1**	**26**	**21**
No persons present	27	27	-	27			-			22	4	1		-
Second residences	22	22	-	22			-			22	-	-		-
Holiday accommodation	4	4	-	4			-				4	-		
Student accommodation	1	1	-	1			-					1		
Persons enumerated but no residents	47	47	-	47			-			-	-	-	26	21
Owner occupied	26	26	-	26			-			-	-	-	26	-
Not owner occupied	21	21	-	21			-				-	-		21

65. Dwellings; household spaces in dwellings

Occupancy type of dwelling	TOTAL DWELLINGS	Unshared dwellings	Shared dwellings	TOTAL HOUSE-HOLD SPACES	Occupancy type of household spaces									
					Households with residents		Vacant accommodation			Accommodation not used as main residence				
										No persons present			Persons enumerated but no residents	
					Persons present	Absent household	New	Under improve-ment	Other	Second residences	Holiday accomm-odation	Student accomm-odation	Owner occupied	Not owner occupied
a	b	c	d	e	f	g	h	i	j	k	l	m	n	o
					Northavon									
ALL TYPES OF OCCUPANCY	**51,086**	**51,052**	**34**	**51,137**	**47,677**	**1,398**	**451**	**220**	**1,202**	**55**	**10**	**2**	**54**	**68**
Dwellings with residents	**49,032**	**48,999**	**33**	**49,082**	**47,677**	**1,398**	**-**	**-**	**5**	**-**	**-**	**-**	**-**	**2**
Dwellings with person(s) present	47,641	47,609	32	47,690	47,677	6	-	-	5	-	-	-	-	2
Dwellings with no person(s) present	1,391	1,390	1	1,392		1,392	-	-	-	-	-	-	-	-
Vacant accommodation	**1,867**	**1,866**	**1**	**1,868**			**451**	**220**	**1,197**	**-**	**-**	**-**	**-**	**-**
New, never occupied	451	451	-	451			451							
Under improvement	220	220	-	220			-	220	-	-	-	-	-	-
Other	1,196	1,195	1	1,197			-		1,197	-	-	-	-	-
Accommodation not used as main residence	**187**	**187**	**-**	**187**			**-**			**55**	**10**	**2**	**54**	**66**
No persons present	67	67	-	67			-			55	10	2		-
Second residences	55	55	-	55			-			55	-	-		-
Holiday accommodation	10	10	-	10			-				10	-		
Student accommodation	2	2	-	2			-					2		
Persons enumerated but no residents	120	120	-	120			-			-	-	-	54	66
Owner occupied	54	54	-	54			-			-	-	-	54	-
Not owner occupied	66	66	-	66			-				-	-		66

Table 65 Occupancy of dwellings and household spaces – **continued**

65. Dwellings; household spaces in dwellings

Occupancy type of dwelling	TOTAL DWELLINGS	Unshared dwellings	Shared dwellings	TOTAL HOUSE-HOLD SPACES	Occupancy type of household spaces									
					Households with residents		Vacant accommodation			Accommodation not used as main residence				
										No persons present			Persons enumerated but no residents	
					Persons present	Absent household	New	Under improve-ment	Other	Second residences	Holiday accomm-odation	Student accomm-odation	Owner occupied	Not owner occupied
a	b	c	d	e	f	g	h	i	j	k	l	m	n	o
					Wansdyke									
ALL TYPES OF OCCUPANCY	**31,914**	**31,891**	**23**	**31,957**	**29,802**	**849**	**175**	**200**	**728**	**74**	**32**	**1**	**36**	**60**
Dwellings with residents	**30,615**	**30,593**	**22**	**30,656**	**29,802**	**849**	**-**	**-**	**1**	**-**	**-**	**-**	**-**	**4**
Dwellings with person(s) present	29,775	29,753	22	29,816	29,802	9	-	-	1	-	-	-	-	4
Dwellings with no person(s) present	840	840	-	840		840	-	-	-	-	-	-	-	-
Vacant accommodation	**1,100**	**1,099**	**1**	**1,102**			**175**	**200**	**727**	**-**	**-**	**-**	**-**	**-**
New, never occupied	175	175	-	175			175							
Under improvement	200	200	-	200			-	200	-	-	-	-	-	-
Other	725	724	1	727			-		727	-	-	-	-	-
Accommodation not used as main residence	**199**	**199**	**-**	**199**			**-**			**74**	**32**	**1**	**36**	**56**
No persons present	107	107	-	107			-			74	32	1		-
Second residences	74	74	-	74			-			74	-	-		-
Holiday accommodation	32	32	-	32			-				32	-		
Student accommodation	1	1	-	1			-					1		
Persons enumerated but no residents	92	92	-	92			-			-	-	-	36	56
Owner occupied	36	36	-	36			-			-	-	-	36	-
Not owner occupied	56	56	-	56			-				-	-		56

65. Dwellings; household spaces in dwellings

Occupancy type of dwelling	TOTAL DWELLINGS	Unshared dwellings	Shared dwellings	TOTAL HOUSE-HOLD SPACES	Occupancy type of household spaces									
					Households with residents		Vacant accommodation			Accommodation not used as main residence				
										No persons present			Persons enumerated but no residents	
					Persons present	Absent household	New	Under improve-ment	Other	Second residences	Holiday accomm-odation	Student accomm-odation	Owner occupied	Not owner occupied
a	b	c	d	e	f	g	h	i	j	k	l	m	n	o
					Woodspring									
ALL TYPES OF OCCUPANCY	**73,116**	**72,887**	**229**	**73,644**	**67,159**	**2,495**	**453**	**402**	**2,454**	**280**	**192**	**9**	**97**	**103**
Dwellings with residents	**69,237**	**69,024**	**213**	**69,737**	**67,159**	**2,495**	**-**	**5**	**58**	**3**	**6**	**2**	**-**	**9**
Dwellings with person(s) present	66,806	66,594	212	67,304	67,159	64	-	5	56	3	6	2	-	9
Dwellings with no person(s) present	2,431	2,430	1	2,433		2,431	-	-	2	-	-	-	-	-
Vacant accommodation	**3,224**	**3,210**	**14**	**3,248**			**453**	**397**	**2,396**	**2**	**-**	**-**	**-**	**-**
New, never occupied	453	453	-	453			453							
Under improvement	397	394	3	400			-	397	3	-	-	-	-	-
Other	2,374	2,363	11	2,395			-		2,393	2	-	-	-	-
Accommodation not used as main residence	**655**	**653**	**2**	**659**			**-**			**275**	**186**	**7**	**97**	**94**
No persons present	466	465	1	468			-			275	186	7		-
Second residences	275	275	-	275			-			275	-	-		-
Holiday accommodation	184	183	1	186			-				186	-		
Student accommodation	7	7	-	7			-					7		
Persons enumerated but no residents	189	188	1	191			-			-	-	-	97	94
Owner occupied	97	97	-	97			-			-	-	-	97	-
Not owner occupied	92	91	1	94			-				-	-		94

66. Shared dwellings; household spaces in shared dwellings

Number of household spaces within dwelling	TOTAL HOUSEHOLD SPACES	Type of not self-contained household space in shared dwellings				TOTAL SHARED DWELLINGS
		Not self-contained flat	Not self-contained 'rooms'	Bedsit	Not self-contained unoccupied	
a	b	c	d	e	f	g
		AVON				
TOTAL SHARED DWELLINGS	**5,878**	**1,064**	**626**	**3,997**	**191**	**1,695**
2	1,624	737	326	498	63	812
3	891	166	122	553	50	297
4	844	63	77	670	34	211
5	720	38	25	645	12	144
6	540	24	13	495	8	90
7	329	20	23	280	6	47
8 or more	930	16	40	856	18	94
		Bath				
TOTAL SHARED DWELLINGS	**912**	**221**	**86**	**576**	**29**	**263**
2	286	161	47	59	19	143
3	114	36	22	53	3	38
4	108	12	11	82	3	27
5	95	2	4	89	-	19
6	54	2	-	52	-	9
7	70	5	1	63	1	10
8 or more	185	3	1	178	3	17
		Bristol				
TOTAL SHARED DWELLINGS	**3,934**	**623**	**403**	**2,802**	**106**	**1,109**
2	1,022	416	212	365	29	511
3	555	98	73	358	26	185
4	572	39	48	466	19	143
5	535	31	17	478	9	107
6	432	20	12	393	7	72
7	161	8	7	144	2	23
8 or more	657	11	34	598	14	68
		Kingswood				
TOTAL SHARED DWELLINGS	**124**	**20**	**7**	**91**	**6**	**37**
2	28	15	2	11	-	14
3	42	3	1	36	2	14
4	20	-	1	15	4	5
5	5	-	-	5	-	1
6	6	1	1	4	-	1
7	7	-	-	7	-	1
8 or more	16	1	2	13	-	1
		Northavon				
TOTAL SHARED DWELLINGS	**85**	**21**	**15**	**46**	**3**	**34**
2	50	20	13	14	3	25
3	15	1	1	13	-	5
4	8	-	1	7	-	2
5	-	-	-	-	-	-
6	12	-	-	12	-	2
7	-	-	-	-	-	-
8 or more	-	-	-	-	-	-
		Wansdyke				
TOTAL SHARED DWELLINGS	**66**	**18**	**13**	**31**	**4**	**23**
2	26	15	6	5	-	13
3	18	2	3	10	3	6
4	8	-	4	4	-	2
5	-	-	-	-	-	-
6	6	1	-	4	1	1
7	-	-	-	-	-	-
8 or more	8	-	-	8	-	1

66. Shared dwellings; household spaces in shared dwellings

Number of household spaces within dwelling	TOTAL HOUSEHOLD SPACES	Type of not self-contained household space in shared dwellings				TOTAL SHARED DWELLINGS
		Not self-contained flat	Not self-contained 'rooms'	Bedsit	Not self-contained unoccupied	
a	b	c	d	e	f	g
		Woodspring				
TOTAL SHARED DWELLINGS	**757**	**161**	**102**	**451**	**43**	**229**
2	212	110	46	44	12	106
3	147	26	22	83	16	49
4	128	12	12	96	8	32
5	85	5	4	73	3	17
6	30	-	-	30	-	5
7	91	7	15	66	3	13
8 or more	64	1	3	59	1	7

Annex A Changes of boundary (between 5th April 1981 and 21st April 1991)

County, districts

Date of change	Authority for change	Existing area i.e. as constituted at 21st April 1991 (names or descriptions not existing on 5th April 1981 are marked *)	Composition of existing area in terms of areas as constituted at 5th April 1981 (names or descriptions of counties/districts which have now ceased to exist are marked #)	Present population 1981	Existing areas in which the balance (if any) of the area named in col d is now situated
a	b	c	d	e	f
1st April 1983	The Avon and Somerset (Areas) Order 1983	AVON		914,636	
			Avon	915,176	
			except:		
			Woodspring (pt)		†Somerset
			Hutton Ward (pt)	−30	
			Winscombe Ward (pt)	−12	
			Somerset (pt)		
			viz:		
			Sedgemoor (pt)		†Somerset
			Shipham Ward (pt)	-	
1st April 1990	The Avon, Somerset and Wiltshire (County Boundaries) Order 1990		Avon		
			except:		
			Northavon (pt)		†Wiltshire
			Badminton Ward (pt)	-	
			Hawkesbury Ward (pt)	-	
			Wansdyke (pt)		†Somerset
			Hinton Charterhouse Ward (pt)	−9	
			Woodspring (pt)		†Somerset
			Winscombe Ward (pt)	-	
			Somerset (pt)		
			viz:		
			Mendip (pt)		†Somerset
			Stratton Ward (pt)	-	
			Sedgemoor (pt)		†Somerset
			Axe Vale Ward (pt)	-	
			Wiltshire (pt)		
			viz:		
			North Wiltshire (pt)		†Wiltshire
			No 16 Ward (pt)	+13	
			No 30 Ward (pt)	-	
1st April 1991	The Avon and Gloucestershire (County Boundaries) Order 1991		Avon		
			except:		
			Northavon (pt)		†Gloucestershire
			Charfield Ward (pt)	−9	
			Hawkesbury Ward (pt)	−493	
			Gloucestershire (pt)		
			viz:		
			Stroud (pt)		†Gloucestershire
			No 31 Ward (pt)	-	

†See relevant County Report

Notes:- Hectare measurements for those areas affected by boundary changes have not been included because the figures are not routinely available.
Changes of boundaries may involve areas of land with no population present in 1981, this is shown by a dash in Column e.
With reference to paragraph 4.1 and Table B, changes to the district boundary of Bristol were minor and did not involve 1981 district population counts.
Where changes have affected ward or parish boundaries and/or names, details can be obtained from the Office of Population Censuses and Surveys, Census Customer Services, Titchfield, Fareham, Hants. PO15 5RR.

Annex A Changes of boundary (between 5th April 1981 and 21st April 1991)

County, districts

Date of change	Authority for change	Existing area i.e. as constituted at 21st April 1991 (names or descriptions not existing on 5th April 1981 are marked *)	Composition of existing area in terms of areas as constituted at 5th April 1981 (names or descriptions of counties/districts which have now ceased to exist are marked #)	Present population 1981	Existing areas in which the balance (if any) of the area named in col d is now situated
a	b	c	d	e	f
1st April 1990	The Avon, Somerset and Wiltshire (County Boundaries) Order 1990	Northavon		118,808	
			Northavon	119,297	North Wiltshire †(Wiltshire)
			except:		
			Badminton Ward (pt)	-	
			Hawkesbury Ward (pt)	-	
			North Wiltshire (pt)		North Wiltshire †(Wiltshire)
			viz:		
			No 16 Ward (pt)	+13	
			No 30 Ward (pt)	-	
1st April 1991	The Avon and Gloucestershire (County Boundaries) Order 1991		Northavon		Stroud †(Gloucestershire)
			except:		
			Charfield Ward (pt)	−9	
			Hawkesbury Ward (pt)	−493	
			Stroud (pt)		Stroud †(Gloucestershire)
			viz:		
			No 31 Ward (pt)	-	
1st April 1984	The Bristol, Wansdyke and Woodspring (Areas) Order 1984	Wansdyke		76,728	
			Wansdyke	76,733	
			Woodspring (pt)		Woodspring
			viz:		
			Winford Ward (pt)	+4	
1st April 1990	The Avon, Somerset and Wiltshire (County Boundaries) Order 1990		Wansdyke		Mendip †(Somerset)
			except:		
			Hinton Charterhouse Ward (pt)	−9	
			Mendip (pt)		Mendip †(Somerset)
			viz:		
			Stratton Ward (pt)	-	
1st April 1983	The Avon and Somerset (Areas) Order 1983	Woodspring		163,137	
			Woodspring	163,183	Sedgemoor †(Somerset)
			except:		
			Hutton Ward (pt)	−30	
			Winscombe Ward (pt)	−12	
			Sedgemoor (pt)		Sedgemoor †(Somerset)
			viz:		
			Shipham Ward (pt)	-	
1st April 1984	The Bristol, Wansdyke and Woodspring (Areas) Order 1984		Woodspring		Wansdyke
			except:		
			Winford Ward (pt)	−4	
1st April 1990	The Avon, Somerset and Wiltshire (County Boundaries) Order 1990		Woodspring		Sedgemoor †(Somerset)
			except:		
			Winscombe Ward (pt)	-	
			Sedgemoor (pt)		Sedgemoor †(Somerset)
			viz:		
			Axe Vale Ward (pt)	-	

†See relevant County Report

Notes:- Hectare measurements for those areas affected by boundary changes have not been included because the figures are not routinely available.
Changes of boundaries may involve areas of land with no population present in 1981, this is shown by a dash in Column e.
With reference to paragraph 4.1 and Table B, changes to the district boundary of Bristol were minor and did not involve 1981 district population counts.
Where changes have affected ward or parish boundaries and/or names, details can be obtained from the Office of Population Censuses and Surveys, Census Customer Services, Titchfield, Fareham, Hants. PO15 5RR.

Annex B How to obtain 1991 Census results

The products described in this Annex become available in the period May 1992 until mid-1994. Dates of availability are not given, to avoid any confusion as this Report continues to be used during and after the period 1992-94. All products are described as if available, but, in any case of doubt, a check should be made with OPCS Census Customer Services at the address given at the end of this Annex.

The form of results

The statistical results of the Census are made available in two ways:

(a) in printed *reports* sold by HMSO bookshops (or, in a few cases, directly from the Census Offices); or

(b) in *statistical abstracts* available, on request and for a charge, from the Census offices.

The *reports* take three general forms:

- volumes - such as this Report - containing substantial and detailed tables;
- *key statistics*, which give around 200 summary statistics for particular types of areas throughout the country, with national and regional figures, laid out for easy comparison between areas; and
- *Monitors*, pamphlets which either give between 20 and 60 summary statistics for particular types of area in parts of the country, sometimes issued before main reports to give early results, or provide summaries for the country as a whole.

Statistical abstracts are supplied mainly in machine-readable form, although small quantities can be supplied as hard copies, and are generally either:

- in a standard form, commissioned by a number of customers sharing costs, particularly to provide results for areas and populations smaller than those covered in reports; or
- specially designed output commissioned by individual customers.

The Census Offices also supply supplementary products, for example to provide information on the geographical base of the Census, and documentation in a series of OPCS/GRO(S) *1991 Census User Guides*.

There are two broad types of results:

(a) *local statistics*, which cover the full range of census topics - such as this Report; and

(b) *topic statistics*, which focus on particular census topics in more detail, mainly at national and regional level.

All the main statistical results and products are described in *Prospectuses* in the *User Guides* series, available from the addresses given in section 13 and at the end of this Annex. Prospectuses for reports and abstracts contain complete outlines of the tables which will become available.

All areas for which results are provided in reports and abstracts are as at the time of the 1991 Census (unless otherwise indicated).

Local statistics

Local authorities

Results for smaller areas within the local authorities covered in this Report, or within local authorities elsewhere, are available as:

Ward and Civil Parish Monitors (England) or *Ward and Community Monitors* (Wales): pamphlets for each county in England and Wales which give some 30 statistics for each ward and civil parish/community, with figures for counties and districts/boroughs for comparison (see *Prospectus/User Guide 32).*

Local and Small Area Statistics are standard abstracts available from a variety of areas throughout Britain from the smallest - the Census Enumeration District - upwards. They are introduced in section 3 of this Report, and further information is available in *Prospectus/User Guide 3*. Further *User Guides* give: the file specification (number 21); the cell numbering system (24 and 25); and explanatory notes (38).

Results for local authorities in other parts of the country are available, with full comparability, as:

County Reports (England and Wales) and *Region Reports* (Scotland): issued separately in two parts for each County in England and Wales and for each Region in Scotland.

Key Statistics (Great Britain): a single report giving around 200 summary statistics, with some 1981/91 comparisons, for each local authority (see *Prospectus/User Guide 29*).

County Monitors (England and Wales) and *Region Monitors* (Scotland): pamphlets issued separately for each County or Region in advance of the main *Reports*, with contents as section 15 of this Report. Welsh County Monitors will be produced in bi-lingual format (Welsh and English).

Local and Small Area Statistics are also available at local authority level.

Results for other types of area, in forms comparable with those for local authorities listed above, are available for:

Health authority areas

Health Regions Report: a single report, in the form of a County Report, for Regional Health Authorities in England (elsewhere in Britain health authority boundaries coincided with those of local authorities at the time of the 1991 Census).

Key Statistics: a single report giving some 200 summary statistics for each Regional and District Health Authority in England (see *Prospectus/User Guide 30*).

Health Authority Monitors: pamphlets, in the form of County Monitors, for Regional and District Health Authorities.

Local and Small Area Statistics are also available at health authority level.

Urban and Rural Areas

Key Statistics: a single report for the larger urban areas and the rural areas in Great Britain, giving some 200 summary statistics for each area, with six 'regional' reports covering urban areas of all sizes and the rural areas in various parts of England and, separately, for Wales and Scotland (see *User Guide/Prospectus 31*).

Urban and rural areas have been specially defined for both the 1981 and 1991 Censuses, and a further report will give figures on change over the decade. 'Urban areas' cover conurbations, cities and towns of all sizes defined on a land use ('bricks and mortar') basis, so, for example, Census results are available for smaller towns *within* the larger local authority areas.

Small Area Statistics are also available for each urban and rural area.

Parliamentary and European Constituencies

Parliamentary Constituency Monitors: pamphlets, in the form of County Monitors, but with some additional '10 per cent' statistics, with results for each Parliamentary Constituency (and with figures for Britain for comparison). There are separate Monitors for each standard statistical region in England, and for Wales and Scotland (see *User Guide/ Prospectus 34*). A single pamphlet in the same form is available for the European Parliamentary Constituencies in Great Britain.

Postcode areas

Postcode Sector Monitors: pamphlets for counties or groups of counties in England and Wales, giving some 30 '100 per cent' and '10 per cent' summary statistics at postcode sector level (see *Prospectus/User Guide 33*).

Small Area Statistics are also available for postcode sectors.

The 1991 Census records for England and Wales are re-sorted to give exact counts for postcode sectors. Results for a wide range of postcode based areas are available in Scotland.

National versions of local results

Results for Great Britain, regions in England, and Wales and Scotland, for these areas as a whole in forms comparable with those for local authorities and other types of area listed above, are available as:

National Reports: issued in two parts, on the lines of this Report, for Great Britain as a whole, including results for standard statistical regions in England and for Wales and Scotland; there is also a *Report for Wales*, bi-lingual in Welsh and English, and a *Report for Scotland.*

National and Regional Summary Monitor: pamphlet for Great Britain, including results for standard statistical regions in England and for Wales and Scotland, with contents as section 15 of this Report. Similar summary Monitors will be issued for Wales (bi-lingual) and Scotland, including summary results at County/Region level.

Topic statistics

Results for particular census topics are available in a series of reports summarised in the table on the following page. The reports present results mainly at the national level, but the following table shows those which have results at regional level, or at a county or district (or equivalent) level. Prospectuses should be checked for detailed information. The Regional Migration Reports comprise separate volumes for each standard statistical region of England, and for Wales and for Scotland.

Workplace and migration statistics

The analysis of the Census questions on 'address of workplace' and 'usual address one year before the Census' gives results on journeys from residences to workplaces and on migration moves, together with figures on people with workplaces in an area and out-migrants from an area, not only for the larger areas covered by the Reports listed above but also for smaller local areas. The latter are:

Special Migration Statistics: which provide information (in machine-readable form only) on migrants within and between local areas (see *Prospectus/User Guide 35).*

Special Workplace Statistics: which provide information (in machine-readable form only) on workforces in areas of workplace and residence for customer defined zones, and on journeys from residence to workplace between the zones (see *Prospectus/User Guide 36*).

Other products

Commissioned tables

In addition to the standard tables prepared for the local and topic statistics, the Census Offices also supply tables, on request, to a customer's own specification, at a charge which meets the marginal cost of production. *Prospectus/User Guide 14* explains how customers may specify and order commissioned tables, and provides guidance on estimation of costs.

Topic	Processing level (per cent)	Prospectus (number)	With some results for:		
			Standard Statistical Regions*	Counties/ Scottish regions	Districts
Sex, Age and Marital Status (GB)	100	2	yes	yes	no
Historical Tables (GB)	100	4	yes	yes	no
Usual Residence (GB)	100	7	yes	yes	yes
Persons Aged 60 and Over (GB)	100	6	yes	no	no
Housing and Availability of Cars (GB and S)	100	12	yes	yes	yes
Communal Establishments (GB)	100	15	yes	no	no
Household Composition (GB)	100	11	yes	no	no
Limiting Long-term Illness (GB)	100	5	yes	no	no
Ethnic Group and Country of Birth (GB)	100/10	9	yes	yes	yes
Welsh Language in Wales	100/10	10	n/a	yes	yes
Gaelic Language in Scotland	100/10	18	n/a	yes	yes
National Migration (Part 1) (GB)	100	17	yes**	no	no
National Migration (Part 2) (GB)	10	17	yes**	no	no
Regional Migration (Part 1)	100	22	yes**	yes	yes
Regional Migration (Part 2)	10	22	yes**	yes	no
Report for Health Areas (GB)	100	39	n/a	n/a	n/a
Economic Activity (GB and S)	10	16	yes	no	no
Workplace and Transport to Work (GB and S)	10	20	yes	yes	yes***
Household and Family Composition (GB)	10	23	no	no	no
Qualified Manpower (GB)	10	8	yes	no	no
Children and Young Adults (GB)	100/10	13	yes	no	no

GB Volumes for Great Britain
GB and S Volumes for Great Britain together with additional volumes for Scotland

* includes Metropolitan Counties in England
** includes main urban areas
*** includes city centres

Enumeration District/Postcode Directory

This Directory provides a means of associating enumeration districts to postcodes to enable users to undertake their own linkage between census and other datasets. It is available, on magnetic media only, separately for each county. Alternatively, customers may purchase a National Directory. Further details of the file specification, information on availability, cost and ordering are provided in *Prospectus 26*.

User Guide Catalogue

This catalogue is available from the Census Customer Services at the address given below. The catalogue is regularly revised to provide up-to-date information on all Prospectuses/User Guides.

Census Newsletter

The Newsletter is published several times a year to provide a link with users. It gives information on many aspects of the 1991 Census, including details of relevant publications and census-related activities. The Newsletter is a major source of information about the availability of census results and also reports on the main findings from evaluations of coverage and quality. Customers wishing to be included on the mailing list for future copies of the Newsletter should contact Census Customer Services.

Information on all products described in this Annex may be obtained from

Census Customer Services
OPCS
Segensworth Road
Titchfield
Fareham
Hampshire
PO15 5RR

Telephone 0329 813800

Please mention this Report when making an enquiry.

Annex C Explanatory notes on the summary and main (part 1) tables

Summary tables

References to the '*Definitions* volume' are to the publication described in section 7.

Tables A and B

Tables A and B are the only summary tables which refer to the present population. In Tables A and B, and in the accompanying diagram, *preliminary counts of the population present* for 1981 have been used because they are felt to be generally more accurate than the final 1981 counts of the population present which were inflated by a processing error (see *1981 Census Monitor CEN 82/3*). The 1981 preliminary counts have been corrected for a few errors (also reported in *1981 Census Monitor CEN 82/3*), and for boundary changes between 1981 and 1991. Because of the preliminary nature of these figures, they have been rounded to the nearest hundred before presentation.

Tables C, E, F, G, I, K, L, and M

Tables C, E, F, G, I, K and L (also M - Wales only) include comparisons between the numbers of residents, and households with residents, in 1981 and 1991. These comparisons are made using the 1981 resident population base (that is, the 1991 statistics used in the comparisons exclude wholly absent households in the same way that the 1981 statistics do) to give a valid picture of intercensal changes.

Tables F and K

The 1981-91 comparisons in Tables F and K use the 1981 definition of students, in which all students are categorised as economically inactive. The remaining sections of these tables use the 1991 definition, in which students who were in employment or seeking work in the week before the Census are categorised as economically active and are included in the relevant economically active categories.

The 1981-91 comparisons of residents and households with residents in section 15 also use the 1981 population base. Some intercensal changes are expressed in terms of *'percentage points'*. This is the arithmetic difference between the 1991 percentage and the 1981 percentage.

All Tables

The following terms appear in the *Summary* tables - see the *Definitions* volume for full details:

(i) A 'hectare' is equivalent to 2.471 acres.

(ii) A 'household' is either one person living alone; or a group of people (who may or may not be related), living, or staying temporarily, at the same address with common housekeeping - that is, sharing at least one meal a day or sharing a living room or sitting room.

(iii) 'Communal establishments' comprise:

- NHS and non-NHS hospitals,
- local authority homes,
- housing association homes and hostels,
- nursing homes,
- residential homes,
- children's homes,
- prison service establishments,
- defence establishments,
- educational establishments,
- hotels and boarding houses,
- hostels and lodging houses,
- other miscellaneous establishments,
- campers and people sleeping rough, and
- civilian ships, boats, and barges.

(iv) A 'person of pensionable age' is a man aged 65 or over or a woman aged 60 or over.

(v) 'Economically inactive' includes:

- students without a job in the week before the Census,
- permanently sick people,
- retired people, and
- people looking after the home or family and not in paid employment.

(vi) A 'dwelling' consists of one or more household spaces, which may be occupied or unoccupied. A *shared dwelling* consists of two or more household spaces in a multi-occupied building which share access and are not self-contained.

(vii) A 'lone parent' in the Summary tables is a person who is the only adult (person aged 16 or over) in a household with children aged 15 or under.

(viii) A 'dependant' is either a dependent child, or a person with limiting long-term illness *and* permanently sick or retired.

(ix) A 'dependent child' is defined as either a person aged 0-15 in a household; or one aged 16-18, never married, in full-time education, *and* economically inactive.

Percentages in the tables do not necessarily add up to exactly 100 per cent, because each is individually rounded.

Vertical lines in the tables separate different analyses. Percentages or counts should only be summed *within* vertical lines.

In the tables a count or percentage of zero is shown by a dash (-). In Tables A and B percentages of less than 0.005 per cent are shown as 0.00 per cent. In other tables percentages of less than 0.05 per cent are shown as 0.0 per cent.

In Tables E, F, I, K, and L a blank means that no relevant 1981 Census data exist.

In Table G the 1981 percentages for household amenities straddle two columns because no information on central heating was collected in the 1981 Census.

Main tables

References to the '*Definitions* volume' are to the publication described in section 7.

I Demographic and economic characteristics

Table 1

Definitions of populations counted on rows 1 to 5 are:

1. Present residents - residents and persons of no fixed abode or no usual residence who were present on Census night (that is, for whom the response to Question 6, whereabouts, was 'at this address').

2. Absent residents (part of household present) - residents for whom the response to Question 6, whereabouts, was not 'at this address' in households where one or more persons were enumerated as present 'at that address' on Census night.

3. Absent residents (wholly absent household - enumerated) - residents in households where nobody was enumerated as present at that address on Census night (wholly absent households), where a Census form was returned under the voluntary arrangements for the enumeration of such wholly absent households.

4. Absent residents (wholly absent household - imputed) - residents in households where nobody was enumerated as present at that address on Census night (wholly absent households), but where no Census form was returned. Details for the households and residents have been imputed - see the *Definitions* volume paragraphs 1.48-1.54. This category also includes imputed residents of households reported to have residents but where no contact could be made, and also imputed residents in households that refused to complete a Census form.

5. Visitors - persons present at an address for whom the response to Question 7, usual address, was 'elsewhere'.

   The components in rows 1 to 5 are used to compile counts on three population bases - those used in the 1971, 1981, and 1991 Censuses. This allows comparison with Small Area Statistics (SAS) results from previous censuses:

   PERSONS PRESENT 1991: 1971 BASE (1+5) - this is the sum of lines 1 and 5; that is all present residents plus all visitors. This is equivalent to the count 'Total population present' in 1971 SAS Table 1, from which other sub-populations of persons were drawn for the 1971 SAS.

   RESIDENTS 1991: 1981 BASE (1+2) - this is the sum of lines 1 and 2; that is all present residents plus all absent residents in households where someone was enumerated as present on Census night. This is equivalent to the count ALL RESIDENT 1981: 1981 BASE in 1981 SAS Table 1, which formed the base for most 1981 SAS Tables, most tables in the 1981 Reports, and many other 1981 Census Tables.

   RESIDENTS 1991: 1991 BASE (1+2+3+4) - this is the sum of lines 1, 2, 3, and 4; that is all present and absent residents. This is the count which forms the base for most 1991 100 per cent tables in the Reports/LBS, SAS, and most other 100 per cent tables.

Table 3

(i) 'Persons present not in households' are all persons enumerated in communal establishments, plus persons sleeping rough and campers.

(ii) 'Number of establishments' is the total number of each type of establishment in the area at which persons were enumerated on Census night. No counts of 'establishments' are given for persons sleeping rough or for campers.

(iii) 'Residents: Staff' includes residents returned on the Census form as relatives of the manager or other staff, and other people who are not guests (in hotels, etc) or inmates. It should be noted that staff **on duty** in an establishment on Census night whose usual addresses were elsewhere were **not** enumerated in the establishment unless they were temporarily residing in the establishment.

(iv) 'Residents: Other' will, in general, include only those persons who were resident guests (in hotels, etc) or resident inmates. However, **all** persons resident on ships and all persons resident in defence establishments are included in this category.

(v) 'Non-NHS/LA/HA' means that the establishments are not under the management of the National Health Service, a local authority, or a housing association. 'Non-HA' means not under the management of a housing association.

(vi) For the full definition and classification of communal establishments see Chapter 4 of the *Definitions* volume.

Table 4

(i) 'Residents (non-staff) present not in households' will, in general, include only those persons who were resident guests (in hotels, etc) or resident inmates. However, **all** persons resident on ships and all persons resident in defence establishments are included in this category.

(ii) 'Non-NHS/LA/HA' means that the establishments are not under the management of the National Health Service, a local authority, or a housing association.

Table 5

(i) See note (i) to Table 4.

(ii) 'Non-HA' means not under the management of a housing association.

Table 7

(i) The 'Europe' sub-total comprises UK, Channel Islands, Isle of Man, Irish Republic, Ireland (part not stated), and all countries under 'Remainder of Europe'.

(ii) The 'European Community' sub-total comprises UK and all countries listed under 'European Community'.

Table 10

Because the County Reports are published for each county soon after processing of the Census data for each is completed, this table counts only those students who are resident in the area and those who are not residents but were present on Census night. Students who normally live in the area during term-time but are not residents of the area and were not present in the area on Census night are excluded from the table. A complete matrix of area of residence and area of term-time address for students is being prepared by the Census Offices when processing all areas of Great Britain is complete. More information on the availability of statistics from this matrix can be obtained from the Census Offices at the addresses shown in section 13.

Table 11

(i) 'Residents: Staff' includes residents returned on the Census form as relatives of the manager or other staff, and other people who are not guests (in hotels, etc) or inmates. It should be noted that staff **on duty** in an establishment on Census night whose usual addresses were elsewhere were **not** enumerated in the establishment unless they were temporarily residing in the establishment.

(ii) 'Residents: Other' will, in general, include only those persons who were resident guests (in hotels, etc) or resident inmates. However, **all** persons resident on ships and all persons resident in defence establishments are included in this category.

Table 13

(i) 'Other' establishments comprises 'Detention, defence, and education' establishments, and 'Other groups' including persons sleeping rough and campers.

(ii) For the full definition and classification of communal establishments see Chapter 4 of the *Definitions* volume.

Table 15

'Neighbouring counties/neighbouring districts' are areas with common boundaries. This concept is used in tables counting 'migrants' (usual residents of an area with a different usual address one year before the Census). The counts in these columns represent the number of migrants resident in an area who lived in neighbouring areas one year before Census night. For each local government district the counts represent those migrants who formerly lived in the counties/Scottish regions neighbouring the county containing the area in question, or those formerly living in the local government districts neighbouring the district in question. For the county as a whole the counts will represent the sum of all migrants who moved from neighbouring counties/ Scottish regions and neighbouring districts. (All areas/boundaries are as on 21 April 1991.)

All areas which share a section of land boundary, including those which touch at a point, are included as neighbours. Areas which are separated by water (a river, or larger body of water) are included as neighbours if there is a transport link (rail or road bridge, or tunnel, or vehicle ferry) between the two areas. Areas which are separated by land belonging to a third area are not included as neighbours, no matter how close together the areas are. The lists of neighbouring areas were compiled in consultation with the local authorities.

The full lists of neighbouring counties/Scottish regions and neighbouring districts are shown in a *User Guide* available from the Census Offices.

Table 16

(i) See note to Table 15.

(ii) Counts of persons and households in the section for 'Wholly moving households with dependent children' may include a small number of households with no adults.

Table 18

(i) This table includes counts of all imputed residents in wholly absent households which did not return a form under the voluntary arrangements for the enumeration of wholly absent households, plus imputed residents in households where people were reported to live, but where no contact could be made, plus imputed residents of households which refused to complete a Census form.

(ii) 'Other ethnic groups' comprises Black-Caribbean, Black-African, Black-Other, Indian, Pakistani, Bangladeshi, Chinese, and Other groups.

(iii) See paragraphs 1.48-1.54 of the *Definitions* volume for details of the imputation of wholly absent households.

II Housing

Table 19

(i) This table gives imputed counts of all wholly absent households which did not return a form under the voluntary arrangements for the enumeration of such wholly absent households, plus households where people were reported to live, but where no contact could be made, plus households which refused to complete a Census form.

(ii) See paragraphs 1.48-1.54 of the *Definitions* volume for details of the imputation of wholly absent households.

(iii) The range of tenure categories in this table is incomplete; the category 'rented with a job or business' is omitted because it would contain only very small numbers. The counts can be derived by subtracting the sum of the given tenure categories from the table total.

Table 21

(i) 'Number of persons aged 17 and over (with and without others)' is a classification of residents aged 17 and over in households regardless of whether any other residents in the household are aged under 17.

(ii) The rows 'ALL HOUSEHOLDS' and 'TOTAL PERSONS (ALL AGES)' may include a small number of households with no person aged 17 and over, and residents in such households. Such households and residents are not included elsewhere in the table.

Table 22

(i) 'Households with the following rooms' counts the number of households with the stated number of rooms.

(ii) 'Households with the following . . . persons' counts the number of households with the stated number of residents.

Table 24

(i) 'Households with the following persons' and 'Households with the following number of persons aged 18 and over' count the number of households with the stated number of residents, and residents aged 18 and over respectively.

(ii) The column 'TOTAL HOUSEHOLDS' may include a small number of households with no person aged 18 and over, and residents in such households. Such households and residents are not included elsewhere in the table.

Table 25

(i) This table counts households which were enumerated with persons present but which had no residents, whether present or absent; that is households consisting entirely of visitors. The table will include occupied second homes, holiday accommodation, and student residences (excluding halls of residence and other communal student accommodation).

(ii) 'Students' in this table are defined as those aged 18 and over to exclude schoolchildren enumerated with their parents.

(iii) The range of tenure categories in this table is incomplete; the category 'rented with a job or business' is omitted because it would contain only very small numbers. The counts can be derived by subtracting the sum of the given tenure categories from the table total.

Table 26

(i) This table counts households enumerated with residents (whether present or absent) in which at least one student (aged 18 or over) was resident (whether present or absent) or a visitor.

(ii) 'Students' in this table are defined as those aged 18 and over, to exclude schoolchildren enumerated with their parents.

(iii) The range of tenure categories in this table is incomplete; the category 'rented with a job or business' is omitted because it would contain only very small numbers. The counts can be derived by subtracting the sum of the given tenure categories from the table total.

Table 27

(i) This table counts households, persons in households, and rooms, according to the population bases used in the 1971, 1981, and 1991 Censuses.

(ii) Row 1 counts households with at least one person present on Census night 1991, whether a resident or not, sub-divided by the number of persons present on Census night. The 'TOTAL PERSONS' column counts the total number of persons present in households.

(iii) Row 2 counts households with at least one person present on Census night 1991, whether a resident or not, sub-divided by the number of residents, whether present or absent on Census night. The entry in the column headed '0' counts households with no residents but at least one person present on Census night. The 'TOTAL PERSONS' column counts the total number of residents present in households, and absent residents in households where at least one person was present.

(iv) Row 3 counts households with at least one person present (whether a resident or not), plus wholly absent households (enumerated and imputed), plus imputed counts for households where people were reported to live, but where no contact could be made, or which refused to complete a Census form, sub-divided by the number of residents, whether present or absent on Census night. The entry in the column headed '0' counts households with no residents but at least one person present on Census night. The 'TOTAL PERSONS' column counts the total number of residents in households, whether present or absent.

III Households and household composition

Table 30

In the columns classifying households by the age of the youngest and oldest dependant, households with only one dependant are classified by taking the dependant as both the youngest and the oldest in the household.

Table 31

The row 'ALL HOUSEHOLDS' may include a small number of households with no adults, and residents in such households. Such households and residents are not included elsewhere in the table.

Table 32

(i) This table is given alongside Table 31 to provide comparative statistics with 1981 County Report Table 34.

(ii) The row 'ALL HOUSEHOLDS' may include a small number of households with no persons aged 16 and over, and residents in such households. Such households and residents are not included elsewhere in the table.

Table 33

(i) A 'couple' is a male aged 16 and over and a female aged 16 and over, whether or not both were returned as 'married' (whether to each other or not), resident in a household with no other residents aged 16 and over.

(ii) 'Other' economically active females comprise females on a Government scheme, and those unemployed.

Table 36

'Households with the following adults' and 'Households with the following dependent children' count respectively households with the stated number of resident adults, and resident dependent children.

Table 37

(i) Lone 'parents' are the sole *residents* aged 16-24 (with no residents aged 25 or over) in households with a child or children aged 0-15 in the household. The 'lone parent' is not necessarily a parent of the child, for example, a woman aged 21 living alone with her 15 year old sister will be included in the counts. The counts will not include all lone parent families; those in households with other adults will be excluded - see Table 87 in Part 2 of the County Report for 10 per cent sample counts of *lone parent families*.

(ii) The range of employment position categories in this table is incomplete; the category 'self-employed' is omitted because it contains only very small numbers. The counts can be derived by subtracting the sum of the given economic position categories from the table total.

Table 39

The two total rows 'All ages 16 and over' may include a small number of heads and residents in households where the head is aged under 16. Such households and residents are also included in the rows for ages 16-19.

Table 40

(i) Lone 'parents' are the sole *residents* aged 16 or over in households with a child or children aged 0-15 in the household. The 'lone parent' is not necessarily a parent of the child, for example, a woman aged 21 living alone with her 15 year old sister will be included in the counts. The counts will not include all lone parent families; those in households with other adults will be excluded (see Table 87 in Part 2 of the County Report for 10 per cent sample counts of all *lone parent* families).

(ii) 'Other' economically active comprises those on a Government scheme, and those unemployed.

Table 42

(i) The range of 'persons per room' categories in this table is incomplete; the categories 'up to 0.5 persons per room' and 'over 0.5 and up to 1 person per room' are omitted. A total for these two counts can be derived by subtracting the sum of the given 'persons per room' categories from the table total.

(ii) The range of categories of dependent children by age in this table is incomplete; the category 'dependent children aged 18' is omitted. The counts can be derived by subtracting the sum of the given categories from the total for all dependent children.

(iii) The range of categories of cars in this table is incomplete; the categories '1 car' and '2 cars' are omitted. A total for these counts can be derived by subtracting the sum of the given categories from the table total.

(iv) The total row 'ALL HOUSEHOLDS' may include a small number of households with no resident adults. Such households are not included in the other household composition categories.

Table 43

(i) The total row 'ALL HOUSEHOLDS' may include a small number of households with no resident adults. Such households are not included in the other household composition categories.

(ii) The range of categories of residents by age in this table is incomplete; ages 19 up to pensionable age are omitted. A total for these ages can be derived by subtracting the sum of the given categories from the total. (**Note**: the age categories 0-4, 5-15 and 0-17 are all sub-categories of 'All dependent children aged 0-18' and therefore should be omitted from any calculation of the number of residents aged 19 up to pensionable age.)

Table 44

The total row 'ALL HOUSEHOLDS' may include a small number of households with no resident adults. Such households are not included in the other household composition categories.

Table 45

The columns 'Total migrant heads' and 'TOTAL HOUSEHOLD HEADS' may include a small number of households where the head is aged under 16. Such households are also included in the age 16-19 columns.

Table 46

(i) The range of 'persons per room' categories in this table is incomplete; the categories 'up to 0.5 persons per room' and 'over 0.5 and up to 1 person per room' are omitted. A total for these two counts can be derived by subtracting the sum of the given 'persons per room' categories from the table total.

(ii) The range of tenure categories in this table is incomplete; the category 'rented with a job or business' is omitted because it would contain only very small numbers. The counts can be derived by subtracting the sum of the given tenure categories from the table total.

Table 47

The final six cells in the last column of this table are blank to avoid needless repetition of the counts in the last three cells of the first column.

Table 49

(i) The range of 'persons per room' categories in this table is incomplete; the categories 'up to 0.5 persons per room' and 'over 0.5 and up to 1 person per room' are omitted. A total for these two counts can be derived by subtracting the sum of the given 'persons per room' categories from the table total.

(ii) The range of tenure categories in this table is incomplete; the category 'rented with a job or business' is omitted because it would contain only very small counts for most ethnic groups. The counts can be derived by subtracting the sum of the given tenure categories from the table total.

(iii) Counts for households with head born in the New Commonwealth are included to provide some statistics to compare with 1981 Report Table 33.

Table 50

In the columns, 'Inside UK' **does not** include Channel Islands and the Isle of Man.

Table 52

This table is included as a proxy measure of the population not having English as a first language.

Table 53

A 'couple' household is a household with one male resident aged 16 and over and one female resident aged 16 and over, whether or not both were returned as 'married' (whether to each other or not), with no other residents aged 16 and over in the household.

IV Household spaces and dwellings

Table 54

(i) 'TOTAL HOUSEHOLD SPACES' for households with residents, and with persons enumerated but no residents, include as 'household spaces' the accommodation of any households living in non-permanent accomm-odation. The other occupancy types shown comprise only accommodation in permanent buildings.

(ii) 'TOTAL ROOMS' in 'Hotels and boarding houses' include only those rooms used by guests or staff for living, eating or sleeping.

(iii) 'TOTAL ROOMS' in absent households (imputed), in vacant accommodation, and in accommodation not used as main residence in which no persons were present (that is, second residences, holiday accommodation, and student accommodation), are totals of estimates made in each such case by the enumerator.

Table 56

(i) 'Absent households' includes both enumerated and imputed absent households.

(ii) 'Other' vacant accommodation includes vacant accommodation 'under improvement'.

(iii) The distinction between 'not self-contained flat' and 'not self-contained 'rooms'' in columns j and k, and columns m and n is made with reference to whether basic household amenities are shared. For household spaces where nobody was enumerated (vacant accommodation etc), this distinction is not possible, and only a single count can be given to cover 'not self-contained flat' and 'not self-contained 'rooms''. This also affects any totals which incorporate unoccupied accommodation. Some counts in this table therefore straddle columns.

Table 57

'Households with the following rooms', 'Households with the following persons', and 'Households with the following persons per room' count the number of households with the stated number of rooms, residents, and residents per room respectively.

Table 59

(i) The range of categories of residents by age in this table is incomplete; adults up to pensionable age are omitted. A total for this group can be derived by subtracting the sum of the given categories from the total. (**Note**: the age categories 0-4 and 5-15 are all sub-categories of 'All dependent children' and therefore should be omitted from any calculation of the number of resident adults up to pensionable age.)

(ii) The total row 'ALL HOUSEHOLDS' may include a small number of households with no resident adults. Such households are not included in the other household composition categories.

Table 60

'TOTAL CONVERTED OR SHARED ACCOMMODATION' is a count of buildings containing converted or shared household spaces; that is, a count of multi-occupied buildings.

Table 61

The distinction between 'not self-contained flat' and 'not self-contained 'rooms'' in columns k and l is made with reference to whether basic household amenities are shared. For dwellings where nobody was enumerated (vacant accommodation, etc), this distinction is not possible, and only a single count can be given to cover 'not self-contained flat' and 'not self-contained 'rooms''. This also affects any totals which incorporate unoccupied accommodation. Some counts in this table therefore straddle columns.

Table 64

(i) The tenure of a dwelling is chosen with reference to the tenure(s) of the household space(s) making up the dwelling. For a dwelling of one household space the tenure will be the same for both the dwelling and the household space. For a multi-household space dwelling the tenure is chosen according to a priority order:

1 Owner occupied - owned outright
2 Owner occupied - buying
3 Rented from a housing association
4 Rented from a new town
5 Rented from a local authority
6 Rented privately - unfurnished
7 Rented privately - furnished
8 Rented with a job or business

(Items 4 and 5 are always taken together in England and Wales.)

The highest ranked tenure among the household spaces becomes the tenure for the dwelling. For example, a dwelling consisting of one 'owner occupied - buying' household space and one 'rented privately - furnished' household space will be classified as an 'owner occupied - buying' dwelling.

Impossible combinations of dwelling and household space tenures (where the dwelling would have a lower priority tenure than a household space) are shown in the table as blank cells.

(ii) 'Other unoccupied accommodation' comprises second residences, holiday accommodation and student accommodation.

Table 65

The occupancy type of a dwelling is chosen with reference to the occupancy type(s) of the household space(s) making up the dwelling. For a dwelling of one household space the occupancy type will be the same for both the dwelling and the household space. For a multi-household space dwelling the occupancy type is chosen according to a priority order:

1 With residents - persons present
2 With residents - absent household (no persons present)
3 Vacant - under improvement
4 Vacant - other
5 Persons enumerated but no residents - owner occupied
6 Second residences
7 Persons enumerated but no residents - not owner occupied
8 Holiday accommodation
9 Student accommodation
10 Vacant - new, never occupied

The highest ranked occupancy type among the household spaces becomes the occupancy type for the dwelling. For example, a dwelling consisting of one 'second residence' household space and one household space 'with residents - persons present' will be classified as a dwelling 'with residents - persons present'.

Impossible combinations of dwelling and household space occupancy types (where the dwelling would have a lower priority occupancy type than a household space) are shown in the table as blank cells.

V Wales only table

Table 67

The question on the Welsh language is asked only of persons aged 3 and over.

Imputed data

A Tables 18 and 19 show counts of residents in imputed households, and imputed households for a selection of key variables (these tables include imputed wholly absent households and the other categories of imputed households and residents described in section 5). Table 71 in part 2 of the Report shows a comparison of the numbers of households processed at 100 per cent, and the number included in the 10 per cent sample.

B These counts will aid any comparison of grossed-up estimates from 10 per cent sample tables with 100 per cent processed tables, and to calculate percentage distributions of 10 per cent items based on an estimate of the total population. The imputed households and imputed residents form, in effect, 'not stated' cases for each census topic in the 10 per cent sample tables.

Printed in the United Kingdom for HMSO
Dd295707 1/93 C6 G3397/7 10170